Who's Who

IN CONTEMPORARY GAY AND LESBIAN HISTORY

Who's Who
IN CONTEMPORARY
GAY AND LESBIAN
HISTORY

From World War II
to the Present Day

Edited by
Robert Aldrich
and Garry Wotherspoon

London and New York

First published 2001
by Routledge
11 New Fetter Lane, London EC4P 4EE

Simultaneously published in the USA and Canada
by Routledge
29 West 35th Street, New York, NY 10001

Routledge is an imprint of the Taylor & Francis Group

Typeset in Sabon by RefineCatch Limited, Bungay, Suffolk
Printed and bound in Great Britain by
TJ International Ltd, Padstow, Cornwall

British Library Cataloguing in Publication Data
A catalogue record for this book is available from the British Library

Library of Congress Cataloging in Publication Data
A catalogue record for this book is available from the Library of Congress

ISBN 0–415–22974–X

Contents

Introduction

At the end of the twentieth century, it seems a not inappropriate time to put together a *Who's Who in Contemporary Gay and Lesbian History* covering the period from 1945 to the present.

First, and probably most importantly, this relates to the massive – and in the long sweep of human history, relatively rapid – changes that have occurred in the Western world in the situation of those with same-sex desires. We have only to look back a generation or two to see the magnitude of these changes: anyone born prior to World War II in most European countries and their overseas offshoots was born into a world where their homosexual orientation was usually seen as a crime, or a medical pathology, and – where Judeo-Christian values held sway – a sin. In contrast, for those born in the last several decades, the emphasis in Western pluralistic societies on human rights has seen (at least in an increasing number of countries) decriminalisation of previously proscribed sexual activity, and the passing of anti-discrimination and anti-vilification laws to protect gays and lesbians, as well as the extension, to them, of relationship and immigration rights. The great festivals that now annually draw hundreds of thousands of participants, from the Europride celebrations to the Sydney Gay and Lesbian Mardi Gras, would have been unthinkable even a generation ago. So too would have been the proliferation of bars and saunas, bookshops selling gay 'classics' and erotica, and the hundreds of other services that openly and loudly hawk their wares in gay 'ghettos' from the Castro to the Marais.

Such dramatic changes did not occur in a vacuum, and there are a variety of reasons for this changed situation, not least being the work of homophile activists working to change both laws and attitudes.

Activism for lesbian and gay rights, although it has a long history, has only really been a 'success story' for the post-World War II era, and here it ties in with the emergence of a range of 'new social movements' and their advocates. Partly emerging from the counter-cultural revolution, and linked with such developments as second-wave feminism, the anti-war and anti-nuclear movements, black power and anti-colonial movements (including the American civil rights movement and anti-apartheid efforts in South Africa) and the ideas of the 'New Left', activists for gay liberation were able to tap into the widespread discontent with, and questioning of, the values and moralities of their forebears. All of these social movements had an impact, though of varying degrees; in the case of homosexual emancipation, then gay liberation, it meant the start of an era of dramatic change.

Activism on its own is not sufficient, and so another point to note is the changed mental climate since World War II, which has allowed this activism both to occur and to be successful. New ideas issued from various sources – Freudian explanations of human sexuality, the debate in many countries about sex education (often associated with the birth-control debate, and attempts to stabilise marriage), the impact of cross-cultural studies indicating that many societies had for long accommodated people with same-sex desires, the notion that 'the personal is political' – all drew together a range of people to contest old ideas about what homosexuality represented.

Other developments were also important, and they could be quite diverse. Kinsey's famous sexological research of the 1940s showed that, far from being an indulgence of a small minority of deviants, same-sex sexual activity amongst males was far more common than had been presumed; moreover, the advent of the contraceptive pill allowed for sexual activity to be effectively separated from reproduction, encouraging large-scale sexual activity outside the old norms.

Another major driving force in the re-evaluation of those with same-sex desires has been scholarship. Both within and outside the academy, there has been an enormous growth in the level and quality of scholarship on sex and gender issues. Historical studies indicated that a major cultural fount of the West, classical Greece, had a set of institutionalised arrangements for same-sex relations. Works by such researchers as Evelyn Hooker in sociology, Jeffrey Weeks, Gert Hekma, Alan Bray, Wilhelm von Rosen and Giovanni Dall'Orto on the history of male homosexuality, and Martha Vicinus, Lillian Faderman, Karla Jay and Marie-Jo Bonnet in lesbian history have greatly enhanced our knowledge of sexuality in general, and how it is historically constructed. Pioneering work in women's studies by such scholars and theorists as Monique Wittig, Mary Daly and Kate Millett provided a new, feminist reading of culture. Many of the myths surrounding those with same-sex desires have been demolished (though they unfortunately persist in some quarters and have been resurrected by apostles of the radical right). Indeed, it would not be drawing too long a bow to say that activism and scholarship have played complementary roles in the past few decades. The activities of gay and lesbian scholars – in rediscovering the lives of homosexuals 'hidden from history', in undermining received medical and psychiatric notions about the pathology of homosexuality, in documenting the frequency of same-sex behaviour throughout different social milieux, in providing new readings of art and literature – have contributed greatly to contemporary gay and lesbian emancipation.

This volume has, therefore, been fortunate in being able to draw on several decades of pioneering scholarship. Indeed, the fact that there are 125 contributors, drawn from around the world, is in itself an indication of the progress that lesbian and gay studies have made, and the legitimacy that they have earned, over this period. While, as one might expect, many of these contributors come from the academy, it is important to note that not all do: in fact, much scholarship on gay and lesbian issues has been conducted outside the university.

The form chosen for this work – biographies – allows us both to focus on the individual and to set that individual in a social context. Apart from being interesting individual stories, these biographies are also a lens through which to view wider issues: at their most basic level, they tell us much about attitudes and behaviours, and how these have changed in the recent past. Even today in the West and within its various cultures, as these entries show, attitudes to same-sex relations vary considerably.

In looking back over some three thousand years of same-sex desires, it seemed to us that a major change, though by no means the only one, occurred from the mid-twentieth century, whence the beginning date of this volume. Several major reasons may be highlighted. First was the impact of World War II; extreme right-wing political movements had curbed or ended the vibrant public gay and lesbian life of many European cities, and the war led to greater persecution, including the gay holocaust in Nazi death camps. The war was also a general dislocator of values and behaviour and a stimulus to individual 'self-discovery'. Furthermore, the impact of new knowledge – as with the dissemination of Freudian ideas or of the work of Kinsey – provided a base from which to contest the old views.

One should also note a range of other factors affecting ideas about homosexuality, from increasing urbanisation and the disappearance of the old 'communitarian' societies, to the improving levels of education in post-war Western societies, and the growth of travel and how this brought an accompanying awareness of how homosexuality was accommodated elsewhere. More recently, the growth of burgeoning consumerism and the pursuit of the newly identified 'pink dollar', and the development of worldwide audio-visual mass media, have further helped break down barriers of ignorance, prejudice and isolation.

But one other factor was also important, and the irony in all this relates to the role of oppression. It was from the late 1940s that the cold war escalated, and with it came increasing oppression of those with same-sex desires. Along with communists, foreigners and other 'outsiders' – all seen as risks to national security in certain Western countries – homosexuals experienced persecution. In the US, as in the UK and Australia, there were campaigns to remove all such outsiders from government positions where they might constitute a security risk; these campaigns often spilled over into wider purges in society. In Australia, for example, one New South Wales Police Commissioner in the 1950s claimed that homosexuality was the 'greatest social menace facing Australia', and instituted wide-ranging campaigns against homosexuals, utilising everything from *agents provocateurs* to entrap them to the introduction of new laws to further criminalise them. Many politicians in other countries held similar, if less extreme, views.

Even in societies which did not experience McCarthyism, the old oppressive laws – such as the infamous Paragraph 175 of the German penal code, the criminalisation of homosexuality in Britain which dated back to the early modern age but was strengthened by the Labouchere amendment of the 1880s, a crack-down on homosexual activity imposed by the Vichy regime in France – increasingly rankled in the post-war world. In many non-English-speaking countries, the homophobic hysteria was far less, but a heightened negative awareness of homosexuality did make life difficult for those with same-sex desires. Whereas previously a lack of awareness might have allowed those with such desires to live their lives quietly, now the spotlight of public discussion made for sometimes uncomfortable and difficult experiences.

While the initial impact of often negative public awareness was undoubtedly much misery and even the destruction of human lives, in the long run this activity led to a raised profile for homosexuality, a widespread debate about what its 'causes' were, and whether homosexuals were in fact evil or sinful or sick. This in turn led to a coalescing of those so designated into an opposition – in effect, the oppression created an identity that drew together all those so labelled, and these formed the nucleus of reformers, with ongoing activism in many countries from the late 1940s and early 1950s. Homophile groups were set up in Norway and Denmark in 1948, in Holland in 1949, in Sweden in 1950, and in France in 1954. For the English-speaking world, in the US the Mattachine Society was set up in 1950, the Daughters of Bilitis in 1955 and the Society for Individual Rights in 1964, while in the UK both the Homosexual Law Reform Society and the Albany Trust were established in 1958. Indeed, the Stonewall Riots in 1969, when patrons of a gay bar in New York famously fought back against police harassment, should be seen from this longer-term perspective as a symbolic moment in, rather than the start of, the push for change.

Although it may seem evident to many readers, particularly those from North America, northern Europe and Australasia, that a public gay culture of a still familiar sort – bars and discotheques, backrooms and saunas, social and political groups, law reform campaigns – flourished by the mid-1970s (or even before), this was not the case for a significant part of the Western world. In most parts of the US, for instance, 'sodomy' continued to be illegal, and remains so in some states. In South Africa, until the end of the apartheid regime, homosexual relations (especially involving interracial couples) were also strictly forbidden. In Eastern Europe and the Soviet Union, until the collapse of communist regimes at the end of the 1980s and early 1990s, homosexuality was similarly illegal, gay and lesbian life was clandestine, and expressions of dissent (including sexual dissent) were muzzled. Though some countries of Eastern Europe now have progressive law codes – even with recognition of same-sex couples – and a lively public gay life, this is a very recent development indeed.

In southern Europe, the regimes that ruled Spain and Portugal until the 1970s – marked by fervent Catholicism, social conservatism and authoritarian politics – stifled public gay and lesbian life. Only since the 'carnation revolution' in Portugal has an open gay life bloomed there, though it is yet to be mirrored in literature, art and film. The death of Franco, by contrast, led to 'la movida', an intense period of social freedom and creative innovation in Spain, and to an explosion of gay life in that country's major cities. In Greece, the rule of the colonels in the late 1960s and early 1970s, in a similar way, staunched public gay life, but Greece has yet to see the emergence of a more 'Western'-style subculture.

Furthermore, as several writers in this volume suggest, a 'Mediterranean' type of same-sex activity continued to mark southern European countries along with the absence of a more public gay culture. Same-sex relations between men (or often, between older and younger males) were said to be commonplace, though most men married and fathered children. Openly gay bars and other commercial gathering places were scarce, even when homosexual cruising was common in public parks, railway stations, cafés and other venues. Few people openly identified themselves as 'gay' or showed an interest in participating in gay movements or gay associations. Whether this situation was simply the survival of the closet, coupled with social and cultural hypocrisy, or whether it represented a different approach to sexuality – one which rejected exclusive homosexuality or heterosexuality, and one which refused to be bound by affirmations of identity – is a matter of interpretation.

In any case, the spectrum of sexual attitudes and subcultures which come to light in these entries is again a warning against assumptions that the Castro or Christopher Street, or Soho or the Marais, are the ultimate or ideal incarnations of homosexual life and loves.

Several aspects of this book engage with some of the more important intellectual debates of the late twentieth century. One of these relates to identity. It is of course ironic that, when many postmodernists decry the idea of identity, even a passing knowledge of history would indicate the critical role that 'identity' has played for so many groups, whether national or international. In this context, we merely note that a 'homosexual' identity was created by religion, the law and the medical profession, to incriminate those with same sex desires. Yet in the post-war period, a new articulation of same-sex orientation – as gay and lesbian – formed a rallying point from which those with homosexual desires and their supporters could set out to change the world's conceptualizations of them. What all this indicates is not only the importance of ideas, but that ideas on their own are not enough: what is also required are the activists to put these ideas into action.

This Who's Who records the progress (in a chronological and, for many, moral sense) towards greater acceptance of gay men and lesbians as equal members of pluralistic societies since 1945. It also records examples of those whose careers and lives were destroyed by homophobia, whether of the past or present – those victimised by the political witch-hunts and sexual entrapment trials of the 1950s, those arrested for consensual relations with adult partners of the same sex into the 1990s, those who felt unable to come out of the closet as homosexuals in the 1950s and 1960s, and those stigmatised because they suffered from an illness viciously termed the 'gay plague' in the

1980s and 1990s. The lives profiled here are a reminder of how recently homosexual acts have been decriminalised in many parts of the Western world, and how insecure gay and lesbian human rights remain in numerous societies. The other side of the contestatory and affirmative 'gay pride' of marches and demonstrations and the jubilant social life of the post-World War II period is the story of the arrests and imprisonments, religious condemnations and attempted 'cures' for homosexuality, the physical and mental violence, exile and shame experienced by many, and the horror of AIDS. If few of the figures from the 1950s and 1960s who appear in this volume were not affected by homophobia – from jokes in school or workplace about 'sissy boys' or 'bull dykes', to raids on such meeting places as private parties or pubs and saunas – none from a later generation have not grieved for a friend or a lover who died prematurely; the number of entries which conclude by noting that a particular individual died from an AIDS-related illness is poignant testimony.

The editors faced a number of issues in putting together this *Who's Who*. One was the distribution of entries among various countries. Much of gay and lesbian history has been written about Western Europe and the United States. We have made an effort, in particular, to bring to the attention of English-speaking readers the biographies of many men and women from other non-English-speaking countries, and to give due attention to those from Australia, New Zealand, Canada and South Africa as well. (This *Who's Who*, however, does not include entries on people from non-Western societies other than Yukio Mishima.) We decided, after considerable consultation with women scholars, that an effort to achieve gender parity in this volume would be artificial, if not impossible; the amount of research done on male homosexuality, the criminalisation of homosexual acts between males (when lesbian sex was not illegal), and the greater public role of men in Western societies which remain patriarchal help explain the gender imbalance. Another important issue that this book had to negotiate was the balance between the living and the dead. Choosing which figures of the past to include was difficult enough, but the problem grew larger with the living. This is not linked so much with questions of defamation, or of the unrevealed homosexuality of some well-known figures, as to the question of whether 'fifteen minutes of fame' is enough reason for someone to be included. A hard-and-fast rule was impossible to formulate, and a case-by-case approach was necessary. This book is weighted to figures who have had a sustained or major presence on the public stage over the past fifty years, rather than those who have emerged into the spotlight in the last few moments. Many noteworthy (and sometimes notorious) people of the present instant may well become significant to a wider public or over a longer run, but, as historians, we feel that a rush to include every recent – and perhaps transitory – star would be ill-advised. Any attempt to provide an exhaustive coverage of every recognised figure of significance to contemporary lesbians and gay men in four continents and several other countries would be an impossible effort. We can only hope that more specialised directories – for example, of lesbian and gay writers – will provide material on worthy individuals whom space and a necessary and proper attention to balance among many countries and fields of endeavour make it impossible to include here.

This *Who's Who in Contemporary Gay and Lesbian History*, as we remarked in the earlier *Who's Who in Gay and Lesbian History: From Antiquity to World War II*, shows how much gay and lesbian history, including current history, there is to explore, how many individuals need to be brought to greater public attention, how many figures have not received appropriate full-length studies, how much archival work, primary research and empirical history remains to be done. Secondly, it also suggests how unfamiliar many of us are with the gay and lesbian history of such regions as Scandinavia, or the Iberian peninsula, or Australia, despite the significance and importance of a number of figures from those regions. Thirdly, it provides convincing evidence of the merits of biographical study as a lens through which to view the history of sexuality and gender, and the usefulness of studies of individuals as a way to see into entire historical milieux and epochs. Furthermore, such a compilation of material from different societies allows for interesting comparisons, and speculation as to what any similarities and differences might signify. Finally, it confirms the vitality of gay and lesbian studies throughout the Western world today.

Note: Those figures in the history of homosexuality who are most often associated with the period before World War II, or whose major activities of relevance occurred in the years before 1945, are included in a companion volume, *Who's Who in Gay and Lesbian History: From Antiquity to World War II*, even when they lived past 1945. Those who have come of age since the war, those whose major activities have occurred in the period since 1945, and living figures are included in the present volume. This division across two volumes has necessitated some difficult decisions, such as placing Auden and Spender in the first volume but placing their colleague Isherwood in the second volume, as Isherwood went on to write gay-relevant works into the second half of the twentieth century.

This work of reference covers figures who have had an impact upon gay and lesbian life throughout recent history, and not merely individuals who were or are themselves homosexual. Unless explicitly stated, no inferences should be made about subjects' sexual orientation.

Contributors

Stephen Bourne, London, United Kingdom

Roger Bowen, University of Arizona, United States

Jason Boyd, University of Toronto, Canada

Fiona Buckland, London, United Kingdom

Peter Burton, London, United Kingdom

Lucille Cairns, University of Stirling, United Kingdom

Andrea Capovilla, Oxford University, United Kingdom

Chistopher Capozzola, Columbia University, United States

Adam Carr, Melbourne, Australia

Susana Chavez Silverman, Pomona College, United States

Vitaly Chernetsky, Columbia University, United States

Joseph Chetcuti, Melbourne, Australia

Beate Lønne Christiansen, Oslo, Norway

John Connell, University of Sydney, Australia

Ken Davis, Sydney, Australia

Dennis Denisoff, University of Waterloo, Canada

Karen Duder, University of Victoria, Canada

Ianthe Duende, London, United Kingdom

Mattias Duyves, Amsterdam, The Netherlands

Wayne R. Dynes, Hunter College, City University of New York, United States

Karin Enderud, Oslo, Norway

C. Faro, University of Sydney, Australia

Maureen FitzGerald, University of Toronto, Canada

Ruth Ford, La Trobe University, Australia

Krzysztof Fordoński, Adam Mickiewicz University, Poznań, Poland

Barbara M. Freeman, Carleton University, Canada

Jan Olav Gatland, University of Bergen, Norway

Franceso Gnerre, Rome, Italy

Ken Gonzales-Day, Scripps College, United States

Laurent de Graeve, Brussels, Belgium

Haukur F. Hannesson, Gavle, Sweden

Melissa Hardie, University of Sydney, Australia

Linda Heidenreich, University of California, San Diego, United States

Jörg Heinke, University of Kiel, Germany

Michael Hendricks, Toronto, Canada

David Hilliard, Flinders University, Australia

John Howard, University of York, United Kingdom

Keith Howes, Sydney, Australia

Susan Humphries, University of Sydney, Australia

Olivier Jablonski, Paris, France

Nancy Johnston, Ryerson Polytechnic University, Canada

James W. Jones, Central Michigan University, United States

Tuula Juvonen, University of Tampere, Finland

Marita Keilson-Lauritz, Bussum, The Netherlands

Lasse Kekki, University of Turku, Finland

Hubert Kennedy, San Francisco State University, United States

Pirkko Koski, University of Helsinki, Finland

Laurie Kruk, Nipissing University, Canada

Alice A. Kuzniar, University of North Carolina, Chapel Hill, United States

Roger Leong, National Gallery of Australia, Canberra

Andrew Lesk, University of Montreal, Canada

Margareta Lindholm, Gothenburg University, Sweden

Svend Erik Løken Larsen, Oslo, Norway

Karin Lützen, University of Roskilde, Denmark

Ian Maidment, Adelaide, Australia

Robert K. Martin, University of Montreal, Canada

William Martin, University of Texas, Austin, United States

Elena M. Martinez, Baruch College, City University of New York, United States

Alfredo Martínez Expósito, University of Queensland, Australia

Donald W. McLeod, Canadian Lesbian and Gay Archives, Canada

Martin Meeker, San Francisco State University, United States

Kevin Moss, Middlebury College, United States

Michael J. Murphy, Washington University, United States

Stephen O. Murray, San Francisco, United States

Trent Newmeyer, University of Toronto, Canada

Juliet Nicolet, McGill University, Canada

Lisbeth Nilsen, Oslo, Norway

Salvador A. Oropesa, Kansas State University, United States

Karen Lee Osborne, Columbia College of Chicago, United States

Annette Oxindine, Wright State University, United States

Johanna Pakkanen, University of Tampere, Finland

David Parris, Trinity College, Dublin, Ireland

Kate Pearcy, University of Sydney, Australia

Aleš Pečnik, Ljubljana, Slovenia

David L. Phillips, University of Western Sydney, Australia

George Piggford, Tufts University, United States

Gerald Pilz, Korwestheim, Germany

Ryan Prout, Oxford University, United Kingdom

Robert Pryde, Sydney, Australia

Neil A. Radford, Sydney, Australia

Tim Reeves, Canberra, Australia

Graeme Reid, University of the Witwatersrand, South Africa

Adrian Renzo, University of Western Sydney, Australia

Miriam Reumann, Brown University, United States

Philippe-Joseph Salazar, University of Cape Town, South Africa

Carlos Schröder, Washington, United States

Juan Antonio Serna, Rockford College, United States

Mark Seymour, Trinity College, Rome, Italy

Charley Shively, University of Massachusetts, Boston, United States

Gary Simes, University of Sydney, Australia

Graeme Skinner, Sydney, Australia

William J. Spurlin, Columbia University, United States

Marja Suhonen, University of Helsinki, Finland

Gerard Sullivan, University of Sydney, Australia

Ira Tattelman, Washington, United States

Susan Taylor, Dunedin, New Zealand

Deborah Thomas, Nelson Muncipal Library, British Columbia, Canada

Nancy C. Unger, Santa Clara University, United States

Helen Waite, Central Queensland University, Australia

Shelton Waldrep, University of Southern Maine, United States

Hans Warmerdam, Amsterdam, The Netherlands

A. M. Wentink, Middlebury College, United States

David West, Australian National University, Australia

Graham Willett, University of Melbourne, Australia

Carolyn Williams, University of Technology, Sydney, Australia

Elizabeth A. Wilson, University of Sydney, Australia

Michael Wooliscroft, University of Otago, New Zealand

Garry Wotherspoon, University of Sydney, Australia

Timothy Yap, Toronto, Canada

Acknowledgements

We would like to thank, at Routledge, Kieron Corless for having suggested this volume, and Roger Thorp, Kate Chenevix Trench and Hywel Evans, who encouraged us through the work and saw the book to publication. Our Editorial Advisers, in addition to writing a large number of entries themselves, have provided regular counsel on which figures ought to be included here, helped us locate contributors, and aided greatly in sorting out questions about the appropriate balance between various countries, periods and domains of activity. A particular word of thanks should go to Wilhelm von Rosen for helping us to put together a group of Nordic entries and contributors and to David William Foster for advising us on Latin American entries. Henny Brandhorst at Homodok in Amsterdam helped line up writers and entries on the Low Countries, and Vicki Feaklor, in the United States, kindly circulated our draft lists and appeals for contributions through the e-mail list of the Committee on Gay and Lesbian History. The contributors themselves have written entries which, while confined by strict word limits, often provide small-scale essays not just on the individuals about whom they have written but on general historical contexts. Many contributors have willingly taken on extra entries at our request – sometimes when other authors, alas, did not come through with the pieces they promised – and we are most grateful.

Robert Aldrich translated entries by Giovanni Dall'Orto and Laurent de Graeve, Mark Seymour translated those by Francesco Guerre, and Michael Sibalis translated the one by Olivier Jablonski.

Jonathan Cape has given permission for a quotation from *Patrick White: A Life* by David Marr. Julie Manley, at the start of this project, and Ruth Williams, during the last stages of editing, provided truly invaluable secretarial assistance, and cheerfully and efficiently handled various versions of entries, countless changes made while we edited them, and a constantly evolving list of contributors and entries. Patrick Ferry kindly helped in checking and collating the manuscript.

A

Abba, Swedish pop group. Unleashed on to an unsuspecting world by the Eurovision Song Contest in 1974, the Swedish group Abba became one of the most enduring of the 1970s pop sensations. Garbed in a glam-trash 1970s aesthetic, with a long list of eminently singable tunes, they acquired a cult following among gays and lesbians which both pre-dated and outlived their mass appeal.

Formed in Stockholm in 1972, the group consisted of Agnetha Faltskog, Anni-Frid Lyngstad, Bjorn Ulvaeus and Benny Andersson. Despite some early chart success, it was really the 1974 hit 'Waterloo' that propelled them to European prominence. By the late 1970s the Abba sound had reached a worldwide audience with hits such as 'Money, Money, Money' and 'The Name of the Game'.

In many ways the initial appeal of the group to gay audiences derived from the sheer straitlaced image projected by the foursome. The quintessential boys-and-girls-next-door, they were so straight they were camp!

However, two Abba songs more than any others also endeared the group to gay audiences: 'Dancing Queen' and 'Gimme! Gimme! Gimme! (A Man after Midnight)'. To the general bewilderment of the group, these songs quickly became disco anthems amongst gay audiences, their lyrics playfully subverted into paeans of sexual marginality and freedom. Meanwhile the Abba aesthetic – with its glitzy 1970s sheen, elaborate costuming, and liberal application of blue eye-shadow – has been gleefully appropriated (and satirised) by many a drag queen.

The Australian movie *The Adventures of Priscilla, Queen of the Desert* (1994) riotously captured the gay cult of Abba, and ushered in a huge revival of interest in the group.

Peter Gammond, *The Oxford Companion to Popular Music* (Oxford, 1991); *Contemporary Musicians*, vol. 12 (Detroit, 1994).

C. Faro

Abse, Leo (b. 1917), British politician and law reformer. Abse was born in Cardiff, the son of a Jewish solicitor. He served in the RAF during World War II and became a lawyer himself. In 1958 he became Labour MP for the safe Welsh mining seat of Pontypool. Abse saw himself as a crusader for liberal reforms. He worked for abolition of the death penalty, reform of the laws relating to suicide, adoption, vasectomy and divorce, and for prison reform. He remained, however, violently opposed to abortion.

The year before Abse's arrival in Parliament the WOLFENDEN Report had recommended the decriminalisation of consenting sex between adult males in private. Abse, whose brother was a psychiatrist, took a strict Freudian view of homosexuality: that it was an unfortunate disorder caused by a hostile father and dominant mother. This enabled him to support homosexual law reform while generally disliking and disapproving of homosexuality. Married with two children, and fond of the publicity that came with associating himself with unpopular causes, he was well positioned to take up the case for law reform in the House of Commons.

In 1960 Labour MP Kenneth Robinson had moved a motion calling on the government to implement the Wolfenden Report's recommendation. He was supported by, among others, Margaret THATCHER, Roy Jenkins, Tony Benn, Enoch Powell, Keith Joseph and Barbara Castle, by the majority of Labour and Liberal members, and by younger and better-educated members generally, but the motion was defeated by the conservative mass of Tory backbenchers. The party leaders on both sides remained silent. Nevertheless this debate set the stage for the long campaign to repeal Britain's anti-homosexual laws.

In March 1962 Abse moved the first of his private member's bills on the subject. This would not have led to full decriminalisation, but would have required all prosecutions to be approved in advance by the Director of Public Prosecutions, would have required offences to be prosecuted within twelve months of their commission, and would have required a psychiatric report before sentencing in all cases. These proposals were intended to curb the zeal of homophobic chief constables and introduce uniformity in prosecutions: in practice they would have greatly reduced the number of prosecutions. The bill was 'talked out' by Tory backbenchers led by Sir Cyril Osborne.

The issue then lapsed for three years, despite the campaigning efforts of the Homosexual Law Reform Society, the Albany Trust and a galaxy of supporters from the universities, the press, the churches and the arts. The problem was not marshalling parliamentary numbers but securing parliamentary time, since the Conservative government controlled the House of Commons timetable. No such problem existed in the House of Lords, and in 1965 the Earl of Arran, an eccentric Scottish peer whose homosexual elder brother had died tragically after being committed by his family, moved a private peer's bill which was passed after a prolonged debate. The real importance of the Lords debate was that the Archbishop of Canterbury, Michael Ramsay, took the opportunity to announce his support for reform.

By 1965 there was a Labour government and a number of Cabinet ministers, notably Roy Jenkins, were determined to move the issue forward, although Prime Minister Harold Wilson, a Yorkshire puritan, was unsympathetic. In February 1966 a Conservative MP, Humphrey Berkeley, moved a private member's bill which passed the second reading stage by 164 to 107, but which lapsed when the 1966 election – at which Berkeley lost his seat – intervened. In April 1966 Arran tried again in the Lords and again gained support for his bill. The 1966 election gave Labour a large majority, bringing in a flood of younger and more liberal MPs, making the passage of a bill in the next Parliament a near certainty.

In July 1966 Abse brought in another bill, drafted by the Home Office under instructions from Jenkins. Abse's crucial contribution was to persuade John Silkin, the government whip, to allow parliamentary time. Abse's bill set an age of consent of 21 and provided severe penalties for sex with persons under that age. This, Abse noted, 'aroused anger among supporters of the Homosexual Reform Society, who considered 21 far too high an age: but I would not accommodate them, both because I was unconvinced they were right and for tactical reasons'. Abse's bill was carried on the first reading by 244 to 100, with 70 Tories and 30 Labour MPs opposed. The second reading passed by 194 to 84. Thereafter parliamentary opposition faded and the bill became law in July 1967.

Paradoxically, Abse's views on homosexuality were backward even by the standards of the 1960s. He supported decriminalisation in the hope that this would allow 'a diminution in the incidence of homosexuality' through better education and support for fatherless boys, whom he believed were the most likely to fall victim to 'the curse, for such it must be, of a male body encasing a feminine soul'.

Despite his good works on a variety of subjects, Abse stayed on the backbenches until his retirement in 1987.

Leo Abse, *Private Member* (London, 1973); Patrick Higgins, *Heterosexual Dictatorship: Male Homosexuality in Post-War Britain* (London, 1996).

Adam Carr

Abzug, Bella (Savitsky) (1920–98), American politician and activist. Born in New York City to Russian Jewish immigrant parents, Abzug was educated in New York public schools and at Hunter College, where she graduated in 1942 as president of the student council. She then entered Columbia University Law School, dropping out during World War II to work in a shipbuilding factory. Returning to law school after marrying stockbroker Martin Abzug, she graduated in 1947 and began to specialise in labour law. She did *pro bono* work for the American Civil Liberties Union and defended individuals accused of subversive activities. Often dismissed or ignored because of her sex, Abzug began wearing flamboyant hats, a signature style that increased her visibility and public notoriety.

In the early 1960s, Abzug was active in the peace and women's movements. She helped form Women Strike for Peace in 1961, served as its Legislative Director from 1961 to 1970, and worked closely with Senator Eugene McCarthy's 1968 anti-war campaign for the US presidency.

In 1970, Abzug, a Democrat, was elected to represent New York's ethnically diverse 19th District in Congress. Abzug actively included women in her campaign, offering day care at her headquarters so that mothers could work on her behalf. In the House, Abzug challenged the chamber's complex seniority system, led the House peace movement (introducing on her first day in the House a resolution calling for the removal of all US troops from South Vietnam), opposed the draft, supported women's rights legislation (including the Equal Rights Amendment), and helped write the Freedom of Information Act. Abzug served three terms in the House, narrowly losing the 1976 Democratic Senate primary to Daniel Patrick Moynihan and the 1977 New York City mayoral primary to Edward I. Koch.

Abzug was a leading supporter of equal rights for gay and lesbian people. As early as 1971, she had made public statements of support for gay rights at a New York City hearing, and Abzug and twenty-three co-sponsors introduced H.R. 5452, known as the Civil Rights Amendments of 1975, the first proposed national gay rights legislation in American history. The bill aimed to extend the protections of the Civil Rights Act of 1964 and the Educational Amendments of 1972 to end discrimination on the basis of 'affectional or sexual preference'. The bill failed to pass, but has been reintroduced in every session of Congress since then.

Although Abzug's electoral defeats were more numerous than her victories and her legislative accomplishments were few, she wielded a great deal of influence among legislators, within social movements for peace and gender equality, within the Democratic Party and in New York City politics. Her high profile, long-time commitment to social justice, and safe position in a very liberal constituency allowed Abzug to raise gay and lesbian equality as an issue when few other political leaders were willing or able to do so.

Bella Abzug, 'Seeks Equal Protection',

Congressional Record, vol. 121, pt. 7 (25 March 1975), pp. 8581–2; Bella Abzug with Mim Kelber, *Gender Gap: Bella Abzug's Guide to Political Power for American Women* (Boston, 1984); Doris Faber, *Bella Abzug* (New York, 1976); Mel Ziegler (ed.), *Bella!* (New York, 1972).

Christopher Capozzola

Achmat, Zackie (b. 1961), South African writer, filmmaker and activist. Born in Fietas/Vrededorp in Johannesburg, Achmat grew up in Salt River, Cape Town, in a conservative Muslim family. As told in his autobiographical story *My Childhood as an Adult Molester*, he abandoned the *madrassa* and Islam at age ten, and began toilet sex with older white men. He was arrested in student riots following the 1976 Soweto rebellion and was later active in underground Trotskyist organisations. From the mid-1990s he was a key advocate for the rights of people with HIV through the University of Witwatersrand-based AIDS Law Project and the National AIDS Convention of South Africa (NACOSA). He has made several films including *Scorpion under a Stone* (1996), which reframes the history of the Afrikaans language, *Gay Life is Best*, and *Die Duiwel Maak My Hart So Seer* (1993). In 1994 he became a founding leader of the National Coalition for Gay and Lesbian Equality, and was a key figure in the inclusion and retention of sexual orientation in the equality clauses of the Bill of Rights in the Constitution of 1994, the subsequent striking down of the anti-sodomy laws, and the recognition of same-sex couples in immigration regulations. He publicly announced his HIV-positive status in mid-1998, and became a key activist in the campaign to make HIV treatments available in South Africa.

Ken Davis

Ackerley, J(oe) R(andolph) (1896–1967), British writer. Born in London, the second son of Roger and Netta, brother to Nancy Ackerley, his father was a prosperous businessman, his mother an actress. The family was peculiar in more than one respect. Roger and Netta did not marry until 1919. Netta was a depressed hypochondriac, his father a *bon vivant* away from home a good deal on business and pleasure. Ackerley discovered after his father's death that one of those pleasures was a second family – he had two half-sisters – that his father had established soon after he settled down with Netta. During World War I, his brother Peter was killed and Ackerley himself was wounded and taken prisoner; his experience became the basis for his first foray into literature, his only play, *The Prisoners of War* (1925). It was an artistic but not financial success. While there are no explicit homosexual references in the play, it was obvious that two of the prisoners were homosexuals, one of the earliest unapologetic presentations of gay men on the English stage. The play influenced other gay writers like Siegfried Sassoon and especially E. M. Forster, who wrote a note of admiration to the author. Thus began their life-long friendship, one of the most important relationships for both men. Forster arranged for Ackerley to go to India as a secretary to a rich maharajah who was flagrantly homosexual. That experience was recorded as *Hindoo Holiday: An Indian Journal* (1932).

Ackerley was the literary editor of *The Listener* between 1935 and 1959 and turned his section of the magazine into one of the most prestigious and intellectual voices in book reviewing, soliciting work from every important writer of the time, from T. S. Eliot to W. H. Auden. But the demands of his position kept Ackerley from writing much himself. He wrote a remarkable memoir about his dog Queenie which he called *My Dog Tulip: Life with an Alsatian* (1956) and a novelisation of the same material, *We Think the World of You* (1960). His masterpiece, the autobiography *My Father and Myself* (1968), was published posthumously, as were his letters (1975) and his diaries (1982).

The memoir about his father was begun

thirty years before its publication, but he delayed its public appearance because it was both too intimate and too bold. The book is regarded as one of the best examples of modern autobiography. In it, Ackerley details his own homsexual life, one beset with disappointment and unhappiness, as well as the astonishing life of his father, which he reconstructs to tell the story of both of Roger Ackerley's marriages as well as his experience as a male prostitute when he was a young man in the Guards. The book is a unique exploration of the journey towards self-discovery of a talented, handsome homosexual at a time when most gay men were constrained if not silenced on the subject, a document about gay life when closetry caused gay men and women much pain personally and professionally.

Peter Parker, *Ackerley: The Life of J. R. Ackerley* (London, 1989).

Seymour Kleinberg

Adam, Barry (b. 1952), Canadian academic and activist. Teaching sociology at the University of Windsor (Ontario) since 1976, Adam has been a pioneer in the comparative analysis of lesbian/gay political movements, and prominent in developing networks among sexual minority academics in Canada and the United States.

Adam is well known internationally as one of the very few social scientists to examine lesbian/gay/bisexual/transgendered movements cross-nationally. He first established a significant profile by writing *The Rise of a Gay and Lesbian Movement* (1987, rev. edn 1995), a wide-ranging and widely cited analysis of oppression and activist response in Europe and North America from the early twentieth century to the present. More recently, he has edited an important collection of original essays on gay activism in a variety of countries – *The Global Emergence of Gay and Lesbian Politics* (1998). He has also authored significant articles on AIDS

activism, social-movement theory and other topics.

Adam's activism dates from 1970, when he was a member of Vancouver's Gay Liberation Front. In 1976, he was a founding member of the American Sociological Association's Gay Caucus (now Lesbian, Gay, Bisexual, Transgender Caucus). He was a key member of the founding committee of the Canadian Lesbian and Gay Studies Association, and has served as its president. He was also a founding member and first president of Windsor's AIDS Committee.

Janice L. Ristock and Catherine G. Taylor (eds), *Inside the Academy and Out: Lesbian/Gay/Queer Studies and Social Action* (Toronto, 1998).

David Rayside

Aggleton, Peter (b. 1952), British gay health educator and co-editor of the *Social Aspects of AIDS* series of books and of the journal *Culture, Health and Sexuality*. Aggleton is Professor of Education and Director of the Thomas Coram Research Unit at the Institute of Education, University of London.

HIV/AIDS is a very modern disease which has produced a response appropriate for the times in which it has emerged. It is a disease which has transcended the traditional medical barriers of an epidemic, and particular attention has been placed on the non-medical aspects of the disease. For instance, many social and political issues associated with the disease have been highlighted, particularly as these relate to attempts to contain the spread of the virus. Thus, the epidemic has spawned an industry beyond the scientific and medical communities. Each polity has produced a group of non-medical experts and commentators relevant to their respective needs – in many fields there has been extensive international collaboration in these non-medical aspects of AIDS.

An example of this international collaboration can be found in the work of

Peter Aggleton in his role as editor of the book series *The Social Aspects of AIDS*, published by Taylor and Francis. Aggleton's involvement with HIV/AIDS commenced with the development of AIDS-related health-education materials at the former Bristol Polytechnic (University of the West of England) in the 1980s. Aggleton has worked internationally in HIV/AIDS health promotion and provides technical support for research projects in developing nations under the United Nations AIDS Organisation (UNAIDS). He was Chief of the Social and Behavioural Studies and Support Unit within the World Health Organisation's former Global Programme on AIDS between 1992 and 1994.

Scientific American (March 1991), p. 96; *The Australian* (9 September 1998), p. 15; V. Berridge, *AIDS in the UK* (Oxford, 1996).

Mark Edwards

Al Berto (1948–97), Portuguese poet. Al Berto, whose real name was Alberto Pidwell Tavares, was born in the university city of Coimbra but soon moved to the coastal town of Sines, south of Lisbon, where he grew up and to which he returned in later life. He attended art school in Lisbon but in 1967 he left Portugal and went into self-imposed exile in Belgium, where he continued his art education. In 1971 he finally gave up the idea of becoming a painter and turned to writing. He returned to Portugal in 1975, following the redemocratisation of the country, and worked as a cultural outreach worker, writer and publisher, dividing his time between Lisbon and Sines. During the 1980s he published a series of books of poetry and was recognised as one of the major poets of the decade. A collected edition of his works was first published in 1986 under the title *O Medo* (*Fear*). Subsequent editions with the same title included later poems. He died of AIDS.

During the course of Al Berto's lifetime, Sines was transformed from a small fishing harbour to a major oil terminal and petrochemical industrial complex. Images of the sea, nature and, occasionally, pipelines, together with a concern for ecology, are important elements in his poetry. He also retained a strong interest in the visual arts from his early training. One of his most successful books was *A Secreta Vida das Imagens* (*The Secret Life of Images*, 1991), a series of poems inspired by famous paintings, which has been translated into English and French.

Al Berto was completely out as a gay man, discussing his sexuality in interviews and incorporating references to the gay experience in his poetry. His early works, published in the aftermath of the Revolution of 1974 which swept away the repressive authoritarian regime which had ruled Portugal for fifty years, are essentially poems in prose, incorporating an aggressively explicit sexual imagery and a marked physicality. His poetry of the 1980s, notably *Trabalhos do Olhar* (*Works of Gazing*, 1982) and *Salsugem* (*Saltiness*, 1984), is more relaxed, conveying the excitement of nocturnal cruising and casual encounters or delicately evoking nostalgia for a lost love. Some of Al Berto's poems are suffused with images of great beauty drawn from nature while others aim to shock through their sordid associations. A few key words such as 'sperm' and 'semen' come to symbolise sexual experience and are made to stand for a whole complex of feelings and experience. Although the homosexual context is clear, the experiences described seem to apply to sex in general. While many poems are upbeat and use positive or sensual images, others are imbued with pessimism, evoking an excess of sex which leads to a sense of loss, self-disgust and a preoccupation with death. His last work, *Horto de Incêndio* (*Garden of Fire*, 1997), published the year he died, is more resigned.

Al Berto is best known as a poet but he also wrote a novel, *Lunário* (*Lunar Calendar*, 1988). This work, which appears to be influenced by the author's experience of living in Belgium, is an existentialist novel in which the hero, Beno, moves from one unidentifed snow-bound city to another, living in a world of enclosed rooms, nightclubs, smoking marijuana and having sexual experiences. In sometimes poetic language, the novel describes Beno's relationships with a man, Nému, a woman, Alba, and other characters.

Al Berto was one of a number of Portuguese poets whose writing came to maturity in the years after 1960 and who have incorporated homoerotic themes into their works. These include Armando da Silva Carvalho (b. 1938), João Miguel Fernandes Jorge (b. 1943), Gastão Cruz (b. 1941) and Luís Miguel Nava (1957–95).

Al Berto, Interview in *Ler/Livros & Leitores*, no. 5 (Inverno 1989), pp. 12–15; Álvaro Manuel Machado (ed.), *Dicionário de Literatura Portuguesa* (Lisbon, 1996); Fernando Pinto do Amaral, *O Mosaico Fluido: Modernidade e Pós-Modernidade na Poesia Portuguesa Mais Recente* (Lisbon, 1991).

Robert Howes

Aleixandre, Vicente (1898–1984), Spanish poet. Assessment of the work of Nobel Prize-winning poet Vicente Aleixandre is a pending issue in Spanish literary criticism. His poems are often obscure, filled with violent, organic imagery organised in vivid surrealist compositions; his biography (at least in its official version) is not particularly helpful in attempting to give a meaning to his poetic work. Biographical and literary studies are filled with personal testimonies that seem to emphasise a fairly uneventful life. As one of the members of a left-leaning generation of Spanish poets who not only survived Francoism but decided to stay in Spain after the Civil War, he seems to have decided to go into an 'inner' exile. Increasingly tolerated by the authorities, he seems not to have had a public life at all. Yet he often welcomed young poets and critics into his residence, and shared with them experiences, opinions

and advice. And in a deep misunderstanding of the meaning of the whole issue of 'respect', critics have aggressively defended Aleixandre, even after his death, from prying eyes and attempts to discuss the poet's sexual identity. There are at least two honourable exceptions, namely the poet Luis Antonio de VILLENA and Vicente Molina FOIX, a journalist, a novelist and a playwright, who knew Aleixandre personally. They have insisted that the issue of sexual identity was a delicate matter with him (he stopped short of identifying himself as a homosexual) but nevertheless that he did not make a secret of (and he was not embarrassed by) the fact that his sexual orientation was mostly homoerotic. He did discuss homosexuality openly and was among the very few Spanish intellectuals who did not hesitate in emphasising that Lorca's homosexuality was central to a full understanding of his work.

Aleixandre was among the very few representatives of Spanish surrealism in the 1920s, as shown by his *Pasión de la tierra* (1935). He was acquainted with other homosexual or bisexual poets such as García Lorca, Emilio Prados and Luis CERNUDA. Cernuda, as close to an 'out gay man' as existed at the time, seems to have had little patience with Aleixandre's attempts to cover his sexual orientation with a veil of mystery, and this may indeed be one of the interpretive keys to his work. He spent the Civil War on Republican soil. His poor health prevented him from going into exile after Franco settled in power, and from 1944 he was slowly rehabilitated by the regime. He became a member of the Real Academia de la Lengua (Spain's top cultural institution for issues concerning language) in 1950. During this period, he developed a network of friends and acquaintants who benefited from his knowledge. Many of the poets and critics seem to have been homosexual, and one may safely guess that it is not just Aleixandre's own closet that is being preserved when his sexual orientation is silenced. A reliable and un-censored edition of his correspondence should shed light on the issue. Among his friends was the leading literary critic and poet Carlos Bousoño. Between master and pupil there seems to have developed a strongly emotional relationship, later reflected in Bousoño's poems. After the Francoist era, Aleixandre was awarded the Nobel Prize in 1977, maybe a belated recognition for the work of the poetic 'Generation of '27', to which he belonged, scattered by exile after the war or killed off by the fascists. Among his later works, *Diálogos del conocimiento* (1973) contains probably the only clear expressions of homoeroticism in Aleixandre's work.

Vicente Aleixandre, *Antología total* (Barcelona, 1975); Carlos Bousoño, *La poesía de Vicente Aleixandre* (Madrid, 1977); José Luis Cano, *Vicente Aleixandre* (Madrid, 1977); Luis Antonio de Villena (ed.), *Vicente Aleixandre: Pasión de la tierra* (Madrid, 1977).

Alberto Mira

Aliaga, Juan Vicente (b. 1959), Spanish critic. Critical theory and gender-based criticism have not found much favour in Spanish academia until very recently. Partly this has to do with a certain resistance to change quite noticeable in the arts departments of universities (there are, of course, exceptions), but there is also a certain prejudice in society at large as to whether 'gender' issues are 'political'. A new generation of critics needed to overcome such inertia in order to produce criticism that showed awareness of theoretical developments abroad: given that resistance in Spain extends to any open discussion of homosexuality, Anglo-American criticism could be a starting point by providing a discursive frame that was not being produced by Spanish intellectuals. It is a complex balancing act: obviously, the transfer of concepts created to account for homosexuality in one culture is not always possible, and the accusation of cultural colonialism is frequent.

Juan Vicente Aliaga is one of the young Spanish critics who have rigorously introduced awareness of new discursive readings of sexuality, inspired by Michel FOUCAULT and Judith BUTLER and, to a lesser extent, the work of Eve Kosofsky SEDGWICK, Jonathan DOLLIMORE or Leo Bersani. Other important figures in this still budding panorama include José Miguel García Cortés (a university lecturer and essayist who has worked with Aliaga in several projects), Ricardo Llamas (a sociologist who has published a collection of articles on homosexuality in the media called *Miss Media* and edited a volume on the cultural politics of AIDS), Fefa Vila (among the very few out lesbian critics in Spain, she has carried out valuable research on the history of the Spanish gay movement) and Xosé M. Buxán (who organised one of the first lesbian and gay studies conferences, at Vigo University in 1995). All of them introduce a strongly political element to their work. Aliaga is probably the best known among these critics and he has often worked to strengthen the network that connects them. His ability to straddle several disciplines and his skills in bringing people together give him a special relevance.

The son of a Spanish migrant domestic worker, he spent part of his childhood in Paris, a city that became very important both personally and professionally and where he spent long periods during the 1990s, often to carry out work on authors such as Bataille, GENET and Artaud. He is a graduate in art history from the University of Valencia, and during his years as a student he was active in an extreme left (Troskyist) political movement. These were the years of the Spanish transition, which on some fronts was probably less smooth than is now acknowledged. Troskyists at the time were the only left-leaning party to accept homosexuality, and Aliaga had occasion to experience incomprehension and homophobia from the left. During the mid-1980s, for two years he held a lectureship in Spanish at Oxford

University. These were years of learning and establishing contacts with the British artistic milieu. He became acquainted with the work of Jeffrey WEEKS, Guy HOCQUENGHEM and other gay critics, and travelled extensively, getting to know the work of several contemporary artists who had so far been ignored in his country. It was about that time that he started publishing art criticism for several national and international publications, such as *Artforum* (New York), *Art press* (Paris) or *Lápiz* (Madrid). On returning to Spain, he gained a position as a lecturer in art theory in the Valencian Faculty of Fine Arts, where he still teaches. Among his most important influences, he quotes the work of Georges Bataille.

Although his work was always theoretically informed, it was the onset of AIDS and the silence on the topic in Spain that meant a turning point in his career. Together with García Cortés, who worked at the same institution, he edited and wrote a number of contributions for *De amor y rabia* (1993), one of the earliest examples of the culturalist approach to AIDS attempted in Spain. The book included an essay on the work of the artist Pepe ESPALIU, Aliaga's close friend, who died of AIDS-related illnesses that year. *De amor y rabia* was a necessary book, and Aliaga realized the need to raise awareness on the topic. The exhibitions he curated in the following years also did much to break taboos on sexuality and make homosexuality visible as an artistic position. A selection of his gender-oriented criticism can be found in *Bajo vientre* (1998), where he brings to the general reader's attention the work of young artists such as Jesús Martínez Oliva and Alex Francés, who take risks in their artistic exploration of dissident sexualities. This book caused bitter polemics both because of the topic and the images it contained. In 1997 he published, again with Cortés, *Identidad y diferencia*, one of the earliest attempts to discuss the specificity of homosexuality, as a lifestyle and representation, in Spain. The book

includes a discussion with several representatives of the Spanish gay movement and intellectual world.

Juan Vicente Aliaga and José Miguel García Cortés, *De amor y rabia* (Valencia, 1993), and *Identidad y diferencia* (Madrid, 1997); Xosé Buxán (ed.), *ConCIENCIA de un singular deseo* (Barcelona, 1997); Ricardo Llamas, *Miss Media* (Barcelona, 1997).

Alberto Mira

Allen, Paula Gunn (b. 1939), American writer and scholar. Born in Cubero, New Mexico, Allen grew up near the Laguna Pueblo reservation. She is of Laguna/ Pueblo, Sioux and Lebanese descent and is a prominent scholar of Native American literature. Her 1986 collection of essays, *The Sacred Hoop: Recovering the Feminine in American Indian Traditions*, is a landmark study that has influenced many scholars and teachers; a new edition was published in 1992. Another groundbreaking work was *Studies in American Indian Literature: Critical Essays and Course Designs* (1983). She has also edited anthologies featuring her own lively introductions to the work of other Native American writers as well as her feminist perspective on Native American traditions. In *Grandmothers of the Light: A Medicine Woman's Sourcebook* (1991), she retells goddess stories from several Native American traditions and discusses the importance of these stories, often emphasising a respect for the feminine principle as central to the earth's spiritual and physical survival. Her other anthologies are *Spider Woman's Granddaughters: Traditional Tales and Contemporary Writing by Native American Women* (1989); *Voice of the Turtle: American Indian Literature, 1900–1970* (1994); and *Song of the Turtle: American Indian Fiction, 1974–1994* (1995).

Allen was married and had three children before she came out as a lesbian during the 1970s, the same period during which she began to publish poetry. She acknowledges Judy GRAHN, her former partner, as an influence on her work. Her poetry collections include *The Blind Lion* (1974); *Shadow Country* (1982); *Skins and Bones: Poems 1979–1987*; and *Life Is a Fatal Disease: Selected Poems 1964–1994*. In poems such as 'He Na Tye Woman' and 'Transitions' in *Shadow Country*, Allen, according to Grahn, writes of 'her coming out into a consciousness of the possible bonds and beauty, the possible love and wisdom, of all women'. Allen also published a lesbian novel, *The Woman Who Owned the Shadows* (1983). Like many novels written by Native Americans, it experiments with narrative form and challenges conventions such as linear time. The novel explores different aspects of Indian, female and lesbian identity: like those of Mohawk author Beth Bryant, her Indian heroines often must negotiate identity through their multiple subjectivities.

Allen has received various awards and grants. She received her Ph.D. from the University of New Mexico and has taught at several universities, including the University of California, Los Angeles, where until recently she was a Professor of Literature.

Joseph Bruchac, *Survival This Way: Interviews with American Indian Poets* (Tucson, AZ, 1990); Judy Grahn, *The Highest Apple: Sappho and the Lesbian Poetic Tradition* (San Francisco, 1985): Annette Van Dyke, 'The Journey Back to Female Roots: A Laguna Pueblo Model', in Karla Jay and Joanne Glasgow (eds), *Lesbian Texts and Contexts: Radical Revisions*, (New York, 1990) pp. 339–54.

Karen Lee Osborne

Allen, Peter (1944–92), Australian singer and songwriter. Born Peter Woolnough and growing up, gregarious yet guarded, in Armidale, an Australian country town, he and his friend Chris Bell formed The Allen Brothers and became highly successful singers on television. While on tour in Hong Kong in 1964, he met Judy Garland, who saw in him both great potential and a possible boyfriend for her daughter, Liza Minnelli. He married Minnelli in 1967, soon thereafter resuming having sex with men.

In the 1970s Allen's song-writing was parlayed into a nightclub and concert act which involved two parts romantic ballads with one part high octane camp. Styling himself with Panama hat, Hawaiian shirt and white linen suit, he gradually emerged as the one true star of the 1970s cabaret revival in America. His own early albums met with muted appreciation but, with Jeff Barry, he had an international hit with 'I Honestly Love You', sung by his compatriot Olivia Newton-John.

'I was out on stage before anyone else,' he would later claim, but his teasing Liberace-style stage persona and evasiveness in speaking and singing about his sexuality did not endear him overmuch to gay critics or audiences. Neither was he accepted as a mainstream leading man, being labelled too camp and unmanly. 'Too straight for the gays and too gay for the straights,' he concluded.

The more perceptive realised that Allen possessed a beguiling and sometimes sublime song-writing gift ('Don't Cry Out Loud' with Carole Bayer Sager; 'Tenterfield Saddler', 'Once Before I Go'), as well as blasting away with blowsy numbers like his signature 'I Go To Rio' (with Adrienne Anderson). However, it was on concert and nightclub stages that he achieved popular acclaim; he was possibly the only performer of the last half century to pack Radio City and Carnegie Hall without exposure on television or in films or singing Top Ten hits. Allen returned fairly frequently to Australia, and in 1980 debuted 'I Still Call Australia Home', now regarded by some as that country's true national anthem. The national airline Qantas used it for their advertising campaign.

When Gregory Connell, his partner since 1973, was diagnosed with HIV/AIDS, Allen worked ever more tirelessly until his own death from the disease in 1992. His dream of starring in a big

Broadway musical was realised, then shattered with the $7 million flop, *Legs Diamond*, in which Allen uneasily played a womanising gangster.

Celebrating all aspects of Allen's life – including a chastely handled gay relationship – the 1998 musical *The Boy from Oz* successfully gift-wrapped Australiana, family tragedy, the Garland/Minnelli connection, the Stonewall riots and AIDS with glitz, dynamic dancing and powerful songs. The show presented Allen as something more than a high-kicking campy tunesmith with a fey drawl who had once been Garland's son-in-law. 'In his own way', said Allen's biographer, 'he bridged four cultures: Australian with American, gay into straight'.

Stephen MacLean, *Peter Allen, The Boy from Oz* (New York, 1996).

                                        Keith Howes

Allison, Dorothy (b. 1949), American writer. Allison received popular and critical acclaim for *Bastard Out of Carolina* (1992), a novel which was nominated for the American National Book Award. This vivid and unsentimental novel is narrated by 'Bone' Boatwright, an illegitimate 13-year-old daughter, and recounts her life in an extended family and the trauma of incest and physical abuse. Much of this story of survival is a fictional reworking of Allison's own complicated biography. Allison grew up in Greenville, South Carolina, where she and her sisters suffered poverty, incest and abuse. In her own words, Allison suggests that this novel 'became, ultimately, the way to claim my family's pride and tragedy, and the embattled sexuality I fashioned on a base of violence and abuse'. The 1996 film, *Bastard Out of Carolina*, was adapted from a screenplay written by Allison and Ann Meredith, and marked the directorial debut of Anjelica Huston. The film, which was greeted with critical attention at international film festivals, became embroiled in a censorship debate when Ted

Turner, who financed the film, decided not to air *Bastard* on his television network because of its graphic subject matter.

Well before the publication of *Bastard Out of Carolina*, Allison was known to lesbian and feminist communities for her essays (collected in *Skin: Talking about Sex, Class and Literature*, 1994), her poetry (*The Women Who Hate Me*, 1983), and her short stories (*Trash*, 1988, which won her two Lambda Literary Awards for Best Small Press and Best Lesbian Book). In *Skin*, Allison declares her commitment to writing and embraces her diverse identities as a lesbian, femme, feminist, mother, incest survivor and working-class woman. Further, she insists that these and other categories of gender, sex and class should be actively engaged and 'excavated from the inside'. After the success of her first novel, Allison published a moving memoir, *Two or Three Things I Know for Sure* (1995), about the men and women of her extended family; it is richly illustrated with intimate photographs. This book, which was originally intended for performance, has since become the basis of a biographical documentary about the author. *Cavedweller* (1998) is Allison's breathtaking and powerful novel about the lives of four women: Delia Byrd, a mother who abandons her daughters to escape abuse, and her daughters Cissy, Dede and Amanda, who try to forgive her and redeem themselves.

Allison's literary influences and mentors include poet Irene Klepfisz and novelist Bertha Harris. She also credits Toni Morrison, especially her uncompromising but beautiful novel *The Bluest Eye*, with giving her the courage to write her fiction. Her other influences include Southern writers Flannery O'Connor, Carson MC-CULLERS and Tennessee WILLIAMS. Her writing, she says in her introduction to *Skin*, has offered her a means to resist and to live: 'To resist destruction, self-hatred, or lifelong hopelessness, we have to throw off the conditioning of being despised, the fear of becoming the they that is talked about so dismissively, to refuse lying myths and easy moralities, to see ourselves as human, flawed, and extraordinary. All of us extraordinary.'

Nancy Johnston

Almendros, Néstor (1930–95), Spanish cinematographer. Almendros's father, Herminio Almendros, was a liberal pedagogue who worked for the Spanish Republic's educational institutions then went into exile to Cuba in 1938, when Francoism became a threat for left-leaning intellectuals. Young Néstor was left behind until the Spanish political climate became asphyxiating and he decided to follow his father's footsteps in 1948. He trained as a cinematographer in both France and Italy, although Cuba remained very close to his heart throughout his professional career. Almendros embraced Castroism enthusiastically, as did other intellectuals, only to become deeply disenchanted with the growth of bureaucracy and political repression. As early as 1961, his documentary *Gente en la playa (People on the Beach)* attracted government disapproval because it dared to show 'a place where the blacks gathered'. As a homosexual in an explicitly homophobic country, he experienced a menacing climate that would finally force him to leave his adopted homeland definitively in 1963. He is representative of a generation of Cuban homosexual intellectuals (Reinaldo ARENAS is the other relevant figure) who were trapped in the contradiction between politically revolutionary ideals and sexually reactionary attitudes. Almendros previously had collaborated actively with Castro's cultural project as a director and film critic.

Almendros then moved to France, where he became François Truffaut's favourite cinematographer during the 1970s and also collaborated with Eric Rohmer on several features. With Truffaut, he worked on *The Wild Child* (1969), *Two English Girls* (1971), *The Last Metro* (1980) and

Confidentially Yours (1982); with Rohmer he photographed *nouvelle vague* classics such as *My Night with Maud* (1969) and *Pauline at the Beach* (1982). Hollywood beckoned in the late 1970s and he became a highly esteemed professional after his Oscar for Terence Malick's *Days of Heaven* (1978). This was followed by sensitive compositions for Robert Benton's blockbuster *Kramer versus Kramer* (1979) and the glossy, sun-drenched images he photographed for *The Blue Lagoon* (1980). Almendros has given a full account of his ideas for his films in his autobiographical memoir, *A Man with a Camera* (1980). Equally at home with Hollywood glamour and European art film, Almendros kept combining both when undertaking projects.

Almendros's relevance from the point of view of gay cinema lies especially in the documentary *Mauvaise Conduite* (1984) he directed in collaboration with Orlando Jiménez Leal. It was among the earliest attempts to show the world Castro's government's stern attitudes toward sexual dissidence. Through personal testimonies and other documents, the film presents the plight of homosexuals in Cuba and tackles the issue of 'concentration camps' where they were interned. A passionate debate has surrounded this film: for some it is just part of a capitalist campaign against Castro and his regime, for others, a relentless exposé that shows the cracks in revolutionary ideology. Attitudes seem to have softened somewhat and evidence now seems to show that the work-camps presented in the films were not intended just for homosexuals, but for all kinds of political dissidents. Almendros died of an AIDS-related illness.

Néstor Almendros, *A Man with a Camera* (London, 1984); Paul Julian Smith, *Vision Machines: Cinema, Literature and Sexuality in Spain and Cuba, 1983–1993* (London, 1996).

Alberto Mira

Almodóvar, Pedro (b. 1949), Spanish filmmaker. For somebody who has become something of an international gay icon, Almodóvar is notoriously reluctant to discuss homosexuality (either his own or as a general topic) in the Spanish media. Almodóvar is such a clear representative of Spanish attitudes towards homosexual identities that perhaps rather than criticising his position (as several critics, both in Spain and abroad, have done), some justification for it must be provided.

Gay identity in Spain has never worked in the way it has in English-speaking countries. Whether this is a good or a bad thing is open to debate. A different conception of gender issues means that homosexual identities are more resistant to discursive fixation than in, say, the United Kingdom. One of the unavoidable side-effects of this situation has been ignorance by intellectuals of ways to deal with homosexuality. The traditional psychoanalytic framework was until very recently the most widely used conceptual system to tackle sexual identities. Otherwise, as elsewhere, there are homophobic jokes and gossip. Almodóvar, together with many other artists closer to the libertarian social and cultural group that became known as 'La movida' from the late 1970s, resists homophobic delimitations and decide they are not playing a game that will eventually turn against them and limit the reach of their work. To be fair, this view of sexuality as resisting political identity, as something eminently fluid and never fixed, is apparent in Almodóvar's early work and, on the other hand, he did attempt to be relatively open about homosexuality at the beginning of his career, only to find incomprehension that led to interpretations he did not think were enriching his work.

From a gay perspective, there is something 'wrong' here, but maybe Almodóvar's 'gay' work deserves attention precisely as an alternative to the Anglo-American gay model of homosexual identity. And no doubt, rejection of any influence of the homosexual artistic tradition is going too far; whether the director explicitly acknowledges the fact or not, there are many elements in his films that cannot but be inserted in the tradition of Spanish camp: boleros, 'coplas' and other musical forms favoured in his soundtracks, drag, women-oriented plots.

Almodóvar was born in a small town in rural Spain and the cultural wasteland surrounding him was in later years evoked with some horror. So was the climate of repression the country was going through: Catholicism was one of the main culprits, and like other Spanish libertarians who endured the Church's reactionarism, Almodóvar took some pleasure in mocking religious institutions. But he also feels a strong attachment to his homeland, which provided a continuous source of inspiration for his films, both in the creation of characters and the depiction of habits and images: emotionally, the countryside provides comfort to the long-suffering protagonist of *The Flower of my Secret* (1995), and also features as an enticing utopia in *What Have I Done to Deserve This?* (1984).

Born near Ciudad Real, he moved to Madrid in 1967, where he first worked in the National Telephone Company. There he started working on a series of iconoclastic amateur shorts, helped and inspired by the libertarianism of the times. Sexual heterodoxy had already become a recurrent element in his work, as shown by his first film to achieve commercial distribution, *Pepi, Luci, Bom y otras chicas del montón (Pepi, Luci, Bom and Other Girls Like Mom*, 1980). It is important to read the film in the context of the period: after forty years of sexual repression, there was a lot to catch up on, and films such as this were indeed a breath of fresh air. The *mise-en-scène* is shoddy, performances careless and some of the contents plainly gross. There is a clear rejection of traditional narrative and topics, and, as in many of his later works, references to popular culture are frequent. The Spanish like to call this 'postmodernism'. From that moment, there was a progression towards coherence and homosexuality in his work, and other 'perverse' behaviours became less and less relevant with every new effort. *Labyrinth of Passion* (1982) features a fragmented narrative and plays fast and loose with sexual orientations. *Dark Habits* (1983) is a melodrama of lesbian passion set in a convent, maybe the peak of Almodóvar's expression of irreverence and camp sensibility. Later films still featured homoeroticism: there is the aestheticising of bullfighting and the obsession with masculinity in *Matador* (1986) and a homosexual pederast in *What Have I Done to Deserve This?*

Homosexuality was never again as central as it became in *Law of Desire* (1987), a gay love story told in the style of high melodrama, with garish colours and visually striking art direction. *Law of Desire* was a confusing film for audiences and also critics, who attempted to underplay the role of homosexual relationships in the plot: 'postmodernism' was again a favourite way to refer to the sexual flexibility shown by some of the characters. From the point of view of gay politics, as Paul Julian Smith has rightly pointed out, it is a far from satisfactory film: homosexuality is mostly liberating, but the emphasis on death and repression, together with the apparent inability to produce anything resembling a politically correct 'identity' makes it difficult for the film to project any 'positive' images. Yet it did something no other film had done before and therefore deserves its status as a milestone in gay filmmaking: sexual heterodoxy was presented with a sense of humour, with no fuss and in a very relaxed way. Shock and pathology were blatantly avoided: no wonder critics did not know what to make of it.

At this point Almodóvar had gathered a team of actors and collaborators that drew comparisons with Warhol's 'Factory', and even though some (like leading actress Carmen Maura) left in something of a huff, the sense of a group of friends or an 'extended family', sharing more than work, has been carefully projected by the Almodóvar PR department. *Women on the Verge of a Nervous Breakdown* (1988) was a huge popular success and in many ways Almodóvar's watershed film. His style became more classical and, looking back, one realises how much Almodóvar tried to get his narrative into more traditional moulds. Again, the central character is Gloria, a woman abandoned by her boyfriend. *Tie Me Up, Tie Me Down* (1989) followed, yet another story of obsessive passion with the usual kinky elements. Homosexuality only made short appearances from that moment: the lesbian maid in *Kika* (1993) and the lesbians in prison in *High Heels* (1991).

Almodóvar's attitude towards sexual politics also became more confusing. Although never too forward in identifying himself as gay in his own country, by the mid-1990s he refused explicitly to be drawn into a discussion on the topic. Again, this has been more frequent whenever the interview is aimed at the Spanish market. Accusations that he caters to gay audiences internationally and then will not acknowledge their support have some justification. Charges of misogyny have also been made. Recent work includes *The Flower of My Secret* and *Live Flesh* (1997). They show a better command of technique and are actually brilliantly polished works. Almodóvar's sense of fun is becoming unimportant, and some of his more personal touches are also disappearing: one may wonder whether something may have been lost along the way and whether that wacky shoddiness did not convey a more liberating perspective through irony than do excellent but rather serious products such as *Live Flesh*.

Paul Julian Smith, *Desire Unlimited* (London, 1994); Nuria Vidal, *El cine de Pedro Almodóvar* (Barcelona, 1988).

Alberto Mira

Altman, Dennis (Patkin) (b. 1943), Australian scholar and writer. Altman was born in Sydney, the only son of Jewish émigré parents. In 1950 the family moved to Hobart and a middle-class, provincial environment, enlivened by the interests of Altman's engineer father. An intellectually precocious child who disliked sports, Altman attended a Quaker school before taking an honours degree at the University of Tasmania, where he immersed himself in student politics. He won a scholarship to Cornell University, wrote a master's thesis and was active in the anti-Vietnam War movement. Here he began an irregular expatriate existence and became a sexual and political adult; he confesses that 'much of what I am has been shaped by America'.

In 1967 Altman took up a lectureship at Monash University, Melbourne, later teaching at the University of Sydney. While on leave in New York in 1970, he joined the emergent gay liberation movement and conceived the first book which would describe and theorise it. *Homosexual: Oppression and Liberation* (1971) utilised Herbert MARCUSE's Marxist interpretation of Freud and the writings of BALDWIN, ISHERWOOD and others to argue for a sexual fluidity which refuted categories of human sexuality. Its underlying emphasis on the historical shaping of the homosexual identity anticipated the work of many later academics. While short of practical strategies to create the common community it advocated, it is regarded as a defining text of gay politics.

With this book Altman was launched into a career as a 'public homosexual' and spokesman, a contentious role in Australia's burgeoning gay movement. He addressed, with Germaine Greer, the launch of Sydney Gay Liberation in 1972; took part in the first gay demonstrations, and later, Mardi Gras, in Sydney; and in activities in other parts of Australia, criticising the first bill to decriminalise homosexual acts as 'totally inadequate and probably even dangerous'. A collection of Altman's essays, *Coming Out in the Seventies* (1979), appeared with the trademark

fusing in his writing of the analytical and personal, and the traditions of radical sexual politics, liberalism and socialism. *The Homosexualization of America* (1982) examined the emergence of homosexuals as a new minority and its impact on broader society; the author later noted that the book was better described by its subtitle, *The Americanization of the Homosexual.*

After five years at a number of American academic institutions, Altman returned in 1985 to teach at La Trobe University, Melbourne, where he is now Professor of Politics. He had been commissioned to write on the social and political issues surrounding gay men and AIDS, and in 1986 published *AIDS in the Mind of America.* He has since served on a variety of national and international advisory committees on HIV/AIDS, including the Global AIDS Policy Coalition, and has documented the development of the community sector response to the disease in *Power and Community: Organizational and Cultural Responses to AIDS* (1994). Altman has also published a novel, *The Comfort of Men* (1995), and a memoir, *Defying Gravity: A Political Life.*

Altman has charted some of the major international issues affecting homosexuals and sexual politics. His most recent work has focused on the internationalisation of gay and lesbian identities, and he is currently writing a book, *Global Sex*, about the political economy of globalisation and its impact on sexuality.

Dennis Altman, *Defying Gravity: A Political Life* (Sydney, 1997); Michael Hurley, *A Guide to Gay and Lesbian Writing in Australia* (Sydney, 1996).

Tim Reeves

Alving, Barbro (1909–87), Swedish journalist and writer. Born in Uppsala, Alving moved to Stockholm in her early twenties. Her mother was a writer and her father a teacher. Alving started to work as a journalist in 1928 and continued in this profession (to Alving almost a vocation) for the rest of her life. During the 1930s she became one of the most famous reporters in Sweden, mainly due to her articles on the Spanish Civil War and the 1936 Olympic Games in Berlin. At this time she developed her specific journalistic style where the journalist speaks as one in a crowd, reporting about the realities of ordinary people.

Alving's daughter Ruffa was born in 1938. Alving decided to raise the child as a single mother. In the early 1940s she met her partner, Loyse. They lived together for more than forty years, until Alving's death. With Loyse, Ruffa got a second mother, which was probably a necessary condition permitting Alving's travels around the world with her typewriter.

In 1946 Alving published *Käringen mot strömmen*, a selection of *causeries*, and after that she published a volume almost every year for the next thirty years. With these volumes she became not only one of the most famous journalists in Sweden, but also one of the most loved and popular. The *causeries* are still worth reading, both for the style and the humour: here we also find descriptions of same-sex family life from the 1940s onward. Alving was quite open about the fact that she lived with another woman, but she never publicly declared herself to be lesbian or homosexual.

During the 1950s Alving engaged in both the women's movement and the peace movement. Thus she took up the heritage from her friend and mentor, the writer and radical feminist Elin Wägner. Alving worked against Swedish nuclear weapons, and she was a radical pacifist. In 1956 she spent a month in gaol for her refusal to take part in the Swedish civil defence. At this time Alving also became more and more interested in religious topics, and later she converted to Catholicism.

Apart from the *causeries* Alving published a diary from gaol and selections of her most famous articles. In 1990 her daughter, Ruffa, issued four volumes of selections from Alving's diaries and letters from 1927 to 1957, *Personligt*. These give a touching testimony of a person who faced many conflicts in her private life while she publicly and bravely took a stand on several controversial questions of her time.

After her death Alving's letters and diaries were transferred to the Women's History Collection at Gothenburg University Library.

Margareta Lindholm

Anderson, Patrick (1915–79), British–Canadian writer. Born in England, the Oxford-educated Anderson moved to Montreal in the early 1940s, where he was employed as a teacher. His interest in writing led to his involvement in poetry newsletters, but he found his metier as the founder of *Preview*. His first collection, *A Tent for April* (1945), includes the unmistakably homoerotic 'The Drinker', ostensibly about a sweating and thirsty man in need of water, signified as a 'column of pure love'. Anderson's evident influences include W. H. Auden and Hart Crane, and his political views were notably of the left.

But Anderson was not without his detractors. In 1943, John Sutherland, in the rival journal *First Statement*, attacked Anderson, accusing him of a literary representation of 'some sexual experience of a kind not normal'. Anderson left Canada at the end of the decade, and subsequently published a number of autobiographical works. He co-edited, in 1961, *Eros: An Anthology of Male Friendship*.

Andrew Lesk

Andrade, Eugénio de (b. 1923), Portuguese poet. Andrade was born into a farming family in central Portugal. In his early years he moved around the country, living in Coimbra and Lisbon, but in 1950 he settled in Oporto, with which city he is closely associated. He worked as an inspector of medico-social services. Leaving aside juvenile works, his first book of verse, *As Mãos e os Frutos* (*Hands and Fruits*) appeared in 1948 and he continued to publish regularly up to the 1990s. Andrade is considered one of the major poets of the post-war generation and has given his name to a foundation which publishes his collected works. As well as poetry, Andrade has written some prose works and translated fragments of Sappho and the poems of the gay Spanish poet Federico García Lorca into Portuguese.

Andrade is a lyric poet who uses a simple but elegant style. Many of his images are drawn from nature, evoking the countryside or the sea, or referring back to his childhood. His poems are carefully crafted, using a language which is accessible but not excessively colloquial. His mood is usually gentle, suggesting melancholy and yearning rather than passion. Together these qualities give his verse a wide appeal. Many of his works are love poems addressed to someone, 'tu' (you), whose sex is not revealed. He frequently uses the words 'amor' (love) or 'corpo' (body), which are masculine in Portuguese although not necessarily specifying a male beloved, thus increasing the ambiguity. The use of this recourse was to a large extent a necessity, given the harsh censorship of the repressive Salazar/Caetano regime. Enough could be read between the lines, however, to give Andrade's verse a special appeal to gay readers. In his later works, such as *Rente ao Dizer* (*Close to Saying*) (1992), written after the return to democracy and the lifting of censorship, Andrade is more open. Although still reticent to some degree, some of these poems are more sensual and refer clearly to sex.

Eugénio de Andrade, *Poesia e Prosa, 1940–1989* (Lisbon, 1990); Paula Morão (ed.), *Poemas de Eugénio de Andrade: o Homem, a Terra, a Palavra*, (Lisbon, 1981); Álvaro Manuel Machado (ed.), *Dicionário de Literatura Portuguesa* (Lisbon, 1996).

Robert Howes

Andrzejewski, Jerzy (1909–83), Polish writer. Born in Warsaw, after four years of studies Andrzejewski left Warsaw University without a degree. Attempting to continue his studies in France, he went to Paris in 1931. Much later he commented upon this period: 'When you are twenty years old, transgressing moral norms can be so pleasant'. He travelled widely with Eugeniusz Biernacki who remained a friend of the writer until his suicide in 1941, after which Andrzejewski refused to leave his home for a month.

In the 1930s Andrzejewski worked for various (mainly right-wing) cultural journals. In August 1934, Andrzejewski married but left his wife on their wedding day. After 1935, he underwent a religious conversion which led him to write *Ład serca* (*The Order of the Heart*, 1937), which won an award from the Polish Academy of Literature in 1939. During this period, Andrzejewski was an active member of the Warsaw literary elite, a friend of Witold GOMBROWICZ, Józef Czechowicz, Czesław Miłosz (the poet, writer and future winner of the Nobel Prize for literature) and Jarosław Iwaszkiewicz.

During the war Andrzejewski took part in the Polish resistance movement. The period was also important in his personal life. He fell for Maria Abgarowicz (whom he married only in 1945, after the death of his first wife, who refused to divorce him), and in 1942 he fell in love with Krzysztof Baczyński, a lyrical poet, whose position in Polish literature can only be compared to that of Wilfred Owen in British letters. Although this passion was not reciprocated, Andrzejewski claimed that Baczyński remained forever 'the greatest love of his life'.

Shortly after World War II, Andrzejewski joined the social realist literary movement supporting the newly formed communist government. In 1948, he wrote his most famous novel, *Ashes and Diamonds* (which won him international fame, thanks to the film of the same title directed by Andrzej Wajda in 1958). In the early 1950s his support for the communist cause began to wane, and in October 1956 Andrzejewski stood on the side of the reform movement. Afterwards he remained an active member of the democratic opposition. His later novels, *The Inquisitors* (1957), *Bramy raju* (*The Gates of Paradise*, 1960), *The Appeal* (1963) and *He Cometh Leaping Upon the Mountain* (1963), deal with the most vital moral and humanist issues of our century. Homoerotic motifs, which can already be found in his early short stories, are overtly present in his last published novel, *Miazga* (*Pulp*, 1981).

Andrzejewski was one of the moral and intellectual authorities of the Polish democratic opposition. Although decidedly an active bisexual, he was married with two children and certainly not a gay activist. When in 1976, Andrzejewski took part in Komitet Obrony Robotnika (Committee for the Defence of the Working Man, the first democratic opposition organisation in Poland), the secret police published a fake appeal he supposedly signed in which he demanded equal rights for sexual minorities. Andrzejewski left an unfinished novel about the homosexual Roman emperor Heliogabalus.

Anna Synoradzka, *Andrzejewski* (Kracćw, 1997); Andrzej Selerowicz, *Leksykon kochających inaczej* (Poznań, 1994), p. 106.

Krzysztof Fordoński

Anger, Kenneth (b. 1929), American filmmaker. Born Kenneth Wilbur Anglemyer in Santa Monica and growing up in Hollywood, Anger made his first film, *Fireworks* (1947), when he was 19. Vito Russo suggests that 'Anger dared to film one of his own wet dreams'; its surrealist imagery earned him an invitation to visit Jean Cocteau in France, where he lived and made short movies during the 1950s. He then returned to the US, where his movies, because of their content and style – described by authority Leslie Halliwell as 'short, inscrutable and Freudian' – remained designated as 'underground':

Scorpio Rising (1963), with its imagery of motor-cycle gangs, the leather scene and homosexual sex, exemplifies this. Other films include *Inauguration of the Pleasure Dome* (1954), *Kustom Kar Kommandos* (1965) and *Invocation of My Demon Brother* (1969).

Anger is also well-known for the *Hollywood Babylon* books (1960, 1984), exposés of major Hollywood scandals. Of most interest to gay readers were the revelations of which of the major stars had led closeted lives.

Bill Landis, *Anger: The Unauthorized Biography of Kenneth Anger* (New York, 1995).

Garry Wotherspoon

Arbasino, Alberto (b. 1930), Italian writer. Born into a well-to-do family in the northern Italian region of Lombardy between the wars, Arbasino came of age as a writer during the 1940s. His career spans the profound transformations that Italy has undergone since the end of World War II, and his acute observations of this process have made him one of the most authoritative observers of contemporary Italian society.

Arbasino's career had a fitful start. He began by studying medicine at the University of Pavia, but soon transferred to Milan to study jurisprudence, in which he eventually took his degree in 1955. He also studied at the Sorbonne in Paris for two years while his Italian professor taught there. From 1957 he worked for the same professor at the University of Rome as a research assistant, the first rung of the Italian academic ladder. In 1965 Arbasino abandoned the idea of an academic career because of the 'insupportable conditions' of the Italian university system. By that date he already had a degree of literary and journalistic success. He had contributed many essays, often inspired by his travels, to such important journals as *Il Mondo* and *Tempo presente*, and he had also published several volumes of fiction, including his first novel, *Fratelli d'Italia*

(1963). By the time he discontinued his university career he evidently felt ready to devote himself to writing on a full-time basis.

Arbasino's early fiction immediately marked him as one of Italy's most interesting young writers. His work was recognised as representing a shift from the neo-realism of the post-war period to what was dubbed *neo-avangardismo* – a literary movement centring around the 'Gruppo 63', founded by Arbasino and others in Palermo in 1963. Neo-realism had dominated Italian culture since the end of the war, and was associated with the expectation of a thoroughgoing transformation of society along socialist lines. Indeed, neo-realist art conceived of itself as being directly involved with the process of social and political renewal. By the late 1950s, however, not only had bourgeois and Catholic values become entrenched in Italian politics, but socialist culture found itself less and less able to offer a credible alternative. This was particularly the case after the mid-1950s, with Khrushchev's revelations about Stalin's purges, and then the Soviet invasion of Hungary. Neo-avant-gardism was a literary response to these changes in the political and social landscape, and its representatives tended to withdraw from the ideological battlefield, instead placing increasing emphasis on the autonomy of language, literature and the arts. In Italy, Arbasino was at the forefront of this movement.

This does not mean that his work affected a complete disengagement from social commentary. Arbasino's writing represents a passionate critique of modernity, especially the way it was manifested in Italy. But it is a wry and perhaps slightly cynical critique, far removed from the unalloyed hopes of the immediate post-war period.

In view of the epoch, one of the remarkable features of Arbasino's early work was its seemingly unproblematic portrayal of gay characters. But where PASOLINI had sought to escape social strictures by focusing on a 'pure' sub-proletariat, Arbasino escapes the same strictures by ascending the social scale to a level where the conventions of sexuality no longer seem to pertain. His gay men consume champagne and caviar, wear cashmere, and drive Mercedes sports cars around Europe in search of cultural and sexual adventures. Even in 1959, the stories in *L'Anonimo Lombardo* had portrayed the daily post-prandial trysts of two young men who had met at Milan's opera-house, La Scala. And *Fratelli d'Italia* (the title echoes the first words of the Italian national anthem) follows the adventures of four men and a woman who amuse themselves with teddy-boys and soldiers in their travels around Italy.

At another level, Arbasino was deeply concerned about the corruption of values brought about by consumerism in a country that was undergoing an 'economic miracle'. A good illustration is provided by the novel *La bella di Lodi* (1972) – also made into a film – in which a rich young woman, using gifts and money, seduces and marries a virile working-class man. This clear metaphor for the bourgeois 'purchase' of the protelariat through consumerism was also one of Pasolini's preferred themes.

Throughout Italy's troubled 1970s, Arbasino became increasingly well known as an essayist and critic. His views were aired regularly in prestigious newspapers such as *La Repubblica* and *Il Corriere della Sera*, and from 1977 he also became known to a broad audience as the compère of a television show called 'Match', which featured debates between various protagonists of culture.

Arbasino has continued to publish volumes of critical essays, the better known among which are *In questo stato* (1978), a series of essays prompted by the assassination of Aldo Moro, and *Un paese senza* (1980), further observations on consumer society. His most recent works are travelogues: *Mekong* (1994) and *Passeggiando tra i draghi addormentati* (1997), travel notes on Southeast Asia, Sicily and South America.

It would be wrong to search for the traces of a 'gay writer' in everything that Arbasino has produced, but he is significant for being one of the earliest Italian authors to write about gay characters in a country where gay liberation, even in fiction, was a long time in coming.

Francesco Gnerre, *L'Eroe negato* (Milan, 1981); Maria Luisa Vecchi, *Alberto Arbasino* (Florence, 1980).

Mark Seymour

Arenas, Reinaldo (1943–90), Cuban poet, essayist, playwright, short-story writer and novelist. Arenas learned to write and read from his mother, and when 15 years old, he joined the rebel forces against the military dictator, Fulgencio Batista. After the Revolution, he returned to his home town, Holguín, where he obtained a scholarship to study agricultural accounting, after which he moved to the Sierra Maestra to work at a poultry farm. Unhappy with his job and pastoral life, Arenas left for Havana to attend a training programme for economic planners. In 1963, he started working as a staff member of the national library, where he realised that he wanted to become a writer.

Arenas received several international awards and fellowships for his novels *Celestino antes del alba* (*Singing from the Well*, 1967), *El mundo alucinante* (*The Hallucinating World*, 1969) and *El portero* (*The Doorman*, 1989). He taught at several universities in the US, including Florida International University and Cornell University (1985). His last literary work was an autobiography entitled *Antes de que anochezca* (*Before Night Falls*, 1992), a text that deals with three issues important to the author: his personal experiences in and anecdotes of Cuba and abroad, his country and the melancholy he experienced while in exile, and the history of Cuba and its literature. The work also represents a search for a voice, a need for a

space and a level of tolerance for subaltern individuals within Cuban society. Under Castro's regime the oppression and the silencing of the needs and the rights of individuals who had a different lifestyle and a different political ideology was commonplace.

Arenas's writing has focused on three major aspects: an innovative literary voice; a social denunciation of injustice, marginalisation, harassment, exploitation, abuse of power, lack of liberty and lack of tolerance for homosexuals under Castro's regime; and a voice to narrate the unofficial and the untold history of Cuban society. His concerns are reflected throughout his work in, among other themes, homoerotic needs and fantasies, sex, incest, promiscuity and suicide – a means of deconstruction, nostalgia, dehumanisation, myths and love.

Arenas, as an open homosexual, began acting on his sexual desires and homoerotic fantasies as a child and through his adolescence in his home town. Once he learned that Castro's regime was persecuting homosexuals, he felt betrayed and used by the Revolution whose ideology prohibited the practice of homosexuality in the 'Island of Paradise'. During this era Cuba tried to build a society where the ideology and power were based on a male chauvinistic model, in which the image of manhood was used to combat imperialism. Thus Arenas, as both a homosexual and a subversive writer, met neither of the two requirements for the 'new society', making him a bad example for Cuba. This issue made Arenas feel a lack of freedom and self-expression, so led him to turn away from the Revolution and its ideologies. This, along with the government's finding out about his homosexuality, brought him under surveillance and persecution.

Arenas's employment situation was unstable and forced him to take odd jobs to survive. After a few attempts to escape from Cuba, Arenas – as a result of a bureaucratic blunder – finally managed to escape from the island via the Mariel boatlift in 1980. Having found success in his literary career, particularly outside of Cuba, he lived in exile in Miami and in New York; suffering from AIDS, he committed suicide on 7 December 1990. Nevertheless, his death can be viewed as both a way of escaping from his life and as a means through which he finally reached liberty and peace – on both levels, an escape from Castro's oppressive regime.

Arenas is one of the most important writers that Cuba has produced since the Revolution of 1959, and his work has been translated into a number of languages. Furthermore, he was one of the few Cuban writers to attain international recognition for his contributions as both a prolific writer and a pioneer of innovative Hispanic literature.

In Arenas's literary work appear not only his personal anecdotes and experiences as a human being and as a homosexual, but also an anger and desire for social justice. In most of his works, the theme of homosexuality is present, whether in an implicit or explicit way.

The theme of homosexuality and the depiction of homosexual individuals appears particularly in *Otra vez el mar* (*Farewell to the Sea*, 1982), *Arturo la estrella más brillante* (the second part of *Old Rose: A Story in Two Stories*, 1984), *Viaje a la Habana* (*Journey to Havana*, 1990), *El color del verano* (*The Colour of Summer*, 1991) and *Antes de que anochezca*. Arenas's gayness is reflected in his texts, as he wishes to expound on his homosexuality and personal sexual experiences, while he is challenging the 'masculinised world' made by Castro. Nevertheless, what his gayness or queer practice represents on a metaphorical level is a form of resistance and a struggle, not only against Castro's internal *modus operandi*, but also against any repressive societies and dictators.

Though homoeroticism is present in the works of other Cuban writers like Severo SARDUY, José LEZAMA LIMA, Guillermo Cabrera Infante, Virgilio Pereyra and Senel Paz, it is not until Arenas's work that homosexuality became a symbol of rebellion, resistance, independence, personal crisis, and particularly, a strategy to acquire a voice and a space for homosexuals. However, his literary contributions are well known and appreciated in the literary world today. His struggle as a homosexual writer bore some fruit. Nowadays Castro and Cuban society seem to be more open about homosexuality: an example of this newfound openess is the popular film *Strawberry and Chocolate* (1991), which is based on the short story 'El lobo, el bosque y el hombre nuevo' ('The Wolf, the Forest and the New Man') by Senel Paz.

David William Foster, *Gay and Lesbian Themes in Latin American Literature* (Austin, 1991); Francisco Soto, 'Reinaldo Arenas', in David William Foster (ed.), *Latin American Writers on Gay and Lesbian Themes: A Bio-Critical Source Book*, (Westport, Connecticut, 1994), pp. 24–36; Roberto Valero, *El desamparado humor de Reinaldo Arenas* (North Miami, 1991).

Juan Antonio Serna

Aron, Jean-Paul (1925–88), French author. A French intellectual and the first public figure in France to reveal that he had AIDS, Aron was born into a large Jewish family of medical doctors in Strasbourg. He studied philosophy and psychology before beginning in 1951 an illustrious career as teacher, scholar, journalist and author. *Le Pénis et la démoralisation de l'Occident* (*The Penis and the Demoralization of the West*, 1978), written with Roger Kempf, examined repressive middle-class attitudes toward masturbation and homosexuality in nineteenth-century France. *Les Modernes* (*The Moderns*, 1984), an influential collection of Aron's essays, attacked recent French intellectual trends and affirmed 'real-life experience and good sense' against 'theory and structures'. A socialist by background and temperament ('I'm left-wing in the same way that I like Mozart'), Aron served as adviser to the

Minister of Culture in the socialist government elected in 1981.

Aron, known for both his intellectual brilliance and his dandyism, was an intensely private man, who concealed his homosexuality, although he did participate in gay rights demonstrations in the early 1980s. In any case, as he later confessed, his was a very limited sex life. But in 1985 he began feeling unwell and in January 1986 his brother, a doctor, diagnosed AIDS. In late October 1986, the magazine *Le Nouvel Observateur* carried as its cover story an interview with Aron entitled 'Mon Sida' ('My AIDS'), in which he soberly recounted the story of his private life and 'his' disease. Aron explained that, now that he was dying, 'I do not see why I should continue to hide'. He hoped that the interview 'will allow me to advance along the road toward a partial self-liberation ... It's probably foolish ... but I have never considered myself homosexual. This disease alone forces me to admit that I belong ... to that category'. Aron also criticised his former friend and rival, Michel FOUCAULT, who had failed to speak out when dying of AIDS in 1984: 'His silence in the face of the disease irritated me, because it was the silence of shame, not the silence of an intellectual'.

Aron's printed interview and a televised version in June 1988 caused a sensation in France at a time when most sufferers still did not admit to AIDS and when obituaries usually attributed their deaths to 'a long and painful illness'. Aron remarked on his newfound celebrity status, 'I have been writing and teaching for 30 years, and then 25 pages make me famous'. He died in Paris on 20 August 1988. Numerous obituaries hailed Aron for his dignity and bravery in breaking a social taboo by revealing his illness. For the *Nouvel Observateur*, '[Aron] will remain "he who dared",' while the newspaper *Libération* declared that '[his] courage has probably changed for ever the public perception of the disease [in France]'.

Who's Who in France 1986–87; *Libération*, 22 August 1988; *Le Monde*, 23 August 1988; *Nouvel Observateur*, 30 October–5 November 1986, 26 August–1 September 1988.

Michael Sibalis

Augiéras, François (1925–71), French author. Augiéras was born in the US to a French mother of Polish origin and a French father. His parents had emigrated in 1922 to the US, where his father, a well-known pianist, had been teaching at the Eastman School of Music in Rochester. Just before their first and only child was born, the father died. Within a few months, his mother migrated back to Paris, where the young Augiéras passed his early youth and acquired his life-long loathing for the city. In 1933, mother and child moved to Périgueux in the Dordogne, where Augiéras felt much more at ease. At the age of 14, he left his mother, whom he found tyrannical. During the years of World War II and the German occupation, he lived a nomadic life. His first social activities were with the Vichy youth movement, which he liked for its pagan views but not for its Nazi ideology. He continued with road theatre and worked in a shelter for boys with learning disabilities. In 1944, he joined the French navy in the hope of getting to his uncle, a retired colonel who lived in the Saharan oasis of El Golea; meeting this uncle once in Paris had made a deep impression. The uncle lived in an old fortress that was transformed into a desert museum. After stays in a psychiatric asylum and in a monastery, the nephew finally arrived in El Golea.

The experience of El Golea transformed Augiéras from an erratic young man into a nomadic peripatetic author. His first book, *Le Vieillard et l'enfant* (*The Old Man and the Child*, 1949), is a romanticised version of his life at the 'bordj' of his uncle. Although he was 19 years of age when his relations with his uncle started, he imagined it as a pederastic union, his uncle taking him on the roof of the fortress under a clear sky of stars. Sex is clearly present in most of his novels, including incest, homosexuality, sadism and bestiality, all described in a very decent way. The characteristics of the first book, male-bonding, homoeroticism, an overwhelming presence of nature, nomadism, paganism and a dreamy but vital style, set the tone for his life, writing and painting. Augiéras loathed women, whom he regarded as living only to procreate, while men lived to create art. The worlds of men and women are antagonistic, and he made a radical choice for a world of men. Women were largely absent in most of his books. He himself entered, however, an unhappy marriage with a woman.

The first novel was self-published by the author and sent to the luminaries of French literature of the time. Gide responded in a very positive way to the first book, as did others. The novel was published two years later in a shorter version by Minuit. *Le Voyage des morts* (1959) continues the story of his life in the Maghreb. He roamed through North Africa and went to Greece, but always returned to the Dordogne. From this vantage point he would tell similar stories to the earlier ones from the Sahara: *L'Apprenti sorcier* (1964), *Domme, ou l'Essai d'occupation* (1981) and *Les Barbares d'Occident* (1990). Another novel is set on the renowned Greek peninsula where only monks live, *Un voyage au Mont Athos* (1970). *Une Adolescence au temps du maréchal, et de multiples aventures* (1968) is a kind of autobiography, and meanders through all the locations of his life. Augiéras spent his last years in his beloved Dordogne and died in a local hospital, exhausted by the strains of a nomadic life. A small stream of biographical material continues to appear, drawing attention to his work and life. No work of his has ever been translated into any other language.

Philippe Berthier, *François Augiéras, l'apprenti sorcier* (Seyssel, 1994); Jean Chalon *et al.*, *François Augiéras ou Le Théâtre des Esprits*

(Poitiers, 1998); *Masques*, no.13 (Spring 1982), special issue on François Augiéras; Paul Placet, *François Augiéras: un barbare en Occident* (Périgueux, 1988); Paul Placet and Pascal Sigoda (eds), *Augiéras, une trajectoire rimbaldienne* (Charleville-Mézières, 1996); Christian Rodier and Georges Monti (eds), *François Augiéras* (Cognac, 1984).

Gert Hekma

Axgil, Axel (Johannes) (b. 1915), Danish activist. Born Axel Johannes Lundahl Madsen – he changed his name in 1956 – he was a Danish homophile emanicipist. Inspired by the United Nations Declaration of Human Rights of 1948, Axel Axgil and a small group of friends in the provincial town of Ålborg in June 1948 founded the first formal organisation in Denmark for homosexuals, Forbundet af 1948 (The Association of 1948), later the National Union of Gays and Lesbians, with Axgil as its first president. In January 1949 the Forbundet af 1948 launched the first magazine in Denmark for homosexuals, *Vennen* (*The Friend*), under the editorship of Helmer FOGEDGAARD. A few months later the founding of the organisation was reported in the press and Axgil was fired from his job and excluded from various positions (e.g. membership of the Youth Committee of the Town Council where he represented the Georgian Party). Axgil moved to Copenhagen and was president of the Forbundet af 1948 until 1952. In 1954 he took over as editor of *Vennen*, which in 1952 had become an independent venture.

Since 1950 Axgil and his companion, Eigil Axgil, had owned a small publishing company, the International Modelfoto Service (IMS), which produced and discreetly sold photos of nude men. The IMS was run from premises which also housed *Vennen*. In March 1955 Axgil and his companion were arrested. They were confined in isolation for eleven months and then sentenced to twelve and eighteen months of prison, respectively, for distribution of material which, 'although not obscene may be deemed a commercial speculation with a sensual intent'. The police search of the premises of *Vennen* and the IMS led to the arrest of a large number of sexually active homosexuals and triggered the so-called Pornography Scandal. The press highlighted Axgil's and *Vennen*'s (former) association with the Forbundet af 1948 which as a consequence lost its credibility within the homosexual subculture and suffered dramatically, financially as well as politically. The Axgils' membership of the Forbundet af 1948 was revoked.

In 1954 the Axgils founded The International Homosexual World Organisation (IHWO) which mainly worked through correspondence between individual members. In 1968–69 the IHWO published the magazine UNI (with articles in seven languages). To a certain extent the IHWO was a network for the distribution in Europe of 'male physical' magazines (*International Male*), and after the liberalisation of the Danish statute on pornography in 1967–69, of pornographic material produced by the Axgils. In 1970 the IHWO succesfully appealed to Willy Brandt, the German Federal Chancellor, to discontinue seizure by the German authorities of pornographic material mailed from Denmark to individuals in Germany. The International Committee for Sexual Equality (ISCE) and the Danish and the Dutch national organisations for homosexuals kept a certain distance from the IHWO, which ceased its activities in 1970.

From 1967 to 1980 the Axgils owned a large house in the countryside near Ringsted, 'Axelhus', which housed printing facilities and served as an international holiday resort for homosexuals.

In the second half of the 1960s the Forbundet af 1948 regained its position as the Danish national organisation of homosexuals and in 1970, after a generational renewal of the leadership of the organisation, the Axgils were allowed to become members. In 1974 they became honorary members of what was now called the National Union of Gays and Lesbians.

On 1 October 1989, at the Town Hall of Copenhagen, Axel and Eigil Axgil were the first homosexual couple in Denmark (and in the world) to enter a registered partnership according to the Danish statute on registered partnership between persons of the same sex.

His life-companion since 1950 was Eigil Axgil (1922–95), an accountant, born on Eskildsen, who also changed his name in 1956.

Axel Axgil and Helmer Fogedgaard, *Homofile kampår. Bøsseliv gennem tiderne* (Rudkøbing, 1985); Raimund Wolfert, 'Skandinavien: Grundsteinlegung und Konsolidierung', *Goodbye to Berlin? 100 Jahre Schwulenbewegung* (Berlin, 1997), pp 233–7.

Wilhelm von Rosen

B

Bachmann, Ingeborg (1926–73), Austrian writer. One of the most important women writers in German this century, Bachmann was born in Klagenfurt; her father was a secondary school teacher and her mother a housewife. In her writing she repeatedly treated the theme of growing up during the war, particularly in the short story 'Jugend in einer österreichischen Stadt' ('Growing up in an Austrian Town'). After the war, Bachmann studied psychology, German literature, art history and philosophy, in particular that of Ludwig Wittgenstein. She wrote her doctoral thesis on the existential philosophy of Martin Heidegger. In 1948 Bachmann published her first poems in journals, and in 1953 she was awarded the renowned prize of the 'Gruppe 47' (a group of young German-language writers formed in 1947) for her first volume of poetry, *Die gestundete Zeit* (*Time Suspended*, 1953).

In the 1950s and 1960s Bachmann moved around considerably, living in Rome, Naples, Zurich and Berlin. She had made a name for herself as a poet, but her first volume of short stories, *Das dreissigste Jahr* (*The Thirtieth Year*, 1961), was not well received by the critics. Her initial failure as a prose writer and the end of her long relationship with the Swiss writer Max Frisch plunged her into heavy depression and illness. In 1966 she moved permanently to Rome, where she worked on her *Todesarten* (*Death Styles*) cycle until her early death. During her life, only the first part, *Malina* (1973), was published.

In 1973 Bachmann's flat caught fire, the cause of which was never established, and she died as a result of the burns she received. Further parts of the *Todesarten* cycle, the novel fragment *Der Fall Franza* (*The Franza Case*) and *Requiem für Fanny Goldmann* (*Requiem for Fanny Goldmann*) appeared posthumously.

The cycle navigates the themes of female identity and the difficulties and possibilities of female writing. In a similar way to Charlotte Perkins Gilman's *The Yellow Wallpaper*, the female first person of *Malina* disappears into a crack in the wall in the novel's famous ending. As she gazes upon the worn-down markings on an ancient temple of queens, Franza, the female protagonist of the second part of the cycle, ascertains that traces of female identity exist more strongly in places were they have been destroyed: 'She [the Queen] can be traced because there is nothing there, where she ought to be'.

Bachmann's work is of crucial significance to feminist literary studies. Her story 'Ein Schritt nach Gomorrah' ('A Step towards Gomorrah') is remarkable in its depiction of lesbian love, given the prudery of the post-war period. Catholicism left its mark on Bachmann, and the Bible, saints and martyrs frequently figure in both her poetry and prose. 'A Step towards Gomorrah' can be read as a 'female creation myth' (Achberger). The patriarchal and heterosexually fixated Western tradition is toppled, and in the relationship between Charlotte and Mara the text hints at a utopia of a love without conquerors or vanquished.

Ingeborg Bachmann, *Songs of Flight: The Collected Poems of Ingeborg Bachmann* (New York, 1994); Karen A. Achberger, *Understanding Ingeborg Bachmann* (New York, 1995); Karin Bauer, 'That Obscure Object of Desire: Fantasy and Disaster in Ingeborg Bachmann's "A Step Towards Gomorrah", in Christoph Lorey and John L. Plews (eds), *Queering the Canon: Defying Sights in German Literature and Culture* (New York, 1998), pp. 222–33.

Andrea Capovilla

Bacon, Francis (1909–92), British painter. Born of English parents and brought up in Ireland and England, Bacon received little formal education due to his asthma. In 1927 he travelled to Europe, living in Berlin and Paris, before returning to London in 1929, where he aimed to become an interior decorator and furniture designer working within the art deco style. Although Bacon did not pursue this career, his interest in these aspects of design carried over into his paintings. Experimenting with both cubism and surrealism in his earliest work (most of which he destroyed), Bacon was entirely self-taught as a painter. Arguably, however, this lack of formal training enabled him to develop a technique of painting, as well as a subject matter and style, which were unique.

Dismissive of the abstract art which dominated post-war painting, Bacon was essentially a painter of the human figure, and his paintings frequently depict violently distorted or dismembered figures, usually men, isolated in brightly lit but windowless interiors. The violence in Bacon's art was evident early on in the disturbing half-human, half-animal creatures of *Three Studies for Figures at the Base of a Crucifixion* (1944), and in the memorable series of heads culminating in the *Study after Velázquez's Portrait of Pope Innocent X* (1953) in which the pope is given a screaming mouth. Such paintings are also examples of Bacon's frequent practice of producing paintings in series and his use of the triptych format. Never working from life, Bacon instead used photographs (especially the motion studies by Eadweard Muybridge), film stills (the nurse's head in Eisenstein's *Battleship Potemkin* being a source for the Innocent X series), medical illustrations and pictures from newspapers (including images of Hitler), while his portraits (almost invariably of close friends) were painted from memory.

Not surprisingly perhaps, Bacon's paintings were typically viewed as existential commentaries on the alienation and violence of the modern 'human condition', a perception reinforced by various statements by Bacon himself such as, 'We live, we die, and that is all'. In recent years, however, these now somewhat clichéd views of Bacon as a painter of nihilism and bleakness have been superseded by more nuanced analyses of the body and gender in his work, although the theme of homosexuality has yet to be fully explored. Although Bacon's homosexuality was well known amongst his circle, it was only in his later years and after his death (with the publication of two biographies) that it became known to the wider public – for example, the stormy relationship between Bacon and his lover George Dyer is the subject of a film, *Love Is the Devil* (1998), directed by John Maybery. Despite the strong personal dimension to Bacon's art, writers and critics glossed over his homosexuality, referring instead to his drinking and passion for gambling. However, homosexuality was an aspect of Bacon's work as early as the 1950s in paintings such as *Two Figures* (1953), sometimes nicknamed 'The Buggers' by friends, and *Two Figures in the Grass* (1954); and male couples (often on a bed) were a recurrent motif. So too, some of Bacon's most poignant paintings, e.g.

Triptych May–June 1973, were of George Dyer whose suicide in 1971, on the eve of the opening of a major retrospective of Bacon's work at the Grand Palais in Paris, uncannily echoed the death in 1962 of a former lover, Peter Lacy, on the day Bacon's exhibition opened at the Tate Gallery in London.

Offered a knighthood, and then the Order of Merit, Bacon turned down both. When he died in Madrid, he was widely recognised as one of the major artists of the post-war era and, indeed, was judged by some to be one of the most important painters of the twentieth century.

Ernst van Alphen, *Francis Bacon and the Loss of the Self* (London, 1992); John Russell, *Francis Bacon* (London, 1971, rev. 1979); Andrew Sinclair, *Francis Bacon: His Life and Violent Times* (London, 1993); David Sylvester, *Interviews with Francis Bacon, 1962–1979* (London, 1982).

David L. Phillips

Badinter, Robert (b. 1928), French lawyer and politician. Born in Paris, Badinter studied law and literature in Paris and New York (at Columbia University) before taking up a career as lawyer and law professor. In the mid-1970s, at the request of François Mitterrand, leader of the French Socialist Party, Badinter put together a committee to draft a Charter of Liberties for the party. The Charter recognised 'the free use of one's body' and 'the right to pleasure' as fundamental human rights. It concluded that 'everyone is free to have the sexual relations of his or her choice' and that 'homosexuality is a sexual behaviour like any other. It is an expression of the fundamental freedom of the body'.

During the presidential campaign of 1981, Mitterrand courted the homosexual vote. After Mitterrand's electoral triumph in May, Badinter became Minister of Justice from 1981 to 1986. In June 1981 he told the National Assembly that 'it is not for the legislator to define what is normal and what is not', and called for extension of

'the principle of non-discrimination' to sexual matters. He steered through parliament important legal reforms, one of the most notable of which, in 1982, lowered the age of consent for homosexual relations from 18 to 15, the same as for heterosexuals. More recently Badinter has served as president of France's Constitutional Court (1986–95) and as a senator (since 1995). He has written several history books, sometimes in collaboration with his wife, Elizabeth Badinter. His play about the imprisonment of Oscar Wilde, entitled *C.3.3* (the number of Wilde's prison cell), premiered in Paris in October 1995.

Who's Who in France; *Liberté, libertés: Réflexions du comité pour une charte des libertés animé par Robert Badinter* (Paris, 1976).

Michael Sibalis

Baldwin, James (1924–87), American writer. Baldwin became one of black America's most articulate spokespersons in the 1960s, and is now regarded as one of the best American essayists. Son of Emma Berdis Jones and stepson of David Baldwin, James Baldwin wrote plays, novels and short fiction, but his lasting fame is as an essayist and non-fiction writer, whose collections include *Notes of a Native Son* (1955), *Nobody Knows My Name* (1961), *The Fire Next Time* (1963) and *The Price of the Ticket: Collected Nonfiction* (1985). His plays include *The Amen Corner* (1954, produced in 1968) and *Blues for Mister Charlie* (1964). Among his fiction are *Go Tell It on the Mountain* (1953), *Another Country* (1962), *Tell Me How Long the Train's Been Gone* (1968), *If Beale Street Could Talk* (1974) and *Just Above My Head* (1979). *Giovanni's Room* (1956) was a groundbreaking novel about homosexuality. Baldwin's publisher rejected the manuscript, and he was warned that the book would damage him among the black community and among white liberals at a time in his career when he was being looked to as a spokesman for civil rights and as one of the most gifted writers to articulate the experience of black Americans. At the 1963 Civil Rights March on Washington, he was excluded from the list of speakers because civil rights leaders were so uneasy about his outspokenness on the subject of homosexuality.

For Baldwin himself, the subject of his sexuality was not compelling; he devoted his thought to the much more central issue of racism which had sent him abroad after his first literary successes, first to France, later to Turkey and back again to Paris and Provence, where he finally settled. He returned to the United States when the struggle for civil rights began and produced some of the most trenchant literature about the movement, but he remained primarily a writer. He disliked labels, finding them irrelevant to how he felt about himself, and did not want to be thought of as a gay writer or a black writer; his lasting significance is certainly as one of the great journalists who recorded the struggle against racism in the United States, but his courage and forthrightness about the experience of being homosexual were also notable.

James Campbell, *Talking at the Gates: A Life of James Baldwin* (New York, 1991); Randall Kenan, *James Baldwin* (New York, 1994); David Leeming, *James Baldwin, A Biography* (New York, 1994).

Seymour Kleinberg

Bandler-von Frenckell, Vivica (b. 1917), Finnish theatre director. Bandler, born in Helsinki in the year Finland gained its independence, worked as a movie director's assistant in France in the 1930s and planned a director's career for herself, but her gender and finally the war prevented this. She studied agriculture at the University of Helsinki and graduated in 1943. Working on her farm, the Saari manor, was in accordance with her training, but theatre, which had replaced film-work, became her occupation. Bandler became one

of the best-known theatre directors in the Nordic countries.

Bandler's prominent public career started in 1955 when she purchased the Little Theatre (Lilla teatern) and made it one of the most important avant-garde theatres in the Nordic countries. Bandler sold her theatre a little over ten years later and had a period as a theatre manager in Oslo and then as an executive director and administrative reformer of the Stockholm City Theatre. Since 1980 she has also worked as freelance artist and an authority on theatre in Sweden and Finland, and represented the Nordic countries throughout the world. Bandler's international links and expertise proved important in the 1990s as the chairperson of the Tampere Theatre Festival. Throughout her long career as a director, and especially as a manager-director, she reformed the Nordic theatre sphere markedly.

Vivica von Frenckell was married in the early 1940s to Kurt Bandler, a Jew from Vienna who was a volunteer in the Finnish Winter War. Their childless marriage lasted for two decades. Typically for the time, the father of the bride saw it as necessary to hide the Jewish background of the groom from the Germans. Nevertheless, the marriage conformed with the norms of a bourgeois family.

Bandler brings her memoirs *Vastaanottaja tuntematon* (*Receiver unknown*) to an end with a letter to her mother: 'Now that you are dead I can finally talk with you . . . Every now and then, for a blink of an eye, I am at home, when in the arms of a woman. That is when I am at home. It is said now . . . That, which was never allowed to be said aloud while you were alive.' In Bandler's life homosexuality was never a dominating factor, despite being a generally known fact. Its collision with her social background did, however, influence her general attitude until old age. Bandler's father, Erik von Frenckell was, among other things, city manager of Helsinki, Member of Parliament and a member of the International Olympic

Committee; her mother, Professor Ester-Margaret von Frenckell, was especially distinguished as a researcher in the Swedish-speaking Finnish theatre. Bandler's work has no trace of loyalty to her upper-class Swedish-speaking background. The disapproval and hostility of her father, who stood for those ideals, has however been a painful matter throughout her life. Her relationship with her mother was warm, although apparently not completely open. These phases are portrayed in the film based on her memoirs, *Jäähyväiset* (*Farewell*), directed by Tuijamaija Niskanen. Bandler is in fact the other scriptwriter of this early lesbian movie.

Bandler's memoirs indicate that she kept her lucid and individual attitude to life through various political trends. She did not deny her patriotism, which grew during the experiences in the Winter War. However, she associated herself with the cultural radicalism and generally sympathised with those who were marginalised in various ways. She united without conflict an aristocrat's upper-class attitude, a provocative defiance of conventions, and a sense of economic responsibility and artistic innovativeness. The public image of a strong woman covered the anxiety of youth which she claims still isolated her from others and linked her with friends in the 1940s. 'Friendship, insecurity and an open fright are a firm base for friendship,' she wrote about Tove JANSSON, an important soulmate in her youth, who decisively supported and encouraged her to choose a career as an artist. Her way of avoiding homosexuality as a topic may reflect a desire to preserve her privacy.

Bandler developed a repertoire model for the Little Theatre, popular plays subsidising the more experimental ones which often challenged the values of the regular audience. Many of her productions were staged in Finland, and many of her administrative innovations were made in Sweden. From the beginning Bandler was deeply and broadly international. She knew how to manage her staff and she carried her responsibilities boldly. She has a special talent in evaluating performances. Her special interest in absurdist drama after the war – GENET's *The Maids* was an early staging – brought friends among writers and an enduring reputation as an innovator. This interest sat well with the shattered post-war atmosphere. She also used irony and satire while criticising the bourgeois way of life or attitudes. One link with this world was the dramatisation of Klaus Mann's *Flykt mot norr* (*Journey into Freedom*), co-directed with Raija-Sinikka Rantala. She mastered the civilised manners and attitudes in the social context of the play, and knew what everyday life for a refugee was, as well as woman's love for a woman, which was central in this production.

Vivica Bandler, *Adressaten okänd. I samarbete med Carita Backström* (Helsinki, 1992); Vivica Bandler, *Vastaanottaja tuntematon. Yhteistyössä Carita Backström kanssa* ed, Juha Siltanen (Helsinki, 1992); Lasse Pöysti, *Jalat maahan* (Helsinki, 1991).

Pirkko Koski

Bang-Hansen, Arne (1911–90), Norwegian actor. Bang-Hansen made his debut at the National Theatre in Oslo in 1932, and was a member of that state company for almost all his career, becoming popular for his many comical and grotesque character parts. His speciality was the secondary lead (the hero's best friend) in the classical Norwegian/Danish plays by Ludvig Holberg.

Among his best-remembered parts at the National Theatre are Gibbs in *The Cocktail Party* (T. S. Eliot), Leonid in *The Cherry Orchard* (Chekhov), Kroll in *Rosmersholm* (Ibsen) and the lecturer in *The Trial* (Kafka). His national fame however, was secured by his many important co-starring parts in popular Norwegian comedy movies, especially in the late 1950s and early 1960s. In the movies, he also did well-noticed character parts in the historical epic *An-Magritt* (1969) and the internationally well-known Ingmar Bergman film *Autumn Sonata* (1978), both starring his good friend Liv Ullmann. In 1985, when he retired, he became the first well-known Norwegian actor to come out of the closet with his warm and open autobiography *From My Bent Corner*.

Svend Erik Løken Larsen

Barr, James (Fugaté) (1922–95), American author. Barr was born in either Texas or Oklahoma; he died in Claremore, Oklahoma. Barr's illegitimate birth haunted him as a child, but his adoptive parents gave him 'a loving, devoted upbringing and a pretty good education'. His best-known work, the novel *Quatrefoil* (1950), is based on his experience in the US Navy during World War II, but a central character is patterned after a man Barr had sex with as a university student. It was followed by *Derricks* (1951), a collection of short stories.

In 1952 Barr re-enlisted in the Navy during the Korean War, but when it became known that he was the author of *Quatrefoil*, an eight-month interrogation followed that resulted in his discharge. This event politicised him and he became active in the homosexual cause, writing articles and stories for *One* (Los Angeles), *Mattachine Review* (San Francisco) and *Der Kreis* (Zurich). In 1955, in telling the story of his discharge from the US Navy, he revealed that his name was Fugaté; it appears as James (Barr) Fugaté in his only published play, *Game of Fools* (1955). However, his second novel, *The Occasional Man* (1966), was published with the name James Barr and it is by this name that he continues to be known.

Although Barr considered *The Occasional Man* to be better written, he remains best known for *Quatrefoil*, whose portrayal of a manly, ethically responsible homosexual relationship struck a strong chord in the gay movement of the 1950s. A French translation (*Les amours de l'enseigne Froelich*) appeared in 1953; a German

translation was prepared, but no publisher was found who would print such a positive picture of male–male relations. Following the publication of his second novel, Barr lost contact with the (post-Stonewall) gay movement. When *Quatrefoil* was reprinted in 1982, the publisher was unable to locate the author; a later reprinting (1991) contained a new epilogue by him, and the novel continues to gain new readers.

Hubert Kennedy, '*Quatrefoil* Broke New Ground', *The Harvard Gay & Lesbian Review*, vol. 3, no. 1 (1996), pp. 22–4.

Hubert Kennedy

Barthes, Roland (1915–80), French writer. Roland Barthes is credited with effecting a major revolution in twentieth-century literary criticism. He championed structuralism and accommodated it to the analysis of 'texts' (of any provenance, as opposed to 'literary texts'). He is also responsible for having acclimatised psychoanalysis to literary studies, and in this was a true inheritor of Georges Bataille (1897–1962) whose books on transgressive sexuality are benchmarks (*The Story of the Eye*, 1928, 1979). Barthes, together with Jacques Lacan, Michel FOUCAULT and Claude Lévi-Strauss, reshaped the European and American intellectual landscapes. The very concept of 'studies' (such as 'gay and lesbian studies') superseding traditional disciplinary boundaries is very much his brainchild.

An eminently public figure, a tremendously successful essayist engaged, in true Sartrean fashion, in political strifes, an honoured academic who also knew how to manoeuvre, in true Parisian style, on the margins of the university establishment, Barthes taught at the idiosyncratic Ecole des Hautes Etudes then at the prestigious Collège de France. One of his mottos was: 'Institutions are by nature abusive, let's abuse them in turn'.

Barthes was a well-known figure in Parisian homosexual circles, so much so that his life may serve as a yardstick to measure the deep changes that affected French, and European homo-society before the advent of massification of gay commodities and its neo-capitalist packaging of behaviours and identity politics.

For one thing, Barthes's private life was studiously severed from his public one. However 'homo' (the then-accepted term) his life, it was only known to close friends and gigolos, the Belle Epoque equivalent to our merchandised era's euphemistic 'escorts' or 'masseurs'. Barthes's haunts belonged, in fact, to a Parisian geography of gay life that has been nearly obliterated by the 1980s ghetto phenomenon, Le Marais. Barthes frequented (as did Foucault) bars like the famous One Rue Keller or Saint-Germain neighbourhood bars (the Rue du Dragon now belongs to mythology), he hired gigolos, sometime students, who were busy 'picking up johns' at the Drugstore Saint-Germain (still an emporium of sorts, albeit an Armani store), went to the saunas and bars around Rue Sainte-Anne (a street near the Opéra that turned Japanese and is now recovering its past flavour) and did forays to the *bains turcs*. Barthes's gay and private Paris was essentially still that of Proust, Gide and Cocteau – a Gaullist-era gay life, largely secure from police harassment, a Paris not really carved out of its fabric, like today's specialised era, but embedded in its traditional industries of luxury and pleasures for all. Many of the boys who sold themselves to Barthes and his fellow writers would congregate on the first floor of the famous coffee-house, the Café de Flore, where trade took place, and where Barthes was a regular – he also entertained some of his students at the downstairs dining-room. Intellectual homosexual life in the heyday of the structuralist revolution was also made of such geography, too evanescent to be recalled unless one pays attention to it.

Barthes only lifted the veil on his private 'homo' life in a few of his works. In particular, in that most genial gesture that left the literary world once more amazed at his skills, he published his autobiography in 1975. In *Roland Barthes par Roland Barthes*, he chose a university press series, where modern writers write the lives of dead ones, to 'come out', treating himself as an object for analysis. The arresting volume is divided into alphabetically listed entries which all hinge on the entry HOMO, what he calls 'the goddess homo' – punning on the fact that, at once, he was composing a 'homo or auto-biography' and the biography of 'Barthes homo'. It is noteworthy that, Greek pun aside, he picked 'homo' out of the whole glossary (*tante, pédé, folle*), as that term had just been hurled in an act of defiance by crooner Charles Aznavour in a song that startled everyone.

However Barthes's work is, to some extent, a reflection on this play on private and public spheres, on the entrapments of bought sex, and the French love for talking about love, even paid 'love', on the emmeshing of a writer's desire to succeed with his desire to be loved. Being a writer, some of his major works (beside his epoch-making books on fashion and advertising – a gay man's preoccupation?) cross over from private desires to public admission. In *S/Z* (1970), Barthes gives the first account ever in literary theory of how gender functions, *à propos* of a *castrato* – since then, a staple of gay fiction. With *Fragments d'un discours amoureux* (1977) he casts himself as Goethe's Werther to explicate what he calls 'a lover's speech' or love-as-the-love-of-one's speech-about-love, 'a modern illness', he said (as opposed to pleasure, as in Foucault's notion of care of the self). This was another pathbreaking book. In *Sade, Fourier, Loyola* (1971) he had already compared the workings of desire in three oddly matched authors.

As a professor, he made no mystery that teaching was for him an act of seduction. He would have dismissed the entanglements of 'sexual harassment' as 'repressive'. As most of his books were in part the outcome of seminars he gave at the Ecole des Hautes Etudes, some open to packed audiences, some restricted to a few carefully chosen students (with a high quota of *pédés* and *gouines*, queers and dykes), one must insist on the fact that Barthes's teaching was primarily about the trappings of desire, including the seminarroom itself – he often remarked that *seminar* and *semen* have a common root. His seminars were rituals of seduction, rarely seen since. One of his first texts had been in fact on Socrates and he extolled Proust, the arch-introvert student of seduction, as his master.

As a result he never aligned himself with the burgeoning gay movement. 'Gay visibility' was too much of a code of *embourgeoisement* for someone trained in both the resistance to the Algerian War and the refusal to play up to any sort of power, especially that of self-styled 'communities' or 'identities'. Yet 'Barthes' has become part of the French gay vocabulary, and 'reading Barthes' is a rite of passage for young gay men – as recognised by Edmund WHITE. Paradoxically, he has become what he hunted down in all his books, a 'code name'. He has also given impetus to a new literary style of fiction, in France at least, where matters sexual are turned into cameos of events, and not confessional-style narratives that are the trademark of contemporary American gay fiction. The best example of it remains the 1979 book *Tricks* by Renaud CAMUS.

His preface to *Tricks* sums up Barthes's views on homosexuality. He assigned the real place of the gay man to the 'intensity without regret' of cruising, it being a denial given to the social requirement of defining oneself: 'Just say 'I am' [this, or that] and you will be socially saved'. There are no politics of identity or community in Barthes's thinking. And this may be a reason why, in the post-capitalist *embourgeoisement* of gay men and women, the revolutionary weight of his message has been somewhat lost.

Roland Barthes, *S/Z* (Oxford, 1975); *Roland*

Barthes by Roland Barthes (London, 1977); *A Lover's Discourse* (New York, 1978); *Incidents* (Berkeley, 1992); Renaud Camus, *Tricks* (New York, 1981); D. A. Miller, *Bringing out Barthes* (Berkeley, 1992).

Philippe-Joseph Salazar

Baudry, André (Émile) (b. 1922), French activist. Born in Rethondes, Baudry studied at a Jesuit college and then a seminary, but never actually entered the priesthood. He became a philosophy teacher in a Paris secondary school. His early religious education always coloured his later homosexual militancy.

In 1952 Baudry began writing under the pseudonym André Romane for the homosexual review *Der Kreis* (*The Circle*), published in Switzerland since 1932. This brought him into contact with a new generation of post-World War II homosexual militants organised around COC in the Netherlands and the International Committee for Sexual Equality, founded in 1951 and based in Amsterdam. He became the latter's French correspondent and in 1953 a member of its executive committee. Like many others at the time, Baudry saw the need for an organised homosexual movement in France. Although homosexuality between consenting adults in private was fully legal in France and Paris was the capital of European gay life after 1945, the state still repressed homosexual 'proselytism' in the press, and the police arrested hundreds of men every year for 'gross public indecency', particularly in public urinals.

Baudry started holding regular meetings of French subscribers to *Der Kreis* in Paris in 1952. In January 1954 he launched his own monthly review, named *Arcadie* after the mythical Eden of ancient Greek shepherds. It went out to subscribers by mail and was not sold at news-stands. *Arcadie* at its peak published about 10,000 copies a month, although Baudry claimed three times that number of subscribers in the 1970s. Austere in appearance and sober in both tone and content, *Arcadie* tried to attract readers by inserting in each issue (until 1960) a 'special sheet' with personal advertisements as well as photographs of attractive young men. The government banned *Arcadie*'s sale to minors in May 1954 (an interdiction lifted only in May 1975), which meant that it could not benefit from the reduced postal rate accorded most periodicals. In 1956, moreover, the courts condemned Baudry for offending morals in his review and fined him 40,000 francs. The judges described *Arcadie* as a 'veritable profession of faith in favour of homosexuality', constituting 'a danger for readers and in particular for youth'.

Baudry always preferred the term 'homophile' to 'homosexual': 'The word "homosexual" refers to sexual relations between partners of the same sex,' he said, 'while "homophile" refers to persons who can find their erotic fulfilment (. . . physical, psychological, emotional and intellectual) only with someone of the same sex.' He wanted to encourage the formation of a unified homophile community that would not renounce its differences while nonetheless refusing to create a separate ghetto and merging with the wider society. 'Alongside the others, with the others', was Baudry's motto. *Arcadie* aimed to educate homosexuals to accept themselves and to behave in such a way as to be acceptable to heterosexuals; for Baudry, the outrageous behaviour of certain homosexuals caused public hostility. Baudry's homophile was to be a new man: brave, moderate, determined, discreet and virtuous, with a strict morality based on respectability, solidarity and self-control. 'We cannot tolerate excesses,' Baudry said. This restrictive and reactionary morality was not accepted by all French homosexuals and caused conflicts between Baudry and other French gay groups, like the short-lived *Le Verseau* (1952–56).

In 1957 Baudry established a commercial association under the name Clespala (Club littéraire et scientifique des pays latins: Literary and Scientific Club of the Latin Countries). Clespala offered an alternative to those Parisian homosexuals who did not want to cruise the streets, parks and urinals or who disliked the gay bars and restaurants of the Saint-Germain-des-Prés district. Members could attend weekend dances, listen to Baudry's monthly speech ('the word of the month'), and take part in conferences and other cultural activities. Baudry regularly invited the police to come and observe the members' exemplary behaviour. Members of Clespala were of every age and social class, but the lower middle class, teachers, and above all clergymen, were over represented. Baudry tried to establish similar groups outside Paris, but these did little more than hold monthly dinners.

Baudry controlled *Arcadie* and Clespala like a true autocrat. '[A]mong the French homophile people as I know them', he said in 1979, 'democracy pushed to the extreme would sow doubt. The homophile groups need a leader; not a dictator, of course, but someone who is backed up.' Baudry maintained that the homophile movement that he headed was non-political, but it was in fact legalist and fundamentally conservative. Much about his activities still remains mysterious, especially his close relations with the police and the Church, and his political contacts and lobbying behind the scenes.

After May 1968, with the appearance of a more radical homosexual movement influenced by American gay liberation, Baudry found his authority challenged from within Clespala by a group composed principally of lesbians. This eventually led to the foundation of FHAR (Front Homosexuel d'Action Révolutionnaire: Homosexual Front for Revolutionary Action) in 1971. There would be other breakaway groups in the 1970s. At the same time, *Arcadie* faced competition from new erotic homosexual publications (from 1968), gay magazines offering information and entertainment (from 1975) and then, from 1979, the famous weekly *Gai Pied*.

Baudry could not adapt to the new situation created in France in the 1970s and 1980s by the liberalisation of society and the growing power of the political left. He complained that homosexuals were now interested only in 'their little immediate pleasures'. 'They no longer have a soul, they have only a body.' 'My spiritual aid is no longer required,' he lamented. Baudry nonetheless remained an important presence on the gay scene throughout the 1970s, notably with his first appearances on radio (1970) and television (1973) and the important congresses that he organised in 1973 (Paris), 1975 (Marseille), 1977 (Metz) and 1979 (Paris).

In the early 1980s, Baudry ran into financial difficulties after a tax audit. Clespala had been selling its drinks at a very low price in order to attract a clientele and the government decided that the club had not paid enough tax on these sales. Baudry liquidated both the club and the review in 1982 and at the age of sixty retired to Italy, where he still lives near Naples.

Baudry's complex personality – mixing courage and tenacity with arrogance and ambition – left no one indifferent. Many homosexuals followed him devotedly during his thirty-year career, but others, exasperated by his difficult character and hegemonic ambitions, ridiculed him as 'pope of the homophiles' or even 'His Holiness'. In the letter announcing his retirement, Baudry, true to his ideals, declared serenely: 'And as for me, André Baudry, far from the tumult of this beloved people ... I shall await death, somewhere, uttering only a single wish: "Oh, all of you, be happy in a homophile life constructed out of courage and dignity".'

Jacques Girard, *Le Mouvement homosexuel en France 1945–1980* (Paris, 1981); Frédéric Martel, *Le Rose et le noir: les homosexuels en France depuis 1968* (Paris, 1996).

Olivier Jablonski

Ben, Lisa (b. 1921), American activist. The daughter of apricot ranchers in northern California, Edith Eyde studied the violin and completed two years of university. However, her overbearing parents insisted that she fit their mould of a docile young woman and take a secretarial course and prepare for marriage. While she knew she felt attracted to women, she felt alone and had no words to describe her sexual interest.

In 1945, she left her parents' plans behind and settled in Los Angeles. She found that this city, like other urban areas in the US, had established homosexual communities centred around bars and had recently blossomed with the relocation of people wrought by World War II. She created a new name for herself, formed from the word 'lesbian', Lisa Ben. Sparked by the occasional newspaper article that described homosexuals as perverts, and employed at RKO studios as a secretary with little to do, Ben began typing ten copies of a magazine she called *Vice Versa*.

According to Jim Kepner, founder of the international Gay and Lesbian Archives, *Vice Versa* established the basic format for the general gay and lesbian magazines. The nine issues included editorials, short stories, poetry, book and film reviews and a letters column. Its distribution network consisted of friends passing copies on to other friends and acquaintances. Rodger Streitmatter notes that the magazine maintained a positive tone, communicated political messages in its fiction, and established a forum for gay and lesbian issues.

After the studio closed the division in which she worked, Ben took a variety of secretarial jobs over the next three decades. In the 1950s, she attended performances of female impersonators and became inspired to create entertainment that was not demeaning or filthy. She wrote gay parodies of popular songs and sang them in clubs like the Flamingo, which had Sunday afternoon dances for a gay clientele. Ben joined the Daughters of Bilitis, the country's first lesbian organisation, but elected to stay on the sidelines. Ben supported the political struggles of the community, but considered herself apolitical and enjoyed her retirement in her Burbank bungalow.

Eric Marcus, *Making History: The Struggle for Gay and Lesbian Equal Rights, 1945–1990* (New York, 1992); Rodger Streitmatter, *Unspeakable: The Rise of the Gay and Lesbian Press in America* (Boston, 1995).

Brett L. Abrams

Bernstein, Leonard (1918–90), American musician. One of the most extraordinarily gifted of twentieth-century musicians, Leonard Bernstein towered over the American musical landscape from the 1940s. Flamboyant, mercurial, inventive, charismatic, Bernstein was one of a rare breed: the serious-music celebrity.

In characteristically theatrical style he first came to public prominence when on 14 November 1943 he took over at very short notice to conduct the New York Philharmonic as replacement for the ailing Bruno Walter. A live-to-air broadcast ensured that the artistic triumph of the occasion quickly became a personal success also, the first of many which contributed to his status as a 'personality', the legend that became Lenny.

The son of immigrant Russian Jews, Bernstein's musical education was financed – albeit reluctantly – by his family's beauty parlour business. Quite early he established his gifts as a pianist. However, it was at Harvard in the 1930s, under the influence of Dimitri Mitropoulus and Aaron Copland, that he began to look to composition and conducting as his vocation. It was during this early period too that he established friendships with other leading figures in the classical music scene, several of whom were homosexual. These included the winsome and affable Ned ROREM as well as Paul BOWLES, who was at the time a promising young composer.

One of Bernstein's enduring legacies, dating from the period of his earliest successes was the way in which he bridged the gulf between 'serious' and 'popular' music. In 1943, for example, shortly after his conducting debut in New York, he composed the music for *Fancy Free*, a ballet choreographed by Jerome ROBBINS about three young sailors on twenty-four-hour shore leave in New York. It was so successful that by 1944 the work was expanded into a musical retitled *On the Town*. In 1956 came another widely admired composition, *Candide*, a reworking with Lillian Hellman of the Voltaire classic which featured amongst its numbers the classic song 'Glitter and Be Gay'. These successes were, however, eclipsed by his greatest triumph, *West Side Story*. Premiered in 1957, this retelling of the Romeo and Juliet story set in 1950s New York, with lyrics by the young Stephen Sondheim and choreography by Jerome Robbins, was an unqualified critical and popular success.

Alongside these achievements, Bernstein continued to carve out a career as one of America's foremost conductors. In 1958 he also began the first of a series of music education programmes on television which eventually ran for fifteen years. A generation of young Americans were educated through these 'Young People's Concerts', as Bernstein engagingly and intelligently presented 'serious' and 'difficult' music on the then-still-new medium of television.

By the 1960s and 1970s Bernstein's public persona increasingly threatened to engulf his artistic life. In the heady 1960s, for example, he and his wife were photographed lavishly supping with the Black Panthers in their New York apartment – an event which bequeathed the term 'radical chic' to the lexicon. Meanwhile his all-round extravagance, colourful retinue of followers and sexual indiscretions saw an increasingly hostile reception accorded to his work.

Since his death a series of biographers

have assiduously been stripping away the mythology surrounding the Bernstein legend. Yet, despite all the revelations – many of them, it has to be said, exceedingly unflattering – Bernstein's contribution to American cultural life remains unassailable. Behind the high velocity life of a music superstar lay a seriousness of purpose and depth of talent which has never been equalled. As a conductor he was an interpretive giant, championing not only the music of his contemporaries but also of symphonic predecessors such as Mahler, and younger composers such as Carter, Cage and Babbit. His most important book, *The Unanswered Question* (1976), based on a series of lectures delivered at Harvard in 1973, constitutes one of the most imaginative and bold pieces of contemporary critical writing about music. As a composer his most daring achievement remains the confounding of musical genres, wherein he accorded to popular idioms a seriousness and musical complexity that paved the way for composers like Sondheim. Even his personal life – an egotistical, bravura performance in its own right – showed a heady disdain for the strictures of American bourgeois convention.

L. Bernstein, *The Joy of Music* (London, 1960), *The Unanswered Question* (Cambridge, 1976); B. Hadleigh, *The Vinyl Closet: Gays in the Music World* (San Diego, 1991); M. Secrest, *Leonard Bernstein: A Life* (New York, 1994).

C. Faro

Best, Mireille (b. 1943), French writer. Born in Le Havre, France, to working-class parents, Best was beset by ill-health during her school days, and never sat the *baccalauréat* giving access to higher education. After leaving school, she spent a brief period working in a factory before joining the French civil service. She lives with her partner Jocelyne Crampon, whom she met at the age of 15, and hopes to marry if and when French law makes this possible. She has achieved public recognition as a writer

of short stories and novels, all published by the prestigious Éditions Gallimard. Virtually all of her works, several of which have been translated into Dutch, English and German, explicitly thematise amorous and sexual relationships between women. The following four texts are of particular interest to lesbian readers.

Her first book, *Les Mots de hasard* (*Random Words*, 1980), consists of five short stories, four of which depict thwarted lesbian desire. Although characterised by an apparent lack of politicisation or even the vocabulary of lesbian identity, each narrative in fact forms an oblique critique of heteronormativity, through emphasis on the discursive and self-imposed censorship of desire between women and on the absence of a socially legitimised space for lesbian relations within women's lives.

Best's first novel, *Hymne aux murènes* (*Hymn to the Muraena*, 1986), again portrays an abortive lesbian relationship, but contains a more positive, lesbian-affirmative ending. Seventeen-year-old Mila is sent to a nursing home for girls with a medical condition in which wings grow beneath the shoulder-blades, whose optimal treatment is ablation. The centre of narrative gravity is Mila's doomed passion for Paule, a junior member of staff, but the novel uses the image of wings, generally considered aberrant in human beings, as symbol for a sexual and existential difference (and, given the obvious allusion to angels, for a transcendence) which Mila ultimately embraces. The interplay between the literal and the figurative serves to subtextually vindicate same-sex love, normatively considered, like wings, to be an abnormality, but one with which, by the end of the novel, Mila is perfectly comfortable.

On the surface, *Camille en octobre* (*Camille in October*, 1988) seems to plunge back into a gloomy view of lesbian relations as ill-starred. Working-class adolescent Camille's love and desire for bourgeois, married Clara runs up against not just Clara's erratic resistance but also barriers of class and age, belying the idealised fallacy that same-sex love has only homophobia to overcome. Yet despite the failure of the affair, this novel gives more than a glimpse of hope in Camille's encounter with a harmonious community of self-accepting, sensually dynamic lesbians, and also in Camille's own violent revolt, towards the end, against the normativising pressures of straight society.

Best's most recent novel, *Il n'y a pas d'hommes au paradis* (*There Are No Men in Paradise*, 1995), shows an upbeat evolution in the author's take on the prospects for lesbian identity and relationships. Despite a degree of ideological and gut opposition, from the Communist Party to which they once adhered and from one of their mothers respectively, lovers Josèphe and Rachel simply live rather than problematise their lesbianism. Further, the novel contests the model of lesbianism as based on a narcissistic quest for the same instead of enriching espousal of difference (read heterosexuality), through its insistence on the profound differences between the two women. Finally, a valorising link between art and lesbian desire is made, which functions to aestheticise same-sex love and to position it high above the utilitarian, reproductive plane of straight relations.

Asked about the importance of lesbianism in her writings, Best avers that the theme 'establishes itself without drawing attention to itself, without being provocative, but without masking itself either. That's the way I am, I've the right to be like that, just as some people are naturally blond or dark-haired. That's all there is to it.' Such comfortable, uncompromising acceptance and de-dramatisation of lesbian identity sums up both the writer and her principal protagonists, yet Best's work is far from naive or unreflecting; it may not militantly indict, but it certainly exposes the constructedness of heterosexuality, along with the disciplinary, impoverishing effects of its regime on female subjectivities and lives.

Anne Garréta, 'French Lesbian Writers?', in *Same Sex Different Text? Gay and Lesbian Writing in French*, Yale French Studies, no. 90 (1996), pp. 239–41; Catherine Gonnard, 'Des mots sans hasard', *Lesbia Magazine* (November 1988), p. 24.

Lucille Cairns

Bieber, Irving (1908–91), American psychiatrist. Bieber was educated at New York University, where he completed degrees in science and medicine. Active both as a clinician and a researcher, his areas of expertise included the psychoanalysis of homosexuals and the psychological impact of cancer and cancer surgery. He was a clinical professor of psychiatry at New York University Medical College and an attending psychiatrist at numerous hospitals in the New York City area.

In 1952, Bieber formed a research committee on male homosexuality, composed of psychoanalysts and psychologists. The committee's research was published a decade later as *Homosexuality: A Psychoanalytic Study* (1962) with Bieber as primary author.

The committee itself did not see homosexuality as posing a 'key problem' in their psychoanalytic theory since its members were in agreement at the outset regarding the genesis of homosexuality: they all 'assumed that the dominant sexual pattern of the adult is the adaptive consequences of life experiences interpenetrating with a basic biological tendency toward heterosexuality'. Implicit in this assumption was a rejection of Sigmund Freud's concept of instinctual and constitutional bisexuality.

Bieber's decision to research homosexuality seemed less to do with the desire to explore an uncharted territory and more to do with the confirmation of preconceived ideas, then being challenged by other researchers, such as Evelyn HOOKER and Alfred KINSEY.

The project was the first time that a large number of individual psychoanalytic histories of male homosexual patients had been subjected to a systematic statistical and clinical analysis. Moreover, it was a long-term study over nine years that involved successive stages of data collection on patients in psychoanalytic treatment and a monitoring of the success rate of readapting homosexual patients to a heterosexual way of life. Bieber diagnosed homosexuality as originating in the behaviours of both dominating, binding and seductive mothers and hostile, detached fathers who did not provide adequate role models. While not all homosexuals were produced by this particular family configuration, Bieber argued, it was the most common combination. The production of a homosexual son occurred, according to Bieber, in the Oedipal phase when the assumed innate heterosexual drive appears but is made latent by the interventions of the mother and rejection by the father. Therefore, Bieber could argue that 'every homosexual is a latent heterosexual'. This had major repercussions for the validity of 'curing' homosexuals.

Bieber's study was flawed in a number of fundamental ways which he never seriously addressed in his later work on homosexuality. Colleagues, for instance, questioned whether it was valid to rely on data gathered from analysts who presumed heterosexuality to be innate and homosexuality a pathology produced by a particular family configuration, instead of gathering information directly from the patients. Moreover, Bieber's research was based on individuals who were seeking to change and, therefore, it was invalid for Bieber to generalise his findings and conclusions as being applicable to all homosexuals.

Despite these problems, Bieber urged psychoanalysts to work towards a transformation to heterosexuality rather than helping patients to adjust to homosexuality. Bieber's conclusions offered not only a solution to the homosexual 'problem' vis-à-vis the maintenance of the family (and thus American society) – a topic of great concern in the 1950s – but posited a model of a healthy family dynamic that would prevent homosexuality. Bieber subsequently opposed the removal of homosexuality from a list of mental disorders maintained by the major psychological association. He argued, 'I never said homosexuals were sick … I don't want to oppress homosexuals; I want to liberate them, to liberate them from that which is paining them – their homosexuality'. Bieber's opposition was unsuccessful, and his attitudes remained unchanged, though he continued to do research, consult patients and give lectures which were often targets of demonstrations by gay activists. His particular psychoanalytic interpretation of homosexuality was progressively discredited within the psychiatric community. Bieber's work continues to be used by religious and reactionary psychiatric groups who espouse that homosexuals can successfully change and become heterosexuals.

Gary Alinder, 'Gay Liberation Meets the Shrinks', in Karla Jay and Allen Young (eds), *Out of the Closets: Voices of Gay Liberation* (New York, 1972); Richard Friedman, *Male Homosexuality: A Contemporary Psychoanalytic Perspective* (New Haven, Connecticut, 1988).

Trent Newmeyer

Blais, Marie-Claire (b. 1939), Canadian writer. Perhaps the best-known of Quebecois writers, Blais burst into the literary world at age twenty with the publication of her first novel, *La Belle Bête* (*Mad Shadows*) in 1959. In 1961 she received a Canada Council grant and spent a year in France. By 1963 she was friends with Edmund Wilson and living in Massachusetts on a Guggenheim Fellowship. It was a long way from her early working-class roots in Quebec city. Her family was typical Quebecois: large and Roman Catholic. After several years at convent school, she left at age fifteen and eventually studied French literature at Laval University. It was there that she caught the attention of Jeanne Lapoint (the first female professor of literature at Laval) and Georges-Henri Lévesque (vice-president of the Council of Arts). Both encouraged her to continue writing and she followed *La Belle Bête* with *Tête blanche* (*Whitehead*). Then came *Une saison dans la vie d'Emmanuel* (*A Season in the Life of Emmanuel*) and a highly autobiographical trilogy: *Les Manuscrits de Pauline Archange* and *Vivre! Vivre!* (together translated as *The Manuscripts of Pauline Archange*) and *Les Apparences* (*Dürer's Angel*).

But it was through Wilson at Cape Cod (Massachusetts) that Blais met a lesbian couple, Mary Meigs and Barbara Deming (Blais and Meigs would eventually become lovers). Blais writes (in *American Notebooks: A Writer's Journey*, 1996) of Wilson: 'Edmund told me: "I'll introduce you to two extraordinary women . . . . You'll see that Virginia Woolf's world is not so far removed from ours".' While both *Le Loup* (*The Wolf*) and *David Sterne* have elements of gay male content, it was not until *Les Nuits de l'Underground* (*Nights in the Underground*) that she wrote about lesbianism. It was also a departure from writing about sociopaths and people with chronic lung infections. In an interview with the Canadian Broadcasting Corporation in the early 1980s, she called *Nights in the Underground* her first happy book. It focuses on the lives of several women in a Montreal lesbian bar called the Underground, during a blizzard.

Blais has written about AIDS; in her play *L'Ile* (*The Island*), based on an actual gay bar in Key West, Florida, there is a menacing plague (though not stated, it is understood as AIDS). Blais is familiar with both Key West and Provincetown (Massachusetts) – both with large gay male communities, both hit by AIDS. She writes (in *American Notebooks*) of Provincetown before AIDS as 'a joyful town humming with the love of boys for each other'; afterwards, 'the streets of Provincetown no longer ring with the confident joviality of those voices, those healthy voices unconcerned with health'.

She returned to the theme of lesbian collectivity with her novel *L'Ange de la solitude* (*The Angel of Solitude*) in 1989. Here, a community of young lesbians deal with death, political and social struggles, and relationships within and without the group. Like *L'Ile*, the spectre of AIDS plays a role in the lives of these characters. Besides being a novelist and playwright, Blais has published several volumes of poetry. In her later prose, she has adopted a writing style that eschews paragraph breaks and full stops. Some readers consider this a brilliant use of stream-of-consciousness writing; others find it symbolic of the chaotic lives of her protagonists; still others find it simply hard to read. Blais has received numerous literary awards in both Canada and Europe.

Mary Jean Green, *Marie-Claire Blais* (New York, 1995).

Lee Arnold

Blewett, Neal (b. 1933), Australian political scientist, politician, diplomat and architect of the Australian response to the HIV/AIDS epidemic.

Born in Tasmania, Blewett was a Rhodes Scholar in 1957 and holds a D.Phil. from Oxford University. He was Professor of Politics at Flinders University in South Australia until his election to the Australian Parliament in 1977. He held several ministerial posts in the years 1983–93, including the health portfolio from 1983 to 1987. He resigned from Parliament in 1993 and served as High Commissioner for Australia in London from 1994 to 1998. Blewett was made a Companion of the Order of Australia in 1995 for his parliamentary service.

The first case of AIDS in Australia was reported in March 1983; within two years it had become a major preoccupation of government policy. Blewett, the Federal Minister for Health, has been described as playing 'perhaps a more significant role than any other health minister in the world' in the field of HIV/AIDS policy. In particular, Blewett is credited with incorporating the involvement of affected community groups in addition to that of the medical community in the development of HIV/AIDS policy. As gay men have been the major group affected by the virus, representatives of that section of the community have played an integral role in the development and implementation of the Australian response to the epidemic. Blewett was obviously comfortable working with gays. Not only did he incorporate members of the gay community into the AIDS policy process: he also appointed an openly gay man as his chief policy adviser when he was Minister for Health.

Blewett can also be credited with putting in place mechanisms within the Australian Parliament to encourage a bi-partisan approach to the emerging policy debate. He established a multi-party parliamentary liaison committee to handle issues relating to the epidemic, which enabled informed debate within Parliament. The Australian 'model' has been lauded as exemplary in the international community – many other national and regional governments have incorporated aspects of the model into their respective approaches.

Without exception, in all countries the first responses to AIDS were developed at the community level within the affected communities, notably within the gay male community. They quickly developed a pool of expertise and contacts which governments were later able to put to good use in the fight against the disease. The Australian government, under Blewett's direction, was the first government in the world to adequately fund the operations of the community sector. Today these organisations are the repositories of considerable knowledge; their skills and expertise remain in high demand from both governments and the medical profession.

The position of gay men within the Australian community has improved considerably since the advent of HIV/AIDS. Whilst this development has resulted from a number of other factors, including homosexual law reform and the general maturation of society, the epidemic has ironically proved beneficial to the gay community. The visibility of gays has increased significantly – not only in terms of actual exposure but also in terms of wider community perceptions. Having been incorporated into mainstream policy-making, gay community representatives have been reported and photographed meeting with 'respected' politicians, bureaucrats and community leaders. These representatives, and in turn the communities which they represent, have gained improved public acceptance. That an improvement in the position of lesbians flowed from their involvement with the epidemic is less clear. Some commentators have suggested that lesbians have 'piggy-backed' on the AIDS issue to gain increased community exposure for their cause. There is considerable evidence to support the case that lesbians have contributed significantly to the fight against AIDS in Australia; that is, they have contributed by assisting gay men, asking nothing in return. The Australian community response to AIDS can then best be considered as a gay and lesbian response – the epidemic has contributed significantly to closer political and social coalition-building between gay men and lesbians in Australia. Blewett 'came out' in early 2000 and, now retired, lives with his partner in the Blue Mountains west of Sydney.

Mark Edwards

Blunt, Anthony (1907–83), British scholar and Soviet spy. Blunt was born in Bournemouth, the son of an Anglican minister. He was the younger brother of the artist and writer Wilfred Blunt, who was also gay. He was educated at Marlborough, where he displayed a precocious brilliance and developed the passion for art history that was to dominate his professional life. His school friends included John Betjeman and Louis MacNeice. In

1926 he went to Trinity College, Cambridge, where he graduated with a double first in mathematics and languages, and in 1932 he was elected to a Trinity Fellowship. His doctoral thesis was on the Italian Renaissance theory of art, and in 1933–34 he travelled in Italy. By 1937 he was already a recognised authority on modern art (especially Picasso), on the Italian Renaissance and on the work of the French artist Poussin.

At Cambridge Blunt met communists such as John Cornford, James Klugman and particularly Guy BURGESS, who was a major influence on Blunt personally and politically. Burgess and Blunt were probably lovers, though Blunt later denied this. This was a period in which many intellectuals, alarmed by the rise of fascism and the failure of the Western democracies to resist Hitler, were sympathetic to communism, and Blunt, like many others, became fully convinced at the time of the Spanish Civil War. It is not clear whether Blunt actually joined the British Communist Party: certainly he was never an 'open' member. The Party was at this time following Stalin's 'united front against fascism' policy and was actively recruiting intellectuals. Some, like Blunt and Burgess, were homosexual, though it seems unlikely there was a deliberate policy of recruiting gay men given Soviet attitudes to homosexuality under Stalin. The most important Cambridge recruit, Kim Philby, was aggressively heterosexual.

In 1939 Blunt volunteered for military service and, through the 'old boy network,' got himself into a military intelligence training course and thence, by mid-1940, into MI5, the British secret intelligence agency, where Burgess was already ensconced. Here his linguistic skills were put to good use and he worked on matters dealing with neutral countries and analysing the results of various forms of diplomatic spying. He passed on whatever he learned to Burgess, who passed it on to the Soviet Union. Blunt was therefore technically a spy, but he was not spying directly on Britain or harming the British war effort. The Soviet Union was a neutral power until July 1941, when Hitler attacked it, and from then on it was an allied power. Burgess and Blunt supplied information to the Soviet Union with clear consciences, confident that Soviet and British interests were now identical, and that in any case helping the Soviet Union was the best way to defeat Hitler.

By 1944 Blunt was sufficiently trusted to be appointed as liaison between MI5 and Anglo-American staff planning the D-Day invasion of France. He again passed on what he learned to Burgess, but again it is hard to see how this could have harmed the Allied cause: the Soviets were desperate for the western allies to launch the Second Front. In 1945 he left the secret service and thus lost his usefulness to the Soviet Union, but he remained in contact with the Soviets via Burgess. In 1951, when Burgess and Donald Maclean, fearing exposure, fled to Moscow (possibly with Blunt's assistance, though this is unclear), Blunt was contacted directly by the Soviets and urged to follow. He declined, thus ending his career as an agent. He later said that he had become disillusioned with communism as early as 1945, but this seems to be a little generous. Burgess's defection left Blunt exposed to suspicion, but through the 1950s he defied all MI5's attempts to prove anything against him.

Meanwhile he resumed his career as an art historian, as professor of fine art at both Oxford and Cambridge, and in 1947 he became Director of the Courtauld Institute. He published *Art and Architecture in France 1500–1700*, *Picasso: The Formative Years*, *The Art of William Blake*, *Artistic Theory in Italy 1450–1600* and a five-volume edition of *The Drawings of Poussin*, among many other works. In 1952 he was appointed to the honorary position of Surveyor of the Queen's Pictures: by virtue of his long-standing friendship with the Duke of Kent he had already been an adviser to the Royal Family on art matters for some years. In 1956 he was knighted. When he retired from the Courtauld in 1974, he was generally regarded as Britain's leading art historian, and was highly regarded in France for his work on Poussin.

Blunt was finally undone when MI5 received new and undeniable evidence in 1964, after the defection of Philby made it clear that all the wartime Cambridge recruits should be regarded with suspicion. Blunt had already been interrogated eleven times by the formidable MI5 investigator William Skardon, but had denied all with an impressive *sang-froid*. Now, in exchange for an offer of total and permanent immunity from prosecution, he confessed. Not that there was much to confess. It was twenty years since he had passed information to the Soviet Union, and none of what he had passed related directly to British or Allied security in the cold-war context. If he knew the names of any 'fifth' or 'sixth' men, he did not reveal them. Compared to Maclean or Philby, Blunt was a very small-time spy, though a singularly well-connected one. The decision not to expose or prosecute him seems to have been taken partly out of concern not to embarrass the Queen.

It was inevitable, however, that the facts about Blunt's wartime actions would come out sooner or later. The defections of Burgess, Maclean and Philby left an obvious trail for journalists to follow, and the gentleman's agreement to keep Blunt's confession quiet could not last for ever. In 1979 the BBC journalist Andrew Boyle published *The Climate of Treason*, in which he extensively described the career of the long-sought 'Fourth Man' in the Cambridge spy ring, but referred to him only as 'Maurice'. Following questions in the House of Commons, Prime Minister Margaret Thatcher confirmed that 'Maurice' was in fact Sir Anthony Blunt. A typically British media hurricane followed, and Blunt was stripped of his honorary positions and his knighthood. Branded as a 'traitor' (though against what was never quite clear), Blunt appeared at a press

conference at which he expressed some regret for his actions, while maintaining that they were excusable in the political context of the 1930s. He then maintained a dignified silence until his death in 1983.

There has been a vast amount of ink spilled on the 'Cambridge spies' and their activities. In the fevered atmosphere of 1979, when the Soviet invasion of Afghanistan had revived the cold war, it seemed that the 'unmasking' of Blunt was an event of major importance, and many journalists and writers of paperback instant histories appeared convinced that the activities of a handful of intellectuals during the 1930s and 1940s had changed the course of history. Twenty years later it all seems rather less momentous. The fall of the Soviet Union and the subsequent revelations of its incompetence and corruption have put this petty cold-war saga in a clearer perspective. Nothing that Philby, Blunt and the rest of them did, or could have done, would have made much difference to the Soviet Union's slow slide into bankruptcy and disintegration, and the devotion that Philby at least gave to the Soviet cause until his death now seems more pathetic than sinister. The 'unmasking' of a harmless 72-year-old art historian as though he were one of the master criminals of the century also seems in retrospect to have been tawdry and pointless.

This is not to exonerate entirely those intellectuals of Blunt's generation who succumbed to the lures of communism. It is true that the rise of fascism in the 1930s made it appear that the Soviet Union was the world's only hope and that the Western democracies were hopelessly decadent. But World War II proved that this was not the case: it was, after all, Stalin who signed a non-aggression pact with Hitler in 1939, not Chamberlain. And the evils of Stalin's regime, if not quite as gothic as those of Nazi Germany, were apparent to people on the left who took the trouble to find them out, even in the 1930s, as the careers of George Orwell, Arthur Koestler and

Malcolm Muggeridge, to name a few, testify. Communist intellectuals in the 1930s developed a peculiar kind of myopia that made them blind to the mounting evidence of Stalin's crimes – in some cases until the Soviet regime itself denounced them in 1956.

Much has been made of the fact that some of these Cambridge recruits to the Soviet cause were homosexual: Blunt and Burgess certainly, Maclean less certainly (he appears to have been bisexual in practice). In his 1984 film *Another Country* (memorable for introducing the talents of Rupert Everett and Cary Elwes), Julian Mitchell suggested that Burgess became a spy because of the beastly way he was treated at school. In other words, as Mitchell put it in an interview, 'If you treat any minority unfairly, at some stage it will turn on you'. This seems dubious even in relation to Burgess, and it is ludicrous to suggest it in the case of Blunt, who excelled at school and whose homosexuality was if anything an asset in winning glittering prizes in scholarship and the art world. For discreet establishment gay men like Blunt, sexuality was never a barrier. Blunt must be taken at his word when he says he worked for the Soviet Union because he felt 'that I could best serve the cause of anti-fascism by joining [Burgess] in his work for the Russians'.

Andrew Boyle, *The Climate of Treason* (London, 1979); Barrie Penrose, *Conspiracy of Silence: The Secret Life of Anthony Blunt* (London, 1986).

Adam Carr

The Body Politic Collective Members (1971–87), Canadian magazine writers, editors, and activists, including John Allec, Chris Bearchell, Rick Bébout, Gerald Hannon, Edward Jackson, Michael Lynch, Paul Macdonald, Tim McCaskell, Jearld Moldenhauer, Ken Popert, Gillian Rodgerson and Merv Walker.

For fifteen years, *The Body Politic* (*TBP*) was Canada's most important gay newspaper/magazine, and for most of that time its quality gave it an international profile. Its first issue, twenty-four pages in tabloid format, appeared in November 1971. Within it, typewritten like the rest, was a listing of twenty-two community organisations across Canada, many of them recently formed political groups. It was conceived of as a gay liberation journal – to promote a cause in addition to chronicling and analysing it. It was wary of the emerging gay commercial scene, for a time spurning paid advertisements.

It developed a substantial reputation for its writing and its coverage, attracting contributions from the likes of Jane RULE, John D'EMILIO, James Steakley, Andrew Hodges and Vito RUSSO. It was certainly Toronto-based, reporting on community events and local political developments, but also attempting to cover national and international events. For some time, one-third of its subscribers were outside Canada.

Jearld MOLDENHAUER, a driving force among the founding members, was an American who was also responsible for founding two of the earliest and most important gay bookstores in North America – Glad Day Books in Toronto and Boston. He had the organisational talent, determination and intellect required to get a political magazine off the ground and sustain it in its first years. It was his house that initially served as the magazine's office. He could be bluntly direct, even brutal, drawing some people to *TBP* but driving others away – and eventually he was driven away by other collective members.

Paul Macdonald was another of the key founding members, having already become involved in the Community Homophile Association of Toronto. During the four years of his involvement, he developed a 'community' page, in addition to working on other fronts.

Ken Popert was first to develop the news department, and though he left for a few years, he returned as one of the mainstays until the paper's end. At that point, he continued at the helm of *Xtra!* magazine, a smaller and more commercial offshoot of *TBP* distributed free in Toronto every second week since its birth. John Allec had been crucial in the development of that publication, having coordinated features and reviews and the complex events listings in the main paper until his mid-1980s departure.

Ed Jackson joined *TBP* for their second issue, at the beginning of 1972. He was mostly a journalist during the dozen years he spent there, and arguably the most thoroughly professional of the talented journalists associated with the magazine. He went on to the AIDS Committee of Toronto, where he presided over educational/awareness programming for several years during the group's formative period.

Michael Lynch was involved in the paper for a number of years after 1973, writing for the magazine regularly while also teaching English at the University of Toronto and raising gay issues within the Modern Languages Association.

Tim McCaskell joined in 1975, bringing to the collective unwavering socialist convictions and deep experience in issues of immigration and race. Until the mid-1980s, he managed international news, always as a volunteer.

Chris Bearchell came to the magazine first as a writer in 1976, and as a collective member three years later. She had already accumulated experience in other activist milieux, including the Lesbian Organization of Toronto. For years she was the only woman on the collective, and was one of Toronto's most prominent lesbian activists. Like McCaskell, she was a superb public speaker, and fired up street rallies more than once. Gillian Rodgerson became involved after Bearchell did, and was a high-profile writer and editor until the end, eventually moving to Britain and establishing herself in gay/lesbian journalism there.

Rick Bébout, another migrant from the US, joined later, in 1977, on the recommendation of Merv Walker, until then responsible for design. Bébout soon became central, and arguably the most influential person on the collective – editing, designing, compiling, administering and writing. Through much of the late 1970s and the 1980s, he was as close to an overall editor as the magazine ever had, managing production and design over impossible odds.

Gerald Hannon joined the paper on its second issue, was one of its first paid staffers, and stayed until the last issue. As much as any collective member, Hannon's writing focused on the sexuality in gay liberation, pushing against envelopes of disapproval and censoriousness. His 'Men Loving Boys Loving Men' article in late 1977 produced criminal charges that put the magazine into mainstream press headlines, ending in final acquittal only in 1983. An article on fisting in 1982 resulted in a further court battle, that too ending in acquittal. During those legal battles, *TBP* was an important centre for activist mobilisation (and fundraising), something that had been true from its beginnings.

When Toronto police launched a massive raid on the city's gay bath-houses in February 1981, *TBP* was a central rallying point for activist response, though by then there were also other activist nodes in the city taking up that and other struggles. In some ways its standing and certainly its political centrality diminished in the years to follow. The difficult tensions between serving as a Toronto publication and a national voice – always substantial in a country with marked regional and linguistic divisions – increased. Rising costs and declining subscriptions contributed to the pressures on staff and volunteers, and important figures left in the mid-1980s. In early 1987, the last issue was published.

Xtra! magazine, lighter, more commercial and exclusively for a Toronto audience, continued and prospered, and eventually developed sister publications in Vancouver and Ottawa.

Ed Jackson and Stan Persky (eds), *Flaunting It!*

A Decade of Gay Journalism from The Body Politic (Vancouver, 1982).

David Rayside

Bogarde, Sir Dirk (1921–99), British actor and writer. Born Derek van den Bogaerd, the son of a Dutch-born art editor of *The Times*, his first major role was on television, playing one of the murderous gay lovers in a production of *Rope* (1947). Such was his impact that the handsome newcomer was immediately signed to a long-term contract with the Rank Organisation. A series of mainly lightweight thrillers, comedies and costume melodramas gradually established him as the number one British star of the mid-1950s. His subtle talent was finally given full rein – destroying his carefully nurtured matinée idol image in the process – in *Victim* (1961), and two years later as the decadent valet in *The Servant*, which won him a British Film Academy award.

Although no longer at the height of his popularity, Bogarde's decision to play a homosexual man in *Victim* was courageous. 'I realised it was a risk. I knew a lot of people would rather see me kill my wife on the screen than play this barrister . . . But I decided it was a risk worth taking . . . This was a film about a real person with a real problem.'

His career became increasingly international from the mid-1960s and reached its pinnacle with his portrayal of von Aschenbach, besotted with a youth in visconti's *Death in Venice* (1971), based on Thomas Mann's novella of the same name. He then became a consistently successful writer: a number of novels and seven volumes of autobiography beginning with *A Postillion Struck by Lightning* (1977) and ending with *Cleared for Take Off* (1995). He was knighted for services to cinema in 1992.

Although clearly relishing his position and reputation as both 1950s box-office star and latterday respected character actor, Bogarde's writings and appearances on television, before a disabling stroke re-moved him from public life, revealed him to be acutely self-protective, aloof and brittle. In the mid-1980s he took great pleasure in saying that he had burned his letters and personal papers to stave off biographical prying.

His relationship with his agent, Anthony Forwood, who shared his life for forty years, remains a subject for speculation. Despite Bogarde's pronouncement that 'People are far too obsessed nowadays with homosexuality. Ours was a totally platonic relationship,' he did, however, write movingly of his friend's long illness and death.

Sheridan Morley, *Rank Outsider* (London, 1999).

Keith Howes

Bønnelycke, Per Kleis (b. 1942), Danish politician and activist. Bønnelycke grew up as an only child of fairly old parents. Poverty prevented him from attending high school. In 1959 he was apprenticed as a clerk at the Scandinavian Airlines System (SAS) and after graduating from night school as a correspondence clerk in German in 1962, he moved to Hamburg, where he worked as a computer operator until 1964. Back in Copenhagen Bønnelycke worked as a programer and computer consultant for various companies until in 1976 he returned to the SAS. He is now (2000) vice-president for sales in a subsidiary company, SAS Data.

In 1959 Bønnelycke won the national first prize in an essay competition arranged by the Council of Europe and was awarded a journey to the Federal Republic of Germany where, at the central railway station of Nuremberg, he had his debut as a practicing homosexual. His move to Germany three years later was motivated by his desire to distance himself from his parents' poverty and the psychiatric illness of his mother, and by a need to lead a private life. A few months earlier he had been picked up by the Copenhagen Vice Squad for having sex in the gateway of a building in central Copenhagen. After his return to Copenhagen, Bønnelycke became actively involved in the National Union of Homophiles, later of Gays and Lesbians. He was elected vice-president in 1968 and served as president 1970–77, after coming out in 1969 as the official spokesman for the National Union.

Bønnelycke's period as president of the National Union of Gays and Lesbians was felicitous in many ways. It coincided with a general and historical breakthrough of sexual permissiveness in Denmark, with an explosion of the discourse on sex and gender, the rise of the new radical women's movement, and with the evolution of the homosexual subculture from Stonewall and the Gay Liberation Movement. In spite of genuine anxiety and grumbling from the older members of the National Union, Bønnelycke succesfully established and maintained informal cooperation with the Copenhagen Gay Liberation Front, which in its early days met on the premises of the National Union. The generational renewal of the Executive Committee made it possible to revoke the exclusion since 1955 of the founder and first president of the National Union, Axel AXGIL, and his companion, Eigil, who had been vilified as the irresponsible mainspring of the so-called Pornography Scandal. The ensuing crisis and long-term financial and political paralysis of the organisation was definitively reversed during Bønnelycke's presidency. The National Union became a high profile organisation which lobbyed for societal acceptance of homosexuals. Bønnelycke's and the National Union's adroit and competent approach to the mercurially shifting political constellations in Parliament in the 1970s was an important factor, if not the decisive cause, in the lowering of the homosexual age of consent in 1976 from 18 to 15 years.

As president of the National Union of Gays and Lesbians, Bønnelycke effectively took advantage of the social and political opportunities which opened up in the period of the 'youth revolt'. His approach was pragmatic; although he skilfully promoted the politicising of homosexuality, he had no inclination to theorise on homosexuality or gay politics, nor did he inspire as a speaker. But he demonstrated a formidable ability to handle a swiftly expanding and changing organisation.

From 1985 to 1988 Bønnelycke was a member, appointed by the Minister of Justice, of the Royal Commission on the Situation of Homosexuals in Society, whose report broke the ground for the statute of 1989 on registered partnership.

Bønnelycke was originally a member of the Conservative Party. His contacts, however, as president of the National Union of Gays and Lesbians made him receptive to the arguments of the prominent pro-homosexual politician Else-Merete Ross, MP, who in 1971 persuaded him to join the small but influential Social Liberal ('Radical') Party. Since 1978 he has been a member of the Tårnby Town Council (a suburban municipality where the Copenhagen airport is located), since 1994 a member of the Copenhagen County Council, from 1994 to 1997 chairman of the Copenhagen County Council's Committee on Infrastructure and Environment, and from 1986 to 1993 member of the Governmental Central Committee on Ethics in Science. Bønnelycke is currently a member of the Executive Committee of the Social Liberal Party and chairman of the Committee on Local Politics. He was chairman of the Social Liberal Party's Committee on Judicial Politics, 1978–88.

He has a registered partnership (1989) with his companion since 1978, schoolteacher Per Møller Sørensen (b. 1943).

Per Kleis Bønnelycke, 'Pæne mennesker', in Anette and Jørgen Johansen (eds), *Rapport om homofile* (Copenhagen, 1973), pp. 144–9.

Wilhelm von Rosen

Bonnet, Marie-Jo (b. 1949), French activist and scholar. Born in Deauville, Bonnet moved to Paris at 16, where she joined the MLF (Mouvement de Libération des

Femmes, Women's Liberation Movement) in February 1971 and became a founding member of both FHAR (Front Homosexuel d'Action Révolutionnaire, Homosexual Front for Revolutionary Action) in March 1971 and the Gouines Rouges (Red Dykes) in April 1971. The Gouines Rouges began as a liaison group between FHAR and the MLF, but broke with FHAR in June 1971 in reaction against the 'misogyny' of the men, who, more and more numerous, had come to dominate the meetings: 'We [lesbians] felt dispossessed of FHAR .... We spoke, [the men] no longer listened to us.' Bonnet remained a feminist and lesbian militant throughout the 1970s: 'Sisterhood is powerful, said American women; we [French women] experienced it, thrilled finally to be able to join with other women regardless of our social origin, our sexual practices or the colour of our skin.'

Bonnet meanwhile pursued postgraduate studies in history and in 1979 completed her doctoral thesis (at the University of Paris-VII) on love between women from the sixteenth century to the present. This was the first thesis in the history of homosexuality written in France. The topic emerged directly from her political convictions: 'I needed to reflect on love between women. It was a way of extending and deepening my militant activities as both feminist and lesbian.' She published an extended version of the thesis in 1981 as *Un Choix sans équivoque* and a revised edition in 1995 as *Les Relations amoureuses entre les femmes du XVIème au XXe siècle.*

Although Bonnet temporarily gave up militancy in the early 1980s for 'a long period of interiorisation of [her] years of action', she continued to work as a teacher, journalist and independent scholar. She is currently researching artistic creation by women from antiquity to the present. She took up political militancy again in the mid-1990s in order to defend (in her words) 'the dual equality between men and women and between heterosexuals and homosexuals'.

Interview in *Homophonies*, no. 8/9 (July/August 1981); interview with author (January 1998); Marie-Jo Bonnet, 'De l'émancipation amoureuse des femmes dans la cité', *Les Temps Modernes* March/April 1998.

Michael Sibalis

Bory, Jean-Louis (1919–79), French writer, journalist, broadcaster and activist. The anti-gay psychiatrist Henri Amoroso described Bory as 'a veritable Goebbels of homosexual propaganda'. Bory was born and died in the village of Méréville in the Beauce region not far from Paris. His father was a pharmacist; his mother, a schoolteacher. Bory had a happy childhood, despite initial anguish when he realised at 16 that he was a homosexual. An understanding teacher assured him that the minority to which he belonged was 'not monstrous', while his father told him, 'As long as you don't hurt anybody, you have no reason to be ashamed'. During World War II, Bory served in the French army (1939–42) and participated in the Resistance (1944). He graduated from university in 1945 with a degree in classical literature. He was a highly successful and popular teacher of Greek, Latin and French literature in secondary schools until 1962, when he decided to devote himself to his literary pursuits.

Bory's first novel, *Mon village à l'heure allemande* (*My Village on German Time*), won the Prix Goncourt, one of France's most prestigious literary prizes, in 1945. Although none of his later novels ever earned him comparable critical esteem, he published thirty volumes of fiction, history and film criticism over the next three decades. He was best known as a film critic, both in the press and, from 1964, on a popular weekly radio show, *Le Masque et la Plume.*

Bory once described the four stages through which every homosexual must pass as 'recognising yourself, accepting yourself, getting others to recognise you, getting others to accept you'. Having recognised and accepted his homosexuality as a teenager, he made it public in a radio broadcast in 1969. In 1973 he published a short autobiography, *Ma Moitié d'Orange* (*My Half of the Orange*), and the Swiss review *Accord* carried an interview with him under the title 'I am a homosexual'. 'I can no longer claim ... to be crusading against such and such a conformity, prejudice or taboo', he explained, 'if ... I keep silent about the truth of my personal life!' On 21 January 1975, Bory took part in a landmark television broadcast in the series *Les Dossiers de l'Écran*: a live debate on homosexuality. He told 19 million viewers, 'I do not confess that I am homosexual, because I am not ashamed of it. I do not boast that I am homosexual, because I am not proud of it. I state that I am homosexual, because it's a fact'.

Bory became the best-known homosexual in France, with a readership and radio audience in the millions. Although never primarily a gay militant, he used his fame and prestige to advance homosexual liberation in France. 'I do not plead [a cause]. I inform ... Homosexuality is an aspect of life that people should know – and understand.' Bory advocated a middle way between the Catholic conformism preached by André BAUDRY, who headed the 'homophile' organisation Arcadie, and the revolutionary radicalism of the gay liberation movement, represented by Guy HOCQUENGHEM and FHAR (Front Homosexuel d'Action Révolutionnaire: Homosexual Front for Revolutionary Action). Bory wanted homosexuality and homosexuals to be 'banal' – that is to say, ordinary. 'A homosexual', he said, 'is simply a heterosexual who loves men'. He was not interested in 'bourgeois homosexuality', generally tolerated by the French elite, and defended instead 'the homosexuality of the truck driver or of the unskilled worker at the Renault car factory'. His message was simple: 'Homosexuality must be recognised and accepted as a social and sexual lifestyle as valuable as all others. ... One can be homosexual without being a pervert ... or a criminal; one can be a

homosexual and still pay one's taxes. ... In short, one can be homosexual and ... find happiness.' He wanted for homosexuals not the *droit à la différence* (the right to be different), but rather the *droit à l'indifférence* (the right to be treated with indifference).

Bory was cultured, witty and charming, yet rarely happy. His ugliness tormented him, and he once told his mother, 'I would give ten years of my life to be handsome'. By the end of the 1970s Bory was in deep depression and under heavy medication. Discouraged by his literary failures, weary of his role as 'the homosexuals' Joan of Arc' (his phrase), and dispirited at the end of an unhappy love affair with a young actor, Bory took his own life on 11 June 1979.

Jean-Louis Bory and Guy Hocquenghem, *Comment nous appelez-vous déjà?* (Paris, 1977); Daniel Garcia, *Jean-Louis Bory* (Paris, 1991); Marie-Claude Jardin, *Jean-Louis Bory* (Paris, 1991).

Michael Sibalis

Boswell, John (1947–94), American scholar. For most gay folk of faith, and gay men in particular, Boswell burst on to the scene with his 1980 monumental book *Christianity, Social Tolerance, and Homosexuality: Gay People in Western Europe from the Beginning of the Christian Era to the Fourteenth Century*. The book and the author brought new life and new pride to those gay men and women who identified themselves as Christian. Many modern Christians have condemned and excluded gays who claim to be believers, while many gays condemn and exclude Christians who claim to be gay. Like many gays of faith, Boswell himself was a devout Catholic (having converted in his teens). But his book was not without critics, some of whom thought that by emphasising the tolerance of the early Church towards homosexuality, he was letting them off the hook for both the anti-homosexual attitudes and violence that followed and its equally insidious legacy of emotional (and still at times physical) terror. Boswell's second major work was *Same-Sex Unions in Premodern Europe*, published in 1994. In reviews which appeared widely, historians and theologians, as well as gay critics, disputed his findings that same-sex marriage-like religious ceremonies were performed between the eighth and sixteenth centuries. They questioned his methodology, his translations from the original languages and his interpretations. Many thought, furthermore, that he had a personal agenda and was bending facts to prove it.

Born in Boston, Massachusetts in 1947, Boswell received his doctorate in history from Harvard University and in 1975 became a full-professor (and eventually department head) at Yale University. It was, perhaps ironically, a piece in the *New Republic*, after his death, that summed it up the best. Jacob Weisberg, a student of Boswell, wrote: 'Though Boswell wrote several wonderful books, his public recognition is based on the controversy over his final one, *Same-Sex Unions in Premodern Europe* ... The book's scholarship is as meticulous as Boswell's always was, but so incendiary ... It is characteristic of Boswell's argumentative brilliance that he sought tolerance for homosexuals not by decrying the Church's long persecution of them, but by demonstrating that the Church once accepted them. In time, his book will prove enormously influential.' Boswell died of AIDS.

'Rites: A Yale Historian Sets Off an Uproar by Claiming Catholicism Once Blessed Same-sex Marriages', *People Weekly*, vol. 41, no. 24 (1994), p. 57; Jacob Weisberg, 'Dirty Books', *The New Republic*, vol. 212, no. 3 (1995), p. 46.

Lee Arnold

Botha, Kevan (b. 1962), South African activist. Botha has been active in South African gay and lesbian politics since the early 1980s, when he was a member of the Gay Association of South Africa (GASA). In 1986 he represented GASA at the International Lesbian and Gay Association convention, where he argued against GASA's expulsion from the international body. Botha subsequently played a key role in the Convention for Democracy in South Africa (CODESA) – the preliminary negotiations that led to South Africa's first democratic elections and ushered in the interim constitution. At CODESA he acted on behalf of the Equality Foundation, a trust established to promote legal equality for lesbians and gay men in South Africa. He led the successful lobby to include 'sexual orientation' in the Equality Clause of the Interim Constitution formulated at CODESA. In 1994, the National Coalition of Gay and Lesbian Equality (NCGLE) was formed – the first national umbrella body of its kind in South Africa. The NCGLE was established in order to protect the inclusion of 'sexual orientation' in the constitution, and to ensure that legislation was brought into line with the new constitution, which would be ratified after South Africa's first democratic elections. During this period the NCGLE launched an intensive lobbying and public awareness campaign, during which Botha acted as parliamentary lobbyist for the NCGLE.

Gay and Lesbian Archives, University of the Witwatersrand Libraries, Johannesburg.

Graeme Reid

Boulerice, André (b. 1946), Canadian politician. Boulerice was the first politician in any of Canada's provincial legislatures to be openly gay, eventually followed by two British Columbians elected in 1996. In the 1970s, Boulerice had been an organiser for the sovereigntist Parti Québécois (PQ). He was first elected to Quebec's National Assembly in 1985, representing a constituency of central-south Montreal that includes the substantially gay *Village de l'Est*. He was then re-elected three times, in 1997 becoming Deputy House Leader for the PQ government of Premier Lucien Bouchard. He had been an opposition spokesman on various portfolios, including culture and communications, though he has not yet been a cabinet minister during the times when his party has formed the government. Like other sovereigntists, Boulerice has argued that Quebec society is more accepting of sexual diversity than the other Canadian provinces, and that such acceptance is reflected in Quebec being the first to add sexual orientation to its provincial human rights legislation (in 1977). Public opinion surveys do reveal a relatively liberal pattern of public beliefs on the subject, although Quebec government policy has always not been ahead of other provinces (e.g. British Columbia). In 1999 Quebec legislated wide-ranging recognition for same-sex relationships, though adoption rights were excluded, and passage occurred at a time when courts elsewhere were forcing similar change.

David Rayside

Bowie, David (b. 1947), British singer/songwriter. Born David Robert Jones in London, he changed his name to David Bowie in order to avoid confusion with Davy Jones of The Monkees. Bowie tried for several years to break into the pop charts with various incarnations of bands that played everything from Motown-influenced sax to Anthony Newley-inspired light commercial pop, until he finally became famous with the precocious hit 'Space Oddity', which came out in time for the first Apollo moonwalk.

During the 1970s he wrote and produced a string of albums beginning with *The Man Who Sold the World* (1971) and ending in 1980 with *Scary Monsters (and Super Creeps)*. For each album he created a new persona that often included elements of gay, bisexual and lesbian identity that he used when promoting the album and performing the songs. Influenced by gay Scottish mime Lindsay Kemp, Bowie was able to bring a minimalist sexiness to his concert performances. In 1972 as Ziggy Stardust he climaxed each show by imitating fellatio with Mick Ronson's guitar. Bowie not only performed in leotards and pancake powder, but also in the same year caused a controversy by casually admitting his bisexuality in an interview, which he reaffirmed in *Playboy* in 1975.

Although he has since moved away from this position, he has continued to raise questions in his music about both sexuality and gender. An important contribution came with the album *Lodger* (1979) for which Bowie created several striking videos. One, for the song 'DJ', shows Bowie being kissed by a man as they walk down a crowded city street, while another features a self-conscious use of drag to put a bitterly ironic political edge on 'Boys Keep Swinging', a song about male privilege. *Lodger* updated and expanded his comments on sexuality and gender and gave to his ideas a political cohesion they had lacked. His albums in the 1980s and 1990s, though musically interesting, have added little to his image as a bisexual artist. He married the model Iman in 1992 and claimed that he was, during the 1970s, 'a closet heterosexual'. Since the release of *Outside* (1995) and *Earthling* (1997) – and the reconsideration of his early 1970s work that they seem to suggest – he has said that he does not regret his forays into the gay demi-monde.

Roy Carr and Charles Shaar Murray, *David Bowie: An Illustrated Record* (New York, 1981); Kenneth Pitt, *Bowie: The Pitt Report* (London, 1985); Elizabeth Thomson and David Gutman (eds), *The Bowie Companion* (London, 1993).

Shelton Waldrep

Bowles, Paul (Frederick) (1910–99), American writer. Born in New York, Bowles made Tangier, Morocco, his home for over half a century, and helped to shape the Western fascination with Tangier and Morocco.

Bowles's early career was as a composer and he wrote music for the New York theatre scene, including scores for the Tennessee WILLIAMS plays *The Glass Menagerie* and *Sweet Bird of Youth*. He studied music with Aaron Copland and Virgil Thomson. While in the United States, Bowles met Jane Auer, a writer, and the two were married in 1938.

Bowles's greatest legacy, perhaps, is his involvement with Tangier, its storytellers and musicians, and with the American and European expatriates and tourists who made it their residence and playground. His first trip to Tangier was in 1931, at the suggestion of Gertrude Stein and Alice B. Toklas, who thought that an encounter with non-Western culture would help him determine his own artistic style. Bowles was captivated by Morocco, its people, culture and landscape.

The Bowles took up semi-permanent residence in Tangier in 1938. During this period, Bowles wrote *The Sheltering Sky* (1949), about an American couple travelling in the North African desert. The novel was so stylistically unconventional that Doubleday, which had commissioned it, refused to publish it. It was eventually published by New Directions and has since been exalted as a great work of existentialist literature.

After World War I, Tangier increasingly became a haven for a wide range of Western adventurers and tourists, from millionaires to artists to homosexual men. For the last group, Tangier was popular for its cheap cost of living and the availability of drugs and young male prostitutes. Bowles eventually became the 'American resident' whom Western homosexual writers and artists would visit and whom they called upon for his services as host and guide to Tangier and the rest of Morocco; as such, he met Tennessee Williams, William BURROUGHS, Allen GINSBERG, Truman CAPOTE, Brion Gysin, Rupert CROFT-COOKE, Cecil Beaton and Gore VIDAL.

Bowles's love for Tangier can be witnessed in his considerable corpus of writing, much of it concerned with North Africa. He published six novels, fourteen short story collections and three volumes of poetry. In addition, he recorded, transcribed and translated Moroccan oral stories in collaboration with Mohammed Mrabet and Driss Ben Hamed Charhadi (Larbi Layachi), and he translated works of the contemporary Moroccan author Mohammed Choukri, including the latter's memoirs, *Jean Genet in Tangier* (1974) and *Tennessee Williams in Tangier* (1979). Bowles also took an interest in the preservation of Moroccan folk music. In 1959, he spent five weeks travelling around Morocco recording Moroccan 'andaluz' music. Only two of the recordings have been commercially released, but the full set is kept at the American Library of Congress.

In recent years there has been a rebirth of interest in Bowles with reprints of his book of travel essays, *Their Heads Are Green* and *Their Hands Are Blue* (1990), and his autobiography, *Without Stopping* (1991). He also published *In Touch: The Letters of Paul Bowles* (1994) and *Two Years beside the Strait: Tangier Journal 1987–89* (1990). Perhaps most popularly known is Bernardo Bertolucci's film adaptation of *The Sheltering Sky* (1990), in which Bowles had a cameo role.

Jennifer Baichwal, *Let It Come Down: The Life of Paul Bowles* (film, 1998); Iain Finlayson, *Tangier: City of the Dream* (London, 1993); Michelle Green, *The Dream at the End of the World: Paul Bowles and the Literary Renegades in Tangier* (New York, 1991); Christopher Sawyer-Lauçanno *An Invisible Spectator: A Biography of Paul Bowles* (London, 1989).

Trent Newmeyer

Boy George (b. 1961), British singer. George O'Dowd was born and grew up in London. Early on, he found himself the object of ridicule among his peers; according to his 1995 autobiography, *Take It Like A Man*, George's interest in women's clothing, Shirley Bassey and his demeanour in general quickly marked him as different, and the nicknames 'pansy' and 'poof' were his first.

George's early years were spent dodging authority, and at 15 he found himself out of school and frequenting nightclubs. He entered London club culture as a punk; musical aspirations shortly followed, and his association with Mikey Craig, Bow Wow Wow and John Moss, drummer and lover, paved the way for the formation of Culture Club in 1981. Culture Club's third single and first hit, 'Do You Really Want To Hurt Me?' (1982) was a huge success, and signalled the recasting of the punk aesthetic in the popular imagination as a more palatable 'new wave'. A string of hits followed, and then the release of their successful albums *Kissing To Be Clever* (1982), *Colour By Numbers* (1983), and *Waking Up With The House On Fire* (1984).

Culture Club toured their idiosyncratic blend of pop, soul and reggae in the US, and George became an infamous figure as he parlayed Wildean soundbites in a manner not unlike Wilde's on his tour of a century earlier. George renovated the mass perception of British culture following punk as acceptably *outré*, most significantly through an insistence on locating questions of gender ambiguity along with a distinctive stylistic heterogeneity in their string of hits. The success of Culture Club was accompanied by the kind of mass-market merchandising more traditionally associated with teenage heart throbs; the production of a now highly collectible Boy Geoge doll epitomised the mass-media appeal of the group, and especially of its lead singer. George's succes initiated a flurry of interest in 'gender-bending' in the mid-1980s, an interest capitalised upon by both George's friend and fellow singer Marilyn, and by the 'androgynous' explorations of Annie Lennox, lead singer of the Eurythmics. More distantly, the ambiguity surrounding sexuality which was a hallmark of Boy George's persona paved the way for the decadence-inflected, James Dean-styled sexual bewilderment of a

Morrissey. In turn, Boy George's stylisations owed much to the precedent of David BOWIE and glitter rock, if not to their aesthetics. Despite George's elaborate drag and camp persona, the 1980s saw no explicit avowal of gay identity by the singer.

When George's personal life was clouded with escalating drug use, he became the focus of a brief but massive tabloid frenzy. Culture Club unofficially disbanded in 1986. George's subsequent career as singer, writer and DJ was followed by his developing interest in Buddhism, and the completion of his autobiography; Culture Club have recently reformed. George's singing career was revitalised in 1993 with the success of the single of the title song from the film *The Crying Game*. Appropriately, that combination of lachrymose and lyrical nostalgia and a secret sexual 'identity' which the song and movie celebrate serves to capture some of the poignancy and transitoriness of a quixotic 'gender-bending' which had held many in thrall.

Boy George, *Take It Like A Man* (London, 1995).

Melissa Hardie

Boyd, Malcolm (b. 1923), American priest and religious author. Born in Buffalo, New York, the only son of wealthy parents, he was raised in New York City and attended high school in Denver, Colorado. After graduation from the University of Arizona in 1944, he worked in Hollywood in advertising, radio, film and television, and with the film actor Mary Pickford and her husband 'Buddy' Rogers formed a company, Pickford, Rogers and Boyd. In 1951 he began study for the ministry of the Episcopal Church at the Church Divinity School of the Pacific in Berkeley, California, where he graduated in 1954. This was followed by a year's study at Oxford University and a postgraduate degree in theology at Union Theological Seminary in New York. He was ordained priest in Los Angeles in 1955. After two years as rector of a downtown parish in Indianapolis, Indiana, he became a college chaplain. From 1959 he was chaplain to Episcopal students at Colorado State University and from 1961 at Wayne State University in Detroit. There he became involved in the black civil rights movement. He wrote a weekly column in a national black newspaper, took part in demonstrations and later assisted with the registration of black voters in the South.

During these years he became, he recalled in his autobiography, 'the image of a rebel priest and an angry young man'. Distrusted by conservatives, he was labelled as 'controversial'. His book *Are You Running with Me, Jesus?* (1965) reflected the religious activism and cultural ferment of the period. It went through many editions and made its author famous. In 1965 Boyd became the national field representative of the Episcopal Society for Cultural and Racial Unity, based in Washington, DC. In the late 1960s he was active in the peace movement and from 1968 to 1971 was a writer in residence at Calhoun College, Yale University. During these years he wrote many books and articles.

Boyd experienced his first sexual relationship with another man in New York in the mid-1950s, but he was slow to accept his homosexuality. In 1976 he decided to come out in an interview with the religion editor of the *Chicago Sun-Times*. This was followed by the publication of his autobiographical works *Take Off the Masks* (1978) and *Gay Priest* (1986). He was the first prominent priest in the US publicly to disclose his homosexuality. From 1982 to 1995 Boyd was on the staff of St Augustine-by-the-Sea Episcopal Church in Santa Monica, California, and active in the AIDS ministry of the Episcopal diocese of Los Angeles. In 1996 he became poet/writer in residence at St Paul's Episcopal Cathedral in Los Angeles. Boston University has established the Malcolm Boyd Archive. In 1984 Boyd formed a partnership with a writer, Mark Thompson, author of *Gay Spirit*, *Gay*

Soul and Gay Body, and editor of *Leatherfolk* and *Long Road to Freedom: The Advocate History of the Gay and Lesbian Movement*.

Malcolm Boyd, *Take Off the Masks* (New York, 1978, rev. edn, 1993) *Gay Priest: An Inner Journey* (New York, 1986).

David Hilliard

Brant, Beth (b. 1941), Canadian-American writer. A Bay of Quinte Mohawk from Ontario, Canada, Brant was born in a suburb in Detroit. She has lived much of her life in Michigan, and divides her time between Michigan and Canada. She married at 17 and had three daughters; the marriage – to an abusive, alcoholic husband – ended in divorce. As a single mother who had not completed high school, she worked in various jobs to support herself and her children. At the age of 33, Brant began to identify herself as a lesbian. She did not identify herself as a writer until she was forty.

Her major works are *Mohawk Trail* (1985), *Food & Spirits* (1991) and *Writing as Witness* (1994). She also edited *A Gathering of Spirit: A Collection of North American Indian Women*, (1983; expanded edition, 1988). *Mohawk Trail* is a collection of stories, poems, autobiographical sketches and creative reinventions of folktales. It explores issues of Native American identity, gay and lesbian identity and working-class struggles. In many of her works, Brant establishes thematic links among homophobia, racism and sexism. In 'Coyote Learns a New Trick', she re-imagines a traditional coyote trickster tale; in Brant's version Coyote is a female who dresses as a man, planning to play a trick on Fox, and Coyote discovers the joys of lesbianism. In 'Danny', a young gay man finds it difficult to disguise his identity in a hostile, heterosexist patriarchal environment. He becomes a nurse in a hospital, cross-dresses at night and eventually becomes a victim of gay-bashing. 'Her Name Is Helen' describes a working-class Indian lesbian with low self-esteem. In 'A Long Story', Brant juxtaposes two narratives, both involving 'child stealing'. One story takes place in 1890 and describes the kidnapping of Indian children by the white authorities; the other takes place in 1978, when a lesbian mother is denied custody of her child.

In *Food & Spirits*, Brant continues exploring themes of Indian identity, gay and lesbian identity, working-class struggles, abusive relationships and recovery from abuse and alcoholism. In 'This Place', a gay Indian with AIDS comes home to the reservation to die. In 'Turtle Gal', an elderly gay man cares for a young Indian girl when her alcoholic mother dies. In 'Swimming Upstream', a lesbian recovering alcoholic must struggle with the temptation to drink after her son dies.

Brant refers to Native American gays and lesbians as 'Two Spirits'. She believes that homophobia, sexism and racism were brought to North America by the European invaders. In 1995, Brant wrote: 'Faced with homophobia from our own communities, faced with racism and homophobia from the outsiders who hold semblances of power over us, we feel that desire to make connections between oppressions in a primal and necessary way.' She also believes that writing is a conscious political act.

Beth Brant, 'Giveaway', *Off Our Backs*, 1 (Nov., 1995), and *Writing As Witness: Essay and Talk* (Toronto, 1994).

Karen Lee Osborne

Brantenberg, Gerd (b. 1941), Norwegian novelist, lesbian feminist and activist. Brantenberg was born in Oslo, but grew up in the coastal town of Fredrikstad in south-eastern Norway. She graduated from the University of Oslo with a degree in English language and literature in 1970, and then worked as a high school teacher for several years, before she made her literary debut in 1973. She has been a full-time writer since 1982.

Brantenberg's literary production includes eight novels, all translated into other languages, and numerous short stories, essays, articles, plays and songs. She has done a number of reading tours in countries outside Norway. Her true-to-life books on the themes of lesbian life and awakening have undoubtedly contributed greatly to the self-confidence of two generations of lesbians and gay men, in Norway as well as in other countries where her works are known.

Her first book, *Opp alle jordens homofile* (*What Comes Naturally*, 1973, transl. 1986), is a gay coming-out story in the form of a sarcastic monologue. *Egalias døtre* (*The Daughters of Egalia*, 1977, transl. 1985) is a satire about the fantasy country Egalia, where the women are in power and oppress the men. The book was an international bestseller, and has been translated into thirteen languages. Her trilogy on the Norwegian post-war generation, *Sangen om St. Croix* (*The Song of St Croix*, 1979), *Ved fergestedet* (*At the Quay*, 1985) and *For alle vinder* (*The Four Winds*, 1996), portrays young Inger, who gradually comes to realise her love for other women. *Favntak* (*Embraces*, 1983) tells the love story of a married woman and a lesbian in the feminist Scandinavian setting of 1978. *Eremitt og entertainer* (*Hermit and Entertainer*, 1991) is a collection of essays, articles and lectures on feminist, gay and literary topics.

In 1986, she published *På sporet av den tapte lyst* (*In Remembrance of Lusts Past*; with co-writers), a literary motif study of love between women in European literature translated into or originally written in one of the Scandinavian languages in the period 1900–85. Her most recent book, *Augusta og Bjørnstjerne* (1997), is an historical novel of the mid-nineteenth century about the author's great-grandmother and her secret engagement to the Norwegian national poet Bjørnstjerne Bjørnson.

In addition to her outstanding authorship, Brantenberg also is known as a remarkable feminist and lesbian activist. She was instrumental in the founding of the Lesbian Movement in Denmark (1974) and Norway (1975), and has also been a board member of the main gay organisations in the two countries. She has also been a co-organiser of Feminist Book Fairs, and a contributor in writing on feminist, gay and literary topics in newspapers and periodicals.

Lisbeth Nilsen

Bray, Alan (b. 1948), British scholar. Bray was born in Hunslet, a working-class district in Leeds in the north of England, where his father was a worker in the engineering industry. He joined the Gay Liberation Front in 1970 and the later Gay Activists Alliance and helped to found the Lesbian and Gay Christian Movement. This political activism was the background to his book *Homosexuality in Renaissance England:* a book written at the time in isolation from academia (and mostly late at night after a day's work as a British career civil servant). Its appearance in 1982 had a formative influence on the early mapping-out of the history of homosexuality then emerging; its conclusion was to argue that the modern homosexual identity was a product of history, something radically new, and not immutable and outside historical change. The book appeared in Japanese in 1993 and was republished in a new edition in 1995. He was elected a research fellow of Nuffield College, Oxford in 1984 and is now an Honorary Research Fellow of Birkbeck College in the University of London. He has been an editor of *History Workshop Journal*, a journal of socialist and feminist historians, where his later research appeared. He lives in Notting Hill, in London; and his book is dedicated to his life-long friend Graham Wilson, whom Bray met when they were both thirteen, together at their school in Leeds.

Robert Aldrich and Garry Wotherspoon

Briggs, John V. (b. 1930), American politician. Briggs was born in South Dakota, moved to California in 1935, was a veteran of the Korean conflict, established a business as an insurance broker, and was a Republican California State legislator representing Orange County from 1976 to 1981.

He gained notoriety in June 1977 when he sponsored Senate Bill 1253 in the California legislature. The bill proposed that local school districts be given the right to suspend and dismiss teachers who engaged in homosexual acts, whether or not this behaviour was considered criminal in California. The bill also proposed that school boards be allowed to require applicants for teaching jobs to furnish a statement that the applicant had not engaged in homosexual activity. From the outset, SB1253 had little chance of becoming law. Even fellow Republicans regarded Briggs as a 'loose cannon' and Senator Richardson, a religious, conservative ally who led Senate opposition in 1975 to decriminalisation of sexual acts between consenting adults in private, remarked that Briggs was of the 'drop-your-pants school of political issues' and more interested in promoting himself than the issue at hand. (Briggs was a Republican gubernatorial candidate in 1978 but withdrew before the primary.)

SB1253 failed in the Senate, as did a resolution introduced by Briggs commending Anita BRYANT for 'her national, religious crusade [and] courageous stand to protect American children from exposure to blatant homosexuality'. The resolution was voted down, 36 to 2 votes on 15 June 1977, and a second attempt to have the resolution passed was killed in committee a week later. Around the same time Briggs also sponsored in the Senate a bill to prohibit homosexual marriages in California which passed both houses and was signed into law by Governor Jerry Brown in August 1977.

When SB1253 failed, Briggs organised an initiative petition to hold a referendum on the issue. A technicality prevented the vote from being held in June and it was delayed until November 1978. Officially titled, 'Proposition 6: School Employees Homosexual Initiative', informally it was known as the 'Briggs' Initiative'. The California Defend Our Children (CDOC) organisation was primarily responsible for supporting the initiative. It was chaired by Briggs, with Rev. Louis P. Sheldon, an Anaheim Presbyterian minister, as executive director. Sheldon is still active in the anti-gay movement in southern California and nationally. CDOC ran short of all sorts of resources (funds, endorsements, credible leadership, volunteers) long before the vote. Although US Senator S. I. Hayakawa (a Republican from California) gave tacit approval to the proposal, it was supported by few other well-known conservatives, and even Ronald REAGAN opposed it. Proposition 6 was soundly defeated with 58 per cent voting against it. After this, Briggs's political fortunes began to wane. In 1981 he seemed to lose interest in politics and resigned with three years left in his current term.

A massive effort was made by the gay and lesbian community to fight the initiative. Gay leaders such as David Goodstein, publisher of *The Advocate*, and Troy PERRY, founder of the Metropolitan Community Church, began raising funds to hire professional lobbyists and campaigners, and a string of grassroots organisations also appeared, headed by long-time activists such as Morris Kight and Harvey MILK. Conflict about appropriate strategies to combat the initiative were inevitable but the groups became more cohesive as the election approached.

Gerard Sullivan, *A Study of Political Campaigns of Discrimination Against Gay People in the United States, 1950–1978* (Ann Arbor, University Microfilms International [8729425], 1987).

Gerard Sullivan

Britten, Benjamin, Baron (1913–76), British composer, and **Pears, Sir Peter** (1910–86), British singer. One of the most gifted

British composers, Benjamin Britten met Peter Pears in 1936. Together they forged a personal and professional relationship which produced some of the most important British music and performance of the century. A talented symphonist and orchestrator, Britten was most successful in writing vocal music of great subtlety and power in which he achieved an idiomatic style which had eluded so many other British composers. In Pears, Britten found the ideal collaborator who inhabited many of his most important musical creations and brought to them interpretive skills of unparalleled intensity and intelligence.

Born to a middle-class family in Lowestoft, Britten started composition lessons with prominent British composer Frank Bridge at the age of 13. By 1930 he was studying at the Royal College of Music of London, where he produced a number of early chamber works. By the 1940s Britten's most important work was written for the stage, and a series of operas established him as one of the dominant figures in post-war British music. He went on to produce a large body of chamber music, musical parables and symphonic works, such as the *War Requiem*. Set to the poetry of Wilfred Owen, this piece is widely regarded as one of the most powerful and moving compositions of the twentieth century.

Pears originally began his career as an organist at Hertford College, Oxford, but by the 1930s he was also studying at the Royal College of Music, where he began to concentrate instead on voice. After his meeting with Britten, his repertoire centred on Britten's compositions. His plangent voice, with its distinctive timbre and clear diction, was ideally suited to the musical textures created by Britten, and Pears was the first – and often definitive – interpreter of many of the most important roles in the operas as well as other vocal compositions.

Apart from Britten's meeting with Pears, by then a promising young tenor with the BBC Singers, the 1930s also saw the composer develop an important association with poet W. H. Auden. Both of them homosexual and pacifist, their friendship blossomed in the climate of 1930s Britain, and their partnership yielded several early works, including *Paul Bunyan*, an operetta on which they collaborated while in the US during World War II.

It was Auden who also stimulated Britten's interest in English poets, in particular the work of Suffolk poet Henry Crabbe. This, in turn, sparked an interest in English folk music and customs more generally, which were to become a preoccupation throughout Britten's life and work. The first flowering of these concerns came with Britten's composition of the most important British opera of the postwar period, *Peter Grimes*. First performed in London in 1945 with Pears in the lead, this work revolutionised the British opera stage. Not only was the music powerful and dramatically charged, but for the first time idiomatic treatment of the English language had been achieved for the opera stage.

In 1948, along with librettist Eric Crozier, Britten and Pears founded an annual Music Festival in Aldeburgh, the town where they lived. Once described by E. M. Forster as a town that 'generally seemed to have got a good allocation of paint', Aldeburgh – through its festival – became a cultural focus for post-war Britain where new music in particular was fostered. In later years the Aldeburgh Festival became part of the mainstream of British cultural life, and Britten and Pears held court there each year in ever grander style. Those who fell out of favour were barred from the inner sanctum of the festival. Others prospered in the intensely creative atmosphere, and the influence of the festival and of Britten and Pears's work more generally remains a testament to one of the most enduring and fruitful partnerships in musical history.

Britten's works for the operatic stage were probably his most challenging – both musically and in their subject matter. In 1953, for example, he composed *Gloriana* in celebration of the new British monarch, Queen Elizabeth II. It was, however, rather tersely received by the Queen, who approved of neither the angularity of its musical language nor the treatment of Elizabeth I, the opera's protagonist.

Many of Britten's other operatic compositions communicated complex and sometimes quite radical ideas, and the gilded opera audiences of the 1950s were confronted by dark, brooding pieces, often involving matters of sexuality or unconventionality. As early as *Peter Grimes*, for example, Britten (and Pears) had produced a subtle treatment of outsiderness, captured within the setting of 'quaint' English village life. Even the most obtuse of critics realised that the work could be read as a metaphor for a more general social hostility towards difference – sexual or otherwise. In 1951 came *Billy Budd*, an all-male opera based on the Herman Melville novella which was suffused with homoerotic desire. Four years later Britten adapted a Henry James 'ghost story', *The Turn of the Screw*: in this opera he gave an already eerie tale an extra charge by adding an explicitly pederastic dimension. Themes of homosexual attraction and thwarted desire featured again in Britten's last opera, *Death in Venice* (1973), in which he adapted the Thomas Mann novel and wrote for Pears the central part of Aschenbach. Even today, performances of many of these works often leave audiences in a stunned silence at their conclusion, the dramatic charge of the music and the disquieting sexual politics intruding upon the familiar and often facile rituals of a night at the opera.

A. Blyth, *Remembering Britten* (London, 1981); Donald Mitchell, *Britten and Auden in the Thirties* (London, 1981); Christopher Palmer (ed.), *The Britten Companion* (London, 1984); M. Thorpe (ed.), *Peter Pears: A Tribute on his 75th Birthday* (London, 1985).

                                                                    C. Faro

Brongersma, Edward (1911–98), Dutch activist. Born to a well-to-do Protestant family from Haarlem, Brongersma became enamoured of Catholicism and of right-wing governments in southern Europe, specifically Salazar's corporative state in Portugal. After studying law, he wrote his dissertation on 'The Making of the Corporative State'. Its ideal was not socialist struggle but cooperation between workers and capitalists. In the years of World War II he did not, however, take the side of right-wing groups but started to move towards social democracy. After the War he joined the Labour Party as one of its most prominent leaders to come from a Christian background. He was elected to the Dutch Senate and the provincial council of Northern-Holland. In 1950, he disappeared suddenly from the political scene after he was indicted for having sex with a 16-year-old young man. (This act became a crime in the year he was born; since 1971 it is no longer illegal.) Brongersma was sentenced to ten months in prison. He afterwards took up the cause of liberalising Dutch sex laws, especially concerning age of consent and pornography. From 1963 to 1977 he was back in the Senate for the Labour Party. From the 1950s on, he was involved in the COC (the Dutch homosexual organisation) as one of its main spokesmen on legal affairs. Both he and his colleague Frits Bernard were however removed from the COC journal in 1963 when the gay movement wanted to show its respectability and get rid of unwelcome minorities. They both started their own foundations for research and documentation on paedophilia. Brongersma's two-volume magnum opus, *Boy-Love: A Multidisciplinary Study of Sexual Relations between Adult and Minor Males*, appeared in 1986 and 1993. The text offers rich material but is hampered by the author's old-fashioned perspectives in defence of the love between men and boys. At the end of his life, Brongersma had to face the gradual demonisation of paedophilia. Just before his death, he was accused in the media of encouraging child abuse.

It is expected that his significant estate, consisting of letters, unpublished texts, an important library and many objects all related to man–boy love, will be the basis of a research and archival centre on child sexuality. Considering the negative climate surrounding the subject, it may be some years before Brongersma's last ideal is realised.

Gert Hekma

Bronski, Michael (b. 1949), American writer. Born in New York City, Bronski attended Rutgers University at Newark (where as a member of a student group he organised opposition to the Vietnam War) and Brandeis University. His play *Man for Man* (1974) went on stage at Harvard's Loeb Theatre; the work demonstrated a capacity to fracture oppressive characters, images and dialogues only to reunite them in another gay structure.

In Bronski's most recent book, *The Pleasure Principle: Sex, Backlash, and the Struggle for Gay Freedom* (1998), he describes himself 'as a writer, political activist and organiser, critic, cultural maven, reader, moviegoer, and general consumer of culture'. He was a founder of the *Boston Gay Review* and *Fag Rag*, a co-ordinator for 'OutWrite: Lesbian and Gay Literary Conference', and a mainstay writer for the *Gay Community News*. He has written for a number of other publications, and nearly forty of his essays have appeared in anthologies.

Bronski proudly maintains his status as an independent writer. While never a member of the sectarian left, he has always sought to incorporate class into his gender and sexual analyses.

Neither his first book, *Culture Clash: The Making of Gay Sensibility* (1984), nor *Pleasure Principle* succumb to the current fashion to write obscurely and obtusely. Bronski attempts to locate 'gay history and politics in broad historical cultural context'.

For many years Bronski lived with Good Gay Poet Walta Borawski, whose poetry, scarves, cats and death from AIDS kept him close to the heart of a living/loving culture. He has also mingled with the new generation of gay thinkers such as Michael Lowenthal and Joshua Oppenheimer, who, as he notes, continue to spark 'a renewed sense of intellectual excitement and an idealistic commitment to truth'.

Charley Shively

Brossard, Nicole (b. 1943), Canadian writer. One of Quebec's best-known literary figures, Brossard is widely known and respected in the rest of Canada and in France. Much of her work has been translated into English, and some into German and Italian.

Her work has always embraced the unconventional and transgressive. That has been evident in the form and content of her writing, in her blurring of the lines between fiction and non-fiction. She regularly places herself as woman, feminist, lesbian and writer in the midst of a kind of 'hall of mirrors' that her overall body of more than twenty books seems to constitute.

From her first writing in the 1960s, Brossard has helped in the development of vehicles for literary and political challenge. In the mid-1960s, she co-founded *La Barre du jour*, an avant-garde literary magazine that published for more than a decade. In the mid-1970s, she was active in a feminist journal, *Les Têtes de pioche* (at about the same time co-directing *Some American Feminists* for the National Film Board of Canada). In 1977, she was elected to the first board of directors of the Union of Québec Writers, and in 1988 she presided over the International Feminist Book Fair. In the early 1980s, she founded *l'intégrale* – a feminist publishing house. In all, she was a profoundly influential voice in reshaping Quebec literature.

The first ten years of her published poetry is gathered in *Le centre blanc: poèmes 1965–75* (1975). Her *Mécanique jongleuse suivi de masculin grammaticale* (*Daydream Mechanics*) won the Governor-General's Award in 1974. Much of her poetry, particularly from the mid-1970s on, is influenced by her feminism and lesbianism, including *Under Tongue* (1987) and *La nuit verte du parc labyrinthe* (1992). Her volumes of poetry now number more than seventeen.

Her fiction has been constantly experimental, and regularly taken up with issues of identity – identity based on language, gender and sexuality. Among those works appearing in both French and English are: *A Book* (1970), *French Kiss* (1974), *These Our Mothers; or The Disintegrating Chapter* (1977) and *Surfaces of Sense* (1980). *Picture Theory* (1982), thought by some to be her most important prose work, mixes fiction and essay in treating the relationships between women on a utopian lesbian island. Ideas emergent from lesbian feminism are explored in numerous other works, including essays gathered in *Double Impression: Poèmes et textes, 1967–1984*, a work which won her a second Governor-General's Award.

Brossard has herself translated poetry and prose from English to French, and her best-known novel, *Mauve Desert* (1987), takes up themes of translation and cross-cultural understanding. In *She Would be the First Sentence of My Next Novel* (1998), Brossard presents English and French side by side in a work of autobiographical fiction that centres on a woman writing a novel. Here as elsewhere she struggles to represent female subjectivity in the midst of male-shaped language and literature forms, challenging modernist claims to universality.

Brossard has been awarded honorary degrees from the University of Western Ontario and the Université de Sherbrooke. In 1989 she was awarded the *Grand Prix de la Fondation des Forges*. In 1991, she was honoured by the Quebec government for her work, and in that same year received the Harbourfront Festival Prize in Toronto for her overall contribution to literature.

Oxford Companion to Canadian Literature, second edition (Toronto, 1997); Barbara Goddard, 'Nicole Brossard', in *Profiles in Canadian Literature* (Toronto, 1986).

                                                    David Rayside

Brown, Rita Mae (b. 1944), American writer. Brown's first disappointment in life perhaps came at the time of her birth: not that she was born to an unwed mother, not even that she was given up for adoption, but rather perhaps that she was born just north of the Mason-Dixon Line (symbolic of the traditional division of the United States into North and South). Despite her biological mother's Southern family roots, Brown was a Pennsylvanian and Northerner. By age eleven, her parents moved to Florida, and with the exception of stints in Boston, New York and Los Angeles, she has been a Southern woman (and Virginian) ever since, as well as the best-known writer who is a lesbian in the United States.

Brown is known for her off-the-page activities perhaps as much as for her literary work. She has been lovers with the first openly gay person elected to an American state legislature, Elaine NOBLE, comedienne and author Fannie Flagg, tennis diva Martina NAVRATILOVA, and socialite Judy Nelson. Brown met Noble, also born in Pennsylvania, in Boston. Noble's rising star fell as she was caught up in an FBI sting. According to Brown, 'While my romance with Elaine was short-lived, I wasn't upset. I rarely was, because I neither understood romantic love nor wished to understand it. It looked like neurosis shared by two . . . Elaine, however, could not have cared less. She was wrapped up in what appeared to be the beginning of a good career and was meeting lots of women who were falling all over her. My southern worldview, with its emphasis on honour in capital letters and underlined three times, wearied her.'

Brown met Flagg in Los Angeles at a fund-raising party: 'I was hardly the only lesbian or bisexual in the crowd. I was the only one honest about it. After thanking my host two hours later, I walked down the long drive to the valet parking area. Standing there, waiting for her car to be driven up, was one of the most beautiful women I'd ever beheld. I fell in love with Fannie Flagg at first sight.'

Navratilova was twenty-two when she first met Brown. They eventually moved in together, but the pressures of Navratilova's very public career, and her constant need for love, made the relationship tense.

As well-known as she is for her association with these women, Brown is first and foremost a writer. Indeed, it was her scandalous classic *Rubyfruit Jungle* which put her on the literary map, though the book was initially rejected by the large publishing houses. She writes about women and their social situations. While some of her protagonists may be lesbian, with the exception of *Rubyfruit Jungle* (and perhaps *In Her Day*), lesbianism is not the main issue. Lately she has turned to mystery writing, 'co-authoring' the books with her cat, Sneaky Pie.

Rita Mae Brown, *In Her Day* (Plainfield, Vermont, 1976), *Rita Will: Memoir of a Literary Rabble-Rouser* (New York, 1997), *Rubyfruit Jungle* (Plainfield, Vermont, 1973), *Starting from Scratch: A Different Kind of Writers' Manual* (New York, 1989).

                                                    Lee Arnold

Brown, Roger (1925–97), American scholar. Brown was born in Detroit, Michigan. After US naval service, he earned degrees from the then ultra-behaviorist, experimental psychology programme at the University of Michigan. From 1962, he taught psychology at Harvard University. He was elected to the National Academy of Science and to the American Academy of Arts and Sciences, and received the Distinguished Scientific Contribution Award of the American

Psychological Association in 1971. Brown was a pioneer in 'the cognitive revolution' in human sciences and a founder of the social psychology of language in his work on reference (*Words and Things*, 1958), democratisation of terms of address (*The Pronouns of Power and Solidarity*, 1960, with his lover Albert Gilman, a professor of English at Boston University), different individual styles (*Personality and Style in Concord*, 1966, also with Gilman), and young children's acquisition of language (*A First Language*, 1973). His magisterial 1965 book, *Social Psychology*, was very widely used; a second version, published in 1986, contained the only analysis of research on homosexuality that Brown published. He had 'gone public' about his own homosexuality in the seventh volume of *A History of Psychology in Autobiography* (1989). After his retirement, Brown published *Against My Better Judgment* (1996), a memoir of several frustrating years of trying to find love by hiring rent boys after his lover of forty-two years died in 1989.

Stephen O. Murray

Bruce of Los Angeles (1909–74), American photographer. Bruce of Los Angeles was born Bruce Harry Bellas, in Alliance, Nebraska, and taught chemistry there before moving to California in the 1940s, when a wide range of fitness or physique magazines – such as *Strength and Health*, *Muscle Power* and *Tomorrow's Man* – began to emerge. Produced for a variety of audiences, these magazines primarily catered to fitness buffs and a growing gay subculture. Always a dabbler in photography, Bruce began to work as a freelance photographer at body-building competitions. By the late 1940s he was a staff photographer for Joe Weider publications and travelled to body-building contests across the country. In the 1950s even more photo studios began to open, including the likes of the Athletic Model Guild, the Western Photography Guild and Spartan of Hollywood. They explored a wide range of motifs usually settling on images of cowboys, Indians, construction workers, buccaneers and more than a few Spartan wrestlers, frequently frolicking in hotel rooms, makeshift studios and an occasional suburban backyard.

By the 1960s Bruce was able to publish his own magazine, *The Male Figure*, in which shimmering weight-lifters were frequently transported from the gym to the public park. Interspersed between short articles on proper weight-training were images of young boys wrestling or engaged in mock sword fights along secluded creek beds or in grassy fields, clad in g-strings and bending before the camera's lens. These publications frequently included articles on the manly virtues of bachelor life. Unfortunately, due to US Postal Service regulations, Bruce was forced to sell most of his magazines and prints from a roadside hotel room. These photographs trace the cultural and economic evolution of the early gay movement in America while at the same time marking the creation of a particular kind of masculinity, one which has become firmly grounded in the dominant culture's image of masculinity. Until the 1950s this had yet to be fully realised within an overtly gay context. While seemingly innocent by today's standards, the publications were nevertheless recognised as erotically charged, as evidenced by the abundance of post office box numbers and anonymous authors. Clearly, readers understood that risk itself could be enough to transform the mundane into a site of excitation. Bruce of Los Angeles, more than anyone else in his time, was able to suggest the innocence and freedom of a moment that would be shortlived.

Jim Dolinsky (ed.), *Bruce of Los Angeles* (Berlin, 1990).

Ken Gonzales-Day

Bruhn, Erik (Bolton Evers) (1928–86), Danish ballet dancer. Bruhn entered the school of the Royal Danish Ballet in 1937, became a member of the company in 1947, and was promoted to principal dancer in 1949. His career as an international solo dancer began in 1947 and in 1956 he resigned from the Royal Theatre but returned on a regular basis as a guest dancer. Bruhn was a solo dancer at the Ballet Theatre, London (1956–58), then solo dancer and ballet instructor at the Royal Theatre, Copenhagen (1958–60). He was chief of the Royal Opera Ballet, Stockholm (1967–71), then the National Ballet of Canada, Toronto (1983–86).

Bruhn was the most prominent Danish male dancer of the twentieth century. In the first phase of his career as a classical dancer, le danseur noble et sérieux, he became one of the most outstanding of the international elite of dancers, characterised by his flawless technique, harmonious composure and musicality. He danced in the roles of all the princes of the classical repertoire, Swan Lake, the Nutcracker Suite and Sleeping Beauty, as well as in the leading roles of the ballets of August Bournonville. From the mid-1950s Bruhn added new aspects to his interpretation of the roles of the classical ballet princes in order to make these figures relevant and meaningful to contemporary audiences. Bruhn gave up his career as a dancer in 1972, but he returned to the stage later on in character roles, e.g. as the witch in La Sylphide. His most important teachers were Harald Lander and Vera Volkova.

Bruhn wrote two important books on the technique of August Bournonville, Bournonville and Ballet Technique (1961, with Lillian Moore) and Beyond Technique, Dance Perspectives 36 (1968). He was awarded several prizes, among them the Nijinsky Prize in 1963.

In 1961, shortly after defecting from the Soviet Union, the Russian ballet dancer Rudolf NUREYEV arranged a meeting with Bruhn in Copenhagen. They met in the bar of the Hotel d'Angleterre, which at the time was the socially upward-mobile meeting place for Copenhagen's homosexuals and theatre-goers. Thus began a life-long relationship between Erik and 'Rudik'. 'Theirs was as much passion of ideals as of physical attraction. Each was entranced by what he lacked himself, Rudolf by Bruhn's refinement and standing; Bruhn by Rudolf's youth, passion and fearlessness' (Solway). Nureyev moved in with Bruhn, who lived in Copenhagen with his mother. A year later they moved together to a flat in London where both were guest dancers at the Royal Ballet.

In the 1960s Bruhn was probably a better dancer than Nureyev ever became. Nureyev, however, was the darling of the anti-communist West and contrary to Bruhn he revelled in publicity and loved to act off the stage. In the longer run Bruhn could not cope with Nureyev's closeness and promiscuity. He tried to withdraw from the relationship and left London, but Nureyev followed him wherever he went, and inevitably upstaged him in the public arena. Their sexual relationship ended in 1967. Mutual attraction had turned into jealousy. Their friendship, however, lasted. Nureyev was present at Bruhn's deathbed in Toronto in 1986.

Erik Aschengreen, 'Erik Bruhn', Dansk Biografisk Leksikon, vol. 3 (Copenhagen, 1979), pp. 576–7; John Gruen, Erik Bruhn, danseur noble (New York, 1979); Diana Solway, Nureyev – His Life (London, 1998).

Wilhelm von Rosen

Bryant, Anita (b. 1940), American political figure. Bryant was born in Oklahoma and was raised as a Southern Baptist. She showed talent as a singer and performer from an early age and made radio and television appearances. She was Miss Oklahoma in 1958 and second runner-up for the 1959 Miss America title, tying for the Miss Congeniality award. Bryant obtained gold records for her hit songs, 'The Music Man', 'Paper Roses' and 'My Little Corner of the World', and in 1960 married a successful disc-jockey, Robert Einar 'Bob' Green, who experienced Christian 'rebirth' on their marriage and became her manager. Green selected family-oriented engagements for Bryant, and she advertised the products of several companies including Coca-Cola, Kraft Foods and the Florida Citrus Commission. Religion has been intertwined with Bryant's career and her repertoire includes both sacred and popular songs. Bryant travelled with Bob Hope on seven USO Christmas tours; cohosted eight Orange Bowl parade telecasts for NBC in the 1970s; made Florida Orange Juice commercials which aired on national television; and was featured in *People* magazine in 1976. Bryant's name was known all over the United States. She was a wife and mother, religious, patriotic and 'American as apple pie' in that she represented traditional, white, middle-class values.

Bryant was instrumental in repealing legislation in Miami in 1977 which prohibited discrimination on the grounds of sexual or affectional preference. Shortly before what came to be known as Miami's 'gay rights law' was enacted, Bryant's Baptist pastor, William Chapman, encouraged his congregation to become active civically and politically. Bryant responded by endorsing her agent's wife, Ruth Shack, for a seat on the county commission. Shack's first action in office was to introduce the amendment to (greater Miami) Dade County's anti-discrimination ordinance. Bryant was embarrassed and angry, and with other members of her Church opposed the ordinance.

A conservative Christian organisation, Save Our Children (SOC), was formed which aimed to repeal the ordinance. Bryant was elected president and Green, treasurer. Strong local and national media attention throughout the campaign was attributed to Bryant's involvement, but she was in many respects a figurehead and much of SOC's strategy was formulated by its secretary, Bob Brake, and hired public relations consultant, Mike Thompson. The repeal effort was successful and Bryant made guest appearances during similar repeal efforts throughout the

country in the subsequent year, but her involvement quickly subsided. These activities probably had a negative impact on her career and personal life. Gay rights leaders began a boycott of Florida Orange Juice and other products Bryant advertised. While the boycotts did not have a major impact on sales, they highlighted Bryant's controversial status and she began to lose contracts. In 1978 Bryant and Green divorced.

Local Miami activists Bob Basker and Bob Kunst were principals in the formation of the Dade County Coalition for the Humanistic Rights of Gays (DCCHRG), which was responsible for passage of the gay rights amendment to the city's anti-discrimination law, and which was active in defending it after opposition emerged. Jack Campbell, a prominent gay Miami resident who owned the Steamworks chain of gay saunas, helped raise funds and liaised with national gay rights leaders such as David Goodstein, publisher of *The Advocate*, to prepare a defence of the law, which included sending to Miami Jim Foster and Ethan Geto, gay men with experience as political campaigners and aides to San Francisco and New York City politicians, respectively. Almost from the beginning, factionalism plagued the defence. Kunst and his supporters were regarded as radicals and while disputes about strategy and leadership raged, SOC gained considerable popular support.

Anita Bryant, *The Anita Bryant Story: The Survival of Our Nation's Families and the Threat of Militant Homosexuality* (Old Tappan, New Jersey, 1977); Charles Moritz (ed.), *Current Biography Yearbook* (New York, 1975); Gerard Sullivan, *A Study of Political Campaigns of Discrimination Against Gay People in the United States, 1950–1978* (Ann Arbor, University Microfilms International [8729425], 1987).

Gerard Sullivan

Bullough, Vern (LeRoy) (b. 1928), American scholar. Bullough is the author of works on medicine and nursing but a substantial part of his career has been devoted to the study of gender and sexuality, from histories of prostitution, homosexuality and medieval sexuality, to works on cross-dressing, transgenderism and the history of sexology.

Bullough received his degrees from the University of Utah and the University of Chicago. He has held professorships at Youngstown University, Ohio (1954–59) and California State University, Northridge (1959–80), and was Dean of Natural and Social Sciences at the State University of New York at Buffalo (1980–90). In retirement, Bullough returned to California, where he currently resides.

On his own, and with his late wife Bonnie, Bullough has authored, co-authored or edited over fifty books, most of which are on sexual and gender history. In *Homosexuality: A History* (1979), Bullough analyses the ways in which homosexuality has been viewed from the ancient Greeks to modern times. While he agrees with social constructionists like Michel FOUCAULT that each historical period has its own perspective on homosexuality, he contends that 'same-sex behavior has a long and honorable history and that many of the gays and lesbians in the past would be recognizable by their counterparts today if they could read and study their lives'. Bullough stresses this continuity because he believes that contemporary gays and lesbians who seek to change society's view of homosexuality must understand the historical roots of discrimination and prejudice in order to effect any change.

Like Evelyn HOOKER, Bullough's involvement with the homosexual community went beyond academic interest as he became a supporter of the gay liberation movement. With his wife, he helped found the original Parents and Friends of Gays and Lesbians is Los Angeles.

Vern and Bonnie Bullough, 'How We Got Into Sex', in *Personal Stories of 'How I Got into*

Sex' (Amherst, 1997), and 'History, the Historian, and Sex', in *The Sex Scientists* (New York, 1998).

Trent Newmeyer

Bunch, Charlotte (b. 1944), American activist and writer. Bunch was co-founder, with Rita Mae Brown and others, of the most influential lesbian feminist group of the early 1970s, The Furies.

Educated at Duke University, Bunch was involved in campus-based civil rights and New Left groups in the 1960s. As with many women in the Left, Bunch's experience of sexism provoked an analysis of gender relations which led, in 1968, to the formation of the first autonomous women's liberation groups. Subsequent tensions between heterosexual feminists and lesbians in the women's liberation movement, however, led to the formation of lesbian feminist groups such as Washington DC's The Furies in 1971. The Furies, in their newsletter published between 1972 and 1973, advocated the most hardline position on lesbian separatism, with their insistence that feminists must renounce heterosexual privilege and make the political choice to become lesbians. After The Furies disbanded in 1973, Bunch and Brown went on to co-found, with others, the influential journal *Quest: A Feminist Quarterly*.

Bunch co-edited three collections of articles from The Furies' newsletter: *Women Remembered*, *Class and Feminism* and *Lesbianism and the Women's Movement*. Her own influential essays include 'Not for Lesbians Only' (1975) and 'Learning from Lesbian Separatism' (1976). Bunch became increasingly interested in education and feminist pedagogy, publishing several co-edited collections on the subject: *Not by Degrees* (1978) and *Learning our Way: Essays in Feminist Education* (1983). She was a member of the National Gay Taskforce during the 1970s and has more recently been involved in international feminism. In 1989 she founded the Center for Women's Global Leadership at Rutgers

University. Other members of The Furies went on to found significant feminist cultural enterprises such as Diana Press and Olivia Records.

Charlotte Bunch, *Passionate Politics: Feminist Theory in Action* (New York, 1987); Alice Echols, *Daring to be Bad: Radical Feminism in America, 1967–1975* (Minneapolis, 1989).

Carolyn Williams

Burgess, Guy (1910–63), British public servant and Soviet spy. Burgess, along with Donald Maclean and Kim Philby, was a member of the infamous group of Soviet spies in Britain whose activities were uncovered in the early 1950s. Maclean was bisexual, though Burgess strenuously denied that they had ever been lovers. (The activities of another contemporary spy and homosexual, Anthony BLUNT, only became publicly known in the 1970s.) Revelations of his espionnage made Burgess, according to Patrick Higgins, 'the greatest homosexual demon of the decade'. With Maclean, Burgess defected to the Soviet Union in 1951, lived the rest of his life there and died in Moscow.

Born in Devonport, the son of an officer in the Royal Navy, Burgess was educated at Eton, the Royal Naval College and Cambridge, where he was an excellent student (and was elected to the elite Apostles society, known for its significant number of homosexual members). At Cambridge, where he enrolled in 1930, he was introduced to both homosexuality and communism, which had gained increased currency among left-wing intellectuals such as the economics tutor at Burgess's college, Trinity, Maurice Dobb. While a student, Burgess also visited the Soviet Union, though he was little impressed by what he saw, and he renounced his leftist views, at least in public, when he left Cambridge.

After university, Burgess found a position at the BBC (1936–39 and 1941–44); he also worked in the war propaganda office (1939–41) and subsequently at MI5

and the Foreign Office – initially in the ministry's News Department, then in the Far Eastern Department, and later as second secretary under Philby at the British embassy in the United States in 1950. His improprieties – failure to conform to diplomatic etiquette, indiscreet discussions about secret matters (for which he was reprimanded), and various other incidents, such as speeding offences – led to his recall and resignation from the Foreign Office.

Burgess had been recruited as a Soviet spy in the 1930s. His government work and travels, including his service as a courier between the British and French prime ministers of the late 1930s, Chamberlain and Daladier, gave access to material on such issues as Britain's willingness to compromise with Hitler, that was of great interest to the Soviets. Burgess later had access to higher-level information in the Foreign Office, some of which he also gave to Soviet contacts.

Rumours among associates about his homosexual liaisons sometimes masked his 'secret' meetings. According to John Fisher, sexually, 'his liaisons were of a purely physical nature and unclouded by any form of romanticism … transitory and impermanent, but he managed in many cases to retain the goodwill of his former lovers'. He did carefully keep a number of love letters. His other activities – motoring, the theatre, alcohol, friendships with many well-respected people in British public life – also hid his undercover work.

The spy scandal of the early 1950s played a major role in witch-hunts of both homosexuals and 'communist-sympathisers', and led to views in some quarters that sexual and political heresy were intertwined. Scholars judge that Burgess was originally motivated by his idealism in an era of political polarisation, the social effects of the Depression and the drama of the Spanish Civil War. The argument that his homosexuality alienated him from British society and played a part in his willingness to spy for the Soviet Union is dubious, especially given Burgess's straightforwardness and seeming lack of psychological torment about his own proclivities. His reputation remains that of a traitor.

John Fisher, *Burgess and Maclean: A New Look at the Foreign Office Spies* (London, 1977); Andrew Sinclair, *The Red and the Blue: Cambridge, Treason and Intelligence* (Boston, 1986); Patrick Higgins, *Heterosexual Dictatorship: Male Homosexuality in Post-War Britain* (London, 1996).

Robert Aldrich

Burroughs, William (Seward) (1914–97), American author. Few writers have had such an ambivalent reputation as Burroughs, whose work has been greatly admired by many as uniquely imaginative, while reviled by others as 'repellent, nauseating, and sick'. His emphasis on what was seen as the sordid side of life and his often less-than-accessible style – using everything from stream of consciousness to 'cutting up' (reassembling at random a manuscript that had been chopped up for this purpose) – all play their part in this assessment.

Burroughs was born into an affluent family in St Louis, Missouri (his grandfather had invented the adding machine), and educated at Harvard and Vienna universities. He saw brief service in the US army during World War II, and then worked in a variety of jobs – factory worker, private detective, bartender and even pest-controller – his experiences of which would figure in his later fiction, as would his experimentation with drugs, petty crime and a diverse range of sexual activities.

With Allen GINSBERG and Jack KEROUAC, he was one of the founding members of what came to be called the Beat Generation. Like them, he rejected a settled existence, and his wealth allowed him to live in such exotic locales as Tangier, Mexico, South America, Paris and London. He was a prolific writer, producing novels and screenplays, and writing the libretto for a comic opera, *The Black Rider*, with music by Tom Waits. His writings found a ready audience among parts of the gay community, whose own outsiderness made them identify with the outlaw society that Burroughs so well described. Probably his most famous work was *The Naked Lunch* (1959); other books include *Junkie: Confessions of an Unredeemed Drug Addict* (1953) and *The Soft Machine* (1961). There has been a revival of interest in Burroughs's work since the 1990s, as part of a broader – 'retro' – rediscovery of the excitements of the Beat Movement and the Counterculture.

Twice married, his second wife, Joan Vollmer, died in unusual circumstances. While both were drunk, they played at William Tell: unfortunately the arrow that Burroughs shot missed the apple and went through her forehead. Her death was deemed accidental. In his later years, he lived with his long-time companion James Grauerholz.

Graham Caveney, *Gentleman Junkie: The Life and Legacy of William S. Burroughs* (Boston, 1998); Ted Morgan, *Literary Outlaw: The Life and Times of William S. Burroughs* (New York, 1988).

Garry Wotherspoon

Busi, Aldo (b. 1948), Italian writer. One of Italy's most controversial contemporary writers, Busi has had a high profile since the publication of his first novel, *Seminario sulla gioventù*, in 1984. Since then he has published some twenty-one volumes, including six novels. A significant number of these have been translated into various languages, and he is well known in much of the Western world, as much for his innovative literary techniques as for the sometimes scabrous material of his works.

Born in northern Italy near Lake Garda, Busi was a footloose youth. He gravitated towards Milan, where he worked as a waiter, but he also spent several years living in different parts of Europe, earning a living in a variety of jobs. He was always fascinated by language, and while he was abroad he learnt French, German and English. Later he returned to Italy, completed a degree, and began to work as a translator. He had been writing from a young age, and when his first novel was published, he claimed that he had been working on it for twenty years.

Seminario sulla gioventù is a semi-autobiographical novel which follows the central character on a journey, both metaphorical and real, from a difficult childhood in the Lombardy countryside to the lights of Paris. It is constructed out of a sequence of eight episodes, all presenting various adventures and misadventures which show the pain and sadness of youth. The stories clearly articulate several gay themes, and at the time its author saw himself as part of a vanguard of new artists, superseding a generation of Italian gay intellectuals who had hidden or veiled their sexuality. Busi wanted to be identified as an artist without having to hide his gayness. Indeed, one of the main purposes of the first novel was to elaborate cultural models for young gay Italians, partly because it had not really been done before, and partly because Busi felt that northern European and American models were not always appropriate in Italy.

But the relationship between Busi, writing and sexuality has mutated considerably since 1984. Although he has never hidden his own homosexuality, he insists that this should not be read into his works. He rejects the category of 'gay writer' completely, and has distanced himself from the various Italian gay movements. Busi's more recent work aims to overcome the traditional polar opposition between masculinity and femininity, and with it the dualism between homo- and heterosexuality. He laments what he views as a growing trend for gays to see themselves almost as an ethnic group, and does not see the path to liberation leading towards the imitation of heterosexual norms, such as marriage for gays. Instead, he has a more typically postmodern view that the whole concept of normality itself must be overcome, making way for a more fluid spectrum of sexual expression.

Busi's writing was brought to national attention when he was tried for obscenity by the Italian judicial system in 1989, after the publication of his third novel, *Sodomie in corpo 11* (1988). The trial caused a furore because it was the first of its kind in over nine years. Pier Vittorio TONDELLI's *Altri libertini* had attracted similar charges in 1980, and before that PASOLINI had frequently had to stand trial for the same reason. Thus Busi entered the canon of Italian gay writers who ran foul of Italy's obscenity laws. He was absolved, and it is quite probable that the trial had a beneficial effect upon the sale of his books.

Other major works by Busi include *Vita standard di un venditore Provvisorio di collant* (1985), *Vendita galline km. 2* (1993), and *Cazzi e canguri (pochissimi i canguri)* (1994). As well as the prolific production of his own fiction, Busi is also a well-respected translator. He has translated several major works into Italian, including J. R. Ackerley's *My Father and Myself* (1981) and Goethe's *Werther* (1983). He now lives and works in central Italy.

Marco Cavalli, 'Nudo d'autore', *Babilonia*, vol. XI (1998).

Mark Seymour

Bussy, Dorothy (1865–1960), British writer and translator. Dorothy Strachey Bussy was born in 1865 into a large English family that produced a number of early twentieth-century luminaries, including her brother, biographer Lytton Strachey; her sister Philippa, a political activist who organised one of the first marches for women's suffrage in London; her sister Marjorie, also an activist and writer; and brother James Strachey, who with his wife Alix translated Freud's complete works. Dorothy Bussy, also a translator, is responsible for translating most of the novels of French writer André Gide, whom she met in 1918 and with whom she had a life-long friendship. Bussy spent much of her life in France after marrying the painter Simon Bussy in 1903; in 1906 she had a daughter, Jane, who also became a painter and who preceded her mother in death by two weeks in 1960 – a sorrow Bussy was spared due to her senility.

In addition to translating the works of Gide, who was homosexual, Bussy contributed to the gay and lesbian canon with her novel *Olivia*, published anonymously in 1948 and dedicated to the 'beloved memory of V. W.' (Virginia Woolf). The novel is based on the life of Marie Souvestre who co-founded and ran the girls' school Les Ruches, in Fountainebleau, Dorothy Bussy attended as a girl. She developed a deep romantic passion for Mlle Souvestre, who is portrayed as Mlle Julie in *Olivia*. The novel's namesake recounts her 'foolish dreams of adolescence', capturing the rhapsodic ache of a schoolgirl crush: 'how I should save her life at the cost of my own by some heroic deed, of how she would kiss me on my deathbed ... of how I should become famous by writing poems which no one would know were inspired by her, of how one day she would guess it, and so on and so on'. The novel seems to have been largely forgotten by critics, but there may be renewed interest in the work as a chapter has been excerpted in *The Penguin Book of Lesbian Short Stories*, edited by Margaret Reynolds (1994).

Annette Oxindine

C

Cabaj, Robert Paul (b. 1948), American activist. Cabaj has been instrumental in bringing homosexuality out of the psychiatric closet, and into the light of scientific scrutiny. The result has been the dispelling of numerous myths and inaccuracies, the depathologising of homosexuality as a psychiatric diagnosis and the inclusion of homosexuality as a subject worthy of study in training programmes for the helping professions.

Cabaj was born and grew up in Chicago and graduated from Notre Dame University and Harvard Medical School, where he was a staff member until 1991, working, teaching, and supervising at several Boston hospitals. He served as Medical Director of Mental Health and Addictions for the Fenway Community Health Center – one of the largest urban community health centres and the largest centre for the treatment of gay men, lesbians, bisexuals and the HIV-infected in Boston. He relocated to the San Francisco Bay Area to create the Substance Abuse Consultation Service, incorporating the AIDS and Substance Abuse Program for the AIDS Health Project at San Francisco General Hospital; he was associate professor in psychiatry at the University of California there. Since 1995 his full-time work has been as the Medical Director of Mental Health Services for San Mateo County, California.

In addition he has a private practice specialising in the treatment of gay men, lesbians, bisexuals, people facing issues related to HIV and AIDS; cultural and ethnic minority people; and substance-abusing patients. He is co-editor and a major contributor to *Textbook of Homosexuality and Mental Health* (1996) and co-editor of *Same-Sex Marriage: A Supportive Guide to Psychological, Political and Legal Issues* (1997). Cabaj was chairperson of the Committee on Gay, Lesbian and Bisexual Issues of the American Psychiatric Association for nearly ten years. He is Past President of the Gay and Lesbian Medical Association (GLMA).

Robert Pryde

Cadinot, Jean-Daniel (b. late 1940s), French photographer, director and producer of pornographic films. Cadinot, son of a tailor, was born in Paris, probably in the late 1940s (he will not divulge the year). 'My father dressed people', he likes to joke; 'I undressed them later on'. Artistically inclined, the teenaged Cadinot hoped to become a painter and in the face of parental opposition ran away from home at seventeen. He studied industrial drawing at the École des Arts et Métiers in Paris, but his teachers told him that he had no talent. He discovered the camera at nineteen and began taking evening classes in photography, while supporting himself by working during the day as a messenger or a warehouse packer.

Cadinot started his professional career taking studio photographs of actors and actresses. He also took nude photographs of male friends on the side and by 1975–76 he was selling his erotic pictures to homosexual magazines. He published the first of seventeen albums of photographs in 1976 and directed his first pornographic movie, *Scouts #1* (only thirty-nine minutes long), in 1981. By 1998 he had directed fifty-four films and videos (some under the pseudonym Tony Dark).

Cadinot's movies are intensely personal. 'I never try to know what the public will like or not, I don't do market studies . . . I make the films that I want to see'. Directing, he explains, is 'my personal therapy'. 'Through my movies, I settle scores with my parents, with society, with the Church.' He claims that his movies are all autobiographical in origin: 'My movies are my past private life; in my life today I am preparing my future movies!'

Although they include the obligatory (and frequent) scenes of sexual activity, Cadinot's movies always tell a story. Most American porn stars are wooden actors whose well-muscled (and usually shaved) bodies seem artificial. Cadinot's performers are not professionals. They are as young and attractive as their American counterparts, but their bodies are more natural and their acting seems spontaneous. Cadinot dislikes 'clones' and chooses performers 'with swarthy skin, sensual lips, a face that catches your eye'. Above all, he adds, 'I like their personality'. Cadinot has remarked: 'I can't film somebody who doesn't give me an erection, that's evident . . . . but to act on [my desire] is another matter. I express my desire through the lens.' All this contributes to the so-called 'Cadinot look' for which his movies are famous.

Cadinot has no complexes or reservations about either his homosexuality or his career as a pornographer. Although he dislikes the word 'pornography', because of its pejorative implications, he also declares that 'pornography is life, it's sex, and life cannot be pornographic'. He is pleased that his brother holds shares in his film company and his mother has played bit parts in two films. No mere photographer, Cadinot is a shrewd and successful businessman, as well as a genuinely talented artist.

'Jean-Daniel Cadinot fait le point', *Homo*, no. 13 (June 1976); interview in *Samouraï*, no. 4 (Feb. 1983); 'Ne crachez pas sur le porno' and 'Sacre Cadinot', *Gai Pied Hebdo*, 24 Dec. 1983 and 27 Sept.–3 Oct. 1986; interview with author, Paris, 3 Oct. 1998.

Michael Sibalis

Cadmus, Paul (1904–99), American artist. Cadmus has lived long enough to have passed through the representational paintings of social realism of the 1930s, when he began his career, to a late twentieth-century return to representation, now embodied in what Cadmus terms his own 'magic realism'. Throughout these cultural shifts, Cadmus has remained faithful to his exceptionally elegant drawings and draftsmanship, to his reworking of the art-historical tradition since the Renaissance, and to his portrayal of the potential beauty of the (most often male) body.

Like so many utopians, Cadmus expressed his sense of loss through satire. He juxtaposes the ideal, pastoral body, seen in repose, or on display, with the grotesque of the ageing, overweight body that indicates the loss of innocence and beauty. Cadmus played a remarkable part in the emergence and recording of gay urban life as it came into visibility between World War I and World War II. His *YMCA Locker Room* (1933) signals the existence of such spaces of male desire, and at the same time draws upon a tradition of celebration of the body and masculine desire. Among Cadmus's intellectual masters are, in particular, Walt Whitman, with his visions of young men bathing, and E. M. Forster, whose not-yet-published *Maurice* saw the ethical and political potential in male friendship.

Cadmus became notorious in 1934, when his large painting *The Fleet's In* was banned from a Work Progress Administration show. Cadmus's work, with its flagrant bisexuality, said what was known but unsayable: he explored the sexual aura drawn around the body of the sailor. If the sailors are equally available for men and women, the gentleman in the red tie signifies, through his cravat, his sexuality. The painting is thus a brilliant account of the growth of an underworld of urban cruising. A few years later, Cadmus was censored once again, this time for his *Pocahontas Saving the Life of Captain John Smith* (1938), when a fox tail that covered the male genitals was deemed too explicit.

One of Cadmus's great passions was the ballet, a taste he shared with Lincoln KIRSTEIN. He designed the decors and costumes for Virgil Thomson's ballet 'Filling Station', which once again allowed for the celebration of the working-class male body, a theme later developed by playwrights William INGE and Tennessee WILLIAMS. Dancers formed the principal subject for his drawings. In the 1940s Cadmus spent summers on Fire Island, along with his friend Jared French. This idyllic, often gay, scene was in sharp contrast with the vulgar world of Coney Island, recorded in the 1935 painting of that name which still finds ways to insert the virile body in the midst of the excesses of the flesh. During the 1940s Cadmus became, largely through correspondence, a close friend of Forster, and one of his most important paintings is called *What I Believe*, the title of the essay that gives the fullest statement of Forster's humanism. The painting makes explicit Cadmus's recurring theme of the opposition of the pure and the impure, here rendered even more terrifying by memories of fascism.

If gay culture was becoming visible in Cadmus's work, it was not yet exclusive in the ways it became in the 1960s and 1970s. Cadmus was fascinated by the triangular relations of desire, manifest in some of his best paintings, such as *The Shower* (1943) or *Night in Bologna* (1958). Cadmus's Italian paintings often reflect a diverse and polymorphous sexuality with beauty contrasting with ugliness. They also demonstrate his deep indebtedness to Renaissance masters such as Piero della Francesca. Although the framing of many of these paintings was Baroque architecture, Cadmus remained hostile to the contortions of Baroque, which he characteristically viewed ironically. His body of work is impressive, and plays a major role in the creation of gay male iconography.

The Drawings of Paul Cadmus, introduction by Guy Davenport (New York, 1989); Philip Eliasoph, *Paul Cadmus Yesterday and Today* (Oxford, Ohio, 1981); Lincoln Kirstein, *Paul Cadmus* (San Francisco, 1992); Lincoln Kirstein, *Paul Cadmus* (New York, 1984).

Robert K. Martin

Call, Hal (b. 1917), American activist and publisher. Born in Missouri, Harold (Hal) Call moved to San Francisco in 1952 and shortly thereafter became one of the most important, if controversial, figures in the American homophile movement. Prior to heading west, Call attended the University of Missouri, suspending his studies on entering the army in 1941. After serving in the Pacific theatre of the war, Call returned to Missouri to finish his journalism degree and began working for the *Kansas City Star's* advertising department. While on a business trip to Chicago, Call was arrested on a morals charge and, like many gay men of his generation, found his life irreversibly altered even though his case was dismissed. Though Call later claimed that his move to San Francisco had little do with the city's reputation as a 'gay mecca' – he said, 'back then, it wasn't' – he was in fact a refugee from intolerance and persecution, and saw San Francisco as a congenial place to build a new life. In this sense he was a participant in the first wave of gay migrants to the city and within a decade would himself play a considerable role in helping subsequent sexual émigrés.

Both Call's contemporaries and later historians have found many reasons to dislike the man. Aside from his famously contentious personality, much of Call's reputation stems from his participation in dissolving the Mattachine Foundation into the Mattachine Society, Incorporated, in 1953. The Foundation was the brainchild of several gay men in Los Angeles. A number of the founders, including Harry Hay, brought to the organisation a radical critique of society based in part on communist ideology as well as a belief in the fundamental difference of homosexuals from heterosexuals. But, according to Call and several other Mattachine members, the founders' ideology also meant an undemocratic organisational structure and, even more, potential political and legal trouble at a time when anticommunism was costing many their jobs and reputations. After a series of contentious organisational conventions in 1953, the new Mattachine Society took shape in November and in 1957 Call relocated its headquarters to San Francisco.

More accurately a journalist, a public relations consultant and a social service worker than a gutsy political activist, Call's leadership of the Mattachine Society in San Francisco veered from the lofty goals of the Foundation and focused instead on what appear to historians today to be mundane and even conservative tasks. Along with his editorship of the *Mattachine Review* (1955–66), Call founded the Pan-Graphic press in 1954 with Don Lucas (a much neglected figure in the homophile movement). Pan-Graphic published the review and several pathbreaking gay books and, through its profits, helped fund the activities of the Mattachine Society. In public relations, research, education, publications and social services, the Mattachine Society in the late 1950s and early 1960s provided a key source of information about law, religion and counselling to isolated gay men and lesbians throughout the country; by appearing on television, radio and in print, the society's members provided the public with a homosexual's viewpoint where before only the voices of the police, psychologists and clergy were heard. By providing researchers like Alfred KINSEY, John Gagnon and Evelyn HOOKER with an entrée into the gay community, it helped lessen the opprobrium heaved upon 'deviates' by powerful 'experts'; and, in combination, these activities resulted in constructing a steady base for future, more daring organisations to build their agendas, including the second generation homophile groups, the Council on Religion and the Homosexual, the Tavern Guild and the Society for Individual Rights – all of which left their mark on San Francisco's gay world as they survived into the 1970s.

By his own admission, Call was no longer in the activist vanguard by the late 1960s. And though the Mattachine Society still exists (in name only), Call began directing his attentions elsewhere by the 1970s, leaving politics for the next generation. What began as a small, private gathering of men to watch early gay pornography eventually grew into an erotic bookstore and a sex club, which survives today as one of the few remaining gay businesses in the formerly heavily gay Tenderloin neighbourhood in San Francisco. Though historians like John D'EMILIO and Rodger Streitmatter have had harsh words for Call and his 'accommodationist' views, final historical evaluation must await a more detailed and complete consideration of the actual activities of his Mattachine Society, not simply its public ideology.

John D'Emilio, *Sexual Politics, Sexual Communities: The Making of a Homosexual Minority in the United States, 1940–1970* (Chicago, 1983); Eric Marcus, *Making History: The Struggle for Gay and Lesbian Equal Rights, 1945–1990: An Oral History* (New York, 1992); Rodger Streitmatter, *Unspeakable: The Rise of the Gay and Lesbian Press in America* (Boston, 1995).

Martin Meeker

Callas, Maria (1923–77), Greek-American opera singer. Of all opera singers of the modern era, none has so captured the popular imagination as the soprano Maria Callas. At the height of her powers, in the 1950s, she was one of the first superstars, her fame transcending the rarefied world of opera.

Born in New York of recently arrived Greek immigrants, she was named Maria Anna Cecilia Sofia Kalogeropoulos. She made her professional debut with the Athens Opera in 1940, and by the late 1940s was appearing in many of the major Italian opera houses with a repertoire that took in everything from the crystalline *bel canto* roles to heavy-duty Wagner. It was, however, the combination of her vocal craft with dramatic powers of unparalleled intensity that made her a unique figure on the otherwise staid operatic stage of the time.

If her stage personas were unforgettably dramatic, so too was the personal life that she increasingly lived under the scrutiny of the mass media. Highly charged conflicts with opera managements, and personal relationships of soap operatic proportions only served to fuel the myths of personality and the cult of diva worship surrounding her.

Throughout her career, Callas was closely associated with several important gay artists. These included the directors Luchino VISCONTI and Franco Zefferelli, the conductor Leonard BERNSTEIN and the filmmaker Pier Paolo PASOLINI who, late in her career, cast her as the lead in his film *Medea*.

She has also had a loyal following amongst gay and lesbian opera-lovers. (Her mannerisms have, for example, been affectionately satirised by the cross-dressing La Grande Scena Opera Company of New York as 'callasthenics'.) Indeed, it has been said that the cult of Maria Callas has largely been driven by gay men. This diva worship has been most closely deconstructed by Wayne Koestenbaum, who concludes that her enduring fascination for gay audiences lies in her paradoxes: 'she was a mess *and* she was a goddess'.

Wayne Koestenbaum, *The Queen's Throat: Opera, Homosexuality and the Mystery of Desire* (New York, 1994); Catherine Clément, *Opera, or the Undoing of Women* (Minneapolis, 1988).

C. Faro

Cameron, Edwin (b. 1953), South African jurist. Born in Pretoria, Cameron studied there and as a Rhodes scholar at Oxford. A respected advocate of human rights and labour rights, as Professor of Law at the University of the Witwatersrand in Johannesburg he helped establish the AIDS Law Project within the Centre for Applied Legal Studies, was founding convenor of the non-government national AIDS Consortium in 1993, and a leading figure in the national AIDS Convention. He helped draft a Charter of Rights on HIV/AIDS, and was influential in the drafting and defence of the 1994 South African constitution's Bill of Rights, and the inclusion of sexual orientation in its equality clause – a world first. Cameron also edited *Defiant Desire*, an anthology of South African lesbian and gay writing, with Mark GEVISSER. In 1995 he chaired an enquiry into South Africa's armaments industry. Cameron was appointed Judge of the High Court, Witwatersrand Local Division, in 1995. He was elected Chair of the Council of the University of the Witwatersrand in March 1998. In 1999, prior to his appointment to the Constitutional Court, he chose to publicly declare that he was living with AIDS.

Edwin Cameron and Mark Gevisser (eds), *Defiant Desire* (Johannesburg, 1993).

Ken Davis

Cammermeyer, Magarethe (b. 1942), American soldier. Born in Nazi-occupied

Norway, Cammermeyer moved with her family to the US in the early 1950s. After completing college in 1963, she went on active duty in the US Army, taking up nursing as a career. She served in Vietnam, earning the Bronze Star Medal as well as several citations. In 1968, having married, she left the army, although in 1972 she resumed active duty in the Reserves, serving initially in Seattle, Washington. In 1985 she was named Nurse of the Year by the Veterans Administration, and in 1987 she was promoted to full colonel. Hers was a successful career *par excellence*.

However, Cammermeyer, the mother of four sons, divorced her husband in 1980 and, later that decade, met the woman who was to become her long-term partner. In 1989, she revealed to a military investigator that she was a lesbian, and there followed several years of activity as the US Army sought to have her discharged; it was, in mid-1992, successful.

Cammermeyer has been the highest ranking officer in the US military to contest its anti-gay policies, joining others such as Sharon Kowalski and Leonard MATLOVITCH. Her own career certainly challenges the view that lesbians and gays are detrimental to the military ethos; indeed, like the hundreds of thousands of other lesbians and gays who have served their countries in hours of need, she has indicated that one's sexuality need be no bar to both a sense of duty and an ability to command. Since her dismissal, she has become something of a folk-hero; she continues to work with veterans suffering from Post-Traumatic Stress Disorder.

Margarethe Cammermeyer, with Chris Fisher, *Serving in Silence* (New York, 1994).

Garry Wotherspoon

Camus, Renaud (b. 1946), French author. Camus was born near Clermont-Ferrand. Having studied law and political science for his first degree and followed this with a masters in philosophy, he worked as a language assistant for a year at Oxford and then at two universities in America. During the 1970s and 1980s he mostly lived in Paris, although he travelled widely, both elsewhere in France and also in Portugal and Italy. Unlike most of his generation, he has preferred to make a living by writing, his work ranging across a wide variety of genres and styles, from the essays which he contributed for a while to the Parisian periodical *Gai Pied* to travelogues and experimental fiction. His earliest works fall into the category of 'polyphonic' writing, using passages excerpted from other writers to create a patchwork text somewhere between fiction and criticism. Homosexuality as an issue – or a non-issue – came to the fore in *Tricks* (1979), which records a series of autobiographical sexual encounters while cruising, and the essays and 'thoughts' in *Notes achriennes* (1982) and *Chroniques achriennes* (1984), where Camus's use of two neologisms for gay and straight which are more or less anagrams of one another – *achrienne* and *hinarce* – embodies his view of the immateriality of sexual identity. This theme then transfers into his fiction, in a pair of pseudo-historical novels, *Roman roi* (1983) and *Roman furieux* (1986), and has been developed in increasingly complex ways in *Le Chasseur de lumière* (1993), *L'Epuisant Désir de ces choses* (1995) and *P.A.* (1997), all of which are also reflections on the nature of writing in general and fiction in particular. Alongside these more 'objective' works he has continued to produce a series of consciously self-referential works, including *Journal d'un voyage en France* (1981), *Journal romain* (1987) and *L'Esprit des terrasses: Journal* (1990) and another set of volumes of essays classified under the general heading 'Elegies', the first of which, *Elégies pour quelques-uns* (1988), was evidently inspired by the effect of the AIDS crisis.

Lawrence Schehr, *The Shock of Men: Homosexual Hermeneutics in French Writing* (Stanford, 1995).

Christopher Robinson

Capote, Truman (1924–84), American writer. Born Truman Streckfus Persons in New Orleans and later given the name of his stepfather, Capote was raised in southern Alabama by maternal cousins. The Gothic tenor of these years resulted in the emotional autobiography of a gay teenager, *Other Voices, Other Rooms* (1948), his first published book, and eventually *The Grass Harp, A Christmas Memory* and *The Thanksgiving Visitor*. The rest of his writing career involved experimenting with the integration of different forms of reportage and fiction. It was the publication of *In Cold Blood* (1966), an account of the murder of a Kansas family and the subsequent hunt for the killers, that brought him sustained fame and with which he arguably invented the non-fiction novel – widely copied by such prominent writers as Norman Mailer and Tom Wolfe. As a public wit, he became one of the most photographed gay men of his generation as his fame grew and, possibly, peaked with his famous Black and White Ball of 1966, the high society event of the decade.

As a contributor of experimental fiction to *Esquire* and then to Andy WARHOL's *Interview* during the 1970s, he once again returned to more explicitly gay themes, most notably with the bisexual protagonist P. B. Jones who narrates the unfinished novel *Answered Prayers*. Because anyone familiar with his circle of acquaintances could easily identify the characters and the dirty laundry that he aired, the appearance of the first few instalments of this Proust-like *roman à clef* resulted in his banishment from the society set. Although he complained that his being snubbed was merely inconvenient because it separated him from people who were his material rather than his friends, he entered into a dependence upon drugs and alcohol from which he was only free for relatively brief periods during the rest of his life.

In 1980 Capote was able to rally long enough to write a still undervalued book of short writing exercises titled *Music for Chameleons*, which was the preliminary result of an attempt to prepare himself for the completion of *Answered Prayers*. He was never able to work at the height of his powers again, however, and he died from causes as yet unknown. Although his magnum opus remained unfinished at his death, the small portion that remains suggests a new form of novel potentially as influential as the one fashioned for *In Cold Blood*, and his deft retelling of the gossip of the rich could have been a dramatically queer way to end a long reign as one of the US's most visible writers.

Gerald Clarke, *Capote: A Biography* (New York, 1988); George Plimpton, *Truman Capote* (New York, 1997).

Shelton Waldrep

Cárdenas, Nancy (1934–94), Mexican writer, actress, director. Born in Parras, in the northern province of Coahuila, Cárdenas was a student of Polish language and literature as well as of cinema and the dramatic arts. After taking her doctorate at the National Autonomous University of Mexico, she studied at Yale and Lodz. Theatre and agitation were closely related for Cárdenas: her friend and fellow writer Carlos MONSIVÁIS remembers her as someone who 'combined theatre and activism with the eloquence which comes from understanding the positive knock-on effects of all acts which claw back from repression some of the space it occupies'. In the 1970s she won several accolades for her work as a stage-director and was involved with productions of plays by authors as disparate as FASSBINDER and Lope de Vega. Her directorial debut came in 1970 with a production of Paul Zindel's *The Effect of Gamma Rays on Man-in-the-Moon Marigolds*, for which she was awarded the coveted Association of Theatre Critics Prize. Cárdenas was ahead of her time in 1973 when she became the first person to speak out in defence of homosexual rights on Mexican television.

Cárdenas herself directed programmes

on cinema, culture and criticism on Mexican radio and television. Her knowledge of film led in 1979 to her collaboration with Monsiváis on the script of *México de mis amores*, a compilation of highlights from Mexican cinema. Monsiváis recalls Cárdenas as a vivacious woman with an ebullient passion for life. Her manifest *joie de vivre*, he says, had the self-preserving sarcastic edge to it that was called for by the hostile climate which marked the early days of feminist and gay activism in Mexico. Her optimism faltered only once, he suggests, following the Tlatelolco Massacre of 1968. Cárdenas had been a member of the Alliance of Writers, Artists and Intellectuals for the Student Movement, and Monsiváis conjectures that it was after the shocking events of 1968 that her political activism became more sharply defined around issues affecting sexual minorities.

In 1972, her production of Mart Crowley's *Boys in the Band* caused controversy. It was officially condemned as 'immoral and offensive to good taste' but was brought to the stage following a campaign led by other intellectuals and writers. In 1975, as a contribution to the International Year of Women, Cárdenas addressed a conference in Mexico City on lesbianism. As she left she was met with placards calling for the deportation of all 'perverts and degenerates' from Mexico. In the 1980s and 1990s her work was more self-evidently connected with issues of sexuality and identity politics. Her plays *Sexualidades I* and *Sexualidades II* were premiered in 1992 and 1993, and in 1988 she worked on *Sida, así es la vida*, an adaptation of William M. Hoffman's *As Is*. She also brought to the stage an adaptation of Radclyffe Hall's *The Well of Loneliness*.

A book of poetry, *Amor de verano*, was published in 1985. She combined her talents as translator and director in a production of a Spanish version of *Mistero Buffo* by Dario Fo. The *Excélsior* newspaper published selections of her poetry. Shortly after her death in 1994, a compilation spanning four decades was published as *Cuaderno de amor y desamor* (*Falling In and Out of Love: A Notebook*). The evocation of Neruda's *Veinte poemas de amor y una canción desesperada* (*Twenty Love Poems and a Song of Despair*) presents the dynamic of love between women as fully the equal of even the most passionate heterosexual affair. As its title suggests, in this long series of poems Cárdenas muses on the process by which love ebbs away and then grows again. Written in the first person, *Cuaderno de amor y desamor* follows the subject's reconciliation to the loss of her lover and the stirrings of her desire for another woman. In her dialogue between lesbian lovers, Cárdenas vindicates female eroticism whilst also vaunting the value of feelings: 'I exist only in the emotions I produce'. The poem presents the realm of ideas as inseparable from the erotic, refusing to reduce the female lover simply to her body. The lover's bodily presence is celebrated through a holistic perspective: 'Svelte waist refines ideas' and 'Firm muscles sustain emotion'. Emphasis is placed on the equality and reciprocity of lesbian relationships. The spirituality of religious faith is realigned with an erotic mysticism. Through tropical and animal similes, Cárdenas's *Cuaderno* situates homosexuality as an intrinsic part of nature. In a phrase which encapsulates the indefatigable optimism of a pioneering advocate of homosexual visibility in Mexico, Cárdenas wrote that those who persist in seeing homosexuality as aberrant are fossils from another age. 'To love like this, openly and without guilt,' she writes, 'is to live in the twenty-first century.'

Elena M. Martínez, *Lesbian Voices from Latin America: Breaking Ground* (New York, 1996); Maria Elena De Valdes, *The Shattered Mirror: Representations of Women in Mexican Literature* (Houston, 1998).

Ryan Prout

Cardín, Alberto (1948–92), Spanish essayist and activist. Cardín is probably the key figure in Spanish gay culture after Francoism and his case illustrates the pressures and contradictions suffered by Spanish gay intellectuals. Several issues come to mind when thinking about his work. The first is the sheer amount. In a mere twenty years he wrote over twenty books and scores of articles and contributions. He collaborated on a number of cultural journals, worked on translations of gay authors and took part in several cultural debates during the 1970s and early 1980s. But it is the variety of his oeuvre that makes assessment a daunting task: fiction, anthropological essays, sociology, literary criticism, historical research, poetry and journalism are only some of the areas in which he worked. As a result, it is easy to get the impression of lack of discipline or rigour. This is only partly true. Cardín was an enthusiastic writer at a moment when enthusiasm was justified: after Franco there was so much to write about, the whole world had to be rewritten and rethought.

Cardín's research into homosexuality was cutting-edge and he was acquainted with the work of cultural critics such as Michel FOUCAULT at a time when nobody in Spain seemed to be aware of New French Thought. His notion of homosexuality is very much in line with radical formulations carried out in the 1960s and the 1970s by authors such as Guy HOCQUENGHEM and Herbert MARCUSE (and therefore seldom easy to reconcile with the more stable 'gay identity' model). He saw homosexuality as fundamentally transgressive and anti-institutionalistic, and in his life he seems to have shown contempt for any assimilationist agenda. His ideas were too new in Spain's intellectual world and never took root. It did not help that Cardín was a self-confessed troublemaker, always eager to antagonise anybody with a comfortable or even stable vision of the world.

Cardín was born in Asturias and spent a number of years in Mexico during his childhood. It was there that he had his sexual initiation. After a few more years in Spain and London, he moved to Barcelona, where he lived for most of his life, making friends and enemies, keeping his distance from the budding gay movement, lecturing and participating in literary journals. Some of them were ephemeral, but for the scholar they hold special interest and research on them is badly needed. *La Bañera* may be illustrative of his work in this field. He started as a member of this magazine devoted to cultural issues and as his colleagues started to leave, he ended up taking charge and writing most of the contents (including the 'lonely hearts' section) under different pennames. The magazine included fake interviews, outings of canonical writers in the Spanish literary tradition, reviews, camp columns and polemics. His fiction is equally outrageous, and again it is easy to be discouraged by its lack of discipline. His stories give the impression of having been written in a rush, and boast scandalous topics presented in unpolished style, maybe a sign of the times. He wrote several long essays on the philosophy of religion and on sociological issues. As an editor, he compiled the first anthology published in Spain with essays on AIDS as early as 1985. Even if his introduction seems to reflect the confusion of the times around the issue, one must set this in the context of a country where nobody thought AIDS was important, and where silence on homosexuality was and is part of a pact of non-aggression.

Alberto Cardín and Armand de Fluviá, *Sida: Maldición bíblica o enfermedad letal?* (Barcelona, 1985); Alberto Cardín, *Detrás por delante* (Barcelona, 1986), and *Sida: enfoques alternativos* (Barcelona, 1991); Paul Julian Smith, *Vision Machines* (London, 1996).

Alberto Mira

Castells, Manuel (b. 1942), Spanish-American scholar. Castells was born in Spain, and educated there and in France, taking degrees in law and sociology. He is currently Professor of City and Regional

Planning and Affiliated Professor of Sociology at the University of California, Berkeley. After early work on urban problems in South and Central America, he wrote *The Urban Question* (1977), a Marxian analysis of urban issues. This was followed by his magisterial *The City and the Grassroots* (1983), which was heralded as a pioneering study of urban social movements. Chapter 14 of the book was devoted to an analysis of the social, political and spatial organisation of San Francisco's gay community (a preliminary version of which he had written a year earlier with Karen Murphy). This described the emergence and early evolution of the gay movement in the Castro district: the first analysis of the manner in which homosexuality was a critical element in influencing the social and spatial structures of urban change. This study led the way for a series of works by sociologist, geographers and others of urban gay life, but few were as substantial as that of Castells. Subsequently Castells became increasingly interested in information technology, and is widely acknowledged as the world's foremost authority on the emergence of the 'network society', publishing a trilogy of books on the topic between 1996 and 1997.

Stuart Lowe, *Urban Social Movements: The City after Castells* (New York, 1986).

John Connell

Cazuza (1958–90), Brazilian rock singer and song-writer. Cazuza was born in Rio de Janeiro, the only child of a middle-class family. His real name was Agenor de Miranda Araújo Neto but he was always known by the nickname Cazuza (Rascal) given to him by his father, an executive in the recording business. After a stable childhood he became a rebellious teenager, exploring the frenetic nightlife of Rio and cutting school. He dropped out of university in his first year and tried unsuccessfully to find his vocation in the theatre and as a photographer. In 1981 he teamed up with a rock band called Barão Vermelho (Red Baron) and became their lead singer and song-writer. Their first record made little impression, although one of the songs, 'Todo Amor que Houver nessa Vida' (All the Love There Could Be in This Life) was performed by Caetano Veloso, one of Brazil's most popular singers. The band's success began with their second record, *Barão Vermelho 2*, and with the theme music for the film *Bete Balanço*. Their next record *Maior Abandonado* (*Abandoned Adult*), launched in 1984, won a Golden Disc and the band had achieved star status. At this time Cazuza, whose striking good looks always attracted attention, was leading a frenetic lifestyle, partying all night, consuming alcohol, drugs and sex, and frequently acting crazy.

In 1985, Cazuza broke with the band and went solo. His first disc was *Exagerado* (*Over the Top*), a title which summed up his life to that point. In the same year he suffered the first symptom of AIDS. He issued his second LP, *Só Se For a Dois* (*Only If It Is For Two*) in 1986 and went back to doing live shows the next year. In 1987 he suffered a recurrence of an AIDS-related illness. Rumours spread about his health but he denied having AIDS until February 1989, when he publicly acknowledged his illness in an interview. This was a courageous step, helping to break some of the taboos surrounding the illness. From then on his condition was widely covered by the media and Cazuza became the symbol of the person living with and fighting against AIDS. In April 1989 the weekly news magazine *Veja* (*See*), the Brazilian equivalent of *Time* magazine, devoted its cover story to the singer. He was incensed at the caption on the cover, 'Cazuza, a victim of AIDS, is dying in full public view' and wrote to the press to complain.

As the illness took its toll, Cazuza's lifestyle became more restrained. His songs and performances became more serious, reflecting the social issues which concerned the great mass of the Brazilian population. His earlier songs appealed to a rebellious middle-class youth anxious to shock and owed something to punk. Later songs, such as 'Brasil', which became the theme music for a popular TV series, reflected the disenchantment with the chaotic and corrupt administration of President Sarney. In 1988 he produced the album *Ideologia* (*Ideology*), considered by many his best work, and toured the country, to great acclaim. From then on, frequent bouts of illness with spells in hospital made performing more difficult but he insisted on recording his last double-album *Burguesia* (*Bourgeoisie*).

Cazuza died in 1990 in the apartment of his parents. To commemorate him his mother set up the Viva Cazuza Society, a charity which sponsors AIDS prevention work and provides a home for HIV-positive children. Cazuza was openly bisexual and, according to his mother's biography, had an affair with Ney Matogrosso, a famous androgynous singer. He was not close to the gay movement but his public acknowledgement of his position as a person with AIDS helped to change public attitudes and dispel some of the prejudice surrounding the disease in Brazil.

Cazuza, *Songbook* (Rio de Janeiro, 1990); Lucinha Araujo, *Cazuza: Só as Mães são Felizes* (São Paulo, 1997); Antônio Fausto Neto, *Mortes em Derrapagem: os Casos Corona e Cazuza no Discurso da Comunicação de Massa* (Rio de Janeiro, 1991).

Robert Howes

Cernuda, Luis (1902–63), Spanish poet. Cernuda is among the foremost Spanish poets of the twentieth century. Homoeroticism is strikingly obvious in his work, but somehow Spanish literary critics have been reluctant to deal with this aspect of his poetry. Given the fact that it cannot be missed, it is often perfunctorily mentioned, as if its specificity did not even deserve attention. In a perfect world it might not be noteworthy. But the critics' deeply neurotic attitude towards homosexuality cannot be dismissed as progressiveness. Cernuda and García Lorca illustrate Eve Kosofsky SEDGWICK's reflections on attitudes towards homosexuality: when it is obvious, it does not matter and therefore does not deserve discussion, whereas when it is less so (as it is in Lorca's case) then it should not be brought into the open and therefore cannot be discussed.

In biographical portraits and testimonies of acquaintances, Cernuda appears as a self-aware homosexual if not a particularly happy one. In the 1920s he identified with the image of the dandy, and his immaculate attire and manners are often remarked upon. Even if he did not discuss homosexuality (apart from poetic treatment), he seems to have favoured an attitude of dealing with it and identifying with homosexual culture, something that was noticed by his friend Juan GIL-ALBERT. He came from a wealthy Andalusian middle-class family and there is an aristocratic element to his upbringing that was reflected in both his personality and his work. He read André Gide's *Corydon* before he was 20, and his vision of homosexuality was deeply informed by Gide's reflections. Cernuda matured in a country that was becoming more cultivated and progressive, and is very much a man of his time. But, differently from sociable García Lorca, he could not stand fools easily, and his impatient personality did not win him any friends. Many of the negative accounts about Cernuda deal with his 'dandyism', and the author seems to have decided to keep silent about this. He left Spain after the Civil War: as with most other members of the movement known as the 'Generation of 27', his political allegiances were with the left (which could prompt reflection on the supposed lack of political commitment present in homosexual dandies: their sexual dissidence was likely to bring about political dissidence, too) and his obvious homosexuality made him an easy target (for others, like Vicente ALEIXANDRE, sexual orientation was easier to conceal). Cernuda left for Great Britain (he worked as Spanish lecturer in Cambridge), and then for the United States, finally settling down in Mexico. Exile made him into an embittered man and he was often in poor health.

His work gives evidence of an extraordinary lucidness even in the most difficult of times, and his poetry often conveys an almost Zen-like serenity that seems difficult to reconcile with information about the poet. Homoeroticism features in most of his books (his poetical works are collected in a volume entitled *La realidad y el deseo, Reality and Desire*). The poet tends to reflect on the difficulties of attaining an ever-fleeing object of desire, normally incarnated in the figure of a youth, following the patterns of the Hellenistic tradition. Regrets about old age and detached fascination with the male body make it difficult to find a more steely voice in his poetry. Cernuda's erotic poetry, however, goes beyond voyeurism. Homoeroticism is used as a means to convey certain ideas, and it is relevant that the love Cernuda cherishes is forbidden. That is why the poet's attitude towards sexual orientation cannot be dismissed easily: it is a central part of his overall project. His anguish, the distance he feels from the object of desire, his scepticism and even his quiet acceptance of a difficult fate simply would not be portrayed in the same way if the object of desire had been female. Sexual orientation is portrayed not just as subjective desire, but as something deeply rooted in and indebted to social discourse. His bitterness or his feelings of self-defeat do not come just from a personal frustration or internalised homophobia, but from the fact that, open and willing as the poet is to explore his sexuality, indeed to enjoy it, society will prevent him from doing so, tainting the purity of sexual desire.

Cernuda fell in love at last in 1951, during his Mexican exile, and one of his most moving works, *Poemas para un cuerpo* (*Poems for a Body*), can be read in the light of this relationship. The physicality of love is a striking leitmotiv in Cernuda's work, and it is at its most explicit both in this book and in the much earlier *Los placeres ocultos* (1931). Cernuda's last years were unhappy and are painfully recreated in the poetic journey of his last book, *Desolación de la quimera* (1962).

Luis Cernuda, *La realidad y el deseo* (Madrid, 1991); Salvador Jiménez Fajardo, *The Word and the Mirror: Critical Essays on the Poetry of Luis Cernuda* (London, 1989); Philip Silver, '*Et in arcadia ego*': *A Study of the Poetry of Luis Cernuda* (London, 1965); Jenaro Talens, *El espacio y las máscaras* (Barcelona, 1975).
                                                                      Alberto Mira

Chatwin, Bruce (1940–89), British writer. Chatwin was born in Sheffield. After attending Marlborough School, a famous public school in southern England, he began work as a porter at Sotheby's. Chatwin rose quickly in the well-known art-and-antique auctioneering firm to become one of Sotheby's youngest directors. Eight years after joining the firm, he abruptly left the company, to pursue his passion for world travel and continue to study nomads and nomadism. For the rest of his life, he travelled widely in Asia, Africa and Australia, rarely remaining long in any place despite marrying, in 1965, an American, Elizabeth Charrer, whom he had met at Sotheby's. From 1972 to 1975 he worked as a journalist for the *Sunday Times* and announced his next departure in a telegram, 'Gone to Patagonia for six months', which led to his first book, *In Patagonia*. This launched his writing career, which produced five more books, the most famous of which was *The Songlines* (1987), which reflected on the lives and mobility of Aborigines from Central Australia. Chatwin was equally nomadic between sexual partners. Indeed, his unsettled sexual and romantic life may be reflected in his peripatetic professional achievements. His bisexuality posed problems for him and his partners. According to friends, he had numerous one-night stands, with both men and women, and several longer affairs, including one with the Jamaican actor Peter Straker. Chatwin died after a protracted illness – 'a blood disease picked up in China' – at a time when many public figures dying of AIDS chose not to disclose the nature of their illness.

Nicholas Shakespeare, *Bruce Chatwin* (London, 1999); Bruce Chatwin, *What Am I Doing Here?* (London, 1989).

John Connell

Chauncey, George (b. 1954), American scholar. Educated at Yale University, Chauncey has taught at New York University and the University of Chicago, where he is presently Professor of History. In 1989, he co-edited *Hidden from History: Reclaiming the Gay and Lesbian Past*, a pioneering collection of essays. His *Gay New York: Gender, Urban Culture, and the Making of the Gay Male World, 1890–1940* was widely hailed as a major contribution to historical scholarship and a comprehensive study of the development of a gay subculture. The book received several awards and is being translated into French; a film based on the book is being produced by the American Social History Project. Chauncey is now completing *The Strange Career of the Closet: Gay Culture, Consciousness, and Politics from the Second World War to the Stonewall Era*. He is the founding chair of the Lesbian and Gay Studies Project of the Center for Gender Studies at Chicago and a member of the editorial board of *GLQ*; he has served as historical consultant for several exhibitions and broadcasts and as an expert witness in trials concerning sexual discrimination issues.

Robert Aldrich and Garry Wotherspoon

Chicago, Judy (b. 1939), American artist. Chicago holds an important position in the development of feminist art. Born Judy Cohen in Chicago, she adopted the name Chicago in 1970. In response to the sexism and discrimination she experienced

in her art training in Los Angeles, she developed at California State University the Fresno Feminist Art Program which mounted the first feminist art exhibition, *Womanhouse*. In her own art work she endeavoured to represent the experience of female sexuality initially through abstract forms and later through a crude representational style to counter the elitism she perceived in modernism. She developed an imagery based on a central open core, and was consequently criticised for attempting to construct a universal sign for feminity that suggested female experiences could be reckoned simply through the form of female anatomy.

Chicago wanted to reinstall important women in history and, aided by hundreds of assistants, she completed the large-scale, carefully researched sculptural installation, the *Dinner Party*, using traditional female crafts such as embroidery and ceramics. This project valorised over one thousand women including Sappho and Ethel Smyth.

A later ambitious project, *The Holocaust Project: From Darkness into Light*, used feminism and the Jewish tradition of *tikkun*, the traditional process of healing and repairing the world, to depict the struggle of the Jews, women and homosexuals against Nazism.

Judy Chicago, *Through the Flower: My Struggle as a Woman Artist* (Garden City, NY, 1975); Amelia Jones (ed.), *Sexual Politics: Judy Chicago's* Dinner Party *in Feminist Art History* (Berkeley, 1996).

Elizabeth Ashburn

Cliff, Michelle (b. 1946), Jamaican-American-British writer. Michelle Cliff was born in Jamaica, but later moved between Britain and the United States. Throughout her career as a writer and educator, these three countries have formed the backdrop for her investigation of race, class, gender and sexuality. An avowedly political writer, her early work probes the legacies of the English colonisation of Jamaica. In 1980, Cliff published her first prose collectioin, *Claiming an Identity They Taught Me to Despise*. Explicitly autobiographical, this work addresses her early life as a part of the white-identifying Jamaican elite, and her gradual repudiation of this priviledged background. Although she was the co-publisher and editor of the lesbian-feminist journal *Sinister Wisdom* from 1981 to 1983, her engagement with issues of sex and sexuality is underplayed in her novel *Abeng*, published in 1984. This work, like the 1985 anthology of prose and poetry *The Land of Look Behind*, continues to foreground issues pertaining to race, class and colonisation, as does her 1988 novel *No Telephone to Heaven*.

It was not until the 1990 release of *Bodies of Water*, her third anthology of prose writing, that Cliff began to address queer sexuality in more sustained and explicit way. As a consequence, Cliff has been lauded by resident and expatriate Caribbeans as a powerful critic of the entrenched homophobia of the region. This work was followed in 1993 by *Free Enterprise*, which turned to America, and its radical Abolition movement. In 1998, Cliff released a volume of short stories, *The Store of a Million Items*. She continues to write in the United States, where she also teaches.

Belinda Edmonson, 'Race, Privilege, and the Politics of (Re)Writing History, an Analysis of the Novels of Michelle Cliff', *Callaloo*, vol. 16, no. 1 (1993), pp. 180–91; Ramchandran Sethuraman, 'Evidence-cum-Witness: Subaltern History, Violence, and the (De)Formation of Nation in Michelle Cliff's *No Telephone to Heaven*', *Modern Fiction Studies*, vol. 43, no. 1 (1997), pp. 249–87; Timothy Chin, ' "Bullers" and "Battymen", Contesting Homophobia in Black Popular Culture and Contemporary Carribean Literature', *Callaloo*, vol. 20, no. 1 (1997), pp. 127–40.

Susan Humphries

Clift, Montgomery (1920–66), American actor. Clift was breathtakingly beautiful.

He virtually redefined screen acting and, for a time, the world loved him. A precursor of 'the Method' – an acting philosophy he himself never studied – he would totally immerse himself in a character emotionally and physically. His spontaneity and sexual intensity in *Red River* (1948), *The Heiress* (1950) and *A Place In The Sun* (1951) created a sensation. As Chris Huizenga wrote in *After Dark*, bobbysoxers 'weren't sure whether they should mother him or go to bed with him'. It was during this period that he was arrested for 'soliciting' on 42nd Street, but his studio intervened and the charge was dropped without attracting publicity.

Romantic roles were lost to him for ever when, in 1956, a car crash left him physically and mentally damaged, as well as drug- and alcohol-dependent. Increasingly erratic behaviour over the next few years, coupled with sexual recklessness, severely restricted his ability to work and the number of job offers. Moreover, Clift finally found himself totally unemployable (and uninsurable) after the financial and critical disaster of *Freud* in 1962. Rescue came when his friend Elizabeth TAYLOR insisted on 'Monty' as her co-star in *Reflections in a Golden Eye*, where he was to play an overtly homosexual character (though there were already elements of sexual ambiguity running through his performance in Hitchcock's *I Confess* (1953) and *The Misfits* (1961)). However, a few months before filming was to begin he died of a heart attack, joining Tyrone Power and Errol Flynn, beautiful young men who burned themselves out long before 50.

Clift was one of the very few gay men to have a successful career within an industry dedicated to conformity and moral judgements. Clift had his first male regular partner in 1940, when he was 20, and although he had intense relationships with women he was predominantly homosexual. Almost uniquely, he did not go out of his way to cover up that fact. A casual lover, Maurice Leonard, has recently painted him not as a guilt-ridden 'basket case' but as a man at ease with his sexuality who probably would, given the more enlightened 1960s and his own provocative nature, have come out. Despite his early fame, Clift has not become the major male icon of the 1950s. Unlike James DEAN, he did not die young and beautiful; neither did he make films which win the hearts of large numbers of today's young people. However, his early beauty lives on – as does his vulnerability – in a few key films of the era.

Robert LaGuardia, *Monty* (London, 1977); Patricia Bosworth, *Montgomery Clift* (New York, 1978); Maurice Leonard, *Montgomery Clift* (London, 1997).

Keith Howes

Clod, Bente (b. 1946), Danish writer. Born in Copenhagen into a broad-minded left-wing family, Clod went to school in the first 'Small-School' in Denmark, founded by her parents and other pioneer teachers. She left school in her mid-teens and earned her living by odd jobs in factories and restaurants. In 1973 she went back to school, and there met Jeannette, a young married woman with whom she fell in love. It was Clod's first love affair with a woman, and the two of them maintained their intense relationship for ten years during school, the founding of a Women's Press and their working in the editorial group of *Sexual Politics* magazine (a follow-up on an earlier publication with that name, founded by psychotherapist Wilhelm Reich during his stay in Norway in the 1930s). The magazine 'confronted political parties with sexual reality', and counted another well-known Danish gay writer in the circle, Christian KAMPMANN. In 1976 Clod published her first book, *The Authorized Version and Other In-Fights*: articles, poems and fiction about feminism and gender roles. In 1977 she published her autobiographical novel *Brud* (*Break-Up* or *Bride*). In this novel she told with great passion about her relationship to Jeannette

which made her come out as a lesbian – or a 'bisexual' as she first labelled herself – and about her experiences of being a woman in modern society. It became an immense success among younger women who could identify with the protagonist. *Brud* was translated into Norwegian, Swedish, Icelandic and Finnish, and Clod went on a tour of Scandinavia, often with a catalyst effect, as women would come out in the audience during the reading sessions. Together with the books of the Norwegian writer Gerd BRANTENBERG, *Brud* was the most influential book for lesbians in Scandinavia in the 1970s.

In 1974, the Lesbian Movement was founded in Copenhagen as a breakaway group from the new feminist group, 'the Redstocking Movement'. Both movements considered themselves radical feminists, squatted houses and made them into Women's Centres (one of them still exists as a Centre for Battered Women), arranged women-only summer camps, celebrated the 8th of March and were organised into consciousness-raising groups. The Lesbian Movement was, like the Gay Liberation Front (Bøssernes Befrielses Front), an alternative to the more sedate homophile organisation founded in 1948.

After Clod published *Brud* she also joined the Lesbian Movement and took part in many of its activities, reading from her writing at festivals, and supporting the founding of a women's education centre. Together with six other women in 1978 she founded the small publishing house 'Kvindetryk' (Women's Press). The following year she co-founded a Women's Cultural Foundation and a Women's Group in the Danish Writers' Association. In these years she also published an anthology of women's texts, a collection of poetry and a sequel to *Brud* called *Syv Sind* (*In Doubt*). The novel was translated into Norwegian, Swedish and German.

In 1979 Clod entered the Danish Film School to become a screenwriter, and in the following years she wrote several screen- and stage-plays. She also had a love relationship with one of Denmark's leading modernist writers of books, radio, screen- and stage-plays, also working as a director and teacher. Since 1985 Clod has taught creative writing in hundreds of courses, and is now considered an authority in this field, with publications about writing and screenplaying. In some workshops she teaches the art of erotic writing, based on her publication of erotic short stories in English, *Ex Hibition*. Around 1987 she became a member of ALGWE, the Association of Lesbian and Gay Writers in Europe.

Clod's greatest impact on her lesbian readership was in the late 1970s and early 1980s with *Brud*. Her writing has been very influential on many lesbians, especially in their coming-out phase. Today many young gay writers go to her workshops.

Karin Lützen

Close, Roberta (b. 1964), Brazilian hermaphrodite and male-to-female transsexual. Close achieved celebrity status in Brazil and internationally through her striking good looks. An American newspaper summed up her appeal when it announced, 'The world's most beautiful model is really a man'. Her fame raised issues of gender and sexuality with the Brazilian public in a sensational way and highlighted the situation of transvestites and transsexuals, hitherto a highly marginalised group in Brazil.

Born in Rio de Janeiro, Close was given the masculine name of Luiz Roberto Gambine Moreira and brought up as a boy. According to her authorised biography she had defective male genitalia, with a small penis and no testicles. As a child she preferred to play with little girls and as a teenager she began to dress as a woman. Her feminine appearance and behaviour led to conflict with her family and at the age of 14 her father threw her out. Her public career began in 1981 when she caused a sensation at a number of gay balls in the annual Carnival celebrations and was featured almost nude in a magazine called *Close* (from which she took the name by which she is generally known).

The pictures which appeared in the press launched her career as a media personality. With her round face, almond eyes, long dark wavy hair and winning smile, she really looked like a beautiful woman. She appeared in illustrated and soft-porn magazines, in the gossip columns of newspapers, on the stage and in television shows and commercials. At the height of her popularity she became an icon of Brazilian popular culture. A rock song and a traditional chapbook ballad were dedicated to her. The artist Adir Sodré painted a stylised nude portrait in acrylic, complete with male genitals, which was exhibited in the government-sponsored exhibition of Brazilian modern art in Paris in 1987–88. She attracted a following among both gay and straight men and some lesbians, although many women remained at best ambivalent and often hostile towards her. She was also reviled by the more traditional, machista elements, who criticised the way she flaunted her striking androgyny.

As her fame grew, Close travelled to the US and Europe, working as a fashion model and being photographed with the stars in fashionable night clubs. In 1989 she decided to take the final step and undergo a sex-change operation. As such operations were illegal in Brazil at the time, the surgery was performed in London. Photographs published in the biography show her new female genitalia. Afterwards she moved to Switzerland, living under the name of Luiza Gambine. There she met a Swiss man with whom she went to live, although expressing a desire to return permanently to Brazil. During the 1990s she waged a long legal battle with the Brazilian authorities to have the name on her official identity documents changed from the original masculine form to her preferred female name.

In the Brazilian media she was generally

referred to as a transvestite or more latterly as 'the most famous transsexual in Brazil'. In her biography she preferred to be described as a hermaphrodite and tried to distance herself from transvestites and homosexuals, without openly rejecting them. Nevertheless, her fame or notoriety encouraged a more open discussion of questions related to transvestism and transsexualism.

Transvestites, or *travestis*, form a distinct category in the sexual subculture of Brazil, frequently viewed with suspicion by the gay community and repressed with violence by the police. Many *travestis* take hormones, inject silicone and dress as women, sometimes convincingly so. They generally live by prostitution, since their marginalised status and reputation for violence and robbery allow no other occupation. According to some reports their clients are mostly married men who want to play the passive role with a woman. For this reason they retain their male genitalia in working order, even when taking hormones. On other occasions, the *travesti* will be the passive partner. While some may eventually undergo a sex-change operation, others have no wish to take this irrevocable step, preferring to identify as effeminate homosexuals rather than as women.

Brazilian *travestis* have travelled to France and latterly to Italy, where they are able to make far more money as prostitutes than they can in Brazil.

A step above the world of street prostitution in the Brazilian social hierarchy are the *travesti* shows, which feature the more accomplished female impersonators and have been successful as theatrical reviews, sometimes interspersed with camp commentary and male strip-tease acts. Two artistes who achieved success in this genre are Valéria and Rogéria. Close denies ever having engaged in prostitution. Despite her notoriety, she represents the more socially acceptable side of gender-crossing and her high media profile has permitted the discussion of issues of sexual identity previously relegated to the margins of society.

Lucia Rito, *Muito Prazer, Roberta Close* (Rio de Janeiro, 1998); Don Kulick, *Travesti: Sex, Gender, and Culture among Brazilian Transgendered Prostitutes* (Chicago, 1998); Helio R.S. Silva, *Travesti: a Invenção do Feminino* (Rio de Janeiro, 1993).

Robert Howes

Cohen, Steven, aka **Princess Menorah** (b. 1962), South African artist. Born in Johannesburg. Cohen spent much of his conscripted army time in the 'mad house', studied arts at the University of the Witwatersrand, and became a collage silkscreen print artist, focusing on controversial images of apartheid, childhood, anatomy and sexuality, his surreal fabrics used in fashion and furnishing. He has had exhibitions in South Africa, Germany and Luxembourg. After severe illness and incarceration in Rietfontein hospital in 1996, he became South Africa's leading and most disturbing performance artist, choreographing through spectacular gymnastics, drag, butt-plugs and blood enemas, exorcisms of cruelty to animals and hatred of marginalised people: homosexuals, Jews, drug users, ugly girls. For his 'ordeal art', in 1998 he won the premier South African art prize, the First National Bank Vita National Art Award. He was named South Africa's most significant cultural figure by the Johannesburg *Star* newspaper in 1998. He resides with his lover Elu, a dancer and choreographer, in Troyeville, Johannesburg.

Ken Davis

Cohn, Roy (1927–86), American political figure. Cohn was closely linked with Joseph McCarthy (1909–57), Republican Senator from Wisconsin, during the height of the cold-war anti-communist hysteria in the United States later known as McCarthyism. Homosexual men and women were among the principal victims of that hysteria, and the revelation at the time of his death that Cohn had been a secret homosexual all his adult life cast a new light on his activities in the 1950s.

Cohn was born in New York, where his father was a judge of the New York State Supreme Court. A brilliant student, he graduated from the Columbia University Law School and immediately obtained a position as an Assistant United States Attorney. In this role he was involved in the prosecution of Julius and Ethel Rosenberg for espionage. In 1948 the Rosenbergs were executed, and it was later claimed that their conviction had resulted from improper contacts between Cohn and the trial judge. Nevertheless, the case made his reputation, and in 1953 he became chief counsel to McCarthy's Senate investigations sub-committee, which was conducting a wide-ranging purge of real and alleged Communists and leftists from American public life. Many innocent reputations were ruined in this process. By a pleasant irony, Cohn was the unwitting instrument of McCarthy's downfall. He was infatuated with his associate on McCarthy's staff, the handsome young lawyer David Schine, and tried to pull strings to get the Army to exempt Schine from military service (then compulsory). The Army refused, and Cohn in a fit of pique launched his campaign alleging that the Army was riddled with communists, up to and including General George Marshall. This campaign led to the infamous Army-McCarthy hearings, which exposed McCarthy as a paranoid bully and led to his censure by the Senate in 1954. McCarthy died of alcoholism in 1957.

It was alleged then and later that McCarthy was a closet homosexual, and that he was sexually involved with Cohn – the left-wing playwright Lillian Hellman called Cohn and McCarthy 'Bonnie and Clyde' – but this has never been proved. His career in Washington over, Cohn moved to New York and went into legal practice. Although he remained a registered Democrat, he used his political connections to become a sort of legal hatchet-man for the political right, especially during the Nixon and REAGAN administrations, and also became a legal servant of figures associated with the New York Mafia. He successfully defended Carmine Galante and Tony Salerno, and also represented the Catholic Archbishop of New York and Donald Trump. His friends included Rupert Murdoch, Bianca Jagger, Andy WARHOL, Calvin Klein and Estée Lauder. In the 1970s and early 1980s he was one of the most prominent figures in New York high society, holding frequent parties at Studio 54. At the same time, Cohn fought a running battle with the New York State legal authorities and with the Internal Revenue Service over his behaviour as a lawyer and as a taxpayer – or non-payer. He was several times reprimanded for unethical conduct, was sued by clients from whom he had borrowed money, and faced almost continuous attempts to disbar him from legal practice. In 1964, 1969 and 1971 he was tried on various charges including fraud, conspiracy and corporate manipulation, but was acquitted on each occasion. In 1973 a court found that he had improperly profited from an insurance claim resulting from the sinking of a yacht. This issue eventually resulted in Cohn being disbarred shortly before his death.

Cohn never married, but he always denied that he was homosexual. Nevertheless, his extravagant lifestyle of 'boys, booze and drugs' was widely known in New York, and Cohn became increasingly reckless and arrogant during the pre-AIDS 'party years' of the late 1970s. He used his considerable wealth to finance a lavish lifestyle, including cosmetic surgery, to keep a series of handsome young 'aides', and to fight off lawsuits, sue his enemies for defamation and keep his clients out of trouble. He remained a brilliant courtroom performer to the end. 'I sleep well at night', he once said. 'I won't be saying "please forgive me" on my deathbed'. This was a promise he kept. After denying for months the increasingly obvious fact that he had AIDS, Cohn died of the disease in August 1986, supported by his lover, Peter Fraser – whom he had been in the habit of taking to receptions at the Reagan White House.

Cohn was a corrupt lawyer, a cynical exploiter of McCarthyite hysteria, a political reactionary, a liar, a cheat and a fraud: all extensively documented in Nicholas von Hoffman's excellent biography. Yet he was also a compelling personality who retained the friendship and loyalty of many who knew they should have known better, but could not help admiring his combative nature, his brazen effrontery and, it must be said, his legal and political skills. The fact that he died owing US$3 million in unpaid taxes has been regarded by many as more admirable than reprehensible. Attempts to blacken his name posthumously have tended to backfire. He was meant, for example, to be the principal villain in Tony Kushner's 1992 play *Angels in America*, but instead he emerges as the only real fighter in the cast: like Satan in Milton's *Paradise Lost*, he somehow has most of the best lines.

Nicholas von Hoffman, *Citizen Cohn* (New York, 1998).

Adam Carr

Collard, Cyril (1957–93), French author, filmmaker. Collard grew up in Versailles, in a comfortably-off but relatively liberal bourgeois family. From an early age his father's passion for sailing gave him access to the Mediterranean, particularly North Africa, thus nurturing a fascination for 'elsewhere' which is reflected in all his work. It is thus perhaps not so surprising that he eventually rebelled against his Catholic schooling and untroubled upbringing by abandoning the science degree that he was following at the University of Lille. He was already showing an interest in the cinema and the technical aspects of filmmaking, but the decisive factor in his life at this stage was a trip to Puerto Rico with his father in 1979 to attend the

Panamerican games (both of them were sports fanatics). Cyril stayed on alone. It was there that he started to write and to explore a bisexuality of which he was already aware but which was brought to a head when he was gang-banged for a whole night by six Puerto Rican street boys. When he returned to Paris, it was to launch himself into the film world under the aegis of Claude Davy, who introduced him to such directors as René Allio and Maurice Pialat. The early 1980s were passed in a frenzy of sexual indulgence (Collard was given to anonymous sex and multiple partners) and artistic fervour, the latter culminating in the production of a series of brilliant 'shorts', notably *Alger la blanche*, which combined the themes of passionate desire, racial difference and violence, and *Taggers*, a 1986 television feature with Collard's own musical score, portraying conflicts between young graffiti writers and the forces of law and order. His first novel, *Condamné Amour*, published by Flammarion in 1987, reflected the fact that he already knew that he had contracted AIDS: it explores emotional, erotic, social and spiritual disintegration in the context of a symbolic but unnamed 'divine virus'. It was his second novel, *Les Nuits fauves* (1989), and the film of the same name which he made from it, which are his principal artistic legacy. A review of the novel in *France-Soir* described its author as 'the spiritual child of GENET and PASOLINI, convinced like Bataille that eroticism and death are inextricably linked', but the work is not merely the rewrite of a Romantic stereotype which that suggests. It *is* a work, as Collard himself said, intended to convey to others what having AIDS really means, but alongside its expression of tortured bisexuality it is also a classic exploration of modern youth-culture and of the difficulty of finding meaning, personal or otherwise, in contemporary society. As such it helped to launch the 1990s French movement, exemplified by such writers as Vincent Borel and Guillaume Dustan, away from a death-centred attitude to AIDS. Sadly, Collard died a week too soon to see his film win no fewer than four Césars (the French equivalent of Oscars), including that for best film, at the 1993 awards.

G. Médioni, *Cyril Collard* (Paris, 1995).

Christopher Robinson

Collinson, Laurence (Henry) (1925–86), Australian-British writer and artist. Jewish, communist, homosexual, poet and playwright and painter – any one of these was enough to raise eyebrows in 1950s Australia. To be all of them, as Collinson was, seems just perverse. Brought from Leeds to Brisbane by his parents in the 1930s, he soon found himself caught up in that city's post-war cultural efflorescence and at school was a member of the Barjai group, a literary magazine and a cultural circle for youth, and of Miya, the closely associated art society. He both painted and wrote poems. It was during the post-war years that he found himself drawn to communism, and to men (as were several of the Barjai group, including Barrie Reid), though his party membership was better known than his sexual preferences.

After a brief sojourn in Sydney at the Julian Ashton Art School, Collinson moved to Melbourne, where he continued his association with the Communist Party until, in about 1958, during the membership review that followed on from the post-Hungary turmoil, his sexuality came to the attention of certain party officials, who unceremoniously lapsed his membership. He remained close to those who had chosen to leave, especially those around the radical nationalist magazine *Overland*, which published his first major book of poems, *The Moods of Love* (1957). Although the book was widely reviewed and generally praised, Collinson's pleasure was overshadowed by the fact that his lover, to whom the book was dedicated and about whom many of the poems were written, broke up with him. Even his

marriage of convenience, to a fellow member of the New Theatre, failed.

He remained politically committed, serving as president of the Fellowship of Australian Writers. In 1958–59, in communication with the Homosexual Law Reform Society in Britain, he attempted to establish such a group in Melbourne, though without any demonstrable success.

As was the case for many of Australia's creative people, Collinson was drawn to the bright lights of London, travelling to Britain in 1964 and spending the rest of his life there. The arrival of the gay rights movement in 1970 captured his radical imagination and he participated enthusiastically, writing journalism and polemic, especially in *Quorum*, a gay magazine. More and more his creativity was expressed in plays and novels and, although he succeeded in being performed and published, he failed to make the breakthrough for which he had hoped. By the 1980s, his curiosity had been captured by Transactional Analysis and he undertook training and then practised as a counsellor for many years. His finances were never good, his mood varied wildly and a falling out with his landlord added to the pressures of his life. He died from liver disease.

Graham Willett

Comisso, Giovanni (1895–1969), Italian journalist and novelist. In many ways, Comisso's life exemplifies the experience of what one historian has dubbed 'the generation of 1914', the cohort which came of age during World War I, whose lives seemed to represent the struggle to reconcile the feverish hopes of August 1914 with the subsequent experience of the war and the disillusionments of 1918. An aspect of this generation was the everlasting search for the camaraderie of the war years, and in cases like that of Comisso, there was probably only a fine line between camaraderie and sexuality.

Comisso was born into a middle-class family in Treviso in northern Italy. In

1914, at the age of 19, he volunteered for the army even before Italy had officially entered the war. He published his first poems – influenced strongly by Baudelaire, Rimbaud and Nietzsche – in pamphlet form in 1916. After the end of the war Comisso briefly attended university in Rome, where he made friends with the artist Filippo De Pisis. But in September 1919 Comisso decided to participate in the occupation of the Croatian port city of Fiume (led by Gabriele D'Annunzio), as a protest against Italy's poor territorial gains at the Versailles conference. The occupation lasted for fifteen months, and the theatrical political style developed by D'Annunzio was subsequently imitated by Mussolini's fascist government. Comisso's experience in Fiume provided the inspiration for his first novel, *Il porto d'amore* (written in 1921, published privately in 1924). Between 1921 and 1924 Comisso attended university in Genoa, Padua and Siena, graduating with a degree in letters. He spent the next nine years earning a living as a freelance journalist, often travelling for long periods (as far as Japan and China). He also spent time as a crew member of a sailing ship in the Adriatic, and in 1928 published his second novel, *Gente di mare*.

In 1933 Comisso chose to settle near his native Treviso, where he lived simply, grew his own food and wrote. It was also during these early settled years of his life that he had his most significant private relationships. The first of these was with the 16-year-old Bruno Pagan, nephew of the sea-captain for whom Comisso had worked in the Adriatic. Bruno had recently been released from prison (for stealing a bicycle), and Comisso offered to look after him. Their friendship soon took on tones of passion, as one of Comisso's biographers discreetly puts it, and they lived together for several years. In 1937 Pagan went his own way, and Comisso's diary entries show that he was distraught: the young man had been his life, and he lamented Bruno's departure as the symbolic end of his own youth.

Three years later, however, Comisso took in another 16-year-old. He was Guido Bottegal, an unsettled young man who had already run away from his family several times. Comisso dubbed him 'the fugitive' and took him in on the pretext of teaching him to be a writer. Again a youth became the focus of his life, and when Bottegal (true to his nickname) fled briefly, Comisso's diary records the way he paced desperately next to Guido's empty bed. Towards the end of the war Bottegal was mistaken for a fascist spy and was executed by partisans. Comisso never got over his death.

In keeping with the political and social climate of fascist Italy, Comisso only tangentially confronted the theme of homosexuality in his literature. His three major novels – *Un inganno d'amore* (1942), *Capriccio e illusione* (1947) and *Gioventù che muore* (1949) – have no gay characters. Yet careful comparison of their plots with Comisso's diaries and autobiography (*Le mie stagioni*, 1950) suggests that the heterosexual relationships portrayed in the novels are transfigurations of the author's own relationships with men. This is especially clear in *Gioventù che muore*, where the main character dies young, and even has the same name as Comisso's own fugitive youth – Guido.

The only work which openly suggests a homosexual relationship is *Gioco d'infanzia*, and even here the subject is only touched upon fleetingly. Written in the 1930s but held back from publication until the 1960s, it is clearly autobiographical. Its protagonist, Alberto, sets off on a voyage to the Far East, in search of sensual gratification and his childhood friend, Piero. After their reunion in the Italian colony of Eritrea, the two men find themselves in bed together with a woman, and in the process discover each other's own bodies. The novel is intertwined with impressionistic memories of Alberto's childhood, particular his lusty and gratifying games, explicitly physical, with his male friends. Towards the end of the novel the adult Alberto admits to himself that his pleasures in life have really been nothing but an extension of his childhood games.

This admission provides a key to understanding Comisso's view of his own sexuality. He, like many others of his generation, was deeply imbued with the Freudian view of homosexuality as an indication of arrested sexual and emotional development. Comisso's transfiguration of the joys and woes of his homosexual love into heterosexual stories, and in particular his reluctance to publish the only work which treated the subject openly, showed the extent to which he, like many other Italian writers, had internalised society's unwillingness to consider homosexual love as a valid form of human emotional expression.

In 1956 Comisso built a new house closer to Treviso, and employed a secretary–chauffeur. But the new man was middle-aged, and did not take the place formerly occupied by Pagan and then Bottegal; in fact, Comisso adopted his illegitimate children. He continued to write novels, which were enjoyed by a select public and well regarded by critics, until shortly before his death.

Francesco Gnerre, *L'eroe negato* (Milan, 1981); Nico Naldini, *Vita di Giovanni Comisso* (Turin, 1985).

Mark Seymour

Corinne, Tee A. (b. 1943), American photographer. According to *Completely Queer: The Gay and Lesbian Encyclopedia*, Tee A. Corinne is 'one of the most visible and accessible lesbian artists in the world'. She was named by the Lambda Book Report as one of the fifty most influential lesbians and gay men of the 1980s and continues to be a prolific photographer, poet, writer, editor and activist. She was born in St Petersburg, Florida, of mixed European ancestry – Welsh, English, Scotch, Irish, French and Dutch. She

grew up in Florida, North Carolina and the Bahamas in a vaguely Church of England upper-middle-class family. Educated at the University of South Florida and the Pratt Institute in Brooklyn, New York, she has been writing, exhibiting and publishing art since the mid-1960s.

Corinne was an important force in the development and critiquing of lesbian photography in the United States. She was a co-facilitator of the *Feminist Photography Ovulars* (1979–81) and a co-founder of *The Blatant Image, A Magazine of Feminist Photography* (1981–83). Her own work has been published in many photography books such as *Erotic by Nature*, and in two books devoted to her work, *Yantras of Womanlove*, which was the first book of lesbian photographic erotica, and *Lesbian Muse: The Women Behind The Words*, which was also important because of the depiction of a range of ethnic women and women from other races.

She is best known for her photographs of love-making, images of labia and portraits of lesbian writers. Her sexual images are important because they were the first to be circulated so publicly but are also remarkable because they included different body types and images of disabled women. These photographs have been extensively published in many journals such as *Sinister Wisdom* and *Yellow Silk* as well as magazines like *On Our Backs*.

In the 1970s and 1980s many books of her art were published, including *Lesbian Muse: The Women Behind The Words* (1989), *Women Who Loved Women* (1984) and *The Cunt Coloring Book* (1975). More recent publications include *At Six – an Artist's Book* (1990) and *Family* (1990), her show of mixed-media drawings about growing up in an alcoholic family, which is the subject of a video interview by Jane Scott Productions.

Corinne's work is reproduced and discussed in many important collections of lesbian art such as *Nothing But The Girl* (Bright and Posener, eds), *Finger Licking Good* (Tamsin Wilton, ed.); *Stolen*

Glances: Lesbians Take Photographs (Jean Frazer and Tessa Boffin, eds), *Forbidden Subjects: Self-Portraits by Lesbian Artists* (Caffyn Kelley ed.) and *In a Different Light: Visual Culture, Sexual Identity, Queer Practice*, (Blake, Rinder and Scholder, eds), a study of lesbian and gay images in art. She edited and supplied photographs for *Riding Desire and Intricate Passions* (which won a Lambda Literary Award), and edited *The Body of Love and The Poetry of Sex: Lesbians Write the Erotic*, a Lambda Award finalist.

She is also a critic, writer of fiction and poetry. Her best-known work is *Dreams of the Woman who Loved Sex* (1987), a book of lesbian erotic stories which was a small press bestseller; an expanded edition was released in 1999. A co-founder and past co-chair of the Gay & Lesbian Caucus (an affiliated society of the College Art Association), she also co-founded the Women's Caucus for Art Lesbian & Bisexual Caucus. She has curated AIDS awareness shows, Women's History Month shows, exhibits of self-portraits by women artists, and an Internet site about Lesbian Photography on the US West Coast, 1970–97. Her contribution to the arts was recognised in 1997, when she received the Women's Caucus for Art President's Award for service to women in the arts.

Elizabeth Ashburn

Corley, Carl (b. 1921), American writer and physique artist. Corley grew up on a farm in Rankin County, Mississippi. He served in the Pacific as a Marine during World War II, then returned home and took a job as draftsman with the Mississippi Highway Department in Jackson. He was employed there for almost fifteen years.

Early in the morning and at night after work, Corley sketched and painted human figures, many in futuristic settings. He built upon a childhood fascination with Flash Gordon to write and illustrate his own science fiction – both short stories and novels. Though he initially failed to interest publishers, his artwork circulated in the burgeoning realm of soft-core homoerotica. In the late 1950s, Sir Prise of Chicago sold copies of Corley's illustrations by mail. At least ten were reproduced as posters, signalling the rising popularity of distinctive gay archetypes: farm hands, college boys, sailors and hunters, as well as ancient and mythological figures such as princes, gladiators and gods. Similar imagery appeared in mid-century physique magazines, the pocket-size, black-and-white pictorials of near-naked young men. Ostensibly promoting youth fitness and featuring illustrators such as George Quaintance and TOM OF FINLAND, they increasingly relied on photographs, which were increasingly pornographic.

In the 1960s, Corley became chief of the art and model shop of the Louisiana Department of Transportation, earning accolades from several state and federal officials. His moonlighting focused more on fiction. Pad Library of Agora Hills, California, published his first pulp novel, *A Chosen World*, in 1966; he published more than twenty others over the next six years, mostly as part of the French Line series by PEC, (Publishers Export Company of San Diego). A reflection of his vast audience, these works were frequently reprinted. Three were collected as a PEC Classic, *Gay Trilogy*, in 1967.

Clearly autobiographical (one of his many first-person narrators was named Carl Corley), the novels tended to be set either in the rural world of Mississippi or the urban underworld of New Orleans and Baton Rouge. Sadomasochism often figured prominently. White narrators, usually butch bottoms, were partnered with masculine tops of varied European-American descent. Reflecting the racism of the era, Choctaw characters were romanticised, Asians feminised and African-Americans vilified. Misogyny also imbued the works.

But Corley, one of the most prolific of

early gay male erotic fiction-writers and one of the few to use his real name, pushed the limits of the genre. He resisted editors' 'tacked-on unhappy endings' and he elaborated regionally specific narratives that complicated the urban biases of emergent gay cultural production. At a time when gay political forums were insufficient, he used his art and particularly his storytelling as a means to celebrate homosexuality and to argue for equal rights.

John Howard, *Men Like That: A Southern Queer History* (Chicago, 1999); Tracy D. Morgan, 'Pages of Whiteness: Race, Physique Magazines, and the Emergence of Public Gay Culture', in Brett Beemyn and Mickey Eliason (eds), *Queer Studies* (New York, 1997); John D'Emilio, *Sexual Politics, Sexual Communities* (Chicago, 1983); Carl V. Corley Papers, Special Collections Library, Duke University, Durham, North Carolina.

John Howard

Corn, Alfred (b. 1943), American writer. Corn has described his 'unmoneyed' Christian upbringing in Valdosta, Georgia, in essays such as 'A Goya Reproduction' and 'What is the Sexual Orientation of a Christian?' He attended Emory University then Columbia, where he pursued postgraduate studies in French literature. He has taught at Columbia, Connecticut College, Yale and the City University of New York. By the end of the 1990s he made his home in lower Manhattan.

Best known for his superb neo-formalist poems, Corn has also been a reviewer, essayist, art critic, novelist and prosodist. Two of his books, *Notes from a Child of Paradise* (1984) and *Autobiographies* (1992), consist of long narrative poems and deal, at least in sections, with gay issues such as coming out and building monogamous, same-sex relationships. Although he is himself 'out', Corn's work does not treat homosexual themes exclusively or even pervasively. Some of his best work is, however, explicitly gay, such

as the typically wry and mannered 'A Marriage in the Nineties'. Robert K. MARTIN has situated him within a specifically Whitmanian homosexual tradition that also includes Hart Crane and James MERRILL. Corn has also been associated with a circle of formal traditionalists that involves Daryl Hine and J. D. McClatchy. Perhaps the most profound and elusive aspect of his poetry is its spirituality; Corn is a practising Episcopalian whose work often seems, for all its witty candour, infused with divinity.

Robert K. Martin, *The Homosexual Tradition of American Poetry*, revised and expanded edition (Iowa City, 1998).

George Piggford

Cory, Donald Webster pseudonym of Edward Sagarin (1913–86), American scholar. Donald Webster Cory was a pseudonym used by Edward Sagarin, who was born in Schenectady, New York, to Jewish, Russian-immigrant parents. After school Sagarin spent a year in France, where he met André Gide. At City College of New York, as a member of the National Student League, he became interested in the injustices of US race relations. In spite of his homosexual inclinations, in 1936 he married a fellow activist, Esther Liphshitz. Sagarin worked in the cosmetic industry until 1961, when he graduated from Brooklyn College. He was awarded a PhD in sociology by New York University in 1966 and became a professor at City University of New York, specialising in criminology. Sagarin's publications cover the fields of perfumery, sexology, minorities, criminology and psychotherapy. He also published a novel and a play.

It is Sagarin's alter-ego, Donald Webster Cory (a play on Gide's *Corydon*), which is of most interest here. In 1951 he published a groundbreaking book entitled *The Homosexual in America*, which was based in part on 'participation in American life as a homosexual'. Cory took the position that homosexual behaviour is socially constructed, arguing that in most respects homosexuals were like everyone else and that their problems were a result of prejudice and discrimination rather than because of anything inherent to homosexuality. Cory came to see homosexuals as a minority, much like African-Americans, but in some ways worse off because the group had no leaders, publications or philosophy.

Cory's book made a mark, coming not long after the KINSEY Report into male sexual behaviour in 1948 and in the midst of the McCarthy-inspired purges of homosexuals from the civil service. While it was widely reviewed and generated much mail to the author, primarily by people who took comfort from the views it expressed, it also met with some hostility. Its publisher was charged with obscenity and ordered to cease publication of books with a homosexual theme; Sagarin was fired from his job. Nevertheless in 1953 he edited a collection of short stories with homosexual themes, *21 Variations on a Theme*; in 1956 he edited *Homosexuality: A Cross-Cultural Approach*. In 1963 with John P. LeRoy (a pseudonym of Barry Sheer), he published *The Homosexual and his Society: A View from Within*, and in 1964 *The Lesbian in America*. In addition, he set up a book service which mailed books with a homosexual theme to subscribers, and he became active in homosexual organizations, including the Veterans' Benevolent Association, Mattachine Society, ONE Institute and Daughters of Bilitis.

As he grew older, Sagarin, influenced by a psychologist, Albert Ellis, who believed that aspects of homosexuality were pathological and that homosexuals could become heterosexuals, became more conservative and turned his back on his early work.

Martin Duberman, 'Dr Sagarin and Mr Cory', *Harvard Gay and Lesbian Review* (Fall 1997); Jeffrey Escoffier, *American Homo: Community and Perversity* (Berkeley, 1998); Jim Levin, 'The Homosexual Rights Movement in the United States to 1959: Some Basic Questions', *Gay Books Bulletin*, no. 7 (Spring 1982); Ann Evory (ed.), *Contemporary Authors*, New Revision Series, vol. 4 (Detroit, 1984), pp. 520–1.

Gerard Sullivan

Courage, James (Francis) (1903–63), New Zealand writer. James Courage was born in Christchurch, New Zealand, in 1903; his father owned the Seadown sheep station near Amberley (North Canterbury). Courage was educated at Christ's College, Christchurch (1916–21), where he felt he was educated badly, and at St John's College, Oxford (1923–27), which he later described as 'a useless but delightful school'.

While Courage began his literary career early as a poet and dramatist, it is his eight novels and some short stories which show real strength. His first novel, *One House* (1933), was set in England but his next five novels were set in the Canterbury of his birth. Here he explored family relationships, especially relations between sons and their parents, and the conflicts of children growing through adolescence to maturity, focusing on the difficulties of relationships within the family and the home. The problems encountered by young and adult homosexuals is one of the themes which Courage explores in some of his New Zealand novels and in depth in his two last published novels. His first novel set in England also shows his repeated concern regarding the impossibility of one sex ever knowing the other fully.

In the period between his first and second novels, Courage returned to New Zealand in 1934–35, having contracted tuberculosis in 1931. The fresh air of the country was to help him convalesce physically but he also re-encountered a society not tolerant of the elements that made him different – particularly his homosexuality – and so he returned to England for good.

Some view Courage as so determinedly an expatriate that they do not classify him as a New Zealand writer, yet the setting for most of his novels is a rural setting and a provincial city of the New Zealand of earlier years, and some of his best short stories and the novel *The Young Have Secrets* are almost certainly semi-autobiographical.

Courage's first New Zealand novel, and his second to be published, was *The Fifth Child* (1948), shortly to be followed by the rather Gothic *Desire without Content* (1950). In his third novel with a New Zealand setting, *Fires in the Distance* (1952), Courage introduces explicitly amongst the general themes of family relationships problems encountered by those of homosexual orientation. Anticipating PASOLINI's *Teorema*, the handsome visitor, Paul, engages at least romantically and physically with not only Leo, the son of the family, but also Leo's mother and sister. *The Young Have Secrets* (1954) is generally regarded as the most successful of Courage's novels in both commercial and literary terms but in this work homosexuality is not apparent. In *The Call Home* (1956), the last novel set in New Zealand, a principal concern is an individual's maturing and includes the tantalising situation of his being unable to resurrect a past homosexual relationship.

In his seventh novel, *A Way of Love* (1959), set in England, Courage directly explores a homosexual relationship between two men. Its publication represented a milestone in New Zealand gay fiction in that it was the first novel to explore with such candour the homosexual condition as Courage knew it. The book was treated with incredulity and even antagonism by some of New Zealand's literary elite and it was withdrawn from New Zealand bookshops and libraries in 1962 because of its alleged indecency. This only convinced Courage that he was right in not returning to live in a New Zealand which he saw as remaining hostile to his lifestyle.

Curiously, Courage's paternal grandmother, Sarah Amelia Courage, had her satire *Lights and Shadows of Colonial Life* (1896) greeted with outrage by her neighbours, some of whom identified themselves in spite of her use of pseudonyms, and many of the eighteen published copies were destroyed.

Courage's last novel, *The Visit to Penmorten* (1961), explores someone suffering from what was then called a mental/nervous 'breakdown'. Courage was no doubt able to draw on his own experience, for during his last years his periodic bouts of depression became more severe and from 1951 until his death he was almost always undergoing psychiatric treatment. Yet these were the years when he undoubtedly produced his best work, and perhaps the process of counselling assisted his self-knowledge and informed his writing of relationships.

Courage also wrote many short stories, nineteen of which were published, a selection of them appearing in *Landfall* (a New Zealand literary journal) with fifteen of these being posthumously published in one volume as *Such Separate Creatures* (1973).

Courage, never robust, was supported through his years in England by an allowance and then a sum of capital from his father, but he did manage a bookshop in Hampstead for six years from 1946 until his depressive condition made it too difficult to continue in that role. He died of heart failure.

In 1998, the New Zealand Society of Authors (PEN New Zealand) established 14 November as the day on which to hold the first annual public ceremony to highlight matters concerning freedom of expression. The day is known as Courage Day, acknowledging the intolerance shown to the writings of both Sarah and James Courage.

Courage's personal papers are embargoed until the early years of the century. Only then will substantially more be revealed of the man and his life to enable a full exploration to be made of their impact on his writing.

Grant R. Harris, 'A Reading of the Novels of

James Courage' (MA thesis, Massey University, 1990).

Michael Wooliscroft

Courte, Bernard René (1949–91), Canadian activist, educationalist, writer. Raised in the Anglophone village of Weir, Quebec, Courte learned English out of necessity. This and an early traumatic experience with homophobia – the infamous 1977 raid on Truxx bar in Montreal – were defining elements in his life. As an adult, he fought tenaciously for French rights and for lesbian and gay rights.

After the Truxx raid, Courte joined the principal Montreal gay group, the Association pour les Droits des Gais du Québec. He was an effective spokesman and liaison officer, and for two years ran the news section of its paper, *Le Berdache*. When it folded in 1982 he moved to the new monthly, *Sortie*, which he (latterly as editor) helped develop into a very professional magazine. Courte early recognised the threat of AIDS and created controversy by insisting that it be at the forefront of reporting. He made the first of many radio and television appearances on the subject in August 1983, and wrote over twenty articles on it for *Sortie* and then for *RG* magazine.

Courte taught English as a second language in Quebec for a decade before moving to Toronto in 1986. A recognised expert in language and education, he was hired as a research officer in the Franco-Ontarian centre at the Ontario Institute for Studies in Education. Courte focused on AIDS, education and rights for Franco-Ontarians. He was an adviser to a number of government agencies and active in several Franco-Ontarian groups. He penned numerous articles for educational and Francophone journals. He also wrote a column for *Sortie* until it folded in 1988, then for Toronto's *Xtra!* magazine.

Courte directed his work on AIDS awareness in Ontario towards the Francophone community. When the advocacy group AIDS Action Now! was founded early in 1988, he created a francophone section within its media committee. He initiated the translation of its AIDS treatment data newsletter and a French-language index of all medical data relating to AIDS treatment, a resource unique in North America. He helped found a Francophone AIDS support group in Toronto and organized safe-sex workshops for PLWA/HIV. He also made presentations to eight AIDS conferences between 1984 and 1990 and was a consultant at the 5th International Conference on AIDS in Montreal in 1989.

In addition to his columns in the gay press and his television and radio appearances, Courte wrote more than 130 articles and essays (over fifty on AIDS) and numerous reports, and edited one book.

Bernard Courte papers [92–145], Canadian Lesbian and Gay Archives, Toronto; *Xtra!* (#184, 1991), *Our Paper* (July 1986).

Harold Averill

Cowell, Roberta (1918– ?), British engineer, seamstress. Cowell was born in England, the son of a surgeon and military officer. While identified as a male at birth, Cowell had sex-reassignment surgery and was issued a new birth certificate as Roberta Cowell in 1951. Cowell's surgery was one of the earliest successful cases of sex-reassignment surgery and, like similar cases in the 1950s and 1960s, served to clarify differences between homosexuality and gender variance in the press and popular culture.

Cowell spent her childhood in England. At age 17, Robert Cowell joined the Royal Air Force but was discharged due to problems with air sickness. With the outbreak of World War II, Cowell attempted to re-enlist in the Royal Air Force and was successful in doing so in January of 1940. During the war, she served as a Spitfire pilot and was shot down while flying over France. She served the remainder of the war in a German prisoner of war camp. After the war, Cowell became a race-car driver and engineer, was married and had two children. It was after she married that she began to suffer from severe depression and sought psychological help. According to Cowell's autobiography, she was diagnosed as intersexed and presented with the choice of living as a man or living as a woman. She chose to live as a woman and so began hormone treatment. Sex-reassignment surgery was performed in 1951 – one year prior to that of Christine Jorgensen. Unlike Jorgensen, however, Cowell was not subjected to a media blitz and loss of privacy following her surgery. Instead, Cowell gave up race-car driving and studied to become a seamstress.

While Cowell identified as intersexed, rather than as a transsexual or transvestite, her autobiography is very similar to those autobiographies written by some transsexuals in the United States in the mid-to-late twentieth century. This is especially true in the lengths that she went to in order to clarify the differences between homosexuals and people who seek sex-reassignment surgery. In writing of her own sexual orientation, Cowell asserted that before sex-reassignment surgery, 'I was never either a transvestite or a homosexual, my inclinations which were normal, simply died, then when they appeared again, they were re-oriented. By this time I was the opposite sex anyway, so still was not homosexual'. Cowell's autobiography remains important as an artefact for the history of sexuality and gender because it tells the story of one of the first persons in modern times to undergo sex-reassignment surgery and because of the distinctions Cowell makes between gender variance and sexual orientation throughout her work. In addition, for the late twentieth century, her autobiography is important because in it Cowell documents (and presents documents) proving that she was able to legally change her name and gender identification. Because of this, in the 1990s, transsexuals in the United Kingdom used her story to challenge laws that prohibit people from changing their gender identities on legal documents.

Bonnie Bullough and Vern L. Bullough, *Cross Dressing, Sex, and Gender* (Philadelphia, 1993); Roberta Cowell, *Roberta Cowell's Story* (London, 1954).

Linda Heidenreich

Crisp, Quentin (1908–99), British writer and public figure. From 1931, when he moved to London from Surbiton in Surrey, to 1968, when he published his autobiography *The Naked Civil Servant*, Quentin Crisp was the most visible – and therefore the most despised, beaten and spat-upon – gay man in Britain.

He made his living as a prostitute, then an office worker and an artist's model. His crusade was to make people understand that effeminate homosexual men like himself existed. His weapons were hennaed hair, long finger nails, mascara and lipstick. His philosophy was total self-absorption and passivity. His Holy Land lay between Soho and Chelsea. After his story was made into a groundbreaking and acclaimed television film starring John Hurt, Crisp became a sought-after guest on TV chat shows, a book and film reviewer, a character actor and proponent of 'lifestyle'. He has been called a hero and a saint. 'I was, of course, born an alien,' he has said.

At the age of 73 he moved to New York. 'I came to America because my fare was paid. That's the story of my life. I go where my fare is paid.' As before in London, he lived in one room, had few possessions and never dusted.

Crisp remained true only to himself, providing wisdom and aphoristic insights upon request. As a writer he contributed some witty and perceptive film and book reviews to gay magazines such as *Christopher Street*. As an actor he played Queen Elizabeth I and starred opposite Lea de Laria in *Homo Heights* (1997). A living work of artifice, he was featured in a TV advertisement for Levi jeans. 'I never wear denim but I wasn't surprised to be asked by Levi's . . . I'm not surprised by anything that happens in America.'

Crisp, with his signature black Fedora hat, open-necked white shirt and paisley scarf setting off his mask-like face with its post-henna post-blue white coiffure and lugubrious droning voice, remained a dignified outsider, probably still looking for that great dark man who would, of course, reject him (as any real man would).

He was not a political animal: 'With the passing of time, I have come to think that both sex and politics are a mistake and that any attempt to establish a connection between the two is the greatest error of all'. Nor did he like contemporary 'real' gay men, 'gargoyles of masculinity, scorning or regarding with pitying contempt those of us who cannot rise to such manliness'. He was, indeed, whatever one desired him to be: guru, saint, eccentric, right-wing conservative, faggot, pansy, silly old queen . . .

Quentin Crisp, *The Naked Civil Servant* (London, 1968); Quentin Crisp, *Resident Alien: The New York Diaries* (London, 1996).

Keith Howes

Croft-Cooke, Rupert (1903–79), British writer. Croft-Cooke was an extraordinarily prolific author who served a 1953–54 prison sentence for 'gross indecency', recounted in one of his over two-dozen autobiographical books, *The Verdict of You All* (1955). An inveterate traveller and adventurer, Croft-Cooke, who was born in Kent, studied at the University of Buenos Aries (1923–26) and served in the British army, primarily in India (1940–46). After his military service, he returned to Britain, where he worked as a book reviewer and writer.

In the summer of 1953, Croft-Cooke and his Indian secretary and companion, Joseph Alexander, met, in the Fitzroy Tavern (a well-known London gay haunt), two naval cooks, Harold Altoft and Ronald Charles Dennis. As they were on

leave and looking for a place to stay, Alexander suggested to Croft-Cooke that they invite the two men back to their modest Georgian house at Ticehurst, Sussex, and Croft-Cooke agreed. Croft-Cooke later admitted this was unconventional: but, as he pointed out in *The Life for Me* (1952), he made no secret of such 'bohemian' socialising at Ticehurst.

Altoft and Dennis spent an enjoyable if unremarkable weekend at Ticehurst, but en route back to their base, they became drunk and assaulted a roadmender and a policeman. When it was learned where they spent the weekend, the police persuaded them that any allegations they made against their hosts would be to their benefit regarding their assault charges. Although they later recanted their allegations in writing, this was ruled inadmissible during Croft-Cooke's trial, and he and Alexander were convicted of gross indecency. Croft-Cooke was given a nine-month sentence at Wormwood Scrubs, Alexander a three-month sentence at Brixton.

The Verdict of You All is a vivid memoir of prison life: Chapter 8 is an indictment of the effects of the criminalisation of homosexuality and portrays the variety of homosexual prisoners, as well as those incarcerated for homosexual offences and for blackmailing homosexual men; Chapter 14 briefly discusses sex and relationships in prison.

Croft-Cooke was released after serving six months of his sentence. He promptly took up residence with Alexander in Tangier, Morocco (1954–68). His leaving Britain for Morocco and his life there is recounted in *The Tangerine House* (1956) and *The Caves of Hercules* (1974). Croft-Cooke also wrote two idiosyncratic and lively biographies, *Bosie: The Story of Lord Alfred Douglas, His Friends and Enemies* (1963) and *The Unrecorded Life of Oscar Wilde* (1972), as well as *Feasting with Panthers: A New Consideration of Some Late Victorian Writers* (1967), a study of nineteenth-century Decadent writers (Algernon Charles Swinburne, John Addington Symonds, Oscar Wilde and their associates). He died in Bournemouth.

Jason Boyd

Croome, Rodney, (b. 1964), Australian activist. Croome has been the public face of the Tasmanian Gay and Lesbian Rights Group (TGLRG) for the last decade and a key activist in a movement which has transformed Tasmanian laws and social attitudes.

In 1989, inspired by a speech by Bob Brown, a prominent Tasmanian environmental activist and later Senator in the Commonwealth Parliament, Croome and several others formed the TGLRG to take up the struggle for homosexual law reform in Tasmania, then one of three Australian states which still criminalised male homosexuality. A stall at Hobart's Salamanca market set up to distribute information and gather signatures on a petition was banned by the local council. After three months of harassment and 130 arrests, the council backed down, delivering the TGLRG and its supporters their first great victory.

Five attempts at law reform over the following ten years, a major grassroots mobilisation in opposition, a UN challenge, a national boycott of Tasmanian products and a federal law which broke the back of the anti-gay laws ensured that the Tasmanian campaign had national attention. It also turned a law reform campaign into a movement for social change which delivered the best decriminalisation laws and the best anti-discrimination package in Australia, as well as a deeper transformation of attitudes to homosexuality, human rights and social diversity more generally. Through all this time, Croome was a tireless advocate of reform and social justice, travelling, writing, demonstrating. His interest in the broader issues is reflected in his editorship of the journal *Island* between 1995 and 1999.

Croome's role in all this has been acknowledged by his receiving numerous state, national and international awards for human rights activism and in 1999 he was described by a Tasmanian newspaper as one of the six great Tasmanians of the 1990s. He is currently employed by the federal Human Rights and Equal Opportunity Commission's gay, lesbian and bisexual rural youth project.

Graham Willett

D

Daly, Mary (b. 1928), American theologian and philosopher. Born in the US, Daly studied theology and philosophy in Fribourg, Switzerland (1959–65), since at that time Roman Catholic universities in the US did not allow female students. As she was trained in Catholic theology and philosophy, in her works Daly often uses ideas from the Aristotelian-Thomist tradition, but her own thinking is existential philosophy and theology, or process theology. Daly is one of the first, most important and most influential feminist theologians. She has been an important figure also in discussions on radical feminism and lesbian separatism, which she also practises. During the 1980s and early 1990s Daly – with other radical feminists – was strongly criticised, for example, for essentialism. However, lately her work has been read again in a more careful and perhaps less political manner that makes possible more accurate criticism and also realisation of her merits.

In Fribourg Daly wrote her doctoral dissertations both in theology and philosophy and started her first feminist book, *The Church and the Second Sex*. It came out in 1968, when she was back in the US working in Boston College as an assistant professor in theology. The book started her feminist career, but it almost ended her academic career: she was given a one-year terminal contract, which meant that she was fired. However, the students demonstrated for her and on occasion achieved maximum publicity. In the end Boston College granted her promotion and tenure. Since then, Daly has worked as an associate professor in theology at Boston College.

In *The Church and the Second Sex*, Daly took up the issue of defending Christianity against French feminist Simone de Beauvoir's criticisms. Daly tried to show that sexism does not belong to the core of Christianity; rather it is a sin and thus the Church should reject sexism. Her aim was to achieve equality between women and men within Christian churches. However, in her second book, *Beyond God the Father* (1973), Daly had changed her thinking, claiming that Christianity is at its core sexist. Thus feminists should leave it and create new kinds of spirituality outside traditional religion(s).

Beyond God the Father is an important theological book for many reasons. It opened the way to a new kind of feminist theology and it radicalised feminist theology. Daly criticises symbolism that excludes all but male symbols. Perhaps the most famous sentence of the book is 'If God is male, then the male is God'. Also, she starts to talk of God as Verb, as a moving process to be participated in, as something opposite to the traditional, static and hierarchical image of God.

Another merit of the book is that Daly argues for a new kind of normativeness in sexual ethics. She points to the intercon- nectedness of sexism and heterosexism: heterosexism is just another form of sexism. An ethics which claims that het- erosexuality is more valuable than homosexuality is patriarchal, and even the opposition between heterosexuality and homosexuality is a patriarchal classifica- tion. The oppression of women and hostil- ity towards homosexuality are connected: they reflect 'anxiety over losing power that is based upon sex role stereotyping'. Therefore, homosexuality is considered a problem, and lesbian and gay relation- ships are not seen as authentic relation- ships. Daly wants to deny heterosexist morality, but she also thinks that feminists should avoid all other 'dogmas' concern- ing sexual behaviour. Thus, while noting the interconnectedness of sexism and heterosexism, she dismisses the idea that feminists should reject heterosexuality as such. Later, almost all feminist theo- logy has adopted this rejection of heterosexism.

Her later works are lesbian feminist. Daly continues her work on feminist spirituality. To her, feminist spirituality is a question of becoming the being one is in connection to others: to other people, to divinity and to nature. This means that she understands human existence in terms of becoming. Thus, to be human means that one is open to the future, and con- sequently the future is seen as an open field of possibilities. Existence – acting and doing – precedes 'essence'. Thus, one creates one's essence.

Starting from *Gyn/Ecology* (1978) Daly's texts are written in a very personal style. One distinctive feature in her texts is her way of using language: she has tried to create and use a feminist language that overcomes sexist aspects of standard English.

Marja Suhonen

Damata, Gasparino (pseud. of Gasparino da Mata e Silva) (1918–*c*.1980), Brazilian

writer and activist. Born in Pernambuco in north-east Brazil, Damata worked as an interpreter on a US military base in Brazil during World War II and then as a petty officer on an American transport ship sail- ing around Brazil and across the South At- lantic. In 1949 he became a professional journalist and for a time in the early 1960s was the Brazilian press attaché in Ghana. Returning to Brazil, he lived as a bo- hemian, buying and selling pictures and antiques in Rio de Janeiro. Damata was one of the founders of the newspaper *Lampião*, which appeared monthly from April 1978 to June 1981 and acted as the vehicle for the first wave of the Brazilian gay liberation movement. He died in obscurity in the 1980s.

Damata wrote a novel and two collec- tions of stories. He also published three anthologies, one about the Lapa, the former bohemian and night-life district of Rio de Janeiro, and the other two, collections of Brazilian gay short stories and, in partnership with the poet Walmir Ayala, gay poems. The latter two were pioneering endeavours and provided some of the material for the two Gay Sunshine Press anthologies of Latin American gay literature in English trans- lation, *Now the Volcano* and *My Deep Dark Pain is Love*.

Damata drew on his own experience for his fiction, in which homosexuality was a major theme. His first published work, the novel *Queda em Ascensão* (*Fall on Ascen- sion*, 1951) was set in Pernambuco and on an American transport ship sailing to As- cension Island during the war. The narra- tor is a Brazilian sailor who is befriended by a young American soldier on the island but, although fascinated, fails to respond to the latter's veiled declaration of love, leading to a tragic dénouement. There are a couple of explicit references to homo- sexuality, but the nature of the relation- ship between the two main characters is ambivalent. Equally enigmatic is the short story 'O Capitão Grego' (The Greek Cap- tain) in which two young sailors are forced to return to their ship and face the advances of the captain.

Damata's last work, the collection of short stories Os Solteirões (The Confirmed Bachelors, 1976), has been unjustly neglected by critics, although some have been translated into English. Set in Rio de Janeiro in the 1960s, they evoke the thoughts, attitudes and lifestyles of urban male homosexuals in the days before gay liberation. In two of the stories, 'O Crucificado' (The Crucified Man) and 'Fábula' (Fable), the characters reflect on their difficulties in coming to terms with their own homosexuality. In 'Paraíba' (Construction Worker) and 'Módulo Lunar Pouco Feliz' (Unhappy Lunar Module), two male prostitutes explain their attitudes towards their lifestyle.

The remaining stories deal with the power relations between older homosexuals and their younger partners. In 'A Desforra' (translated into English as 'Revenge') a dentist humiliates a boy who has left him to live with a woman, who turns out to be a lesbian, while in 'O Inimigo Comum' (The Common Enemy) an old man berates a woman who has just stood up the boy who lives with him. A strong streak of misogyny runs through both these stories. The two most powerful stories in this book have both been translated into English. 'Muro de Silêncio' (Wall of Silence) describes the last night together of a middle-class homosexual and a young marine with whom he has been having a relationship. The marine has now become a father and although he agrees to have sex and accepts money, he refuses to reveal anything about his private life or his emotions. The story concentrates on the thoughts and feelings of the older man, who suffers a mixture of desire, hurt pride and frustration at not being able to get at the truth.

The hero of the novella 'O Voluntário' (The Volunteer) is a tough marine sergeant, Leocádio, who pursues a young recruit, Ivo. After much initial reluctance, the recruit agrees to sleep with Leocádio,

provided he is not forced to play the passive role. Their relationship continues after the sergeant has left the Army but comes to a bitter end when Leocádio angrily insults Ivo's new girlfriend. Ivo reacts with dignity and leaves him, swearing he will never sleep with another man. Leocádio, in despair, goes out and gets drunk, ending up trying to pick up another boy. The story is remarkable for the openness and self-confidence of the gay sergeant, the submissive but dignified attitude of the soldier and the low-key, non-judgemental ending. It contrasts with the guilt and self-loathing in the American novel The Sergeant by Dennis Murphy (1958) and may well have been intended to provide a Brazilian counterpoint.

The relationships portrayed in these stories are governed by inequalities of wealth, power, social skills and age, with the attractiveness and poverty of the younger men set against the experience and loneliness of the older ones. The characters' attitudes show a struggle for identity and self-esteem interspersed with cynicism, self-oppression and misogyny, which are relieved by occasional moments of tenderness and vulnerability. Many aspects of this world are unappealing but the stories communicate a strong sense of time and place. Mercenary relationships are endemic in societies with extremes of wealth and poverty, while the disparaging expressions about women and homosexual men are characteristic of their period. The feel of the city of Rio is a powerful presence. The stories are well-constructed, with a lively, colloquial narrative-style which counter-balances the detached stance of the author. The best of them deserve to be better known for their portrayal of the psychology of power in personal relationships.

Gasparino Damata, 'Revenge' and 'Wall of Silence', in Winston Leyland (ed.), Now the Volcano: an Anthology of Latin American Gay Literature (San Francisco, 1979), pp. 98–144; 'The Volunteer: a Novella', in Winston Leyland (ed.), *My Deep Dark Pain Is Love: A Collection of Latin American Gay Fiction* (San Francisco, 1983), pp. 171–224; Gasparino Damata (ed.), *Antologia da Lapa* (Rio de Janeiro, 1965; 2nd. edn, Rio de Janeiro, 1978); *Histórias do Amor Maldito* (Rio de Janeiro, 1967); Gasparino Damata and Walmir Ayala (eds), *Poemas do Amor Maldito* (Brasília, 1969).

Robert Howes

Damien, John (1933–86), Canadian activist. Damien worked in horse-racing in Ontario for twenty years, as a trainer, jockey and a racing steward for the Ontario Jockey Commission. He was one of the top three racing judges in Ontario when on 7 February 1975, he was dismissed without notice after his gay sexual orientation came to the attention of the Commission, an independent agency of the Ontario provincial government. Almost immediately a Toronto gay group began to campaign for his reinstatement, as well as an enquiry into his firing and into the status of gay people working in positions under Ontario government jurisdiction. The Committee to Defend John Damien was established soon after, and the Damien case gained attention across Canada. For all of the publicity, though, and the support of civil libertarians, journalists, lawyers, doctors and politicians, court actions launched in 1975 dragged on for years without the case being brought to trial. Damien was ruined financially and supported himself through odd jobs. Finally, in 1986, the first legal action, a suit of wrongful dismissal against the Commission, was settled in Damien's favour; he was awarded one year's wages plus interest, a total of about $50,000. By this time Damien was in poor health, and he died of pancreatic cancer. A second lawsuit, for loss of income, had been filed against the estate of a racetrack doctor who had informed the Jockey Club that Damien was a homosexual; the case had not yet been heard when Damien died. Damien proved that blatant discrimination in the workplace based on sexual

orientation could no longer be tolerated in Canadian society and that court action in such cases would (eventually) succeed.

Mary Gooderham, 'Legal Fight Will Survive Ex-jockey Dismissed for Being Homosexual', *Globe and Mail* (Toronto), 1 January 1987, p. A10; John Hofsess, 'Damien's Exile: What John Damien Represents and Defends Is Not Homosexuality but Human Dignity', *Weekend Magazine* (Toronto), 21 February 1976, pp. 14–17, 19.

Donald W. McLeod

Daniel, Herbert (1946–92), Brazilian guerrilla, writer and activist. Daniel came from the conservative state of Minas Gerais and studied medicine at the university in Belo Horizonte. In 1964 the Brazilian military seized power from the left-wing government of João Goulart and established an increasingly repressive right-wing dictatorship. Having been a student activist Daniel joined the radical leftist guerrilla movement which fought against the military and went underground for six years. He was active in a number of the fragmented guerrilla groups and participated in the sequestration of the German and Swiss ambassadors, which had considerable political and diplomatic repercussions. He was never arrested but, under sentence of death, finally managed to make his way abroad and lived in exile in Lisbon and Paris for seven years. He took a series of jobs to earn a living, including working as a journalist, a waiter and a porter in a gay sauna in Paris. Unlike most Brazilian exiles he was not given an amnesty when the military began to relinquish power, but eventually managed to return to Brazil in 1981.

Daniel met his life-long partner, Cláudio Mesquita, while still living clandestinely in Brazil in 1971. In Paris he began to come out as gay and openly to raise the question of sexual politics among exiled Brazilian left-wingers. Back in Brazil he became a gay activist, writing memoirs, autobiography and works of fiction relating to the gay experience. The three categories are intertwined in his works and hard to separate. In 1986 he stood as a candidate for the Green Party in elections for the State Assembly in Rio de Janeiro but was not elected. As the AIDS epidemic reached Brazil, Daniel became a vocal spokesman for people with AIDS, helping to establish the ABIA (Interdisciplinary Brazilian AIDS Association), which promoted AIDS education and monitored government action, and Grupo Pela Vidda/ RJ, a self-help group for HIV-positive people in Rio de Janeiro. In January 1989 he was diagnosed as suffering from AIDS and from then on he intensified his efforts, writing openly and courageously about his condition and the reflections it inspired in him. He succumbed to the illness at the end of March 1992.

Daniel's writings reflect his eventful life. *Passagem Para o Próximo Sonho* (*Ticket to the Next Dream*) is a mixture of memoirs and reflections written while he was still in exile in Paris in 1981. He recounts his experiences as a guerrilla living underground, his involvement in the sequestration of the two ambassadors and his life in exile in Paris, giving a jaundiced description of the gay ghetto. He describes the repercussions of his coming-out and the reactions of traditional left-wingers to his attempt to discuss homosexuality at a meeting of Brazilian exiles in Paris, which ranged from outright hostility to a desire to avoid discussing the topic. In 1983, in a volume published jointly with the writer Leila Míccolis, he reflected on the homosexual condition and analysed the political implications for gays of AIDS and its treatment by the media.

The following year he published his most ambitious book, *Meu Corpo Daria um Romance: Narrativa Desarmada* (*My Body Would Produce a Novel: Unarmed Narrative*), a work which is part autobiography, part personal reflections and part fiction. It is divided into eleven parts, each inspired by an incident on a nighttime bus in Copacabana, when the passengers saw him kissing his partner and he

became aware that they were each objectifying him as a queer. The incident triggers off a series of reflections about his own homosexuality and Brazilian attitudes to the subject, as he recalls his childhood, his experiences as a guerrilla and an exile, and his different relationships with men and women.

In the novel *Alegres e Irresponsáveis Abacaxis Americanos* (*Gay and Irresponsible American Pineapples*) (1987), Daniel refers to the question of AIDS. His later works deal with AIDS more directly. In *Vida antes da Morte / Life before Death*, with texts in Portuguese and English, written after his diagnosis, he reflects on what it means to have AIDS in Brazil. He describes the inhumanity of the doctor who told him he had the disease, his fear of being subjected to the dictates of the medical profession, the popular prejudice which adds to the suffering of people with AIDS and the lack of government attention to the problem. The book has a courageous, combative tone as Daniel sets out his determination to make the most of the life which remains to him. *AIDS: A Terceira Epidemia* (*AIDS: The Third Epidemic*), written jointly with the American researcher Richard Parker, contains a number of essays and papers about the disease and its effects in Brazil. Most of the essays in these two works have been published in English in *Sexuality, Politics and AIDS in Brazil: In Another World?* Daniel's style in his earlier works is full of word-play and conscious literary artifice. In these later works, as AIDS looms larger, his style becomes more straightforward and direct.

Leila Míccolis and Herbert Daniel, *Jacarés e Lobisomens: Dois Ensaios sobre a Homossexualidade* (Rio de Janeiro, 1983); Herbert Daniel and Richard Parker, *AIDS: A Terceira Epidemia: Ensaios e Tentativas* (São Paulo, 1991); Herbert Daniel and Richard Parker, *Sexuality, Politics and AIDS in Brazil: In Another World?* (London, 1993); Dário Borim Jr, 'Daniel, Herbert', in David William Foster (ed.),

Latin American Writers on Gay and Lesbian Themes: A Bio-Critical Sourcebook. (Westport, Connecticut, 1994), pp. 129–34.

Robert Howes

Davidson, Michael (1897–1976), English journalist and memoirist. Michael Childers Davidson was born into a well-connected upper-middle-class family and was educated at Lancing. He started at Cambridge but, with the outbreak of war, joined up in 1914 and remained in the army until 1919, being wounded in 1916. He became a newspaper reporter, and his socialist and anti-fascist beliefs took him into the Communist Party. In the mid-1930s he translated a number of anti-Nazi books. He also drank a lot and, leading a classic double life, haunted London swimming-baths ('I could have compiled a guide-book to them') in quest of sexual encounters with adolescents. This latter pursuit landed him in Wormwood Scrubs in 1936, and upon his release in 1937 he decided prudently to become a foreign correspondent. He found at length his *métier*, and after World War II had a distinguished career with the *Observer*, *News Chronicle*, *New York Times* and *Christian Science Monitor*, covering eight wars 'of varying size', including the Korean and the Cypriot conflicts.

His autobiography, *The World, the Flesh and Myself* (1962), which provides a fascinating picture of the privileged world in which he grew up and of interwar England, was one of the first of a new outpouring of homosexual memoirs that followed the publication of the WOLFENDEN report, and is a masterpiece of the genre, brutally honest and self-critical. The book begins with the bold declaration, 'This is the life-story of a lover of boys ... a first-hand report, therefore, on that heresy which, in England especially, is reprobated above all'. His success as a foreign correspondent meant that after 1937 he largely dwelt abroad, in places where his sexual predilections were, if not openly approved, tacitly tolerated (he reveals, for example, that when on assignment for the Indonesian government he was provided with young male companions at official expense). He was able to combine his reporting with an active amorous life, which his autobiography records. A later volume of memoirs, *Some Boys* (1970), taking advantage of the relaxation of censorship in the course of the 1960s, recalls in more candid detail particular relationships that he enjoyed over the years. It is probably the frankest and most joyous celebration of pederasty since the *Mousa Paidikē* of Straton (2nd century AD, preserved in the *Greek Anthology*, Book XII).

'Michael Davidson', *Contemporary Authors*, vols. 29–32 (1972), p. 155.

Gary Simes

De Cecco, John P. (b. 1925), American scholar. De Cecco was born in Erie, Pennsylvania. Being Catholic and the son of Italian immigrants set him apart from the mostly Protestant and established American students at Allegheny College, where he took a degree in biology in 1946. But it was there that he began to come to terms with his homosexuality. He continued his studies at the University of Pennsylvania, where he received master's and doctor's degrees in English and Modern European History. He then taught history at the University of Detroit until his doctrinal differences with the Jesuit administration became too apparent. At the same time he pursued post-doctoral studies in psychology at Wayne State University and later at Michigan State University, where he eventually received an appointment in its faculty of Educational Psychology; he taught there from 1955 to 1960, when he left to escape the widespread purges of 'homosexuals'. He has been a member of the Psychology Department at San Francisco State University (SFSU) since 1960; he has also taught at Columbia University.

Author of about ten books (four of them on gay topics: relationships, homophobia, constructionism versus essentialism, and the biology of homosexuality) and over forty articles, De Cecco is perhaps best known as the editor of the long-running *Journal of Homosexuality*, the leading journal of gay and lesbian studies and a major source of information on its subject. This journal was founded in 1974 by the gay clinical psychologist Charles Silverstein, who suggested to the publisher that De Cecco be appointed editor, a post he has held since 1977. At first it published mostly psychological and sociological studies, but under De Cecco's editorship the *Journal of Homosexuality* increased in variety and quality – and pace – of publication to become a widely read, multi-disciplinary journal. He is also the editor of the Gay and Lesbian Studies book programme of the Haworth Press. In 1975, with funding from the National Institute of Mental Health for research on homophobia (the first ever granted by the Federal government), he founded at SFSU the Center for Homosexual Education, Evaluation, and Research (from 1980 the Center for Research and Education in Sexuality), which has continued to be the home of the *Journal of Homosexuality* with De Cecco as its director.

De Cecco's achievements have been recognised both locally – the San Francisco council proclaimed 23 May 1998 'John P. De Cecco Day' in that city – and internationally, for example, by his receiving the Magnus Hirschfeld Medal for outstanding service to sexual science from the German Society for Social Scientific Sex Research in 1992.

He is currently 'working on a philosophy of homosexuality, dealing with the notion of the "gay self" and the typologies that have been used in Gay/Lesbian Studies'.

Hubert Kennedy

Dean, James (1931–55), American film actor. With Marilyn Monroe and Elvis Presley, Dean was a 1950s icon, 'a rebel without a cause'. His death at 24 caused a worldwide shock unsurpassed since the death of Valentino.

Although Dean's career began in television, it was his provocative playing of the small but pivotal role of a bisexual Arab in the stage adaptation of Gide's *The Immoralist* that inspired Elia Kazan to cast him in the part of brooding Cal Trask in *East of Eden*. This was followed by Nicholas Ray's seminal teenage angst drama *Rebel without a Cause*, which was released a few days after his death. He was also featured in the epic *Giant*.

In the space of 18 months and 300 minutes of celluloid, he became the voice of a generation, the idol of both sexes, a mumbling god who shouldered the burdens that many young people felt in the 1950s: parental control and misunderstanding, peer pressure, sexual confusion, the turning away from violence yet being drawn inexorably towards it. Dean was equated with Jesus Christ in Kenneth ANGER's underground gay biker classic *Scorpio Rising* (1964), and Andy WARHOL called him 'the damaged but beautiful soul of our time'.

His brooding, taunting face has been used to advertise banks. He is still the subject of books and documentaries. His photograph appears on walls and locker doors, in TV comedies and dramas. His car accident was scrutinised and re-enacted in *Crash* (1996). His loving tenderness towards the besotted Sal Mineo in *Rebel without a Cause* continues to touch and excite gay audiences by its honesty. The *Gay Times* Readers' Awards cited him as the male gay icon of all time, followed by River Phoenix (whose performance in *My Own Private Idaho* was partly inspired by Dean).

The debate about Dean's sexuality rages as passionately as that about whether he was a good, great or indifferent actor. He told a friend, 'I've had my cock sucked by five of the big names in Hollywood . . . '. When asked if he was gay, he replied, 'Well, I'm certainly not going through life with one hand tied behind my back'. His long-time roommate and first biographer, William Bast, told *After Dark* in 1976: 'Gay, as a descriptive term, would characterise Jimmy in such a limited manner. He tried a lot of things and was always into new experiences. He was so many things and responded so easily to just about any stimulus ... unfortunately Jimmy never lived long enough to realise his full potential.'

David Dalton, *James Dean: The Mutant King* (New York, 1975); Venable Herndon, *James Dean: A Short Life* (New York, 1975); Donald Spoto, *Rebel: The Life and Legend of James Dean* (London, 1996).

Keith Howes

Degeneres, Ellen, (b. 1958), American actor and activist. Her announcement, 'Yep, I'm Gay', on the cover of *Time* magazine on 14 April 1997 served to spotlight the controversial career of comedian Ellen Degeneres as the harbinger of a new openness about sexuality on prime-time television. Born in Louisiana, and educated there and in Texas, Degeneres worked at a variety of jobs whilst pursuing a career in comedy until she won the title 'Funniest Person in America' in 1983. She moved to San Fransisco, then Los Angeles, developing her particular comedy of rambling and quirky semi-philosophical rumination about everyday life and an engaging focus on verbal, physical and situational awkwardness. Degeneres' television career, which began with featured spots on *Open House* and *Laurie Hill*, took off with the premiere of the sitcom *These Friends Of Mine* in 1994; it centred on the character Ellen Morgan, a bookshop owner in Los Angeles, and the show's second series saw it retitled simply *Ellen*.

Degeneres's television career was more prosperous than her cinema efforts: *Mr Wrong*, an indifferently successful film about matrimonial error, did little to boost her career, though it did serve as an uncanny prelude to the kind of changes that were introduced on her sitcom in 1997. Mooted for some time before its occurrence, the decision to introduce a story-line in which Ellen's eponymous character realises that she is a lesbian was leaked from ABC network, and much debated in the popular press, before the fourth series wound its way to the infamous 'Puppy' episode first aired in 1997. Prior to the double episode in which Ellen Morgan announces that she is gay, earlier episodes in the series featured much play on the question of closeting, secrecy and revelation. The 'Puppy' episode featured cameo performances by well-known lesbians k.d. LANG and Melissa Etheridge, as well as spots by others whose performances had touched on the question of sexual preference – for example Gina Gershon, for her roles in *Showgirls* and *Bound*. The potential of Ellen's coming out as a mobilising moment for the mainstreaming of gay and lesbian politics of public self-identification meant that the airing of the issue became a *cause célèbre* in the gay and lesbian community. GLAAD (The Gay and Lesbian Alliance Against Defamation) issued 'Come Out With Ellen' packs and advice on holding house parties to celebrate the episode; ABC weathered considerable pressure from sponsors and right-wing groups to withhold the episode. The concurrent coming out of Degeneres – her headline announcement in *Time* preceeded the airing of the episode by a fortnight – added fuel to the international debate over the significance of the portrayal of a main character in a prime time sitcom as gay. As *Time* noted, the threshold of tolerance on television is significantly lower than other media, and 'Puppy's' frank consideration of the questions surrounding sexual self-identification meant that the episode was seen as a bellwether moment in popular media.

The fifth series of *Ellen* negotiated the question of Ellen's new sexuality through a comic capitulation of stock gay and lesbian experiences. Degeneres's own personal life became the focus of sustained media attention due to her relationship with the movie actress Ann Heche (*Volcano*; *Six Days, Seven Nights*; *Wag the Dog*; *Psycho*), whose own coming out coincided with Ellen's. *Ellen* was cancelled in the face of slipping ratings and conflicts between Degeneres and network executives over the new direction the show had taken. The year 1999 saw Degeneres reanimate her movie career with *Ed-TV* and *Goodbye, Lover*, and she remains a vocal and visible figure for the broad dissemination of a pro-gay message. Degeneres's mother's book, *Love Ellen: A Mother/Daughter Journey* (1999), has furthered discussion of the kinds of relationships that gays and lesbians might enjoy with their families, with Betty Degeneres developing her own profile as a pro-gay advocate.

Melissa Hardie

Delaney, Colin John (1897–1969), Australian police commissioner. Delaney is an excellent example of someone whose religiously inspired phobias, combined with the fears and anxieties of the cold war era, impacted on the lives of homosexuals in a small democracy like Australia.

Delaney was born in rural Victoria, the seventh child of an Irish-Catholic father and an Australian mother, and received a Catholic education in Bendigo. After work as an engine-driver, butter-maker and tram conductor, he joined the New South Wales Police Force in 1919 (and remarried his wife of several months at Sydney's St Mary's Roman Catholic cathedral that same year). His rise in the police force was rapid – constable (1920), detective constable (1927), detective sergeant (1933), inspector (1943) and superintendent (1946). He also had some involvement with security and intelligence work during World War II.

Delaney was appointed police commissioner in 1952, the first Catholic to hold that position. At a time when relations between police and public were at a low ebb, because of allegations of assaults, bribery

and corruption, Delaney attempted to reform the force (but with little apparent effect, as subsequent Royal Commissions into his successors proved). Delaney, a staunch Catholic and conservative, regarded homosexuality as a major problem for Australia: 'the greatest menace' facing Australia was how he saw it. At a time when difference of any sort – social, ethnic, political, sexual – was deemed unpatriotic, he initiated major programmes of surveillance, persecution and prosecution of those suspected of homosexuality (*agents provocateurs* were a common feature of this period). On his urging, new legislation was introduced into the state Parliament, both increasing penalties for existing crimes and creating new crimes (such as asking someone to commit a homosexual act). Other areas of policing suffered from his myopic obsession.

Recent research, such as oral histories and accessing court records of the period, indicates how many lives were blighted or destroyed by the bigotry and ignorance inherent in Delaney's homophobic pursuits. In this, Australia was not alone: the experiences of homosexual men in Britain and the US in this period would have been much the same.

Garry Wotherspoon, 'Colin John Delaney', *Australian Dictionary of Biography*, vol. 13, 1940–1980, A–De (Melbourne, 1993).

Garry Wotherspoon

Delaney, Samuel (b. 1942), American writer. Best known for his science-fiction writing, Delaney has helped push the boundaries of tolerance for sexual diversity, often by creating, in his fiction, characters and plots which step outside the conventions.

Born in Harlem, New York, he was aware of his sexual preference by the age of 10, and recorded his fantasies in a diary. Unfortunately, his mother found the diary, resulting in him – like myriads of other Americans of his generation – having to undergo therapy. His creative energies – in writing and music composition – continued unabated. His first novel, *The Jewels of Aptor*, was published when he was 20, and by the time he was 26 he had won the coveted Nebula Award (for science-fiction writing) four times.

Despite his sexual inclinations, in 1961 he married Marilyn HACKER, a young Jewish poet, who knew of his sexual preferences. They remained married until 1980, although his later memoirs indicate that it was not a successful relationship.

It was with the publication of his autobiographical *The Motion of Light on Water* (1988) that Delaney first publicly disclosed his homosexuality. However, novels such as *Stars in My Pocket like Grains of Sand* (1984) – at whose centre is a gay male relationship – and *Flight from Neveryon* (1987) – in which a serious AIDS-like plague strikes his imagined civilisation – had already paralleled aspects of homosexual reality.

Delaney has, like many other writers, recently become increasingly outspoken on gay issues. He is undoubtedly a role model for young African-Americans still believing they can find a place in American society.

Samuel Delaney, *The Motion of Light on Water: Sex and Science Fiction Writing in the East Village, 1957–1965* (New York, 1988).

Garry Wotherspoon

Deleuze, Gilles (1925–95) and **Guattari, Félix** (1930–92), French philosopher and psychoanalyst/political activist, respectively. Deleuze and Guattari had both worked extensively in their fields prior to meeting in 1969. Perhaps Deleuze's greatest previous endeavour involved his critique of the Hegelian dialectic, most notably in *Nietzsche et la philosophie* (1962). He also wrote *Marcel Proust et les signes* (1964), in which he analyses *À la recherche du temps perdu* as a demonstration of Proust's investigation of the process of signification. In *Différence et répétition* (1968), Deleuze builds on his previous work on Hegelian dialectics and the Platonic model of repetition. He proposes an alternate model of repetition that replaces the notion of an essential ideal with that of a simulacrum. By centring difference, this move challenges philosophical positions that encourage the privileging of sameness or the notion of an ideal. Other works by Deleuze include *Francis Bacon: Logique de la sensation* (1981) and *Foucault* (1986). Guattari studied under Jacques Lacan during the 1950s and 1960s, and his collection of essays *Psychanalyse et transversalité* appeared in 1972. It is primarily for his work with Deleuze that he is now known.

A couple of years before their meeting, Deleuze, in *Présentation de Sacher-Masoch* (1967), had used *Venus in Furs* to propose that masochism offers an escape from the Freudian notion of Oedipal subjectivity. In *L'Anti-Oedipe* (1972), the two theorists expand on this line of enquiry. They argue that people are constituted by 'desiring-machines' that produce desire as an affirming force felt through a 'Body without Organs', a body that is unclassified, unorganised and non-totalised. The conventional centring of desire on genitalia, the two claim, is actually a structure fabricated to control desire so that its self-perpetuating energy does not displace capitalism. Challenging conceptions of desire and sexuality that give primacy to heterosexuality, the traditional family model and procreation, Deleuze and Guattari encourage the perception that desire is protean and unstructured, and that it exists within a social field rather than the psyche. When they describe this desire as 'homosexual' or 'transexual,' they are using the terms to define a distinctly non-humanist notion of desire. Such desire defies the Oedipal model by constituting distinctly different modes of human relations, and attains a negative taint of perversity only through a unifying oedipalisation.

The two theorists expand on these views in *Capitalisme et schizophrénie: Mille plateaux* (1980). In *Homosexual*

Desire (1972), Guy HOCQUENGHEM relies heavily on *Anti-Oedipe* to argue that homosexuals who lack sexual guilt offer a unique potential for sexual-political change. Deleuze and Guattari address lesbianism only briefly in their work, although some poststructuralist feminists see in their focus on difference rather than some universalising ideal a means of destabilising male-privileging, binary models of sexuality and the body.

Gilles Deleuze and Félix Guattari. *Anti-Oedipus: Capitalism and Schizophrenia*, transl. Robert Hurley *et al.* (New York, 1977), and *A Thousand Plateaus: Capitalism and Schizophrenia*, transl. Brian Massumi (Minneapolis, 1987); Guy Hocquenghem, *Homosexual Desire*, transl. Daniella Dangoor (London, 1978).

Dennis Denisoff

D'Emilio, John (b. 1948), American scholar and activist. Born in New York and educated at Columbia University, D'Emilio's early work focused on the struggle of minorities to gain recognition, as in his first book, *The Civil Rights Struggle: Leaders in Profile* (1979).

His groundbreaking *Sexual Politics, Sexual Communities: The Making of a Homosexual Minority in the United States, 1940–1970* (1983) was one of the first works to provide an analysis of the changes that took place in the US leading to the emergence of a gay political movement. With Estelle B. FREEDMAN, he wrote *Intimate Matters: A History of Sexuality in America* (1988), which documented the various forces that had interacted to create American attitudes to sex and sexuality.

He was a founding member of the Gay Academic Union (1973), and Co-Chair, Board of Directors, National Gay and Lesbian Task Force (1989–91). He spent time as a Research Fellow at the Australian National University in 1993.

John D'Emilio, *Making Trouble: Essays on Gay History, Politics, and the University* (New York, 1992); *The Writers Directory* (Detroit, 1999).

Robert Aldrich and Garry Wotherspoon

Detrez, Conrad (1937–85), Belgian writer. Detrez, a Belgian-born French-language writer, authored half-a-dozen essentially autobiographical novels. After completing theological studies, in the early 1960s Detrez went to Brazil, where he was active in Marxist and Christian movements. After a military coup took place there in 1964, he began to take part in clandestine political activities, for which he was arrested, tried, sentenced to two years of imprisonment and finally expelled from Brazil. Returning to Europe, he became a journalist, covering the 1974 Portuguese revolution for Radio-Télévision Belge. He was awarded the prestigious Prix Renaudot for *L'Herbe à brûler*. He became a French citizen in 1982 and died in Paris.

Detrez's work is branded by nostalgia for childhood. For this former Jesuit, childhood represents the harmonisation of differences, the perfect and happy, though fragile, time when soul and body are united, a world without either conflict or lust – beatific tranquillity. For Detrez, desire (basically homosexual desire) ruptures this harmony, and as desires grow strong, the gulf between a soul longing for peace and a lustful body grows wider. The unending task of a literary narrator is to reconcile these irreconcilable urges.

Detrez's main novels – *Ludo* (1974), *Les Plumes du coq* (1975) and *L'Herbe à brûler* (1978) – are the story of this impossible quest, which age makes even more painful. All of the narrators' romances are marked by the original rupture – sad, furtive, tortured and chaotic, desire is always clandestine and illicit, with stolen pleasures rather than shared ones. Paradoxically, desiring means being violated. Plenitude, a trait of childhood, cannot be attained by the living adult. Sex, violence and death are intrinsically linked.

These themes are particularly developed in Detrez's descriptions of Brazilian revolutionary milieux. The individual and history, sex and politics are mixed up and complicit in a mirror game: an incomplete revolution is as much emotional as social;

the chaos in the street harks back to the disorders in the soul.

Laurent de Graeve

Diana, Princess of Wales (1961–97), British AIDS activist. After her marriage to Charles, Prince of Wales, in 1981, Diana was widely credited with having a modernising and humanising effect on British royal tradition. Following her divorce from Charles in 1996, Diana was not only stripped of the 'Her Royal Highness' title, but was also obliged to relinquish her patronage of more than 100 charities.

Diana's involvement with AIDS commenced relatively early in the days of the epidemic in the UK. She was asked to open the first dedicated AIDS Ward in a UK hospital, in Middlesex, in 1987 – she gladly accepted and thus began a close association which continued for the rest of her short life. Not only did she officiate at the opening, she did much more. The Princess was filmed shaking the hands of and talking to AIDS patients, which did much to allay public fears about possible infection through casual contact.

Although Diana did not become involved with the work of the principal AIDS charity in the UK, The Terrence HIGGINS Trust, Garfield notes that she 'rattled buckets elsewhere'. Berridge notes that Diana's continuing involvement with the AIDS cause added not just respectability and regular news coverage, but a sense of style and excitement. AIDS charities in the UK were able to capitalise on her involvement. Further, Berridge argues that AIDS fund-raising activities of the type supported by Diana 'brought a wider range of gay men into alliance with other "names" from a range of society and business backgrounds'.

Diana also 'introduced' other prominent individuals to the world of AIDS. For instance, during an official tour by the American president she escorted a noticeably reluctant Barbara Bush on a visit to an AIDS unit. Perhaps her single most important contribution was the fact that she disregarded royal etiquette by not wearing gloves when shaking the hands of people infected with the virus. According to Garfield, 'The fact that she didn't [do so] gave "royal approval" to the fact that it is impossible to become infected through social contact'. Photos of such meetings were instantly beamed around the world.

Her involvement was not only professional – it was also personal, as a number of her close friends, as well as those of other members of the royal family, had been affected by the virus.

Diana did not limit her AIDS-related work to the UK. On trips overseas she made time to visit both those affected and those working in the AIDS field. The AIDS scientist Luc MONTAGNIER, noted that she 'was generally well informed on the topic'.

S. Garfield, *The End of Innocence: Britain in the Time of AIDS* (London, 1995); P. Beharrell, 'AIDS and the British Press', in J. Eldridge (ed.), *Getting the Message: News, Truth and Power* (London, 1993); V. Berridge, *AIDS in the UK* (Oxford, 1996); *Current Biography Yearbook*, January 1983.

Mark Edwards

Dietrich, Marlene (1901–92), German actress. Born Maria Magdalene Dietrich, she was a film actress and cabaret performer in pre-Nazi Berlin, who invited notoriety by her participation in knowingly lesbian songs in the satirical revue *Two Neckties*. Her appearance as Lola Lola in *The Blue Angel* in 1930 propelled her to Hollywood, where her director-mentor and sometime lover, Josef von Sternberg, transformed her into a goddess. Through gauze and net, wearing ever more outrageous costumes, flirting with sexual ambiguity, Dietrich was one of the most dazzling of Hollywood's stars. With a cruel and mercurial face and creamy but cold voice, she exerted merciless reign over powerless men. Audiences eventually tired of all the flummery that surrounded her. She changed tack and became the bawdy

Dietrich of *Destry Rides Again* singing 'See What The Boys in the Back Room Will Have'.

Surrounding Dietrich – who had married but lived apart from her husband with her daughter – were rumours of lesbianism, which she encouraged by her non-screen attire of suits, berets, slouch hats. (She made trousers acceptable wear for women.) There was talk of an affair with the artist Mercedes De Acosta. Dietrich never spoke publicly about her emotional life. Brought up in an atmosphere of stern Prussian discipline and strict propriety, she said, 'My whole upbringing was to mask my feelings'. Her prickly, stubborn, bigoted personality was well displayed in the documentary *Marlene* (1984) in which she did not appear on camera.

Her aura remained indolently bisexual. Many lesbians and gays continue to delight in her ironic, disdainful attitude towards a hypocritical world, giving all for love, indifferent to consequences. Her iconic stature assured, Dietrich became ever more dismissive of her image, calling her films 'kitsch' and disparaging the 'pansy film-fan writers' who came to fawn, 'only wanting to know about *Blonde Venus* and *Shanghai Express*'. Maria Riva, her daughter, published a book after Dietrich's death which portrayed her as an arch-manipulator, cold, remote, and with a drinking problem. This viewpoint has been vigorously disputed by surviving friends. She remains for many the epitome of café society glamour and poise.

Axel Madsen, *The Sewing Circle: Female Stars Who Loved Women* (New York, 1995); Maria Riva, *Marlene Dietrich By Her Daughter* (New York, 1993).

Keith Howes

Ditsie, Beverley (b. 1972), South African activist. Palesa Beverley Ditsie was one of the founding members of the Gay and Lesbian Organisation of the Witwatersrand (GLOW), which was launched in 1989. The organisation was one of the first lesbian and gay organisations in South Africa to affiliate to the United Democratic Front in line with GLOW's strong anti-apartheid stance. GLOW organised Africa's first Gay and Lesbian Pride March, which took place in Johannesburg in 1990. Ditsie addressed the United Nations on lesbian issues at the 4th World Conference on Women in Beijing in 1995. She also testified at the UN Global Women's Tribunal, in New York City in 1998. She currently works as a journalist and documentary filmmaker.

Gay and Lesbian Archives, University of the Witwatersrand Libraries, Johannesburg.

Graeme Reid

Dlugos, Tim (1950–90), American poet. Raised in East Longmeadow, Massachusetts, then Arlington, Virginia, Dlugos attended LaSalle College and later Yale Divinity School. His poetry was first published in the early 1970s, while he resided in Washington, DC. In 1976 Dlugos moved to New York City, where he established himself as a prominent younger poet of the New York School. Important influences include John Ashberry and Frank O'Hara. His early, consistently wry, verse incorporates settings and characters from popular culture, particularly TV sitcoms. By the early 1980s Dlugos had befriended the poets Dennis Cooper and David Trinidad, whom he frequently visited in Los Angeles, often to participate in Cooper's programming for the Beyond Baroque Literary/Arts Center. During this period Dlugos, enjoying a fast and rather glamorous transcontinental life, drank heavily and struggled with depression.

After joining Alcoholics Anonymous in the mid-1980s, Dlugos decided to pursue a vocation to the Episcopal priesthood and in 1986 moved into the Church of Saint Mary the Virgin, familiarly known as 'Smoky Mary's', in New York. In 1989 he tested positive for HIV and read from his poems on 'Good Morning America' as part of a segment about artists living with

AIDS. His poetry from this period is characterised by grace, simplicity and directness, epitomised by his long poem 'G-9'. His selected poems were published posthumously, edited by Trinidad and introduced by Cooper.

George Piggford

Dollimore, Jonathan (b. 1948), British scholar. Born in Bedfordshire, Dollimore worked in a factory, on a farm and in journalism before attending university as a mature-age student. He then taught at the University of Sussex and is presently Professor of English at the University of York. He is the author of a major study of homosexuality in European letters, *Sexual Dissidence: Augustine to Wilde, Freud to Foucault*, which has been reprinted four times since it was published in 1991. More recently, he has published *Death, Desire and Loss in Western Culture* (1998), and he has edited (with Alan Sinfield) *Political Shakespeare: New Essays in Cultural Materialism* (1985, second edition, 1994), as well as contributing chapters on Wilde, Gide, Shakespeare and bisexuality to various collections. With Alan Sinfield, he established the first MA programme in lesbian and gay studies in the United Kingdom.

Robert Aldrich and Garry Wotherspoon

Donahue, Phil (b. 1938), American talk show host. For over twenty-five years, Donohue provided a regular daytime platform for discussion of sexual and social issues. He has shown abortions, natural childbirth, reverse vasectomy, tubal ligation and male octopi having sex. He hosted the first gay wedding, and conducted debates on the gay gene. He was the first to tackle, on daytime TV, a mysterious cancer which later became known as AIDS.

In 1967 when Donahue, a former journalist and radio presenter, first went on the air, daytime television meant soaps and game shows. No one before Donahue had wrestled with taboo subjects such as abortion, incest, impotence and homosexuality. Donahue's early guests were often people at the political margins, including civil rights activists, war dissenters and members of minorities. Expedience made his show issue-based, being produced from Dayton, Ohio, on a small budget without access to celebrities. Shock and controversy were a substantial part of the mix. Brusque and tenacious, arguing fiercely but diplomatically with guests and audience members, Donahue was sometimes a hyperbolic evangelist for liberalism, sometimes a hyperactive defender of normality. *Newsweek* commented (in March 1979), 'One sometimes suspects that Donahue's idea of the perfect guest is an interracial lesbian couple who have had a child by artificial insemination'. (Such a couple did in fact appear a couple of years later.)

By 1985 the show, now based in New York, was the most watched syndicated show on television and was also being broadcast in the United Kingdom, Australia and elsewhere. In addition to over twenty Emmy Awards and numerous citations, Donahue has received commendations from the lesbian and gay community. Undoubtedly his consistent, if not always cogent, airing of gay and lesbian rights issues, especially AIDS, has been of enormous and widespread value in combatting ignorance and fear. He retired in 1995.

Phil Donahue, *Donahue: My Own Story* (New York, 1981).

Keith Howes

Doty, Mark (b. 1953), American writer. In an essay entitled 'Sweet Chariot', Doty writes that he grew up in Tennessee in two religions: the fundamentalist Christianity of his grandmother and the more worldly and strident Protestantism of his parents. Certainly, a spiritual sensibility pervades all of his work, including the memoir *Heaven's Coast* (1996), which won the PEN/Martha Albrand Award for First Nonfiction. The book deals with the 1994 death from AIDS of his long-time lover Wally Roberts.

Doty's poetry suggests connections with the American transcendental tradition; it is evocative of Elizabeth Bishop in that it is consistently imaginative and lushly descriptive. Many of Doty's poems deal with gay themes, including homophobia ('Charlie Howard's Descent'), bar culture ('Playland'), transvestism ('Tiara'), and most pervasively, AIDS. In a 1999 debate with J. D. McClatchy published in *The James White Review*, he defended the importance of an explicitly gay poetry, as opposed to a mode that eschews homosexuality for a more 'universal' vision. Nonetheless, his poetry suggests universal themes such as love, loss and death. His verse is collected in *Turtle, Swan (1987), Bethlehem in Broad Daylight* (1991), *My Alexandria* (1993) (which won the national Book Critics Circle Award and the T. S. Eliot Prize), *Atlantis* (1995), and *Sweet Machine* (1998). Doty, who has taught at Sarah Lawrence College Brandeis University, Vermont College and the University of Iowa Writers' Workshop, has become something of an inspiration and a mentor for a younger generation of American gay male poets. He has lived for a number of years in Provincetown, Massachusetts.

Robert K. Martin, *The Homosexual Tradition in American Poetry*, revised and expanded edition (Iowa City, 1998).

George Piggford

Doucé, Joseph (1945–90), French cleric. Doucé was a Baptist minister and founder of the first church for homosexuals in France. Doucé's family were Flemish peasants in the Belgian village of Saint-Trond, where he was born. He was a studious boy, who prayed for deliverance on first becoming aware of his homosexuality at the age of 10. At 16 he entered the local seminary to study for the priesthood, but he left it in 1967. He had his first homosexual experience with a teenaged orphan while work-

ing as monitor at an orphanage in Limoges, France. He converted to the Baptist faith in 1968, because (he said) it offered freedom of choice: 'This means that every man has infinite value and the highest dignity before God'. He studied for the ministry in Zurich and became pastor in Lens in northern France in 1971. A scholarship from the Ecumenical Council of Churches of Geneva enabled him to study psychology and sexology at the Protestant University of Amsterdam from 1974 to 1976.

Doucé wanted to minister to 'sexual minorities' – gay men, lesbians, bisexuals, transsexuals, transvestites, sadomasochists – and on 10 October 1976 he founded the Centre of Christ the Liberator (Centre du Christ Libérateur) or CCL in Paris. He held Sunday services in a pornographic cinema until the church got permanent quarters in November 1977. The CCL's goals were 'to give immediate pastoral, psychological, medical and legal aid to sexual minorities' and 'to bring about the evolution of all French-speaking society toward more tolerance, enlightenment and knowledge of real problems through information and the education of people'. The CCL held that 'sexuality is a magnificent gift from God, which we should receive with gratitude and love, and that it is a positive element in human existence, just like eating, sleeping, working and praying'. The CCL was explicitly non-political and served men and women of all races, opinions and religions.

The CCL provided a meeting place for sexual minorities, published a monthly bulletin entitled *Ilia* (for '*Il libère, Il aime*', i.e., 'He liberates, He loves'), and operated a telephone help-line for those in distress (SOS-Homos). Doucé also performed about 100 benedictions for homosexual couples (three-quarters of them lesbian), which the press dubbed 'gay marriages'.

Doucé kept up an exhausting pace of eighteen-hour days at the CCL, which remained very much his personal operation. One of his friends remarked that Doucé 'functioned in a monarchist way: he did everything himself'. Some of his actions, however, were imprudent. He kept up contacts with neo-Nazi homosexuals and defended paedophiles, although not himself either right-wing or a paedophile. The police questioned him for the first time in 1988, and in June 1990 they began an investigation into Autres Cultures, the bookstore opened by Doucé and his lover, Guy Bondar.

On the evening of 19 July 1990, two men came to Doucé's door, identified themselves as police officers and took him away for questioning. He never returned. His body was found on 17 October in the forest of Rambouillet outside Paris; he had been dead since about 20 July. Doucé's death caused a major scandal in France, but has never been elucidated. Were the murderers real police officers? If so, did they act on their own or on orders from above? Was Doucé murdered or did he perhaps die accidentally during an overly vigorous interrogation and was his body then discarded to conceal what had happened?

Françoise d'EAUBONNE summed up Doucé as not a saint, but merely 'a man, yes. With his weaknesses, his limits, his stumbling. But also and especially with his humanity, his fervent faith, his stubborn courage, his immense intellectual power, his unfailing generosity, his flame'. The CCL has survived his death and is now headed by Pastor Caroline Bianco. It is affiliated with the Metropolitan Community Church.

Françoise d'Eaubonne, *Le scandale d'une disparition: Vie et œuvre du Pasteur Doucé* (Paris, 1990); Bernard Violet, *Mort d'un pasteur: L'affaire Doucé* (Paris, 1994).

Michael Sibalis

Dover, Sir Kenneth (b. 1920), British scholar. Born in London and educated at Balliol College, Oxford, Dover became the leading classicist of his generation. He was Professor of Classics at the University of St Andrews from 1955 to 1976 (where he is

at present Chancellor), then President of Corpus Christi College, Oxford, from 1976 to 1986. He is a Fellow of the British Academy and has received numerous awards and honorary degrees for his translations, editions and scholarly studies of ancient Greek culture.

While lecturing on Plato's *Symposium* in the 1970s, Dover – a happily married heterosexual man – became interested in same-sex relations in Greece. In 1978 he published *Greek Homosexuality*, aiming, he stated in the preface, 'to describe those phenomena of homosexual behaviour and sentiment which are to be found in Greek art and literature between the eighth and second centuries BC'. Though interest in Greek sexuality had been one of the standard references – and key justifications for their own desires – for generations of homosexual writers and painters, Dover examined portrayals of homosexuality with greater scholarly rigour than ever before. Previous academic studies, except those by homosexuals, had tended to explain away homosexual behaviour as a shameful blot on the ancient Greek society taken as the very ideal for Western civilisation. Indeed, Dover commented, 'I know of no topic in classical studies on which a scholar's normal ability to perceive differences and draw inferences is so easily impaired'.

Dover investigated pederasty as an integral and accepted part of Greek culture and found omnipresent traces of it in vase painting, poetry, Plato's dialogues, Aristophanes' comedies, political speeches and graffiti. Dover's own interest lay particularly in such evidence as vase paintings, as he steered away from the study of 'great Greeks' such as Plato to show that pederastic behaviour and emotions spread throughout ancient Greek society. Dover argued, however, that same-sex relations must be seen in the context of general Greek attitudes to public and private behaviour, social roles, and masculinity and femininity; he rejected the idea that Greek homosexual practices descended from prehistoric initiation rituals.

Dover's study – though the object of some criticism from both more traditional classicists and, he says, 'some homosexuals [who] did not like to be told that much of their wishful idealisation of "Greek love" was wide of the mark' – established pederasty as a central feature of classical Greece. It led the way for other specialists (including Bernard Sergent, David HALPERIN and Eva Cantarella) to explore homosexuality in the ancient world further. His book, along with others published in the same years (notably John BOSWELL's study of homosexuality and Christianity), inaugurated a new era in gay and lesbian studies, and provided academic legitimacy to the field.

Kenneth Dover, *Marginal Comment: A Memoir* (London, 1994).

Robert Aldrich

Driberg, Thomas (Tom) Edward Neil (1905–76), British politician and journalist. Born into an upper-middle-class family in Crowborough, Sussex, he was educated at a local preparatory school and at Lancing College, where he was a near-contemporary of Evelyn Waugh. In his revolt against the values of his bourgeois upbringing he joined the Communist Party, from which he was eventually expelled in 1942. Several writers on British espionage have claimed that Driberg was a counter-agent, working for the British security service. The evidence is unconvincing. Driberg was also drawn to the Anglo-Catholic wing of the Church of England; he remained a devout Anglo-Catholic.

At the age of thirteen he had his first sexual experience with a man in a public lavatory. From then on sex became his ruling passion. In 1924 he entered Christ Church, Oxford University, where he left three years later without a degree. In 1928 he joined the *Daily Express* as a reporter, and for ten years from 1933 he wrote a wide-ranging and popular daily column under the pen name of William Hickey. During World War II he was also a war correspondent. In 1939 he bought a mansion at Bradwell in Essex, which was his country home for the next thirty years. In 1942 he was elected to Parliament as an Independent for the local constituency of Maldon. Three years later he joined the Labour Party. He was Labour Member of Parliament for Malden from 1945 to 1955, when he did not seek re-election. He served on the national executive of the Labour Party from 1949 to 1972 and was its chairman in 1957–58. In 1959 he returned to Parliament as Labour member for Barking, a seat that he retained until his retirement in 1974. As a member of the party's left wing, he opposed many of the policies of Harold Wilson's government (1964–70). Despite his seniority, he never became a minister.

Driberg was a flamboyant character, with a fruity voice and an endless stream of gossip. Throughout his life he enjoyed many homosexual adventures; he pursued working-class young men for sex and was never discreet about his activities. On several occasions he was caught by the police but successfully avoided public scandal. Nor was his homosexuality used against him by his political opponents. One lucky escape, in Edinburgh in 1943, was fictionalised by Compton McKenzie in his novel *Thin Ice*, about a homosexual politician. To the surprise of his friends and parliamentary colleagues, in 1951 Driberg married Ena Binfield in an elaborate ceremony at an Anglo-Catholic church in London. It turned out to be an unhappy marriage. They increasingly lived apart and in 1971 they finally separated.

Driberg was a skilled journalist. In addition to hundreds of newspaper articles, he wrote several biographies, a critical study of Moral Re-Armament, and an indiscreet autobiography, posthumously published. In 1975, after his retirement from the House of Commons, he was made a life peer, taking the title of Baron Bradwell of

Bradwell juxta Mare in the County of Essex. Driberg's homosexuality was widely known among politicians and journalists; he was among the most prominent homosexuals in British public life.

Obituary in *The Times*, 13 August 1976; Tom Driberg, *Ruling Passions* (London, 1977); Francis Wheen, *Tom Driberg: His Life and Indiscretions* (London, 1990).

                                    David Hilliard

Duberman, Martin Bauml (b. 1930), American scholar and activist. Duberman was born in New York City, the son of a Russian Jewish father from the Ukraine, eventually the founder of a dress-manufacturing company, and a second-generation Jewish Austrian-American mother.

His early interest in theatre discouraged by his parents, Duberman turned instead to academic pursuits. An exceptional student, he entered Yale University in 1948, graduating in 1952, and received his MA and PhD from Harvard University. From 1957 to 1961, he was history instructor at Yale. Following the publication of his first book, *Charles Francis Adams*, winner of the coveted Bancroft Prize (1962), and the offer of an assistant professorship at Princeton University, Duberman's academic rise was meteoric. For the next five years he wrote plays, including the critically acclaimed *In White America* (1963) and historical studies, including *James Russell Lowell*, a National Book Award nominee, and progressed from associate to full professor by 1967.

Until his postgraduate studies at Harvard, Duberman remained closeted and thereafter spent years vacillating between a string of unsuccessful gay affairs and the psychiatrist's couch. In his confessional autobiography *Cures* (1991), this richly gifted scholar chronicles his years of repression and sudden 1971 breakthrough when he abandoned therapy and came out. This liberation was reflected in his plays, including his own favourite,

Payments (1971), dealing with the world of male hustlers, and in his scholarship as well as in his personal life. In exposing a shocking instance of homophobia in his 1972 history *Black Mountain, An Exploration of Commmunity*, Duberman himself was the target of homophobic attacks from his academic peers.

Subsequently, Duberman delved into gay activism on academic, public and private levels. With fellow gay scholars, he founded the Gay Academic Union (1973) and joined the National Gay and Lesbian Task Force. His extensive writings on gay topics include: *About Time: Exploring the Gay Past* (1986); *Hidden from History: Reclaiming the Gay and Lesbian Past* (1989) and *Stonewall* (1993). Dedicated to promoting understanding of gay and lesbian history, Duberman has edited two pioneering series for teens: *Issues in Lesbian and Gay Life* and *Lives of Notable Gay Men and Lesbians*. In 1971, Duberman resigned from Princeton to become Distinguished Professor of History in the field of gay and lesbian studies at Lehman College, the City University of New York. At CUNY he founded the Center for Lesbian and Gay Studies (CLAGS), sponsoring public events and conferences, monthly research colloquia and research grants to academic staff and postgraduate students. His other works include *Visions of Kerouac* (1977) and *Paul Robeson* (1989).

Martin Duberman, *Cures* (New York, 1991) and *Midlife Queer* (New York, 1996).

                                    A. M. Wentink

Duncan, George (Ian Ogilvie) (1930–72), British-Australian academic. Duncan was born in London, the only child of a well-to-do family which moved to Victoria, Australia in 1937. Although an outstanding student, Duncan was forced to withdraw from the University of Melbourne because of tuberculosis, but in 1957 he entered Cambridge University, graduating with a doctorate in law. About 1970 he joined the Gaytime Friendship Society, a London club.

Duncan returned to Australia in March 1972 to take up a lectureship at the University of Adelaide. On 10 May that year he was thrown into the River Torrens and drowned; television news viewers were treated to the spectacle of his body being recovered. The area was a known beat and rumours spread that Duncan had been killed by police engaged in 'poofter-bashing'. At the inquest, nineteenth-century pathology was employed to classify Duncan as a passive homosexual because of his 'funnel-shaped' anus. Two police officers refused to answer questions put to them; three were suspended from the force and resigned.

The case gained nationwide publicity and challenged societal attitudes towards homosexuality. Within three months a private member's bill was placed before the South Australian Parliament to de-criminalise homosexual acts between consenting males over the age of 21. The ignorance and prejudices of even those politicians in support was evident during debate; Premier Don Dunstan referred to homosexuals' 'vulgarity and unpleasant-ness' of behaviour. The bill was heavily amended, and new legislation which provided for a code of sexual behaviour regardless of sex or sexual orientation was introduced in 1973. In 1975 South Australia became the first state or territory in Australia to embrace full decriminalisa-tion; Tasmania only completed the cycle in 1997.

Duncan was held up as a martyr by the gay rights movement in Adelaide because of the many unanswered questions sur-rounding his death. On the basis of a New Scotland Yard report, the crown solicitor had decided against proceeding with any prosecution; in 1988 two ex-members of South Australia's vice squad were acquit-ted of manslaughter. A police task force reported to Parliament in 1990 that there was 'insufficient evidence to charge any other person'. And so the mystery remains.

Malcolm Cowan and Tim Reeves, 'The "Gay Rights" Movement and the Decriminalisation Debate in South Australia, 1973–1975', in R. Aldrich and G. Wotherspoon (eds), *Gay and Lesbian Perspectives IV: Essays in Australian Culture* (Sydney, 1998); Tim Reeves, 'Duncan, George Ian Ogilvie', in John Ritchie (ed.), *Australian Dictionary of Biography*, vol. 14 (Melbourne, 1996); Tim Reeves, 'The 1972 Debate on Male Homosexuality in South Australia', in R. Aldrich (ed.), *Gay and Lesbian Perspectives II: More Essays in Australian Gay Culture* (Sydney, 1993).

Tim Reeves

Dynes, Wayne R. (b. 1934), American scholar. Born in Fort Worth, Texas, and educated at the University of California in Los Angeles and New York University, Dynes is Professor of the History of Art at Hunter College of the City University of New York. In 1987, he published *Homosexuality: A Research Guide*, and in 1990 edited a two-volume *Encyclopedia of Homosexuality*. Both were pioneering works, and remain standard references, in gay and lesbian studies. The encyclo-paedia, particularly noted for the breadth of its coverage, is the first and most com-prehensive compendium in the field. Dynes is currently editing a volume on pioneers of the American gay movement.

Robert Aldrich and Garry Wotherspoon

E

Eaubonne, Françoise-Marie-Thérèse d' (b. 1920), French writer. Born into a well-to-do family in Paris and educated in Toulouse, Eaubonne has pursued a career as reader for various publishers, journalist and woman of letters. She has written novels, biographies, poems, essays and several volumes of autobiography. Eaubonne is also a political militant both by nature and by circumstance: 'I will have fought all my life for my liberty, given the price that society has exacted for [my] being a women, a woman who wrote and who did not want to have a second profession.' 'Ever since I have held a pen, I have been [politically and socially] engaged without even knowing it, because even if you talk about things that don't appear to have political implications, they do.' And she has added, 'I will never cease . . . fighting for all the groups and individuals who are oppressed in any way whatsoever and who are denied the right to be what they are.'

Heterosexual, twice married and mother of two children, Eaubonne has nonetheless participated in the struggle for gay and lesbian rights. In 1970 she published *Eros minoritaire*, a book about homosexuality showing 'the geographical and historical universality of what people still persist in calling a vice'. She has, in her own words, 'always [been] attracted by male homosexuality as the highest form of escape from existential and social constraints,' but lacks 'the same sort of attraction for lesbianism, which [is] less repressed.' She has often declared: 'I'm not a Lesbian, I'm a faggot.' In the mid-1960s André BAUDRY invited her to participate in Arcadie, the 'homophile' movement that he headed, but she came to reject Baudry's advocacy of homosexual respectability. She even told him on one occasion, 'You say that society must integrate homosexuals, but I say that homosexuals must disintegrate society'. As she later explained: 'What's the point of being integrated into a neurotic society that brands homosexuality a neurosis? What's the point, for women, to be equal in an unequal society?'

Eaubonne was one of the prominent figures in the radical break-away movement from Arcadie that created FHAR (Front Homosexuel d'Action Révolutionnaire, the Homosexual Front for Revolutionary Action) in March 1971. She did not join lesbians like Marie-Jo BONNET who soon left FHAR because of its alleged misogyny, but remained active alongside men like Daniel GUÉRIN and Guy HOCQUENGHEM until the movement's demise in 1973–74. In the 1970s she still believed that male homosexuality and feminism were 'natural allies in the war that they wage against the patriarchy'. By the 1980s, however, she was deploring the fact that the homosexual movement had ceased being subversive: 'When there are fifty of you,

you storm the heavens; when there are 50,000 you storm the bath-houses'. Eaubonne nonetheless remains a strong supporter of gay and lesbian rights.

Christiane Jouvet, 'Rencontre avec Françoise d'Eaubonne,' *Lesbia* vol. 10 (September 1983).
Michael Sibalis

Egan, Jim (1921–2000), Canadian activist. Born in Toronto, Egan first came to prominence in 1949 when he began writing letters to the editor to protest sensational or misleading articles on homosexuality that were then common in the North American mainstream press. Egan was determined to challenge the conspiracy of silence that he believed had formed around the true nature of homosexuality. He undertook this campaign at a time when there was no organised gay movement in North America.

By 1951 Egan was publishing a long series of sympathetic articles on aspects of homosexuality in Toronto tabloid newspapers such as *True News Times (TNT)* and *Justice Weekly*. He also began to correspond with early American homophile activists such as Henry Gerber, and later with members of the Mattachine Society in Los Angeles, and ONE, Incorporated. By the close of the 1950s Egan was contributing articles to *ONE Magazine*.

Throughout his life Egan worked as a merchant seaman, biologist, carpenter, farmer, writer and environmentalist. His early gay activism spanned the years 1949 through 1964, during which time he published dozens of articles and letters that dared to present a homosexual point of view, and became a leading figure in the nascent world of gay activism in Toronto. Eventually, Egan grew disappointed with what he perceived to be a lack of community support for his efforts. At the insistence of Jack Nesbit, his partner since 1948, they moved in 1964 to British Columbia, where Egan abandoned gay activism in favour of business, environmentalism and, eventually, politics. Egan was the first openly gay man elected to public office in Canada, serving as Regional Director for Electoral Area B of the Regional District of Comox-Strathcona, BC, from 1981 to 1993.

By the late 1980s Egan and Nesbit had embraced gay activism once more, most spectacularly by fighting for same-sex spousal benefits all the way to the Supreme Court of Canada in 1995. Egan and Nesbit used the Canadian Charter of Rights and Freedoms to challenge the discriminatory exclusion of pension benefits to same-sex couples under the Old Age Security Act. This was the first such claim heard by the Supreme Court under the Charter. Although the claim was ultimately unsuccessful, the Court did rule that 'sexual orientation' must be read into the Charter as a ground of discrimination analogous to existing grounds such as race, gender and religion. This ruling essentially changed the Canadian Constitution and paved the way for further high court challenges based on sexual orientation as a ground of discrimination. Egan is today widely regarded as Canada's pioneer gay activist.

David Adkin, *Jim Loves Jack: The James Egan Story* (film) (Toronto, 1996); Jim Egan, *Challenging the Conspiracy of Silence: My Life As a Canadian Gay Activist*, ed. Donald W. McLeod (Toronto, 1998); Jim Egan papers, Canadian Lesbian and Gay Archives, Toronto; Jim Egan, *Jim Egan: Canada's Pioneer Gay Activist*, ed. Robert Champagne (Toronto, 1987).
Donald W. McLeod

Eikvam, Turid (b. 1948), Norwegian activist and journalist. Born in the town of Ski, near Oslo, Eikvam worked as foreman in a newspaper printing office. She received a degree in criminology in 1991 and has since held the position of office manager at the Institute of Criminology at the University of Oslo.

Eikvam's first involvement in gay politics was in 1978, in a small, radical organisation called 'Working Group for Gay Liberation' (AHF), where, during the first years, she was active as a member of the board and leader of the group. In her work for the gay movement, Eikvam strongly emphasised the importance of ground-work and activism, i.e., to engage as many gay women and men as possible in the work against discrimination and for openness within the family, among friends, colleagues and in society generally.

In 1978, AHF began to publish a journal for gays dealing with cultural and political issues: *Løvetann* is the first and only jour-nal of its kind in Norway. Eikvam has been a member of the editorial collective since the publication of the journal's third issue. She has since contributed actively to this journal which, after twenty years, is still going strong. Its publication continues to be based on the unpaid work of an edi-torial collective. In 1991, *Løvetann* became an autonomous journal, no longer de-pendent on the gay organisation. It has developed into a solid and popular journal with emphasis on cultural and political issues for gays, lesbians and other inter-ested readers. Eikvam has in recent years contributed a series on historical women/lesbians, and has in this way brought to light and described a number of well-known and less well-known female figures from a lesbian angle. She was also the prime mover in the first Norwegian gay film festival in 1986; this has since become a popular annual tradition.

Eikvam has since 1987 been involved in work with HIV/AIDS issues in Norway. She has been one of the few lesbians work-ing in this area. In 1986 she started and participated in the 'Henki-campaign' – a campaign in support of a gay man who was dismissed from his job for being HIV-positive. The campaign was successful and the case was won in the Supreme Court of Justice in 1988. Eikvam was employed for two and a half years in the secretariat of the Public Health Committee for gays. This committee was started in connection with the gay movement. Its main objective was (and still is) to carry out preventative

work among men who have sex with men. In the initial phase, the informative work about HIV/AIDS was carried out ex-clusively by organised gays. However, Eikvam took the initiative, together with two gays, of starting a project which aimed at visiting the places frequented by gays – discotheques, bars and saunas. She also helped to promote drag-shows, as a preventative measure which would reach gays living in all parts of the country. She also organised support groups for people who were HIV-positive and for those with AIDS. Later she became the representative of the gay organisations on the Board of the National Society against AIDS, which is based on collaboration between many federations of trade unions, and other professional and industrial bodies.

Eikvam was co-author of the book *Aids and Society* (1987), which discussed the non-medical social, sociological, eco-nomic and legal aspects of the HIV epi-demic. The authors thereby contributed to a debate on these issues, in addition to the medical aspects which until then had been the focus.

Eikvam has since 1992 been an active or-ganiser of the 'Network for Gay Re-search'. The network was created in 1992 and has established contact between scien-tists, exchanging research findings through monthly seminars about homosexuality. This applies to research at undergraduate level, to theses for doctorates and to re-search carried out by fully qualified phys-icians, psychologists, sociologists and other professional groups.

Karin Enderud

Elliott, Sumner Locke (1917–91), Austral-ian writer. Elliott was born in Sydney, Aus-tralia, the son of Helena Sumner Locke, a playwright and novelist, and Henry Logan Elliott, a freelance journalist. His parents enjoyed only ten days of marriage before his father was sent to England with the Australian army. Nine months later his mother died the day after giving birth but not before naming him, somewhat curiously, after herself. The absent father gave guardianship of the baby to two of his wife's sisters but this led to a difficult and stressful childhood as the sisters fought over his custody, a bitter legal battle only resolved by the death of one of them when Elliott was twelve. He was moved back and forth from one aunt to the other, disrupting his schooling and making it hard to develop friendships, and at one stage a court ordered that he be placed in a boarding school when his aunts could not agree on where he should live. Elliott's first novel *Careful, He Might Hear You* (1963), is based on his turbulent and traumatic early years.

At school he became involved in amateur theatre, both as a writer and actor, and at sixteen he joined the Independent Theatre group in Sydney. He also began acting in radio plays and writing for radio serials. It was an exciting life after a lonely and troubled childhood and the friends he made provided him with a surrogate and supportive family who shared his interests. During his teens and twenties he called himself Sumner Locke-Elliott, which he thought sounded more sophisticated; in later life he admitted that he had been 'terribly conceited' as a young man.

A former colleague from the Independent Theatre produced a play of his in Hollywood in 1938 and this led, unexpectedly, to the offer of a contract to write dialogue for MGM. He declined, but this, and a long-standing fascination with the glamour of Hollywood movies, planted the idea of eventual migration to the United States, an unusual goal at the time, as most Australians who aspired to success in writing or acting made for London. He applied to immigrate to the US, but World War II intervened.

In 1942 he was drafted into the Australian army and spent four boring years as a clerk in army posts in various parts of Australia. After the war he turned these experiences into the very successful stage play *Rusty Bugles* (1948). Police action

over its raw barracks language ensured wide public interest and eventually forced a revision of Australian censorship laws.

Permission to migrate to the US came in 1948 and Elliott seized the opportunity. His interest in that country had been intensified by an affair with a US officer in Sydney after the war. Although he loved acting he soon realised that his abilities were modest, the competition was fierce, and his accent restricted him to 'British' roles. 'I was crazy about acting,' he recalled, 'but I was never really that good . . . I think I always knew that writing was my strength.' At that time television networks broadcast much live drama and Elliott became very successful as a television playwright. He became an American citizen in 1955.

He left television writing in 1962 to write a novel. His mother had been a novelist and all through his childhood and adolescence Elliott had heard from her friends and family what a loss her premature death had been, cutting off such a talent. He was left in little doubt that, as she had died in childbirth, he had an obligation to become as accomplished a writer, yet her shadow inhibited him from attempting to follow the same path. When he finally did he realised immediately that this was his 'true medium of writing'.

Clarke says that in Elliott's novels 'the boundary between fact and fiction is not only blurred, it is almost invisible.' Certainly they illustrate Alberto Moravia's aphorism that fiction is a higher form of autobiography. Most are set in Sydney between World Wars I and II and deal with a child or young man struggling to come to terms with life in the confusing context of a dysfunctional family. Elliott's real family members and their interactions with him are important presences in most of his works, as are loneliness, repressed emotions and desires, and the bewildering difficulty of trying to discover oneself in the absence of normal family relationships. Although strongly autobiographical, none of the novels (before *Fairyland*,

1990) has any significant homosexual flavour.

In *Fairyland*, published the year before he died, Elliott at last 'came out' as a homosexual after a lifetime of avoiding the issue. 'After fifty years of secreting part of myself, writing *Fairyland* was like going to a psychiatrist, like fresh air coming into a room', he said. 'I've been gay all my life and this is about that experience.' It was a very frankly autobiographical, and cathartic, novel, presenting the frustration, alienation and anxiety of being homosexual in pre-war Australia, a time when, as he described it, 'to be openly gay was out of the question, to be privately gay was immensely difficult'. Until he left Australia in 1948 Elliott was uncomfortable about his homosexuality and did his best to keep it secret. There were furtive and sometimes dangerous casual encounters, and a few unsatisfactory affairs, but no stable sexual relationships. The homosexual characters in his other novels exhibit the same feelings of anxiety and uncertainty that Elliott later confessed to in *Fairyland*. Many of the heterosexual encounters and relationships in his novels are in fact replicas of his own homosexual experiences.

Although Elliott found greater sexual freedom and acceptance in New York than he had in Sydney, he still felt unable to be open about his sexuality to the Australian friends with whom he maintained a regular correspondence. They, of course, had already worked things out for themselves, but not until *Fairyland* was published, when Elliott was in his seventies, did he publicly declare his sexuality. It is unclear whether Elliott ever had a significant homosexual relationship in the US, but at about the age of 60 he met Whitfield Cook, a widower, eight years older, and also a writer. For years they spent summers together in rural New Hampshire. They maintained separate apartments in New York City but when Elliott suffered a stroke in 1985 Cook moved in to help care for him for the last six years of his life. The

nature of their relationship hardly matters; Cook gave Elliott the support and companionship which had eluded him for so much of his life.

Elliott wrote ten novels and left an uncompleted manuscript (*Radio Days*, published posthumously in 1993). His first, *Careful, He Might Hear You*, won the Miles Franklin Award, an annual prize for the best Australian novel, and in 1977 he received the Patrick White Award 'for an older Australian writer of distinction for a body of work'. Most of his novels were best sellers; *Careful, He Might Hear You* was later made into a film and *Water Under the Bridge* (1977) became a television mini-series. Another gay novelist, Patrick White, Australia's only Literature Nobellist, and a man not bereft of ego, once said that Elliott was the finest living Australian novelist, apart from himself of course. High praise by any measure.

Sharon Clarke, *Sumner Locke Elliott: Writing Life* (Sydney, 1996).

Neil A. Radford

Elmer, Martin (b. 1930), Danish author and journalist. Born Robert Carl Berg, he changed his name in 1953 to Robert (Bob) Cecil Martin Elmer Berg. From 1954 Martin Elmer contributed articles and short stories to the homophile monthly *Vennen* (*The Friend*). In 1957 he joined the editorial staff, and from 1962 was editor-in-chief until *Vennen* ceased publication in 1970. From 1961 to 1974 he was coordinator of *Vennen* Activist Group which from 1962 was the owner of the magazine. From 1956 till the mid-1970s Elmer contributed to the public debate on homosexuality and argued for the emancipation of homophiles in numerous newspaper articles, lectures, books and novels, some of them aimed at young readers. In 1968 he authored and co-hosted a TV debate on homosexuality, 'Et foragtet mindretal' (A Despised Minority).

The first decade of Elmer's collaboration with and later editorship of *Vennen* was characterized by severe repression of homosexuality and homosexuals. The arrest and subsequent sentencing in 1955 of the editor Axel AXGIL touched the leadership of the Forbundet af 1948 (The Association of 1948, National Union of Homophiles), which as a consequence suffered a severe loss of credibility within the homosexual subculture and was critically weakened, politically and financially. *Vennen*, which had been associated with the Forbundet af 1948, was now published as an independent magazine which under Elmer's leadership became the voice of the homophile subculture during a very difficult period of virulent anti-homosexuality. His editorship of *Vennen* and his participation in the public debate under his own name constitute the beginning of the raising of the political profile of homosexuals in Denmark after the disaster in 1955. When the Forbundet af 1948 gradually regained its strength during the second half of the 1960s, Elmer's fiercely maintained independence, personally and editorially, meant that he began to lose touch with a younger generation. In the early 1970s Elmer publicly and polemically attacked the Gay Liberation Front.

Elmer stood as candidate for Parliament (Georgian Party) from 1972–77. He was a member of the Board of Directors of the State Foundation for the Arts (1972–79), and of the Danish Association of Authors (1971–79). Under the name Robert C. Berg, Elmer has published four volumes of novels and short stories, and been a prolific and regular contributor of short stories (about heterosexual love) mainly to women's magazines. Elmer has won several literary prizes for his short stories and novels and was awarded the prestigious PH-Prize in 1971 for his contribution to homophile emancipation.

In 1966 Elmer and his life-companion since 1963, the textile artist Erik Fink, applied for civil marriage which predictably was declined; they were joined in a registered partnership in 1994. In 1979 they settled in Torremolinos, Spain, where they have played a leading role in the social and cultural organisations of the Danish expatriate colony.

Martin Elmer, *Verden uden drøm* (Copenhagen, 1959), *My Spanish Youngster* (Copenhagen, 1964), *Wurzellos* (Copenhagen, 1968), *Mondays Will Never Be the Same* (Vancouver, 1988).
Wilhelm von Rosen

Emaer, Fabrice (1935–83), French businessman. Emaer was a Parisian nightclub owner who shaped gay life in the city in the 1970s. Francis Paul Emaer (he adopted the Christian name Fabrice as a teenager) was born in Wattrelos near Lille in northern France. In 1949, the death of his father, a travelling salesman for the local spinning-mills, left the family impoverished. Emaer's life before 1964 remains a mystery, but he apparently left his family at seventeen and travelled around North Africa and the French Riviera, where he may have worked as a beautician. In 1964 he opened Le Pimm's Bar, a tiny gay bar at 3 Rue Sainte-Anne near the Paris Opera House. In 1968 he launched Le Club Sept, a ground-floor restaurant and basement discotheque at number 7 of the same street. The restaurant regularly drew celebrities like Diana Ross, Mick Jagger, Andy WARHOL and Yves SAINT LAURENT, while the discotheque gained renown as Paris's classiest gay club. It was very expensive but also democratic because open to everybody irrespective of age, sex, race or sexual orientation. Emaer sought, in his own words, 'to democratise poshness'. As the journalist Frédéric Martel has put it, he also 'invented a new way of being homosexual: chic and stylish to American [dance] music'. Other bars and clubs opened nearby in the early 1970s, and the district surrounding the Rue Sainte-Anne developed into the centre of gay night life in Paris, until displaced by the Marais quarter in the mid-1980s.

In 1977 Emaer acquired Le Palace, a large music hall on the Rue du Faubourg-Montmartre, constructed in 1895. Inspired by New York's Studio 54, he reopened it in March 1978 as a giant discotheque, perhaps the most sumptuous in the world. The philosopher Roland Barthes wrote: 'Le Palace is not a "nightclub" like the others; it brings together in an original setting pleasures that are ordinarily dispersed: ... the stimulus of the Modern, the exploration of new visual sensations, due to new technologies [like lasers]; the joy of the dance, the charm of potential [sexual] encounters.' The clientele was largely mixed, however; Le Palace was exclusively gay only at its Sunday afternoon tea dances, which remained an institution in gay Paris until Le Palace finally closed its doors in 1996.

Emaer described himself as a 'homosexual militant' whose commercial activities helped to build a sense of community among French homosexuals: 'I set up some of their privileged zones, and these, which provide the basis for a family of ideas and interests, are important to the extent that they reinforce a cultural community.' Shortly before his death from cancer, Emaer commented: 'I think that I have been rather successful in life. I am unhappy about only one thing: I have not earned any money ... I often worked for the prestige, but not really for the money.' In fact, generous and spendthrift, Emaer was deep in debt, because, as a friend later remarked, 'Whenever Fabrice earned 100 francs, the next day he gave a party that cost 120.' Obituaries declared that 'Fabrice Emaer ... has left the night of which he was prince' and that 'his departure leaves a black hole in the Parisian night'.

Daniel Garcia, *Les années Palace* (Paris, 1999); Frédéric Martel, *Le Rose et le noir: Les homosexuels en France depuis 1968* (Paris, 1995); 'Fabrice Emaer du 7 au Palace', *Gai Pied*, October 1981; *Libération*, 13 June 1983; *Le Monde*, 14 June 1983.

Michael Sibalis

Engelschman, Nico (1913–88), Dutch actor. Engelschman was the eldest of five sons. His father was a Jew, his mother a Protestant. For both parents the marriage meant that they broke with the past. Engelschman was not brought up in any religious or political way. He started to work in his early teens. He became a union member and through that he also became a member of the social democratic party. He sincerely believed that this was the dawn of a socialist society. In 1932 he left the more moderate social democratic party and became a radical socialist. He was very active in the radical socialistic youth movement; in fact he became the secretary. Here he learned to organise and was politically schooled. In this youth movement, the Leninistic Youth Guard, members in their teens and twenties discussed not only the Russian Revolution and the ideas of Lenin, but also the theories of the sexologist Wilhelm Reich, who combined in his thinking the ideas of Freud and Marx. In these years Engelschman became aware of his homosexuality. In the 1930s one did not speak about homosexuality. There were no magazines and only a few places where men could meet. Most of the time men met through personal ads. Engelschman too in this way came to know other homosexuals. He also met J. A. Schorer, the leading man of the Dutch branch of Magnus Hirschfeld's Scientific-Humanitarian Committee. He realised that if he wanted to change his own position as a homosexual and that of others he had to fight. He left the radical socialist movement and started in the winter of 1940, with some other men, a magazine for homosexual men and women called *Levensrecht* (*Right to Live*). The occupation of the Netherlands by Nazi Germany ended these efforts. Through his old contacts with the radical socialist movement he became involved in the Resistance. Because of this and his Jewish descent, he spent several years in hiding. He spent his time taking acting lessons secretly; after the war, in May 1945 he began to work as an actor.

In the summer of 1946, Engelschman

revived *Levensrecht*, several years later re-naming it *Vriendschap* (*Friendship*). But he wanted to achieve more than just a magazine, so he and several others formed a group around the magazine. It was the beginning of the Dutch homosexual and lesbian movement, COC (Centre for Culture and Recreation). Engelschman wanted to give homosexual men and women the opportunity to meet each other in a suitable way, out of the darkness and away from obscure cruising places. In the eyes of Engelschman homosexuals had the same rights and duties as all other citizens. They could be proud of themselves and should act accordingly. All kinds of activities which society associated with homosexuality in a negative sense such as promiscuous behaviour, brief relationships and unstableness were, according to Engelschman, a result of societal dislike and repression. He never hesitated to state this clearly time after time, especially in his famous New Year statements. The word 'homosexual' had a negative connotation; it placed too much emphasis on sexuality. To make sure that society would understand that homosexual men and women could love each other as any other human being, Engelschman in 1949 introduced the word 'homophile' – the last part of the word meaning 'to love' in classical Greek. 'Step by step the insight will grow', he said, 'that race, colour, religion and political convictions should not be grounds for discrimination and persecution. Very slowly society will be convinced that homophiles are complete normal human beings with the same human shortcomings and feelings of love as all other humans.'

It was a political statement, part of Engelschman's strategy to make homosexuality acceptable to society. For him it was clear that the struggle for the emancipation of homosexuals was a political one. Homosexuals should eventually come out into the open and stop using pen-names as most members of the COC did – even Engelschman used the pen-name Bob Angelo. The COC based its policy on the Universal Declaration of Human Rights by the United Nations: 'All human beings are born free and equal in dignity and rights'. The COC also promoted scientific research into homosexuality. It promoted a just and humane judgement and treatment of homophiles and gave homophiles psychological, moral and legal assistance in the setbacks they experienced as a result of prejudices. Besides that it strived for the abolition of criminal laws – in the Netherlands sexual contacts between adults, male and female, and minors under the age of 21 were forbidden between 1911 and 1971 in Paragraph 248*bis* of the criminal code. From 1946 until the early 1970s he saw this as his life's task as chairman of the board and managing director of the COC office, as editor of *Vriendschap*, and as stage manager of many plays.

During the 1950s and the early 1960s the COC tried to accomplish its goals by manoeuvring very carefully in its contacts with the state, i.e. the police that watched the COC like a hawk, and its contacts with scientists. During the mid-1950s Catholic, Protestant and humanist scientists – a normal coalition in the Netherlands, as members from different religious/political backgrounds worked together in this way – with the help of the COC philosophised about what caused male homosexuality. It created step by step a different atmosphere. Regular contact with the COC made people experience homosexuals as 'normal' other human beings. After a wave of suicides in Amsterdam amongst young Catholic homosexuals Engelschman agreed with Catholic scientists that they would offer actual help; Protestants followed. At the beginning of the 1960s these scientists started to plead publicly for acceptance of 'the homosexual fellow man'. The COC itself had come to believe in the idea that all humans were in essence bisexual, so all humans had more or less homosexual feelings. Homosexuals were no different from heterosexuals except for their choice of a mate. This cleared the road for the COC to more openness and to their policy in the late 1960s of integration.

In 1962 the policy of the association changed officially. Engelschman, having been chairman of the board from 1946 until then, disagreed with the pace of policy changes and resigned.

In December 1986, the fortieth anniversary of the COC, the Dutch government knighted Engelschman, a reward for the way he had given indefatigably of his strength for the emancipation of homosexuals. In 1998 the municipality of Amsterdam honoured Engelschman by naming the bridge near the Homomonument after him.

Hans Warmerdam

Espaliu, Pepe (1955–93), Spanish artist. Pepe Espaliu was probably the first Spanish artist to invest his 'coming out' with political meaning (in 1992). Maybe this statement needs qualification: other intellectuals, like Alberto CARDÍN, or activists, like Jordi Petit or Armand de FLUVIÀ, identified publicly as homosexual long before that. An artist like OCAÑA found inspiration in his homosexuality in more direct and explicit ways than Espaliu. On the other hand, the sexual identity of other public personalities like Pedro ALMODÓVAR was an open secret. What is important in Pepe Espaliu's case is the transition between an attitude that resisted what he called 'confession' and a moment in which he publicly expressed his sexual identity. The political articulation between these two moments can be illustrative of the fate of the 'gay' model in Hispanic culture, and in Espaliu's case the catalyst was AIDS.

Espaliu was born in provincial Cordoba, in Andalusia, in a period of profound sexual and political repression. The Church and other institutions made the atmosphere stifling for an adolescent exploring his sexuality. However, according to a provocative statement he made shortly before his death, the army seems to have provided some relief for this situation: as suspected, all-male environments encourage homosexuality even as they brutally repress it. His personal growth was linked to two very different cities: Barcelona and Paris. Both provided opportunities and anonymity. The references to sexual acts in his work are informed by furtive experiences in cinemas, public toilets and cruising areas. Typically for a Spanish homosexual, Espaliu only became sexually active in the dark; his experiences, as he tells them, were mostly fleeting, and this reflected a certain discomfort with his condition. It would be inaccurate to say that he internalised homophobia, even if he certainly internalised repression. In his development as an artist, Jean GENET was an important reference, and his world – in which homosexuality is proudly presented as marginal and linked with crime and transgression – was one with which Espaliu identified. Psychoanalytic thought, especially Lacan, is another of his influences, and this discipline provides numerous interpretive keys to understanding Espaliu's art. In Paris, he became acquainted with the radical philosophical currents of the 1970s; at the same time, he reacted against post-Stonewall gay identity (maybe following a Mediterranean/French perspective).

Espaliu moved between painting, drawing, sculpture and performance art. As he declared, his earlier works aimed to protect him against the world; they were, he said, 'an alibi'. The topic of art as a mask or as protection was a constant throughout his career. His later work included tortoise shells and other objects that function as a reference both to his vulnerability as an AIDS patient and the shell that artists construct with their work. Direct homoerotic imagery did not find a place (however understated) in his artistic production until his very last works. But before that, his experiences as a homosexual and HIV-positive person determined the meaning of many of his works. Given his background, there is a strong element of violence and even death linked to sex. His later works explore mysticism as a way to make life endurable, as is the case with the performance piece *El nido* (*The Nest*, 1993), inspired by Sufi rituals. Indeed, it was AIDS that gave a new direction to his art: aware of the political consequences of silence, he felt the need to make sexuality a public issue, both for his own and for others' sake. He was among the very first public voices raised in Spain to protest against society's treatment of AIDS patients. One of his last performance pieces, *Carrying*, which took place in San Sebastian and Madrid in 1992, was a call to solidarity with the victims of the disease and required the participation of large numbers of people; many artists, intellectuals and politicians answered the call. If the artist's task was to bring about symbolic change, it is undeniable that somehow in Spain the situation for HIV-positive gay people was different 'before' and 'after' Espaliu's coming out. This does not make him into a hero – he would have been embarrassed at anyone suggesting this – but simply someone who made his point.

Juan Vicente Aliaga and José Miguel Cortés (eds), *De amor y rabia. Acerca del arte y del sida* (Valencia, 1993); Juan Vicente Aliaga, 'De mascaradas y certezas: en torno a la representación de la homosexualidad en la obra de Pepe Espaliu', in Xosé Maria Buxán (ed.), *Conciencia de un singular deseo* (Barcelona, 1997); Paul Julian Smith, *Vision Machines* (London, 1996).

Alberto Mira

F

Faderman, Lillian (b. 1940), American scholar. Interdisciplinary scholar Lillian Faderman has arguably done more than any American historian to date to insure that lesbians are not and do not become invisible to history's selective gaze. Professor of English at the University of California at Fresno, where she has taught since 1967, Faderman was born to a single working mother in the Bronx, New York; the family moved to East Los Angeles before Faderman finished elementary school. She earned her undergraduate degree from the University of California at Berkeley, and her master's and doctoral degrees from the University of California at Los Angeles.

Faderman's work first gained national prominence with the publication of *Surpassing the Love of Men: Romantic Friendship and Love between Women from the Renaissance to the Present* (1981), which examines numerous cultural variables affecting women's social, romantic and sexual relationships with each other – attempting, in part, to determine why certain romantic same-sex relationships were condoned while others were denounced. While many of Faderman's assumptions and hypotheses have been compellingly challenged by other scholars, always a foregone conclusion, Faderman's book remains invaluable, in part because the discussion it engendered is still thriving.

Faderman's *Odd Girls and Twilight Lovers: A History of Lesbian Life in Twentieth Century America* (1991) was nominated for a Pulitzer Prize and the National Book Award and was named 'Editor's Choice' by the *New York Times Book Review* - all of which suggests that Faderman writes books that readers outside academia can also appreciate. She is also the editor of *Chloe plus Olivia: Lesbian Literature from the Seventeenth Century to the Present* (1994), a ground breaking anthology which received the Lambda Literary Award for Best Anthology.

Dedicated 'again' to her partner Phyllis Irwin, with whom she has been since 1971, Faderman's latest work, *To Believe in Women: What Lesbians Have Done for America – A History* (1999), consciously works to overturn the 'almost always tacit assumption [of heterosexuality] we make about those whose actions have been socially useful or heroic'. This most recent book, writes Faderman, 'focuses on how certain late nineteenth- and early twentieth-century women whose lives can be described as lesbian were in the forefront to procure the rights and privileges that large numbers of Americans enjoy today'.

Additional works by Faderman that address lesbian experience are *The Scotch Verdict* (1985) and *Lesbian-Feminism in Turn-of-the-Century Germany* (1980), edited with Brigitte Eriksson. Faderman, who is of Jewish ancestry, has also published in the area of ethnic studies, having co-edited both *Speaking for Ourselves: American Ethnic Writing* (1969)and *From the Bario: A Chicano Anthology* (1973). Faderman's books have been translated into German, Japanese and Italian.

Annette Oxindine

Falwell, Jerry (b. 1933), American political figure. Falwell was born in Lynchburg, Virginia, the son of a pious homemaker and successful businessman involved in a restaurant, a trucking company and service stations, and who died at age 55 as an alcoholic. Falwell was a very good athlete, and an excellent but high-spirited student. In college he became a born-again Christian. His meeting Marcel Pate, a church pianist who became his wife (and with whom he had three children), is said to be an important factor in his conversion. On a shoestring, in 1956 Falwell established the independent Thomas Road Baptist Church in Lynchburg and built the congregration up to 17,000. Falwell became a prominent television evangelist with his weekly *Old Time Gospel Hour*, which was broadcast over nearly 400 radio stations and 400 television stations, mostly in the United States. He established a home for alcoholics, a school, a bus ministry, a seminary and the Liberty [Baptist] University, and engaged in overseas missionary work. In 1973, his church was charged with 'fraud and deceit' and 'gross insolvency' but the charges were dropped.

Falwell was not interested in political activism until the late 1970s, when he began to publicly espouse his views on topics related to sex, such as opposition to abortion, homosexuality and pornography. Falwell promoted 'family values' which, to a considerable extent, involved traditional sex roles. He also opposed gambling, military spending cuts and the Equal Rights Amendment; he supported prayer in public schools, free enterprise,

Israel and a balanced budget. He lent his support to the anti-gay campaigns in Miami in 1977 and in California in 1978. Falwell's quip that God created 'Adam and Eve, not Adam and Steve' is still widely quoted by Christian homophobes.

In 1979 Falwell established the Moral Majority with the assistance of a group of inter-denominational conservatives with political experience. It was a secular enterprise but advocated essentially the same views as Falwell promoted on his *Old Time Gospel Hour*. The Moral Majority was credited with being influential in the defeat of a number of prominent liberal candidates for Congress in the 1980 US elections, and in the success of several conservative candidates, including Ronald REAGAN.

Despite these achievements, Falwell and the evangelical right failed to have their agenda made into public policy. Their cause was not assisted by the well-publicised discrediting of prominent evangelists like Jimmy Swaggart, Jim Bakker and Pat Robertson, and Falwell's pronouncements about economic and foreign policy made him sound more like a fascist than a religious leader concerned with individual morality. Falwell's strong rhetoric alienated people who believed in individual freedom. He slowly moderated his views as he became more powerful, but then began to lose support from conservative hardliners. Contributions began to dwindle and in 1989 the Moral Majority ceased operations. An attempt to revitalise the organisation ended in tax fines against Falwell in 1993 for using profits from the *Old Time Gospel Hour* to fund a political action committee.

Falwell continues to make news. He sued Larry Flynt for comments made about him in *Hustler* magazine. The case eventually went to the US Supreme Court and Falwell lost decisively. Falwell has been outspoken against President Clinton, and he offended many when he said that the anti-Christ is Jewish. He has also expressed concern about the 'Teletubbies', and the Y2K millennium computer bug. In regard to the last threat, Falwell suggested that people stock up on food, water and weapons in case social unrest broke out as a result of the disruption which might occur if computers failed.

Larry Martz with Ginny Carroll, *Ministry of Greed: The Inside Story of the Televangelists and their Holy Wars* (New York, 1988); Charles Moritz (ed.), *Current Biography Yearbook 1981* (New York, 1981); Sean Wilentz, review of Jerry Falwell, *Strength for the Journey: An Autobiography*, in *New Republic*, vol. 198, no. 17 (25 April 1988), pp. 30–8.

Gerard Sullivan

Fashanu, Justin (1961–98), British sportsman. Justin Fashanu was born in London, the elder son of a Nigerian law student and a Guyanese nurse. His parents split up when he was a child and he and his brother, John, also a footballer, were sent to a Dr Barnardo's orphanage before later adoption. After leaving school he became a footballer with Norwich City, and was quickly successful, finishing the 1979–80 season as the club's leading goalscorer. In 1981 he was transferred to Nottingham Forest, becoming the first million pound black player, but never lived up to his early promise, though he played once for England's second team. After short spells with smaller clubs in England and North America he ended his career in Scotland in 1994, eventually being dismissed from Hearts for 'conduct unbecoming a professional footballer'. In the 1980s Fashanu had declared his homosexuality, the first – and still the only – professional football player in Britain to do so, and his career was affected by homophobia in both the black community and in English football, as well as by a serious knee injury. After the collapse of his football career Fashanu went into a self-destructive spiral, falsely claiming that he had sexual relations with senior Members of Parliament, and he eventually went to live in the US. At the time of his death – suicide in London –

he was wanted by American police on a charge of sexual assault.

John Connell

Fassbinder, Rainer Werner (1945–82), German filmmaker. Born in Bavaria, Fassbinder began his professional life working in the theatre in Munich in 1968, but achieved fame as a film director. The last of the forty-three films he made in thirteen years, *Querelle* (1982), remains one of the best known. A dramatisation of Jean GENET's novel *Querelle de Brest*, it featured Brad Davis as a handsome, hunky sailor involved in multiple social and sexual liaisons in the erotic world of a harbour-city; a scene in which Querelle is raped by a black man achieved notoriety. Several of Fassbinder's earlier films had treated homosexual themes as well. *The Bitter Tears of Petra von Kant* (1972), in which not a single man appeared, focused on the life of a lesbian fashion designer who falls tragically in love with one of her female models. *Fox and His Friends* (1975), in which Fassbinder himself played the main role, recounted the story of a crude working-class homosexual who falls in love, again tragically, with a glamorous young man. *In a Year of Thirteen Moons* (1978), dedicated to one of Fassbinder's male lovers (who had committed suicide), centred on the last days of a transsexual who searches for former friends and lovers, including the man for whom she had a sex-change operation but who ultimately rejected her.

Others of Fassbinder's films provided searing views of post-war Germany or focused on recent German history, examining the exploitation of women, migrant workers and other marginal figures. Among those which attracted most attention – often with the actress Hanna Schygulla – were *Ali – Fear Eats the Soul* (1974), *Effi Briest* (1974), *The Marriage of Maria Braun* (1979) and *Veronika Voss* (1982). Fassbinder's films were often visually ugly and intentionally contrived in staging but innovative for their techniques. His characters, viewed with pity, are generally social victims condemned to despair and suffering because of the hypocrisies of capitalist, bourgeois society.

Fassbinder's films were confronting and provocative; he was taken to task by some critics for his insistence on the unhappiness and passivity of his characters (especially the gay and lesbian ones). His somewhat doctrinaire political stance, which Richard Dyer sees as 'left-wing melancholy', now appears naive. Fassbinder's lasting importance resides in his contestatory view of contemporary society, his attention to both present-day and historical issues and, for gays and lesbians, his presentation of strongly drawn and memorable, even if not always likeable, homosexual characters. In this achievement, Fassbinder bears comparison with several other gay filmmakers of the postwar years, Pier Paolo PASOLINI; and Derek JARMAN.

Fassbinder died from an alcohol and drug overdose.

Tony Rayns, *Fassbinder* (London, 1979); Thomas Elsaesser, *Fassbinder's Germany: History, Identity, Subject* (Amsterdam, 1981); Robert Katz, *Life Is Colder Than Death: The Life and Times of Rainer Werner Fassbinder* (New York, 1987).

Robert Aldrich

Fernandez, Dominique (b. 1929), French writer. Fernandez is a novelist, essayist, academic, travel-writer, literary and music critic, translator, author of one libretto and reader for the publishing house Grasset. Born in Neuilly-sur-Seine, France, to a middle-class intellectual family, he is the son of Ramon Fernandez, a renowned writer and critic (of Mexican and French parentage). Ramon Fernandez, who died in 1944, is now remembered mainly for swinging from extreme left-wing politics in the 1930s to collaboration with the occupying Germans during World War II.

Though haunted by the stigma of his father's involvement with fascism, Fernandez scaled French intellectual heights: admission to the top-flight École Normale Supérieure, successful completion of both the *agrégation* (competitive examination giving access to top *lycée* and university teaching posts) and a doctoral thesis (1967) on the gay Italian writer Cesare Pavese. An otherwise successful engagement teaching French at the French Institute in Naples (1957–58) came to an abrupt end after the scandal created by his lecture 'Eroticism and Communism in the Work of Vailland'. From 1966–89 he was Professor of Italian at the University of Haute-Bretagne, contributing significantly to Italianist scholarship. He married in 1961 and had two children, Laetitia and Ramon, by his wife Diane (née Jacquin de Margerie), before divorcing her in 1971 and publicly assuming his homosexuality.

Fernandez has a fairly unusual identity in French society. On the one hand, he is a respected member of the intellectual and literary establishment – author of scholarly works and literary theory (*L'Arbre jusqu'aux racines* (*Right Down to the Tree Roots*, 1972), for instance, elaborates his own method of psychobiographical criticism), as well as sixteen novels, and recipient of seven prestigious literary prizes, including the Goncourt. On the other hand, his novels since 1978 deal directly and affirmatively with homosexuality, and he contributed many articles to the contestatory gay magazines *Gai Pied* and *Masques*. After publishing three homo-erotic but closeted novels, he shot to literary fame with the Médicis' Prize-winning *Porporino ou les mystères de Naples* (*Porporino or Naples' Mysteries*, 1974), the tale of an eighteenth-century castrato. The novel depicts homosexual desire openly, if tentatively, for the first time in his writing, and Fernandez has since commented that in this novel, castration functions as a symbol of the homosexual's fate in a hostile environment. His unequivocal literary coming-out, however, was in 1978 with

L'Étoile rose (*The Pink Star*), a remarkable combination of documentary, essay, autobiography and fiction which historicises and politicises homosexual life in France, and takes issue with a large range of writers and theorists who have pontificated about homosexuality. *L'Étoile rose* is said to have been a favourite bedside book of Gaston Defferre, who as French Minister of the Interior in 1981 banned gay-bashing by the police, and is likely to have had a heavy input in the 1982 law equalising the gay age of consent with the straight.

An increasingly favourite genre adopted by Fernandez is the imaginary autobiography, in which he projects himself into the personae of notable historical personages who are known to have, or thought to have, loved men: writer and film-director Pier Paolo PASOLINI (*Dans la main de l'ange* (*In the Hand of the Angel*), 1982), religious painter Friedrich Overbeck (*L'Amour* (*Love*), 1986), last member of the Medici family Gian Gastone (*Le Dernier des Médicis* (*The Last of the Medicis*), 1994), and composer Tchaikovsky (*Tribunal d'honneur* (*Court of Honour*), 1996). In these works, Fernandez is exploring the largely censored homosexuality of well-known personalities from the past, whilst simultaneously using his immense erudition and love for the arts to paint vibrant portraits of different national societies and histories, united only by their common homophobia.

Younger French gays, however, often brush aside these weighty credentials, tending to view Fernandez as a reactionary who purveys a disempowering image of gay men. Such cold-shouldering arises from Fernandez's regular literary use of homosexuality as a metaphor for what I have elsewhere called 'privileged pariahdom'. Particular wrath was aroused in activist circles by *La Gloire du paria* (*The Outcast's Glory*, 1987), often misunderstood and vilified as a morbid glamorisation of AIDS in the name of heroic martyrdom and gay atonement for past promiscuities. Fernandez set the record straight on this charge in *Le Rapt de Ganymède* (*The Abduction of Ganymede*, 1989), his wide-ranging study of homosexuality and the arts: far from cashing in on a fashionable subject, *La Gloire du paria* used AIDS as a new vehicle for the trope marking much of his previous fiction – the glory of the outcast. It is often ignored that this was one of the very first AIDS novels published in France, and that amongst other things it represents an indictment of both homophobia and social rejection of PWAs.

There is, however, an undeniable tension in Fernandez between an ethic and an aesthetic, between the gay man and his artistic ideal of homosexuality. In an interview in 1995, he summed this up candidly: 'I'm very divided because, as a citizen, I rejoice in the freedom we've gained. . . . That has to be a priority. But as a writer and a reader of novels I'm perplexed because I notice that permissiveness has trivialized homosexual culture. As soon as we can calmly reveal everything, we lose any specificity and often what you get are merely stories about sleeping around which are just as boring as heterosexual stories.'

Fernandez is, then, something of a paradox: a gay, formerly married man who had the courage to divorce and come out, who did his bit for the early activist cause, who strongly supported the campaign in France for the variously named *contrat d'union civile*/*contrat d'union sociale*/*pacte civil de solidarité* (which grants to non-married couples, straight or gay, similar rights to those enjoyed by married couples); and yet also a distinguished writer who, in the artistic sphere, laments the passing of the age of gay marginality as the loss of the pariah's glory. French critic Alain Clerval is surely right in calling him a Romantic.

Robert Aldrich, *The Seduction of the Mediterranean: Writing, Art and Homosexual Fantasy* (London, 1993), pp. 44–5, 192–8, 252; Lucille

Cairns, *Privileged Pariahdom: Homosexuality in the Novels of Dominique Fernandez* (Berne, 1996); Frédéric Martel, *Le Rose et le noir: Les homosexuels en France depuis 1968* (Paris, 1996), *passim*; Christopher Robinson, *Scandal in the Ink: Male and Female Homosexuality in Twentieth-century French Literature* (London, 1995), *passim*.

Lucille Cairns

Fernie, Lynne (b. 1946), Canadian artist, filmmaker. Fernie achieved international recognition as the co-director of two lesbian-specific films, *Forbidden Love: The Unashamed Stories of Lesbian Lives (1992)* and *Fiction and Other Truths: A Film about Jane Rule (1994)* The award-winning *Forbidden Love*, co-directed by Aerlyn Weissman, and made through the National Film Board, interweaves a dramatisation of a formula lesbian pulp novel of the 1950s with a documentary based on the remembered lives of nine 'gay' women. *Fiction and Other Truths* was independently produced by Great Jane Productions, as was the 1997 video 'Schools Out!'. They are good-looking, funny and smart with an subversive intent to educate.

Until 1994, Fernie was known in Canada as a visual artist and cultural animator often working in highly collaborative work. As a co-founder of *Fireweed: A Feminist Quarterly* she helped bring out the first all-lesbian issue of a journal in Canada in 1982. As part of a group of artists curated by Public Access she designed a giant pixelboard that flashed 'Lesbians Fly Canada: Private Desires/Public Sins' over a main Toronto intersection. She curated and wrote the catalogue for an art exhibit, *Sight Specific: Lesbians and Representation*. It is less publicly known that she was also a lyricist with the band Parachute Club (1983–88) with several gold records to her credit.

Fernie has a fierce intolerance of injustice and unfairness as a result of experiencing it first-hand, growing up one of three children of an impoverished sole-support mother on the wrong side of the tracks in Kilowna, a small town in British Columbia. Office work brought her to Toronto, where at the age of twenty-seven she read *The Female Eunuch* and both a feminist and lesbian light bulb went on. She was able to put her mother's life in the context of an historical vision of women and she was able to unearth her own sexual fantasies. Shortly thereafter she had her first affair with a woman.

Maureen FitzGerald

Fichte, Hubert (1935–86), German author. Fichte lived a series of split identities and wrote from the multiple viewpoints they provided him. He was born the son of a German mother and a Jewish father (who fled Germany and never knew his son). Classified as a 'half-breed' according to the Nazi racial scheme, the boy did not fit in and soon Allied bombings made his home in Hamburg unsafe so, although being raised a Protestant, he was sent to a Catholic orphanage in Bavaria. After the war, his work as an actor brought him into contact with the well-known (and probably homosexual) German author Hans Henny Jahnn, who became his mentor. In the 1950s, Fichte worked on farms in France and northern Germany and also at a children's home in Sweden. His life as a traveller and participant observer had begun.

His life as a writer had already started with stories and articles in those years and by the early 1960s he had found his career as an author. He became famous in literary circles with a series of novels written in an experimental style that employed multiple points of view (e.g. *Das Waisenhaus* (The Orphanage, 1965); *Die Palette* (The Palette, 1968); *Detlevs Imitationen 'Grünspan' (Detlev's Imitations*, 1971)). In each, male adolescent homosexuality, often coupled with acts of violence, figures to a greater or lesser degree. Fichte's style made for difficult reading, but he also did not offer his readers easy answers or much, if any, hope for a stable identity or for the integration of the individual into a larger community. Thus, it is not surprising that his works did not appeal to a broad audience.

Fichte also developed a new and unique style in his essays and books of non-fiction. In the essays, he would extract sentences or paragraphs from the writings of the author who was his subject and interpolate them with his own reactions to them. Most relevant here are his two collections called *Homosexualität und Literatur*, vols I and II (1987, 1988). (The first volume has been published in English as *The Gay Critic*, 1996.) In them, Fichte ranges far and wide along and across the margins. The range is remarkable: Henry James, the Marquis de Sade, PASOLINI, to name but a few. He uncovers the different kinds of homosexualities across times and cultures, reinforcing his own credo of deconstructing identity.

His interests led him to over twenty countries in Africa, the Caribbean and Latin America. Most often he was accompanied by his long-time friend Lenore Mau, a photographer who documented these journeys in her own work. Fichte was fascinated by cultures that resisted the obliterating force of his time and wrote about them in such books as *Xango* (1976) and *Petersilie* (1980), two volumes on 'Afro-American Religions'.

Inspired by Marcel Proust's magnum opus, *Remembrance of Things Past*, Fichte aimed, in the 1980s, to write a 'History of Sensibility' by linking his fiction and non-fiction, already published and yet-to-be-written, into one great work. He sketched out its components many times; it would be made up of approximately sixteen to nineteen works (depending on which plan one reads). The epic remains unfinished, as Fichte died before completing it. This parallels perhaps the central role that autobiography played in all Fichte's work, fiction or non-fiction.

Thomas Beckermann (ed.), *Hubert Fichte:*

Materialien zu Leben und Werk (Frankfurt am Main, 1985); Hartmut Böhme, *Hubert Fichte: Riten des Autors und Leben der Literatur* (Stuttgart, 1992); Hubert Fichte, *The Gay Critic*, trans. Kevin Gavin (Ann Arbor, 1996); Wolfgang von Wangenheim, *Hubert Fichte* (Munich, 1980).

James W. Jones

Finch, Peter (1916–77), British-Australian actor. Raised by relatives in France, India and, from the age of 10, in Australia after his parents' divorce, he had a variety of jobs (including working as a swagman travelling across Australia), before going on the stage (1935) and making his first film, *Dad and Dave Come to Town*, in 1938. By the 1940s he was the country's leading radio actor.

Famously heterosexual – his lovers later included Vivien Leigh and Shirley Bassey – Finch was a man with an enormous appetite for life. Taken to Britain as protégé of Laurence Olivier in 1949 he soon established himself as an interesting screen presence; reports of his drunken binges and 'hellraising' added a measure of danger which was lacking in most home-grown stars. Having finally made his international breakthrough as Audrey Hepburn's virile ungodly tempter in *The Nun's Story* (1959) , it was perhaps doubly courageous a year later for him to risk Hollywood stardom to accept the role of Oscar Wilde: he brought great sincerity and some flair to *The Trials of Oscar Wilde*, winning the first of an unprecedented five British Academy Awards.

A decade after playing Wilde, Finch stepped in to replace an ailing actor in John Schlesinger's semi-autobiographical depiction of two love affairs involving a bisexual man. In *Sunday, Bloody Sunday* (1971) he played 'a man with certain emotional problems which have nothing to do with the sex of the person he's involved with. It might just as easily be a girl, but it happens to be a boy . . . Homosexuality is just a fact about a character not presented at all as an issue.' About his groundbreaking kiss and bed scene with Murray Head in the film (for which he was nominated for an Oscar) he airily dismissed any discomfort: 'I lay back and thought of England.'

With these two films, Finch was the first star to play on screen both a sympathetic gay role and then another, equally complex but this time sexually explicit character. He opened the door through which, in the subsequent forty years, only a relatively small number of people, usually heterosexual, have passed. These include Dirk BOGARDE, Richard Chamberlain, Alan Bates, Marcello Mastroianni, Gérard Depardieu, Richard Burton, Marlon Brando, William Hurt, Rod Steiger, John Hurt, Antonio Banderas, Gary Oldman, Rupert Everett and Tom Hanks.

Keith Howes

Findley, Timothy (b. 1930), Canadian writer. Findley was born in Toronto to a well-to-do family of Anglo-Irish origins, although the Depression brought temporary economic setback and childhood sickness cut short his education. His first choice of career was ballet, but a fused disk eliminated that possibility. His next choice was acting. He participated in the first Stratford (Ontario) Shakespearean Festival in 1953, beside Tyrone Guthrie and Alec Guinness, before going to the Central School of Speech and Drama in London. A year later, he toured Britain and the US in *The Matchmaker*, its playwright Thornton Wilder encouraging him to consider writing.

In 1962, after a brief failed marriage, and difficult years as a struggling actor–writer, he met his life-long companion William Whitehead, with whom he moved to a rural Ontario farmhouse where both could more easily write. Findley's first novel, *The Last of the Crazy People* (1967), took the position of the watchful outsider and displayed an attachment to animals and an intrigue with acts of irrational violence that were to be replayed in later

work. His award-winning book *The Wars* (1977) focuses on a World War I soldier who rebels against military authority and its codes of destructive masculinity. *Famous Last Words* (1981) tackles the connection between fascism and aestheticism during World War II. The 'Minna and Bragg' stories in his collections *Stones* (1988) and *Dust to Dust* (1997) probe the special tensions of living as a gay man in contemporary society. His 1993 play *The Stillborn Lover* presents its diplomat-hero as 'stillborn' because of his covert homosexual desires.

Although his novels and most of his other work do not focus on homosexuality, they do raise questions about traditional gender roles and draw sympathetic portraits of women and of various characters on the margin. He is now quite open about his own gayness, but has wanted to avoid being labelled as a gay writer. He has himself said, 'I'm not turning my back on homosexuality ... I just don't think I want to be collected exclusively in gay anthologies ... I want my world to be wider than my sexuality.' Since the early 1990s he has enjoyed wide popularity and critical acclaim.

Findley and Whitehead now divide their time between southern France and Stratford, Ontario.

Carol Roberts, *Timothy Findley: Stories from a Life* (Toronto, 1994); Laurie Kruk, 'I Want Edge: An Interview with Timothy Findley', *Canadian Literature*, no. 148 (Spring 1996, pp. 115–29); Lorraine M. York, 'Timothy Findley', in *Canadian Writers and Their Works*, Fiction Series, vol. 12, ed. Robert Lecker *et al.*, (Toronto, 1995), pp. 71–120.

Laurie Kruk

Fini, Leonor (1908–96), Argentine-Italian artist. Fini was a self-taught painter who exhibited with the surrealists but refused to be so categorised, preferring to maintain her autonomy. She was born in Buenos Aires to parents of mixed Argentinian and European background, but from 1920 grew up in her mother's home in Trieste, Italy. After being expelled from every school she attended, she studied the old and new masters in museums and anatomy at the morgue. She was also involved in theatre design and book illustration and moved to Paris around 1936. Her work explores issues of matriarchy, lesbianism and androgyny, using the subject matter of her personal totem, the cat, alchemical female characters and women as powerful sorceresses. She achieved a considerable reputation in Europe and died in Paris.

Whitney Chadwick, *Women Artists and the Surrealist Movement* (London, 1985); Constantin Jelenski, *Leonor Fini* (London, 1972).

Elizabeth Ashburn

Flanner, Janet (1892–78), American journalist. Flanner was born in Indianapolis, Indiana, where her father was a mortician and her mother was a poet and playwright active in their community. Her mother, in particular, fostered the education and artistic involvement of her daughters during their years at Tudor Hall, a private school. In 1910 the family spent a year in Berlin, and after returning to the US in 1912 her father committed suicide, an event which left Janet depressed for some time afterwards, yet she enrolled at the University of Chicago.

Flanner then took a job working at a model Quaker girls' reformatory in Philadelphia but left to return to Indiana, where in 1917 she was hired by the drama editor of *The Indianapolis Star* to review vaudeville and burlesque shows. Later that year she was promoted to assistant drama editor with her own byline. In 1918 she married William Lane Rehm and moved to New York City, but she stayed with him only briefly, finding that marriage did not suit her. She was physically and emotionally attracted to women, and soon fell in love with Solita Solano, a 30 year-old writer from Boston then living in New York City; Solano remained a major love of hers throughout her life. In 1921 they

travelled to Greece for three months, and then moved to Paris where they lived for the next sixteen years.

In 1925 Jane Ross, a friend, introduced Flanner to her husband Harold's new magazine, *The New Yorker*, and Flanner took over writing the 'Letter From Paris' column, using the pen name 'Genêt'. This column became a key litertary achievement through her career, with a series of profiles of living figures for the magazine. During her first years in Paris, Flanner began work on a novel about sexual freedom and the destructive nature of jealousy, *The Cubical City*, which was published in 1926 to mixed reviews.

By 1932 Flanner had fallen in love with Noel Murphy, an expatriate American woman and a tall, flamboyant arts aficionado and singer, who lived on a farm in France.

Flanner was noted for her timely and insightful cultural and political commentaries. She offered well-developed pieces on new developments in European arts, literature, politics, economics, biography and daily life to readers based primarily in the US. During the years leading up to and during World War II her contributions were particularly sensitive to tensions arising in Europe. She travelled to Germany in 1935, where she became increasingly aware of Nazi persecution of Jews and began drafting a profile of Adolf Hitler. From the end of 1942 to the beginning of 1944 she immersed herself in a four-part profile of Marshal Pétain, the head of Vichy France. These articles were compiled into a book, *Petain: The Old Man of France* (1944), which received a very favourable response.

She resumed work on *The Cubical City* in 1944, seeking more focus on her inner life. In 1948 she resumed writing her 'Letter From Paris' column and initiated work on a similar 'Letter From Naples' column, which drew her more closely to socialism because of its orientation towards women.

In 1952 she was diagnosed with sclerosis of the liver, but nevertheless adroitly testified in her friend Kay Boyle's trial in Germany about the differences she saw between anti-fascist and pro-communist stances. By 1954 she had completed a profile of André Malraux, and in 1956 published *Men and Monuments*, a biography of the art dealer Karl Habenstock; in 1957–58 she encountered legal action when Habenstock's widow claimed the book libelled her husband's reputation, but the claim was dropped. For the latter part of her life Flanner divided her time between France and the US, though Paris remained her spiritual home.

She always maintained close relationships with lesbians in Europe and the US, although she preferred more understated expressions of sexuality. As she grew older she became particularly devoted to her friends' well-being; the year 1960 brought increasing concern about Nancy Cunard's excessive drinking and violent, abusive behaviour. In 1963 she returned to France to assist Alice B. Toklas, who was having both financial and physical difficulties. During the 1960s and 1970s she worked primarily on her books, including *Paris Journal*, which in 1966 won a National Book Award, and *Paris Was Yesterday* (1971). She received numerous awards, but by that point her health was not good and she suffered two heart attacks in 1975 before dying in an ambulance en route to a hospital in New York City.

Janet Flanner, *Janet Flanner's World: Uncollected Writings 1932–1975*, ed. Irving Drutman (New York, 1979); Claude Summers (ed.), *The Gay and Lesbian Literary Heritage* (New York, 1995); Brenda Wineapple, *Genêt: A Biography of Janet Flanner* (New York, 1989).

Sarah Holmes

Flood, Maurice (1941–91), Canadian activist. Flood is best known for pioneering gay liberation activism in Vancouver. He was born in the Bronx (New York) of an Irish Roman Catholic family, and before leaving New York became enamoured of the progressive politics of the Catholic

Workers League. By the time he migrated to Vancouver, in 1970, he had married Cynthia Creighton, a daughter of one of Canada's most eminent historians. It was after moving that Flood told his wife of his homosexuality. They stayed together, parenting two daughters, and she helped support him financially through the years that he threw himself into gay activism – she was herself active in left-feminism.

He was a founder of one of Canada's first left activist groups – the Gay Alliance Toward Equality (GATE) and a leading organiser and writer for the early liberationist magazine *Gay Tide*. For the next eight years, he remained GATE's leading strategist and idea-generator, and one of Canada's most important early activist figures. (He left the group and the city in 1979, and the group disbanded in 1980.) He came to liberationist politics from the socialist left, though in 1974 he severed connections with the Young Socialists because of what he saw as their inadequate understanding of and commitment to gay liberation. He remained loyal to a progressive politics that combined Marxist and feminist analyses throughout his years at GATE, and the group itself remained largely committed to such politics. He argued from the early 1970s that gays and lesbians could and should receive support from the labour movement, and appeared before the executive of the British Columbia Federation of Labour to argue the point. In 1974, he led a GATE contingent in a labour protest against government-imposed wage and price controls.

Under Flood's leadership, GATE was entirely ready to use mainstream political channels to its advantage. From its beginnings, the group lobbied the British Columbia government to include sexual orientation in provincial human rights legislation, though it received no satisfaction even when the social democratic New Democratic Party came to power in 1973. When the *Vancouver Sun* refused to print a GATE advertisement for *Gay Tide* in that same year, the group launched a court challenge that eventually became the first sexual orientation case to be heard by the Supreme Court of Canada. The case was lost, but it gained considerable publicity and politicised many people. The case was an example of GATE's and Flood's conscious strategy of provoking discrimination in order to raise awareness of it and to combat it.

Flood moved to San Francisco after his years of Vancouver activism, retaining close contact with his daughters until his death from AIDS.

Miriam Smith, 'Social Movements and Equality Seeking: The Case of Gay Liberation in Canada', *Canadian Journal of Political Science*, vol. 31 (June 1998), pp. 285–310.

David Rayside

Flores, Joseph (1907–74), Maltese judge, politician. Born at Hamrun, he studied law at the University of Malta, where he later taught.

Flores attempted to enter politics in 1932, but was defeated. In 1950, he was elected to the legislative assembly as a member of the Malta Labour Party through three elections. In 1955 he served as Speaker of the Maltese Parliament; the same year he was appointed a judge. In 1971 he became vice-president of the Constitutional Court. He retired from public life in 1972.

Widely known as a homosexual, Flores appears to have had a soft spot for the working-class homosexual. Flores was a close friend of Herbert Ganado, editor of *Lehen is-Sewwa*, an ultraconservative Catholic newspaper. At Ganado's wedding, Flores was his best man. On the eve of the wedding, Flores dressed up as a woman, and on another occasion, Flores and others put on a drag show sending up Queen Victoria.

Flores regularly visited Queens, a coffee shop and reputed homosexual haunt. He often did the beats either on foot or driving in his car. Flores has been romantically

linked with Ganado and Gerry Zammit, a trade unionist, both deceased.

Some commentators have praised Flores as judge for the way he 'humanised punishment'. Regrettably Flores' concern seldom extended to defendants charged with homosexuality. He invariably handed down very harsh sentences. Flores exemplifies the hypocrisy of the Maltese establishment. So long as he paid lip service to the island's Christian morality, he was allowed the freedom to enjoy a discreet homosexual lifestyle, a lifestyle denied to many others.

H. Ganado, *Rajt Malta Tinbidel*, vol. II (Malta, 1977).

Joseph Chetcuti

Fluvià, Armand de (b. 1926), Spanish activist. Fluvia was one of the key figures in the Spanish gay movement of the 1970s and he has remained an outspoken advocate of the gay cause ever since.

Fluvià's story follows the story of Spanish activism. He was born into a wealthy family and had a sheltered childhood. He grew up in Francoist Barcelona, in Catalonia, a Spanish region that the dictator did his best to degrade and humiliate, banning the Catalan language and expressions of national identity. Political and sexual repression were experienced as interlinked, and even today Fluvià associates Spanish centralism with backward, reactionary attitudes. Being both a nationalist and a homosexual were forbidden until well into the 1970s. Fluvià studied law and started by using his profession to defend the causes in which he believed. He defended victims of sexual intolerance and also established a network of contacts among gay intellectuals. He even organised meetings in his own residence and worked on clandestine publications. Under a pseudonym, he appeared as a Spanish representative in several international fora.

Francoism ended in 1975, but Fluvià's career as a gay activist had hardly started by then. He was among the group of intellectuals to start an unambiguous struggle to eliminate the homophobic 'Ley de Peligrosidad y Rehabilitación Social', an item of legislation that could and did get used against homosexuals, from the penal code. At the same time, a great deal of work was to be done: the 1970s were in Spain the golden age of 'associationism', and homosexuality was no exception. Fluvià helped organise and fund a number of gay groups both in Catalonia and in the rest of Spain. He co-authored the first gay manifesto published in Spain, as the key document of the FAGC (Front d'Alliberament Gai de Catalunya). This is a strikingly 'modern' statement for a country with no gay tradition. The social fate of homosexuals as members of society is linked to other concerns of the left, like the liberation of women and the fight against social repression; the view given of homosexuality dismisses a stable notion of 'gay identity' to follow current, more radical formulations (by Guy HOCQUENG-HEM and others) that point toward boundless libidinal freedom. In the next few years, between 1977 and 1982, he founded several gay groups in Catalonia which often combined both nationalist and sexual concerns. Indeed, gathering together several oppressed groups seems to have been close to Fluvià's heart. He remembers fondly the support lent by the unions and other left-leaning organisations and the enthusiasm shown in demonstrations and other gatherings. If 1982 was a watershed year for the Spanish gay movement, it was also a critical moment. The recent arrival of the Socialist government to power gave the impression that activism was now unnecessary. The oncoming of the AIDS crisis to a country with still weak gay institutions was a serious setback from which the Spanish gay movement would take ten years to recover. Fluvià worked tirelessly in those years for the gay community. He co-edited with Alberto CARDÍN the earliest gay-oriented anthologies of articles on AIDS, and kept on being visible in the media. He also collaborated

with the increasingly rare gay publications during this period, and he became the driving force behind the news magazine *Lambda*. But somehow he did not find the necessary response. Fluvià lives in Barcelona. He is far from inactive: he has taken a clear stance on some issues that more 'respectable' (i.e. 'assimilationist') branches of the gay movement regard as too risky, such as pederasty.

Armand de Fluvià *et al.*, *Manifest. Front d'alliberament gai de Catalunya* (Barcelona, 1977), and 'La represión legal' and 'El movimiento homosexual en el estado español', in José Ramón Enríquez (ed.), *El homosexual ante la sociedad enferma* (Barcelona, 1978).

Alberto Mira

Fogedgaard, Helmer (b. 1907), Danish publicist. Fogedgaard grew up as the son of a wealthy farmer and local politician in Langeland, an island in the western Baltic. He was apprenticed to a shopkeeper, and was then employed at the Ølandenes Frøkontor A/S in Rudkøbing, Langeland, a company trading in seeds. The company was bought by Fogedgaard and his father around 1930, and Fogedgaard was managing director until the company was wound up in 1972.

At the same time that Axel AXGIL and his friends in 1948 made plans to found an organisation for homosexuals, Fogedgaard planned to launch a magazine. Mutual friends made them aware of each other and the two projects were combined. *Vennen* (*The Friend*) was published by the Forbundet af 1948 (the Association of 1948, later the National Union of Homophiles, still later the National Union of Gays and Lesbians) from January 1949 till early in 1952, when a large accumulated deficit made it necessary to form an independent publishing company which was partly financed by Fogedgaard and informally associated with the Forbundet. At first under the pseudonym 'Homophilos', later under his own name, Fogedgaard was the editor of *Vennen* from

1949 to 1953. The magazine was distributed to subscribers and to members of the Forbundet only, until in 1951 it became available at a few newsstands in Copenhagen and the larger provincial towns. From early on, *Vennen* had a fairly large readership in Sweden and Norway. Fogedgaard continued as a regular contributor of comments on homophilia and society until the magazine was taken over in 1955–56 by people not associated with the Forbundet. For some years Fogedgaard's articles appeared in *Pan*, launched in 1954 by the Forbundet as a journal exclusively for its members.

The concept 'homophile' was introduced in *Vennen* in May 1950 by Fogedgaard, who was unaware that the word had also been coined a few months previously by Jaap van Leeuwen in the Netherlands. The intent of the word was to divert attention from genital sexuality and to underline love between adults of the same sex as a respectable emotion and a legitimating quality.

Fogedgaard's fearless and lucid running commentary and criticism of the authorities, the police and the press had an edge which demonstrated that he did not gladly suffer fools. 'The dogs howl at the passing caravan, but the caravan passes by' was his favourite proverb. However, the almost Voltairian viciousness and retaliatory quality of his articles did not reach far. *Vennen* was not cited in the straight press, which concentrated on the immorality and the sexual perversity of *Vennen's* personal ads.

The rebellious character of Fogedgaard's style as editor of *Vennen* mirrored the comparatively unrestrained behaviour of sexually active homosexuals during the period after World War II. However, the heightened visibility of Copenhagen's homophile subculture became a part of the background of the dramatically augmented oppression of homosexuals which followed in the 1950s. In the wake of the efforts of the Copenhagen Police Department to undermine the Forbundet and

Vennen (the so-called Pornography Scandal, 1955–56) a large number of homosexuals were arrested and sentenced for having had sex with minors. The experience of numerous sexually active homosexuals targeted by the police as potential or actual criminals added an element of dread and apprehension of heterosexual society to the mentality of the homophile. Fogedgaard was arrested in July 1955 and briefly held in custody. As a consequence of the events in 1955–56, the Forbundet lost its credibility within the homophile subculture, almost collapsed financially, and was reduced to political impotence for the following ten years.

In 1998 Fogedgaard summed up: 'It was an exciting period. We saw the magazine as an instrument for fighting. At the same time we felt sorry for each other. It was a strange contradiction: outwardly we fought; inside, we were marked by our not daring yet to come out.'

All of his life Fogedgaard has lived in the small provincial town of Rudkøbing, since at least 1955 as a well-known homosexual. He was made an honorary member of the National Union of Gays and Lesbians in 1974. He entered into a registered partnership in 1994 with life-companion since 1955, Johnny Köhler.

Helmer Fogedgaard, *Sådan er jeg. Et liv med mange facetter* (Rudkøbing, 1977); Axel Axgil and Helmer Fogedgaard, *Homofile kampår. Bøsseliv gennem tiderne* (Rudkøbing, 1985); Interview in *PAN-Bladet*, No. 4 (1998).

Wilhelm von Rosen

Foix, Vicente Molina (b. 1946), Spanish writer. Molina Foix is one of the few Spanish intellectuals who openly support homosexuals, people affected by HIV and gay liberation. He used his column in Madrid's daily *El País* to comment on controversial issues such as the 'Arny affair' (involving the mis-reporting of a case of male prostitution in a Seville pub) and institutionalised homophobia. He even dared to refer to Spanish poet and Nobel

Prize winner Vicente ALEIXANDRE as a gay man in a time when homosexuality was taboo. As most intellectuals of his age, he always maintained a clear political attitude of opposition to the military regime of General Franco, who ruled the country for nearly four decades until his death in 1975. Molina Foix's early novels are reminiscent of expressionist aesthetics, where absurdity and the grotesque play a central role. In recent years, a more vivid sense of humour has become one of his narrative landmarks. A mixture of both elements can be found in the comic thriller *La mujer sin cabeza*.

Homosexual themes are prevalent in his literary works, especially in the two-part narrative *La comunión de los atletas* (1979) and *Los Ladrones de niños* (1989), where homosexuality and paedophilia are interestingly combined, although no clear conclusions are advanced. Adolescent homosexuality as a narrative topos is also central to his, perhaps, best novel, *La quincena soviética* (1988). The novel *La comunión de los atletas* focuses on the misadventures of an upper-middle-class mature man, José Lorenzo, involved in a case of paedophilia. The young boy, it is suggested, was willing to have sex with the older man, but his family, the judges and society at large explicitly deny such a possibility. Eventually, the man is found guilty and put in gaol for an excessively long period. He uses his term to recall his relations, as a teenager, with another young boy. Homosexuality is not openly discussed in the novel, as if it was not an issue for the main character nor for the rest of society; paradoxically, homosexual desire is the dramatic base for the whole narrative. As a poet, Molina Foix was anthologised by José María Castellet in his groundbreaking *Nueve Novísimos* (1970). He wrote for the stage 'Don Juan Último' (subsequently directed by Robert Wilson) and 'Seis armas cortas'. He has translated some of Shakespeare's plays into Spanish. Molina Foix is an important voice in Spanish cinema criticism; he currently writes for the popular magazine *Cinemanía*.

Laura Silvestri, 'Vicente Molina Foix o el autorretrato de un novelista', in Alfonso de Toro and Dieter Ingenschay (eds), *La novela española actual: autores y tendencias* (Kassel, 1995), pp. 167–91.

Alfredo Martínez Expósito

Ford, Tom (b. 1963), American fashion designer. Ford is this century's most heroic fashion designer. Not only did he make fashion history in the mid-1990s by single-handedly restoring Gucci, the venerable Italian leather goods company, from near bankruptcy; alongside Miuccia Prada and Helmut Lang, he created some of the strongest influences on contemporary fashion, with sexy, sophisticated and minimalist style. Ford also used his signature cutting, advertising genius and celebrity status to explore the ways in which fashion could make sexuality more inclusive in society.

After a childhood in Texas, Ford attempted a modelling and acting career in Los Angeles and New York, but completed a degree in interior architecture at Parson's School of Design. Interested in fashion, however, Ford pursued work with designer Cathy Hardwick and the Perry Ellis label in New York. In 1990 Ford was hired by Gucci and, by 1994, had become its creative director.

In 1995 Ford dazzled the fashion press with a collection featuring shocking blue, green and chocolate brown, suede, silk and velvet hipster pants paired with satin shirts open to the waist. Glamour, attitude, sex and mod – all reminiscent of disco, funk and the newfound sexual freedom.

The essence of Gucci's success, which led Ford to win the Council of Fashion Designers of America award for Designer of the Year for 1995, was defiance of cultural taboo. The Gucci man was essentially 'soft' and effeminate; his female counterpart 'mannish', 'bitchy' and self-indulgent. Ford created these personas by draping a male torso over furniture or having a male model lie face down on the floor as his counterpart towered above him. Other highly sexualised images were common in his advertising.

Articles in *The Advocate* (in 1997) and *Vanity Fair* (in 1998) made explicit Ford's homosexuality. Ford also admitted to being 'straight' in his adolescent years, and later insisted that 'heterosexuality is still a possibility'.

In 1997 Ford shifted his efforts towards the gay community by using the Gucci name to host an AIDS Project fundraiser in Santa Monica, California. Both dinner and fashion show demonstrated Ford's ethical responsibility towards the fight against AIDS, but more importantly showed how the fashion industry could move past an era of AIDS to revive sexuality in fashion and recognise how sexuality and fashion could never be distinct from the social realities of the day.

Timothy Yap

Foucault, Michel (1926–84), French philosopher. Born in Poitiers, Paul-Michel Foucault (he later dropped 'Paul', his father's Christian name) refused to pursue a medical career as desired by his father, a celebrated surgeon. He studied philosophy in Poitiers and Paris, winning admission to France's elite École Normale Supérieure in 1946. He earned a bachelor's degree in psychology from the Sorbonne in 1949, passed the *agrégation* (France's highest teaching certificate) in philosophy in 1951 and received his doctorate in philosophy in 1961.

After teaching psychology at the University of Lille (1952–55), Foucault served abroad as director of the Maison de France in Uppsala, Sweden (1955–58); the Centre de Civilisation Française in Warsaw, Poland (1958–59); and the Institut Français in Hamburg, Germany (1959–60). He then taught psychology and philosophy at the University of Clermont-Ferrand (1960–68), the University of Tunis (1966–68) and the University of Vincennes (1968–70). In 1970 he was elected to the

Chair in the History of Systems of Thought (created specially for him) at the Collège de France, France's most prestigious institution of higher learning.

As Foucault himself once explained: 'My field is the history of thought . . . The way [one] thinks is related to society, politics, economics and history and is also related to very general and universal categories and formal structures.' He analysed the particular systems of thought that predominated at given historical periods (especially in Europe since the Enlightenment) and the specific institutions that embodied these systems and thereby held society together. For Foucault political and social power was not something imposed directly from above, but was instead widely diffused throughout society ('power is everywhere . . . because it comes from everywhere'). He studied the ideas, institutions and social relationships that constituted this web of power in the past and the present, as well as the resistance that (he believed) power automatically provokes from those subject to it.

Foucault published an impressive list of articles, essays and books, most of them translated into English. His most important books are *Madness and Civilization* (1961, transl. 1965); *The Birth of the Clinic* (1963, transl. 1973), *The Order of Things* (1966, transl. 1970); *Archaeology of Knowledge* (1969, transl. 1972); *Discipline and Punish: The Birth of the Prison* (1975, transl. 1977); and *The History of Sexuality* (3 volumes, 1976–84, transl. 1978–86). Most historians have been critical of the historical dimensions of this work. Lawrence Stone described Foucault's history as 'abstract and metaphoric in expression, unconcerned with historical detail of time or place or with rigorous documentation'. Foucault was indeed much given to sweeping generalisations based on extensive but often unsystematic and incomplete research. On the other hand, he formulated bold, innovative and often brilliant hypotheses that have influenced and inspired philosophers, historians, political scientists and sociologists around the world.

Nor was Foucault an ivory-tower thinker. Over the years, he spoke out against conditions in French prisons; protested the Vietnam War, French racism and police brutality; and actively supported the Solidarity movement in Poland. He also defended gay and lesbian rights, although he was not in any sense an active gay militant. He did not hide his own homosexuality, but he always remained publicly discreet.

Although it is reductionist to consider Foucault's homosexuality the sole or even the principal determinant of his ideas and theoretical positions, his work cannot be entirely separated from his private life. Foucault himself remarked that 'each of my books [has been] fragments of an autobiography. My books are my personal problems with madness, prison, sexuality'. His general conception of the workings of power certainly derived in part from the fact that as a young homosexual in the 1940s and 1950s – a period in France particularly hostile to any manifestation of homosexuality – he saw at first-hand how law, medicine and the Church worked to control people not by outright repression but through a more subtle ideological process of 'normalisation' that transformed the dissident into a criminal, a patient or an outcast.

Foucault's intellectual influence has been strong in the fields of gay and lesbian studies or queer studies, most notably in the English-speaking world (homosexuality is not yet an acceptable subject of academic research in France). In the first volume of *The History of Sexuality* (1976), he advanced the thesis (which he did not originate, but did much to popularise) that homosexuality as we conceive it is a recent social construction. Men and women had always engaged in same-sex relations, but (he claimed) until relatively recently their acts did not confer any specific identity. According to Foucault, medical science 'invented' the homosexual as an 'abnormal' in the years around 1870:

'The sodomite had been a temporary aberration; the homosexual was now a species.'

Foucault's theory has become orthodoxy among so-called 'social constructionists', who oppose the views of 'essentialists', who maintain that homosexuality has existed in one form or another in all cultures across time. As Didier Eribon has written: 'Unfortunately, this [particular] page of *The History of Sexuality* has become a veritable article of faith on the other side of the Atlantic, where books and journals tirelessly repeat that before the late nineteenth century there were not [homosexual] "identities", but only acts between people of the same sex'. Eribon demonstrates, however, that Foucault's opinion on this point was never permanently fixed. In *Madness and Civilization* (1961), he had argued that the homosexual first appeared as an 'abnormal' in the course of the seventeenth and eighteenth centuries and he returned to this view in interviews given in the 1980s. He much admired the study of 'gay people' in the Middle Ages published by John Boswell in 1980 and agreed that 'the feeling [among homosexuals] of belonging to a particular social group . . . goes back to very early times'.

Foucault initially had some trouble dealing with his sexual orientation. He drank heavily as a young man and at least twice attempted suicide, but he came to terms with his homosexuality in the early 1950s and thereafter lived it happily and to the full. He later commented: 'There is objective proof that homosexuality is more interesting than heterosexuality. It's that one knows a considerable number of heterosexuals who would wish to become homosexuals, whereas one knows very few homosexuals who would really like to become heterosexuals'. In 1963 he entered into a romantic relationship with the sociologist Daniel Defert, which lasted until his death. He described his feelings as 'a state of passion toward someone, for someone. Perhaps at some given moment this passion took the form of love'.

Foucault always respected André Baudry and the conservative 'homophile' association, Arcadie, that Baudry founded in 1954. He spoke at a congress organised by BAUDRY in May 1979, declining to accept the fee pressed upon him and declaring that a gay man should not be paid to speak to fellow homosexuals. But he was politically and personally closer to the radicals like Guy HOCQUENGHEM who participated in FHAR (Front Homosexuel d'Action Révolutionnaire, Homosexual Front for Revolutionary Action) in 1971–74. And it was he who suggested the name for *Gai Pied*, France's leading militant gay magazine from 1979 to 1992, founded by Jean Le Bitoux.

By the 1970s, Foucault was an international intellectual celebrity, frequently invited to speak abroad. Having discovered California with its free-wheeling gay subculture and drug scene in 1975, he revisited the state several times, making forays into San Francisco's bath-houses and leather bars. He saw the 'gay ghettoes' of the United States as exciting 'laboratories of sexual experimentation'. He evinced a keen interest in S/M (sado-masochism), which he apparently practised, explaining that 'what all those people are doing is not aggressive; they are inventing new possibilities of pleasure with strange parts of their body – through the eroticization of the body. I think it's . . . a creative enterprise, which has as one of its main features what I call the desexualization of pleasure.'

In the last decade of his life and undoubtedly inspired by what he had seen in the United States, Foucault imagined the possibility of creating new lifestyles through which individuals could both reshape their personal identities and free themselves from the constraints of power. He repeated this idea in numerous interviews in the gay press in the 1980s: 'It is not enough to affirm that we are gay, but it is also necessary to create a gay way of life'. 'To be gay, I believe, is . . . to seek to define and develop a style of life' that 'would give rise to a culture and to an ethic.' 'It's not only a matter of integrating this strange little practice of making love with someone of the same sex into pre-existing cultures; it's a matter of constructing cultural forms.' 'We have to understand that with our desires, through our desires, go new forms of relationships, new forms of love, new forms of creation. Sex is . . . a possibility for creative life.' Like Karl Marx, who never gave any precise description of life under the communism that he advocated, Foucault remained extremely vague about the new gay lifestyle that he desired and predicted, but he apparently saw it as involving the cultivation of friendship and the pursuit of new (sexual) pleasures.

Foucault was at first sceptical about descriptions of a new disease among homosexuals later dubbed AIDS and then, when he accepted its reality, he remained mistrustful of the moralising warnings issued by the press and the public authorities. He typically told a gay American student that it was 'unbelievable' and 'absurd' that gays were 'looking to authorities for lessons: doctors, the Church'. He was 'incensed that a group [gays] . . . are looking to standard authorities for guidance in a time of crisis'. It was probably in California that Foucault himself contracted AIDS. There is contradictory testimony as to whether or not he actually knew that he had the virus, but he certainly suspected as much. He expired in a Paris hospital on 25 June 1984. Family, friends and the press at first concealed the cause of his death, in part because they feared that the truth would somehow discredit his work on sexuality. The left-wing newspaper *Libération* even published an offensive insert expressing dismay at 'the viciousness of the rumour' that the philosopher had died of this 'stylish disease . . . . As if Foucault must have died shamefully'. In contrast, Daniel Defert, Foucault's lover, founded Aides, an association that fights against the disease and promotes safe sex.

David Macey, *The Lives of Michel Foucault* (London, 1993); James Miller, *The Passion of Michel Foucault* (New York, 1993); Didier Eribon, *Michel Foucault* (Cambridge, MA, 1991) and *Réflexions sur la question gay* (Paris, 1999); David M. Halperin, *Saint Foucault* (New York, 1995); Tamsin · Spargo, *Foucault and Queer Theory* (Duxford, Cambridge, 1999).

Michael Sibalis

Francia, John Baptist (1893–1974), Maltese businessman. Francia was a prominent businessman and director of the National Bank of Malta. In 1971, he adopted English-born William Nathaniel Fenton, then aged in his thirties. Fenton possibly reached Malta in the mid-1960s and was probably introduced to Francia by a British officer. In May 1988, Fenton died in the United Kingdom. Francia and Fenton were, in fact, lovers. Their relationship was an open secret notwithstanding their half-hearted attempts to conceal their relationship. At their house, Francia and Fenton also organised formal and informal gay parties at least as early as the 1960s. At the time, Malta's Criminal Code considered homosexual acts criminal yet such laws were seldom enforced against the elite. Fenton's alleged conversion to Catholicism also served to camouflage his homosexuality and to provide him with a convenient reason for wanting to remain in Malta.

Joseph Chetcuti

François, Jocelyne (b. 1933), French poet and novelist. Born in the Lorraine, France, to a petit bourgeois family, François received her secondary education at a convent boarding school, where she latterly fell in love with a fellow schoolfriend, Marie-Claire Pichaud. While studying philosophy at the University of Nancy, she was coerced by the student chaplain – now a bishop – into renouncing this love for the 'good' of her slightly younger partner. Marriage and three children followed swiftly, but after some four years François re-established contact with Pichaud, eventually setting up home with her and one of the children after ending a six-year-long, deadening marriage. Writing, of poetry and of poetic prose, became her foremost activity, earning her critical esteem and the prestigious Prix Fémina in 1980. After many years of tranquil country dwelling, she and Pichaud now live in Paris, where the former writes and the latter paints.

This turbulent trajectory is reflected in François's autobiographical quartet of novels (recently supplemented by a shorter text entitled *Le Sel* (*Salt*, 1992), though proper names are often changed, and order of publication does not follow the chronology of the real-life events recounted therein: François has remarked that 'the autobiographical work obeys . . . the order of inner necessity'.

The first part of the quartet, *Les Bonheurs* (*Kinds of Happiness*, 1970), deals with the private and public dimensions of desire and love between women before the sexual liberation of the post-1968 period. It explicitly depicts erotic relations between two women, and also traces their battle to overcome the various social, institutional and internal barriers to their love, not the least of which is one partner's fear of losing custody of her children. Anne's long battle to free herself from this fear, and also from internalised guilt-feelings, finally results in full reconciliation with Sarah.

Les Amantes (*Two Women in Love*, 1978) recounts the first temptation the couple face – that of François (alias Anne) for a male poet (based on René Char). Initially, she just wants friendship; he wants more. Her motives turn out to be a good deal more complex, and the question of her 'true' sexuality is never neatly resolved, although her final decision is to sacrifice the ambiguous friendship with the male poet in order to preserve the love between herself and her female partner. The text simultaneously inscribes what it is all too easy to compartmentalise as lesbianism and bisexuality, and thus doubly marginalises itself, potentially alienating both a straight readership and advocates of solidaristic lesbian identity-politics.

Joue-nous 'España' (*Play Us 'España'*, 1980) refers to events covered in *Les Bonheurs*, but concentrates on the author's childhood and pre-sexually-aware years. The reduction in her previous focus on love between women may have helped critics to acknowledge François's merit at last, through award of the coveted Prix Fémina.

Histoire de Volubilis (*Tale of Volubilis*, 1986) returns to the more risky business of spotlighting love and desire between women. This time it is François's partner who faces temptation … for another woman. The dynamic of *Les Amantes* is thus reversed, with François (alias Cécile) suffering from her lover Elisabeth's passion for another. Only when the interloper Agatha brutally rejects Elisabeth after four years of prurient interest on her and her male partner's part does the primary, same-sex relationship slowly begin to recover its intimacy and commitment.

François considers the concept of a 'homosexual writer' to be a 'total absurdity'. She abhors the word 'lesbian' and its cognates, claiming that it divides men and women, and dismissing its postulation of a (mythical) hellenic allegiance to the isle of Lesbos and its most famous inhabitant, Sappho. She is generally opposed to any form of segregation. Resistance to any perceived form of recuperation by, or critical assignment to, lesbian or gay interest groups arises from the conviction that her regular contributions to the gay arts review *Masques* in the 1980s led mainstream literary critics to fetishise the sexual thematics of her work, to ignore its aesthetic and philosophical qualities, and to relegate her to a minority group. Further, *Les Amantes* and *Histoire de Volubilis* refuse to place lesbian love in a utopian category, and clearly posit the lesbian couple's permeability to outside attractions, be they gay or straight. Nonetheless, she has openly lived most of her life with a female partner for whom her love and admiration are unmasked, is passionately opposed to any gay individual remaining in the closet, and concedes that 'certainly homosexual readers find in my books a force that gives their choice of love a foundation'. Despite, or perhaps in some adamantly queer cases all the more so because of, François's rejection of identity politics, lesbians and gays may well concur with the author's feeling that her books have had a positive, empowering influence on homosexual readers: 'In clearing homosexual love life of devalorizing and guilt-producing prejudices, I may contribute to the inner restoration of individuals, the strengthening of their being. The many letters I receive year after year from readers confirm this.'

Marguerite de Clézio, 'François, Jocelyne: *Les Amantes*', *French Review*, vol. 56, no. 3 (February 1983), pp. 507–8; Anne Garréta, 'French Lesbian Writers?', in *Same Sex Different Text? Gay and Lesbian Writing in French*, Yale French Studies, no. 90 (1996), pp. 237–9; Jean Royer, 'Jocelyne François: la justesse du regard', *Écrivains contemporains. Entretiens 3: 1980–1983* (Montréal, 1985), pp. 40–7.

Lucille Cairns

Frank, Barney (b. 1940), US politician. In 1997, Frank became the second representative in the United States House of Representatives to come out as gay, the first having been Gerry STUDDS (in 1983). By this time, he had acquired a reputation as one of the smartest and hardest-working politicians in Washington, and had already become an advocate for sexual minority concerns.

Frank was born in 1940 of Jewish parents whose politics were shaped by the period of Franklin D. Roosevelt's 'New Deal'. He himself has been on the left of the Democratic Party, but as a 'prudent liberal', who believes in the free market and who has warned against his party being too closely allied with some of the left causes with which it has been traditionally tied.

Frank first entered politics while a doctoral student in political science at Harvard University, working as an aide to Democratic politicians in Boston and Washington. He first won electoral office in the state legislature of Massachusetts in 1972, and was re-elected in 1974, 1976 and 1978. In 1976 State Representative Elaine NOBLE had come out as a lesbian, the first to do so in the US. That was insufficient inducement to the still-closeted Frank, though he was outspoken in his advocacy for gay/lesbian causes.

In 1980, he ran for the US House of Representatives, in a district that ran south from the suburbs of Boston. His opponent jabbed at his 'bachelor' status and played up 'family' themes, but Frank won the election. He became an extraordinarily diligent representative, and in the elections every two years after that first win, he piled up larger and eventually unassailable majorities.

By the mid-1980s, Frank was half in and half out of the closet, and by now Studds had been re-elected as an out gay man, despite his having been forced out by 'scandal'. The 1987 death from AIDS of a Republican Congressman, provoking media speculation, nudged Frank toward the decision to come out himself, which he did in May of that year. His opponent in the 1988 election had tried to raise the issue of family values, but it failed to dent Frank's majority.

In 1989, a sometime hustler named Steve Gobie talked publicly of a relationship with Frank, and made claims that seemed to jeopardise the Congressman's career. He chose to confront the charges directly and honestly, and survived with a reprimand from the House of Representatives and little damage to his standing at home.

Frank's reputation among fellow politicians quickly recovered, though there are some who speculate that his being openly gay itself might have somewhat slowed his ascent within Democratic ranks. On the other hand, when the Republicans gained

a majority of both houses of Congress in the 1994 elections, Frank was designated one of his party's key spokespeople in debate on the House floor and in the media.

The relative lack of party discipline in American legislative politics gives individual politicians a more significant role than in most other political systems. That has provided room for Frank to play a crucial role in acting as advocate for sexual diversity causes and watchdog for anti-gay initiatives. The anti-gay bent of much of the Republican Party, along with the moral conservativism of a notable minority of the Democratic Party, has made significant legislative advances toward equality difficult to achieve. But the gains that have been made have usually found Frank as an active intervener, and as a near-constant source of advice for activists and lobbyists working for lesbian/gay/bisexual/transgendered organizations. He and his office aides are crucial 'eyes and ears' for the movement inside Capitol Hill. He is also a master strategist, extraordinarily knowledgeable about what compromises are essential to secure gain or avoid defeat.

The 1993 debate over President Clinton's proposal to lift the ban on lesbians and gays serving openly in the US military found Frank once again in the centre of complex political debate, illustrating the difficulty of the role he sought to play. In the face of drastically slipping chances for any progressive movement on the question of the ban, Frank proposed a compromise that came to be labelled 'don't ask, don't tell'. The final legislative outcome acquired that same label, though in fact it represented virtually no change in the pre-existent ban. Frank came under severe criticism from activists for proposing compromise, though his persistent willingness to work on sexual diversity issues in Congress has largely put that controversy behind him among Washington insiders, and among many activists outside the capital.

Between 1993 and 1996, the ranks of

openly gay members of Congress were increased to four, when Repubicans Steve Gunderson and Jim Kolbe came out, though Gunderson and Gerry Studds retired from elective office in 1996. In 1998, Kolbe and Frank were joined by Tammy Baldwin, who became the first lesbian elected to federal legislative office and the first person to run for the first time as openly gay or lesbian and win.

David Rayside, *On the Fringe: Gays and Lesbians in Politics* (Ithaca, 1998); Urvashi Vaid, *Virtual Equality: The Mainstreaming of Gay and Lesbian Liberation* (New York, 1995).

David Rayside

Freedman, Estelle B. (b. 1947), American scholar. Freedman was born in Harrisburg, Pennsylvania, where she was raised in a Jewish community. She graduated from Barnard College, then earned her doctoral degree in history from Columbia University. Freedman taught for two years at Princeton before joining Stanford University's history department. In 1983 Freedman charged that sex discrimination had influenced the administration's decision to reverse her department's recommendation of tenure. Her nationally recognised victory was an important legitimisation of feminist scholarship, an achievement some view as a triumph over unspoken homophobia as well.

Freedman's interest in changing gender boundaries and their impact on women, crime and sexuality led to several influential works: *Their Sisters' Keepers: Women's Prison Reform in America, 1830–1930* (1981) won the Hamilton manuscript prize, followed by *Maternal Justice: Miriam Van Waters and the Female Reform Tradition* (1996). Empathy and identification drew Freedman to the case of prison reformer Van Waters, dismissed from the superintendency of the Massachusetts Reformatory for Women in 1949. The charges that Van Waters had overstepped her authority included accusations of condoning homosexuality among inmates. Enmeshed in her own tenure battle at the time of her research, Freedman dug deep into the professional philosophies as well as the personal life of this important reformer who did not identify as a lesbian but had a deeply romantic relationship with one of her benefactors. Freedman used Van Waters's successful challenge to her dismissal to investigate issues of shifting gender roles in post-war America.

From 1980 to 1985 Freedman was associate editor of *Signs: Journal of Women in Culture and History*. In 1985 she co-edited *The Lesbian Issue: Essays from SIGNS*. Her most influential work, co-authored with John D'EMILIO, is the groundbreaking *Intimate Matters: A History of Sexuality in America* (1988), released in a second edition in 1997. This exceedingly well-researched and fascinating work served as a lynchpin for the explosion of scholarly studies of sexuality. It is especially noteworthy for its detailed study of the evolution of same-sex relationships, particularly as the primary association with sex changed from reproduction to emotional intimacy and sexual pleasure early in the twentieth century.

A full professor at Stanford, Freedman lives with Susan Krieger, her life-partner since 1980. Active in campus politics, Freedman and other scholars have publicly urged Stanford to live up to its commitment to ensure gender and race equity. She has also been a part of the movement lobbying the university to provide gay and lesbian partners of staff members with the same benefits available to spouses. Freedman is nationally recognised for her teaching as well as for her publications. Her most recent honour is the 1998 Nancy Lyman Roelker Award of the American Historical Association, in recognition of Freedman's excellence as a mentor to her many graduate students. She is currently at work on a new book, tentatively titled *No Turning Back: The Historical Case for Feminism*.

Nancy C. Unger

Fretheim, Tor (b. 1946), Norwegian author. Born in Oslo, Fretheim still lives there. He has written some plays, but most of his literary production is fiction for young people. After working for many years as a journalist, Fretheim is now a full-time writer.

Among his homoerotic novels for youth are *Markus kjenner ikke Supermann* (*Markus Does Not Know Superman*, 1982), about friendship and love between two boys, and *Om bare sola ville danse* (*If Only the Sun Would Dance*, 1990), about a love relationship between a Norwegian boy and a North African illegal immgrant boy in Oslo. *Kysset som fikk snøen til å smelte* (*The Kiss That Melted the Snow*, 1991) is a coming-out story, published in an easy-to-read series for young readers; in 1997, the Norwegian film director Frank Mosvold based his short film *A Kiss In the Snow* on this book. Fretheim has been awarded several literary prizes, and a number of his books have been translated into Swedish, Danish and German.

Jan Olav Gatland

Friele, Karen-Christine (Kim) (b. 1935), Norwegian activist. Friele was born in Bergen and, like most people from that city, she has been outspoken in a clear, fearless way. Those qualities were essential for her as a pioneer in the Norwegian gay rights movement from the early 1960s onwards.

After high school, language studies and a short-lived marriage, Friele moved to Oslo and worked as a secretary in the insurance business. In Oslo she made contact with the Norwegian gay rights organisation, Det Norske Forbundet av 1948 (DNF-48), and soon came to play an important role there. Friele was the first person in Norway who came out publicly and 'confessed' her homosexuality using her own name, and she became Norway's Gay Face Number One. She was chairman of the organisation from 1966 to 1971, when she was appointed its first Secretary-General. This post she held until 1989, when she resigned from the organisation,

and soon after moved to her cabin in the mountains, where she continued her activities as a writer and travelling lecturer on gay history and gay rights issues. Since 1989 she has received an annual stipend from the Norwegian government for her work. After the amalgamation of the Norwegian gay rights movements into a new organisation, Landsforeningen for Lesbisk og Homofil Frigjøring (LLH) in 1992, Friele has been once again active in the gay rights movement, as well as in the gay and lesbian caucus in the country's largest political party, the Norwegian Labour Party.

Her excellent and persistent work in the gay rights movement contributed strongly to the abolition, in 1972, of Section 213 in the Norwegian penal code (a semi-dormant clause which had classified homosexual practices between males as a criminal offence, punishable by fines or imprisonment), as well as to the removal of homosexuality from the Norwegian nomenclature of psychiatric disorders (1978). When Norway in 1981 adopted a new anti-discrimination clause in the penal code, giving homosexuals the same rights as ethnic and religious minorities to protection against discrimination, it was largely thanks to the tireless lobbying efforts of Friele and other activists in the gay rights movement. The new law was first tested in 1985, in a lawsuit that the organisation launched against a pastor of a Norwegian charismatic church, who had been making strong anti-gay public statements.

In 1993, Norway (the second country in the world, after Denmark) passed legislation that allows public registration of same-sex relationships (*registrert partnerskap*, in Norwegian). Again, Friele had been advocating this for years, and it was only fitting that she and her long-time companion, Wenche LOWZOW – Norway's first openly lesbian MP – were chosen to be one of the first couples to have their partnerships registered. The ceremony, which included five other couples, was held in the Oslo City Hall, in the same room that is used for marriage ceremonies for heterosexual couples.

Friele is a prolific and proficient lecturer and writer, but, unfortunately, so far none of her books have been translated into other languages. Her production includes four non-fiction books, a great number of newspaper articles and pamphlets, hundreds of lectures and speeches, as well as participation in numerous radio and television programmes, and counselling and information work. Her first book, *Fra undertrykkelse til opprør* (*From Oppression to Revolt, 1975*), is a fiery manifesto about being gay – and proud of it! *De forsvant bare . . . Fragmenter av homofiles historie* (*They Just Disappeared . . . Fragments of the History of Homosexuals*, 1985) recounts the fate of homosexuals in world history, from the time of the Old Testament to Hitler's Germany.

Jon Gunnar Arntzen (ed.), *Med regnbuen som våpen* (*The Rainbow Is her Weapon* [tribute volume to Karen-Christine Friele]), (Oslo, 1995); Bjørn Gunnar Olsen, *To kvinner. Karen-Christine Friele og Wenche Lowzow forteller* (Oslo, 1983).

Lisbeth Nilsen

Friend, Donald (1915–89), Australian painter, illustrator and writer. Born Donald Stuart Leslie Moses in Sydney, and descended by paternal line from the Marquis of Queensbury (the father of Lord Alfred Douglas), the maternal maiden name, Friend, was adopted after a family quarrel in the 1920s. A highly prolific artist who worked as a painter, draughtsman, book illustrator, printmaker, sculptor, diarist and writer, Friend trained under Dattilo-Rubbo in Sydney before travelling to London in 1936, where he studied under Mark Gertler and Bernard Meninsky, who encouraged his lifelong interest in figure-drawing – the youthful male figure, especially, being a recurrent subject for Friend. Leaving London in 1938, Friend settled in Nigeria until the outbreak of war forced

him to return to Australia early in 1940. This Nigerian sojourn was indicative of two traits throughout Friend's life: firstly, a recurrent pattern of escape (often in the wake of a failed relationship) either from Australia (for example, he lived in Sri Lanka in the late 1950s and in Bali between 1968 and 1980) or, within Australia, of flight from Sydney to tropical Queensland and, secondly, a lifelong interest in non-European art and cultures.

Friend enlisted in the Australian army in 1942 and in 1945 was commissioned as an Official War Artist working in Borneo and New Guinea. In 1942 he began a series of illustrated wartime journals entitled, after Goya, *Desastres de la Guerra*, the first three volumes of which were published as *Gunner's Diary* (1943), followed by further edited extracts in *Painter's Journal* (1946). Although further publication was planned, the bulk of the war diaries (comprising twenty-seven extant volumes) remain unpublished. Following the war, Friend moved into 'Merioola', a colonial mansion in the Sydney suburb of Woollahra, which became a focus for Sydney's bohemian and artistic homosexual subculture. Other residents included the religious artist Justin O'Brien,who may have encouraged Friend to study Byzantine, Medieval and early Renaissance art in Italy and to paint allegorical works such as *The Apocalypse of St John the Divine* (1949). Of greater significance, however, was the artistic partnership between Friend and the landscape painter Russell Drysdale in the late 1940s, when they both lived in the deserted gold-rush town of Hill End in outback New South Wales, which soon became an artists' colony of considerable significance within Australian art.

Within Australian art history Friend is closely identified with a group of Neo-Romantic artists dubbed, somewhat dismissively, as the 'Charm School'. The view that Friend's artistic talents were essentially decorative and that, while he was an important artist he was not a great one, has largely endured and was voiced by Robert Hughes in his (largely appreciative) 1965 monograph. Although he judged Friend to be a first-class draughtsman, Hughes also noted that Friend's skill was also his limitation: 'His hand runs away from him, diffusing his output. He is totally fluent . . . As a result, he has become rather unfairly regarded as the last of the journeymen painters, the master craftsman who can produce any effect his audience wants; his problem is not so much over-production as failure to edit his output . . . Nature, heredity, training and experience have endowed Friend with talent enough for six painters, without making a major artist of him.'

In his later years Friend focused increasingly on writing and illustrating limited edition books (eighteen were published in his lifetime), including *Bumbooziana* (1979), *The Farce of Sodom* (1980), *Songs of Vagabond Scholars* (1982) and *Art in a Classless Society and Vice Versa* (1985). Although required at times by his publishers to tone down their content, these books amply demonstrate Friend's wit, and his skill at verbal and graphic interplay, and place him in a tradition of satirical caricature reaching back to Hogarth, Gilray and Rowlandson.

Friend was awarded a University Medal by the University of Sydney in October 1988 for his services to art and died in Sydney just a few months before a major retrospective of his work opened at the Art Gallery of New South Wales.

Gwen Friend, *My Brother Donald* (Sydney, 1994); Gavin Fry and Colleen Fry, *Donald Friend, Australian War Artist 1945* (Melbourne, 1982); Robert Hughes, *Donald Friend* (Sydney, 1965); Barry Pearce, *Donald Friend, 1915–1989 – Retrospective* (Sydney, 1990).

David L. Phillips

Fries, Kenny (b. 1960), American writer. Originally from Brooklyn, New York, Fries holds a Master of Fine Arts from Columbia University. His verse appeared in two chapbooks before the publication of the book-length collection *Anesthesia* (1996). He is also the author of the memoir *Body, Remember* (1996) and has edited *Staring Back: The Disability Experience* (1997), a collection of 'nonfiction, poetry, action, and theatre' by thirty-seven writers who live with disabilities.

Fries writes about the experience of living and coping with a congenital disability, about being Jewish and gay, and, in 'The Healing Notebooks', an exquisite and simple cycle of nineteen poems, about AIDS. His work owes a debt to W.H. Auden, David Bergman, Adrienne RICH, and especially Louise Glück. Fries has taught at Goddard College.

George Piggford

G

Gadda, Carlo Emilio (1893–1973), Italian writer. A major figure of twentieth-century Italian literature, Gadda was the first of three children born into a well-to-do bourgeois family in Milan. His father died when Gadda was young, and his mother and other relatives pushed him into studying engineering, even though he was more interested in literature. He took part in World War I, during which his younger brother died. From 1922 Gadda worked as an electrical engineer not only in Italy, but also in France, Germany and Argentina. During these years he also studied philosophy, and began to work casually as a journalist. In 1936 Gadda's mother died, and he sold the family home. This left him financially comfortable, and his work as an engineer became increasingly sporadic as he devoted himself more and more to writing. He moved to Florence, where by the early 1940s he had established a strong network of friends and cultural contacts. In 1950 he moved to Rome, where he worked for the national broadcasting company until 1955, when, tempted by the assurances of the publisher Garzanti, he devoted himself exclusively to literature.

Bashful, awkward, and neurotically attached to a bourgeois tradition of decorum, Gadda was never at ease with his homosexuality. Judging by the accounts of those who knew him well, he was terrorised by the idea that others might discover his sexual tastes. Piero SANTI recounts that he once procured a young man for Gadda, who said the next day that all had gone well but for the boy's 'heavy shoes' – he was worried about what the lawyer in the apartment below might think. Yet Gadda's work demonstrates a strongly subversive attitude towards bourgeois values, expressed above all by a discordant use of language interspersed with dialect, academic and technical jargon, and dirty talk: a chaotic language to represent a chaotic world, which, under its superficial order, seethed with passion and hidden sentiments, and was dominated by chance and ambiguity. Homosexuality never appeared undisguised in any of Gadda's works, but was referred to through allusions to motives which in turn could be attributed to sexual ambiguities outside the norm. These ranged from violent misogyny to the defence of celibacy, with the occasional listing, in tones ranging from prurient to forgiving, of historical and cultural characters who had been homosexual.

Gadda wrote two of the most important twentieth-century Italian novels: *Quer pasticciaccio brutto de via Merulana* (1957) and *La cognizione del dolore* (1964). The first tells the story of a wealthy married woman, whose frustrated maternal love of her young female servants is mixed with secret erotic desires. Like Hitchcock in his films, Gadda represents himself in a secondary character, Filippo

Angeloni, a gentleman who lives in the same building as the main character. Angeloni is accused of inviting too many delivery boys into his home. His tragi-comic embarrassment when confronted with the police officer's questions clearly reveals the character's sense of guilt. This seems to be the only moment in which Gadda chooses to refer specifically to his own homosexuality, though the word is not mentioned, and it does not go beyond a rather grotesque and self-pitying portrait.

Gadda's other great novel, *La cognizione del dolore*, is an autobiographical work whose central theme is the neurotic relationship between mother and son. Homosexuality is not even alluded to, but the lack of tenderness which has irremediably disturbed the childhood of the protagonist, and the tangle of unresolved emotional conflicts between mother and son which leads to a horror of the female sex, are both suggestive of Gadda's own confused sexuality. Perhaps reading the book only as a metaphor of the drama of a repressed homosexuality is to limit it, but it is certain that the 'invisible ill' which runs throughout the novel cannot be separated from Gadda's own difficult experience of his sexuality. He died in Rome.

Giulio Cattaneo, *Il gran lombardo* (Turin, 1991); Elio Gioanola, *L'uomo dei topazi. Saggio psicoanalitico su C. E. Gadda* (Genoa, 1977); Gian Carlo Roscioni, *La disarmonia prestabilita* (Turin, 1975).

Francesco Gnerre

Galliano, John (b. 1960), British fashion designer. Galliano's project of writing femininity through the language of fashion is not revolutionary in itself. Rather, it is Galliano's use of modern day signifiers of homosexual identity which deconstructs the essence of femininity in order to redefine femininity that makes him one of the most imaginative and important designers in the twentieth century.

Of Gibraltarian and Spanish descent, Galliano, born Juan Carlos Antonio Galliano, moved from Gibraltar to London at the age of six, and experienced an unsettling youth. Yet, as a student at the prestigious St Martin's College of Art in London, Galliano exhibited an unparalleled talent for drawing, styling and incorporating visionary cutting techniques. Galliano blended imaginative impulses with romanticism, literature, music, theatre and the elements of London's night life, and over the course of his career, cemented his reputation as master of bias-cut.

His expertise as a precision tailor earned him appointments as design director at Givenchy in 1995 and Christian Dior in 1996. No longer plagued by financial obscurity, Galliano was finally able to produce couture as extravagant as the imagination would allow: delinquent Victorians, goddesses of the Nile, *belle époque* mistresses, old-world Suzy Wongs, leopard-print temptresses and Masai-accented Edwardians.

In the late 1990s, Galliano continues to evoke the traditional sentimental girl–heroine–victim but to appropriate her sexuality, rough her up, and send her out into the world less diffident about her position and influence in society. If the Golden Age heroine is innocent but also complicitous in her fall from grace, she is so because Galliano does not see her identity as being singular but rather complex, more like a palimpsest. Accordingly, Galliano's use of camp, irony and illusions of history throughout emerge as markers of a homosexual identity in motion.

Timothy Yap

Gallo, Robert (b. 1937), American medical researcher. Along with Luc Montagnier, he is considered to be a co-discoverer of human immunodeficiency virus (HIV) – the virus many believe causes acquired immune deficiency syndrome (AIDS). He has been Director and Professor of Medicine and Microbiology at the Institute of Human Virology, University of Maryland, Baltimore, since 1993.

In the early 1980s a number of young gay men in the US presented with medical symptoms not normally associated with men of their age, prominent among which was the presence of Kaposi's Sarcoma. Further medical investigations showed that many of these men had compromised immune systems. Little was understood about the condition which quickly acquired the name gay-related immune disorder (GRID). A number of other acronyms were coined for this condition – the international community finally agreed on what is now called AIDS.

Gallo is credited with the discovery of the retrovirus Human T-cell Leukaemia Virus (HTLV) in 1978 and other human retroviruses. HTLV can be transmitted from mother to placenta and through sexual contact and contaminated blood; it may lie dormant for many decades. Following laboratory tests in 1982–3, Gallo and his team announced their belief that variants of HTLV (HTLV-I or HTLV -II) were responsible for the cause of the recently termed Acquired Immune Deficiency Syndrome (AIDS). There ensued considerable medical controversy about the efficacy of these findings – the connection between AIDS and HTLV was never proved.

Following Montagnier's discovery of Lymphadenopathy Associated Virus (LAV) in April 1984, which was considered by many in the scientific community to refute Gallo's link between AIDS and HTLV-I or HTLV-II, Gallo and his team returned to the lab and isolated what they called HTLV-III. The scientific controversy continued, as many believed the 'new' HTLV-III to be identical with the already discovered LAV. Transatlantic rivalry was at its peak. Berridge notes that the battle between the two scientists for recognition of the discovery of the virus 'eventually led to a political compromise agreed at Presidential level between [the US and France], a compromise which was legitimated by an official history, agreed by both sides, of the discovery'.

Further research proved that indeed the two viruses were identical and a new double-acronym was developed – LAV/HTLV-III (WHO usage) or HTLV-III/LAV (American usage). In 1986 the use of this cumbersome acronym was dropped in favour of the acronym now used – HIV (Human Immunodeficiency Virus). Gallo alone is credited for developing a test for antibodies to HTLV- III.

Both Gallo and Montagnier noted that HIV may not be the sole cause of AIDS and, according to Garfield, 'that there may be co-factors which determine the rate to which those infected progress to disease (though they both maintain that HIV is paramount)'.

M. D. Grmek, *History of Aids: Emergence and Origin of a Modern Pandemic* (Princeton, 1990); S. Garfield, *The End of Innocence: Britain in the time of AIDS* (London, 1995); V. Berridge, *AIDS in the UK* (Oxford, 1996)

Mark Edwards

Garmeson, Bertram Eugene Joseph ('Joe') (b. 1928), South African activist. Garmeson was the secretary of the Legal Reform Fund which was formed in 1966 in order to oppose new draconian legislation in the form of the Immorality Act Amendment Bill. In introducing the Second Reading of the Bill, in 1967, the Minister announced that it 'seems to be my unenviable task this year to have to present to this House several measures concerned in some way or other with the morals of our people'. These measures governed sexual relations 'between White and non-White', and outlawed all sexual activity between men and, for the first time in South Africa, extended this legislation to include lesbians. Before passing into law, the proposed legislation was referred to a Parliamentary Select Committee for review and to provide an opportunity for public submissions. The Legal Reform Fund was established in order to ensure a coordinated and professional input to the Parliamentary Select Committee on the question of homosexuality, from the perspective of gay men and lesbians. The Legal Reform Fund succeeded in raising sufficient funds to appoint a professional legal team to assist in defeating the proposed Bill. Many lesbians and gay men appeared before the Select Committee to give testimony and throughout the country friendship networks were mobilised in order to raise the necessary funds. As secretary, Garmeson played a key role in fundraising and co-ordinating the activities of the fledgling social movement. The efforts were successful and based on the Select Committee recommendations, a heavily revised version of the Bill was passed, which made illegal 'any act which is calculated to stimulate sexual passion or to give sexual gratification' at a party. A party was defined as 'any occasion where more than two persons are present'.

Gay and Lesbian Archives, University of the Witwatersrand Libraries, Johannesburg.

Graeme Reid

Gaultier, Jean-Paul (b. 1952), French fashion designer. For more than twenty years, Gaultier, the *enfant terrible* of fashion in France, has shocked the fashion press with his irreverent charm. From his personal style of kilt and kitsch to Mongolian exoticism, fourteenth-century knights, space-age chic and beatniks, Gaultier has been an iconoclast. Yet Gaultier remains one of the most important couturiers in the twentieth century, with his innovative approach to design: a mélange of haute couture, street style and the burlesque. He bases his designs on a comprehensive understanding of the body, sexuality and meaning as a product of cultural values.

Gaultier was born in Arcueil. In 1970, he was asked to work with Pierre Cardin, then in the early 1970s with Jacques Esterel and Jean Patou. By 1976 Gaultier launched his first collection. On the one hand, his designs evince a preference for sartorial classicism, recognizable in his form, details, origins and influences. At the same time, they are liberated from convention and unapologetically narcissistic. There are clear elements of male and female dress among Gaultier's Mad Max outfits, kimonos, rap-inspired bodysuits, swashbucklers, neo-punks, eighteenth-century tunics, leather middy blouses, sarongs, trains, cyber-age headgear, tulle jerseys, bustiers, voile and conic breasts. Yet Gaultier subverts and transforms them into a cosmopolitan array of clichés of gender: the male princess, the camp weightlifter, the dandified hooligan, the street-smart Robin Hood and *homme fatal* pretty boy.

Gaultier has said, 'I love freedom and I express it in a mixture of genders, periods, with materials and shapes.' Already, by 1985, Gaultier had designed a skirt to be worn by men, a pair of trousers which had in fact an added 'leg' over the top of another. Repeatedly, Gaultier proves academic Judith Butler's point that 'drag is subversive to the extent that it reflects on the imitative structure by which hegemonic gender is itself produced and disputes heterosexuality's claim on naturalness and gender'. He continues to tease gender with costumes for films such as *The Cook, The Thief, His Wife and Her Lover* (1990), *Kika* (1994) and *The Fifth Element* (1997), in which sexuality and utopia are central, as one might expect from the homosexual fop and muse of his own imagination.

Timothy Yap

Genet, Jean (1910–86), French author. Genet's life has been turned into the perfect embodiment of an arch-Romantic stereotype, the homosexual as pariah: illegitimate and socially disadvantaged, heroically choosing both his criminality and his sexuality as a defiance of bourgeois values. The legend was carefully fostered for different reasons by both Genet himself and by SARTRE and continues to be far more important to his admirers, particularly among anti-assimilationist gay intellectuals, than any biographical reality. The main sources of the Genet legend originated from Genet's novels, particularly *Miracle de la Rose* (1946), *Pompes funèbres* (1947) and *Le Journal d'un Voleur* (1948), the last of which has also been treated as autobiography, and in all of which he presents himself as both writer and character. Additional sources were the statements, oral and written, which he made to other writers and friends, notably Cocteau, Sartre, Simone de Beauvoir and Violette Leduc, and the interviews which he granted in the 1960s and 1970s to such periodicals as *Playboy*, *L'Express* and *Le Nouvel Observateur*. As the legend was created during the writer's lifetime, it is important as affecting his self-image and consequently the development of his work.

Genet's mother abandoned him soon after his birth and he was probably initially brought up in an orphanage. The first that is really known of him is that from the age of six or seven he was fostered by a poor peasant family in the Morvan region. At a young age he started stealing, doubtless because of the deprived circumstances in which he found himself, and seems to have been traumatised by being publicly branded a thief at the age of 10. He claims to have left school when he was 12. Certainly, by 15 he had been in trouble sufficiently often to be sent to the notoriously harsh reformatory at Mettray in the Loire region. It was there that he began to explore his homosexuality, both emotionally and physically, and became fully initiated into the arts of delinquency. In 1929 he volunteered at the army recruitment office which existed inside Mettray and was duly accepted. In January 1930 he was sent to the Levant, where he had his first taste of colonialism. At this period, according to Genet himself, he began to read widely, notably Dostoevsky. A year later he was released from active service, but by June 1931 he was back in the army, this time in Morocco, acting as secretary to General Goudot. (At this point we might ask ourselves how he gained the standard

of literacy necessary to be a general's secretary – and to go on to be one of the most sophisticatedly elaborate writers of literary French in the present century – if he had no formal education after the age of twelve.)

Genet returned to France in 1933 but re-enlisted ten months later, for another year and a half. Meanwhile, in the breaks between army service (a service which is notably suppressed from his autiobiographical narratives), he seems to have begun the European wanderings, first in Spain, later in a variety of countries including Czechoslovakia, Poland, Austria and Nazi Germany, with which he occupied his life until 1940. Keeping himself by theft, mugging and probably by prostitution, he spent most of his time in company similar to that which he had shared at Mettray. Certainly he portrays himself as integrated into the dregs of society. Yet already, in July 1933, he had made personal contact with the eminent (and eminently bourgeois) author André Gide; as his biographer Edmund White observes, how he knew Gide's address or could get himself admitted is a mystery. What we do know is that in the early 1940s Genet was in and out of prison for theft, and that it was at this period that he started writing, particularly in his prison cell at Fresnes. His first major work, the novel *Notre-Dame-des-Fleurs*, was written there and published at the expense of an unidentified patron in 1944. In that year he met Jean-Paul Sartre, to whom he owed the rapid success his work was to enjoy in the 1950s and the relative financial stability attendant on that success. Between 1944 and 1956 Genet wrote most of his poetry and fiction, his 'autobiography', his first two plays and a couple of essays. In 1948 he was condemned to life imprisonment for recidivism, but a group of writers led by Cocteau and Sartre obtained a presidential pardon for him. It was the Sartre–Cocteau open letter to President Auriol published in *Combat* which helped to launch the Genet legend, raising his career of self-indulgent petty crime to the heroic status of the artist-as-outlaw. Sartre then metaphorically canonised him in *Saint-Genet: Comédien et martyr* in 1952.

Genet himself reacted to this with a period of introspective silence which was followed by the production of the series of highly politicised plays – *Le Balcon* (1965), *Les Noirs* (1958) and *Les Paravents* (1961) – on which his broader reputation rests. This transformation was followed by the adoption of an overtly radical stance in matters social and political. In 1970 on a trip to the US he spoke out widely on racial issues and supported the Black Panthers. He then became a militant supporter of the Palestinians, and later still he sided with the Baader-MEINHOF gang in Germany. All three were revolutionary groups whose violent methods had made them unacceptable to liberal intellectuals. His last major work, *Un Captif amoureux* (1986), puts these passions (or at least the first two) into a comprehensible perspective. Genet was fascinated by two societies – American Negroes and Palestinian Arabs – which are entirely male dominated, with a crudely macho ethos which equates masculinity and violence. He identified with their sense of marginalisation and was erotically attracted to the violence which that frustration generated in them. His hero-worship in *Un Captif amoureux* is in fact a re-run of his view of prison life in his youth and is entirely consonant with his willingness to spend time in the army. Hence the continuing attraction which he has for a certain sector of the Western gay world. In France, however, many gay writers of a younger generation, such as Renaud CAMUS and Dominique FERNANDEZ, have found the Genet image of the homosexual-as-outlaw negative and outdated.

J.-P. Sartre, *Saint-Genet, Actor and Martyr* trans. B. Frechtman (London, 1988); J. Savona, *Jean Genet* (London, 1983); E. White, *Genet* (London, 1993).

Christopher Robinson

Gevisser, Mark (b. 1964), South African author. Born in Johannesburg in 1964 and educated at Yale and Columbia Universities in the United States, Gevisser is a prominent South African author, political journalist and filmmaker who has done significant work, in print and in film, in excavating gay and lesbian South African history. He co-edited *Defiant Desire: Gay and Lesbian Lives in South Africa* (1994), the first collection of essays about gay South African history and identity, to which he contributed a lengthy study of the history of the gay subculture in South Africa; an update of this essay is to be found in *Different Rainbows: Same-sex Sexualities in the Developing World*, to be published in 2000. He initiated, wrote and produced 'The Man Who Drove With Mandela' (1998), a feature-length documentary about Cecil WILLIAMS, the gay freedom-fighter and theatre producer who was with Nelson MANDELA when he was arrested in 1962. The film, which was directed by Greta Schiller, has won awards at Berlin and Milan and has played at festivals and been broadcast on television throughout the world. It is in part a history of gay identity in South Africa in the 1940s and 1950s, and features many interviews and rare archival footage. Gevisser has also published *Portraits of Power: Profiles in a New South Africa* (1996), a collection of his celebrated political profiles from the *Mail & Guardian* newspaper. In 1999, he was commissioned to write a six-part biographical series on South Africa's new president, Thabo Mbeki, for the South African *Sunday Times*, and is currently working on a biography of Mbeki.

Gay and Lesbian Archives, University of the Witwatersrand Libraries, Johannesburg.

Graeme Reid

Gil-Albert, Juan (1904–93), Spanish writer. Even if legal prohibition of homosexuality was less explicit under Francoism than in many less repressive regimes (for instance, the infamous Paragraph 175 of the German civil law punishing homosexual practices survived Nazism and was still in force in the early 1990s), possibilities for the expression of homosexual voices were close to non-existent. What the legal system did not enforce was achieved through intense homophobia in every power structure, and by complete silence about the subject on the part of intellectuals and writers. Silence and homophobia complemented each other to make the situation difficult for homosexual writers, very few of whom entertained any hopes of their thoughts on homosexuality ever reaching an audience, with the result that nobody bothered to write on the subject.

Gil-Albert is therefore an exception, and his work becomes more extraordinary for it. He represents what has been called 'inner exile', the isolation forced on intellectuals who had supported the cause of the Republic and/or did not go through a process of rehabilitation after the Civil War. Gil-Albert left for Mexico and Argentina, but returned to Spain in 1947, unable to continue living far from his homeland. He lived for almost thirty years in almost complete isolation, sometimes visited by other dissenting intellectuals, such as Jaime GIL DE BIEDMA or Luis Antonio de VILLENA, but receiving no public attention whatsoever. He is remembered as a fastidious dandy who had no public life.

In those years, he worked constantly on a number or books encompassing poetry, narrative, memoirs and essays, that he felt he would never see published. It was only in the 1980s that he received attention from the critics and many of his books became widely available. In spite of his outspokenness, homosexuality was never an aspect of his life that was dealt with by critics. Oddly, the hushed tones in which reviewers and friends refer to his sexual orientation contrasts with his own open treatment of it. In many of his works he discusses homosexuality openly. For

instance, he is the author of the first long apologia for homosexuality written in Spain, *Heraclés*, a lengthy essay that traces the cultural evolution and social manifestations of love between men (women do not figure in the tract at all). The book was written in 1951, and when it finally saw the light in 1977 it was obviously too late for it to have any impact. Worse still, some of the ideas proposed were old-fashioned in more revolutionary times. *Heraclés*, however, can be read as an attempt to write rigorously and lucidly about a topic that had only been dealt with in terms of prejudice and hysteria until that moment. In those dark years he also wrote a number of narratives with homosexual characters. *Valentín* is set in an Elizabethan theatre company and presents a rather melodramatic homosexual character, whereas *Tobeyo* is a love story with a strong autobiographical element.

In several interviews after Franco's death, Gil-Albert appeared as a witness of his times. He was always willing to discuss his and other people's homosexuality, something that was not even a possibility during Franco's years, and he was very open especially about the feelings of his fellow-poets during the Spanish Republic. Oddly for a man who went through exile and political repression, he showed a remarkably healthy attitude towards his sexual orientation. He never resorted to self-pity and he did not feel 'explanations' or apologies were required: but a need for speaking out after such long silence was present overall. He is especially renowned as a poet, but homoeroticism rarely comes to the fore in his poems. Some of them ('Hyazinthos', 'Una vez el otoño') have a homoerotic focus, but desire in his poetry seem to be a given that never becomes an issue (as it does, for instance, in the work of his admired mentor Luis CERNUDA).

Juan Gil-Albert, *Las fuentes de la constancia* (Madrid, 1984); Angel Sahuguillo, *García Lorca y la cultura de la homosexualidad masculina: Lorca, Dalí, Cernuda, Gil-Albert, Prados y la voz silenciada del amor homosexual* (Alicante, 1991); Luis Antonio de Villena, *El razonamiento inagotable de Juan Gil-Albert* (Madrid, 1984).

Alberto Mira

Gil de Biedma, Jaime (1929–91), Spanish poet. Gil de Biedma's carreer developed mostly under the repressive climate of Francoism. He has become one of the most widely acknowledged poets of his generation and, thanks to his candid memoir, *Retrato del artista en 1956*, and several later contributions to gay forums and publications, one of the key intellectual figures in the discussion of homosexuality under Francoism. After the end of the dictatorship he was invited on several occasions to meetings in the Casal Lambda, a Catalan gay cultural association, and occasionally he became a lucid critic of the role of homosexuality in poetry, especially as it concerned the members of the 'Generación del 27' poetic group. A sense of detachment prevails in his work. The 'invention' of identity is a recurring topic in his writings, and the poetic voice he created in his work is typically distant, lucid and not too emotional. In the repressive times of Francoism, when sex was mostly taboo, he sketches some scenes in an almost Cavafy-like style, featuring raw sex that may be emotionally rewarding but certainly has nothing to do with love. One such poem is 'Loca', translatable both as 'Mad-Woman' or 'Queen'. His relationship to the closet is nevertheless complex. Given the harshness of the times, ambiguity is central to his expression, and the gender of the object of desire is kept in the dark when possible; sometimes the difference between homo- and hetero- desire is ignored, even though the reader may recognise that the situations described come closer to homosexual experience of sex and relationships. Poems like 'Peeping Tom' and 'Auden's At Last the Secret Is Out' hint at heterosexual shock when faced with gay sex, although again this is not made explicit.

Gil de Biedma belonged to a wealthy Catalan family, and put most of his time into the family business. In 1956 he spent time in the Philippines, which he detailed in his memoir of the period. Ostensibly, he was there to write a report on one of the family's companies. But this book reveals his keen interest in sexual exploration. The portrait that emerges is strikingly guilt-free (in stark contrast with images of homosexuality prevailing at the time) and fun-loving. He reveals his experiences with rent-boys and provides a curious account of sexual flexibility in the country. The paradoxes of homosexuality (as a practice or as a sexual identity) are pointed out wittily, as are the mediocrity and dimness of some 'respectable' people around him.

Gil de Biedma's poetic output is relatively small and is collected in *Las personas del verbo*, which he kept updating throughout his life, although he practically stopped writing poetry by 1966. He was also a literary critic. As happens with other Spanish poets, homosexuality has been carefully sidestepped in critical appraisals of Gil de Biedma's work. Critics appear to be embarrassed when discussing it and often resort to tired clichés such as 'love is always love, no matter with whom', which are only partially accurate: after all, Gil de Biedma's world-weary detachment has a lot to do with nights of furtive sex, with the difficulties for commitment that repression produced, threats, one-night stands and the need for anonymity; these features, so close to homosexual experience under Francoism, are still to be studied in his work.

Antonia Cabanilles, *La ficción autobiográfica: la poesía de Jaime Gil de Biedma* (Valencia, 1989); Jaime Gil de Biedma, *Las personas del verbo* (Barcelona, 1985), and *Retrato del artista en 1956* (Barcelona, 1994).

Alberto Mira

Gilbert, Sky (b. 1952), Canadian playwright and theatre director. Born and raised in the US, Gilbert travelled north to study drama at York University and the University of Toronto in the 1970s. He co-founded Buddies in Bad Times Theatre, dedicated to the production and staging of innovative and political gay/lesbian drama, and led it from 1979 to 1997. Through it, he helped launch the Rhubard Festival of new plays, and other initiatives. In 1994, the company took over a disused theatre close to the heart of Toronto's gay/lesbian commercial centre, thereby creating the largest lesbian/gay theatre in North America. He resigned his position as Artistic Director in 1997 in order to concentrate on writing.

Gilbert is a prolific though uneven playwright, his works including *Drag Queens on Trial* (1985), *The Dressing Gown* (1989) and *Play Murder* (1995). One critic has divided his dramatic output into two categories, 'parodic spectacles' and 'historiographic mediations', this reflecting the combination of comedic outrageousness and political edge that are so central to Gilbert's personality. His works typically involve farce, outrageousness, irreverence, biting political commentary and male drag. Gilbert is frequently on stage himself, and often directs his own plays. Off stage, he sometimes adopts the persona of 'Jane', wearing dresses and skirts closely hugging his large-frame figure. He has long been outspokenly radical on sexual politics issues.

The Whore's Revenge (1990) and *Suzie Goo* (1992) have received Dora Awards, prestigious Canadian awards for theatre.

Oxford Companion to Canadian Literature, 2nd edn. (Toronto, 1997); Robert Wallace, *Making Out: Plays by Gay Men* (Toronto, 1992).

                                    David Rayside

Ginsberg, Allen (1926–97), American poet and activist. Ginsberg was born in Newark, New Jersey. His father was a Jewish socialist teacher and a poet of some note; his mother a Russian-born communist who suffered from mental illness most of her life. His early years were dominated by left-wing politics, his mother's frightening episodes of paranoia, and the poetry of Walt Whitman, which he encountered at high school. He began to study law at Columbia University, intending to become a labour lawyer, but he soon fell in with an anti-establishment group including Jack KEROUAC, William S. BURROUGHS and Neal Cassidy, and was suspended for various offences. This group became the core of the 'Beat Generation' of American writers. Ginsberg at this time discovered drugs, Eastern religions and homosexuality, all to be constants in his tumultuous life.

In 1955 Ginsberg moved to San Francisco, where he was encouraged to publish some of the poetry he had been writing since childhood, under the influence of Whitman and the New Jersey poet William Carlos Williams. The result was the epic poem *Howl!*, published in October 1955 and immediately but unsuccessfully prosecuted for obscenity for lines like 'who let themselves be fucked in the ass by saintly motorcyclists, and screamed with joy'. *Howl!* is one the great landmarks of modern American literature, the supreme expression of Beat defiance, marking the emergence of a generation of alienated, non-conforming educated youth, rebelling against the post-war suburban American dream and the intellectual phobias of the cold war. Its opening lines, 'I saw the best minds of my generation destroyed by madness, starving hysterical naked, dragging themselves through the negro streets at dawn . . . ', became instantly famous, as did their author. Ginsberg was living at this time with his lover Peter Orlovsky, and made no secret of his homosexuality. The notoriety of *Howl!* thus made him one of the first openly gay celebrities in the United States. For this he was denounced by press and pulpit, but it was a mark of how American society was changing, even in the later 1950s, that this did not impede his literary career, though he always had battles with censorship.

In 1961 he published *Kaddish*, a long

poem about his mother's insanity and death (she had died in 1956), which he considered to be his best work. This was followed by *Reality Sandwiches* (1963), *Planet News* (1969) and *The Fall of America* (1974), which received the National Book Award. He also won the Robert Frost Medal and an American Book Award for his contributions to literature. His poetry became something of a national institution, particularly for the rebellious youth of the 1960s: he was a major influence on the lyrics of Bob Dylan. But Ginsberg considered himself to be more than a poet, and others shared this estimation. He saw himself as part of a prophetic tradition, expressed through poetry, begun by William Blake and continued by Walt Whitman. 'I want to be known as the most brilliant man in America', he wrote modestly in *Ego Confession* (1974). 'Prepared the way for Dharma in America without mentioning Dharma / distributed monies to poor poets & nourished imaginative genius of the land / Sat silent in jazz roar writing poetry with an ink pen / wasn't afraid of God or Death after his 48th year.' He was an evangelist for Buddhism and pacifism, a courageous opponent of the Vietnam War, a defence witness at trials of political activists and authors facing obscenity charges, and an advocate of the liberatory potential of psychedelic drugs.

He was also an active gay liberationist. He was expelled from Cuba in 1965 for criticising the Castro regime's persecution of gay men, and was present at the Stonewall Riots of 1969.

Ginsberg's personal life was as tumultuous as his public career. It was greatly complicated by his tendency to fall in love with heterosexual men, beginning in the 1940s with Neal Cassidy and Jack Kerouac, by his bouts of depression and high level of drug use, and by the alarming rate of mental illness, suicide and drug-related death among his circle of Beat Generation friends – Cassidy died of a drug overdose in 1968 and Kerouac of alcoholism in 1969. He also suffered from the consequences of his considerable egotism, a personality trait he disliked but could never entirely conceal. His long relationship with Peter Orlovsky, the love of his life, fluctuated on and off from their meeting in 1954 until the poet's death, but its sexual content had faded by the 1960s as Orlovsky became increasingly heterosexual. Ginsberg was a sexual masochist, something he made no secret of, as shown in his startling 1968 poem, 'Please Master', written for Orlovsky: 'Please master order me down on the floor / Please master tell me to lick your thick shaft'.

In his later years Ginsberg's concerns became more and more spiritual, though he never lost his ability to make rather hyperbolic political statements when he chose. His pacifism distanced him from the revolutionary left of the 1970s, and in any case he increasingly considered the concerns of this world to be superficial. He studied Buddhism under the Tibetan guru Chogyam Trungpa, and his commitment to religion was deep and sincere: he took Buddhist vows (not including celibacy) in 1968. After Kerouac's death he devoted himself to getting his friend's work published and recognised. He also worked for the promotion of experimental poetry. In 1973 he and Trungpa founded the Jack Kerouac School of Disembodied Poetics, an institute to promote both Buddhism and poetry, in Boulder, Colorado, and he devoted much of the rest of his life to teaching there and helping young poets financially and professionally.

Allen Ginsberg, *Collected Poems 1947–1980* (New York, 1984); Michael Schumacher, *Dharma Lion: A Critical Biography of Allen Ginsberg* (New York, 1992).

Adam Carr

Girard, David (1959–90), French businessman. Girard was born in Saint-Ouen, a working-class suburb of Paris, where his mother was a prostitute. His autobiography claims that as a young teenager, he regularly turned his grandmother's flat (where he lived) into a restaurant, a beauty salon or a nightclub for his friends – early evidence of a highly developed capitalist spirit. He left school at 15 and travelled across France, hawking candy and then low-quality sheets at country fairs and suburban flea markets. He soon discovered the profits to be made selling his own body on the Rue Sainte-Anne in Paris. A year's study earned him a beautician's certificate and he opened David-Relax, a luxurious beauty salon and massage parlour for gay men, where he continued to prostitute himself. Girard later boasted of turning 13,000 tricks during this first phase of his career.

Girard's empire grew rapidly in the early 1980s to include (among other businesses) two bath-houses, a nightclub (Haute Tension), several gay magazines and a line of poppers (amyl nitrate). Handsome, young, brash and ambitious, Girard seemed to dominate the Parisian gay milieu of the 1980s, even taking virtual control of the annual Gay Pride parade every June. Gay political militants attacked him for promoting commercialism and sexual hedonism, but Girard replied that by creating so many openly gay establishments, 'I think that I have done more for gays than they ever have.'

Girard also earned criticism for his attitude toward AIDS, which was nonetheless typical of how many French gay men initially reacted to the disease. He refused to put up posters on AIDS or to distribute condoms in his bath-houses, because 'people come to saunas to relax, and not to worry'. An infamous editorial in his magazine, G.I., entitled 'Merde au Sida' ('Shit on AIDS'), advised readers to take precautions, but also accused doctors of reviving Judeo-Christian strictures against homosexuals, who happily 'have rediscovered the pleasure of their bodies'. His autobiography declared that 'while awaiting a decisive cure [for AIDS], each person has to make *his own* decision. Do nothing [sexual] at all . . . , keep to a single

"safe" partner (how sad), or pretend that nothing is happening, by saying that Russian Roulette must be a very exciting game'.

Girard died of AIDS. In the words of one obituary: 'Too young, too rich, too famous to die, David streaked like a comet in the gay night.' His life and career were emblematic of the French gay world of the 1980s, a period characterised by an unprecedented expansion of gay commercial venues, fast living and sometimes reckless disregard of the AIDS crisis.

David Girard, *Cher David: Les nuits de Citizen Gay* (Paris, 1986); Frédéric Martel, *Le rose et le noir* (Paris, 1995); *Gai-Pied Hebdo*, 30 August and 6 September 1990.

Michael Sibalis

Gleeson, James (b. 1915), Australian artist and writer. Born in Sydney, Australia, Gleeson grew up in Gosford, a small town north of Sydney. His father died in 1919 during the post-war influenza epidemic and James lived in a household of women – his mother, sister and an aunt who encouraged his artistic talent. Gleeson's mother had a deteriorating heart condition and from 1942 until her death in 1958 James was her main carer.

Gleeson began his study of art at the East Sydney Technical College in 1934 and continued at the Sydney Teachers' College from 1937. There he was introduced to Freud and psychology; he was already familiar with Jung and his concept of the collective unconscious. In 1939 Gleeson was a founder-exhibitor of the Contemporary Art Society, Melbourne. He later lectured at the Sydney Teachers' College and was active in the Teachers' Federation Art Society. As both a painter and poet, his poem-drawings of 1938–39 combined images and words with equal status.

Gleeson is one of Australia's most significant artists and one committed to surrealism throughout his career. In both painting and poetry he explores the conflicts within himself and his disillusionment with the world of so-called reason. In Europe Gleeson responded to Max Ernst's techniques of decalomania, collage and frottage – manipulating the effects of randomly produced patterns of paint, or rearranging cut-out images – and began using these techniques. While his work has consistently progressed and evolved throughout his career, he has never deviated from his central commitment to explore his unconscious mind. He has written and lectured on surrealism, has written books on the Australian artists William Dobell and Robert Klippel and on the history of Australian painting, and from 1949 to 1972 wrote regular art criticism for Sydney newspapers.

In the early years of World War II Gleeson's paintings expressed the tragedy of young mens' deaths. From 1950 there was a complete change of scale and subject due in part to a visit to Italy and his re-evaluation of Michelangelo and the Platonic idea of man's beauty reflecting goodness. In the late 1950s and 1960s Gleeson returned to experiment with techniques which created abstract backgrounds into which he could project realistic elements – usually a naked male.

During the 1970s Gleeson turned to collage and drawing. He was involved with other projects which absorbed his painting time. In 1975 he was made a Member of the Order of Australia. In the 1980s his paintings increased in size. Figures were now rarely seen or used only in part in landscapes of tortured flesh-like shapes. Occasionally he included a glimpse of sea or sky or something recognisable which gives the whole image an illusion of reality. These later paintings, which continued in the 1990s, return to Gleeson's theme of humanity's punishment for unstated deeds.

Christopher Chapman, 'Surrealism in Australia', *Surrealism: Revolution by Night* (Canberra, 1993); Renée Free, *James Gleeson: Images from the Shadows* (Sydney, 1993); Lou Klepac, *James Gleeson: Landscape out of Nature* (Sydney, 1993).

Ian Maidment

Gombrowicz, Witold (1904–69), Polish writer. Born on his family's estate in the Russian partition of Poland, Gombrowicz studied law at Warsaw University, but eschewed practice in favour of writing, and soon became a controversial figure on the literary scene of inter-war Poland. His first book, a collection of short stories titled *Memoirs of a Time of Immaturity*, was published in 1933. A play, 'Iwona, Princess of Burgundia', appeared two years later. And *Ferdydurke*, his best-known novel, was published in 1937, to the bewilderment of critics. In August 1939, largely on a whim, Gombrowicz sailed to Argentina. War broke out in Europe shortly after his arrival; he opted not to return, and instead spent the next twenty-four years in Buenos Aires.

From this position of compounded marginality Gombrowicz continued an *oeuvre* characterised by its provocativeness and opposition to convention. Form and deformation, as categories of intersubjectivity (what he terms the interhuman), are problematised throughout his writing, both explicitly and in terms of his favourite modes of operation: paradox, self-parody and the absurd. In works like *Ferdydurke* and *The Marriage* (1952), he enacts the problem of individual subjectivity, which is constructed in dialectical relation to others and thus exists 'simultaneously at the table and under the table'. Critics have drawn connections to Lacan in this regard, but Gombrowicz is rather more partisan about the matter, championing degradation and inferiority as principles of his aesthetic interrogation of the symbolic.

Homosexuality occasionally surfaces as a representative part of this subaltern consciousness. The conflict in *Transatlantyk* (1952), for example, consists in the narrator's decision whether or not to help his queer Argentinian friend seduce the son of an upstanding Polish émigré, thus delivering the son up to 'the troubled waters of the abnormal, of limitless liberty, of an uncontrollable future'. While none of his other works deals with homosexuality as directly, homosocial and vaguely homoerotic encounters predominate, from the early story 'Mecenas Kraykowski's Dancer' (1928) to his last novel, *Kosmos* (1965).

Gombrowicz nevertheless waxes rather coy on the subject of his own sexuality. In his serialized *Diary* (1953–68), he alludes to his 'experiences with lower class boys' in Buenos Aires, but then discreetly skirts elaboration by instead expressing his diffident critique of gender construction: 'I had to find a different position for myself beyond man and woman which would nevertheless not have anything to do with a third sex. If I could get out of this masculinity openly and decisively, its judgment of me would lose its bite and I could then say much about certain inexpressible things.' In an interview with Dominique de Roux (*A Kind of Testament*, 1973), Gombrowicz extends this critique of masculinity with regard to his 1960 novel *Pornografia*, and another of his hallmark obsessions, youth: 'Is it possible for the most masculine man, who loves women, to remain entirely insensitive to the beauty of a boy? Is homosexuality, that age-old, eternal, recurrent phenomenonon, a mere deviation?'

Gombrowicz published mainly in the Polish émigré press, especially the Paris-based journal *Kultura*. Somewhat censored versions of his works were released in Poland during a brief thaw in 1957, but a renewed ban the following year kept him restricted to underground editions until 1988. He has had an immeasurable influence on post-war writing, theatre and other arts in Poland, and, increasingly, in other countries as well. A lifelong detractor of all '-isms', and shadow adversary of SARTRE and Roland BARTHES, Gombrowicz unabashedly proclaimed himself both the first existentialist and the

first structuralist. His often difficult friendships with writers as far-flung as Czeslaw Milosz and Bruno Schulz, Ingeborg BACHMANN and Virgilio PINERA merit a chapter of their own in the history of twentieth-century intellectual culture. When he left Argentina for Europe in 1961, translations of his major works into Spanish, French and German, and successful performances of his plays in Stockholm and Paris, had already established his international reputation. He never returned to Poland. After estranging himself from literary circles in Berlin and Paris, Gombrowicz married his companion, a French-Canadian student, and spent his last years with her in the south of France.

Hanjo Berressem, *Lines of Desire. Reading Gombrowicz with Lacan* (Evanston, 1998); Tomislav Longinovic, *Borderline Culture: The Politics of Identity in Four Twentieth Century Slavic Novels* (Fayetteville, 1993); Ewa Ziarek, (ed.), *Gombrowicz's Grimaces: Modernism, Gender, Nationality* (Albany, 1998).

William Martin

Gómez Arcos, Agustín (1933–1998), Spanish playwright and poet. Gómez Arcos was born in Almería and most of his childhood was shaped by the experience of the war and the harshness of the post-war years. He witnessed a grotesque society, its members holding tight to prejudice in order to survive. Both his plays and his novels are influenced by a baroque view of this world: Oedipal narratives, repressive figures, sexual misery are recurring topics. He explictly identified with a strand of popular Andalusian culture that stands against any kind of oppression. Clearly these attitudes could hardly be tolerated by the censors in Francoist Spain and he became one among many Spanish artists who decided to go into exile. Before this came about, in the early 1960s, Gómez Arcos was the victim of Francoist double standards concerning culture. On the one hand, the government needed legitimacy and recognition, and awarded the important Lope de Vega prize to his play *Diál-ogos de la herejía* (1964), but performances were subsequently banned. A similar fate was faced by his next effort, *Queridos míos, es preciso contaros ciertas cosas* (1966). Shortly after, he left the country and moved to Paris. His first years in this city were difficult and he took up several minor jobs. Soon he returned to the stage, developing his own cabaret act, and then wrote several pieces in French. Some of his works from this period were not per-formed on the Spanish stage until the early 1990s. He was a keen observer of the roots of repression in Spain and provides a bleaker view of Spanish sexuality than other more optimistic intellectuals.

For Gómez Arcos, the focus of emo-tional sterility and sexual misery is the family, a strongly repressive structure that bribes the individual with highly suspi-cious promises of love and affection. The family as conceived in traditional societies will stifle individuality. The church, organ-ised religion, is the other element that con-spires to annihilate personal self-discovery. This is evident in his most famous work, *The Carnivorous Lamb*, a semi-autobiographical novel originally pub-lished in French in 1975 and which earned him the prestigious Hermès award. Homosexuality is not a central concern in his work, although its presence is con-stant; the male protagonist is trapped in the web of Oedipal relationships and un-able to follow his own desire for another man. For Spanish writers and intellectuals, homosexuality was never an important issue to deal with: even after Francoism, homosexuals found more tacit tolerance than active support, the 'official' version being that it was a personal question and not an ideological problem. Consequently, the homosexual is hardly ever represented as an unfairly oppressed victim of political conservatives, but as a pervert more or less deserving of understanding. The work of Gómez Arcos presents homophobia as a result of political repression and places the homosexual with other dissidents in

Spain. After Francoism, he stood as an often bitter critic of his own country: the mental attitudes encouraged by the dicta-torship were still very much alive, he thought, and there had never been a ser-ious process of understanding and over-coming the past. Some of the silences in Spanish cultural life, according to Gómez Arcos, are not the result of liberal atti-tudes, but of a deeply rooted fear of dealing with certain issues.

Alberto Mira

Gottlieb, Mike (b. ?), American medical doctor and AIDS activist. On 10 Decem-ber 1981 the *New England Journal of Medicine* published a series of articles on a new medical phenomenon which was af-fecting the male homosexual population of the US. Symptoms included *Pneumo-cystis* pneumonia and Kaposi's sarcoma: these conditions had usually only been as-sociated with older men in a state of ill health. The occurrence of these conditions in young adults was considered to be as-sociated with an immune dysfunction in the individuals concerned. Many of those affected were either homosexual men and/ or drug users: the syndrome was con-sidered by many observers at the time to be 'community acquired'. This syndrome is now known as HIV/AIDS.

One of the articles was written by Mike Gottlieb, a gay medical doctor who worked in New York and Los Angeles. The article is universally regarded as the first medical publication to link the as-yet un-known and unnamed syndrome with pos-sible infectious transmission. This was the first time that immune deficiency was con-sidered to be transmissible from one human to another.

Gottlieb was also the physician to American actor Rock Hudson during HUDSON's battle with AIDS. Through this association Gottlieb met Hudson's friend and high profile actor Elizabeth TAYLOR. Gottlieb provided her with factual infor-mation about Hudson's condition – she in turn relayed this information to a wider audience, the American public. In 1985 Gottlieb and Taylor collaborated in the establishment of one of the largest AIDS charities in the US, the American Foundation for AIDS Research (AmFAR).

M. D. Grmek, *History of Aids: Emergence and Origin of a Modern Pandemic* (Princeton, 1990).

                                                    Mark Edwards

Goytisolo, Juan (b. 1931), Spanish writer. Born in Barcelona and growing up against the backdrop of the Spanish Civil War, Goytisolo was further traumatised in 1938 by the loss of his mother, a 'collateral' victim of the fighting. This early tragedy informs Goytisolo's focus on civilian casualties in his meditation on the Gulf War, *La cuarentena* (*Quarantine*, 1991), accounts of the wars in Bosnia and Chechnya and of the unrest in Algeria, and *Cuaderno de Sarajevo* (*Sarajevo Diary*, 1994). Goytisolo's war reports show us a landscape where agency and masculinity, like femininity and powerlessness, often seem to be indivisible. Goytisolo's work also highlights his engagement with the Muslim world. Like his friend and mentor, Jean GENET, Goytisolo had a deep personal and literary affinity with the Arabs; this is most persuasive in *Reivindicación del Conde don Julián* (*Count Julian*, 1970), the work for which Goytisolo is best known.

Though homosexuality was never developed explicitly as a theme in either Goytisolo's earlier realist work or his travelogues (centred on Spain and Cuba), it inflects the infatuation described by *Fiestas* (1958), for example, with its sympathetic descriptions of same-sex affections and its more stereotyped portrayal of individuals socially designated as homosexual. Goytisolo's attitude towards 'ordinary' homosexuals is more pronounced in the earlier works, but does not disappear in the later ones; gay patrons of art-house cinema seem to be scoffed at in *Land-scapes After the Battle* (1987) while readers may wonder how to react to the predatory gay Scandinavian sex-tourist in *Count Julian*.

In the autobiographical *Coto Vedada* (*Forbidden Territory*, 1985), Goytisolo's discovery of Arab culture is intimately connected with recognition of his adult homosexuality, a connection which becomes increasingly complex in later works. Goytisolo came out by writing a letter to Monique Lange, his wife. The letter and the coming out are reiterated in the autobiography, which also evidences the writer's growing conviction that left-wing ideology enshrines an inimical stance towards homosexuals. *Forbidden Territory* and *En los reinos de taifa* (*Realms of Strife*, 1986) capture both the homophobia of Franco's Spain and the exile's perspective on a universal hostility towards any display of non-conformity.

Published in 1980, *Makbara* most effectively articulates the reach of his irony and iconoclasm. In a story of frustrated union, *Makbara* weaves together the sociology of the nuclear family, the inequities of global industrialism and the cynical consumer-oriented construction of gender, to show that sex is never just sex. It is perhaps Goytisolo's most gay novel. Its sense of the interrelatedness of racism, economic inequality and homophobia gives way in subsequent works to a more discreet treatment of political issues where homosexuality is progressively absent. *La saga de los Marx* (*The Marx Family Saga*, 1993) shows a subtle reworking of the place gender and sexuality play in the author's critique of global consumerism.

One of Goytisolo's most poetic works, *Las virtudes del pájaro solitario* (*The Virtues of the Solitary Bird*, 1988), looks back to a time when sexual choices were made in ignorance of AIDS, with a suggestion of regret that pleasure was not already a more organised enterprise. A flight of fancy embracing Juana de la Cruz and Sufi mysticism, the novel turns the cabins of a gay sauna into the cells of religious contemplatives and, by implication, suggests a homosexual fraternity hastily summoned into being by the AIDS crisis.

For Goytisolo, homosexuality is but one facet of a complex sense of being which is deeply uneasy with the classificatory urge to name and define. 'Within the gay movement', Goytisolo observed to an interviewer, 'I have been reproached for not having turned my homosexuality into a political weapon. This kind of militant posture has never interested me. I am only concerned with what I term the sotadic zone and I have never slept with homosexuals, only with heterosexuals who become bisexual on occasion.'

Goytisolo's younger and elder brothers are also significant figures in Spanish literature.

Randolph D. Pope, *Understanding Juan Goytisolo* (Columbia, SC, 1995); Juan Goytisolo, *Forbidden Territory: The Memoirs of Juan Goytisolo, 1931–1956* (London, 1989); *Realms of Strife: The Memoirs of Juan Goytisolo, 1957–1982*, trans. Peter Bush (London, 1990).

Ryan Prout

Grahn, Judy (b. 1940), American writer. Born in Chicago, Grahn grew up in a working-class environment and wanted to be a poet from an early age. She was writing poetry about women by the time she reached her early twenties. While serving in the US Air Force, she burned her notes more than once because such notes 'sometimes were seized by government authorities and used against other people, as happened to me'. By the late 1960s she had moved to the San Francisco Bay area. In 1971 she published her first book, *Edward the Dyke and Other Poems*, when she and her then lover, artist Wendy Cadden, founded the Oakland Women's Press Collective. 'Edward the Dyke' criticises the mistreatment of women by the medical profession, specifically psychoanalysts.

Other books followed from the press: *She Who: A Graphic Book of Poems with*

Fifty-four Images of Women (1972); *The Common Woman* (1973); *A Woman Is Talking to Death* (1974); all of these early chapbook-length poems were collected with new poems in *The Work of a Common Woman: The Collected Poetry of Judy Grahn, 1964–1977*. Adrienne RICH wrote in her introduction that 'A Woman Talking to Death' is 'both a political poem and a love poem ... concerned with powerlessness and power'. The lesbian poet, Rich argues, must reject the conventions of love poetry and instead must 'create a new tradition' in order to ask questions 'about taboo, integrity, the fetishization of the female body, the worldwide historical violence committed against women by men, what it means to love women when that love is denied reality, treated as perversion, or, even more insidiously, "accepted" as a mirror-image or parallel to heterosexual romance'. Rich concludes that 'Judy Grahn, more than any other poet today, has taken up that challenge'.

Grahn's lesbians do not 'fit in', do not want to be 'accepted' as mirror images of heterosexual women. Her poems reject lesbian romanticism and are informed by her experience as a nurse's aide in a military hospital. Like the work of Carson MCCULLERS, whom she admired, Grahn's work explores intersections of race, class, gender and sexuality. In some poems Grahn depicts the failure of members of one oppressed group to overcome their own bias towards other oppressed groups. Grahn's work also confronts taboo subjects such as fat oppression and ageism. She rejects the image of wealthy, privileged, educated, refined lesbians, and instead creates powerful testaments to the experience of working-class lesbians and other women who suffer violence and hatred in a heterosexist, patriarchal world. Her work celebrates bull daggers, dykes and common women. Her poetic language reclaims derogatory words and embraces them with a new, affirming vision of self-acceptance. Similarly, her poetry challenges conventional notions of form and often is written in prose.

Grahn has also edited collections and contributed to anthologies. She became known in the 1980s as an essayist and lecturer. One of her popular works is *Another Mother Tongue: Gay Words, Gay Worlds* (1984), in which she blends autobiography with a quest for traditions in language, myth and history that help establish a gay/lesbian culture and vocabulary. In *The Highest Apple: Sappho and the Lesbian Poetic Tradition* (1985), Grahn discusses the traditions of lesbian poetry from Sappho onwards. A pioneer in gay and lesbian studies, Grahn (who studied at Howard University and San Francisco State University) taught at the New College of California in San Francisco during the 1980s and has been a visiting professor at other universities, including Stanford.

Adrienne Rich, 'Power and Danger: *The Work of A Common Woman* by Judy Grahn', in *The Work of a Common Woman: The Collected Poetry of Judy Grahn, 1964–1977* (New York, 1978), pp. 7–21.

Karen Lee Osborne

Gray, Stephen (b. 1941), South African writer. Born in Cape Town, he completed postgraduate studies at Cambridge University in 1964. Gray has lived in Johannesburg since 1969, when he became Professor of English at Rand Afrikaans University. He has twice been married. Novels with queer themes include *Born of Man* and *Time of Our Darkness* (1988). His autobiography *Accident of Birth* was published by the anti-Apartheid Congress of South African Writers. He has also been a literary historian and editor.

Stephen Gray, *Accident of Birth* (Johannesburg, 1993).

Ken Davis

Great Garlic Girls, The, (1981–), Norwegian Drag Company. The most important members have been Jonny Nymoen (b. 1965), Terje Schroeder (b. 1962) and Olav Klingen (b. 1959). The company was founded as an underground joke in the gay community in 1981, at a time when drag shows were an almost unknown phenomenon in Norway. They rose to national fame when Klingen and Nymoen participated in the Norwegian entry 'Romeo' in the Eurovision Song Contest (1986), being the first drag artists in this ill-famed competition. The same year their TV show 'Ladies, But Gentlemen' was the Norwegian entry in the Montreux Competition.

In the late 1980s their summer shows at the huge nightclub Humla (now called Dizzie) were great hits, and the boys became national figures of real fame. In 1992 Klingen was paralysed in a car crash, and had to leave the company. With new members Kåre Jonny Enderud and Geir Lillejord, the Company has continued throughout the 1990s, although not with the same national attention as in the 1980s. They have, however, had some success in the late 1990s with shows produced especially for the gay community in New York.

Svend Erik Løken Larsen

Green, G(eorge) F(rederick) (1910–77), British writer. Born into a prosperous Derbyshire family, Green was educated at Cambridge, then moved in literary circles in London. Several of his short stories had been published, and received well, when he was called up for military service in 1940. Green was sent to Ceylon, where he edited newspapers which the army published for the local population. In 1944, he was arrested after being caught in bed with a rickshaw-puller. Green's associations with native men had become too indiscreet, and his alcoholism too advanced, for his superiors to tolerate; his criticism of military authorities was also little appreciated. Court-martialled, Green served a sentence in Ceylon and England. He then overcame his alcohol problems and spent the remainder of his life comfortably in the English countryside.

Green's first volume of stories, *Land*

without Heroes (1948), provides harrowing portraits of working-class life in Derbyshire during the Depression. Many speak of male comradeship in homosocial circumstances, though romantic and sexual attractions are seldom consummated. *The Power of Sergeant Streater* (1969), consisting of three interconnected stories set in England and Ceylon, describes the impossibility for the hero to act on his homosexual urges except in a destructive and self-destructive fashion. Several stories with gay themes, published posthumously along with memoirs about Green as *A Skilled Hand*, are set in Ceylon and Morocco and chart the course, and usually tragic end, of homosexual relationships. Though Green himself found contentment in later life, his works illustrate the difficulties faced by men crossing class or racial boundaries in their search for homosexual love.

G. F. Green, *A Skilled Hand*, ed. A. D. Maclean and Chloë Green (London, 1980).

Robert Aldrich

Green, Julien (1900–98), French writer. Green was the first and so far only foreign member of the Académie Française, remarkable for his extraordinary longevity and his ability to reinvent himself. Born into an English-speaking Protestant family in Paris, he never wholly took to his ancestral tongue. His first reinvention was to exchange his American name Julian for the French Julien. Though French in culture and a major French cultural figure, he never severed his links with the United States or took French nationality. After serving as a stretcher-bearer in World War I (all he was allowed to do as a foreigner), he went to the United States to study at the University of Virginia; he spent World War II in America as well. After his mother's death, Green followed his father into the Catholic church. His faith was never simple: even as a Catholic he remained marked by the English of the Bible, and he was a Biblical scholar. Despite one or two

lapses into agnosticism, had he died at a reasonable age, he would have been remembered (or forgotten) as the author of a succession of worthy, but tedious Catholic novels, mostly with a female main character, of a sort not uncommon in the 1920s and 1930s.

In advanced years, though, he reinvented himself yet again, revealing that even as he was penning the novels that earned him a place in the Académie, he was having a turbulent gay sex-life. Religion and homosexuality coexisted uneasily, though. He saw homosexuality as an insoluble problem, adding, 'All you can say is why?' Green kept a diary and wrote voluminous autobiographies, and it is perhaps these personal writings that may come to be seen as the most interesting part of his work, especially for gay readers who may well be put off by the constrained, provincial Catholic atmosphere of the novels that made his early reputation. Green had, for a long while, a partner who, as often in France, became an adopted son. One of the great worries of his later life was finding a church that would allow them both to share a tomb.

Michael O'Dwyer, *Julien Green: A Critical Study* (Dublin, 1997); Louis-Henri Parias, *Julien Green, corps et âme* (Paris, 1994).

David Parris

Grillini, Franco (b. 1955), Italian activist, politician. More than any other figure, Franco Grillini has been a consistent presence in Italian gay politics since the early 1980s. His eleven-year leadership of the country's only national gay organization (from 1987 to 1998) may indeed be a record. Grillini was born to a lower middle-class rural family just outside Bologna, in central Italy. He was a good student and a precocious activist: he got his first taste of social protest in the student uprisings of 1970 at the age of 15. He went on to university in Bologna, and graduated in 1979 with a degree in education. He worked initially as a journalist, but soon became involved in party politics.

Grillini's entry into gay life was less precipitous than his entry into politics. Not untypically in a society that places particular emphasis on marriage and the family, he was 27 and engaged to be married when he came out. Thereafter, he has dedicated himself to gay politics, and took part in the formation of Bologna's Circolo Omosessuale Ventotto Giugno, founded officially on 28 June 1982. This was the first gay group to receive financial assistance from a government body. Grillini was instrumental in the process by which this group subsequently became the nucleus for the formation of Italy's first national gay organization, ARCIGay, and he was elected its first national secretary after the group's formation in 1985. The ARCI insignia, which had been used by a gay group in Palermo in 1980, was already familiar to Italians as the Associazione ricreativa culturale italiana – the cultural organization of the Italian Communist Party. The financial sponsorship of the party was important, but no less so was the recognition engendered by the ARCI prefix, especially at a time when gay issues in Italy still tended to be stifled in a conspiracy of silence.

The phenomenon which effectively broke that silence was AIDS. Media interest in the syndrome meant that the journalists' spotlight naturally sought out the ARCIGay organization, which assumed the role of mouthpiece for Italian gays. As president of ARCIGay, Grillini therefore presided over a period in which gays were transformed from a repressed and silent minority into a recognised social group in Italian society – even if there is still a long way to go. Moreover, ARCIGay has been at the forefront of AIDS education in Italy, and this has also meant combating the particularly dogged obscurantism of the Catholic Church on the issue. Paradoxically, the tragedy of AIDS appears indirectly to have improved the overall position of gays in Italy since the mid-1980s.

Over the years, Grillini has made many appearances on national television, and has been the subject of numerous journalistic articles. In 1990 Grillini was elected a councillor in Bologna's local government, as a member of the principal left-wing party, the Democratic Party of the Left, and he was reappointed in 1995. In 1998 he stepped down from the presidency of ARCIGay but remains as honorary president. He directs an Internet-based journal, *NOI* (Noi omosessuali italiani), and remains dedicated to the cause of gay liberation.

Mark Seymour

Gründgens, Gustaf (1899–1963), German actor and director. Gründgens was born in Düsseldorf. His great dream was to become a famous actor and producer. At the age of 17 he had his first role at a theatre during World War I. After the war he studied acting and dramatic arts in Düsseldorf and became an actor at theatres in Halberstadt and Kiel, where he appeared in dramas by Ibsen, Hebbel and Goethe.

In 1922 Gründgens moved to Hamburg, where he met Erika and Klaus Mann, the children of the novelist Thomas Mann, and Pamela Wedekind, the daughter of a well-known playwright. Although Gründgens and Klaus Mann were gay, Gründgens never came out to the public. In the roaring twenties, homosexuality was fairly open, particularly in Berlin, where more and more gay bars and cafés opened. Klaus Mann's novels and dramas included gay characters and heroes and contributed to the open-minded attitudes of many contemporary writers towards gay men and lesbian women. In 1927 several artists initiated a campaign to repeal the sodomy laws in Germany, but parliament did not pass the bill.

Gründgens married Erika Mann, but they soon divorced. In 1928 he had the opportunity of going to Berlin and joining the theatre ensemble of Max Reinhardt, one of the very important producers of this decade. Gründgens advanced in his career, and his unique talent was appreciated by the public. In 1931 he also played roles in several movies such as Fritz Lang's *M*, *Danton* and *Yorck*.

When President Hindenburg named Hitler as German chancellor in 1933, Gründgens was in Spain producing a movie. Although many friends asked him to stay in Spain, he decided to return to Nazi Germany. Because of the atrocities, cruelties and excesses of the Nazis, a majority of writers, artists and scientists fled the country. The Nazi government did not hesitate to honour the remaining artists, and so Gründgens became the director of the Staatstheater in Berlin. Although he was gay and had several men, including hustlers, who visited him in his luxurious villa, the minister of culture protected him. After the so-called Roehm riot in 1934 the Nazis intensified persecution of gay men and sent them to concentration camps, but Gründgens was not targeted because all other highly gifted actors had emigrated.

Erika Mann, who lived with her father in Switzerland, condemned his opportunistic attitude. Klaus Mann, his former brother-in-law, who had fled to Amsterdam, wrote a novel called *Mephisto*, which characterized Gründgens as an unscrupulous egoist, whose career was based on machinations. The only aspect Mann never mentioned in this novel was that Gründgens was gay; he wanted to suggest that gay men would never co-operate with their hangmen.

After World War II the Soviets imprisoned Gründgens and accused him of supporting the Nazis. But several actors testified that he had helped Jewish actors to flee. In the case of the actor and writer Moritz Seeler, Gründgens had rescued him from deportation and given him enough money to leave the country. Gründgens was released and acquitted and worked at the German Theatre in Berlin. In 1947 he moved to Düsseldorf, where he staged the plays of Tennessee WILLIAMS, Calderón and Goethe. In 1955 his career reached a zenith when he became the director of the theatre in Hamburg. There he became famous by introducing the dramas of Bertolt Brecht, who was an outcast playwright in the atmosphere of this decade, Hans Henny Jahnn, Carl Zuckmayer and Lawrence Durrell.

The McCarthy-like climate in post-war Germany was opposed to all those who returned from exile, and to all those who were different. Thomas Mann and his children refused to go back to Germany and stayed in Switzerland. The aggravated sodomy laws of the Nazis were not repealed, and the witch-hunt against gay men continued. Gründgens was condemned to hide his gay identity. Honoured and appreciated as a unique actor and producer, he died in an accident in Manila.

Heinrich Goertz, *Gustaf Gründgens* (Reinbek, 1995).

Gerald Pilz

Guattari, Félix See DELEUZE.

Guérin, Daniel (1904–88), French journalist and activist. The journalist Frédéric Martel has called Guérin 'the grandfather of the French homosexual movement'. Born into a well-to-do Parisian family, Guérin nonetheless described himself as a 'congenital rebel'. He attributed his socialism both to his extensive reading of radical literature (especially Karl Marx and Pierre-Joseph Proudhon) and to his homosexual tendencies, which drew him to young working-class men ('it was in contact with young oppressed men that I learned to hate the social order').

In 1927–29 Guérin managed a bookstore in Beirut and then travelled in French Indochina. The experience turned him into a lifelong anti-colonialist. In the 1930s he worked in Paris as a journalist and organiser for trade unions and left-wing political parties. He was on a mission in Norway for a socialist organisation when World War II began in September 1939. Although he returned to France in

March 1942, he did not participate in the French Resistance because, as a socialist and internationalist, he refused to fight for either of the 'imperialist' blocs. After the war, he spent almost three years (1946–49) in the United States, which he later described as 'that splendid America, that repugnant Amerika', and where he became interested in the plight of African-Americans. Back in France in the 1950s, he supported the Algerian independence movement and then threw himself into the failed French uprising of May 1968.

Guérin had his first heterosexual experience in 1934, with the woman who became his wife and the mother of his daughter, but he remained a practising homosexual. His first public defence of homosexuality was a short book of essays, *Shakespeare et Gide en Correctionnelle?* (*Shakespeare and Gide in Criminal Court?*, 1959): 'In a society too organized, too planned, too mechanized, too regimented, the liberty of everyone to make love as he pleases, including in the manner of Shakespeare and [André] Gide, is one of the last rights ... that remain to us.' But he kept his homosexuality private for fear of compromising himself in the eyes of his revolutionary comrades. He had to wait for the events of May 1968 'to be delivered from that heavy and daily secrecy'.

He was thereafter outspoken in combining the twin causes of social and sexual revolution. In December 1968, for example, he told an interviewer, 'There is not only an economic struggle against capitalism, but simultaneously there must be ... a struggle for sexual liberation.' In 1971, in his late sixties, he joined the newly founded FHAR (Front Homosexuel d'Action Révolutionâire, Homosexual Front for Revolutionary Action) and became a fixture at its weekly meetings. In numerous articles and interviews and in two autobiographies, he spoke and wrote openly about his life and his loves. He blamed the bourgeoisie for repressing homosexuality in the name of the family and of procreation, and advocated revolutionary

social and political change: 'A gigantic clean sweep is indispensable to achieving the liberation of man in general ... and the homosexual in particular.'

Guérin published books on a wide range of subjects that reflected his varied interests, including anarchism, socialism, the American labour movement, the condition of African-Americans, the French Revolution, the Kinsey Report and homosexuality. He spent a lifetime fighting for socialism, freedom, equality and sexual liberty, and against fascism, authoritarian communism, capitalism and colonialism. His dedication, his impetuousity and his energy inspired militants, including gay activists, decades younger than himself.

D. Guérin, *Autobiographie de jeunesse* (Paris, 1972), *Le feu du sang* (Paris, 1977), *Homosexualité et révolution* (Saint-Denis, 1983); *Le Monde*, 15 April, 22 April 1988; *Libération*, 15 April 1988.

Michael Sibalis

Guibert, Hervé (1955–91), French author. Guibert was 22 when his first novel, *La Mort-propagande*, was published. He had just taken a job with the cultural service of the prestigious Parisian daily paper *Le Monde*, where he was responsible for reporting on photography. Writing and photography were in fact his life-long passions, and inseparable in his eyes from the process of giving meaning to his life. In an interview for *Libération* in 1988, when he was already aware that he had contracted AIDS, he defined the function of his art as the attempt to reduce as far as possible the distance between the truths of experience and those of writing. Hence his choice of himself, his family and his friends as his subject matter – for example, his first published collection of photographs, *Suzanne et Louise* (1980), presented a 'photoromance' of two aunts. But that apparently tender album has to be 'read' against the much blacker account of the same two old ladies in *Les Gangsters* (1988). For the results of Guibert's quest are consistently disturbing and suggest a conscious desire to shock. In 1982, in *Les Chiens*, he gave a detailed account of the sadomasochistic practices in which he and his friends indulged; in 1986, he published an excoriation of his parents and the horrors of family life, *Mes parents*, in which he describes his mother's attempts to get rid of him during her pregnancy and her wish that he would be stillborn; in *Fou de Vincent* (1989) he gives in diary form the story of his passion for a teenage boy who dies while trying, in a drug-induced stupor, to fly from the third floor of his apartment block.

During the 1980s Guibert gradually acquired a small public of informed admirers, and even won a literary award which allowed him to spend a year at the Villa Medici in Rome, a stay which itself became the subject matter of *L'Incognito* (1989). But it was with his seventeenth work, the novel *A l'ami qui ne m'a pas sauvé la vie* (1990), in which he gives an account of his experience of AIDS, that he both found his touch as a writer and finally attracted public attention and critical acclaim. AIDS allowed him both to explore the limits of his relationship with the outside world and to examine brutally his own physical and mental processes. The success of *A l'ami* initially owed something to the fact that in it Guibert gave away the 'inside story' about the death of his friend Michel FOUCAULT. But the legitimacy of that success was confirmed by two further powerful books, *Le Protocole compassionnel* and *L'Homme au chapeau rouge*, which continued its themes, the first on an equally documentary note, the second (which appeared posthumously) with a more self-conscious fictionalising tone. It is notable that in these three works the use of visual art, particularly photography, as a medium of self-analysis is explored, bringing together Guibert's two major artistic interests.

Guibert's work stands at the centre of the first phase of French AIDS writing, when the experience of the disease and the prospect of death were the focal points of interest. *A l'ami qui ne m'a pas sauvé la vie* had a considerable impact simply as an account of coming to terms with the condition – by late 1994, over 357,000 copies of the two French editions alone had been sold and it has been translated into seventeen languages. But Guibert's work transcends even that important focus, raising questions about personal identity, the nature of writing, the relationship between truth and fiction, and the relationship of self-perception to self-representation.

Jean-Pierre Boulé, *Hervé Guibert: Voices of the Self* (Liverpool, 1999).

Christopher Robinson

Gunn, Thom (b. 1929), British poet. Gregory Woods considers Thom Gunn 'a model of the contemporary gay poet in transition ... who has progressed from pre-Wolfenden Cambridge to post-"Liberation" San Francisco'. Born in Gravesend, Kent, Gunn, whose father was a journalist, led a peripatetic childhood, his family finally settling in Hampstead. He attended University College School in London as a day boy and read English at Trinity College, Cambridge. Here he met an American, Mike Kitay, with whom he still lives and to whom he dedicates much of his work. In 1954 Gunn entered Stanford University on a creative writing fellowship where he studied under Yvor Winters, and so began a long and fruitful engagement with American poetry. He abandoned his doctoral programme at Stanford in 1958 after being hired by the English Department at the University of California, Berkeley, where he has held full and part-time appointments ever since. Aside from occasional trips back to England and to New York City, the Bay area and California have shaped his life and art for over forty years. He retains his British passport and identifies himself as an Anglo-American poet.

Though included in the Movement

anthology *New Lines* (1956), Gunn's early work was far removed from the defensive ironies of much post-war British poetry. As a 'Faber poet' he was most often paired with Ted Hughes, a contemporary equally at odds with gentility. His native influences begin with Shakespeare and Donne, Jonson and Fulke Greville, and end with Auden; the American poets he has admired include William Carlos Williams, Gary Snyder, Robert Duncan and James MERRILL. As a formalist or a practitioner of free verse, Gunn balances image with discourse, rule with energy, using autobiography but scrupulously avoiding the confessional mode. His first volumes, *Fighting Terms* (1954) and *The Sense of Movement* (1957), celebrate action – 'one is always nearer by not keeping still' – existential freedom and the heroic, embodied in Elvis Presley's 'posture for combat', the leather-jacketed biker and the 'masterful' Byron. An occluded sexual identity can be detected in poems like 'The Secret Sharer', 'The Looking-Glass' and 'The Allegory of the Wolf Boy', but it was not until *Jack Straw's Castle* (1976) that the intimacies of gay sex came into sharp focus. An erotic candour also informs many of the poems in *Passages of Joy* (1982), though it is the moving elegy 'Talbot Road' that perhaps anticipates the tone of *The Man with Night Sweats* (1992), the volume that brought renewed attention to his work. Here he memorializes friends and former lovers borne away by AIDS, members of 'the largest gathering of the decade', never failing to embrace the familial strengths of gay culture, the authenticity of choice and allegiance.

His other volumes include *My Sad Captains* (1961), *Moly* (1971), *Collected Poems* (1993) and *Boss Cupid* (1999); his critical essays, reviews, and memoirs are collected in *The Occasions of Poetry* (1982) and *Shelf Life* (1994).

Alan Bold, *Thom Gunn & Ted Hughes* (Edinburgh, 1976); Gregory Woods, 'Thom Gunn', in *Articulate Flesh* (New Haven, 1987); 'Thom Gunn at 60', *PN Review* (1989); A. E. Dyson (ed.), *Three Contemporary Poets: Thom Gunn, Ted Hughes, and R. S. Thomas* (London, 1990).
                                                          Roger Bowen

H

Hacker, Marilyn (b. 1942), American poet. Hacker is the author of eight books of poetry including the cult classic, *Love, Death, and the Changing of the Seasons* (1986), a book-length sequence of lesbian love sonnets modelled on Shakespeare's sonnets. She has won many prizes and honours including a National Book Award for *Presentation Piece* (1974), Lambda literary awards for *Winter Numbers* (1994) and *Going Back to the River* (1990), and the Poets' Prize for her *Selected Poems, 1965–1990* (1994). Hacker's poetry is noted for its formal sophistication and elegance, combining a conservative aesthetic with autobiographical candour and explicit eroticism: 'I'd like to put my face between your legs, / lick you, my fingers in you, till you moan' ('Estival Passage 9', *Love, Death*). She lives in New York City and Paris.

Annamarie Jagose, *Lesbian Utopics* (London, 1994); Suzanne Gardinier, 'Marilyn Hacker', in *Contemporary Lesbian Writers of the United States*, eds S. Pollack and D. Knight (Westport, CT, 1993), pp 258–68; Marilyn R. Farwell, *Heterosexual Plots and Lesbian Narratives* (New York, 1996).

Kate Lilley

Hahn, Pierre (1936–81), French journalist and activist. Born in Paris, Hahn, when he was 19, went to see André BAUDRY, head of France's principal homosexual move-ment in the 1950s, and noticing a copy of his monthly review, asked: 'Monsieur Baudry, may I look at *Arcadie*?' 'You do not look at *Arcadie*,' came the reply; 'you participate in it.' Hahn was soon a regular contributor under the pseudonym André Clair.

At 20, Hahn went into a mental hospital at the urging of his father, who hoped to cure his homosexuality. This left him with a horror of every kind of confinement and repression. He embarked on a journalistic career and then in the mid-1960s started writing about homosexuality. Having already studied racism in the periodical *Jeune Afrique*, he wanted (in his own words) 'to link discrimination against homosexuals with the discrimination that victimizes North Africans, for example'. Guy HOCQUENGHEM, who met Hahn in 1967, later recalled: 'It was the first time that I saw a homosexual militant. And for good reason, because he was absolutely the only one in Paris at the time.' In 1971 Hahn was among the founders of FHAR (Front Homosexuel d'Action Révolutionnaire, Homosexual Front for Revolutionary Action), a politically radical movement patterned on American gay liberation groups.

Hahn wrote for the mainline press under his own name, but also for gay publications under pseudonyms (Pierre de Valmore, Gilles Santis). In 1971 he published *Français, encore un effort*, a compendium of quotations about homosexuality from antiquity to the present, followed in 1979 by *Nos ancêtres les pervers*, an historical study of nineteenth-century homosexuals. In early 1981 he successfully defended a doctoral thesis at the University of Paris-VIII on 'The Birth of Homosexuality'. Depressed because of an unhappy love affair, however, he soon afterwards committed suicide. Gay militants took up a collection to pay the funeral costs of a man whom they recognised as a pioneer of their movement.

'Pierre Hahn: la tendresse et l'histoire,' *Gai Pied*, no. 26 (May 1981); 'Pierre Hahn' and 'Pierre Hahn historien,' *Homophonies*, nos. 6 and 7 (April and May 1981).

         Michael Sibalis

Halperin, David M. (b. 1952), American scholar. An eminent classicist and major theorist in gay and lesbian studies, Halperin has published widely on Greek and Latin bucolic poetry, the relations between ancient Greece and the Near East, and various topics in literary history, comparative literature and other fields. His first book was *Before Pastoral: Theocritus and the Ancient Tradition of Bucolic Poetry* (1983), and he then edited, with John J. Winkler and Froma I. Zeitlin, a collection of papers entitled *Before Sexuality: The Construction of Erotic Experience in the Ancient Greek World* (1990). In *One Hundred Years of Homosexuality* (also published in 1990), a collection of his own essays, Halperin provided a major reconceptualisation of sexuality in Antiquity and of Greek love. Historiographical and interpretive essays on such subjects as 'Heroes and their Pals', 'Prostitution and Citizenship in Classical Athens' and 'Why is Diotima a Woman?' emphasise the importance of embedding classical sexual behaviour in the general social and political context of Antiquity. Halperin insisted, in particular, that 'the erotics of male culture in the ancient Greek world' must be closely related to notions of active

and passive sexuality and to broader issues of gender. Although heralded for its scholarly integrity and analytical originality, the book provoked a vehement and lengthy critique from Camille Paglia, who objected to its Foucault-influenced social constructionist starting-point. *Saint Foucault: Towards a Gay Hagiography* (1995) offered a passionate defence of the ideas of Michel FOUCAULT and a rereading of the 'queer politics' of the French philosopher, which Halperin said had often been misunderstood or misrepresented.

Halperin also co-edited *The Lesbian and Gay Studies Reader* (1993) and is a founding editor of *GLQ: A Journal of Lesbian and Gay Studies*. After serving as Professor of Literature and Head of the Literature Faculty at the Massachusetts Institute of Technology for a number of years, he taught at the University of New South Wales, Australia, and now holds a chair at the University of Michigan in Ann Arbor.

Camille Paglia, *Sex, Art, and American Culture* (New York, 1992).

    Robert Aldrich and Garry Wotherspoon

Hanlo, Jan (Johannes Bernadus Maria Raphael Hanlo) (1912–69), Dutch poet. Born in Java to Catholic parents, Hanlo grew up in the Catholic south of the Netherlands. A talented youth, raised apart from his father, he wrote from an early age. His prose debut was in with an article on the London jazz scene. In 1936 Hanlo was awarded a teaching certificate in English. In 1942 he undertook a degree in psychology at the University of Amsterdam. But in early 1943 he was picked up by the Nazis and sent to a factory in Berlin. He escaped back to Amsterdam but, after being detained again, went underground. He now began to write serious poetry, often in a 'jazz' or 'beat' idiom. Most prolific in the post-war period, his work was published in established literary magazines. But Hanlo's repressed love for young boys led to a breakdown, and he spent six months in a Catholic mental asylum, where his erotic attraction towards his students became the focus of barbaric treatment. Released at the end of 1947, he contributed to the magazines of COBRA, the movement which bridged the pre-war Surrealists and the Situationist International. In 1952 his Dadaesque sound-poem 'Oote' caused a literary scandal and was debated in Parliament. Hanlo also wrote love poems to boys – 'Jossie' being anthologised three times. After minor brushes with the law, in 1969 he went to Morocco, where he died in a motorcyle accident.

Before his death, Hanlo's work consisted of around 100 poems, and two collections of prose, *In Een Gewoon Rituig* (1966) and *Moelmer* (1967). Published posthumously were: *Going To The Mosque* (1971), travel letters from Morocco; *Zonder Geluk Valt Neimand Van Het Dak* (*No One Falls From The Roof Unless He's Lucky*, 1972), Hanlo's account of the mental asylum; a further collection of prose, *Mijn Benul* (1972), and the 1,000-page, two-volume, *Letters* (1989).

H. Hafcamp, 'Time Of Youth, Time Of Beauty', *Paidika*, vol. 3, no. 3. (1994), pp. 34–60; J. Hanlo, *Verzamelde Gedichten* (*Collected Poems*) Amsterdam, 1974.

Ianthe Duende

Hannon, Gerald (b. 1944), Canadian writer and activist. An award-winning writer, mostly of magazine features, Hannon first gained national attention as the author of a 1977 article on intergenerational sex that was the object of years-long court action instigated by the Ontario government.

Hannon was born in small town New Brunswick and raised in small town Ontario, moving to Toronto for his university studies. At the end of 1971, he joined the editorial group that produced the fledgling gay liberation magazine *The Body Politic*, and for most of its fifteen-year life, he was one of its most prolific and controversial writers. (Hannon was also active in other groups in the early years of gay liberation, including Toronto Gay Action and the Community Homophile Association of Toronto.) In late 1977, 'Men Loving Boys Loving Boys' brought a police raid and obscenity charges against him and others of the magazine's editorial collective, and considerable criticism (as well as support) from the gay community itself. The legal battle (and accompanying political campaign) was waged for several years, eventually yielding acquital, Hannon continuing his edgy writing throughout (incurring another highly publicised set of charges for a 1982 article on fisting).

After *The Body Politic*'s demise in early 1987, Hannon continued writing freelance for magazines such as *Toronto Life* (one of Canada's most important vehicles for high quality magazine writing), *Canadian Art* and *Chatelaine* (a women's magazine), and for newspapers such as Toronto's *Globe and Mail*. That writing has won him two National Magazine awards and several other nominations. That success also helped secure part-time teaching in journalism at Toronto's Ryerson Polytechnical University, though media-inflamed publicity about his 'Men Loving Boys' article, and about his part-time job as a prostitute, led to an ill-thought-out suspension from the university, and eventually to an undisclosed settlement.

Ed Jackson and Stan Persky (eds), *Flaunting It! A Decade of Gay Journalism from The Body Politic* (Vancouver, 1982); G. Hunt, 'Division of Labour, Life-Cycles and Democracy in Worker Co-Operatives', *Economic and Industrial Democracy*, vol. 13, no. 1 (1992), pp. 9–43; Sandra Martin, 'In Your Face', *Toronto Life*, June 1996.

David Rayside

Hansen, Joseph (b. 1923), American author. Hansen grew up during the Depression years in the upper Midwest and then in California. Despite his family's hard existence, Hansen discovered a love for good literature and a desire to write. Before he could claim writing as a profession, there would be many years of part-time jobs in bookstores, singing folk songs on a local radio station, marrying a lesbian and having a child with her, and serving as an editorial jack-of-all-trades for two magazines written for the growing readership of self-identified homosexuals in the late 1950s and early 1960s, *One* and its offspring *Tangents*.

Writing as 'James Colton', the pseudonym he had taken for his stories, editorials and reviews in these magazines, Hansen's first novels were published by firms that supplied mostly pornography. In the mid- to late 1960s, these were the only publishers willing to print and distribute books that portrayed homosexual characters the way Hansen believed was desperately needed: men who were not psychopathic and did not die by the end of the story (e.g. *Strange Marriage*, 1965). In 1970, however, Hansen finally broke through with his novel *Fadeout*, published by a 'mainstream' house and under this own name. This began a series of twelve novels delineating the life, loves, friendships and cases solved of David Brandstetter, an insurance claim investigator. With this character, Hansen created the first gay detective, and his very successful series fathered what has become one of the most popular genres in contemporary gay literature, the gay (or lesbian) detective mystery. Brandstetter fulfilled his author's wish to give readers, especially non-gay readers, a non-stereotypical gay man with whom to identify – and a protagonist at that. The novels portray a wide variety of gay and lesbian characters, and the plots often centre on topical issues such as the homophobia of the religious right (e.g. *Skinflick*, 1979) and the AIDS crisis (*Early Graves*, 1987).

Since ending the Bradstetter series with *A Country of Old Men* (1991), Hansen has begun another set of novels, also centred on a gay man. The two that have

appeared to date (*Living Upstairs*, 1993; *Jack of Hearts*, 1995) trace the life of Nathan Reed, a teenager in Los Angeles in the early 1940s. Hansen has written several other novels with gay characters, and, as with the Nathan Reed novels, his own life experience plays a large role in their characterisation and atmosphere. Hansen's poetry has also been well received, and he has published many short stories.

Although married for over fifty years, he identifies himself as 'homosexual' (not gay). His fiction, the recognition it has received, and the influence it has had, combine perhaps to illustrate the point that the definitions set by social identities need not limit either the way we imagine, or the way we live, our lives.

Ernest Fontana, 'Joseph Hansen's Anti-Pastoral Crime Fiction', *Clues* 7/1 (Spring/Summer 1986), pp. 89–97; James W. Jones, 'Joseph Hansen,' in Emmanuel S. Nelson (ed.), *Contemporary Gay American Novelists* (Westport, CT, 1993), pp. 189–96; Jim Kepner, 'Joseph Hansen', in Sharon Malinowski and Christa Brelin (eds), *The Gay and Lesbian Literary Companion* (Detroit, 1995), pp. 227–52.

James W. Jones

Hardwick, Michael (b. 1954), American activist. Born in Miami, Florida, to a middle-class family, Hardwick studied horticulture at the University of Florida and worked in several professions before settling in Atlanta, Georgia, as a bartender at a gay bar. In August 1982, a police officer entering Hardwick's apartment to serve him with a warrant for failure to appear in court (later determined to be invalid) found Hardwick engaged in private consensual oral sex with another man, and arrested both under Georgia's sodomy law.

Laws forbidding sodomy have ancient roots. While the individual's sex is rarely stated therein, they have almost always been used to prosecute homosexual conduct. All fifty US states forbade sodomy until 1961, when legal reformers in Illinois first removed the penalty. Movements to repeal the laws continued in the post-Stonewall gay and lesbian rights movement. By the time of Hardwick's arrest, sodomy laws were almost universally unenforced. Some legal scholars believed the laws were therefore unimportant, while many advocates of gay and lesbian equality saw them as a symbolic gesture of hatred and recognised them as obstacles to other goals such as military service, immigration rights or same-sex marriage.

At the same time that sodomy laws were challenged, the American court system expanded its understanding of a right to privacy. Activist judges located the right – nowhere mentioned in the US constitution – in traditions of liberalism and cited it as a precondition of personal freedom. The most notable Supreme Court case was Griswold v. Connecticut (1965), which established a married couple's right to use contraception but specifically stated that these privacy rights did not apply to homosexuals. By 1986, the law seemed ripe for a test.

After prompting by the American Civil Liberties Union, Hardwick agreed to challenge the constitutionality of the Georgia law. A federal district court summarily rejected his claim to a right of privacy, but the federal appeals court in Atlanta agreed with him. The United States Supreme Court heard the case in March 1986. Hardwick's attorneys, including Laurence Tribe of Harvard Law School and numerous gay and lesbian rights lawyers, argued that his privacy rights had been violated. Lawyers for the state of Georgia countered that the right to regulate sodomy was reasonable, claiming in a pre-trial brief that 'It is the very act of homosexual sodomy that epitomizes moral delinquency', and warning that establishment of gay privacy rights would lead to the elimination of bestiality and incest laws. Attorneys also cited the crisis of AIDS as a rational basis for the law (clearly not on the minds of the legislators who passed the original statute in 1816).

In its June 1986 opinion, the Supreme Court upheld the constitutionality of the Georgia sodomy statute by a narrow 5–4 vote. Following the Griswold precedent, the Court held that the right to privacy established in that case did not extend to homosexual activity and that states have a legitimate interest in regulating the consensual sexual behaviour of their citizens. The four dissenting justices focused on the right to privacy and wondered whether 'the Court's failure to comprehend the magnitude of the liberty interests at stake in this case leads it to slight the question'.

The swing vote in the case had come from politically moderate Justice Lewis Powell. Soon after the opinion was released, news media learned that Justice Powell had, in a private conference, originally voted to overturn the Georgia law, but then changed his mind, turning the Court against Hardwick's claim. Justice Powell did not speak about this issue at the time, but in a lecture in New York City in October 1990 admitted that he had been in error and regretted his switch.

Powell's regrets have offered cold comfort to gay and lesbian legal activists. Anger at the Court's decision helped spur organising efforts for the 1987 March on Washington. The case also radicalised the normally quiet Hardwick. Although keeping a low public profile as his case worked its way through the system, his experience as the victim of a hate crime and his frustration at the Court's decision led him to speak out at political gatherings and on national television programmes.

Bowers v. Hardwick 478 U.S. 186 (1986); Peter Irons, *The Courage of Their Convictions* (New York, 1988); Richard Laermer, 'Michael Hardwick: The Man behind the Georgia Sodomy Case', *Advocate*, no. 454 (2 September 1986), pp. 38–41; William B. Rubenstein (ed.), *Lesbians, Gay Men, and the Law* (New York, 1993).

Christopher Capozzola

Haring, Keith (1958–90), American painter. Haring's postmodern primitivism exploded across the 1980s international art scene at the same time that Gay Lib transmuted into Queer Nation. Attuned to the intersection of governmental indifference, evangelical Christian homophobia, mass media conglomerations and the cult of celebrity, Haring exploited these cultural forces to forge a deceptively simple art, both popular and fine, ancient and modern, secular and sexual. Haring's stock in trade was the ludicrously naive, brightly coloured crawling baby, barking dog and jumping man with crude force lines indicating their speech or movement. Haring drew from sources as diverse as childhood comic arts, hip-hop music, urban graffiti, Latin American dance and ancient American pictographs.

Haring's art manifested the power and multiplication of the media in the 1980s. Following on the Pop heels of Andy Warhol, Haring respected no division or distinction between high and low, knowing that all culture is not contained within museums, libraries or galleries. He painted everything: bodies, subway walls, murals, lamp-posts, set designs, buses, t-shirts and album covers. His art was immediate, ephemeral, exuberant, transcendent, energetic and insistent. In 1986 Haring further blurred art and commerce by opening the Pop Shop, a New York outlet for Haring-designed, commercially-produced t-shirts, inflatable animals, posters and other sorts of consumer giddiness.

Haring pioneered a type of personal intervention and resistance to overwhelming cultural monoliths like the faceless city and intractable governmental bureaucracy. As a single force he was determined to shock and cajole complacent New Yorkers into an awareness of their physical and ideological surroundings. For example, Haring would cut up and rearrange the words from *New York Post* headlines, then paste them as posters around New York City. His good-natured yet biting style of agit-prop would be taken up in the late 1980s and early 1990s by AIDS activist

groups like ACT-UP, Gran Fury and Queer Nation, who similarly sought to inject social art and personal sexual politics into art and the public sphere.

Haring unashamedly and unselfconsciously dared to express homosexual sex as SEX, not subtext, oblique reference or innuendo. However, his sexual interest in men conditions an art which – although squirting penises and blowjobs are ubiquitous – rarely shows female figures or unambiguous lesbian sex. Haring's imagery became inseparable from the 1980s and 1990s American renaissance of all things queer. Any march, movement, disease or celebration had its Haring image. The best known are probably his Safe Sex images and his 1989 'speak no evil, hear no evil, see no evil' men over the slogan 'Ignorance = Fear, Silence = Death, Fight AIDS, Act Up'. It multiplied through buttons, posters, bus billboards and bumper stickers. Haring himself died of AIDS related complications.

Barry Blinderman, *Keith Haring: Future Primeval* (New York, 1990); Elizabeth Sussman *et al.*, *Keith Haring* (New York, 1997); Bruce D. Katz, 'Haring's Place in Homoerotic American Art', in Germano Celant (ed.), *Keith Haring* (Munich, 1992); Keith Haring, *Keith Haring Journals* (New York, 1996); Keith Haring, *Against All Odds* (Rotterdam, 1990).

Michael J. Murphy

Harris, Jonathan, (b. *c*. 1919), American actor. Harris played the character of Dr Zachary Smith in 'Lost in Space', an innocuous futuristic Swiss Family Robinson children's TV series. It would most likely be forgotten were it not for the participation of an actor who made gold out of lead, playing a role subverting the very family values the programme was supposed to embody.

Harris had the face of a gargoyle, duck-like and implacable. His voice with its icy cadences and satin sheen could make any dialogue sound like Oscar Wilde. As Dr Smith, a conceited, waspish agent of an enemy power, marooned on a planet with a nuclear family and a robot, he brought a welcome touch of asperity to his bland surroundings. Smith had sneaked on board the Jupiter II to sabotage the planned five-year space exploration mission. However an accident upset his plans and he becomes an unwilling stowaway. Each week the castaways faced new perils, with the conniving Smith being kept in check by a vigilant robot and young Will Robinson.

Harris described his character in *TV Guide*: 'I am deliciously wicked. I am selfish, self-pitying, pompous, pretentious, peremptory, conniving, unctuous, scornful, greedy, unscrupulous, cruel, cowardly, egotistical, and it is absolutely delightful.' When asked directly, Harris denied any gay colouring in his performance. In truth, Dr Smith was a great queen: a man of vaunting conceit, total cowardice, superb personal hygiene and arrant disregard for masculine comradeship. His clipped speech, contemptuous epithets and hatred of children endeared him to many.

Probably his finest hour was being chosen to perpetuate the race on a planet all of whose menfolk had become impotent. This episode, 'The Colonists', was a double joke: Smith successfully avoiding intercourse with the planet's queen, who is presented as a butch dyke, eventually spending the night with the vanilla Mrs Robinson. All of this was queer sensibility, brilliantly nurtured and sustained on children's TV.

Keith Howes

Hay, Henry, Jr ('Harry') (b. 1912), American activist. Hay was born in Worthing, England, into a prosperous family. The family moved to Chile when war broke out in 1914 and to California in 1916. In 1930, aged 17, Hay began his first homosexual relationship with a man who told him about the Society for Human Rights (SHR), which advocated homosexual emancipation (and was established in Chicago by Henry Gerber in 1924). In his first

year at Stanford University in 1931, Hay openly declared his sexual orientation to his friends. Shortly thereafter he dropped out of Stanford to pursue an acting career and returned to Los Angeles, where his family lived. Work was hard to find in the Depression years, and through a friend he became involved in political theatre sponsored by the Communist Party, which he joined in 1933. The Communist Party condemned sexual deviance, and in 1938 Hay married Anita Platky, a party member with whom he worked. He attempted to give up his homosexuality and isolated himself from gay social circles. Between 1947 and 1952 he taught at the Los Angeles People's Educational Center (later renamed the Southern California Labor School). During this period Hay fathered two children. However, Hay found it increasingly difficult to suppress his homosexuality and in 1951 he was divorced.

In 1948, a few months after Kinsey and his colleagues published their surprising findings about human male sexual behaviour, Hay conceived the idea of establishing a homosexual organisation. He discussed the idea with friends then wrote a prospectus, but failed to attract support until the end of 1950, when he showed a revised version to one of his students, Bob Hull, who in turn interested two of his friends, Chuck Rowland and Dale Jennings. In 1951 they formed the Mattachine Society, which marked the beginning of a continuous history of gay political organisation in the United States. Hay suggested the name in reference to a secret Renaissance fraternity 'of unmarried townsmen who never performed in public unmasked, [and] were dedicated to ... conducting dances and rituals ... Sometimes these dance rituals, or masques, were peasant protests against oppression – with the maskers, in the people's name, receiving the brunt of a given lord's vicious retaliation'. Because of their history and the anti-communist climate sweeping the United States at the time – which had widened to include 'moral perverts' – the group felt vulnerable and proposed a secret organisation. Their agenda included trying to get homosexuals to see themselves as an oppressed minority that had common interests with other minorities. In 1951 Hay separated from the Communist Party as a 'friend of the people' and somewhat ironically as a 'security risk'.

Paid employment was a necessity for Hay but was secondary to his interests in political activism, relationships with loved ones, and artistic and scholarly pursuits. Among other jobs, he worked in a foundry, for two aircraft companies, in hi-fi sales, in a TV repair shop and in a business manufacturing boilers.

In 1952, Jennings was arrested for soliciting a policeman. The Mattachine Society took over his defence and he was acquitted. The incident led to rapid growth of the organisation which began to survey candidates for election to public office about their attitudes regarding entrapment and 'social variance', and began a successful monthly magazine, *One*; the first regular publication produced by and about American homosexuals. Mattachine branches were established in other cities. With its success came a push to reorganise the group in an open, democratic form. Hay resisted the move, fearing loss of its political activist agenda, but he was under pressure. In February 1953, Hay was named in a Los Angeles newspaper as a Marxist teacher. This was regarded as a threat to the Mattachine Society, and so Hay withdrew from public association with it. The communist witch-hunt was in full swing at the time and the issue led to a split in the organisation, with the conservatives under Hal CALL, a San Francisco journalist, winning out.

This turn of events devastated Hay. Within a short period, he separated from the Community Party, his marriage broke up, his relationship (with Rudi Gernreich) failed, and leftist organisations which he held dear were reeling under the pressure of House Un-American Affairs Committee investigations. Hay was eventually

called before the Committee and found it difficult to obtain legal representation because of his homophile activities. He established a difficult relationship with Jorn Kamgren, which lasted for almost a decade, and which helped him heal but also isolated him from his former associates. It took years for Hay to regain his confidence to participate in public life. During this period, Hay studied homosexuality in history and became interested in the concept of the *berdache*, or cross-dressing Native Americans.

In 1963 Hay began a brief sexual relationship with Jim Kepner, founder of the International Gay and Lesbian Archives in Los Angeles. Soon after, Hay began an enduring relationship with John Burnside, to whom he was introduced by Dorr LEGG at ONE Inc. In spite of its conservatism, ONE and those involved in it played an important social and intellectual role for the couple, as did its splinter organisation, the Homosexual Information Center. In 1966, Hay organised a protest in Los Angeles against the exclusion of homosexuals from the military.

The peace, love and freedom ideology of the late 1960s suited Hay and Burnside, who were enthusiastic participants, with clothes and hair to match. Around this time, Hay met Morris Kight, a community-oriented gay liberationist, active in gay politics and social services. In 1969, Hay was elected first chair of the Southern California Gay Liberation Front, which held several rallies, demonstrations and protests. Hay did not complete his term as he and Burnside moved to New Mexico, bringing Burnside's kaleidoscope business with them. Hay renewed his investigations of *berdaches* and the couple were active in the local gay community and rights movement. In 1978, Hay combined counterculture and New Age ideas with his interests in mixed gender, spirituality and indigenous values, and he and Burnside moved back to Los Angeles to form the Radical Faeries, which bore some resemblance to the more recent men's movement. The group held successful rural retreats and laid plans to establish a utopian community, but dissatisfaction among younger members about Hay's patriarchal style resulted in division among the group and the commune never materialised. In spite of such a revolt in activist terms, Hay has achieved the status of a 'patriarch' in historical terms.

John D'Emilio, *Sexual Politics, Sexual Communities: The Making of a Homosexual Minority in the United States, 1940–1970* (Chicago, 1983); Jonathan Katz, *Gay American History: Lesbians and Gay Men in the USA* (New York, 1976); Stuart Timmons, *The Trouble with Harry Hay: Founder of the Modern Gay Movement* (Boston, 1990); Harry Hay, *Radically Gay: Gay Liberation in the Words of its Founders*, ed. Will Roscoe (Boston, 1996).

Gerard Sullivan

Heath, Gordon (1918–91), American actor and folk singer. Born in New York, African-American actor Heath first came to prominence with his critically acclaimed appearance in the Broadway play *Deep Are the Roots* (1945). Cast as an Army officer who returns home to the Deep South, he is forced to confront virulent racism after being treated as an equal in Europe. In 1947 Heath went to London's West End with the production and received more critical acclaim. Deciding to stay in Europe, Heath enjoyed popularity in Britain and France. On British television he played leading roles in several important dramas including *Deep Are the Roots* (1950) and Eugene O'Neill's *The Emperor Jones* (1953). In 1954 he narrated Halas and Batchelor's award-winning animation film of George Orwell's *Animal Farm*. The following year he appeared in a BBC radio version of Alan Paton's anti-apartheid novel *Cry, the Beloved Country*.

In 1950 Heath toured Britain in an innovative version of *Othello*. Pauline Henriques, a Jamaican-born actress who was cast as Emilia, recalled in 1992:

'Gordon was a slim, sensitive American actor who had a lot to give the theatre. We were all amazed that he had the range to play Othello, but he was, in fact, a very good and very unusual Othello.' Five years later, Heath played Othello again in Tony Richardson's superb BBC television production, broadcast live on 15 December 1955. In the tele-recording that exists in Britain's National Film and Television Archive, Heath's elegant, soft-spoken and understated Othello is a revelation.

From the late 1940s, Heath lived in Paris with his lover, Lee Payant. For many years they ran a popular Left Bank café called L'Abbaye. One of their friends, Leslie Schenck, remembers: 'In 1949 Gordon's partner Lee Payant joined him in Paris. They'd been having a relationship in America for seven years. Lee was a wonderful guy. A sweetheart. He gave up his life for Gordon. They had a great deal of love for each other and they both liked Paris. It was such an exciting place in those days and, when it came to race and your private life, you were left completely alone. So Gordon taught Lee a few chords and songs, and they stayed in Paris, singing duets in L'Abbaye, a "club" they eventually took over. It became an institution . . . As for his acting career, there were very few roles worthy of his attention and that is why he eventually became a theatre director in Paris, doing American plays by people like Arthur Miller . . . Gordon and Payant were together for a very long time, over twenty years. But when Lee died in 1976, it was a terrible blow for Gordon. In fact he decided he couldn't continue with L'Abbaye.' Heath died in Paris from an AIDS-related illness.

Stephen Bourne, *Black in the British Frame: Black People in British Film and Television 1896–1996* (London, 1998); Gordon Heath, *Deep Are the Roots: Memoirs of a Black Expatriate* (Boston, 1992); Pauline Henriques, *Black and White in Colour: Black People in British Television since 1936* (London, 1992).

Stephen Bourne

Hekma, Gert (b. 1951), Dutch scholar. Born in the province of Groningen, Hekma studied anthropology at the Free University in Amsterdam and completed a thesis on the medicalisation of homosexuality in the Netherlands. Since 1984 he has been a lecturer in gay studies at the University of Amsterdam. In 1975, he joined the radical gay group 'The Red Faggots'. He co-organised the first gay film festival in the Netherlands in 1976 and a gay cultural festival in 1980. Since 1983, he has organised several international gay and lesbian studies conferences in Amsterdam and Paris; the 1986 conference, 'Among Men, Among Women', held in Amsterdam, was notable in particular for developing the concept of 'homosociality'. He has co-edited several books on the sociology and history of (homo)sexuality, including *The Pursuit of Sodomy* (1989), *Gay Men and the Sexual History of the Political Left* (1996) and *Sexual Cultures in Europe* (1999), as well as other works in Dutch. He has been a member of the editorial boards of several journals in the field of sexual sciences and editor of *Thamyris*.

In his private life, he is a confirmed satinist ('one who has a fetish for satin'), Sadian and book collector.

Robert Aldrich and Garry Wotherspoon

Hellbach, Hans Dietrich (b. 1906), German writer. Born in Plauen in eastern Germany, where his father served as a district court judge, he graduated from classical secondary school in 1925, and studied German, musicology, philosophy and journalism at the universities of Innsbruck and Leipzig. It was at Leipzig that he defended his thesis in 1930 on 'The Love of Friends' (*Freundesliebe*) in German literature.

In this study, which was published in 1931 under the name 'Hans Dietrich' ('to spare his parents', as Hellbach wrote to Albert H. Rausch), he sums up what had been said and done concerning literature since the beginning of the gay liberation

movement in Germany. His comments apply especially to the *Jahrbuch für sexuelle Zwischenstufen*, edited by Magnus Hirschfeld from 1899 until 1923, and the journal *Der Eigene*, edited by Adolf Brand from 1896 until 1932. Hellbach offers an overview of love between men in German literature (including an historical look at the Ancient Greeks as well as at Michelangelo's and Shakespeare's sonnets) from the Middle Ages, working his way from eighteenth-century poetry of friendship, Goethe, Schiller and Hölderin, up through contemporary gay works by Wilhelm Walloth, Arnolt Bronnen, Bill Forster, Erich Ebermayer, Stefan Zweig, Thomas Mann and others.

Real homoerotic German poetry began, according to Hellbach, with August von Platen (1796–1835). In fact, an entire chapter of the study is dedicated to him. However, despite Platen's very open love poems to quite a number of men and the very open reflections in his diaries, Hellbach criticizes Platen for 'fighting Eros', i.e. fighting his own homosexuality.

The triumph of Eros in modern German literature, according to Hellbach, was gained by Albert H. Rausch (1882–1949) and even more so by Stefan George, who gave a new 'social-ethical' dimension to the definition of the love of friends.

Eros, another journal published by Adolf Brand side by side with *Der Eigene*, hailed Hellbach's book as the first academic study on homoerotic literature and thus a significant 'social and national recognition of our efforts'.

The flow of letters from the young Hellbach to Rausch (he had sent his book and also a charming photograph), our main source on Hellbach's life, stops in 1932. Hellbach, 26 years old by this time, was in 1932 working as a teacher in Leipzig, later probably taking other teaching posts elsewhere in Germany. In 1940, he married. He appears never to have published anything after that.

Hans Dietrich (Hans Dietrich Hellbach), *Die*

Freundesliebe in der deutschen Literatur,
Marita Keilson-Lauritz, intro. (Berlin, 1996).

Marita Keilson-Lauritz

Hemphill, Essex (1957–95), American
author. Born in Chicago, Hemphill grew
up in Washington, DC. He is one of the
many black American authors whose
work is only now receiving proper recognition, having had to battle against both the
neglect of the predominantly white gay
community and rejection from the black
community.

Hemphill began writing early, and published two chapbooks, *Earth Life* (1985)
and *Conditions* (1986). He first came to
wider public attention as one of the contributors to Joseph Beam's path-breaking
In the Life (1986), an anthology of black
gay male writers. Upon Beam's death,
Hemphill took over as editor of the sequel
*Brother to Brother: New Writings by Black
Gay Men* (1991). He was a co-founder of
the *Nethula Journal of Contemporary
Literature*, one of several little magazines
that began to appear, featuring the work
of black writers such as Audre LORDE,
Michelle CLIFF, Anita Cornwell and Larry
Duplechan, and continuing the tradition
associated with the Harlem Renaissance,
that flowering of black culture that threw
up such luminaries as Ma Rainey, Bessie
Smith, Gladys Bentley, Countee Cullen,
Wallace Thurman, Bruce Nugent and
Langston HUGHES.

Hemphill's work has featured in recent
films by black directors Marlon Riggs,
Tongues Untied (1989) and *Black Is, Black
Ain't* (1995), and Isaac Julien, *Looking
for Langston* (1989), both important
filmmakers examining black gay sexuality
from a black point of view.

Hemphill died of AIDS-related complications in Philadelphia.

Garry Wotherspoon

Herbert, John (b. 1926), Canadian writer.
Best known as a playwright, the most
prominent of his works being *Fortune and
Men's Eyes*, Herbert was born in Toronto

and educated there until the age of seventeen. In 1946 he spent six months in a reformatory, providing him with experience
that he would eventually turn to dramatic
effect. In the 1950s he attended ballet
school, but by the beginning of the next
decade had set himself on a career centred
primarily in the theatre. In the early 1960s,
he was artistic director of three Toronto
companies in succession. Through the
1970s and early 1980s, he taught in various
writing and drama programmes in high
schools, universities and other more specialised institutions, though retaining his
primary interest in directing small and
alternative theatre companies. For years he
helped a small troupe that worked out of
the community centre that stands at the
heart of Toronto's lesbian/gay 'ghetto'.

Over his career, he has been dancer,
stage manager, director, designer, teacher,
and of course playwright. *Fortune and
Men's Eyes* (1967) was widely performed
and turned into a film directed by Harvey
Hart (1971). It is set in a Canadian reformatory, and helped stimulate interest in
prison reform, leading to the establishment of the Fortune Society of America,
on the board of which he sits as honorary
member. It also raises questions about
masculine gender roles, and the intersection of power and sex. The play earned
numerous honours for its writer, including
life membership in the Actors Studio in
New York, and a special award from the
Library of Congress in Washington, DC.
Since then he has written other plays, including *Omphale and the Hero* (1974),
and four gay-themed short plays gathered
together as *Some Angry Summer Songs*
(1976). He has also written articles and
essays, and still resides in Toronto.

Oxford Companion to Canadian Literature,
2nd edn. (Toronto, 1997); *Canadian Who's Who.*

David Rayside

Herdt, Gilbert (b. 1949), American
scholar. Herdt was born in Oakley, Kansas, in 1949 and educated in Wichita and

the University of California, San Francisco. His first fieldwork was with Japanese-Americans in the San Francisco Bay area, and his Master's thesis was based on field-work in a hospital psychiatry ward, study-ing the rituals of psychotherapy. In 1974 he was awarded a Fulbright scholarship to study at the Australian National University (Canberra), where he spent two years studying the Sambia people of Papua New Guinea. At the end of the 1970s he was a postdoctoral fellow at the Neuropsychiat-ric Institute at UCLA, where he was a member of the Gender Identity Research Team. He subsequently became Professor of Human Development at the University of Chicago, and is currently Professor of Sexuality and Anthropology and Director of the Human Sexuality Studies Program at San Francisco State University.

He wrote two books on the Sambia, the first of which, *Guardians of the Flutes: Idioms of Masculinity – A Study of Ritual-ized Homosexual Behavior* (1981), began a long process of challenging deeply-held western assumptions about sexual devel-opment and the meaning of homosexual experience. His subsequent books include *Ritualized Homosexuality in Melanesia* (1984), *Culture and Sexual Risk: Anthro-pological Perspectives on AIDS* (1995) and the edited volume *Third Sex, Third Gender: Beyond Sexual Dimorphism in Culture and History* (1994). Herdt demon-strated how important culture is in the formation of gender identity and in the display of sexuality in social contexts; the practices of the Sambia showed that it was possible, indeed required, for individuals to move from exclusive homosexual behaviour to exclusive hetero-sexuality. His work brought together his-torical, psychological and anthropological studies to explore the boundaries of sex-ual difference, the fluidity of the relation-ships between the two biological sexes and the nature of sexuality and eroticism in different societies. He is the most promin-ent anthropologist working in these areas.

John Connell

Hertoft, (Helge) **Preben** (b. 1928), Danish sexologist. Preben Hertoft became a med-ical doctor in 1955 and specialised in neurology and psychiatry at the University Hospital in Copenhagen; he was assistant consultant at the Glostrup Mental Hos-pital (1969–73), consultant at the Uni-versity Hospital Psychiatric Department (1973–98), director of the Sexological Clinic (1986–98), assistant professor of sexology at the University of Copenhagen (1970–73), associate professor of psych-iatry (1973–83), then of clinical sexology (1984–93), and professor of clinical sexology (1994–99).

From his dissertation on the sexual be-haviour, knowledge and attitudes of young men in Denmark (for his higher doctorate in medicine, 1968) through the extra-ordinary professorship in sexology which crowned his career, Hertoft was the un-disputed authority in Scandinavia on sex. From this position Hertoft supported homosexual emancipation, not least by providing the medical and scientific legit-imation for the lowering of the homo-sexual age of consent from 18 to 15 years in 1976, and in general by furthering sex-ual toleration, if not directly permissive-ness and sexual eclecticism. In his widely acclaimed textbook, *Klinisk Sexologi* (1976, 3rd edn. 1987; Italian, German and Swedish translations), Hertoft suggested that homosexuality should be defined with a view to 'enlarging the concept of normality.'

In the 1970s and 1980s Hertoft was psy-chiatric adviser for the National Union of Homophiles, later National Union of Gays and Lesbians. From 1984–88 he was a member of the Royal Commission on the Situation of Homosexuals in Soci-ety which prepared the statute on regis-tered partnership of persons of the same sex (1989). At this point in the history of homosexuality in Denmark, medical and scientific legitimation was no longer seen as a necessary condition for the societal emancipation of homosexuals and Her-toft's task now was to provide the moral and political support of sexological expertise. It should be added that Hertoft's allegiance to sexual minorities has covered the whole range of divergence from heterosexuality, including pleas for a more gentle and differentiating understanding of paedophiles.

Among Hertoft's achievements, mention should be made of the long and continous series of seminars on sex (The Sexological Seminars 1971–98), which were truly interdisciplinary, open to the general public, and often drew a large audience. In 1983 Hertoft was co-founder of the journal *Nordisk Sexologi* (from 1998, *Scandinavian Journal of Sexology*). His creation in 1986 of the Sexological Clinic, which specialised in the treatment of sexual dysfunctions, gender identity problems and forensic sexology, provided the institutional framework for a fertile research milieu.

In 1955 Hertoft married the textile artist Nanna Heerup.

Thorkil Sørensen, 'Preben Hertoft', *Dansk Biografisk Leksikon*, vol. 16 (Copenhagen, 1984), pp. 298–9.

Wilhelm von Rosen

Higgins, Terrence 'Terry' (1945–1982), British AIDS figure. After Terry Higgins died of AIDS in London in 1982 his lover, Rupert Whittaker, and prominent British activist Martyn Butler started a trust to raise funds for medical research and to support other members of the gay community in London affected by AIDS. These funds were used to establish the Terry Higgins Trust (THT) in early 1983. By the end of 1983 it was a registered company with charitable status. It was the first non-government AIDS service organisation in the UK. In the face of government inaction, the Trust also became involved in the dissemination of information to the London gay community about the 'new' disease.

Throughout the industrialised world the formation of such groups has become a hallmark of the community effort to provide financial and emotional support to those affected by HIV. They are usually organised on a city-specific basis and often take the name of an individual in the relevant community who has died of AIDS: often the name of the first known person in a community who has died is used for the group. For example, in Sydney, Australia, the Bobby Goldsmith Foundation was established following the death of one of the first men to die of AIDS in that city. These organisations have stepped in to fill gaps in service provision for those affected by AIDS; in many cases such groups were established prior to recognition by government that any problem existed. Some of these organisations have received government funding to support their activities; others remain totally community-funded. Where government funding has been received, many AIDS service organisations have been criticised for moving away from their community base in an effort to maintain and improve government support.

Initially formed under the name Terry Higgins Trust, the UK organisation was reformed in August 1993 under the name Terrence Higgins Trust. The change in nomenclature provides insight into wider community attitudes surrounding the issue of HIV/AIDS. The name change was a deliberate attempt on the part of members of the gay male community to 'raise' the public perception of the Trust. The initial trust was formed by a group of concerned community members who had no experience in organising or managing such a group. Garfield notes that 'Terrence sounded more formal, more serious'. Berridge notes that their politics were seen to be too 'left'. In the days of Thatcherite Britain these traits were considered negatives when it came to attracting government support and public donations. Hence the name and the *modus operandi* were altered to make the organisation more appealing and less confronting to mainstream Britain.

S. Watney, *Practices of Freedom: Selected Writings on HIV/AIDS* (London, 1994); S. Garfield, *The End of Innocence: Britain in the Time of AIDS* (London, 1995); V. Berridge, *AIDS in the UK* (Oxford, 1996).

Mark Edwards

Hill, Charles C. (b. 1945), Canadian art curator, activist. Born in Ottawa, Hill studied art history at McGill University and the University of Toronto. At the latter, in 1969 he was a founder and first chairman of the University of Toronto Homophile Association (UTHA). UTHA was the first openly gay organisation in Canada and the first group formed after the proclamation of Bill C-160 that decriminalised same-sex relationships between consenting adults in private. Hill was also involved with the Community Homophile Association of Toronto (CHAT), which grew out of UTHA. CHAT's advocacy group, Toronto Gay Action (TGA), organised, on 20 August 1971, the first demonstration by lesbians and gays in Canada. It was in support of a rally in Ottawa on 28 August, at which Hill delivered a stirring speech in support of the famous 'We demand' brief to the federal government, written by TGA and backed by groups from across Canada.

Hill moved back to Ottawa in 1972 and in 1973 assumed the presidency of Gays of Ottawa, which he had helped to conceive 18 months previously. He was an organiser of the 3rd national gay conference in 1975 and assisted the National Gay Rights Coalition with its 1976 brief on dangerous sexual offender legislation. He then dropped out of the gay movement, though he appeared in a feature magazine article, 'Gays in the Seventies', in 1977, and has occasionally addressed community fundraising events. He was honoured at the Ottawa Pride festival in 1997.

Hill was hired as an assistant curator at the National Gallery of Canada in 1972, and in 1980 was appointed its curator of Canadian art. Challenges to conventional wisdom still interest him. In a 1995 exhibition he reassessed the early years of the Group of Seven artists when they threatened the established perceptions of still 'colonialised' Canadians. His 1998 exhibition marking the fiftieth anniversary of the United Nations Universal Declaration of Human Rights examined the positions Canadian artists took on the economic and political issues of the 1930s and the 1940s.

Robert Fulford, 'Regrouping the Group', *Canadian Art*, vol. 12, no. 3 (1995); *Weekend Magazine*, 17 December, 1977; Charles C. Hill papers [82–015] and Toronto Gay Action records [89–058], Canadian Lesbian and Gay Archives, Toronto; Donald W. McLeod, *Lesbian and Gay Liberation in Canada* (Toronto, 1996).

Harold Averill

Hill, Lister (1894–1984), and **Wherry, Kenneth S.** (1892–1951), American politicians. Hill was born in Alabama, and was elected to the US House of Representatives in 1923 and served until 1937, then served in the Senate until 1968. Wherry was born in Nebraska. He was elected to the Senate in 1942. Both were from middle-class families and were university educated. Hill was a Democrat; Wherry, a Republican. Each held local political offices before being elected to the US Congress, where Hill was generally progressive, while Wherry was arch-conservative. In 1947, Senator Wherry informed the Secretary of State that 'admitted homosexuals and suspected perverts' were employed in the State Department in both high and low positions of authority, and provided the names of alleged 'lawbreakers'. Investigations were conducted and over the next three years 91 employees were requested to resign from the State Department. In 1950, police officers estimated that the number of homosexuals in the District of Columbia was at least 5,000, 75 per cent of whom were probably employed by the government, of which about one-quarter were bad security risks and very susceptible to communism.

The statements sufficiently alarmed Hill and Wherry that they decided to conduct further investigations into the employment of homosexuals by the federal government. In response to their inquiries, State Department officials compiled a list of 3,000 people in the United States and abroad who were alleged homosexuals. Existing employees and applicants for positions in the Department were to be checked against this list. Other departments established procedures for dismissing homosexuals. The Civil Service Commission reported that it was denying appointment to homosexuals and dismissing homosexual employees, whose behaviour it considered to fall within the category of 'criminal, infamous, dishonest, immoral or notoriously disgraceful behavior'.

A report issued by Hill in 1950 on 'Subversive Activity and Homosexuals in Government Service' made recommendations that laws, regulations and procedures be changed to prevent retention, employment or transfer of homosexuals. Wherry submitted a similar report. Hill sponsored a Senate resolution 'to make a thorough and comprehensive study and investigation' of 'the alleged employment by the departments and agencies of the Government of homosexuals and other moral perverts'.

A Senate subcommittee did not take the view that what government employees did outside the office on their own time was their own business, arguing that this 'does not apply to sexual perversion or any other type of criminal activity'. It was also critical of the practice of allowing homosexual employees to resign rather than being fired, because they might be re-employed in other branches of government.

Investigations continued – and several hundred homosexuals were dismissed from government employment – between 1950 and 1952. In 1953, one of the first executive orders of the new Republican president, Dwight D. Eisenhower, required that all government employees be subject to a security investigation. Sexual perversion was stipulated as one grounds for ineligibility for government employment. Under McCarthyism, persecution of homosexuals further continued the witch-hunt which owed much to the earlier efforts of Hill and Wherry.

Virginia V. Hamilton, *Lister Hill: Statesman from the South* (Chapel Hill, 1987); Marvin E. Stromer, *The Making of a Political Leader: Kenneth S. Wherry and the United States Senate* (Lincoln, 1969); Gerard Sullivan, *A Study of Political Campaigns of Discrimination Against Gay People in the United States, 1950–1978* (Ann Arbor, University Microfilms International [8729425], 1987).

Gerard Sullivan

Hislop, George (b. 1927), Canadian activist. Born in the village of Swansea (later part of Toronto), Hislop graduated from the Royal Conservatory of Music at the University of Toronto in 1949 with a Diploma in Speech Arts and Drama. During the 1950s he worked as a freelance actor in television and theatre in Toronto and London, England, before running a design and display company with his lover, Ron Shearer, between 1959 and 1971. Although part of the gay scene in Toronto since the late 1940s, and a member of the University of Toronto Homophile Association from 1969, Hislop did not come to public prominence until 1971 when he helped to found the Community Homophile Association of Toronto (CHAT), the first community-based gay liberation group in Canada. Hislop soon became president of CHAT, and remained so until the group disbanded in 1977. CHAT was in the forefront of developing a visible lesbian and gay community in Toronto. It co-operated with various social agencies, sent speakers to high schools, monitored gay-related court cases, provided legal, medical, and psychiatric referrals, and lobbied government and police officials. Through his full-time work as the president and spokesperson for CHAT, Hislop was dubbed the 'unofficial mayor' of Toronto's gay community and became one of the most visible and respected gay leaders in Canada during the 1970s and early 1980s. He used this visibility, as well as his experience on various boards and committees, including the City of Toronto Planning Board, to run for alderman in the Toronto municipal election of 1980. Though unsuccessful, Hislop was the first openly gay man to run for public office in Canada. The following year Hislop was again unsuccessful when he ran as an independent candidate for member of the Ontario legislature in the provincial riding of St George. Hislop's candidacy was in part to protest recent human rights abuses, particularly the 6 February 1981 bath-house raids, in which Toronto police raided four saunas and charged almost 300 men in one of the largest mass arrests in Canadian history. Hislop was one of the founders of the Toronto Lambda Business Council and spent much of the 1980s and 1990s engaged in business pursuits, including running saunas, magazines, a restaurant and a series of bars in Toronto.

Val Edwards, 'The Time, the Place, and the Person', *Body Politic*, no. 68 (1980), pp. 22–5; Bill Gladstone, 'Out in the Open: Like It or Not, George Hislop Won't Go Away', *Quest* (Toronto), September 1981, pp. T7–T12; 'Ron and George Have Been Trying to Get Along for 14 Years, Just Like a Lot of Other Couples', *Canadian Magazine*, 27 May 1972, p. 6, George Hislop papers, Canadian Lesbian and Gay Archives, Toronto.

Donald W. McLeod

Hockney, David (b. 1937), British painter, printmaker, photographer and stage designer. Born in Bradford into what he has described as a 'radical working-class family', Hockney studied at Bradford School of Art between 1953 and 1957. In 1959 he commenced three years of postgraduate study at the Royal College of Art in London and was awarded the Royal College of Art gold medal in 1962. At that time the Royal College was a centre for Pop Art and Hockney produced a number of works that drew upon an eclectic range of references and pictorial styles. Most notable, perhaps, was a series of paintings, produced between 1960–61, addressing the subject of homosexuality, e.g. *We Two Boys Clinging Together* (1961), which combined graffiti-like text from a poem by Walt Whitman with a deliberately naïve figurative style comprised of crudely-drawn, almost caricatural figures.

Although this early work was also influenced by abstract art, naturalism (based upon his skill as a draughtsman) is Hockney's principal idiom and, following his move to California in 1963, he soon established his signature style. Settling in Santa Monica, Hockney produced some of his most well-known paintings depicting a sun-drenched urban landscape of swimming pools, palm trees and boulevards. Rendered in flat expanses of smoothly handled and brilliantly coloured acrylic paint, the paintings nonetheless remain coolly detached – a consequence in part of their often being based on photographs. In contrast to England, Los Angeles appeared to be a gay paradise and contemporary gay life is represented in many of these Californian paintings, e.g. *Domestic Scene, Los Angeles* (1963), which depicts two men in a shower and is derived from photographs from physique magazines, while the male nude was the motif in other paintings, e.g. *Boy About to Take a Shower* (1964), *Peter Getting Out of Nick's Pool* (1966), and *The Room, Tarzana* (1967). During this period Hockney began painting pictures of swimming pools, e.g. *A Bigger Splash* (1967) – a fascination that culminated in the later *Paper Pools* series. Although intrigued by the visual play of their reflective surfaces, swimming pools were perhaps also a metonym for Hockney of a specifically Californian sexual hedonism as suggested in the scene of nude swimmers in the film *A Bigger Splash*, directed by Jack Hazan in 1972, which focused on the break-up of

Hockney's relationship with Peter Schlesinger.

In 1967 Hockney produced a series of etchings titled *Illustrations for Fourteen Poems by C. P. Cavafy* to accompany a selection of homosexual poems by the Greek poet. Aside from the actual subject-matter of the etchings, the prints are a fine example of Hockney's skill as an etcher and lithographer (he has illustrated a number of books) and, more generally, as a graphic artist, and drawing from life remains the basis of Hockney's art as evidenced, for example, in his many portraits. However, Hockney has worked in a range of media including stage design for opera, e.g. *The Rake's Progress* (1975), *The Magic Flute* (1978), *Tristan and Isolde* (1987), *Turandot* (1992), and photography. His photographic works in particular, which include composite images made up of multiple individual prints, are indicative of his interest, partly inspired by Cubism and Picasso, in perspective, multiple viewpoints and the structures of perception. Hockney has also explored the use of new forms of technology such as photocopiers, fax machines, video and computers in the production of images and these various experiments in pictorial construction have in turn influenced his painting style, e.g. the 1992 series of *Very New Paintings*.

David Hockney: A Retrospective (Los Angeles, 1988); Marco Livingstone, *David Hockney* (London, 1981, 3rd rev. edn 1996); Nikos Stangos (ed.), *David Hockney by David Hockney* (London, 1976), *That's the way I see it* (London, 1993); Lawrence Weschler, *David Hockney Cameraworks* (New York, 1983).

David L. Phillips

Hocquenghem, Guy (1946–88), French writer and activist. Born into a large middle-class family (ten children) in the Paris suburb of Boulogne, Hocquenghem was sexually and politically active at an early age. At 15 he began an affair with one of his male teachers, the philosopher René Scherer, who remained a life-long friend. Hocquenghem belonged in turn to the Communist Party (1962–65), the Trotskyist Jeunesse Communiste Révolutionnaire (Revolutionary Communist Youth) (1965–68) and the Maoist Vive la Révolution (Long Live the Revolution) (from September 1968 into the early 1970s).

His was otherwise a traditional French middle-class intellectual upbringing. He entered the élite École Normale Supérieure in 1965 to study Greek epigraphy, and he participated in the student occupation of the Sorbonne during the 'events' of May-June 1968, when protests by students and workers almost brought down the regime of Charles de Gaulle. But Hocquenghem initially kept his sexual life and his political activism strictly separate. On at least one occasion he felt obliged to publicly deny his homosexuality at a political meeting. Disillusioned with the homophobia of the traditional left, he joined FHAR (Front Homosexual d'Action Révolutionnaire, Homosexual Front for Revolutionary Action) in the spring of 1971. FHAR was a radical group founded by lesbians in March 1971 to agitate and demonstrate for gay rights. It took up the emphasis established by the Women's Liberation Movement on direct anti-authoritarian action and on linking issues of gender inequality and oppression to the prevailing politico-economic system.

Hocquenghem co-ordinated the historic issue No. 12 (23 April 1971) of the leftist newspaper *Tout* (nominally directed by the philosopher Jean-Paul SARTRE). This was a special number that reported on the sexual revolution and devoted four pages to homosexuality and to FHAR. The government seized the newspaper and charged Sartre with 'an outrage against public morals', but he was acquitted.

On 10 January 1972, the mass-circulation magazine *Le Nouvel Observateur* published an article by Hocquenghem in which he recounted the story of his life and his involvement with FHAR. The seductive Hocquenghem (who had youth, brilliance, eloquence and angelic beauty) was immediately a public figure in France: an irresistibly attractive spokesman for a new generation of French homosexuals. Many mistakenly considered him the founder and leader of FHAR, although FHAR had begun without him and its radical ideology rejected the very idea of organisational structure, formal membership or even leadership. Hocquenghem himself wrote at that time that 'FHAR belongs to nobody ... It is nothing more than homosexuality on the march. Everyone conscious of his homosexuality belongs to FHAR'. FHAR's radical politics and advocacy of total sexual liberty created an intoxicating brew that inspired young gays throughout the country and launched the modern gay movement in France. As someone recalled of Hocquenghem himself in those days, 'He could leave us for two hours for frenetic cruising, get fucked by five or six guys one after the other, and come back calm and eloquent to resume the conversation.' Hundreds of gay men and a few women attended FHAR's Thursday evening meetings at the Paris School of Fine Arts until the group collapsed in 1973–74.

Hocquenghem went on to teach philosophy at the University of Vincennes and then to pursue a journalistic career, notably on the staff of the left-wing newspaper *Libération* from 1977 to 1979. Always faithful to his youthful ideals, Hocquenghem was increasingly marginal to the gay rights movement as it gradually evolved, changing its tactics and becoming more politically respectable in the 1970s and 1980s. In *La Dérive homosexuelle* (*The Homosexual Drift*, 1977) he attacked gay consumerism and criticised contemporary gay politics and the demand for legal protection as 'organising, rationalising ... , becoming the herald of new repressions ... '. In *Lettre ouverte à ceux qui ont passé du col Mao au Rotary* (*An Open Letter to Those Who Have Moved on from the Mao Collar to the Rotary*

Club, 1986) he denounced his former comrades-in-arms, 'the maoist-leftists-protestors' of the 1960s who had become 'the new middle class of the eighties' and who had rallied to 'the national hypocrisy that is socialist power' (he accused the French socialists, who came to power in 1981, of being 'more right-wing than the Right').

Always provocative, Hocquenghem often took positions that dismayed his friends and allies: he defended paedophilia, attacked the feminist view of rape ('I cannot get it into my head that the slight wound inflicted by the blunt instrument known as a cock is more serious than painful burns or dangerously violent acts') and approved certain ideas of the 'New Right' (such as its opposition to 'universalism' and its theory of racial differences). But, as Hocquenghem explained in 1979, 'You have to play with fire, because that's how you learn to use it.'

Hocquenghem's most important theoretical work was *Le Désir homosexuel* (*Homosexual Desire*, 1972) in which he set out his application of the concept of polymorphous desire and his critique of the ways in which society seeks to control it by imposing categories of difference upon it. Against this social control Hocquenghem promoted the rehabilitation of homosexual promiscuity, particularly in the form of anonymous cruising, and the valorizing of the anus over the phallus, the two together leading to what he calls 'the collapse of both the sublimating phallic hierarchy and the individual/society double-bind'. It is a dual recipe for sexual and social anarchy in a positive sense, but one which is hostile to any notion of individual or social identity.

In 1979 Hocquenghem collaborated with the director Lionel Soukaz to produce an interesting but amateurish and sloppy film, *Race d'Ep* (*Race of Faggots*, in slang), which traced the history of homosexuality in the twentieth century. Its four parts dramatised the life of the photographer Willhelm von Gloeden; the work of Magnus Hirschfeld, and the Nazi repression of homosexuality; the sexual liberation movement of the 1960s; and cruising in Paris of the late 1970s.

In the 1980s the focus of Hocquenghem's writing shifted towards fiction. He turned out a series of fine novels in which he explored the relationship between desire and revolt, incorporating social observation and satire into a much broader canvas of aesthetic experiment and reflection on French intellectual and cultural traditions. Particularly important are *L'Amour en relief* (*Love in Relief*, 1982), *La Colère d'Agneau* (*The Anger of the Lamb*, 1985), and *Eve* (1987). The first of these, which follows the adventures of a beautiful Tunisian adolescent who is blinded in a scooter accident, questions our assumptions about identity, sexuality and literary/linguistic representation. *La Colère d'Agneau*, is a historical novel centred on the shadowy biblical figure of St John, explores the relativity of revolt and the nature of authority, particularly intellectual authority. *Eve*, which is perhaps the most powerful of all his novels, looks at the whole range of these issues in the heightened context of AIDS. Centred upon a pair of twins called Adam and Eve, it is a remarkable blend of realistic critique of contemporary (including gay) society, the expression of the experience of contracting AIDS (Hocquenghem was diagnosed HIV-positive in 1985) and reflection upon a whole series of fundamental Western myths and the discourses which they deploy. Other fiction works include *Les Voyages et aventures extraordinaires du Frère Angelo* (*The Extraordinary Voyages and Adventures of Fra Angelo*, 1988), set in fifteenth-century Europe and America, and the posthumously published *L'Amphithéatre des morts* (*The Amphitheatre of the Dead*, 1994), set in 2018.

Hocquenghem died of AIDS in August 1988.

Frédéric Martel, *Le Rose et le Noir: les homosexuels en France depuis 1968* (Paris, 1995); Bill Marshall *Guy Hocquenghem: Beyond Gay Identity* (London, 1996).

Michael Sibalis

Hogan, Desmond (b. 1951), Irish writer. Born in Galway, Hogan helped found the Irish Writer's Co-op. By the end of the 1990s he was based in London but continued to travel extensively. His stories and novels evince an understated tone and an elegant, spare style. Beginning with collections such as *Diamonds at the Bottom of the Sea* (1979) and *Children of Lir* (1981), his fiction is often concerned with the complex relationships between politics, religion and homoerotics. His style and thematics are exemplified by queer – or more properly 'quare' – stories such as 'Ties' and 'Jimmy'. Hogan's writing, which suggests close affinities with fellow Irish exiles Oscar Wilde, James Joyce and Samuel Beckett, has been embraced by a faithful audience in Great Britain and the United States, but is widely ignored in his native land, a country whose gay rights movement was still in its nascence at the turn of the twenty-first century.

George Piggford

Hollinghurst, Alan (b. 1954), British writer. At a time when the British writing establishment is coming to terms with overt gayness, Hollinghurst can be seen as representative of the new wave, a serious writer addressing a wide audience, for whom the sexual orientation of the *personae* is of little import for plot or character development (although a review in the *Guardian Weekly* rather snootily commented that 'women are largely absent here, class distinctions give way to a new aristocracy of beauty, and the richest and cleverest of boys can be laid low by sexual desire').

Born at Stroud, England, and educated at Magdalen College, Oxford, he taught English at his *alma mater* (1977–8), then at other colleges until 1981. In 1982, he took a similar position at the University of London, but later that same year began work as an assistant editor at the *Times Literary Supplement*.

His first published work was a book of poems, *Confidential Chats with Boys* (1982). He is the author of several acclaimed books which have chronicled aspects of gay life: *The Swimming Pool Library* (1988), *The Folding Star* (1994) – which was shortlisted for that year's Booker Prize, and won the James Tait Black Memorial Prize – and *The Spell* (1998). His work has been acclaimed for its unsensational treatment of what the British press seem to regard as scandalous and salacious topics – life in a gay subculture, the workings of homosexual friendship networks and the sexual activities of gay males (including intergenerational sex).

Contemporary Authors, vol. 114 (Detroit, 1985).

Garry Wotherspoon

Holmes, James S (pseudonyms: Jim Holmes, Jacob Lowland) (1924–86), American-Dutch poet, translator. Holmes was born and raised on a farm in central Iowa. He was educated at William Penn College, Haverford and Brown University. In 1949, he went to the Netherlands as a Fulbright exchange teacher to teach English at an international Quaker college. In 1950, he moved to Amsterdam, where he began working as a freelance editor and translator of Dutch poetry. In 1956, he became the first non-native speaker of Dutch to be awarded the Marinus Nijhoff Prize, the leading Dutch award for literary translation. In 1964, he became a lecturer (and later, a senior lecturer) in Translation Studies at the University of Amsterdam.

In 1978, he co-founded a new discipline, Dutch Gay Studies (*Homostudies*). He helped to launch numerous academic and non-academic gay emancipation initiatives, such as the Amsterdam Documentation Centre *Homodok* and the gay journal *Homologie*. His workshops on gay literature at the General Literary Studies Department of the University of Amsterdam

gained much renown. He retired in 1985 and died from AIDS in 1986. He was buried in Amsterdam, which had been his home for thirty-six years.

In Holmes's work, translating poetry went side by side with theories of translating poetry. Thus, as he translated Baudelaire from one sex into another (*La Géante* became *A Giant* in what he called a 'sex-change version'), and Martial into modern gay lifestyle (with 'window shopping' and lines such as 'Listen, Rick: learn to live!'), he ruminated on how one could translate Virgil's *Eclogue Two* (on Corydon and Alexis) today without dropping most of the history of the gay (and mainstream) reception of this famous core of the gay canon.

In addition to being an openly gay academic, teacher and translator, Holmes was also a poet. As Daniel Weissbort put it, he was a poet 'of exquisite sensibility and, in his later years, of the frankest self-exposure'. And like the teacher and translator, the poet, Jim Holmes (also known under his pen-name, 'Jacob Lowland'), functioned much like a link between American and Dutch culture. Some of his poems were included in American gay anthologies such as *The Son of the Male Muse* (1983). Others appeared in Dutch publications such as *A Gay Stud's Guide to Amsterdam* (1978, 1980) and *Early Verse, Selected Poems 1947–1957* (1985).

Jana Beranova, 'James S(tratton) Holmes, A Flicker of Light behind the Dikes', *Rotterdam mooi* (Spring, 1987), pp. 9–12; James S. Holmes and William Jay Smith, *Dutch Interior: postwar Poetry of the Netherlands and Flanders* (New York, 1984); James S Holmes, *Translated! Papers on Literary Translation and Translation Studies* (Amsterdam, 1988); James S Holmes, 'Translating Martial and Virgil: Jacob Lowland among the Classics', in Daniel Weissbort (ed.), *Translating Poetry: The Double Labyrinth* (Iowa City, 1989).

Marita Keilson-Lauritz

Hooker, Evelyn (1907–96), American psychologist and sexologist. Born Evelyn

Gentry in North Platte, Nebraska, she moved with her family to Colorado, where she studied at the University of Colorado. She went on to complete her doctorate at Johns Hopkins University in 1932, a time when women were exceptions within doctoral programmes. She taught at the Maryland College for Women and Whittier College, where she was fired for being 'too liberal'. Hooker was then hired in 1939 by the University of California at Los Angeles as a research associate in experimental and physiological psychology. She remained at the university until 1970. In Los Angeles, she married her second husband, Edward Hooker. On her retirement in 1970, she engaged in private clinical practice in Santa Monica and died in Los Angeles.

Hooker's early research focused on neurotic behaviour in rats. During World War II, one of her students, Sam Fromm, introduced her to his lover, his network of friends and the homosexual subculture. Fromm's group of friends included professors, writers, artists, engineers, clerks, sailors and salesmen. Hooker was fascinated by the diversity of the group 'who led relatively stable, occupationally successful lives'. Fromm, after a trip to San Francisco with his lover, Hooker and her husband, urged Hooker to study homosexuals: 'It is your scientific duty to study people like us, homosexuals who function very well and don't go to psychiatrists.' Hooker, at first, was reluctant to do research on this topic as it would involve scientifically evaluating people she knew and regarded as friends, but, with the persistence of Fromm, she finally relented.

In 1954, Hooker received a grant from the National Institute for Mental Health (NIMH) to study homosexuality. Hooker obtained her homosexual sample from members of the Mattachine Society and One, Inc. (two homophile associations in Los Angeles committed to, in Hooker's words, 'the development of a homosexual ethic in order to better integrate the homosexual into society') and from friends of members of these organisations. Her heterosexual comparison group was gathered from various community organisations in the Los Angeles area. The composition of the homosexual sample was ground-breaking in that it excluded those individuals who had formed, almost exclusively, the samples in previous research on homosexuals: those seeking therapy or in mental institutions, those in the disciplinary barracks of the military or those who were incarcerated. These pathological and/or criminally deviant populations were popular as samples as they were easily accessible to psychologists and other researchers, but, because Hooker had homosexual friends and approached the topic in a non-prejudicial way, she was able to obtain a sample to which other researchers had never had access.

Hooker eliminated those subjects who were currently in therapy or who clearly exhibited psychological problems and limited her sample to subjects who could be defined as 'exclusively' heterosexual or homosexual. Her final sample consisted of thirty homosexual and thirty heterosexual men. Each homosexual was matched with a heterosexual on three criteria: age, education and intelligence quotient. Hooker administered three standard personality tests to the sixty subjects, including the Rorschach Test (generally viewed as a useful tool to assess personality structure and used by many clinicians to diagnose homosexuality), and also conducted intensive life history interviews with them.

Hooker scored the results for the personality tests and then assembled profiles of each of the subjects, omitting all identifying markers as to sexual orientation. These profiles were then given to three clinical psychologists who were told to judge the general personality structure and adjustment of each subject individually (two-thirds of both groups were rated as having an average or above average overall adjustment). The judges were then given the thirty matched profiles and were asked to distinguish which one was the homosexual. The results were surprising and countered the notion that homosexuality was inherently and manifestly pathological, since the judges could not distinguish homosexuals from the heterosexuals with any more certainty than chance. Given these results, Hooker tentatively concluded that homosexuality as a clinical entity does not exist, but has forms as varied as those of heterosexuality; that homosexuality may be a deviation in sexual pattern which is within the normal range, psychologically; and that the role of particular forms of sexual desire and expression in personality structure and development may be less important than has frequently been assumed.

Hooker's findings were so challenging to 'widespread and emotional convictions' that the editors of the *Journal of Projective Techniques* pressed her to publish her preliminary findings between 1957 and 1959. Their publication challenged the generally held views that homosexuality was easily identifiable and that homosexuals were emotionally and socially maladjusted. She demonstrated that the current belief that homosexuality, by itself, was an illness was simply not supported by evidence.

Hooker continued to conduct research on the homosexual community, publishing various articles in the 1960s. She examined the role that 'institutions', such as gay bars, play in providing various means of support for the gay community. These ethnographic studies reveal that Hooker realised it was important not only to study the psychology of homosexuality but to understand how psychology was affected by homosexual life experience. In her last article, 'Reflections of a 40-Year Exploration: A Scientific View on Homosexuality', she said that 'it was essential to know and understand everything I could about the gay social milieu that they created'.

Hooker's foray into the field of ethnography research was unusual for a psychologist as was the way in which she, in her research, blurred the artificial lines between subject and researcher by establishing relations of trust with her homosexual subjects.

Hooker also felt the need to give something back to those that she researched. She gave speeches to the Mattachine Society members, published in its newsletter, attended meetings and received honours from the Society, though her personal links never 'tainted' her research.

In 1967, Hooker was appointed to lead the NIMH Task Force on Homosexuality, where her double role as researcher and advocate came into play. Its final report, issued in 1969, was severely critical of therapeutic 'treatments' of homosexuals and placed great emphasis on the alleviation and elimination of social discrimination through the implementation of a modern penal code, involving the repeal of sodomy laws, better public education on homosexuality and the establishment at NIMH of a centre to study sexuality. The recommendations of Hooker's Task Force were never implemented, but her work eventually played a significant role in the American Psychiatric Association's deletion of homosexuality from its list of mental illnesses in 1973.

Hooker's work was therefore important in changing scientific and social attitudes, and was much valued on a personal level by gays and lesbians. A documentary, 'Changing our Minds: The Story of Evelyn Hooker', charted her research and influence.

Evelyn Hooker, 'Reflections of a 40-Year Exploration: A Scientific View of Homosexuality', *American Psychologist*, vol. 48, no. 4 (1993), pp. 450–4; Edwin Schneidman, 'Evelyn Hooker', *American Psychologist*, vol. 53, no. 4 (1998), pp. 480–1; Judd Marmor, 'Evelyn Hooker', *Archives of Sexual Behavior*, vol. 26 (Oct. 1997), pp. 577–8; Paul Chance, 'Tolerance is Condescending: Facts that Liberated the Gay Community', *Psychology Today* (Dec. 1975), pp. 52–4.

Trent Newmeyer

Hoover, J(ohn) Edgar (1895–1972), American governmental administrator. Born in Washington, DC, to middle-class government bureaucrats, J. Edgar Hoover's boyhood ambition was to be a minister. He worked his way through George Washington University at night, earning a Bachelor of Laws in 1916 and a Master of Laws in 1917. Soon after law school, he entered the newly formed Bureau of Investigation, a branch of the United States Department of Justice charged with investigating interstate crime. At a time when law enforcement was mostly a state and local affair, the Bureau (it would not be called the Federal Bureau of Investigation until 1934) was a relatively unimportant government agency. Hoover's leadership transformed the Bureau and made Hoover himself the leading figure in the national campaign for 'law and order'.

Hoover's first assignment was in the General Intelligence Division's antiradical division in 1919, where he handled deportation proceedings during the first Red Scare in the US. Following a series of political corruption scandals that he carefully avoided, Hoover was named Director of the Bureau in 1924, a position he kept until his death nearly fifty years later. Hoover was a skilled bureaucrat and technician who professionalised the force and brought criminal investigation and law enforcement techniques into the modern era through the introduction of such procedures as wiretaps and fingerprinting. He was also deft at public relations, actively promoting the figure of the 'G-Man' as a cultural hero beginning in the 1930s; often he took credit for the FBI for work done by local law enforcement officers.

Perhaps Hoover's greatest skill was at politics in the Machiavellian sense: deeply loyal to his friends, willing and able to destroy his carefully selected enemies, at once paranoid and over-confident, Hoover's personality dominated the FBI and gave him greater power and influence in Washington than most elected officials, including the eight presidents under whom he technically served. In 1947, at the height of cold-war anti-communism, President Harry Truman authorised the FBI to investigate the loyalty of federal employees; Hoover and his enthusiastic agents were the footsoldiers of this Red Scare. At times, however, Hoover knew the limits of the accusatory culture he helped foster. Senator Joseph McCarthy sought additional FBI assistance as his own investigation began to draw criticism in the press, but the media-savvy Hoover stepped back and refused to aid McCarthy.

In 1951, Hoover created the Sex Deviates Program, an FBI initiative designed to uncover homosexuals in government positions at all levels. Hoover's programme was part of a larger movement in American public life in the post-World War II period that cost thousands of diplomats, bureaucrats, professors and teachers their jobs – more than those who lost their positions over allegations of communist sympathy. Irony abounds in the fact that thousands of homosexuals were persecuted by a man who was almost certainly one of their own, and there is a temptation to chalk the 'Pink Scare' up to Hoover's own tortured psyche. Yet in pursuing this task, Hoover, ever vigilant of public opinion, did no more than fulfil the wishes of a mainstream 1950s America obsessed with normalcy; his actions reflect the tenor of the times and the political purposes to which homophobia could be put in the cold war era.

Hoover's personal life was shrouded in secrecy and deeply complex. A life-long bachelor, he lived with his mother in his childhood home until her death in 1938, yet also probably lived with FBI Assistant Director and his right-hand man Clyde Tolson for the last forty-four years of his life (although they maintained separate residences) and is buried next to Tolson. A hidebound conservative who ate the same breakfast every day of his life, he also enjoyed a flamboyant and glamorous lifestyle, particularly in the 1930s, when he spent winters at Florida resorts and frequented fashionable New York night-clubs. During Hoover's lifetime, rumours circulated widely about his homosexuality. One unknowing FBI agent even passed a set of allegations directly on to Tolson's office. Hoover was particularly ruthless in his pursuit of those who spread rumours about him, attacking not just critical journalists; a Washington hair salon operator and an Ohio woman who questioned Hoover's sexuality at her bridge club both found themselves under the lamp of FBI investigators.

Stories continued after Hoover's death in a series of tell-all biographies. One repeats a tale of Hoover and friends cross-dressing and participating in group sex at a private party organised by his associate Roy COHN at the Plaza Hotel in New York City. Some authors have questioned the authenticity of the more salacious stories and even the likelihood that Hoover was a homosexual, but offer no contrary evidence. The image of the FBI Director in heels and a feather boa has predominated popular media representations of Hoover since the mid-1990s, allowing mild amusement (and no small dose of homophobia) to obscure a long career as an arch-conservative government servant and a legacy of ruined reputations and destroyed careers.

Curt Gentry, *J. Edgar Hoover: The Man and the Secrets* (New York, 1991); Richard Gid Powers, *Secrecy and Power* (New York, 1987); Anthony Summers, *Official and Confidential: The Secret Life of J. Edgar Hoover* (New York, 1993); Athan Theoharis, *J. Edgar Hoover, Sex, and Crime: An Historical Antidote* (Chicago, 1995).

Christopher Capozzola

Horwitz, Jerome (b. ?), American medical scientist. Whilst working at the Michigan Cancer Foundation in 1964, Horwitz developed a possible treatment for cancer called azidothymidine (AZT). But the experimental drug proved to be useless in the fight against cancer and Horwitz lost his chance of fame. In April 1987 the Wellcome group of companies made AZT famous when it announced the release of the drug as the first HIV-specific treatment. As with all HIV-related drugs, AZT was considered a treatment only – it was never touted as a cure.

It appears that the commercial release of AZT for the treatment of HIV was pushed heavily by individuals within the US government, eager to find a treatment for the new disease. Sam Broder, the Director of the US National Cancer Institute, approached the American branch of the Wellcome group, Burroughs Wellcome, for an anti-viral drug. He convinced the company that development and release of AZT would be commercially viable. Initially, Burroughs Wellcome baulked at the lengthy drug approval processes stipulated by the US Food and Drug Administration, which could easily take up to ten years. In the event, approval for Burroughs Wellcome to release AZT took only twenty months.

The Wellcome group has been widely criticised by HIV-positive peoples' organisations and governments from the developing world for putting profits before people. Garfield notes that 'the first report of the human use of AZT coincided with the flotation of Wellcome shares on the London stock market'. The Wellcome group was a particular target of members of AIDS Coalition to Unleash Power (ACT UP) throughout the world. As with most HIV-related drugs, AZT carries a very high price tag, making it inaccessible for patients who are not lucky enough to have adequate health insurance or access to highly-subsidised public health pharmaceutical programmes. Other drug companies entering the HIV/AIDS field have experienced similar reactions to that directed at Wellcome.

S. Garfield, *The End of Innocence: Britain in the Time of AIDS* (London, 1995).

Mark Edwards

Hudson, Rock (1925–85), American actor. Born Roy Fitzgerald Scherer, in person Hudson appeared to be as uncomplicated as his screen performances. He led a fairly open gay private life after his brief – and arranged – marriage. The gay writer Armistead Maupin met him in the 1970s when Hudson, his film career over, was a popular TV cop: 'Rock was manly, he was successful, kind-hearted and funny and he was gay. He'd been able to surmount the obstacles that face a gay person and had made it big'.

Top box office stars who were gay or bisexual – Tyrone Power, Clifton WEBB, Montgomery CLIFT and possibly Cary Grant – made their individual accommodations to their sexual orientation. If they did not marry, they were discreet. In the late 1950s Hudson was the most popular star in the world yet he was ever fearful of shattering his heterosexual image, purpose-built by Hollywood and which he carefully nurtured in public for over thirty years.

In 1985, just weeks before he died, Hudson was revealed to be not only a homosexual but a homosexual who had AIDS. Supposedly, Hudson allowed his status to be announced to the world, and thus gave the epidemic a human face, focusing worldwide attention on treatment and finding a cure. It is likely, however, that the star died believing that only a handful of intimates knew about his disease.

In the last year of his life, diagnosed with an incurable and probably communicable disease, he continued being Rock Hudson, kissing a female co-star when he supposedly had open sores in his mouth, planning to reunite with Doris Day for a 25-years-later *Pillow Talk*, and turning down the lead in *La Cage aux Folles*. Increasingly exhausted and emaciated, he told a reporter, 'I have the energy of a teenager.' But he also said, 'I am now relaxed enough to go ahead and do whatever I want and not be self-conscious and not be uptight, be unafraid.' A few weeks before he died he apparently authorised a biographer to talk to his friends so that 'the truth' would finally be told.

Though there are no more manufactured stars like Hudson, the pressures that compelled him to deny his inner reality, even on the point of death, are apparently still abroad. Sir Ian MCKELLEN, who only felt able to come out as gay in later life, chillingly spoke about them: 'In Hollywood the pressures are so strong on actors of all generations to keep their sexuality secret that people go to the most extraordinary lengths. They get married – they pretend to be in a relationship with someone of the opposite sex when they are really having a relationship with their own gender . . . There are no really famous actors who are openly gay in Hollywood. People who are earning fabulous amounts of money and are the top of their trees feel that they can't do that. It's an indication of the sort of pressure that's on us all.'

Sara Davidson, *Rock Hudson: His Story* (New York, 1986); Jerry Oppenheimer and Jack Vitek, *Idol Rock Hudson: The True Story of an American Hero* (New York, 1986); John Parker, *The Trial of Rock Hudson* (London, 1990).

Keith Howes

Hughes, Langston (1902–67), American poet and writer. Born in Joplin, Missouri, Hughes spent most of his boyhood years in Lawrence, Kansas, where he was raised by his maternal grandmother and sporadically by his mother. While attending high school in Cleveland, Ohio, he began to pursue the poetic and literary interests that would become his career. Drawn to Harlem as the emerging Negro capital of the world, Hughes attended nearby Columbia University in 1921 but left after a year to take a series of jobs including a position on a ship bound for Africa. His travels to Africa, and later Europe, the Carribean and the Soviet Union, influenced his literary development, though the majority of his work focused on black people in America.

A prolific writer, editor, and translator, Hughes was a central figure in the Harlem Renaissance, a period of exceptional cultural production by African-Americans in the 1920s. His career lasted another four decades, yet Hughes's subsequent work maintained an interest in the concerns of his earliest writings. Traversing the wide varieties of African-American cultures and experiences, his *Montage of a Dream Deferred* (1951) encapsulates passionately but with quiet, sometimes ironic reserve Hughes's engagement with daily life, popular culture and resistance, racism, class inequalities and the hypocritical fiction of the 'American Dream' always postponed for the disenfranchised while being built on their backs and by their labours. In 1953, during the anti-communist McCarthy era, Hughes's literary investigations, combined with his political affiliations and sympathetic assessment of some aspects of Soviet society, earned him a subpoena to testify before the United States Senate. Worried about the costs to his career of remaining silent, Hughes appeased his interrogators by capitulating but more by reframing his criticisms of the United States to evoke the radical potential of an American-style democracy.

Hughes never had a significant lover-relationship, though the poem 'F.S.' (1921) suggests otherwise, and his autobiographical writings briefly mention sex with men. Sexually reticent in most of his literary output, some of his writings do include gay characters, show an interest in the social context of homosexuality, or make reference to the popularisation of Freud and other sexologists characteristic of this century's cultural modernism. During the latter years of his life, as rumours about his homosexuality circulated freely, Hughes guarded his privacy – perhaps to retain the respect and support of black churches and organisations, certainly to avoid exacerbating his precarious financial situation. He died in New York City.

In recent years, Hughes has become an important icon in the intersections of black and gay cultures. While his two major biographers come to opposite conclusions regarding his sexuality, others (such as Isaac Julien in his film *Looking for Langston: A Meditation* (1989)) have approached the question more provocatively by refusing the imperative to name his sexuality in set terms. Preventing a final resolution, whether affirming or refuting his homosexuality, Hughes's evasiveness on the topic troubles the certainty of contemporary categories of identity and has enabled important debates that have enlivened literary and historical study.

Faith Berry, *Langston Hughes: Before and Beyond Harlem* (Westport, CT, 1983); Langston Hughes, *The Big Sea* (New York, 1940) and *I Wonder as I Wonder* (New York, 1956); Arnold Rampersad, *The Life of Langston Hughes*, 2 vols (Oxford, 1986 and 1988).

Scott Bravmann

Hulme, Juliet See Pauline PARKER.

Humphreys, Laud (1931–88), American scholar. Christened Robert Allan Humphreys by his Oklahoma-state-legislator father, Humphreys was ordained as an Episcopalian (Anglican) priest in 1955. He undertook postgraduate work in sociology. His 1968 Ph.D. thesis on impersonal sex in St Louis public toilets was supervised by Lee Rainwater. It outraged the most famous member of Washington University's sociology department, Alvin Gouldner, who sought to have Humphreys's degree revoked because the observation of felonious consensual sex was felony itself (misprision). After physically attacking Humphreys, Gouldner was demoted, and moved overseas. Humphreys's thesis research was published to much controversy in 1970, and won the C. Wright Mills Award of the Society for the Study of Social Problems.

Humphreys taught at Southern Illinois University. In an anti-war demonstration involving the occupation of a draft board office, he destroyed a picture of President Richard Nixon, and was convicted of destroying government property. He was then hired by Pitzer College, one of the Claremont Colleges in southern California, in 1972, becoming a full professor in 1975. At a session on 'labelling' during the 1974 annual meeting of the American Sociological Association, within a wider critique of 'essentializing "the homosexual"', Edward Sagarin (who earlier had published homophile advocacy under the pseudonym Donald Webster CORY) criticised sociologists 'hiding behind' the safety of wives and children while advocating that lesbians and gay men 'come out of the closet'. Humphreys had dedicated *Tearoom Trade* (but not *Coming Out*) to his wife and children, and was likely an instance of what Sagarin had in mind. Humphreys certainly felt that he was being accused of hypocrisy and duplicity, and very publicly avowed a gay identity in his response. Humphreys was then active in founding the Sociologists' Gay Caucus and in challenging the deviance conceptualization of homosexuality. Like his protégé-beloved, Brian Miller, Humphreys subsequently largely abandoned research to focus on providing counselling and on testifying as an expert witness in the years preceding his death from lung cancer.

In the early 1980s, however, the two sociologists co-authored articles on proliferating gay subcultures and on victims of homophobic violence. Although his study of early gay organising in the US Midwest has been largely ignored, Humphreys's research on straight-identified and gay-identified males who have sex with males in secluded 'public' places is of continuing relevance.

Laud Humphreys, *Tearoom Trade* (Chicago, 1970); and *Out of the Closets* (Toronto, 1972).
Stephen O. Murray

Humphries, Barry (b. 1934), Australian actor. Humphries is best known for having created the character of Dame Edna Everage, self-styled Australian housewife and superstar. With her signature wisteria-tinted hair and diamanté upswepts, she has run amok (in the nicest possible way) in her native Australia, in England and, increasingly, in the United States. Fleeing her Humouresque Street, Moonee Ponds home the year after the Queen visited Australia, the Melbourne housewife, formerly Mrs Norm Everage, became a valued social commentator, first on stage and then on television. Her comments related to such matters of suburban moment as sandblasted reindeer on glass double doors, burgundy Axminster carpet squares and a pink chenille bedspread. She has dominated both live performance and the electronic media, pricking and teasing the most intimate bathroom secrets out of the most reticent ordinary folk and superstars alike.

Accompanied by her former bridesmaid, Madge Allsop, with whom she sometimes enjoyed an intimate relationship, she has always kept abreast of social trends (colonic irrigation, liposuction) and shared the joys and heartbreaks of motherhood. Her unmarried son, Kenny, has always been her special favourite. Her only daughter, Valmai, left her marriage to become a leather dyke.

Barry Humphries, himself a critic of middle-class mainstream Australia, sees Edna as in between pantomime dame and drag, 'closer really to character acting . . . making points about life'. Eschewing the foul mouth, but not the innuendo and the misogyny, of drag queens with whom she is sometimes compared, Edna attacks Australian and European alike in the same fundamentally caring manner. Similarities may be observed to the late Divine (aka Harris Glenn Milstead), star of John Waters's films, and the foul-mouthed Lily Savage (aka Paul O'Grady), whose recent success on British television, coupled with that of the sweetly sadistic Julian Clary, has threatened to steal some of the Dame's thunder.

Dame Edna Everage, *My Gorgeous Life* (London, 1989); Barry Humphries, *More, Please* (London, 1992).
Keith Howes

I

Iglesia, Eloy de la (b. 1944), Spanish film-maker. Risk-taking is one of de la Iglesia's trademarks. Ever since his earliest feature films, he has consistently tackled sensitive issues; homosexuality and politics, ideological inconsistences in left-wing parties, juvenile delinquency, drugs, Basque nationalism and violence, law and order, prostitution, corruption and rape constitute an explosive cocktail which, at first sight, points toward scandal-mongering and sensationalism. But this is definitely the wrong approach to the work of this politically commited, socially aware film-maker who has preserved a distinctive style and a hard-edged approach to his work in the face of criticism and even mockery from the establishment. His best work is characterised formally by immediacy and socially by a sense of urgency. Far from excessive intellectualising or empty aestheticism, his films attempt to be eminently popular but never populist. His style is raw, unadorned, rough-edged, and this has not helped his critical fortune in Spain at a time when aping the polished look of 'classic' (that is, American) products seemed to be the only accepted practice. Of course his polemical approach has also been the source of some discomfort among critics, who find it hard to accept so much dissidence. Explicit representation of homosexuality and homoeroticism in his films has always been a favourite target for de la Iglesia's critics: somehow sexual transgression is still easier to use against an artist when attacks on merely ideological grounds become too sensitive.

De la Iglesia's family belonged to the Basque bourgeoisie, and nothing in his background pointed towards filmmaking. In the early 1960s, art was hardly a respectable endeavour, especially if it did not follow ideologically conservative institutional paths. He started as a scriptwriter and then made a number of cheap feature films before finally directing his first important film with Carmen Sevilla, *El techo de cristal* (1970). From that point and until the end of Francoism in the 1970s, he suffered censorship. Some of his earlier features had to be re-edited or otherwise altered to satisfy the strict codes of the times. His commitment to the left led him to become a member of the Communist Party, and in a long interview published in the volume *Conocer a Eloy de la Iglesia* he discusses the homophobia within Spanish left-wing parties and how it affected his sense of militancy. Among his films the following have special relevance in representations of sexuality in Spain: *La semana del asesino* (1972), *Juego de amor prohibido* (1975), *Los placeres ocultos* (1976), *El diputado* (1978), *Navajeros* (1980), *El pico* (1982), *Colegas* (1983), *Otra vuelta de tuerca* (1985) and *La estanquera de Vallecas* (1986). Although homosexuality is only central to the plot of two of them (*El diputado* and *Los placeres ocultos*), it becomes a recurring issue in many of the others. In *El techo de cristal*, the director attempted an understated lesbian subtext (given the political situation, he went as far as he possibly could here). *Navajeros*, *El pico*, *Colegas* and *La estanquera de Vallecas* all have in common the presence of young José Luis Manzano, de la Iglesia's friend, whose death was to leave the director completely shattered with grief. Manzano's body is presented erotically (his raw, sometimes dangerous beauty, fills the screen) and his roles are sexually charged: de la Iglesia's own sexuality is in this way projected onto his images. Even playing strongly heterosexual characters, Manzano projects a strong homoerotic appeal, which is often integrated into the plots. In *El pico*, this is done through an ambiguous relationship with the artist played by Enrique Sanfrancisco, whereas in *Colegas* the friendship between Manzano and Antonio Flores has subtle homoerotic touches. *Otra vuelta de tuerca* is adapted from Henry James's *The Turn of the Screw*, but de la Iglesia brings it closer to his own concerns by replacing the character of the governess by a male seminarian: religious repression and homosexuality are then foregrounded and James's characteristic ambiguity undone.

De la Iglesia is typical of Spanish attitudes to homosexuality in his rejection of the 'identity' model, something all of his films reflect. He is on record as questioning a fixed 'gay identity' which he finds limiting and may actually help to reinforce stereotypes and homophobia. *Los placeres ocultos* is among the very earliest examples of unambiguous homosexual representations in Spanish cinema, and among the very few examples that show an anti-homophobic attitude. The homosexual (Simón Andreu) is shown under pressure coming both from conservative society and other homosexuals who accept stereotypical lifestyles. In a country where homosexuality was depicted exclusively in terms of fluttering, effeminate, unlikable characters, *Los placeres ocultos* was almost unreadable as a pro-gay statement. Because homosexuality was not considered political and because a political discourse is never made explicit in the film, audiences tended to regard this effort as something close to pornography. A fresh viewing reveals a clear-sighted attitude, an intelligent approach to the 'problem' of homosexuality: it is not the homosexual who is at fault, but society in condemning him.

In *El diputado*, de la Iglesia went even further, depicting the double life of a homosexual (José Sacristan) who was a left-wing member of parliament in the years following the democratic transition in Spain. Homosexuality is firmly placed in the agenda of the left, and the political repercussions of outing are considered. The protagonist is baited by corrupt extreme right politicians, who intend to use his sexual orientation to destroy his reputation. Given that he is in the closet, concerned by the lack of support his colleagues would show, this is fairly easy to do. In the end, he decides to come out and fight his battle in the open. This is represented both as an individual step forward and as a political statement.

De la Iglesia holds an important place in the history of Spanish cinema and his role in broadening the limits of expression and introducing complex political debate in film cannot be questioned. Following the death of Manzano, he went through a period of profound crisis, from which he started to emerge in the mid-1990s. He still has a strong contribution to make in the lively but intellectually somewhat shallow panorama of contemporary Spanish filmmaking.

Carlos Aguilar *et al.*, *Conocer a Eloy de la Iglesia* (San Sebastián, 1996); Paul Julian Smith, *Laws of Desire* (London, 1992).

Alberto Mira

Ihimaera-Smiler, Witi Tame (b. 1944), New Zealand writer. Ihimaera was born in Gisborne, New Zealand, with Maori tribal affiliations to the Te Aitanga a Ma-haki, Rongowhakaata, Ngai Tamanuhiri, Tuhoe, Kahungunu, Ngati Porou, Te Whanau a Apanui and Te Whakatohea. His original surname is Smiler, which he retains for general use, but the name he uses as a writer is Ihimaera, the Maori transliteration of Ishmael, the first name of his great-grandfather. In common with many Maori growing up in the 1940s and 1950s, Ihimaera was brought up not speaking Maori but studied the language when he completed his tertiary education at Victoria University of Wellington.

Ihimaera was a journalist in the Post Office Headquarters when the Prime Minister read his first collection of short stories, *Pounamu, Pounamu* (1972), which was also the first to be published by a Maori writer, and suggested that Ihimaera would be well placed in the Ministry of Foreign Affairs. Shortly afterwards, he was seconded there. Ihimaera later became a career diplomat, spending four years in the United States; the last two as New Zealand Consul in New York (1988–89). He then returned to New Zealand.

Ihimaera's novel *Tangi* (1973) was the first novel to be published by a Maori and revolves around the imagined death of and mourning for his father (still alive). It was shortly followed by another, *Whanau* (1974). *The New Net Goes Fishing* (1977) was his second collection of short stories. He then began a major task of co-editing an anthology of Maori writing in six volumes. *The Matriarch* (1986) a novel centred on his grandmother followed. During his time in New York, he wrote both *The Whale Rider* (1987) and *Dear Miss Mansfield* (1989). Later he wrote *Bulibasha: King of the Gypsies* (1994) and *The Dream Swimmer* (1997).

In 1975 Ihimaera was awarded the Robert Burns Fellowship in creative writing at the University of Otago. In 1990, he received a New Zealand Scholarship in Letters. Three years later he spent time as the Katherine Mansfield Memorial Fellow at Menton in France, and he was appointed

Distinguished Creative Fellow in Maori Literature at the University of Auckland. Ihimaera has been winner in the Wattie Book of the Year Awards and the Montana Book Awards. He has taught at the English Department at the University of Auckland since 1990.

Ihimaera has stated that his endeavour as a writer has been 'to convey an emotional landscape for Maori people'. The Maori Renaissance, which has been evidenced by a huge output of considerable quality by Maori writers, artists, musicians and other creative people, Ihimaera sees as more of a revolution so great is its impact on the culture of New Zealand both *pakeha* (non-Maori) and Maori. He has stated that 'just as all literature is politics, so too am I not only a writer but a political person'. In spite of his considerable output as a writer and significant commercial and literary success, Ihimaera's first love is music and this interest has seen him bring elements of opera into his novels and also to write libretti for opera.

While Ihimaera has largely been seen as a Maori writer and a writer for Maori his contribution has been one of encouraging greater understanding of Maori culture not only among Maori but also among other cultures and races. He sees Maori as a sacred language and English as a profane one, but recognises that both are necessary and desirable.

In the mid-1990s Ihimaera published a novel, *Nights in the Gardens of Spain* (1995), which, like many of his fictional works, was semi-autobiographical. In *Nights* he described the coming-out of a married father of two daughters, confirming what had been sensed by some in the gay community, that he was essentially gay. In *Nights* we hear the same voice which has spoken for the Maori minority speaking this time for the homosexual minority. David, the 'hero', is *pakeha* and in this novel we find a more spunky, witty and crisper telling as befits the subject. Ihimaera first envisaged this novel in

1984 when he accepted that his particular sexuality could not or should not be denied, but he decided not to give flesh to this idea principally out of sensitivity to his daughters. (He married in 1970 and has two children.) Then, in 1990, he wrote the first draft of *Nights*, a 'more explicit and ruthless' version than the final one, but he decided to wait until his daughters were older before finishing and publishing it.

Ihimaera sees *Nights* as marking a new beginning in his writing. Until 1995 he saw his priority as being to witness his time as a Maori but now he sees the matter of sexual identity becoming a higher priority, though he is looking for a particular Maori definition for gay Maori men that is more inclusive of options rather than exclusive. He also sees parallels between the Maori and the gay striving for respect and sovereignty, the need for space, for recognition of culture and the right to maintain one's integrity.

Ihimaera plans to publish another two books on male sexuality, the second dealing with issues of being a gay Maori within a *pakeha* gay culture. The indications are that if he is able to draw as fruitfully on his life and experience in this area as he has on Maori themes, there is a rich store to come indeed.

Ihimaera is a founder member of Te Waka Awhina Tane, a support group for gay Maori men and women, a member of the Te Haa, a Maori writing committee, and publisher in a Maori Writing Series.

John Beston, 'An Interview with Witi Ihimaera', in *World Literature Written in English*, vol. 16 (1977); Mark Williams, 'Witi Ihimaera', in *In the Same Room: Conversations with New Zealand Writers* (Auckland, 1992); Mark Amery, 'Witi Ihimaera', in *Quote Unquote* (Feb. 1995).

Michael Wooliscroft

Inge, William (1913–73), American playwright and novelist. Inge was born in Independence, Kansas, in the heart of the American Midwest that forms the landscape of his major plays. During the decade of the 1950s, he was second only to Tennessee WILLIAMS in the critical acclaim and commercial success his work enjoyed in the New York theatre.

A quartet of dramas forms the basis for Inge's reputation: *Come Back, Little Sheba, Bus Stop, The Dark at the Top of the Stairs*, and *Picnic*, which won both the Pulitzer Prize and the New York Drama Critics Circle Award in 1953. All later became successful films. While homosexuality is not overtly present in these plays, there are undercurrents of gay eroticism conveyed in the depiction of several male characters. In his later, minor dramas and two novels, Inge was more explicit in his exploration of gay themes.

Although he won the Academy Award in 1962 for his screenplay of the Elia Kazan film *Splendor in the Grass*, Inge did not again achieve the successs of his earlier works. Troubled throughout his adult life by depression and alcoholism, he committed suicide in Los Angeles, California in 1973.

R. Baird Sherman, *William Inge* (Boston, 1989); Ralph F. Voss, *A Life of William Inge: The Strains of Triumph* (Lawrence, KS, 1989).

David Garnes

Ioannou, Yiorgos (1927–85), Greek author. Born Yiorgos Sorolopi, the son of refugee parents from Eastern Thrace, Ioannou was born and brought up in Thessaloniki, where as a teenager he was a friend of the most outspokenly gay writer of his generation, Dinos Christianopoulos. In his adolescence he became a member of a Christian Youth movement, which he only finally left at the age of 21. He studied history and archaeology in the Arts Faculty of the University of Thessaloniki, gaining his degree in 1950. Thereafter his career was marked by a great restlessness for several years. After his two years' military service he taught in a private school for a few months, but in

1954 he was appointed as a lecturer in the ancient history department at the University of Thessaloniki. In the same year he published his first collection of poems, *Iliotropia*. In 1955 he formally changed his surname to Ioannou. Later that year he resigned his university post and took up a teaching job at a smart private boarding school in Athens, which he also resigned from after a few months, moving into state-sector teaching instead. As Greek school-teaching posts are centrally organised, and Ioannou had no particular leverage at the relevant ministry, for several years he was moved around schools in rural central and northern Greece. He seems to have contrived to use the time to write, because between 1959 and 1963 he regularly published poems and short prose pieces in periodicals, and his second collections of poems, *Ta hilia dendra*, came out in 1963. But it was only in 1964 that his first important collection of prose texts, *Yia ena filotimo*, appeared. Though he continued his teaching career, moving to Athens in 1971, he was henceforth primarily a writer, producing stories, articles, literary criticism, translations and a variety of short prose works which are difficult to categorise generically. Among his more interesting later works are *I sarkofagos* (1971), *I moni kliromonia* (1974) and *I protevousa ton prosfigon* (1984). A volume of his collected prose writings was assembled in 1976 under the flat title *Pezografimata*, and he received the State prize for his prose works in 1980. He died after a prostate operation.

Though Ioannou's homosexuality is very important to his work, it is largely suggested rather than discussed. A sense of isolation and marginalisation which he himself had experienced as a teenager, coupled with a fascination for the beauty of the male body which he himself translates in terms of a religious adoration, are constants in his work. It is a hunted and haunted eroticism in which the intense pleasure of desiring with the eyes is often as far as contact goes. The most elaborate

and overt of his writings in this respect is *Omonoia 1980*. Omonoia Square in central Athens was for decades the centre of the Greek underworld, a place where the unemployed and soldiers on leave would gather and a major place for cruising. Ostensibly a nostalgic reflection on the square's past, Ioannou's text has two more important dimensions: it is both an attack on a policy of social control which destroyed an environment because it harboured values at odds with those of the governing class, and an experimental text in which commentary on the history and geography of the square is linked to photographs of young men frequenting it and to a separate commentary on the erotic implications of all this for the author. The experimentalism of the text is representative of the way in which, more widely, Ioannou's sense of difference led him to write in forms which are difficult to characterise generically, a feature of much twentieth-century European gay writing.

Christopher Robinson

Isherwood, Christopher (1904–86), British–American writer. Isherwood was the author of ten novels, many plays, screenplays and translations. Born in England to upper-class parents, Francis Edward Isherwood and Kathleen Bradshaw, he emigrated with his close friend W. H. Auden to the United States in 1939 and became an American citizen in 1946. He wrote a number of memoirs about his parents, his life as a gay man, and his conversion to Indian religion in *Lions and Shadows: An Education in the Twenties* (1938), an autobiography he said was intended to be read as a novel, *Kathleen and Frank* (1972), *Christopher and His Kind, 1929–1939* (1976), in which he first came out publically as a homosexual, *My Guru and His Disciple* (1980) and *October* (1983) which was illustrated by his lover Don Bachardy, with whom he lived from 1954 until his death. In addition, his diaries, edited by Katherine Bucknell, have begun to appear; the first volume covering 1939–60 was issued in 1996. His first novel, *All the Conspirators* (1928) was followed by *The Memorial: Portrait of a Family* (1932), and after a three-year stay in Berlin (1930–33), he published *Mr. Norris Changes Trains* (1935) and *Goodbye to Berlin* (1935), which were later adaped by John Van Druten into the play *I am a Camera* (1951), the source of the stage musical *Cabaret* (1966) and the film (1972). Some of his other work includes *Prater Violet* (1945), about his experiences in Hollywood. Among his novels, those that deal with homosexuality are *The World in the Evening* (1954), *Down There on a Visit* (1961), *A Single Man* (1964) and *A Meeting by the River* (1967).

His stay in Berlin in the last years of the Weimar Republic, sometimes in the company of his close friends the poet W. H. Auden and Stephen Spender, inspired the works which transformed him as a writer, bringing him to the attention of American audiences. His reputation for raffishness began with his bemused portrait of decadent Berlin torn between the radical political ideas of left and right, by the free-wheeling bohemianism of its cultural life, and most of all by his own sympathetic view of Berlin's gay life.

He was one of the first writers of international reputation to champion gay rights as minority rights, as well as a supporter of the rights of all minorities. By the late 1970s, he had become a champion, if not cult figure, among gay men for his insistence that sexual preference needed no apology, no stance of contrition or remorse. His own dignity, his egalitarianism and good humour, and his domestic happiness made him a post-Stonewall role model.

Francis King, *Christopher Isherwood, A Bibliography* (London, 1976); Jonathan Fryer, *Eye of the Camera: A Life of Christopher Isherwood* (Garden City, NY, 1977, 1993); Robert H. Funk, *Christopher Isherwood, A Reference Guide* (Boston, 1979); John Lehmann, *Christo-pher Isherwood: A Personal Memoir* (New York, 1988).

Seymour Kleinberg

Israel, Franklin D. (1945–1996), American architect. Born in Brooklyn, New York, Israel grew up in New Jersey. His highly creative life ended at the age of 50 when he died of AIDS-related pneumonia. Among the many architects who have died as a result of AIDS, Israel is perhaps the best known. His work was original and provocative, and while there are few public buildings to his credit, the houses and offices he did design have been well documented and highly regarded both during and after his life.

Drawn to architecture at an early age, Israel studied with Louis Kahn at the University of Pennsylvania, did postgraduate work at Yale University and received a Master in Architecture from Columbia University. He studied for two years at the American Academy in Italy after winning the Rome Prize in Architecture. Shortly thereafter, he moved to southern California, where he became part of an artistic community willing to take in the culture of Los Angeles, comment on its disruptions, and experiment with its traditions.

Israel initially found work in the Hollywood studios, designing sets for such Paramount movies as *Night Games* and *Star Trek*. Taking advantage of his film connections, he soon began designing homes for gay and straight Hollywood figures. As his fame grew, he helped create the image of a new Los Angeles run by young independents. The headquarters for Propaganda Films (1988), Limelight Productions (1991), and Virgin Records (1991) were all designed by Israel. Often developing personal relationships with his clients, Israel understood their values and concerns. He was one with them, using architecture to challenge and transform everyday life, juxtaposing contemporary materials and disarming shapes with the remains of older structures. He created interior spaces with the variety, colour and surprise of the city. Corridors became urban streets; rooms were broken into fragmented forms; walls changed into fractured textures.

Israel was influenced by the city's aesthetics and heterogeneity, and attuned to its promises and limitations. His candid life brought him greater design freedom, addressing issues of chaos, change and resilience. 'I do think there is something in the mentality of a gay person that you can see in the work. The idea of openness . . . the inclusion of places to work out – I think all of these can be representative of a gay lifestyle.'

While his battle with AIDS caused him anger and confusion, it pushed him to take risks. Many who might not encounter his architectural work were able to experience its effect during a retrospective at Los Angeles' Museum of Contemporary Art entitled *Out of Order: Franklin D. Israel* (1996). Reworking the museum into a self-created environment, Israel made something that was beautiful, innovative, sculptural and inviting.

Revered as a teacher at the University of California's architecture school in Los Angeles, Israel had begun at the time of his death to obtain commissions for large public projects, at an age when most architects are just beginning to come into their own.

Steven Arnold, *Franklin D. Israel* (New York, 1993); Garrett Glaser, 'Designs of a Decade', *The Advocate*, 9 July 1996, pp. 51–3.

Ira Tattelman

J

Jääskeläinen, Raimo (1932- 1992), Finnish makeup artist. Raimo Jääskeläinen, a.k.a. Monsieur Mosse, was the first to openly announce his homosexuality in Finland. He came out in an interview he gave to a popular magazine in 1971, the same year homosexual acts were decriminalized for both women and men.

Having married early and become a father, Jääskeläinen decided to divorce after his boyfriend outed him to Jääskeläinen's wife and mother. His wife moved to Sweden, and the 25-year old Jääskeläinen moved to live at his mother's with his son. He worked as a make-up artist for the country's first commercial television channel in the mid-1950s. The new glamourous media soon created celebrities, and Jääskeläinen earned and enjoyed his share of the publicity as well.

In 1964 Jääskeläinen became 'Monsieur Mosse' when he opened his own salon, which soon became the place to go for female celebrities or for those who wished to get a glimpse of the high life. Monsieur Mosse had a good eye for talented and beautiful women, and many of his discoveries went on to make careers in TV or in international modeling. The late 1960s were the high point for him: he bought houses with golden toilet seats, American cars and long fur coats, and he threw wild parties, all of which was duly reported in the women's magazines.

At the beginning of the 1970s, his business started to decline due to financial ineptitude. It was then that he chose to take up an offer from the country's biggest gossip magazine, *Hymy*, to make his secret open to public knowledge by coming out in the May 1971 issue, in an interview entitled 'Why should I hide it: my happiness is different'. In the three succeeding issues, he told about his life, career and loves. He travelled to gay Amsterdam to 'marry' his young lover, and was also ready to name names and out his peers. Such public outing was prevented by the self-censorship of the magazine. All the famous names dropped by Mosse in his interview were blacked out.

Despite – or perhaps because of – his coming out, Mosse lost his business, and by September 1972 the same gossip magazine which profited from his confession dryly commented that Mosse was about to move to Mallorca, which, according to them, was 'no doubt a relief to many'. He lived at his friends' homes in Spain and the US for several years, yet returned to Finland in 1982 when he published his memoirs. Until his death, he continued to be 'Monsieur Mosse', the party animal, enjoying his circle of wealthy women friends and younger lovers. He died after his sixtieth birthday, from complications after a long overdue heart operation.

Before Mosse, knowledge about male homosexuality was very sparse in Finland, mostly derived from court cases of faceless paedophiles. The public figure of Mosse created the image of gay men in Finland for the heterosexuals. His witty comments, permed and bleached hair, plump figure, and, in particular, the golden champagne whisk he wore around his neck, are etched in the memory of the nation. For *Psyke*, the newly-founded gay organisation, his figure proved to be more problematic. On the one hand, Mosse was open about his homosexuality, which was one of the things *Psyke* envisioned to be possible for other gays as well. On the other hand, Mosse's lifestyle and behaviour were seen as detrimental to the efforts of gay activists who tried to present themselves as participants in a serious social debate with the government, the church and the medical profession. These gay activists were also ambivalent about his effeminacy, which they feared would project an unreal and stereotypical representation of gay men. However, it took twenty-three years for the lesbian and gay organisation SETA to follow Mosse's lead. In 1994, as a part of their Pride festivities, they speeded up political demands for same-sex registered partnerships by staging a public lesbian and gay 'wedding'.

Monsieur Mosse, *Voi pojat, kun tietäisitte! Eli Raimo Jääskeläisen uskomattomat seikkailut* (*Oh boy, if you only knew! Or the unbelievable adventures of Raimo Jääskeläinen*) (Tampere, 1981).

Tuula Juvonen

Jansson, Tove Marika (b. 1914), Swedish-Finnish writer and artist. Jansson is best known internationally for her 'Moomin' books children's literature, the first of which, *Småtrollen och den stora översvämningen* (*Little Troll and the Big Flood*, 1945), she wrote during World War II. The Moomin family is a large group of characters with strong personalities. Moomintroll himself is a childish boy who is dependent on both his mother (Moominmamma) and his friend Snuffle. Their harmonious family life in the Moominvalley, however, is often endangered by forces of nature – a flood, a comet, etc. Moomintroll and his family and friends have also appeared in comic books, on stage and in animation films. Jansson has made comic strips together with her brother, Lars Jansson.

Late in the 1960s, Jansson published *Sculptor's Daughter* (1968), an autobiography about her childhood in a family where both parents were artists. In the 1970s Jansson began to write novels and short stories. Homosexual characters, both female and male, appeared first in her short stories in *Dockskåpet* (*The Doll House*, 1978). Her novel *Rent spel* (*Fair Game*, 1989) was seen by literary critics as an autobiographical novel because there are many similarities with her own life. For example, the main characters, two elderly female artists, live in the same house but not the same flat: it is not a romantic love story but rather a story about getting old and sharing life together.

It has been an open secret that Jansson shares her life with Tuulikki Pietilä, also an artist. Pietilä is also the model for the character Too-ticky in the book *Moominland Midwinter* (1957), a bittersweet story about Moomintroll becoming independent with the helping hand of Too-ticky. It is noteworthy that amongst elderly women, born in the early twentieth century in the metropolitan cultural circles in Finland, there have been several women couples coming out as lesbians in their literary work in the 1990s: apart from Jansson, one can note theatre manager Vivica BANDLER and poet Mirkka REKOLA. It was also noted with some interest in the media that Jansson took Pietilä as her escort to the Independence Day Ball at the Presidential Palace in 1992. Kanerva Cederström has directed a documentary film, *Matkalla Toven kanssa* (*Travelling with Love*, 1993), on Jansson and Pietilä's travels in Japan and in North America. The film is partly based on home-movies filmed by Pietilä. The home movies are narrated by Jansson and Pietilä themselves.

A number of Jansson's books have been translated into English.

Suvi Ahola, 'Towards the Empty Page', *Books from Finland*, no. 2 (1991), pp. 131–7; Virpi Kurhela (ed.), *Muumien taikaa: tutkimusretkiä Tove Janssonin maailmaan/The Magic of Moomins: Exploring Tove Jansson's World* (Saarijärvi, 1996); Riikka Stewen, 'The Light of Seeing', *Books from Finland*, no. 1 (1993), pp. 21–4.

Johanna Pakkanen

Jarman, Derek (1942–94), British film-maker, artist, writer. Because of his pro-tean talents, the renown of his films, which often focused on homosexual themes, his writing, including an account of his struggle with AIDS, and his political activism, Jarman is one of the most significant figures in gay life of the two decades after the mid-1970s. He was born in Middlesex, the son of a Royal Air Force officer. He studied at the University of London, taking a BA at King's College and a diploma in art from the Slade School. By the late 1960s, Jarman was an up-and-coming artist, soon known for what Roger Wollen has described as his 'sparing and austere approach to landscape' and for his innovative design for such productions as Frederick Ashton's staging of *Jazz Calendar* at the Royal Ballet, John Gielgud's *Don Giovanni* at the English National Opera and Ken Russell's film *The Devils*.

During the 1970s, Jarman published a book of poems, successfully exhibited his paintings, undertook further designs for the ballet and – showing his enjoyment of humorous provocation – won first prize as Miss Crepe Suzette in the Alternative Miss World Competition. In 1976, Jarman made his first feature-length film, *Sebastiane*, a homoerotic account of the early Christian martyr. Jarman turned his attention increasingly to the cinema. *Caravaggio* (1986) explored the voracious bisexuality and social deviance of the Italian painter; *Angelic Conversation* (1987) focused on the homoeroticism of Shakespeare's sonnets; *Edward II* (1991) highlighted the king's relationship with Piers Gaveston; and *Wittgenstein* (1992) portrayed the sexual ambivalence of the Austrian philosopher. Such films, and more particularly *The Last of England* (1987), also contained biting social commentary on the politics of Thatcherite Britain.

In 1986, Jarman was diagnosed as HIV-positive, and his work thereafter more clearly dwelt on his homosexuality and his medical situation. *At Your Own Risk* (1992), the third volume of his auto-biographical writings, discussed being gay and having AIDS, as did the movie *Blue* (1993). Jarman's paintings of this period – bright canvases overwritten with such words as 'blood', 'scream' and 'queer' – manifested his anger at the lack of sufficient public attention to the plight of those with HIV, points also made in his participation in demonstrations mounted by gay activist groups. A gentler side was shown in the garden Jarman created at a cottage he bought in Kent, where he created artistic assemblages of *objets trouvés* and made a film, also called *The Garden* (1990).

Jarman's cinematic work was often bold – the dialogue of *Sebastiane* was in pig Latin, *Edward II* included scenes of contemporary gay demonstrations as well as stylised historical images, and *Blue* consisted only of a blue screen with text and music – though some critics felt the effects contrived. Jarman himself became a very public figure with his appearances in the media and his work with such popular music groups as the PET SHOP BOYS, though his paintings (and writings) are less well known than his films. Commentators compared him to PASOLINI (whom Jarman had himself once portrayed in one of several film appearances) for his historical interests, the variety of his cultural endeavours and his political activism. By the 1990s, he was one of the best known openly gay figures in the Western world, providing homosexual takes on historical figures and a critique of contemporary society.

Roger Wollen (ed.), *Derek Jarman: A Portrait* (London, 1996); Chris Lippard (ed.), *By Angels Driven: The Films of Derek Jarman* (London, 1996).

Robert Aldrich

Jay, Karla (b. 1947), American scholar. Born in Brooklyn, New York, and educated at Barnard College and New York University, Jay has spent her teaching career at Pace University in New York. She is Director of Women's and Gender Studies and Professor of English, and coordinates women's studies for two campuses of the university. Her numerous publications have established her reputation as one of the pioneering and leading scholars of lesbian studies, particularly in the field of history, as well as a commentator on contemporary gay and lesbian issues. They include *After You're Out: Personal Experiences of Gay Men and Lesbian Women* (co-edited with Allen Young, 1975), *The Gay Report* (with Allen Young, 1979), *The Amazon and the Page: Natalie Clifford Barney and Renée Vivien* (1988), *Lesbian Texts and Contexts: Radical Revisions* (co-edited with Joanne Glasgow, 1990), *Out of the Closets: Voices of Gay Liberation* (with Allen Young, 1972, reissued in a twentieth-anniversary edition in 1992), *Lavender Culture* (with Allen Young, 1978), *Dyke Life: From Growing Up to Growing Old – A Celebration of the Lesbian Experience* (1995) and *Tales of the Lavender Menace: A Memoir of Liberation* (1999). With Yvonne M. Klein, she has also translated and introduced *The Woman of the Wolf* (1983), a selection of the short stories and prose poems of Renée Vivien, an American lesbian expatriate in Paris in the early twentieth century. She is the general editor of a series on 'The Cutting Edge: Lesbian Life and Literature' published by New York University Press; twenty-one volumes of new scholarship and biography, as well as reprints of

classics and first publication of 'lost' works have now been issued. Her works have won numerous awards, and she has been elected to the editorial board of several journals. Her papers have been acquired by the rare books and manuscripts division of the New York Public Library.

Robert Aldrich and Garry Wotherspoon

Jersild, Jens (Christian) (1903–78), Danish police officer. Jersild graduated in law in 1929. The same year he became a constable in the Copenhagen Police Department. Various promotions followed. In 1939 he was appointed Police Inspector and deputy chief of the Third Division (vice, sanitation and veterinary affairs) of the Copenhagen Police Department. Police control and supervision of homosexuality was not part of the Third Division but divided between other divisions. In 1948 the Royal Commission on the Civil Service strongly recommended that the Third Division be dissolved at the retirement of the current chief of divison two years hence.

In 1949 the press highlighted the rise of homosexual prostitution in Copenhagen and a police task force was formed in order to clean up the Town Hall Square. When Jersild in 1950 became temporary Police Superintendent and acting chief of division, the task force was transferred to his division where 'police control of homosexuality' was now united in a new Section D, comprising control and supervision of homosexual prostitution, indecent public conduct (cottaging), sexual intercourse with minors (i.e. those under 18 years of age), and 'the supervision of homosexual associations, clubs and other gathering places'. The latter resulted from the founding in 1948 of the first formal organization for homophiles in Denmark, the Forbundet af 1948 (The Association of 1948). The concentration of police control of homosexuality within one section of the police force was probably not Jersild's idea, but inspired by the Police Commissioner's desire to retain the Third Division. In the eyes of the public, 'the homosexual problem' had become a major concern and Jersild turned out to be the right man to exploit this addition to his division. In 1953 his appointment was made permanent.

Until the mid-1960s Jersild was Denmark's principal authority on homosexuality. He very soon gained a high profile in the press by publishing books, by giving lectures and interviews, by presenting radio and television broadcasts, and by acting as adviser for a feature film, *Bundfald (Dregs)*, in 1957, on the evils of homosexual prostitution. In Jersild's opinion homosexuals were mainly attracted to the young. Consequently prostitution was caused by the demand of homosexuals. This might have grave consequences since, according to Jersild's widely disseminated 'Theory of Seduction', boys and young men would sometimes become homosexuals themselves from being sexually used by older homosexuals. In 1960 Jersild thus commented on the murder of a middle-aged homosexual man by two 15– 16 year-old male prostitutes, 'Nice grown men are often dangerous. Every hour of the day a boy is led astray . . . all over Copenhagen, in backyards, on staircases, in parks, and in cemeteries.' Furthermore, when male prostitutes became too old to exercise their profession, they would continue their criminal and anti-social behaviour and become common criminals. These arguments persuaded the Royal Commission on Prostitution, of which Jersild was a member, to recommend in 1955 that it be made a criminal act to obtain sex for payment with a person of the same sex under the age of 21. Until 1961 when this provision, the so-called 'Ugly Clause', was enacted by Parliament, it had not been a crime to pay for sexual favours. Now, Jersild's zealousness and the courts' interpretation of 'payment' meant that the age of homosexual consent was in practice raised from 18 to 21 years in sexual encounters between males of different age.

At the same time Section D pressured Copenhagen's homosexuals to the extent that practically all sexually active homosexuals came into contact with its staff and were followed, interrogated, warned, called as witnesses, arrested, had their homes ransacked and were sometimes convicted. By the early 1960s Section D had the names of about 10,000 homosexuals on its files. To a large extent this had its background in a severe lack of housing which compelled younger homosexuals to cruise in public areas and to indulge in various types of non-private sex, but also in the tendency of homosexuals of that period to seek sexual gratification with prostitutes who often were minors. The economic hardship imposed on the large contingent, in and around Copenhagen, of conscripted naval personnel added to the number of potential and actual male prostitutes.

In 1955 Jersild dealt a serious blow to organised homosexuality by raiding the premises of a publishing company that sold photos of naked young men. Through the seized lists of customers and models, a large number of male prostitutes and men who had had sex with minors were identified and convicted in the so-called 'Pornography Scandal'. The owners of the publishing company were closely but informally connected with Forbundet af 1948, which as a consequence suffered a serious loss of credibility within the homophile subculture and was severely weakened politically and financially.

In the early 1960s public opinion began to change. Jersild was criticised in the press and the 'Theory of Seduction' was questioned. In 1965 the 'Ugly Clause' was repealed.

It should be added that Jersild, as a prelude to his public statements on the growth of homosexual prostitution, seduction of boys and abuse of minors, generally mentioned the existence of law-abiding homosexual citizens. Also, in 1955 he opposed a proposal to raise the age of consent from 18 to 22, which he regarded as an unenforceable and unjust measure.

It is not surprising that, in popular gay

history, Jersild has been represented as the villain incarnate. He was, however, primarily a civil servant who, with professional vigour, acted according to the laws of his day and faithfully gave voice to the attitudes and anxieties of the population he served.

Within a year after Jersild's retirement in 1971, the Third Division was dissolved.

Jens Jersild, *Den mandlige prostitution. Årsager. Omfang. Følger* (Copenhagen, 1953), *Boyprostitution* (Copenhagen, 1956), *Barnet og det homoseksuelle problem* (Copenhagen, 1957), *The Normal Homosexual Male Versus the Boy Molester* (Copenhagen, 1967).

Wilhelm von Rosen

John, Sir Elton (b. 1947), British entertainer. Born in Middlesex, England, Reginald Kenneth Dwight showed an early talent for music, winning a Royal Academy of Music scholarship. He played piano in a local bar, and formed a group, The Corvettes, later reformed as Bluesology, which by 1965 was playing in London's clubland. Bluesology became the regular backing group for blues singer Long John Baldry, and moved on to the UK cabaret circuit, a move which disheartened Dwight, who, in May 1968, both quit the band and changed his name to Elton John. He released his first album, *Empty Sky*, in 1969.

From the early 1970s, John began to make a name for himself, with a series of now legendary songs (written with Bernie Taupin) such as 'Bad Side of the Moon', 'Your Song', 'Rocket Man', 'Candle in the Wind', 'Island Girl', 'Major Tom' and 'The Last Song'. As well, many of his albums – he has released nearly thirty in as many years – have gone gold or platinum; some of the best-known are *Honky Chateau* (1972), *Goodbye Yellow Brick Road* (1973), *Victim of Love* (1979), *Too Low for Zero* (1983), *Live in Australia* (1987) and *The One* (1992). Not only has he been a prolific songwriter, but he has also been enormously successful as a live performer,

with increasingly flamboyant and outrageous costumes and shows over the years.

Like many of the great rock stars of the 1970s, he has admitted to having a drug problem; unlike many of them, he has been a survivor. His growing celebrity status saw him move into new circles, and he became close to DIANA, PRINCESS OF WALES, whose funeral *epicedium* he wrote.

John is one of the few superstars to be openly gay: his well-publicized fiftieth birthday party saw him appearing in full eighteenth-century drag, with ornate gown and powdered wig, on the arm of a handsome young man – his lover, a movie producer – but it appears to have done his career little harm. His records still sell extremely well, and he was knighted for his services to the world of music.

Barry Toberman, *Elton John – A Biography* (London, 1988); Philip Norman, *Elton John* (London, 1991).

Garry Wotherspoon

Johnson, Philip (Cortelyou) (b. 1906), American architect. Johnson was born in Cleveland, Ohio. While his sexuality was never totally secret (he has been with David Whitney since 1960), he did not officially come out of the closet until 1993. At the age of 87 Johnson, one of the most recognisable faces in architecture, created little controversy with his announcement (the catalyst for which was the publication of his biography by Franz Schulze).

Being honest about his sexuality, however, did not go unnoticed. Johnson appeared on the cover of the gay and lesbian magazine *Out* (May 1996) and released images of his design for the Cathedral of Hope. Should the Cathedral be built, it will serve as a new sanctuary for the Dallas, Texas, branch of the Universal Fellowship of Metropolitan Community Churches, the largest gay and lesbian religious denomination in the US. The 2,500-seat sanctuary, over 100 feet tall, is a grand civic statement, imagined as a spiritual centre for gay and lesbian Christians around the world, by a man who helped shape and influence architecture in the US during the twentieth century.

At the age of 24, Johnson became the founding director of the Department of Architecture at the Museum of Modern Art in New York. In collaboration with Henry-Russell Hitchcock, he curated the exhibit *International Style: Architecture since 1922* (1932), which proved highly persuasive in introducing modernist European architecture to North America.

After a brief period in the 1930s during which he moved to Europe and became enamoured of Hitler's Nazi movement, Johnson returned to attend Harvard University's Graduate School of Design. (He received a Bachelor's Degree in Architecture in 1943.) By 1949, he built a much publicised glass house in New Canaan, Connecticut; the large property with the glass house, windowless guest house or bedroom suite and numerous other outbuildings has served as an experimental playground during Johnson's life. Catapulted into the architectural elite, Johnson spent the 1950s and 1960s designing houses and institutional buildings as well as teaching, primarily at Yale University. In the late 1960s, Johnson formed a partnership with John Burgee and began to work on more commercial buildings. He also moved away from the modernist style he had once championed, borrowing from others, experimenting with form, and attempting to move beyond what had become banal modernist boxes. After a number of mediocre buildings in a wide range of styles, Johnson began to perfect an architectural image that offered glass and steel sculptural forms to the increasing number of corporate clients who hired him. Awarded the American Institute of Architecture's Gold Medal in 1978 and the Pritzger Prize in 1980, Johnson became increasingly influential.

In the 1980s Johnson again changed, helping to popularise postmodernist architecture with its direct, ironic and sometime humorous allusions to historical forms and classical devices. He appeared on the cover of *Time* magazine holding a model of the AT & T Building (1984) and designed some kitschy structures for highly visible urban sites throughout the US. The flamboyance and artificiality of his buildings are either loved or hated but they gained him additional fame and notoriety.

By the 1980s and 1990s, Johnson had moved on. He curated a show, *Deconstructivist Architecture* (1988) in New York, and created a new firm with his name. He began working on smaller, more personal projects, leaving the larger ones to many of the architects he had mentored or promoted, including Peter Eisenman, Frank Gehry, Michael Graves and Robert Stern.

Johnson has constantly shifted his identity to match the times. Called a chameleon, whore, salesman and dilettante, he has used his work to keep the architectural community guessing and his fame to keep an interested public entertained.

N. Miller, *Johnson/Burgee Architecture* (New York, 1979); Franz Schulze, *Philip Johnson: Life and Work* (Chicago, 1994).

Ira Tattelman

Johnston, Craig (b. 1951), Australian activist. Johnston has been one of the Australian gay movement's most prolific and thoughtful theorists since he joined Gay Liberation in Sydney in 1973.

An activist who joined the Australian Labor Party at the age of 17, he participated in the anti-war movement and student activism and was a communist within four years. As a gay liberationist, he retained his radical perspective, working to maintain the links between the various social movements of the time. His writings on effeminism (a variety of countercultural radicalism which placed women's liberation at the centre of the radical project), his role in authoring the Manifesto of the Socialist Homosexuals, and his rejection of gay rights in favour of liberationist goals are testament to the radical imperative of the time.

In the late 1970s, he was among the first to detect a sea change among gay men, in particular, which made building a gay community a viable strategy for activists, and he argued strongly in articles and conference papers to persuade the gay left of the need for a rethinking of tactics and strategies. The shift from 'oppression' to 'discrimination', from 'liberation' to 'rights', from 'movement' to 'community', was put into practice most notably and with some success in the New South Wales law reform campaign of 1981–84 which aimed to mobilise the gay scene behind a leadership that did not push its radicalism too far. Johnston's primary work during the mid-1980s was as a Labor and then independent green member of the Sydney City Council. In the 1990s, he has maintained a watching brief on the community that he did so much to construct with articles on leather pride, drugs, the gay press, the gay dollar, the disadvantaged and queer.

Craig Johnson, *A Sydney Gaze: The Making of Gay Liberation* (Sydney, 1999).

Graham Willett

Johnston, Jill, (b. 1929), American activist. Johnston was a radical lesbian who wrote for the *Village Voice* in New York City during the 1960s and early 1970s. Born near London, England, and abandoned by her father, Johnston moved with her unwed American mother to the US as a child. By the 1960s, she had become a well-known art and dance critic in New York. In private life, she was briefly married, and had a son and a daughter, but then suffered three mental breakdowns that she later attributed to her struggles over her identity.

Johnston came out as a lesbian a few months before the Stonewall riots in 1969, later making the connection between her personal revolution and that of the women's movement. But in her book *Lesbian Nation*, she made it clear that she did not believe in fighting for women's equality with men within the mainstream capitalist political system, as did many liberal feminists. She declared that it would take a radical 'lesbian nation' to undermine the patriarchy, which she identified as a male-dominated system of gender relations that oppressed all women. Drawing on the current catchphrase among radicals, 'the personal is political', she maintained that every woman was born a lesbian, and women who slept with men were collaborating with the patriarchy in keeping women down.

Many feminists, especially straight and bisexual women, objected to her views, but Johnston did not see heterosexuality as natural to women. Using current psychological theories, she traced love between women to the love that all infants feel for their mothers. In the interests of the patriarchy, she argued, adolescent girls are forced to shift that love to males rather than to other women. 'ON A CLEAR DAY YOU CAN SEE YOUR MOTHER', she wrote, using capital letters and her particular style of wordplay on a popular song.

She not only wrote frankly, she also staged attention-getting 'happenings' that expressed her sentiments. In May 1971, she was invited to join writers Germaine Greer, a feminist, and Norman Mailer, an anti-feminist, on a panel discussion about women's liberation. Johnston felt that the issue belonged to women and was not debatable, especially by a man. As prearranged, two lesbian friends showed up on stage just as she was concluding her remarks, and they and Johnston rolled across the floor, embracing passionately, in front of the audience and the new media. She later described the scene to her readers: 'And I made love before notables and my circuitry got overloaded and the men in the audience dint [*sic*] want to hear me no more and I don't remember too much except leaving and wishing later I'd kissed Germaine before we walked off.'

Despite her unconventional behaviour, Johnston was not entirely at home as a mascot of the radical feminist movement.

Other women accused her of deliberately being disruptive or acting like a 'star' who was mainly interested in drawing media attention to herself. At the time, they were trying to accomplish a feminist revolution on the basis of group consensus, a socialist ideal, rather than relying on leaders or official spokeswomen, which they regarded as hierarchical.

To today's generation, Johnston's lesbian separatist views may seem alien and counterproductive, given the current 'queer' vision of a united rainbow movement of gays, lesbians, bisexual and transgendered people. But her experience and viewpoint must be seen in the context of the radical politics of the 1960s and 1970s. Many groups, including feminist women, were fiercely challenging the sexual conservatism, misogyny, racism and capitalist supremacy of the post-World War II era, and working out new ideas of their own.

Eventually, Johnston returned to writing about arts and culture, and also published her memoirs. Looking back on the activist years, she wrote, in *Admission Accomplished*, that she still believes that her basic ideology was right, even though she is sometimes embarrased at the vehemence of her political diatribes. In her words, 'The centrality of the lesbian position to feminist revolution – wildly unrealistic or downright mad, as it still seems to most women everywhere – continues to ring true and right.'

Alice Echols, *Daring to Be Bad: Radical Feminism in America, 1967–75* (Minneapolis, 1989); Jill Johnston, *Admission Accomplished: The Lesbian Nation Years 1970–75* (London, 1998); Jill Johnston, *Lesbian Nation: The Feminist Solution* (New York, 1973).

Barbara M. Freeman

Jones, Bill T. (b. 1952), American dancer, choreographer. Jones has long been an openly gay African-American dancer and choreographer, and more recently an openly HIV-positive one, slandered as perpetrating 'victim art' (by a *New Yorker* dance critic long hostile to him, who condemned while refusing to see 'Still/here', his 1993 attempt to craft a piece about living with terminal diseases). In *Last Night on Earth* Jones is acutely aware of his body and the fetishisation of the body of the big, black stud. He plays with that objectification on-stage and off without forgetting its cost. In the era of sexual liberation before AIDS, Jones was mostly a passively available top: 'There were times when I saw someone and pursued him, but most of the time I positioned myself as a "desirable".' Going to the East Village baths during the late 1970s with his partner (in dance and in life), Arnie Zane, 'we had the impression that we were perhaps godlike, desirable, and eternally young. The promised revolution was happening, it would go on forever'. Alas, Zane sickened and died of AIDS, as Jones expects to do.

Jones's father was the boss of a migrant crew of farmworkers based in Florida and working north to New York. Working in the fields and orchards is where some of Jones's muscles developed. Until he began school, he lived in a wholly black world, having never before been close to a white person. Naturally, the first dancing he saw was that of Southern black workers 'getting down' on Saturday nights. His solo dance career began in a high school production of 'The Music Man' because no one could 'deal with a black fifteen-year-old playing the randy lover of a white ingénue'. The teacher who directed the play remained his mentor and supporter until her death. Jones also excelled as a high school sprinter, was generally popular and dated white girls, while being aware of his desire for male bodies, not least that of his older brother. Recognising his curiosity about having sex with a man, in 1971 he enrolled at the State University of New York at Binghamton, where he found a gay liberation group. No one spoke to him, but one non-student tried to pick him up as he was leaving. The next night he met

Zane, beginning their personal and later public collaboration in the Bill T. Jones/Arnie Zane Ensemble Company. Some of the other major dances Jones choreographed include 'Last Supper at Uncle Tom's Cabin' (1990), 'Forsythia' (1989) and 'Last Night on Earth'(1992).

Bill T. Jones with Peggy Gillespie, *Last Night on Earth* (New York, 1996).

Andrew Wentick

Jones, Cleve (b. 1954), American activist, co-founder of the San Francisco AIDS Foundation and originator of the NAMES Project AIDS Memorial Quilt. Jones was born in Indiana and moved to San Francisco in the early 1970s.

Jones conceived the Quilt in 1985. Following the assassinations of gay San Francisco City Supervisor Harvey MILK and Mayor George Moscone in 1978, Jones had organised an annual candlelight march to honour the men. By the time of the 1985 march, the number of San Franciscans who had died from AIDS reached the 1,000 mark: Jones asked each of the marchers to write on placards the names of those lost to AIDS. Levine notes that 'At the end of the march, Jones and others stood on ladders, above the sea of candlelight, taping these placards to the walls of the San Francisco Federal Building. The wall of names looked to Jones like a patchwork quilt'. Thus the AIDS Quilt was born.

Jones later created the first panel of the NAMES Project AIDS Memorial Quilt in memory of one of his friends: in June 1987 Jones and others formally created the NAMES Project Foundation. The aim of the group was to create a memorial for those who had died of AIDS. The Foundation coordinates the display of the Quilt worldwide. The Quilt deliberately aims to attract mainstream attention and appeal. The Foundation does not use the rhetoric of gay liberation. In particular, it is not a political organisation: it is not a lobby nor does it endorse political candidates.

The Quilt consists of individual three-by-six-foot panels sewn together by friends, family and loved ones. The first public display took place in Washington, DC, in October 1987 during the National March on Washington for Lesbian and Gay Rights: 1,920 panels were displayed. Following an extensive national tour of the Quilt, some 8,000 panels were displayed in Washington DC in October 1998. Levine observed, 'Celebrities, politicians, families and friends read aloud the names of the people represented by the Quilt panels. The reading of names is now a tradition followed at nearly every Quilt display.'

The creation of memorial quilts to commemorate the lives of those who have died from AIDS has become a universal phenomenon. There are forty-four NAMES Project chapters in the US and thirty-nine independent quilt affiliates internationally. Different countries have adopted similar names for their quilt memorials: the NAMES Project in the UK and the AIDS Quilt in Australia. The Quilt is considered to be the largest community art project in the world. Since 1987 some nine million people worldwide have viewed the Quilt. In addition to providing a memorial to those who had died from AIDS, the Quilt has also raised community awareness about the disease and raised monies for AIDS community service organisations throughout the world.

Jones has received a number of awards for his work, including being named 'Person of the Week' by ABC News following the Quilt's inaugural display in Washington (October 1987), and in 1993 he received the Harvard AIDS Institute's second annual AIDS Leadership Award.

S. Garfield, *The End of Innocence: Britain in the Time of AIDS* (London, 1995); The NAMES Project homepage (www.aidsquilt.org), 10 April 1998; D. Levine, 'Cleve Jones', in M. Bronski, *Outstanding Lives: Profiles of Lesbians and Gay Men* (Detroit, 1997).

Mark Edwards

Jordan, Barbara (Charline) (1936–96), American politician. Born in Houston, Texas, to a Baptist minister and a domestic worker, Jordan was educated in the city's segregated public schools and encountered racism on a daily basis while growing up; her grandfather was wrongly convicted of killing a white police officer. She graduated in 1956 from the historically black Texas Southern University, and earned a law degree from Boston University in 1959. After teaching political science at Tuskegee Institute in 1959–60, she returned to Houston to set up her own legal practice, briefly using her parents' kitchen table as an office.

Jordan's interest in Democratic Party politics began with John Kennedy's 1960 presidential campaign. She ran unsuccessfully in 1962 and 1964 for the Texas House of Representatives. After federally mandated redistricting guaranteed more equitable election districts, Jordan won election to the Texas State Senate in 1966, the first African-American woman ever to do so. In Texas, she was a very successful legislator, guiding through expanded racial equality legislation and raising the minimum wage.

In 1972, she won the 18th US Congressional seat from Texas after a bitterly contested election in which her black opponent accused her of being an 'Uncle Tom' due to her support from white Democratic party leaders. As a first-term House member, Jordan drew national attention in her position on the House Judiciary Committee during the impeachment of President Richard Nixon. In a moving speech, she noted that 'My faith in the Constitution is whole, it is complete, it is total.' Jordan was re-elected to Congress in 1974 and 1976, and in three terms developed an impressive record of legislative accomplishment, pushing for consumer protection, the extension of social security benefits to women, and increased spending for cities, education and health research. Jordan was under consideration for a cabinet position in President Jimmy Carter's administration in 1976, but was passed

over when she refused to consider 'traditionally black' positions such as Housing and Urban Development or Health, Education and Welfare.

Multiple sclerosis led Jordan to retire from the House in 1979, and eventually confined her to a wheelchair. After leaving office, she taught at the University of Texas, helped found the liberal lobby group People for the American Way, and chaired President Bill Clinton's Immigration Reform Commission from 1993 to 1996. Jordan was widely admired for her power as a public orator. Blessed with a strong and sonorous voice and a gift for language, Jordan electrified the 1976 and 1992 Democratic National Conventions, where she gave the keynote addresses.

Jordan was an extremely private person who revealed little of her personal life and never openly addressed her sexual orientation, although she shared a home in Houston with educational psychologist Nancy Earl from 1976 until her death. Her autobiography portrays a long-term committed relationship, but her authorised biographer claims Jordan had no sexual relationships.

LaVerne McCain Gill, *African American Women in Congress: Forming and Transforming History* (New Brunswick, NJ, 1997); Barbara Jordan and Shelby Hearon, *Barbara Jordan: A Self-Portrait* (Garden City, NY, 1979); Mary Beth Rogers, *Barbara Jordan: American Hero* (New York, 1998).

Christopher Capozzola

Jorgensen, Christine (1926–89), American photographer, performer. Born into a lower middle-class/working-class family, Jorgensen grew up attending public schools, and was ultimately drafted into the military during World War II. She underwent sex reassignment surgery (SRS) in the 1950s and because of the publicity surrounding her surgery, is often thought of as the first person in modern history to undergo SRS. While Jorgensen was not the first person to undergo SRS, the publicity surrounding her surgery and life changes did bring a new understanding of the differences between homosexuality and transsexualism to the United States public.

Jorgensen's childhood was not exceptional; in her autobiography she wrote of a loving family. She was sometimes teased for being a 'sissy', and had a grandmother who stood by her when times were difficult. As a young person in the 1940s, she had difficulties finding regular work. She applied to serve in the armed forces twice and both times was rejected for not weighing enough. Finally, in 1945 she was drafted. In the Army she was assigned clerical work and was honourably discharged in 1946. Following the war, Jorgensen used her Government Issue benefits to take classes in medical technology. At the same time, she suffered from depression, and became convinced that her emotional problems were based in her body. Recognising that she was attracted to men, but convinced that she was not homosexual, she began to read up on endocrinology – which in the 1940s was a new science. It was at this time that she began to administer oestrogen to herself and to seek medical advice. Ultimately, Jorgensen decided to travel to Europe in the hope of obtaining sex reassignment surgery. Through friends in Copenhagen, she was able to find physicians who were willing to provide counselling and surgery in return for using her as a test case.

Jorgensen's surgeries became international news while she was still in Copenhagen. While still undergoing hormone treatment, she had written letters to her parents in the US, explaining the treatment she was undergoing and her reasons for doing so. A friend of the family, in turn, leaked the story to the press. While still in the hospital, Jorgensen was bombarded by phone calls from American reporters – when she returned to the US in 1953, the publicity blitz continued. News reporters were relentless in their pursuit of information from Jorgensen, her family and even distant acquaintances. Finding it

impossible to pursue a normal lifestyle, Jorgensen took up what seemed to be one of the few paths available to her. She became a stage performer. While the end to her private life made it impossible for her to pursue any kind of normal lifestyle, it also provided other transsexuals with a figure with whom to identify, and a person to whom they could write for advice. In the years following her surgery, Jorgensen was bombarded with letters from people in situations similar to her own. It was only decades later that she was finally able to blend in to society, as just another old woman trying to make her way.

While Jorgensen was not the first case of SRS known to historians, it was her surgery and her life that brought the news of sex reassignment surgery and the phenomenon of transsexualism to the wider public. Earlier in the century, in Europe, several instances of SRS were performed. Lili Elbe's surgery was performed in the early 1930s, as was that of Margrith Businger. Arlette-Irene underwent sex reassignment surgery in 1945, and Roberta COWELL did so in 1951 – just one year prior to Jorgensen. In at least three of these histories, the patients were able to legally change their names, find work as women, and quietly blend back into society. Jorgensen's story differs from theirs in several ways. The first of these has to do with the publicity surrounding her surgery – clearly she was not allowed to blend back into society. Even after the initial news coverage, many newspapers and periodicals continued to carry retrospectives of Jorgensen's story. Yet the relationship of Jorgensen to the press is also unique in the history of sexuality because of Jorgensen's role in presenting her own story. Initially, the press determined the story that they would tell to the public. But upon her return to the US Jorgensen chose to speak to a reporter from the *American Weekly* – the articles printed by the magazine were written with Jorgensen's approval, and for perhaps the first time in modern history, a person undergoing SRS was able to define herself to a larger public. Finally, Jorgensen's surgery was performed at a time when some medical communities were beginning to make more of a distinction between homosexuals, transvestites and transsexuals. The publicity surrounding Jorgensen made it possible for members of medical communities, such as Dr Harry Benjamin, to make further contributions to this shift. Benjamin began using the word 'transsexual' immediately following the Jorgensen publicity. While he did not coin the word, it was Benjamin's work, in conjunction with the publicity surrounding Jorgensen that brought understandings of transsexualism as a distinct phenomenon from transvestism and homosexuality to discourses of sex and gender.

Bonnie Bullough and Vern L. Bullough, *Cross Dressing, Sex, and Gender* (Philadelphia, 1993); Pat Califia, *Sex Changes: The Politics of Transgenderism* (San Francisco, 1997); Linda Heidenreich, 'A Historical Perspective of Christine Jorgensen and the Development of an Identity', *Gender Blending* (New York, 1997); Christine Jorgensen, *Christine Jorgensen: A Personal Autobiography* (New York, 1968).

Linda Heidenreich

Jouhandeau, Marcel (1888–1979), French writer. The son of a butcher, Jouhandeau, under the influence of assorted female relatives, retired nuns, frustrated fanatics and elderly spinsters, fell early into a kind of sickly religiosity from which, after a life as a well-liked Latin master, he was just emerging in old age. From his teenage years, when he could watch his father's apprentices bathing nude under his window, he discovered his homosexuality, which he later attempted to repress by marrying a dancer, Élisabeth Toulemon: his wife ('Élisa') is an important figure in many of his hundred or so publications.

No clear view of homosexuality emerges from his writing: *De l'abjection* (first published anonymously in 1939) sees it as an appalling vice; *Monsieur Godeau marié* (1933) recounts an attempted escape from homosexuality through marriage; *Les funérailles d'Adonis* (1948 in a first edition limited to seventy copies) tells of an elderly aristocrat's passion for a dead lover; *L'Imposteur* (1950) tells of a gay married man's double life; *L'Éloge de la volupté* (1951) is a defence of physical pleasure; *L'École des garçons* (1953) is a homosexual epistolary novel, while *Du Pur amour* (1955) shows how a perfect homosexual passion at last achieved what marriage could not – the sublimation of desire. He discovered passive sodomy in old age as a widower. He was opposed to Arcadie, the French homophile association, nowadays often derided for its timidity, as being too public. His work contains everything from hints on Latin syntax to stories about his pets.

Marcel Jouhandeau and Daniel Wallard, *Le moi-même* (Arles, 1994); Henri Rode, *Marcel Jouhandeau: son oeuvre et ses personnages; suivi de, Jouhandeau sur le vif* (Paris, 1972).

David Parris

K

Kameny, Frank (b. 1925), American astronomer and activist. Born in New York, Kameny served in World War II, returning to complete his studies and receiving a Ph.D. from Harvard University in 1956. The following year he was sacked from his job at the US Army Map Service for alleged homosexuality. He fought his dismissal for four years, finally losing the case in 1961, when the US Supreme Court declined his appeal for review.

In the same year, with friends he formed the Washington chapter of the Mattachine Society, a 'civil-liberties, social action organization dedicated to improving the status of the homosexual citizen through a vigorous program of action'. A strong advocate of militancy, at a time when this was seen as both brave and foolhardy, he even had the group's newsletter, *The Gazette*, mailed to the FBI. Rejecting the view that homosexuals needed to adapt to a homophobic society, he focused on legal reforms and re-educating society. Towards this end, in 1963 he helped set up ECHO (East Coast Homophile Organizations), an alliance of the Daughters of Bilitis, various chapters of the Mattachine Society and the Janus Society of Philadelphia.

In line with his contestation of the view that homosexuality was a pathology, in 1971 he led a zap of the American Psychiatric Association's annual meeting, and in the same year became the first openly gay person to run for Congress. He was a founder and board member of the National Gay Task Force and the Gay Rights National Lobby.

Eric Marcus, *Making History: The Struggle for Gay and Lesbian Equal Rights, 1945–1990* (New York, 1992).

Garry Wotherspoon

Kampmann, Christian (Peter Georg) (1939–88), Danish author. Kampmann was the son of a wealthy businessman. He was educated in journalism in Denmark and at the Columbia Graduate School of Journalism (1963–64); he worked as a television news reporter for the Danmarks Radio (State Broadcasting Agency) and was a freelance reviewer of French, English and American literature for the daily *Information* (1964–70). From 1971 Kampmann lived from his literary production. He was a co-editor (1975–78) of the magazine *Seksualpolitik* published by the Gay Liberation Front in Copenhagen.

From his debut in 1962 with the collection of short stories, *Blandt venner* (*Among Friends*), until his sudden death in 1988 Kampmann published 19 volumes, mainly novels. As an author he was a naturalist who decribed close relations, friendships, families and love, always within a concrete social setting, often the upper middle class. His style was consciously non-ornamental, the temper always cool and neutral. From his earliest novels he portrayed homosexual characters that were locked in conflict by the demands of their social environment. *The Gregersen Family*, a four-volume family saga published from 1973 to 1975, was a huge critical success and a best-seller in which Kampmann described the dissolution of a family from the 1950s to the 1970s. One of the leading characters is a gay man who comes out in stages from boyhood to active involvement in the Gay Liberation Front and a debauched gay lifestyle in Manhattan. From the publication of the first volume, Denmark's gay subculture was enthralled and left in breathless waiting for the publication of the sequel. Kampmann himself was still in the closet when, halfway into the tale, he was contacted by the Gay Liberation Front and invited to visit the Gay Summer Camp of that year. Kampmann immediately joined up, added a programmatic ending to the third volume of *The Gregersen Family*, and came out publicly late in 1975. Kampmann's joining the Gay Liberation Front in a flare of publicity was a boost to post-Stonewall gay liberation in Denmark.

In 1977–80 three autobiographical novels followed, in which Kampmann penetrated his own youth and adulthood, existentially and politically. Through these novels his work as a whole can be read as a continuous emancipation from oppressive norms, a permanent search for realness.

In September 1988, Kampmann was murdered by his lover, the author Jens Michael Schau. In 1962 he had married the pianist Therese Herman Koppel (b. 1936); the marriage was dissolved in 1972.

Christian Kampmann, 'The Gregersen Saga': *Visse hensyn* (1973), *Faste forhold* (1974), *Rene linjer* (1975), *Andre måder* (1975) and *Fornemmelser* (1977), *Videre trods alt* (1979), *I glimt* (1980); John Chr. Jørgensen, 'Christian Kampmann', *Dansk Biografisk Leksikon* vol. 7, (Copenhagen, 1981), pp. 585–6.

Wilhelm von Rosen

Katz, Jonathan Ned (b. 1938), American scholar and activist. Concerned, as he told *The Advocate* in 1976, that young people with homosexual desires 'would think that they were the first gay people on earth', he published *Gay American History* (1976), a documentary history covering three hundred years of same-sex behaviour and 'identity' in the US.

Katz was born and grew up in New York, and worked initially as a textile designer, while writing radio documentaries during the 1960s. With the advent of gay liberation, in 1970 he became involved in Gay Activists Alliance, and in 1973 he was one of the founding members of the Gay Academic Union.

In 1972 he presented *Coming Out!*, hailed as the first successful, overtly gay political play in the US. He also oversaw the 69-volume Arno Press reprint project *Homosexuality: Lesbians and Gay Men in Society, History and Literature* (1975), for which he won the annual gay book award from the American Library Association. Other works include the *Gay/Lesbian Almanac* (1983) and *The Invention of Heterosexuality* (1995).

Contemporary Authors, vols 85–8 (Detroit, 1980).

Robert Aldrich and Garry Wotherspoon

Kellendonk, Frans (1951–90), Dutch author. Franciscus Gerardus Petrus Kellendonk was born in Nijmegen into a Catholic family. He studied English at the university in his home town, where leftist and Catholic right battled each other. In 1971 he met his lifelong best friend. He visited Birmingham and London as a student. After he received his MA from Nijmegen, he moved in 1975 to Amsterdam, where he made a living by teaching English and translating novels. In 1977, his first novel, *Bouwval (Ruin)*, was published. The following year with friends he founded the literary journal *De Revisor*, devoted to an academic kind of literature. The same year *De nietsnut (The Good-for-Nothing)* was published, followed by *Letter en geest* (*Letter and Mind*, 1982) and *Namen en gezichten* (*Names and Faces*, 1983). His major work, *Mystiek lichaam* (*Mystical Body*), appeared in 1986. He continued to translate and wrote several major essays. He taught Dutch for one year in Minneapolis and travelled extensively in the US. His life in Amsterdam was of an astonishing regularity; almost every night at the same hour he visited a certain gay pub to have a drink and some small talk. He died of AIDS, and his burial service was a requiem celebrated by barefoot Carmelite monks.

Mystical Body is a very academic novel about a Dutch family. The father is an avaricious rack-renter. The gay son lives in New York and makes a fortune in the art world. The daughter, whose name indicates stupidity, is coming home from Switzerland to give birth to a baby. She is not married to the father, a Jewish doctor. After the art market has crashed, the lost son also comes home. The family is unhappy together once more. The plot of the novel is a comparison of procreative heterosexuality and barren homosexuality. The world of women and reproduction makes the world proceed, while gay aesthetics are at best a funny side-show. A disease that already killed the lover of the son will also kill him. Stereotypes of straight and gay, the family and the Jew, are played out with great ingenuity. While the daughter bears a baby from an unbeloved father, the gay son is absolutely sterile. Straight equals life; gay equals death. As could be expected, the novel raised a storm of protest in the Netherlands, in particular because it was taken to be anti-Semitic. Something similar could have been said about the gay theme, but the point was not raised, probably because the author was himself gay. In the end, all commotion was suppressed because the novel, it was said, did not support, but played on, racism.

In 1992, the complete works of Kellendonk appeared in one volume. *Mystical Body* is still the most important AIDS-novel in Dutch, although the name of the disease is not mentioned. It offers an early example of a postmodern perspective turned conservative, that looks, with some ambivalence, for a return to the eternal values of Catholicism.

Jacob Groot (ed.), *Frans Kellendonk 1951–1990*, special issue of *De Revisor*, vol. 18, no. 1/2 (1991).

Gert Hekma

Kerouac, Jack (1922–69), American writer. Kerouac is best known as a member of the Beat Generation and as the author of *On The Road* (1957), the text which, more than any other, defined a generation, a milieu and even an era in American culture. Kerouac seems to epitomise the characters that he made famous in his novels, with their unceasing travelling, talking, drinking, drug-taking and sexual adventures: he certainly cultivated an image of the hunky, hip, yet brooding author.

Born in Lowell, Massachusetts, into a working-class French-Canadian family, Kerouac's athleticism earned him entrance to Columbia University. He made friends with William BURROUGHS, whose experimentation with literary form probably influenced Kerouac's own style. Like his mentor, he travelled widely (including to Mexico, France and Morocco) and experimented with drugs. Catapulted to fame by *On The Road*, for a brief period he was a quite successful novelist, with works such as *The Subterraneans* and *Dharma Bums* (both 1958), and *Vanity of Duluoz* (1968).

It is only in recent years that evidence has surfaced that Kerouac's sexual 'adventures', particularly with his buddy Neal Cassady, might have been more than mere polymorphously perverse play. Indeed, it is more than probable that Kerouac was in love with Cassady, a love that, for such a man as Kerouac – the epitome of the footloose, woman-chasing, uncommitted macho man – could never be fully expressed. Perhaps his decline into alcoholic despair is explained.

Gerald Nicosia, *Memory Babe: A Critical Biography of Jack Kerouac* (New York, 1983).

Garry Wotherspoon

Kharitonov, Yevgeny (1941–81), Russian writer, director, choreographer. Born in Novosibirsk, Kharitonov moved to Moscow to enroll in VGIK, the state film school. There he studied and then taught acting and pantomime. In 1972 he defended his doctoral dissertation on 'Pantomime in Teaching Acting'. He ran a pantomime studio theatre, 'The School of Non-traditional Stage Behaviour', worked in small groups and clubs, and directed plays at the Theatre of Mime and Gesture, a theatre for the deaf in Moscow. As a specialist in movement on stage, Kharitonov was much in demand. He staged an opera at the Moscow Conservatory, choreographed the first Russian rock musical film, and organized a rock group called 'Last Chance' that existed into the 1990s. At the same time he held a part-time position at Moscow State University in psychology, where he studied speech defects. But all this was merely the official side of his life. His true calling was writing.

Like many underground writers in the Soviet Union, Kharitonov led a kind of double life: their writing was shared with a small circle of writers and dissidents, while their official life served to keep food on the table and the authorities out of their apartments. Kharitonov was exceptional, though, even among these dissident unpublished writers: not only was he more successful in this official life than most, but he also led a third life, as a gay man in Moscow. Kharitonov's writing, in fact, often deals with his gay identity, which made it difficult even for the other writers who shared his outcast dissident status.

While he was never published while he was alive, Kharitonov developed a cult following among other writers. Beginning in the late 1960s, he wrote verse, short stories, essays and plays in a free-flowing postmodern style. Stream of consciousness internal monologues incorporate sound-and wordplay in ways that contrasted both with official Socialist Realism and with the styles of his dissident contemporaries. Because of his style, Kharitonov is claimed as an influence by many of the most respected writers today. They have been influenced by his form, though not by his content. Kharitonov was also innovative in his treatment of his own gayness.

Homosexuality lies at the centre of much of Kharitonov's writing, and he had a remarkably healthy approach to his sexuality, given the virulently homophobic society in which he lived. He claimed and celebrated his homosexuality as a gift, as something that set him apart from others and gave him special insight. In one work, he compares himself to John the Evangelist and Oscar Wilde, who are better than Joyce: 'Joyce wasn't a homosexual, which didn't let him be as heartfelt as Oscar Wilde, for all his artistic gifts impossible for the mind to grasp.' Yet Kharitonov must have been as good at concealing this side of himself from his writer friends as he was at concealing his writing from the KGB: most of them say that as a devout Russian Orthodox believer he felt his gayness to be a sin. There is no evidence for such an interpretation in his writing.

Among his best works is the early story 'Dukhovka' ('The Oven'), which tells the tale in diary form of the narrator's frustrated infatuation with a presumably straight boy he meets at a *dacha* settlement. Other stories and poems also analyse complex emotions and machinations to get close to an unsuspecting object of lust or make a bored lover return. *Roman (Novel)* is a long experimental work in which wordplay and the arrangement of letters on the page are as important as the content. 'Listovka' ('Leaflet') is a short gay manifesto in which Kharitonov compares the position of gay people to that of the

Jews, explaining that straights are right to consider us a threat.

Kharitonov's gayness did get him into trouble. He was completely open about homosexuality and completely frank in his language, which led to some problems with the *samizdat* typists, since those who were not working for the KGB were for the most part puritans in this regard. And he had trouble with the authorities as well: when a gay acquaintance was murdered in 1979, Kharitonov was called in, interrogated and threatened with arrest and a humiliating examination; he fainted. The shock of this harassment may have begun the process that eventually led to Kharitonov's death of a heart attack two years later. Shortly before his death, Kharitonov agreed to be published in *Katalog*, the sequel to the 1979 *Metropol* collection that had resulted in several writers being excluded from the Union of Writers. The KGB again began to put pressure on Kharitonov, threatening him with exposure and arrest.

When Kharitonov died of a heart attack in 1981, the pages of his manuscript collection, which he titled *Pod domashnim arestom* (*Under House Arrest*) flew down into the street in Moscow. Fortunately a few copies survived (though several were discovered in KGB searches of writers' apartments and destroyed), and the first publication of the complete text came in 1993, twelve years after his death. It was the literary event of the year at a time when Russians were preoccupied with non-literary events: politics and the dissolution of the Soviet Union. Publication of Kharitonov's works has ensured him a place in Russian literature as the best gay writer since Kuzmin.

Evgenii Kharitonov, *Slezy na tsvetakh*. (Moscow, 2 vols, 1993); Yevgeny Kharitonov, four stories in Kevin Moss (ed.), *Out of the Blue: Russia's Hidden Gay Literature* (San Francisco, 1997), pp. 196–225.

Kevin Moss

Khumalo, Thokozile [MaThoko] (1947–93), South African activist. Thokozile Khumalo or MaThoko, as she was affectionately known to the township youth of KwaThema, played an important role in gay and lesbian community organisation in the 1980s. Initially in support of her gay nephew, MaThoko opened her heart and her home to lesbian and gay youth in her community. Her address, 32 Legodi Street, became synonymous with the local chapter of the Gay and Lesbian Organisation of the Witwatersrand (GLOW), an organisation committed to lesbian and gay liberation, under the broader banner of the anti-apartheid movement. The KwaThema chapter of GLOW was one of the strongest township-based chapters of GLOW and played an important role in the development of a generation of young black activists. 32 Legodi Street became a refuge, meeting place and social centre for the gay and lesbian youth of KwaThema. All GLOW's mailing to members living in this East Rand township was addressed to 'No. 32'. In commemoration of the significance of the address, the postbox was donated to the Gay and Lesbian Archives of South Africa in 1997. MaThoko led the KwaThema delegation to successive Gay and Lesbian Marches until her untimely death in 1993 in her forty-sixth year.

Gay and Lesbian Archives, University of the Witwatersrand Libraries, Johannesburg.

Graeme Reid

Kihlman, Christer (b.1930), Finnish novelist. Acclaimed as one of the most notable writers in contemporary Finland, Kihlman has characterised himself as a stranger in his own land in many respects. He belongs to the at-one-time privileged Swedish-speaking minority in Finland and he writes in Swedish. Yet he abandoned the bourgeois heritage of his family and became a proponent of a socialist worldview. He has also 'betrayed his own' by challenging the chauvinist aspects of Finnish society and not fitting into conventional heterosexual marriage, as he has also had relationships with men. Moreover, he has even dared to write about these relationships.

Kihlman was one of the first writers in Finland to write openly on homosexuality. He did this in his partly autobiographical work, *Människan som skalv* (*The Man Who Collapsed*, 1971). The book is divided into three sections, 'Alcoholic', 'Homosexual' and 'A Certain Marriage'. The 'Homosexual' triggered public discussion on homosexual relationships which were decriminalised in Finland in 1972. The book sheds light on the closeted life of elderly cultured gay people in the city of Helsinki before the sexual revolution at the end of the 1960s.

Kihlman's novels *Se upp Salige!* (*Pay Heed, O Blessed*, 1960), *Den blå modern* (1963; *The Blue Mother*, transl. 1990) and *Dyre prins* (1975; *Sweet Prince*, transl. 1983) are considered especially noteworthy and valuable. They reveal the dark side of the privileged bourgeoisie that held economic power in Finland. Kihlman became an icon as a socially-engaged writer who did not hesitate to write about the flaws of capitalist society, in pamphlets, essays, plays and fiction. Kihlman has been considered a social critic in his novels, but another important theme in his books, modernity, has often gone unrecognised. For example, *Den blå modern* psychoanalytically examines violence and sex, culminating in long sequences on boy prostitution in Auschwitz. In its modernist style the novel resembles the works of André Gide and Samuel Beckett.

In the beginning of the 1980s Kihlman published several novels in which he diverted from his earlier pattern. He travelled in South America, and in the novels that he wrote about his experiences as, for example, in Argentina, he studied the differences in the masculine codes of Western Europe and Latin America. How West Europeans have constructed gay identity is not relevant to the lives of the Latin American men who can sleep with men without

considering themselves as gay. Finnish critics found it difficult to accept these 'South American diaries', and they also had difficulties in placing them in the totality of Kihlman's *œuvre*.

In the late 1980s Kihlman published his major novel, *Gerdt Bladhs undergång* (1987; *The Downfall of Gerdt Bladh*, transl. 1989). This is a powerful history of a man whose career and marriage are destroyed when his closeted life is revealed. The background for the novel was the Finland of the 1980s where yuppies and the *nouveaux riches* were fighting for power by means fair or foul. The book was also one of the first Finnish novels on AIDS, which here metaphorically destroys the old world and its values.

A measure of Kihlman's significance is that his work has been translated into more than ten languages. Finnish literary critics have so far studied his novels either in a Marxist or in an autobiographical framework; however it is clear that questions of homosexuality, bisexuality, masculinity and gender will be examined in the future. Kihlman wrote on these issues before they were brought to the limelight in gender studies, gay and lesbian studies, and men's studies.

Pirkko Alhoniemi, *Isätpojatperinnöt. Bertel Kihlmanin ja Christer Kihlmanin kirjallisesta tuotannosta* (Helsinki, 1989); Seppo Toiviainen, *Christer Kihlman ja hänen maailmansa* (Jyväskylä, 1984).

Lasse Kekki

King, Billie Jean (b. 1943), American athlete. King was born Billie Jean Moffitt in Long Beach, California. She was raised in a not particularly well-off middle-class family and remembers saving change to buy her first racquet for eight dollars. She played her first tennis match at the age of 11, was at Wimbledon at age 17 and by 1979 had won a record twenty Wimbledon titles, including six singles and seven doubles titles. At the age of 39 and 40 she still reached the semi-finals at Wimbledon.

When King first played internationally, tennis was still organised on an 'amateur' basis with some women and men touring together. In 1971 she joined the new professional women's circuit created by Virginia Slims. In the same year she had an abortion as well as becoming the first woman athlete to make over $100,000 in a year. In 1972 she appeared on the cover of *Sports Illustrated*, as their first-ever sportswoman of the year. During Wimbledon in 1973, King was instrumental in forming the first Women's Tennis Association, to which she was elected president from 1973 to 1981. She established the magazine *Womensports* in 1974, in partnership with her husband. The years 1971–74 were the peak of her playing career, with sporting journalists and women's magazines alike representing her as the spokesperson and epitome of women's liberation in tennis and sports. She was named one of the ten most powerful women in America by *Harper's Bazaar* in 1977. King wrote her first autobiography in 1975, which contained far more expressions of support for liberal feminist ideals than her second one, released in 1982, shortly after widespread publicity surrounding the end of her relationship with Marilyn Barnett.

In 1973, King defeated Bobby Riggs in a $3 million spectacle/match. In this 'match' with 55-year-old Riggs, she was attempting to demonstrate that women players could be entertaining and that they could be just as competitive as male athletes. Much of her off-court time was spent in gaining equality in terms of financial reward for professional women tennis players and laying the foundations for the modern form of the game and sports business for women.

At the age of 21 she married Larry King who, seeing the growing professionalism in men's sport and the potential of women's tennis to move on to the same commercial footing, became a sports promoter and sports businessman. Her relationship with Barnett developed in 1972 after Barnett had done her hair. Barnett in 1973

found and arranged the purchase of the Malibu beach house which became the focus of a later court action; King also employed Barnett as her travelling secretary. In 1979 Barnett, still living at the beach house, was offered $125,000 to move out, remain silent about their relationship and not publish any of King's love letters to her.

In a 1981 lawsuit, Barnett sued for lifelong support on the basis of her seven-year relationship and promises by King during that time. It was a critical moment in contemporary lesbian history for many reasons: the use of the courts to pursue 'rights' normally reserved for heterosexual couples, the prolonged public discussion and scrutiny of the sexuality of a much-admired and loved sporting 'star', and the opportunity it could have afforded lesbians and gays for some public affirmation. When this 'crisis' hit, King initially denied the relationship and then went on to publicly reaffirm both the desirability and superiority of heterosexuality and marriage over lesbian sexuality, in a number of ways, including the writing of her second autobiography. She said of Larry King, 'He is my lover, my husband, and my best friend and has been for nineteen years.' It was also reported she said she always knew she preferred a man's body even when she was with Marilyn and that she had 'made a mistake'. Much of her second autobiography is written not from a lesbian feminist angle but one which emphasises marriage, romantic love, heterosexuality and the family – 'now might be the time for me to have a baby, or for us to adopt one'. King had always claimed to be a conservative, so it is not surprising that she minimised the significance of her lesbianism and feminism. This needs to be seen not only in historical terms of the stage of development of gay liberation but also in terms of her structural location in professional tennis, her business interests and those of her husband, and the fact that she was at the end of her playing career and looking to endorsements as a major source of income. The lesbian case caused her financial losses of more that $1.5 million and her husband had losses of a further $500,000.

Since professional sport is an area of cultural production based heavily on physical skills and attributes, it is an important site for the construction and contesting of ideologies, discourses and practices about gender, the body and its sexuality. The challenge of lesbian femininity (where femininity is taken to mean simply the continuous expression of the experiences of being female) to the power of the institution and ideology of heterosexuality was likely to be greater if it had come from a married heterosexual player than a more 'stereotyped lesbian' such as Martina NAVRATILOVA. However, this was not to be and it took Navratilova's open lesbian sporting life to create this ongoing challenge – a challenge remaining dormant until just recently with the playing success of the young French player Amélie Mauresmo, who talked freely about and was happily photographed with her lesbian lover at the Australian Open in January 1999.

Billie Jean King, *Billie Jean King: An Autobiography* (London, 1975); Billie Jean King with Frank Deford, *Billie Jean King: The Autobiography* (London, 1982).

Helen Waite

Kinsey, Alfred (1894–1956), American sexologist. Kinsey, the primary author of the twentieth century's most famous studies of human sexual behaviour, grew up in a middle-class Methodist family in Hoboken and South Orange, New Jersey. After receiving a bachelor of science degree from Bowdoin College in 1916 and a doctoral degree from Harvard in 1919, he joined the zoology department of Indiana University, where he devoted the next two decades to teaching, raising a family with his wife, Clara, and studying the gall wasp.

Kinsey would be best known not for his work on insect life but for his research into, and scandalous conclusions about, human sexual behaviour. While teaching a course on marriage in 1938, he began to collect sexual case histories from students and colleagues. The process expanded to include a growing pool of informants, and interviews grew to encompass a wide range of information on respondents (organised by sex, race, marital status, age, familial and class backgrounds, childhood and adolescent practices, number of partners and much more). Kinsey soon began networking with other sex researchers, obtained funding from the Rockefeller Foundation's Committee for Research in Problems of Sex, and with co-workers travelled around the country to interview members of groups including club women, prisoners, college students and New York bohemians. In 1947, as he and his colleagues prepared to publish their data, he founded the Institute for Sex Research (renamed the Kinsey Institute for Sex Research in 1981).

Sexual Behavior in the Human Male (1948), which presented information based on the sexual histories of 5,300 white American men, revealed that virtually all subjects interviewed had violated both existing laws and prevailing moral standards en route to orgasm. Virtually all male subjects masturbated, and well over half engaged in premarital and/or extramarital sex. Perhaps Kinsey's most shocking finding, however, was that '37 percent of the total male population has at least some overt homosexual experience to the point of orgasm between adolescence and old age'. Upon the appearance of this volume, Kinsey was simultaneously hailed as a liberator and scientific martyr and denounced as a pornographer and a communist bent on destroying the American family. His much-anticipated companion volume, *Sexual Behavior in the Human Female* (1953), caused a similar sensation even though women reported lower rates of same-sex, premarital and extramarital sex.

Kinsey based his conclusions about sexuality in America on interviewees' reported behaviours rather than upon religious doctrine or psychoanalytic theories of sexuality. Taking the orgasm as his central unit of measurement, he refused to label any sexual behaviour as 'abnormal' or 'unnatural', argued against existing sex laws, and created a 7-point scale ranging between exclusive heterosexuality and homosexuality, emphasizing that most Americans fell in between the extremes of exclusive hetero- and homosexuality. Commentators on homosexuality were especially attentive to Kinsey's work, using his findings variously to plead for tolerance, claim status as a significant minority, or fulminate about the alleged threat that increasing numbers of homosexuals posed to American life. These two books struck a nerve with the American public. Despite their complex graphs and charts and abstruse scientific language, both became bestsellers and spurred an unprecedented public discussion of national sexual practices and ideologies, with Kinsey's conclusions and implications debated exhaustively in the popular and scientific press.

The public uproar over the volumes spread well beyond the worlds of science, medicine and psychiatry, as millions of Americans purchased and discussed them, rendering their vocabulary and sensational findings a part of everyday knowledge. Public response focused on sensational issues – the likelihood of a national moral breakdown, the spread of homosexuality and the future of marriage – while ignoring issues that Kinsey's team saw as important, such as the vast divergence between working-class and upper-class sexual patterns and ideologies. Most commentators also ignored the Reports' focus on whites only, with the exception of African-American journalists who were amused by the controversy.

The Reports' statistics on pre- and extramarital sex prompted a national forum on the state of the nation's morals and marriages, and their findings on the extent of same-sex sexual behaviors spearheaded debate about the increase in and cause of homosexuality in America. These controversies would cost Kinsey dearly: during the last few years of his life, he saw his research questioned by a congressional committee, his funding withdrawn and his plan for a series of studies falter.

Kinsey's work is important to the history of homosexuality for several reasons. Despite continuous challenges, his estimates of the extent of same-sex sexuality remain influential, as does his model of a sexual continuum. His work provided a valuable source for homophile and gay activists, and spurred new commentary and research on homosexuality. To many, Kinsey's work still remains troubling more than fifty years after its initial appearance. A recent biography argued that Kinsey's research agenda and findings were shaped by his own conflicted sexuality, and as of the late 1990s conservative organisations continued to protest his findings and call for another Congressional investigation of his work.

Julia A. Ericksen, with Sally Steffen, *Kiss and Tell: Surveying Sex in the Twentieth Century* (Cambridge, MA, 1999); Janice Irvine, *Disorders of Desire: Sex and Gender in Modern American Sexology* (Philadelphia, 1990); James H. Jones, *Alfred Charles Kinsey: A Public/Private Life* (New York, 1997); Miriam Reumann, 'American Sexual Character in the Age of Kinsey, 1946–64' (Ph.D. thesis, Brown University, 1998).

Miriam Reumann

Kinsman, Gary (b. 1955), Canadian writer and activist. One of Canada's most prolific gay/lesbian academic and political writers, and a leading activist in several cities, he was born and educated in Toronto. Kinsman has lived in Nova Scotia, Newfoundland, and most recently in Sudbury, Ontario, where he teaches sociology at Laurentian University.

Kinsman's most important scholarly work has been *The Regulation of Desire: Sexuality in Canada*, first published in 1986, an historically informed analysis substantially shaped by both socialist and feminist perspectives. He has also written many articles on AIDS politics and on state regulation of gay and lesbian lives in Canada, most recently gaining national attention for scholarly analysis of 'McCarthyite' anti-gay persecution in the three decades after World War II. His work has been included in a number of American and Canadian anthologies dealing with issues of gender and sexuality.

Kinsman was also a central figure in the publication of *Rites*, a national gay and lesbian magazine published for most of the 1980s out of Toronto (other leading figures in that venture including Mary Louise Adams, Doug Stewart and Doug WILSON). He was an activist prominent in such groups as Gay Alliance Toward Equality, the Right to Privacy Committee and the Canadian Committee Against Customs Censorship. All three were Toronto-based but the latter two had national significance. He helped found Gays and Lesbians Against the Right Everywhere and the Lesbian and Gay Pride Day Committee of Toronto. During the 1990s, he took a high profile in activist groups in the Atlantic provinces and northern Ontario, helping to organize Sudbudy's first Lesbian and Gay Pride march.

G. Kinsman, *The Regulation of Desire: Homo and Hetero Sexualities*, rev. edn (Montreal, 1996).

David Rayside

Kirby, Michael (b. 1939), Australian High Court Justice. Kirby is one of the few homosexuals at the top of the Australian establishment who have 'come out'.

Born in Sydney, Kirby was educated at a selective high school and the University of Sydney. Since then, he has had a distinguished legal career, including time spent as a state Law Reform Commissioner, several stints as Acting Chief Justice of the Supreme Court of New South Wales, Chairman of the Australian Law Reform Commission and President of the New South Wales Court of Appeal. He also has a considerable international reputation, having served as the Special Representative of the UN Secretary-General for Human Rights in Cambodia, as a member of UNESCO's International Bioethics Committee and as President of the International Commission of Jurists. Publications such as *T. G. H. Strehlow and Aboriginal Customary Laws* (1980), *Reform the Law: Essays on the Renewal of the Australian Legal System* (1983), *The Rule of Law in Hong Kong after 1997* (1992), and *Lionel Murphy and the Power of Ideas* (1995) give some indication of the diversity of his interests and concerns.

In 1996 Kirby was appointed to Australia's highest legal body, the High Court. His 'coming out' two years later, by the simple expedient of naming a man as his partner in his annual *Who's Who in Australia* entry, merely confirmed what was widely rumoured – and widely known among the *cognoscenti* – for many years. It drew surprisingly little response from the wider community, except for the predictable responses of those who claimed that, since he was admitting to living with his 'partner' since 1969 – any sexual activity in NSW would have been illegal until decriminalisation of male homosexuality in 1984 – he was a confessed criminal and therefore unfit to hold the office.

Kirby has also been willing to speak out, from a 'progressive' stance, on a range of social issues, incurring the dislike of conservatives and reactionaries, but garnering the approbation of a broad spectrum of minority groups, for whose rights he has long been a strong champion. For example, his enormously supportive stance on HIV/AIDS, particularly at a time when the AIDS panic and conservative backlash dominated Australia, epitomises his life as a public figure.

Who's Who in Australia 1999 (Melbourne, 1998).

Garry Wotherspoon

Kirstein, Lincoln (1907–97), American impresario, writer, art patron. Born the son of Louis Kirstein, chairman of Filene's Department store, Boston, and the daughter of a successful clothing manufacturer in Rochester, New York, despite a caustic and introverted personality, Kirstein managed to become one of the most influential forces in twentieth-century American dance.

Kirstein was educated at Harvard,where he was-co-founder and editor of the *Hound and Horn* literary magazine, for which he reviewed dance and theatre. Coming from Boston aristocracy, he and friend E.M. Warburg were socially well-connected and he found his way through Boston and New York society with ease. After moving to New York City, his first artistic endeavour was assisting in exhibitions for the Museum of Modern Art but his desire to establish an American form of classical dance equal to the Russian tradition became his life's ambition. His interest in dance was influenced by seeing performances of Diaghilev's Ballets Russes in London, his introduction to Romola Nijinsky, and ballet lessons with Michel Fokine at his New York City studio. While working as ghostwriter for Romola on her husband's biography, Kirstein toured Europe, where he met George Balanchine, then ballet master/choreographer of the short-lived Les Ballets 1933.

A forceful communicator, Kirstein convinced Balanchine, whose work, including *Apollo* and *Prodigal Son*, he had seen during the Ballets Russes 1929 London season, to come to America to found an American ballet. Soon after Balanchine arrived in the United States, he established, with the assistance of Kirstein and Warburg, the School of American Ballet (1934) and the American Ballet (1935). So committed was Kirstein to establishing an American ballet at the grass roots level that, while Balanchine was occupied with the American Ballet in residence at the Metropolitan Opera and choreographing for Broadway, he formed Ballet Caravan, a touring company for which he presented and wrote librettos for ballets on American themes (*Billy the Kid*, *Filling Station*, *Pocahontas*), by American choreographers (Eugene Loring, Lew Christensen, William Dollar), with scores by American composers (Aaron Copland, Virgil Thomson, Elliott Carter).

In his effort to promote the new American ballet, his writings in the 1930s, including *Dance* (1935) and *Blast at Ballet* (1938), are clearly polemical. Following his directorship of the American Ballet Caravan goodwill tour to South America and wartime work recovering art works stolen by the Nazis, Kirstein again collaborated with Balanchine on the founding of Ballet Society (1946–48), predecessor of the New York City Ballet, which he and Balanchine moulded into one of the world's great ballet companies and co-directed until the choreographer's death in 1983. In 1989, Kirstein retired as General Director of the New York City Ballet and President and Director of the School of American Ballet. He retained emeritus status in both positions until his death. Kirstein wrote poetry, fiction, essays and several scholarly books on dance and art, including the classic works *The Classic Ballet, Basic Technique and Terminology* (1952), *Movement and Metaphor* (1970) *Nijinsky Dancing* (1975), and his autobiographical memoirs, *Mosaic* (1994). Kirstein was awarded the Presidential Medal of Freedom (1984) and the National Medal of Arts (1985).

Although he married Fidelma Cadmus, sister of his friend, the gay artist Paul CADMUS, in 1941, Kirstein exhibited and later admitted homosexual inclinations throughout his life. His most important gay love affair, with minor writer Carl Carlsen, a companion of poet Hart Crane, occurred in 1932.

Nicholas Fox Weber, *Patron Saints: Five Rebels Who Opened American to a New Art, 1928–1943* (New York, 1992).

A. M. Wentink

Klippenvåg, Odd (b. 1951), Norwegian author. Klippenvåg was born and grew up in northern Norway, but now lives in Oslo. After having worked as a high school teacher for many years, he is now a full-time writer. He has written novels and short stories.

Among his books are *Otto, Otto* (1983), a gay love novel about a male couple in Oslo striving for self-confidence and acceptance, but the two differ in how they see themselves as gay. *Triptykon* (1989) is a fascinating novel about three men's different positions in life, about love, guilt and longing for forgiveness and reconciliation. *Body & Soul* (1998) is a collection of short stories, mostly dark and desperate with a language that is at the same time concealing and revealing the characters' desire for contact.

Jan Olav Gatland

Knuth, Count Eigil (1903–96), Danish sculptor and explorer-archaeologist. Knuth was educated at various technical schools and workshops in Denmark and Italy and earned a physical education teacher's diploma (Ollerup Physical Training College) in 1932. He participated in excavations in West Greenland in 1932, 1934 and 1945, in the Courtauld Expedition to East Greenland in 1935, and in the Expédition Française Transgroënland in 1936, which crossed the Inland Ice from West to East; he was leader of the Danish Northeast Greenland Expeditions, 1938–39, leader of the Danish Peary Land Expeditions, 1947–50 and several expeditions to Peary Land, 1963–89. Knuth's discovery of two prehistoric cultures in the now empty land at Independence Bay and Danmarksfjorden (Independence 2000 BC and Independence II 1000 BC) was a pioneering achievement.

Knuth's artistic production includes paintings, water-colours, ceramic works and sculptures. His portrait busts of East Greenland Eskimos (now in Nuuk) executed in Angmagssalik in the winter of 1935–36 are considered outstanding; he had several exhibitions, e.g. at the World's Fair in New York in 1939. Knuth published a large number of books on life in Greenland, early Greenland explorers and the archaeology of Greenland. Among the honours bestowed on Knuth were the Hans Egede Medal of the Royal Danish Geographical Society (1951), the Patron's Medal of the Royal Geographical Society, London (1953), the Royal Scottish Geographical Society's Mungo Park Medal (1953), an honorary degree from the University of Copenhagen (1979), and the Government of Greenland's Nersornaat Gold Medal (1993) which Knuth received at the Cap Moltke Station in Peary Land, the northernmost land on earth, on his ninetieth birthday.

Knuth in his old age privately regretted that he did not at some point in his earlier life come out publicly as a homosexual.

Mads Lidegaard, 'Eigil Knuth', *Dansk Biografisk Leksikon*, vol. 8 (Copenhagen, 1981), pp. 100–1.

Wilhelm von Rosen

Knutsen, Per (b. 1951), Norwegian author. Knutsen was born and grew up in northern Norway, but now lives in Bergen. He has written for children, youth and adults; his production includes fiction and plays, as well as scripts for radio and television.

Among his novels, *Mordere* (*Murderers*, 1984) is a love story between two boys, set in a small fishing village in the north of the country, where homosexuality is not supposed to occur. For a younger audience, Knutsen has written *Svart cayal* (*Black Cayal*, 1988) in which the main character, Jonny, falls in love with his best friend, and *Svømmersken* (*The Female Swimmer*, 1994), about young Khalid, a second generation Moroccan immigrant in Norway, who is thrown out of his home because he is gay and because he wants to be an actor.

Jan Olav Gatland

Komrij, Gerrit (b. 1944), Dutch author. Komrij was born in Winterswijk in the eastern part of the Netherlands. He came to Amsterdam to study literature. Here he met his lover Charles Hofman with whom he still lives. In the 1980s, the couple moved to a 'quinta' (palatial country-house) in northern Portugal.

Komrij's major work is in poetry and criticism, but he also wrote novels and plays and did a series of television talk-shows. His edited collections of Dutch poetry of all ages were bestsellers. After the free poetry of the 1950s, Komrij returned to the classical forms which made his work quite controversial among poets but popular among the public. His criticism of literature, architecture and television for newspapers and weeklies went against the grain and made his reputation in the 1970s: his cracking voice and old man's looks also contributed much to his fame. He wrote a funny and imaginative biography *Verwoest Arcadië* (*Destroyed Arcadia*, 1980). His main novels are *Over de bergen* (*Over the Mountains*, 1990) on renting and losing his 'quinta' in Portugal, and *Dubbelster* (1993) on the hollowness of stardom in the media. His best play is *Het chemisch huwelijk* (*The Chemical Marriage*, 1982). With two gay instead of straight couples, it is a gayification of Goethe's *Wahlverwantschaften*.

The financial rewards he received for the major literary prize of the Netherlands were used to publish his collected poems (1994). His many essays, some gay, some campy, were published in half a dozen books. His translations and criticism indicate a preference for decadent writers: Oscar Wilde, Fernando Pessoa, Ronald Firbank. He also translated Shakespeare and wrote the text for Peter Schat's gay opera *Symposion* (on the life of Tchaikovsky). He was the first to recover forgotten Dutch gay novels from the early twentieth century. Little of his very Dutch and ironic work has been translated. Although he does not function as a gay spokesman, no doubt has ever existed as to his sexual preference. Gerard REVE's *Lieve jongens* (1972) has a superb sarcastic portrait of Komrij and his lover.

Gert Hekma

König, Ralf (b. 1960), German cartoonist. Born in the Westphalian city of Soest, König was training to become a carpenter when he attended a gay pride rally and dance in Frankfurt (the 1979 'Homolulu'). That weekend opened his eyes and put him in the arms and beds of several men. Soon after, König left carpentry and heterosexuality behind. He studied at the Academy of Art in Düsseldorf from 1981 to 1985. Both prior to and during his training, König was already publishing individual comic strips and comic stories in gay publications and with small publishing houses.

Within a reasonably short time, König has become both a widely respected cartoonist and one of the best-selling authors in Germany. His almost two dozen volumes have been widely translated and also adapted for the stage and the screen. He has received several national and international awards, including 'Best Foreign Cartoonist' from the international 'Comic-salon' in 1992.

König's work is immediately identifiable: his characters all have 'potato noses' ('*Knollennasen*'). This quirk makes them a rather endearing lot as they cruise each other, have sex, fall in love, fight and endure the idiocies and inanities of the heterosexuals who live around and about them. He is best known for three series of books depicting life from a uniquely gay point of view. One series follows the lives of two lovers, Konrad and Paul, who have been 'on together' for over a decade. Konrad makes a living giving piano lessons to teenagers with whom he often becomes infatuated. Paul never seems to work; instead, he spends most of his time pursuing hairy-chested, butch men who may or may not be gay. The two lovers do get together, in and out of bed, and their contrasting personalities allow König to satirise a wide range of gay foibles, as well as their relationships with their respective families, friends and neighbours.

Two comic novels, *Der bewegte Mann* (roughly translated: *Moved/Movement Man*, 1987) and *Pretty Baby* (1988), tell the story of Norbert Brommer, an average gay guy who gets mixed up with a hetero hunk, Axel. Norbert is a good samaritan with lust in his heart, but always does his best to help first Axel and then his wife, Doro, when they are in trouble. The film made from these books, *Der bewegte Mann (Maybe … Maybe Not,* 1994) became the highest grossing German comedy, but König, and many gays, were disappointed in the adaptation because it not only shifted the focus away from Norbert and his gay friends but gave what several critics called 'a heterosexualised version' of gay life, the very opposite of what König portrays in his work.

Two more comic novels, *Kondom des Grauens (Killer Condom,* 1987) and *Bis auf die Knochen (Down to the Bones,* 1990), were also turned into a film, *Kondom des Grauens (Killer Condom,* 1996), but this time König co-wrote the script and maintained more control over the production. A mix of noir and horror film, the stories have Luigi Makaroni, a hunky, gay New York City detective, solve two cases in which a fundamentalist Christian sect has gone amok and devised ways to destroy gay men.

The success of the film adaptations is not surprising as König employs a variety of cinematic techniques in his art, e.g. close-ups, 'voice-overs' and intercutting. Drawing humour from real-life situations, his world is one viewed from the perspective of an urban gay man. Bloated egos as well as homophobic attitudes are deflated. He makes fun of what we fear: hateful heterosexuals, never finding love, having to use condoms.

That so many non-gay people read his books still perplexes König. With his growing success, he has had to make choices as to publishers. His mass-market works (e.g. *Der bewegte Mann*) are published by one of the major publishing houses, Rowohlt, and have less explicitly sexual scenes. He places his 'most gay' works (i.e. those with more explicit drawings) with smaller, usually gay-run, publishers. No matter the publisher, however, Ralf König's work remains centred on gay life in all its sexiness, seriousness and silliness. As König said in an interview: 'I just want to tell stories that I and other gay men think are funny and hot. And I just like to draw big dicks, because it's fun.'

Joachim Bartholomae (ed.), *Mal mir mal einen Schwulen: Das Buch zu Ralf König* (Hamburg, 1996); Ralf König, *The Killer Condom,* transl. James Steakley (New York, 1991), *Konrad and Paul* (Northampton, MA, 1997).

James W. Jones

Kramer, Larry (b. 1935), gay community leader, AIDS activist and writer. Born in Bridgeport, Connecticut, Kramer graduated from Yale University in 1957. Following a brief time in the US army he entered the film industry in 1960. In 1969 he adapted and produced D.H. Lawrence's *Women in Love*: his first foray into utilising homosexuality in his professional work.

In the period 1975–78 Kramer produced his autobiographical novel *Faggots* (1978), which portrays the life of gay men in New York during the mid-1970s. Although *Faggots* was savaged by some gay critics at the time, it has remained in print ever since. DeMatio observes that Kramer was disenchanted with the sexual promiscuity of the period and lost favour with the gay community for his criticisms of the lifestyle offered by the new-found sexual liberation. The release of *Faggots* placed Kramer in the public arena: a place he has coveted ever since.

With the discovery of Kaposi's sarcoma in a number of gay men in New York and

San Francisco in 1981, Kramer was the first person, and remained for several years the leading gay figure, to publicise the dangers of a possible 'gay plague': his vehicle was the *New York Native*. Many gay men at the time were indifferent to Kramer's message, and DeMatio notes that some critics accused Kramer of 'inciting panic and of instilling gay homophobia and anti-eroticism'. Regardless of this criticism, it soon became apparent to Kramer and some of his friends that the public health system in New York was not willing or able to provide services for the increasing number of gay men affected by what came to be known as AIDS. Thus, in 1982 Kramer helped to establish in New York the Gay Men's Health Crisis, the world's first true gay community health and advocacy service. In March 1983 Kramer wrote his now famous '1,112 and Counting' article for the *New York Native*. This article urged the gay community to take AIDS seriously, using the evidence of 1,112 cases and 418 deaths as the basis of his argument. Rather than galvanising gay community activity against AIDS, the article engendered renewed criticism of Kramer to the extent that he was forced to resign from the Board of the Gay Men's Health Crisis.

During his time with the Crisis, Kramer had little time for his creative writing as he had become preoccupied with the organisation and was closely involved in its day-to-day management. Following his resignation from the Board, he turned to writing as a vehicle for AIDS activism. His next effort was a play, *The Normal Heart*, which addressed his anger at society's inability to combat AIDS. It opened in early 1985 to positive acclaim: a film version of *The Normal Heart* was later released. The *Destiny of Me*, Kramer's sequel to *Heart*, opened in New York in 1992. Kramer's latest work is a novel entitled *The American People*.

During this time of creative endeavour, Kramer had not moved away from hands-on activism. His emotional speech at New York's Gay and Lesbian Community Center in 1987 inspired the establishment of the AIDS Coalition to Unleash Power (ACT UP). ACT UP has proved to be one of the more powerful mechanisms of AIDS activism in the US and internationally. In his search for a 'cure', Kramer has maintained a close contact with a wide variety of people in the AIDS industry – he continues to be very vocal about those with whom he disagrees. Kramer is described in *The Gay 100* as 'rude, opinionated, inconvenient, invaluable, and irreplaceable, he is the most influential gay man in America today. The organizations he helped found have become some of the most important institutions in contemporary gay America's struggle to survive. If the community does in fact survive, it will owe that survival in no little degree to Larry Kramer'.

L. Kramer, *Reports from the Holocaust: The Making of an AIDS Activist* (New York, 1989); J. E. DeMatio, 'Larry Kramer', in M. Bronski, *Outstanding Lives: Profiles of Lesbians and Gay Men* (Detroit, 1997); Paul Russell, *The Gay 100: A Ranking of the Most Influential Gay Men and Lesbians, Past and Present* (Secaucus, New Jersey, 1996)

Mark Edwards

Kushner, Tony (b. 1956), American playwright. Born in Manhattan, Kushner currently lives in Brooklyn. He was educated at Columbia University and New York University.

Writer of a number of plays since 1985, Kushner is best known for his *Angels in America: A Gay Fantasia on National Themes*. Part I, 'Millennium Approaches', published in 1992, was awarded the Pulitzer Prize for Drama and the Tony Award for Best Play. Part II, 'Perestroika', was released in 1993 and awarded the Tony for Best Play in 1994.

Angels in America was the first AIDS-related art form to receive widespread mainstream acceptance and acclaim. Other examples of mass entertainment include the movies *Longterm Companion* and *Philadelphia:* the latter won an Oscar in the Best Actor category for Tom Hanks.

Numerous novels and autobiographies/ biographies/memoirs with HIV and AIDS as major themes have been written since the mid-1980s. A number of important publications have either chronicled or analysed policy responses to the epidemic in various countries. Randy Shilts's *And the Band Played On*, which highlighted the lack of action by the American political and bureaucratic system, was important in galvanising the input of AIDS community organisations throughout the industrialised world.

http://members.xoom.com/hypesite/kushner. html; E. Nelson (ed.), *AIDS: The Literary Response* (New York, 1992).

Mark Edwards

L

lang, k.d. (b. 1961), Canadian singer. In 1997, at a record release party in New York, k.d. lang promoted *Drag*, a torch-blues compilation of reinterpreted classics. At this point, lang seemed to have achieved many of her ambitions, dreams and desires, including the one of finding reciprocal love with another woman, in this instance Leisha Hailey.

Kathryn Dawn Lang was born in Edmonton, Alberta, but was raised in the tiny township of Consort; her parents were a teacher and a pharmacist. She began performing music as a teenager, aided by a natural ability and extraordinary voice. By January 1982 she scored her first singing role in an Edmonton production; it linked her into country music. More work followed and she took the name k.d. lang to uphold her stage confidence and protect her private identity. She soon moved to Toronto and great success, then produced a country-music album in the US, *Angel With a Lariat* (1987), which was a disappointment, though young Nashvillians, along with many professionals, were excited by k.d.'s innovative approach and image, even if US country radio stations were less accommodating to a singer whom they considered an outsider, upstart and leftist. By the late 1980s, k.d. lang moved away from country music and returned to Canada.

In Vancouver, she made a 'Meat Stinks' advertisement, alienating the massive Canadian meat industry, and boycotts of her music ensued. Bad publicity, however, sold records and in 1990 she was named Canada's Female Artist of the Decade. In 1992 she issued *Ingénue*, which has been described as jazz-ballad meets pop-cabaret, and it presented lang singing, with bittersweet beauty, of unrequited love – love, it seemed, for a woman. The album and its single, 'Constant Craving', made her a star and a lesbian cult hero. *Ingénue*, along with her lesbian role in the film *Salmonberries*, brought the issue of lang's sexual orientation to the fore. *Ingénue* outed lang emotionally and fed into existing gossip. Subsequently she has won a gold record, two American Music Award nominations and five Grammy nominations.

Victoria Starr, *k.d. lang: All You Get is Me* (London, 1994); Brendon Lemon, 'k.d. lang', *The Advocate*, June 1992.

Susan Taylor

Lapinsky, Sheila (b. 1944), South African activist. Lapinksy is a South African human rights activist of many years' standing, having first become involved in the anti-Apartheid struggle in the mid-1960s. As a result of her activities as General Secretary of the National Union of South African Students, she was banned from 1973 to 1978. After her banning order expired, in the early 1980s, she became involved in South Africa's fledgling gay and lesbian rights movement and was part of the small group of activists who were influential in persuading the African National Congress in the early 1990s to adopt gay rights as part of their platform. Lapinsky was chairperson of the Cape Town branch of the Gay Association of South Africa in 1984–85, and subsequently was a founder member of the Cape Town organisation Lesbians and Gays against Oppression (1985–87) and the Organisation for Lesbian and Gay Action (1987–92). She was also active in the End Conscription Campaign in the period 1987–88 and served on the executive of the National Coalition for Gay and Lesbian Equality from 1994 to 1997. She now occupies official positions in both the provincial structures of the African National Congress and the South African Communist Party.

Gay and Lesbian Archives, University of the Witwatersrand Libraries, Johannesburg.

Graeme Reid

Laurencin, Marie (1883?–1956), French painter and designer. Laurençin was born in Paris to a creole mother and never knew the identity of her father. She began her art career as a porcelain painter and later exhibited her paintings at the Salon des Indépendants. She was introduced by Georges Braque to Picasso and the circle of friends who met at his studio. She lived with Guillaume Apollinaire and is the best known of the women associated with the Cubist movement. She was briefly married to a German painter but divorced him and returned to Paris in 1920. Her most admired work was made during the 1920s and 1930s and is distinctive for the use of strong pastel colours and her focus on a dreamlike fantasy world of women in close, loving situations. Her images of fashionable adolescent women created an idealised image of quintessential femininity.

Gill Perry, *Women Artists and the Parisian Avant-Garde*, (Manchester, 1995).

Elizabeth Ashburn

Lavoie, René (b. 1955), Canadian activist. Born in Pohénéhamook, Quebec, Lavoie became a community worker after university studies in fine art, developing a special interest in substance abuse among young people.

In 1979, he began his long involvement in building Montreal's gay community by forming discussion groups and information services for gay men with addiction problems. At the same time, he was an active member of the Androgyny Collective, which founded and operated the city's first and only lesbian/gay bookstore. He was also an active participant in early community publishing efforts and was an editor of *Le Berdache*. This newspaper had a life of several years, difficult to sustain despite being in a community setting that has long had a substantial commercial 'scene'.

Lavoie was a key organiser in the arts. In 1987 he co-founded Quebec Gay and Lesbian Diffusion, still going as an annual Montreal film festival, and in 1995 he organised an International Festival of Films on HIV/AIDS. He created or organised several art exhibitions aimed at confronting HIV/AIDS, including *SIDART* in 1989 (at the 5th International Conference on AIDS in Montreal), *Revoir le Sida (Revisiting AIDS)* in 1991, and *Sida Souvenir* in 1995 (a retrospective of local artists who had died from AIDS).

In 1990, Lavoie immersed himself in AIDS activism and community research. He has led several research projects on AIDS prevention and on community activism. In 1994, he became director of *Action Séro Zéro*, Montreal's HIV prevention programme for gay men. From 1995 to 1997 he was treasurer and then president of *COCQ-Sida*, the Montreal-based coalition of AIDS service organisations.

R. Lavoie, 'Two Solitudes: AIDS Organizations and the Gay Community', in *Sortir de l'ombre, Histoires des communautés lesbiennes et gaies de Montréal* (Montreal, 1998).

Michael Hendricks

Le Bitoux, Jean (b. 1948), French activist and journalist. Born the son of a career naval officer in Bordeaux, Le Bitoux began his career as a concert pianist and music teacher. In the late 1960s and early 1970s, he took part in various left-wing movements in Bordeaux and Nice. When FHAR (Front Homosexuel d'Action Révolutionnaire, Homosexual Front for Revolutionary Action) started up in Paris in 1971, Le Bitoux began attending some of its meetings. He even co-founded a small chapter of FHAR in Nice and edited its local newspaper, *Le Doigt au Cul*. He moved to Paris in 1974 and became active in the GLH (Groupe de Libération Homosexuelle, Group for Homosexual Liberation), a national gay rights organisation formed in late 1974 after FHAR's collapse.

The GLH split into three factions in late 1975. The GLH-14 December, which took a strongly anti-feminist position, soon disappeared, while the GLH-GB (Groupes de Base, i.e., Base Groups), which sought to rally all homosexuals around a reformist political programme, stagnated at about thirty activists. Le Bitoux was one of the moving spirits of the largest faction, the GLH-PQ (Politique et Quotidienne, Politics and Daily Life), which had about 100 members. The GLH-PQ followed a radical political line: 'No socialist revolution without sexual revolution; no sexual revolution without socialist revolution'. Although the GLH-PQ did not survive beyond 1978, it anchored the gay liberation movement firmly on the political left and its militants learned how to use demonstrations, political lobbying and journalism to gain public attention and to advance their cause.

In March 1978 Le Bitoux stood for election to the National Assembly in Paris's sixth district as one of only two openly homosexual candidates seeking a seat in the French Parliament (the other being Alain Secoué, a construction worker, who ran in Paris's eighteenth district). Le Bitoux won only thirty votes (0.11 percent of the total cast), but his candidacy served its purpose: to bring homosexuality to the attention of the media and to put homosexual rights on the political agenda after the government had recently banned much of the gay press.

Le Bitoux was principal founder of the periodical *Gai Pied* in 1979. 'My first plan was for a review dedicated to theoretical reflection,' he has explained, 'but that did not interest publishers. Then, looking at the situation of the French homosexual movement, I thought that launching a widely distributed monthly magazine would be a way to inform homosexuals as a group, to increase their [political] consciousness and to free them of their sense of shame.' *Gai Pied* was the first militantly gay periodical in France to achieve commercial success and the first homosexual publication to be sold at news-stands throughout the country.

The title *Gai Pied* – literally, 'gay foot' – is an untranslatable pun devised by the philosopher Michel FOUCAULT. *Gai Pied* came out monthly in black-and-white newspaper format from February 1979 until November 1982, then as a coloured weekly magazine renamed *Gai Pied Hebdo*. Staffed largely by veteran gay activists under Le Bitoux as 'director of publication', *Gai Pied* initially adopted a radical political tone. But editorial policy gradually changed as the magazine became more financially successful, more commercially oriented and more professional.

In part because of pressure from advertisers, *Gai Pied Hebdo* began diluting its advocacy of political and social change, and instead tried appealing to a new generation of well-to-do gay consumers by glorifying a youthful and costly 'gay lifestyle' centring on bars, nightclubs, bathhouses, travel and fashionable clothes. In Le Bitoux's bitter words at the time: 'Militancy gave way to a discourse of seduction and pretty pictures. The twenty-year-old homosexual who [now] buys *Gai Pied*, what does he get? If he is not provided with a social analysis of his condition, all is lost.' Le Bitoux resigned in protest in July 1983, taking many of the magazine's journalists and regional correspondents with him. The magazine henceforth juxtaposed serious articles (about the gay rights movement, health issues like AIDS, etc.) with more and more erotic photographs and personal advertisements by men looking for sexual partners. Sales peaked at 30,000 copies a week in the mid-1980s, but eventually declined to 9,000 as readers turned away from a magazine that no longer said much of importance. *Gai Pied* died in October 1992.

Le Bitoux himself has remained omnipresent on the French gay scene. He has written countless articles for the French press (both gay and straight), helped launch a number of French gay publications (with varying success), contributed as foreign correspondent to gay periodicals around the world, worked as a technical adviser to the French government in 1985–86, presided over the organization of the annual Gay Pride parade in 1989–90, co-founded Paris's Gay and Lesbian Centre in 1991, and headed the committee that since 1990 perpetuates the memory of the deportation and imprisonment of French homosexuals during World War II. Le Bitoux is especially involved in the ongoing fight against AIDS (he was diagnosed HIV-positive in 1986) and currently works for Aides, an association to promote safer sex, founded in 1984 by the sociologist Daniel Defert after the death of his partner, Michel FOUCAULT.

A thirty-year career as political activist and journalist makes Le Bitoux one of the most representative figures among that generation of gay militants who emerged out of the political struggles of the late 1960s and the 1970s to establish and run the associations and edit the periodicals that together provided the indispensible basis for the development of a French gay community in the 1980s and 1990s.

Jean Le Bitoux, 'De la misère relationnelle en milieu mili-tante', *Libération*, 6 May 1978, and 'Le Groupe de libération homosexuel (1975–1978)', *La Revue h*, no. 5/6 (Spring/Summer 1988), pp. 43–8; Frank Arnal, 'The Gay Press and Movement in France', in *The Third Pink Book* (Buffalo, NY, 1993), pp. 38–45; Jacques Girard, *Le mouvement homosexuel en France 1945–1980* (Paris, 1981).

Michael Sibalis

Lemon, Denis (1945–94), British activist. Lemon achieved international celebrity (notoriety) when he became the focus of a prosecution for a blasphemous libel heard at the Central Criminal Court (the Old Bailey) in London in 1977. The prosecution, initiated by anti-pornography campaigner Mary WHITEHOUSE, was brought as a result of Lemon publishing, in *Gay News* in 1976, the poem 'The love that dared to speak its name' by James Kirkup; the poem suggested homosexual intimacy between the crucified Christ and one of the Roman soldiers at the site of execution. Expert testimony on the literary, social or theological qualities of the poem was disallowed, and Lemon and *Gay News* were found guilty. Lemon's was the first such conviction in fifty years, and he was fined £500 and sentenced to nine month's imprisonment (suspended for eighteen months), subsequently quashed on appeal.

A British gay press had come into fitful being in the wake of the 1967 Sexual Offences Act, which had partially decriminalised homosexual acts between consenting males over the age of 21 and which took place in private. Early publications, such as *Timm, Spartacus, Jeremy* and *Follow-Up*, tended to rely on showbusiness features, fashion and/or pin-up spreads and short stories. *Gay News* was different, a *news*paper which devoted as much space to serious and political issues as it did to the arts and literature. Lemon was part of the short-lived collective which launched *Gay News* in June 1972; by August of that year he had become sole editor, a position he retained until he sold the paper almost a decade later. It did not long survive his departure.

Though hardly a journalist, Lemon was a far-sighted administrator and entrepreneur who was hard-nosed enough to get a gay newspaper up-and-running and to turn it into an essential component of British gay life and a well-respected publication with the mainstream. Between 1972 and his departure in 1981, *Gay News* boasted contributions from a wide range of international, distinguished, forceful and activist gay men and lesbians.

In a (vain) attempt to retrieve the anonymity he had lost as a result of the blasphemy trial, Lemon moved to Exeter, becoming a restaurateur and a contributor to *Gay News*' natural successor, *Gay Times*, writing mostly about crime fiction. It was for *Gay Times* that he wrote his only published account of the blasphemy prosecution.

Somewhat ironically, he became reconciled to religion, and at the time of his death from an AIDS-related illness, he was a practicising Christian; his death and achievements were widely noticed in the national press.

Peter Burton

Le Vay, Simon (b. 1943), British-American scientist. LeVay came to international recognition in 1991 when he published an article in the influential journal *Science* that presented evidence of a neurobiological substrate for sexual orientation in men. The neuroanatomy literature had already established that the hypothalamus (a small sub-cortical structure in the brain) is implicated in the generation of male-typical sexual behaviour and that a specific region of the hypothalamus (the interstitial nuclei of the anterior hypothalamus [INAH 3] is larger in men than in women. LeVay hypothesised that this size dimorphism was linked, not to sex, but to sexual orientation: 'INAH 3 is large in individuals sexually oriented toward women (heterosexual men and homosexual women) and small in individuals sexually oriented toward men (heterosexual women and homosexual men)'. This hypothesis was supported: LeVay found that INAH 3 was more than twice as large in the postmortem brains of the heterosexual men as in the post-mortem brains of the homosexual men in his sample.

LeVay's results were rapidly disseminated by the media and – along with research by Dean Hamer and Richard Pillard on the genetics of sexual orientation in homosexual men – reignited public and academic debates about sexuality, nature and nurture. Some activists welcomed this research, claiming that if sexual orientation was biologically determined then it would have to be given the same anti-discrimination protection as race and gender. Others were less enthusiastic about LeVay's research; there have been criticisms of the methodology (e.g. the absence of homosexual women in the sample) and the theoretical presumptions (e.g. a confusion of the categories of gender and sexuality) of the original research, as well as concerns that biological accounts of sexuality are politically retrograde. While acknowledging that research such as his own could be put to homophobic ends, LeVay has always advocated the homophilic possibilities of biological research into sexual orientation.

LeVay was born in England in 1943, the son of a psychiatrist and a physician. He attended Cambridge University as an undergraduate and received his doctorate in neuroanatomy from the University of Göttingen. His research expertise was in the structure and function of the visual system in the brain. In the early 1970s LeVay was a researcher in the Harvard University laboratory of David Hubel and Torsten Wiesel, who were later awarded the Nobel Prize for their work on the brain's visual system. From the mid-1970s he was an associate professor of neurobiology at Harvard Medical School; he took up a position at the prestigious Salk Institute for Biological Sciences, at La Jolla, California, in 1984.

The death, from AIDS, of his partner of twenty-one years, in 1990 prompted LeVay to redirect his empirical focus and contribute to the neurobiological research on sexuality: 'I had an emotional need to do something more personal, something more connected with my gay identity.' The 1991 study on INAH 3 was the only empirical research LeVay published on the neuroanatomy of sexual preference. Shortly after the publication of this study, LeVay left the Salk Institute to help establish and manage the Institute for Gay and Lesbian Education (based in Los Angeles). He has written two popular books on sexuality and science (*The Sexual Brain*, 1993; *Queer Science*, 1996) and a novel (*Albrick's Gold*, 1997), and co-authored an introduction to gay and lesbian life in the US (*City of Friends*, 1995) and a popular science text on geological cataclysms (*The Earth in Turmoil*, 1998). LeVay lives in Los Angeles, where he continues to work as an educator and a writer.

Simon LeVay, 'A Difference in Hypothalamic Structure Between Heterosexual and Homosexual Men', *Science*, vol. 253 (1991), pp. 1034–7; David Nimmons, 'Sex and the Brain', *Discover* (March 1994), pp. 64–71.

Elizabeth A. Wilson

Leavitt, David (b. 1961), American writer. The youngest of three children, Leavitt grew up in the upper-middle-class world of academia and ideas. His father was a professor of organisational behaviour at Stanford University and his mother was a homemaker and sometime political activist. Leavitt left the northern California, suburban world of his adolescence for a university education on the opposite coast. He graduated from Yale in 1983 with a degree in English, having studied creative writing and literary history. He won the O. Henry Award for fiction in 1984 and Guggenheim Fellowship in 1989. Since the late 1980s, Leavitt has lived in Italy with his lover, Mark Mitchell. They have co-edited two anthologies of gay fiction, *The Penguin*

Book of Gay Short Stories (1994) and *Pages Passed from Hand to Hand* (1997).

While still at university, David Leavitt made his name as an author: not only was he one of the youngest writers ever to have a story published in the *New Yorker* magazine (he was 21), but 'Territory' was the first with an openly gay theme to be published by this prestigious journal. That story and eight others became Leavitt's first book, *Family Dancing* (1984), which garnered critical acclaim for his insightful characterisations of the intricacies of family relationships and for his surprisingly masterful evocations of the secrets and boundaries that define those relationships.

His next work, *The Lost Language of Cranes* (1986), a novel, explores those themes within one particular family that experiences a double coming out: that of the son to his parents and of the father/husband to his son and his wife. Another family and its crisis – this time the terminal illness of the wife/mother – are at the heart of his next novel, *Equal Affections* (1989). A gay son who seems to be trying to replicate heterosexual ideals in his relationship with his lover (as unsuccessfully as his mother had with his father) contrasts with his lesbian sister, who wants to break out of such traditions. Leavitt's second collection of stories, *A Place I've Never Been* (1990), might be seen as the end of Leavitt's first stage of development as an author. These tales are perhaps the culmination of his interest in the collisions of post-1970s definitions of love and family. Indeed, it is the disintegration of the 'traditional' family that fuels Leavitt's early fiction, which seems to both mourn and welcome its passing. The ambivalence may lie in the very cultures that critics attack in Leavitt's work: they read him as not depicting enough the 'out', gay, self-aware culture of the 1980s and as depicting too much the culture of upper-middle-class, white privilege.

Leavitt's success and skill at his craft led him into new avenues in the mid-1990s, but also provoked controversy. With *While*

England Sleeps (1993), he tried to show that he could create a fiction about a world not his own. In the 1930s, two Englishmen of different classes fall in love, separate out of fear of that love, become involved in the Spanish Civil War, and find each other again, but too late. Unfortunately, Leavitt's fiction was inspired by – or too closely based on – an episode from Stephen Spender's life, and Spender sued for copyright infringement. Leavitt brought out a revised edition in 1995 with a different publisher.

Leavitt's confidence may have been shaken (he did not publish another book of fiction for four years), but that did not prevent him from taking on 'some sacred cows' of gay literature (as he put it) in his introduction to *The Penguin Book of Gay Short Stories*. He chastises Gordon Merrick's *The Lord Won't Mind*, Andrew Holleran's *Dancer from the Dance* and Robert Ferro's *The Family of Max Desir* as the wrong kind of literature for impressionable gay boys (such as he was when he had read them) because they depict a world of sexual depravity, impossible excess and eternal marginality. His attack provoked vigorous responses, of which Michael Schwartz's is perhaps exemplary.

He returned to fiction with three novellas collected as *Arkansas* (1997). The first, 'The Term Paper Artist', is a quite funny riposte to the attack he suffered on his last novel. The novella tells of a character named 'David Leavitt' who breaks out of his writer's block (caused by a 'publishing scandal') by writing term papers for college boys in exchange for sex with them. His most recent work is *The Page Turner* (1998), which follows the love between a middle-aged concert pianist and the 18-year-old boy who turns the pages of his music. The novel explores the question 'Why can't people have what they want?', a theme one can find throughout David Leavitt's essays, stories and novels.

D. S. Lawson, 'David Leavitt', in Emmanuel S. Nelson (ed.), *Contemporary Gay American Novelists* (Westport, CT 1993), pp. 248–53; Kevin Ray, 'David Leavitt', in Sharon Malinowski and Christa Brelin (eds), *The Gay and Lesbian Literary Companion* (Detroit, 1995), pp. 309–12; Michael Schwartz, 'David Leavitt's Inner Child', *Harvard Gay and Lesbian Review*, vol. 2, no. 1 (Winter 1995), pp. 1, 40–4.

James W. Jones

Legg, W. Dorr (1904–94), US activist. One of the founders of the modern American gay movement, Legg continued to sustain it until his death. From his base in Los Angeles, he tenaciously fostered the rise of the American gay movement, guiding ONE Inc., its most durable organisation, through many unanticipated storms and discouraging setbacks. Only in his late forties, however, did Legg assume his role as a pillar of what he preferred to term 'homophile' activism and scholarship.

A founder of what was to become the Log Cabin Club, the gay Republican group, Legg was sometimes underestimated as a conservative old fogey. But he anticipated the rise in the 1990s of the non-left gay theorists, including Bruce Bawer and Andrew SULLIVAN. A key component of Legg's Republicanism was his libertarian distrust of government. This distrust led him to throw two FBI agents out of the ONE offices when they sought to intimidate him. In an effort that led to a key US Supreme Court decision (1958), he reversed attempts by the Post Office to keep *ONE* magazine from the mails.

Legg also ranked as a pioneer of interracial understanding. The Knights of the Clocks, his first organisation, was biracial (black and white). As a rule his own partners were either African-American or Asian.

Legg was born in Ann Arbor, Michigan. He studied at the University of Michigan, where he took a double major in landscape architecture and music, and afterwards worked for an architectural firm in New York. In 1935 he took up a position at the State University of Oregon in Eugene. Returning to Michigan to look after his aging parents during World War II, Legg developed a relationship with a young African-American man. To minimise the effects of racial discrimination and harassment, the two moved to Los Angeles, where a black friend suggested that they form a social organisation. Meeting for the first time apparently in early 1950, the Knights of the Clocks attracted blacks and whites in fairly equal numbers. Later in the same year Dorr joined a political gay group, the Mattachine Society, founded by Harry HAY.

Two years later Legg attended a private meeting where the participants took the decision to start a monthly maganzine, *ONE*. Dorr quit his regular job and became business manager of the new publication. ONE Inc. also fostered educational efforts, including the giving of classes. In these and in his publications Legg favoured an interdisciplinary methodology, emphasising the joint contribution of the humanities, social sciences and natural sciences in the study of homosexuality. Finances remained a constant problem, and several major donors proved capricious.

In 1965 a serious schism occurred in ONE Inc., leading to the secession of a faction led by Don Slater. Coping tenaciously with the ensuing legal problems, Legg rebuilt the organisation. He founded ONE Institute *Quarterly of Homophile Studies*, and served as a co-editor of the *Annotated Bibliography of Homosexuality* (1976), still the largest reference work of its kind. ONE Institute obtained a charter from the State of California, offering graduate work leading in some cases to the awarding of the Ph.D. degree.

Shortly after Legg's death, ONE merged with Jim Kepner's International Gay and Lesbian Archives. The new group, termed ONE/IGLA, enjoys the support of the University of Southern California.

W. Dorr Legg, 'Exploring Frontiers: An American Tradition', *New York Folklore*, vol. 19 (1993), pp. 217–36; W. Dorr Legg *et al.*, *Homophile Studies in Theory and Practice* (Los Angeles, 1994).

Wayne R. Dynes

LePan, Douglas V. (1914–98), Canadian diplomat, soldier, academic and poet. LePan was born in Toronto, where he was also schooled. He was widely known on several fronts, not least for poetry. For most of his adult life, he had been married, and had two sons, but by the late 1980s he was more and more open about his homosexuality.

He taught at the University of Toronto and Harvard University before enlisting in the armed forces during World War II. After the war, he served in the Department of External Affairs, attending a number of international conferences. In the late 1950s, he was Secretary and Research Director of the Royal Commission on Canada's Economic Prospects, and then Under-Secretary of State for External Affairs. He afterwards returned to teaching English literature, first at Queen's University (Kingston, Ontario) and subsequently at the University of Toronto, where he was named Principal of University College (1964–70), and honoured with the title of University Professor (1970).

His writing included *The Net and the Sword* (poetry, 1953), *The Deserter* (fiction, 1964), *Bright Glass of Memory* (memoirs, 1979) and further volumes of poetry that culminated in his most ambitious poem – *Macalister, or Dying in the Dark* (1995) – a verse drama on the life of a young Canadian soldier executed behind enemy lines in World War II. The exploration of Canadian landscape and the search for a national mythology featured in some of his poetry, the destructiveness and despair of war in much of the other poetry and in *The Deserter*. He received the prestigious Governor-General's literary awards for *The Net and the Sword* and eleven years later for his novel. In 1976 he received the Lorne Pierce Medal of the Royal Society of Canada for literary contributions. He was granted honorary degrees and just after his death was promoted to the rank of Officer in the Order of Canada.

LePan has said that he wanted to be remembered most for his love poetry, which in his later years was more and more centred on gay relationships. The collection *Far Voyages* (1990) consisted of poems written for and to Patrick Fabbi, a young lover of his who had died in 1985, ending a thirteen-year relationship. Late in life he spoke of his regret at never having authored a gay novel.

Oxford Companion to Canadian Literature, 2nd edn (Toronto, 1997); Robert Martin, Review of *Far Voyages*, Arc (Spring 1994); Jeffrey Round, 'Douglas Valentine LePan', *Xtra! Magazine*, 31 Dec. 1998.

David Rayside

Lešnik, Bogdan (b.1952), Slovenian activist. Lešnik, together with Aldo Ivančić, started the gay movement in Slovenia. In 1984, they organised an exhibition on the gay and lesbian press of the world, historical and current. The exhibition was accompanied by a variety of events and presentations (the guests included Guy HOCQUENGHEM). It evolved into an annual 'Magnus festival', later transformed into the Ljubljana Gay and Lesbian Film Festival.

Later in 1984, Lešnik and Ivančić founded a unit at Ljubljana Students' Cultural Center (ŠKUC) named Magnus (partly after Magnus Hirschfeld), whose purpose was 'socialisation of homosexuality through culture'. It had strong connections with other non-governmental organisations promoting the new social movements (such as the feminist, peace and green movements). Magnus was a gay organisation but it also prompted the establishment of a lesbian organisation called LL. To create a common forum, Lešnik later initiated a new organisation called 'Roza klub' (Pink Club) that deals with overlapping issues.

The work of Magnus, Magnus' strategic links to other 'marginalised groups' and the debates in which Lešnik participated considerably changed Slovenian public opinion regarding homosexuality.

Ales Pečknik

Lezama Lima, José (1910–76), Cuban author. Born to a middle-class family in Havana on 19 December, 1910 (according to some sources, 1912), Lezama Lima lost his father, an army officer and military engineer, at an early age and spent most of his life in his mother's house. After residence in the US, when the family lived in a military camp in Pensacola, Lezama attended the Instituto de Havana until 1928, then the University of Havana, where he obtained a degree in law. After graduation, he decided to abandon the law and devote himself to cultural activities. His earlier literary production can be found in different Cuban cultural journals such as *Verbum* (1937), *Espuela de plata* (*Silver Spur*, 1939–41) and *Nadie parecía* (*It Seemed Like Nobody*, 1941–44). Lezama was also the founder and editor of the famous *Orígenes* (*Origins*, 1944–56). His initial support of the Cuban Revolution won him one of the vice-presidencies of the UNEAC (the Cuban Union of Writers and Artists). His writings include six books of poetry, eight books of essays, and two novels, *Paradiso* (1966; rev. edn, 1968), and its complete continuation, *Oppiano Licario*, published posthumously (1977).

In 1965 he married María Luisa Batista, thus carrying out his mother's last wish. Acording to different accounts, the marriage was never consummated, but the couple lived together harmoniously. Reinaldo ARENAS and Guillermo Cabrera Infante share the same view about Lezama's homosexual identification. Comparing him with another prominent Cuban writer, Virgilio PIÑERA (1912–79), who was in no way closeted, they maintain that Lezama lived a mostly discreet sexuality, dominated by his aesthetic interest in finding the Hellenic ideal form, which explains his interest in intellectually talented and beautiful adolescents and young men. Both Piñera and Lezama were victims of the campaigns sustained by the Cuban government against homosexuals and, even though the latter did not spend time in gaol, he lived his last years in a sort of internal exile. His personal situation worsened after the publication of *Paradiso*. The novel was severely criticised because of its erotic content and, although it is in no way a panegyric of homosexuality, it was taken as such by the Cuban bureaucracy. According to Cabrera Infante, the novel could circulate because of the direct intervention of Fidel Castro, who authorised its publication but forbade any reprinting of the text.

Actually, *Paradiso* reports the formative years of José Cemí, in a sense an alter ego of Lezama Lima, until the end of his adolescence, when he achieves a poetic understanding of the world. The novel exhibits all manifestations of sexual activity, from heterosexual to homosexual relationships, from voyeurism to sadomasochism, from adultery to incest, but sexuality is presented as a natural constituent of life. There is no doubt that as represented in Lezama's fiction, sexuality is a force that has the capability of destroying individuals and, consequently, it must be kept under control.

Due to his laborious and obscure style, oriented towards the search for a baroque expression, the complexity of his poetic system and the accumulation of cultural references, his works stand out among the most difficult and inaccessible in Latin American literary history.

Daniel Altamiranda, 'José Lezama Lima', in David W. Foster (ed.), *Latin American Writers on Gay and Lesbian Themes: A Bio-critical Sourcebook* (Westport, CT, 1994); Reinaldo Arenas, *Antes que anochezca. Autobiografía* (Mexico City, 1992); Guillermo Cabrera Infante, 'Vidas para leerlas', *Vuelta*, vol. 41 (1980), pp. 4–16; Allen Young, *Gays Under the Cuban Revolution* (San Francisco, 1981).

Daniel Altamiranda

Li, Alan (b. 1960), Chinese-Canadian activist. Born in Southern China, raised in Hong Kong, Li moved to Canada in 1976 (first to Winnipeg and in 1981 to Toronto). Since then he has become one of the most prominent Chinese activists for lesbian and gay equality in the world.

He was trained as a doctor, and has practised medicine and served as health promotion advocate within culturally diverse community settings since 1987. His practice has long included people with HIV/AIDS, and in 1992, he became medical director of Casey House, a high-profile AIDS palliative hospice in Toronto. He has served on various advisory committees on AIDS, including the Ontario Ministry Advisory Committee.

Li was a prominent member of Gay Asians Toronto, one of the largest such organisations in the world, serving as president in the mid-1980s, and as a director for most of the years since then. The group created an award in his name to honour lesbian and gay Asians for leadership and community service. He has also served prominently in other community groups, including the Toronto Centre for Lesbian and Gay Studies. He helped found, in 1994, Asian Community AIDS Services, and in 1996 the Coalition Against Homophobia (the latter to combat anti-gay coverage in the Chinese media in Canada).

During a one-year stay in Hong Kong in 1986–87, Li co-founded the Hong Kong 10% Club, the first publicly incorporated lesbian and gay community organisation in that state. While there, he also met his partner Keith Wong, also a founder of the group, and active on sexual orientation and other issues since migrating to Toronto.

Li has played a leadership role among Chinese-Canadians across the country, from 1988 onward serving on the executive of the Chinese Canadian National Council (CCNC) and as president from 1994–98. He has been the only openly gay person to head a mainstream Chinese organization in Canada. The CCNC has long been active on issues of discrimination, and Li has helped secure its participation in programmes and campaigns targeting anti-gay and lesbian sentiment.

In 1983, Li founded and produced 'Celebrasians', an annual lesbian/gay cultural and musical variety show, and since then has performed in several of them as actor, dancer, singer and master of ceremonies. He sings/performs in Cantonese opera productions, and has written, acted in and produced his own play, *Story of Two Boys* – performed path-breakingly in Hong Kong in 1987.

Song Cho (ed.), *Rice: Explorations into Gay Asian Culture and Politics* (Toronto, 1998).

David Rayside

Liberace (Wladziu Valentino) (1919–87), American entertainer. Known for his flamboyance – on stage, dripping with jewellery, swathed in furs, at a white grand piano with his signature candelabra – Liberace epitomised high camp – and made a fortune doing it.

Born of Italian and Polish ancestry in Wisconsin to a grocer father and pianist mother, he showed early talent as a pianist, playing in honky-tonk bars by the age of 14. At 17, he had his debut as a soloist on the concert stage, with the Chicago Symphony Orchestra, but within a few years had relocated to New York and developed the 'style' that was to be his trademark: as he called it, the '*Reader's Digest* versions' of popular classics. While many criticised what they saw as his low-brow approach to music, he became an immensely popular entertainer. Television and Liberace seemed made for each other, and by the mid-1950s he was one of America's most popular stars, with his own TV show.

Despite ongoing rumours and accusations, and a palimony suit brought against him by his chauffeur in 1982, Liberace continued to deny that he was homosexual. Yet, for many, he exemplified what

an effeminate flamboyant homosexual was, at a time when it was not permitted to be a public homosexual.

His death was due to AIDS-related complications.

Scott Thorson with Alex Thorleifson, *Behind the Candelabra: My Life with Liberace* (New York, 1990); Bob Thomas, *Liberace: The True Story* (New York, 1987).

Garry Wotherspoon

Lindstad, Gro (b. 1960), Norwegian activist. Lindstad has been one of the most noteworthy individuals in Norwegian gay and lesbian politics during the 1980s and 1990s.

The first Norwegian organisation for gays and lesbians, Det Norske Forbundet av 1948 (The Norwegian Confederation of 1948), was established in 1950. It underwent a serious division in 1977, mainly due to a radical movement among younger members, and after this date two separate, national organisations for gays and lesbians were in existence.

Linstad started her career as a lesbian activist in 1983 as a member of the women's group in the more radical of the two organisations, but soon became a member and an activist in both organisations. This position would have been unthinkable only a few years earlier, but with Lindstad a new generation of gay and lesbian activists evolved. Active in one or both organisations, they were often friends outside politics and they tried to cooperate where possible and relevant. This was often the case in lesbian politics and in international politics, and it was also the case when Helseutvalget for Homofile (Gay Men's Health Forum) was established in 1983.

Lindstad was one of the strongest defenders of this approach to gay and lesbian politics. During the 1980s she was active in the women's committees in both organisations and in ILIS (International Lesbian Information Service), she was elected to several positions on the central committee of DNF-48 (among them vice-president), she took the initiative to arrange the first national conference on lesbians and health issues, and she sat on the committee of the organisation working against HIV and AIDS.

In 1988 she moved from Oslo to Bergen and there she soon became leader of the local branch of DNF-48. Here she also initiated a counselling service for lesbians and gay men. In 1990 Lindstad was elected as a member of the international committee of DNF-48; she represented the organisation at a number of International Lesbian and Gay Association conferences and she participated in the Scandinavian caucus, working for a clearer position against paedophilia in this organisation. At the Paris conference in 1992, she stood unsuccessfully for the post of general secretary in ILGA.

Lindstad moved back to Oslo in 1992 and participated actively in the work leading to the amalgamation of the two national organisations for gays and lesbians in Norway. A new organisation, Landsforeningen for Lesbisk og Homofil Frigjoering (Norwegian National Organisation for Lesbian and Gay Liberation), was established in 1992 and she was elected its first leader.

After years of lobbying work for equal rights to marriage for gays and lesbians, a partnership law was passed in the Norwegian Parliament in 1993 and the new organisation could celebrate its first victory. The central committee, with Lindstad as its leader, continued intense lobbying in Parliament, and, amongst other things, it worked for asylum rights for gay and lesbian refugees, legal rights for gay and lesbians in labour matters, legal rights for gays and lesbians to adopt children, and against the discrimination of gays and lesbians in the Church. The new organisation held a high media profile, and Lindstad became 'the national lesbian', though this was not accepted readily in all circles. Amongst other things she had to put up with typical anti-female antagonism from the predominantly gay male newspaper

Blikk. They especially gave her a hard time when she, outside the organisational sphere, was appointed as political adviser for the Socialist Left Party in Parliament. Despite this, she was popular both in the national media and amongst gays and lesbians, and is known as a caring and extremely helpful person, able and willing to shoulder a large workload.

Lindstad resigned as a leader of LLH in 1998. Later the same year she married her partner of five years, Bente Vinaes.

Beate Lønne Christiansen

List, Herbert (1903–75), German photographer. The son of a prosperous coffee importer, List studied art history in Heidelberg before working for the family company. During business trips to the Americas, he began to take photographs; in Germany, he associated with the avant-garde, other bright young things, handsome sailors and foreign visitors. (Among his acquaintances was Stephen Spender, who turned him into the character Joachim in the novel *The Temple*, written in 1929.) List moved to Paris in 1935, the year of his first photographic exhibition. For the remainder of the decade he travelled widely in Italy and Greece taking photographs. He returned to Germany in 1940; although known as homosexual and partly Jewish, he worked as a freelance photographer until drafted into the army and being sent to work in a cartographic division in occupied Norway. After the war, he resumed his travels in Europe and overseas, photographed a number of famous figures for *Life* and other magazines and published photography books on the Caribbean, Naples and Nigeria.

During his lifetime, List was best known for his photographs of celebrities; he also took pictures of the ruins of wartime Munich and scenes of daily life in post-war Italy. Among his most artistically accomplished works, however, are photographs of young men, shot unawares on the beach in Capri or posed against monuments in Rome or Athens. In stark and clean but erotically charged works, such as a photograph of a handsome bare-chested youth nestled against a classical statue in Rome, taken in 1949, List summed up the conjoined attraction of the Mediterranean of antiquity and the youths of contemporary southern Europe.

Herbert List, *Junger Männer* (London, 1988), and *Italy*, ed. Max Scheler (1995); Günther Metken, *Herbert List* (Munich, 1980).

Robert Aldrich

Lorde, Audre (1934–92), African-American writer and activist. Lorde was born in New York City to West Indian parents who had emigrated to the US and settled in Harlem. In an essay on women redefining difference, published in the collection *Sister Outsider: Essays and Speeches* (1984), Lorde writes: 'As a Black lesbian feminist comfortable with the many different ingredients of my identity . . . I find I am constantly being encouraged to pluck out some one aspect of myself and present this as the meaningful whole, eclipsing or denying the other parts of myself. . . . My fullest concentration of energy is available to me only when I integrate all the parts of who I am. . . . Only then can I bring myself and my energies as a whole to the service of those struggles which I embrace as part of my living.'

These words are at the heart of Lorde's thinking on identity and difference; she exposes the myth of self-sameness within particular groups, which both elides differences of race, gender, sexuality, class and ethnicity within them, and eclipses the ways in which any one axis of difference is mediated by individual and collective identities that are always situated in shifting, contingent relations to one another. She vehemently believed that differences must be respected as they are a catalyst for social change. Theoretically and politically, as a writer, as an activist, and as a teacher, Lorde was committed to dialogue *across* differences; in her writing, she herself refuses to settle on any one of her particular differences. Her commitment to dialogue is also evident in the various genres in which she wrote, spoke and performed – pamphlets, novels, poetry, speeches, interviews, poetry readings, essays – and these, in turn, reflected and created the range of audiences she addressed through her spoken and written words.

However, race and gender do not hold positions of privilege in Lorde's work; she also writes of how, when working with social liberals on the Committee to Free the Rosenbergs from execution as Soviet spies in 1953, American leftists in the 1950s remained suspicious of homosexuality because it made lesbians and gay men 'more susceptible to the FBI', and she similarly tells of how her lesbianism impeded her full acceptance among blacks. Lorde's best-known work, her biomythography *Zami: A New Spelling of My Name* (1982), is an attempt to recreate the experience of growing up as a black lesbian while making connections to cultural and historical roots as they inscribe subjectivity. In the book, Lorde writes that 'Zami' is 'a Carriacou name for women who work together as friends and lovers'. Yet *Zami* is more than simply a search for identity as a black lesbian – it is similarly an act of re-examination and re-vision.

Lorde published several volumes of poetry including *The First Cities* (1968), as well as *New York Head Shop and Museum* (1974), *The Black Unicorn* (1978), which contains many of her best poems, including 'The Litany for Survival', *Chosen Poems: Old and New* (1982) and *The Marvelous Arithmetics of Distance: Poems 1987–1992* (1993). Essays and addresses from 1976 to 1983 appear in *Sister Outsider: Essays and Speeches*; other essays appear in *A Burst of Light* (1988). In 1978, Lorde was diagnosed with breast cancer (the disease from which she died), and in 1980 she published *The Cancer Journals* where she writes of her mastectomy, her anger at the medical establishment and women's lack of choices, and her personal response to the disease. She lectured extensively in Europe, Africa and Australia. She was given the Walt Whitman Citation of Merit for her poetry in 1991, and was appointed Poet Laureate of New York State. Lorde died in 1992 in St Croix where she had lived with her partner Dr Gloria I. Joseph.

Katie King, 'Audre Lorde's Lacquered Layerings', and Anna Wilson, 'Audre Lorde and the African-American Tradition: When the Family is Not Enough', in Sally Munt (ed.), *New Lesbian Criticism: Literary and Cultural Readings* (New York, 1992), pp. 51–74 and 75–93; Yvonne M. Klein, 'Myth and Community in Recent Lesbian Autobiographical Fiction', in Karla Jay and Joanne Glasgow (eds), *Lesbian Texts and Contexts: Radical Revisions* (New York, 1990), pp. 330–38.

William J. Spurlin

Louganis, Greg (b. 1960), American athlete. Of Samoan and European ancestry, Gregory Efthimios Louganis grew up in San Diego with his adopted parents. A sickly child, considered a sissy at school, he turned to gymnastics and later diving to appease his father. His outstanding talent and graceful athleticism saw him competing in his first Olympics at the age of 16. He went on to win Olympic Gold for both the springboard and platform diving in 1984, a record he repeated in 1988.

Louganis came out as gay at the opening ceremony of the 1994 Gay Games, although his sexuality had long been a matter for speculation. But probably his most public 'coming out' was on TV in 1995, when he informed Barbara Walters – and millions of fellow Americans – that he was HIV-positive. This was a brave admission in a country that often holds back recognition and rewards to those outside the acceptable conventions: Louganis was certainly never able to trade on his name in the way other sporting heroes did, with lucrative remuneration for product endorsements. However, his candidness about living with HIV has undoubtedly been inspirational to many around the world.

Louganis has since attempted a career as an actor, appearing in the off-Broadway play *Jeffrey* (1995), in which he played an HIV-positive character.

Greg Louganis, with Eric Marcus, *Breaking the Surface* (New York, 1995).

Garry Wotherspoon

Lowe, Chris see PET SHOP BOYS.

Lowzow, Wenche Bryn (b. 1926), Norwegian educator and politician. Lowzow was born in Oslo, and worked as a teacher and headmistress in elementary schools there until 1977. During this period, she also served several terms on the Oslo City Council. In 1977, she was elected to the Norwegian Parliament (Stortinget) on the Conservative Party ticket, and served for two four-year terms. However, after she came out as Norway's first (and so far only) openly lesbian MP, she was not renominated in 1985. She was groundlessly accused of 'having maintained an insufficiently high political profile' and was deprived of all her tasks in the party.

Together with her life companion, the pioneer gay rights activist Karen-Christine FRIELE, Wenche Lowzow was invited to a hearing in the US Congress in 1982. In order to enter the US, they had to get a dispensation from the visa regulations, since homosexuality was, at that time, still classified as a contagious disease by the American authorities. Their travel permit was also limited to the area of Washington, DC. While in America, they both spoke out in public against these hypocritical rules in the American immigration laws, and thus contributed to the changing of the law in 1988.

Lowzow and Friele were among the first same-sex couples in Norway to have their partnership registered, when this law was enacted in 1993.

Bjørn   Gunnar   Olsen,   *To   kvinner.*

Karen-Christine Friele og Wenche Lowzow forteller (Oslo, 1983).

Lisbeth Nilsen

Lynch, Michael (1944–91), American-Canadian teacher, activist and writer. A native of North Carolina, Lynch received a Bachelor of Arts degree from Goddard College in 1967. In 1971 he moved to Toronto with his wife, Gail Jones, and joined the English department at St Michael's College in the University of Toronto. In 1972 he was awarded a Ph.D. from the University of Iowa for his study of the poetry of Wallace Stevens. Lynch came out as a gay man by 1973 and for almost twenty years was a leading Canadian gay rights activist and AIDS organizer.

Lynch's life was consumed by several overlapping fields of interest: teaching, scholarship, activism, writing and, especially, fatherhood. Lynch taught modern poetry, fiction and writing at the University of Toronto from 1971 to 1990. He was an early advocate for lesbian and gay studies, and in 1974 taught 'New Perspectives on the Gay Experience' at the University of Toronto School of Continuing Studies, one of the first gay-themed courses offered at a Canadian university. He was the co-organizer of 'Whitman in Ontario', a conference held in Toronto in 1980. His paper, 'Here is Adhesiveness: From Friendship to Homosexuality', was awarded the first Crompton-Noll Award from the Lesbian and Gay Caucus of the Modern Language Association (MLA) in 1981. From 1981 to 1990 Lynch edited the MLA Lesbian and Gay Caucus's *Gay Studies Newsletter* (later known as *Lesbian and Gay Studies Newsletter*), which had a major impact in connecting the growing network of scholars in the field of lesbian and gay studies. At his death he left unfinished an historical study, 'The Age of Adhesiveness', an examination of male–male intimacy in New York City between 1830 and 1880.

Lynch was founder or early organiser of numerous gay organisations in Toronto, including The Gay Alliance towards Equality (GATE) (1973–76), the (Toronto) Gay Academic Union (1975–77), the Committee to Defend John DAMIEN (1977–79), and Gay Fathers of Toronto (1978); he was also a member of the editorial collective that published *The Body Politic* (1976–78).

When AIDS first came to public attention in 1981 Lynch was in the forefront of activists in Toronto to respond to the impending health crisis. His article 'Living With Kaposi's', published in *The Body Politic* in 1982, caused a stir in that it dared to analyse AIDS from a sex-positive, gay liberationist perspective. Lynch was a co-founder of the AIDS Committee of Toronto (1983), and chairperson in 1984. He originated the idea of Toronto's AIDS Awareness Week in 1983. After learning he was HIV-positive in 1988, Lynch helped to found AIDS Action Now!, a group devoted to lobbying the Canadian government for improved access to treatment for people with HIV and AIDS.

Lynch continued to be fully engaged in teaching, writing and activism as his health began to fail. He was the organiser of the Toronto AIDS Memorial (1988) and the founder of the Toronto Centre for Lesbian and Gay Studies (1988–89). In 1989 his first book of poetry was published. *These Waves of Dying Friends* memorialised a generation of gay men struck down by AIDS, including his friend and former lover Bill Lewis, a Toronto AIDS researcher and gay activist.

Lynch loved to dance at discos and to party, and was proud to be the first gay academic ever to pose as a centrefold for both *Honcho* and *Mandate* magazines. He is memorialised by the Michael Lynch History Grant of the Toronto Centre for Lesbian and Gay Studies and by the Michael Lynch Service Award of the Lesbian and Gay Caucus of the MLA.

'Michael Lynch: A Memorial', *LGSN: Lesbian and Gay Studies Newsletter*, vol.18, no. 3 (Nov. 1991), pp. 1–13; Eve Kosofsky Sedgwick, 'White

Glasses', in *Tendencies* (Durham, 1993), pp. 252–66; Michael Lynch papers, Canadian Lesbian and Gay Archives, Toronto.

Donald W. McLeod

Lyon, Phyllis (b. 1924) and **Martin, Dorothy** (Del) (b. 1921), American activists. Martin and Lyon first met in 1950 in Seattle where, after a long courtship, they became lovers and, within five years, founders of the first lesbian civil rights organisation in the US, the Daughters of Bilitis. Martin was born in San Francisco, where she grew up, married a man and became a mother; her conventional life, however, began to disintegrate as she started exploring San Francisco's lesbian world and dating another woman. After divorcing and giving up custody of her daughter, Martin moved to Seattle to work for a publisher. Lyon was born in Tulsa, Oklahoma, and moved with her family to the San Francisco Bay Area where she grew up and attended college. After graduating with a degree in journalism from the University of California at Berkeley, Lyon moved to Seattle, where she found herself working alongside Martin. The two became friends, confidants and eventually lovers – and it was not too long before the two returned to San Francisco to set up a household and blaze what seemed an uncharted lesbian path.

The options available for lesbians to socialise in the early 1950s were few and those that did exist were not very attractive. Though some historians have since reconsidered the political foundations of lesbian bar culture, the truth remains that police harassment, legal strictures, public disdain and the danger of alcohol abuse combined to make the lesbian bar as much a 'well of loneliness' as a site of 'prepolitical' resistance. While not completely rejecting bar culture (as some historians have charged), Martin and Lyon sought out alternatives. In September 1955, a group of four lesbian couples from diverse backgrounds convened with the goal of forming an alternative to the bars, where women could dance with each other without the threat of exposure and arrest. This meant that several of the founders wanted the nascent organisation to be secret, closed to outsiders. Four meetings later, the group of women agreed on a name, the Daughters of Bilitis, which came from a poem by the decadent poet Pierre Louÿs about a fictional contemporary of Sappho. The name was chosen, according to a founding member, because ' "Bilitis" would mean something to us, but not to any outsider. If anyone asked us, we could always say we belong to a poetry club'.

The first official meeting of the Daughters of Bilitis was held on 19 October 1955. The organisation grew slowly in its first year, gradually evolving from a secret social club to an organisation increasingly devoted to education and publicity. Consequently, several of the founding members became unhappy with the change and left to form other organisations whose function was primarily social, remaining invisible to the outside world. Meanwhile, the Daughters of Bilitis progressed towards achieving its goals of education and publicity when it began publishing the monthly magazine, *The Ladder*, in October 1956; the organisation attained full status as a non-profit organisation in California in January 1957. By the early 1960s, *The Ladder* had a circulation of about 1,000, yet because many copies were passed around from person to person, its readership was undoubtedly higher. Though it was the nation's first known lesbian civil rights organisation and was founded in an era of great repression against homosexuals, historians such as John D'EMILIO and Nan Boyd have criticised the Daughters of Bilitis for being too conservative and 'accommodationist'. Martin and Lyon have been challenged because of their stated goal of helping the lesbian in her 'adjustment to society' (rather than the other way around) and their desire, through suggestions about sartorial conventionality, to make the lesbian appear 'non-threatening' to heterosexual America. Similar to the historical critique of the San Francisco Mattachine Society, such commentary needs to be tempered by a more nuanced consideration of the organisation and Martin's and Lyon's role within it. In particular, historians have traditionally given far too much attention to Martin's and Lyon's philosophical conventionality while neglecting the work that absorbed the majority of their time: publishing, publicity and, most importantly, social service activities. The papers of Martin and Lyon, recently made available by the Gay and Lesbian Historical Society of Northern California, reveal that Martin, Lyon and other members of the Daughters of Bilitis spent the vast majority of their time assisting isolated lesbians across the country by providing them with information, counselling (about employment, marriage, divorce, child custody and other legal problems), and, most profoundly, creating a symbol of the larger lesbian world, which helped ease the pain of isolation countless women experienced. Years later, Martin and Lyon declared that the primary goal of 'the organisation was to encourage and support the Lesbian in her search for her personal, interpersonal, social, economic, and vocational identity'. Future historians should use those words to guide an assessment of Martin's and Lyon's and their organisation's success or failure.

About ten years after the founding of the Daughters of Bilitis, the homophile movement began heating up in San Francisco. Such milestones as a media spectacle surrounding the 1959 mayoral race, the candidacy of a drag queen (José SARRIA) for county supervisor and the unfortunate police harassment of a New Year's day drag ball in 1965 provided increased media attention to the homophile movement and along with it much more legitimacy and power. Whenever reporters began an article on homosexuality, they usually found themselves in the offices of the Daughters of Bilitis, interviewing Martin or Lyon

about 'the lesbian'; while the results of such interviews were rarely flattering, they did spread word of the organisation to millions of readers, as was the case with Jess Stearn's best-selling 1964 book, *The Grapevine*. As the 1960s wore on, however, both Martin and Lyon started to lose interest in the homophile movement, which they saw as male-dominated and, thus, not concerned with the special problems of the 'female homophile'. Perhaps the swan-song of Martin's and Lyon's participation in the homophile movement was the fourth biennial convention of the Daughters of Bilitis held in San Francisco in August 1966. The media coverage was generally favourable, police harassment of gay and lesbian institutions (including bars) had virtually ceased, and San Francisco was witnessing the birth of yet another, more determined generation of activist organisations and publications.

The birth of this next wave of homophile activism was in many ways brought into being by Martin, Lyon and their associates. Lyon and Martin assisted in the founding of the Council on Religion and the Homosexual in 1964, and worked closely with San Francisco's most activist church, Glide Memorial, and with its charismatic, radical pastor, the Reverend Cecil Williams. Despite such progress, the middle and late 1960s was a time of change and realignment. In their political memoir first published in 1972, *Lesbian/ Woman*, Martin and Lyon noted that by 1968 they began to withdraw from the homophile movement, moving toward a more particular identification with the emerging feminist movement, turning their attention to women's issues such as employment security, job training and family rights. Moreover, 1968 was also the first year since they founded the Daughters of Bilitis that neither Martin nor Lyon held an office at the national or local level; it was also the first year that the two joined the National Organisation for Women, the organisation that attracted most of their attention over the next several years. Shortly after joining, Martin was elected secretary of the San Francisco chapter and, in 1973, she was elected as the first openly lesbian member of the national board; it is important to note that while involved with the National Organization for Women, Martin and Lyon played key roles in reforming that organisation's less than appreciative stance toward lesbians. As they devoted more attention to the women's liberation movement, the Daughters of Bilitis began to wither; by 1970 the national organisation dissolved and soon after, many chapters did the same (even as they had recently begun to grow due to the rise of gay liberation following Stonewall). In 1972, after an impressive sixteen-year run, *The Ladder* ceased publishing. In some cities chapters did survive (a Boston chapter was still alive in 1999), though barely so; the San Francisco chapter was viable until the late 1970s and from 1970 to 1975 published its own magazine, *Sisters*. But, by the middle 1970s, after about twenty years of life, the Daughters of Bilitis virtually disappeared, a victim of both generational conflicts as well as the culture wars that besieged the internal life of lesbian and feminist organisations during that tumultuous decade.

At the dawn of the 1970s, Martin and Lyon had shed most of the accommodationist tendencies of the early Daughters of Bilitis for a more radical demand: 'Not toleration – lesbian liberation', as the concluding chapter of *Lesbian/Woman* announced. Though Martin and Lyon moved toward radical feminism, they never did embrace its most pronounced philosophy: separatism, or what has been called 'cultural feminism' by the historian Alice Echols. They wrote, 'We never could understand the animosity some separatist Lesbians displayed toward heterosexual women. We all grew up in heterosexual homes and experienced the same early training and oppression as women . . . We are bothered, too, by the contradictions of

Lesbian separatists who reject conformity to women's roles in larger society but impose on Lesbians another conformity in dress, thought, and behavior. To us it is trading one form of tyranny and oppression for another.' Even as politics changed, Martin and Lyon managed to remain active and vital. Martin wrote what many consider the founding text of the 'battered women's movement', *Battered Wives* (1976). Meanwhile, Lyon served as co-director of the National Sex Forum for a number of years. In 1978, on Martin and Lyon's twenty-fifth anniversary, the San Francisco Board of Supervisors voted to honour their relationship; the two votes against the honour were cast in protest by noted homophobes.

Throughout the 1980s and 1990s, Martin and Lyon have been honoured time and again for their contributions to both the homosexual and women's movements. In 1980, the lesbian physician Patricia Robertson founded a non-profit health clinic for lesbians in San Francisco and named it the Lyon–Martin Women's Health Services clinic. In the 1980s, Lyon was appointed to the San Francisco Human Rights Commission. The two received lifetime recognitions from organisations like the Society for the Scientific Study of Sexuality. In March 1999, after forty-six years as a committed couple, Martin and Lyon finally relented to requests that they participate in San Francisco's public domestic partners commitment ceremony at city hall. Jokingly, Lyon told reporters that they had not done it earlier because 'We liked living in sin'.

Del Martin and Phyllis Lyon, *Lesbian/Woman* [1972] (Volcano, CA, 3rd edn, 1991); Del Martin, *Battered Wives* [1976] (Volcano, CA, rev. edn, 1989); Nan Alamilla Boyd, 'San Francisco Was a Wide-Open Town: Charting the Emergence of Gay and Lesbian Communities through the Mid-Twentieth Century' (Ph.D. Thesis, Brown University, 1995); John D'Emilio, *Sexual Politics, Sexual Communities:*

The Making of a Homosexual Minority in the United States, 1940–1970 (Chicago, 1983); Lillian Faderman, *Odd Girls and Twilight Lovers:* *A History of Lesbian Life in Twentieth-Century America* (New York, 1991).

Martin Meeker

M

Mac Liammóir, Mícheál (Alfred Will-more) (1899–1987), Anglo-Irish actor. After a London debut roughly contemporaneous with Noel Coward's (1912) he went to Ireland and joined the Nationalist Gaelic League, and reinvented himself, acquiring a much envied knowledge of Irish and the name by which he became known. He founded the Gate Theatre in 1928 and continued to manage it with his life-long partner Hilton Edwards (1903–82) almost until his death, still appearing on stage even when sight and memory were beginning to fail.

Mac Liammóir wrote a dozen or so plays, often on patriotic themes, and sometimes wrote in Gaelic. His contributions to gay culture were essentially two: the entertainment *The Importance of Being Oscar* in which his face curiously resembled Toulouse-Lautrec's portrait of Wilde (and which was one of the earliest manifestations of an up-turn in respect for Wilde) and his dignified, high-profile life with Hilton Edwards, with whom he shared a huge city house: although neither of them lived to see homosexuality decriminalised in Ireland, their funerals were important public events, and the occasion of much genuine affection. Gay readers attracted by the title of his book *Fairy Nights* (1922) may be disappointed to discover it deals with Celtic mythology; more revealing are *An Oscar Of No Importance: Being an Account of the Author's Adventures with his One-Man Show about Oscar Wilde* (1968) and *Enter a Goldfish: Memoirs of an Irish Actor, Young and Old* (1977). A curious footnote is that Mac Liammóir and Edwards launched Orson Welles' stage career. Mac Liammóir died in Dublin.

Christopher Fitz-Simon, *The Boys: A Double Biography* (London, 1994).

David Parris

Madonna [Veronica Louise Ciccione] (b. 1958), American singer. A performer of inimitable ubiquity, Madonna has saturated the pages of glossy teen-magazines and academic journals alike over the past decade. Even more unusually, her dalliances with queer communities have, more often than not, been deliberately and calculatedly cultivated, though the explanations for this vary from one commentator to another.

Born in Rochester, Michigan, into a Roman Catholic family, Madonna briefly studied music and dance in Michigan and North Carolina. The song 'Holiday' (1983) and its parent eponymous album were her first international hits. The following album, *Like A Virgin*, cemented Madonna's emerging image as independent, knowing and raunchily provocative. She has subsequently reinvented herself again and again: now a saint; now a slut; now a repentant sinner.

Though many pop stars of Madonna's ilk have made titillating use of queer themes in their work, her music and music videos are idiosyncratic insofar as they appeal to both lesbian and gay cultures simultaneously. She appropriates the style and mannerisms of gay male culture on the one hand, while flirting with 'lesbian chic' and actress Sandra Bernhard on the other.

Nevertheless, her relationship with queer cultures has been ambivalent at best. Simon Reynolds and Joy Press decried how the vogueing subculture of black and Hispanic drag queens was 'sold to the world as a titillating freak show' in the video for the song 'Vogue' (1990). The *Sex* book – published in conjunction with the release of the *Erotica* album (1992) – gave impressive exposure to (softcore) images of sadomasochism and sex with gay men, all in the name of purveying her sexual 'fantasies'. But at the same time the book purveyed some of Madonna's racial and sexual prejudices; for example, she informs the reader that sex with a Puerto Rican boy virgin 'gave me crabs'. In other sections of the book, she expresses disgust at the sight of lesbian sex. For one reviewer, the book portrayed homosexuals as 'clearly fabulous, but that's "fabulous" as in "fantastical"'.

Discounting the routine remixing of Madonna's songs for niche dance markets (and hers are often overtly marketed for the gay club scene), she would appear to be shying away from queer culture. A starring role in *Evita*, and several albums tinged with R&B influences rather than the dance music of New York's black gay clubs, all suggest she is becoming a rather common type of queer icon: one careful to eschew association with the communities she pilfers ideas from.

Lisa Frank and Paul Smith (eds), *Madonnarama: Essays on Sex and Popular Culture* (Pittsburgh, 1993); Susan McClary, *Feminine Endings: Music, Gender, and Sexuality* (Minneapolis, 1993); Cathy Schwichtenberg (ed.), *The Madonna Connection: Representational Politics, Subcultural Identities, and Cultural Theory* (Sydney, 1993).

Adrian Renzo

Malouf, David (b. 1934), Australian writer. Born in Brisbane as a grandchild of Christian-Lebanese and British grandparents, Malouf graduated from Queensland University. From 1959 to 1968 he taught English in Britain, and was a lecturer at the University of Sydney from 1968 to 1978 before turning to writing full-time. He lived in Italy between 1978 and 1985 and now resides in Sydney.

Malouf began writing poetry in the 1960s but is best known for his prose, such as *Johnno* (1975), *An Imaginary Life* (1978), *The Great World* (1990) and *Remembering Babylon* (1993). Among numerous national and international prizes he was short-listed for the Booker Prize in 1993 for *Remembering Babylon* and received the inaugural IMPAC Award for the same novel in 1996. He has also written short fiction, one play, opera libretti and music and literary criticism.

A recurring theme in Malouf's writing is the relationship between Australia and Europe and its impact on the Australian cultural development represented in the individual's search for identity. To accomplish this Malouf makes use of the motifs of change and continuity, rebellion and alienation and the difficulties of language as a mediator of experience. His perspective on society, culture and history is one from the edge, considering topics such as wartime Australia, immigration, artists and society, and his own life growing up in Queensland.

Malouf's characters are in line with Patrick White's use of two male figures; both authors, according to Peter Pierce, write 'of the sense of incompleteness in the lives of some men who seek intense and dependent relationships with other men'. In contrast to fellow Australian author Frank Moorhouse, Malouf, says Stephen Kirby, 'celebrates the subversive possibilities of such [homosexual] desire in a way that obliterates its sexual component'. The relationship between men is seldom as overtly sexual as in Malouf's short story *Southern Skies* or in young Gemmy Fairley's fate in *Remembering Babylon*. In *Johnno*, Johnno's desperate plea to the narrator Dante, 'Please, please come . . . I've loved you – and you've never given a fuck for me, except as a character in one of your funny stories', has yet a different quality: homosexuality is used here, according to Kirby, 'as a catalyst to raise the possibility of escape from the strictures of provincial Australia'. Other close male relationships represent a general human closeness of two people, such as Digger who serves as the human conscience of his counterpart Vic in *The Great World*, or Ovid's platonic love for the boy in *An Imaginary Life*. The close relationship between two men in Malouf's writing is 'in some ways suggestive of opponent aspects of a single self' for Helen Daniel. Homosexuality in the writing of David Malouf represents, therefore, *another* way of existence and in that respect carries neither positive nor negative connotations.

Helen Daniel, 'Interview with David Malouf', *Australian Book Review* (Sept. 1996); Stephen Kirby, 'Homosexual Desire and Homosexual Panic in the Fiction of David Malouf and Frank Moorhouse', *Meanjin*, vol. 16, No. 3 (1987), pp. 385–93; Peter Pierce, 'David Malouf's Fiction', *Meanjin*, vol. 41, no. 3 (1982), pp. 526–34.

Jörg Heinke

Mandela, Nelson (Rolihlahla), also referred to by his clan name, Madiba (b. 1918), South African political leader. Born into a branch of the royal house of the Xhosa-speaking Thembu people in Qunu in the Transkei, he studied at Fort Hare University and then studied law at the University of the Witwatersrand, later opening the first black lawyers' office with Walter Sisulu. Mandela was a founding leader of the African National Congress

(ANC) Youth League. Arrested in 1956 and tried for treason, after his release in 1961 he went underground, establishing Umkhonto we Sizwe as the armed wing of the ANC. Mandela was arrested driving with a white gay man, Cecil Williams, in Natal in 1962. He was tried with other ANC leaders and sentenced to life imprisonment on Robben Island. Released in February 1990, he won the Nobel Peace Prize in 1993, and as leader of the ANC Alliance won South Africa's first democratic elections in 1994, becoming the first president of 'democratic non-racist non-sexist South Africa'. As president he held meetings with gay activists, and maintained ANC policy support for lesbian and gay rights, particularly when inclusion of sexual orientation in the equality clause of the constitution was under fire from US-sponsored Christian groups. Mandela married Graça Machel, widow of Samora Machel, first president of Mozambique, on his eightieth birthday in 1998. In contrast, his former wife, Winnie Madikizela-Mandela, several times denounced homosexuality as un-African. Accusations of homosexual activities with a white churchman were central to her rationale for taking Stompie Seipei into custody at her home in Soweto and allegedly torturing him to death in December 1988.

Meredith Martin, *Nelson Mandela, A Biography* (London, 1997).

Ken Davis

Mandelson, Peter (b. 1953), British politician. Mandelson was born in London, a grandson of the late Lord Morrison, a former Labour cabinet minister. He was educated at Oxford University, where he read politics, philosophy and economics. After university he worked for the Trade Union Congress and was a Councillor for the London borough of Lambeth before becoming Labour MP for Hartlepool in 1992. He became an opposition whip. Before the 1997 general election, at which the Labour Party swept to power, he had been one of the most prominent organisers of the reconstruction of the Labour Party and was extremely close to the leader of the party, Tony Blair. After the election he became Minister without Portfolio and was the most senior and influential of a small number of gay Labour Party politicians, though he has never officially declared his sexuality. In 1998 he was targeted in the tabloid media's attack on a 'gay mafia' within government. In the following year he resigned from his ministerial position after the revelation that he had received a secret loan from another MP, but he remained a prominent politician, and is now Secretary of State for Northern Ireland.

Donald Macintyre, *Mandelson: The Biography* (London, 1999).

John Connell

Mann, Jonathan (1947–98), American epidemiologist, medical doctor and human rights activist. Mann founded the Global Program on AIDS within the World Health Organisation (WHO). The programme was established in 1987, reporting directly to the Director-General of the organisation. Through the programme, WHO became, according to Berridge, the 'international standard setter in the AIDS-policy arena, and the disseminator of a type of global ethic of non-discrimination, of voluntarism and a non-punitive response'. Prior to his appointment to the programme, Mann had worked as director of an AIDS research programme in Zaire. Thus he was well placed to comment on the social, political and medical aspects of the AIDS epidemic in Africa.

Mann sought to present the human face of the disease and to co-opt the support of national and international leaders in the fight against HIV/AIDS. He travelled extensively in 1987 and 1988 aiming at and succeeding in establishing a global consensus on policy responses to the epidemic. Through the programme, WHO was able to provide national governments, even those in the industrialised world, with an international benchmark of appropriate policies to which they could refer in this new field of health policy. In making the international community familiar with AIDS, the programme was able to counter the potential stigmatisation of individuals and groups from marginalised communities affected by AIDS. This was particularly the case in the industrialised world where WHO activities alerted governments to the severity of the new pandemic and encouraged governments to look beyond the negative stereotypes often applied to affected communities, particularly gay males, in the development of their policies to combat the disease.

In 1990 Mann left WHO in disgust, following disagreements with a newly appointed Director-General. *The Australian* commented that 'WHO was subsequently said to have removed Mann from its documents and videos'. He was later appointed to the Chair of Public Health at Harvard University and as director of the Harvard International AIDS Center.

Mann's involvement in HIV/AIDS went well beyond medical and scientific issues, as he was acutely aware of the human rights implications of the disease. He highlighted the inequalities in medical treatments between rich and poor nations and called for the establishment of global human rights for people discriminated against on the basis of AIDS. Concurrent with his Harvard appointment, Mann established the François-Xavier Bagnoud Centre for Health and Human Rights and also established the international journal *Health and Human Rights*. Following his death, the International AIDS Society commented that 'AIDS was an instrument to highlight prejudice and social inequality'.

Together with his second wife, Mary-Lou Clements-Mann, he was killed in the crash of a Swissair flight from New York to Geneva in 1998. Mann's passing received considerable international media attention, indicating the level of his contribution to the international community in the fight against HIV/AIDS.

Scientific American, March 1991, p. 96; The Australian, 9 Sept. 1998 (obituary), p. 17; V. Berridge, AIDS in the UK (Oxford, 1996).

Mark Edwards

Mapplethorpe, Robert (1946–89), American photographer. Born in New York into a middle-class Catholic family, Mapplethorpe studied at the Pratt Institute in Brooklyn between 1963 and 1970, majoring in advertising design and graphic arts. In his final years there he began making collages and assemblages incorporating found objects and images from pornographic magazines. In 1971 he began using a Polaroid camera to make his own black-and-white photographs (including self-portrait sequences and portraits of the poet and singer Patti Smith) which were exhibited at his first solo show, 'Polaroids', at the Light Gallery in New York in 1973. Encouraged by John McKendry, a curator at the Metropolitan Museum of Art, and by the curator and collector Sam Wagstaff, with whom he formed a long-term relationship, Mapplethorpe became increasingly interested in photography, which he also started to collect, and began working with a large format camera and negative film. By 1977 he was able to mount two solo shows at the Holly Solomon Gallery in New York and a show of 'Erotic Pictures' at The Kitchen, and was also invited to participate in Documenta 6 in Kassel, West Germany.

From the late 1970s Mapplethorpe was exhibiting regularly both in the US and internationally. Although producing portraits and still-lives, his most well-known, indeed infamous, work during this period depicted gay men engaged in sado-masochistic sex acts, e.g. the seven photographs of the X Portfolio which included an image of a man urinating in another's mouth in Jim and Tom, Sausalito (1977–78), the fisting portrait of Helmut and

Brooks (1978), and Self Portrait (1978), in which Mapplethorpe anally inserts a bullwhip. Describing his S&M photographs as merely 'documenting a certain thing that was going on in New York at a certain moment', Mapplethorpe also observed that he 'was one of the first to really approach sexuality with an eye for lighting and composition and all the other considerations relative to a work of art'.

Typically employing neutral backdrops, clear lighting and sharp focus (heightened by the fine surfaces and rich tonalities of gelatin silver and platinum prints), these photographs combine 'extreme' or shocking subject-matter (e.g. close-ups of genital and bodily mutilation) with a rigorous sense of design and structure. Indeed, despite his frequently confronting imagery, Mapplethorpe maintained a classic modernist stance of cool detachment. Stripped of psychological presence or personality and unlike, for example, the empathetic individualising portraits and nudes by the contemporary gay photographer Peter Hujar (who was also based in New York), Mapplethorpe presents bodies as iconic types or emblems. This overriding, and ultimately aesthetically conservative, classicism and abstract formalism became more pronounced in the less overtly sexual work of 1980s, such as the figure studies of the female body-builder Lisa Lyon and the photographs of black men, e.g. Ajitto (1981). For some critics, however, the latter photographs, such as Man in a Polyester Suit (1980), simply perpetuated fetishistic racist stereotyping of black men as phallus. During these years Mapplethorpe continued to produce portraits of friends and celebrities (particularly from the art world) and still-lives (imparting an uncanny sexual aura to his floral arrangements), and also began working in colour using dye transfer prints.

In May 1986 Mapplethorpe was diagnosed with AIDS, and in 1988 he established the Robert Mapplethorpe Foundation to provide grants for medical research and photographic projects. A few months after his death in Boston, in 1989, a touring exhibition of Mapplethorpe's photographs, entitled 'The Perfect Moment', became the focus of a heated political controversy over freedom of speech and public arts funding when the Republican Senator Jesse Helms cited the exhibition, along with artworks such as Andres Serrano's *Piss Christ*, in his (unsuccessful) attempt to restrict funding of the National Endowment for the Arts (the so-called 'Helms Amendment'). Bowing to political pressure, the Corcoran Gallery in Washington, DC, cancelled the show just prior to its opening, provoking widespread protests. However, the exhibition was staged at other venues, including the Contemporary Arts Center in Cincinnati in April 1990, where the museum and its director were indicted for obscenity and the display of child pornography, but were subsequently acquitted when the case went to trial.

Richard Bolton (ed.), *Culture Wars* (New York, 1992); Germano Celant, *Mapplethorpe* (Milan, 1996); Mark Holborn (ed.), *Mapplethorpe* (London, 1992).

David L. Phillips

Marcuse, Herbert (1898–1979), German philosopher. The philosopher, political theorist, social critic and guru of the 1960s counter-culture, Marcuse was born in Berlin to a middle-class Jewish family. In 1934, to escape Nazi persecution, he emigrated to the US with other members of the Frankfurt Institute of Social Research or 'Frankfurt School', which he had joined a year earlier. Marcuse was inspired by German Romanticism and the philosophers Hegel, Lukács and Heidegger, but his own wider influence stems from his distinctive synthesis of the ideas of Marx and Freud.

The basic outlines of this synthesis emerge most clearly in *Eros and Civilization* (1955). Freud presented a largely ahistorical and pessimistic view of the 'repression' of individual 'eros' as the inevitable price of civilisation. In order to survive, human beings must delay and even sacrifice immediate pleasures. The unmitigated 'pleasure principle' of the child must give way to the 'reality principle' of the responsible adult. Marcuse accepts this basic picture, but insists that the price exacted by the reality principle – the degree of repression necessary for 'civilisation' – varies historically and between different societies. As Marx's materialist conception of history implies, the *degree* of repression required by society depends on both its class relations and its level of economic development. Most societies involve inequality and exploitation; in those societies some individuals are more repressed than others. On the other hand, as the productivity of labour increases with improved technology, it is possible to produce the same goods with less work and less repression. If the degree of repression demanded by society is greater than what is strictly necessary, then there is, in Marcuse's terms, '*surplus* repression'.

Applying this model to contemporary Western societies, Marcuse has little doubt that they involve a great deal of surplus repression. In the first place, capitalist societies exploit their workers, which is unnecessary. In addition, the 'consumer society' promotes more and more unnecessary consumption and 'false needs', requiring even more unnecessary labour. Surplus repression is maintained by what Marcuse calls the 'performance principle', which demands endless activity in the name of productivity, efficiency and growth, but with little regard for genuine human fulfilment. The performance principle is particularly lethal for our erotic lives. It is not just that sex can only take place on the rare occasions when we are not working. Even when we are not working, our 'free' time is organised by the leisure and culture industries, which help to maximise the profitable consumption of commodities. Erotic pleasures are also restricted to the biologically productive and 'mature' genital form of sexuality sanctioned by conventional morality. Other parts of the body must be dedicated to productive labour. Even within the narrow confines of 'normal' sexuality, this is more about performance than pleasure.

Against the bleakly puritan demands of the performance principle, Marcuse proposes a radical liberation of eros. Unlike other sexual radicals, such as Wilhelm Reich, Marcuse goes far beyond the idea that we should simply have more orgasms. Sexual 'perversions' such as homosexuality are potentially liberating violations of the performance principle, putting human fulfilment above the goal of reproduction. Nor is Marcuse a straightforward advocate of the 'permissive society' or 'playboy culture'. He warns of the dangers of a 're-pressive desublimation' of eros, which may escape from the repressions of conventional sexual morality only to be put to other repressive purposes. Some forms of sexuality, such as non-consensual sadism, are aggressive manifestations of the 'death instinct'. Eros may also be harnessed to the performance principle in another guise. Sex has been turned into a profitable commodity. Other commodities are increasingly marketed with the help of sex. And sex itself is still about performance rather than pleasure. In fact, Marcuse's utopian vision of a 'libidinous civilisation' requires a very different liberation of eros. Eros is surely playful, subversive and 'poly-morphously perverse', but it is also potentially sociable, creative, loving and moral – even rational. A liberated eros can still be civilised, only not in repressive ways. It does not mean the end of civilisation, only the end of conventional oppositions between work, art and play, between reason or sense and sensibility, between love, friendship and sex.

Herbert Marcuse, *Eros and Civilization: A Philosophical Inquiry into Freud* (Boston, 1955); Douglas Kellner, *Herbert Marcuse and the Crisis of Marxism* (London, 1984); Vincent Geoghegan, *Reason and Eros: The Social Theory of Herbert Marcuse* (London, 1981).

David West

Martin, Dorothy. See LYON

Martin, Robert K(essler) (b. 1941), American scholar. Martin's *The Homosexual Tradition in American Poetry* (1979; expanded edition, 1998), reclaimed Walt Whitman as a 'gay' poet from an academic tradition that denied and obfuscated the sexuality in his poems, and argued that Whitman's poetic voice enabled Hart Crane's work and provided a sense of continuity and tradition for gay poets of the 1960s and 1970s (and, in the expanded edition, African-American poets). Martin's study elucidates the ways in which poets like Whitman and Crane developed a poetic rhetoric for a social identity, how they were able to express and celebrate their self-conception as 'homosexuals' in a repressive milieu. Martin has also edited a collection, *The Continuing Presence of Walt Whitman* (1992), which contains reflections about Whitman's relation to Native and African-Americans, gay men and women, as well as responses from the poet Thom GUNN and the composer Ned ROREM.

Martin's *Hero, Captain, and Stranger: Male Friendship, Social Critique, and Literary Form in the Sea Novels of Herman Melville* (1986) was the first full-length study of sexuality in Melville's writings. It elucidates, in *Typee, Redburn, White-Jacket, Moby-Dick* and *Billy Budd*, a triangular paradigm in which the Hero is confronted with and must choose between two conflicting erotic forces, 'a democratic eros' (the Stranger) and 'a hierarchical eros' (the Captain). Melville's exploration of this conflict reflects his disillusioning struggle to concretely imagine, articulate and sustain a viable homosexual relationship in his work, given the utter lack of any contemporary social models. For Martin's recent rearticulation of the issues of this book, see 'Melville and Sexuality' in *The Cambridge Companion to Herman Melville* (1998).

Martin's work evinces his commitment to elucidating the complex, coded and often conflicted ways in which writers have articulated and celebrated homosexual desire in homophobic and heterosexist societies. For Martin's reflections on what constitutes 'gay writing' and the myriad ways in which homosexual desire finds textual expression, see his 'Roland Barthes: Toward an "Ecriture Gaie"' in *Campgrounds: Style and Homosexuality*, (1993).

Jason Boyd

Mascarenhas, João Antônio de Souza (1927–98), Brazilian activist. Mascarenhas was born into a prosperous cattle-ranching family in Pelotas, in the southern state of Rio Grande do Sul, an appropriate birthplace since Pelotas has a reputation as a gay city in Brazilian folk mythology. He trained as a lawyer and spent some time in Paris after the war before settling in 1956 in Rio de Janeiro, where he spent the rest of his life, although always retaining strong emotional links with his native state. He worked for a time as an official in the agrarian reform institute but resigned after the military coup of 1964. Apart from a brief return to the civil service following the redemocratisation of Brazil, he lived on his private means, which allowed him to devote much of his time to the gay movement.

Unusually among middle-class Brazilians, where reticence was the norm, Mascarenhas was completely open about his homosexuality, arguing that this was the best defence against blackmail. In 1972 a friend lent him some British gay liberation pamphlets and copies of *Gay Sunshine* (published in San Francisco), which acted as a revelation. Later he joined the International Lesbian and Gay Association (ILGA) and for many years he was the unofficial 'foreign minister' of the Brazilian gay movement, attending the ILGA conference in Oslo in 1988 and maintaining links with groups abroad. His legal training and knowledge of languages allowed him to follow developments in the more progressive European countries and propose campaigns for the fledgling Brazilian movement. He backed up his campaigns with a comprehensive archive of newspaper cuttings and correspondence.

Mascarenhas helped the head of Gay Sunshine Press to compile two anthologies of Latin American gay writing, *Now the Volcano* (1979) and *My Deep Dark Pain is Love* (1983), by arranging meetings with writers. As a result of these contacts, a group of activists founded a gay newspaper, *Lampião da Esquina* (*The Lamp-post on the Street Corner*), which appeared regularly between 1978 and 1981. It acted as a catalyst for the Brazilian gay movement, which flourished briefly in the heady days accompanying the retreat of the military from government. An attempt by the Ministry of Justice to ban the paper was dropped in the face of protests from within Brazil and abroad. Mascarenhas was one of the founding members but later left the editorial board.

Mascarenhas worked closely with Luiz MOTT of the Grupo Gay da Bahia in the successful campaign of the early 1980s to get the Brazilian medical authorities to reject Paragraph 302.0 of the World Health Organisation's International Classification of Diseases, which described homosexuality as a sexual deviation and disorder. In 1985 Mascarenhas founded the Triângulo Rosa (Pink Triangle) group in Rio de Janeiro. Though relatively small – it met in Mascarenhas's apartment in Ipanema – it fought successfully to get the National Congress of Journalists to include a ban on discrimination for sexual orientation in its code of practice.

Triângulo Rosa was the leading organisation for the campaign in the late 1980s to insert a clause prohibiting discrimination on the grounds of sexual orientation into the new democratic federal constitution then being debated. In 1987 Mascarenhas was invited to address two of the subcommittees of the Constituent Assembly in Brasília, the first time an open homosexual had talked about homosexuality in the country's legislature. Despite a sustained campaign and the support of a number of politicians, the proposal was finally rejected, although a quarter of the constituent delegates voted in favour. The most vociferous opponents were a group of conservative evangelical Protestants. Nevertheless, a number of municipalities, including most of the major cities and many small towns in the interior, adopted similar clauses for local constitutions. The campaign brought gay issues into the mainstream of Brazilian politics and paved the way for later initiatives, such as the proposal to recognise gay partnerships. Mascarenhas then withdrew from active involvement in the gay movement, apart from a brief return when a revision of the federal Constitution was being debated.

Mascarenhas was criticised for his failure to recognise the pressing nature of the AIDS crisis as well as his rather conservative concentration on what appeared a narrowly legalistic interpretation of gay rights rather than the broader perspectives of gay liberation. In the longer term, however, his legal training, broad culture and familiarity with developments abroad enabled him to address the Brazilian political and administrative elite in language which it understood. His emphasis on the importance of sexual orientation in terms of human rights laid the groundwork for a change of attitude whose ramifications ultimately promise to benefit everyone. Mascarenhas was honoured by the City Council of Rio de Janeiro for his contribution to gay rights and by the time of his death he was recognised as one of the major pioneers of the gay movement in Brazil.

João Antônio de Souza Mascarenhas, *A Tríplice Conexão: Machismo, Conservadorismo Político, Falso Moralismo* (Rio de Janeiro, 1998); James N. Green, 'More Love and More Desire: The Building of a Brazilian Movement', in Barry D. Adam, Jan Willem Duyvendak and André Krouwel (eds), *The Global Emergence of Gay and Lesbian Politics: National Imprints of a Worldwide Movement* (Philadelphia, 1999), pp. 91–109; Cristina Luci Câmara da Silva, 'Triângulo Rosa: A Busca pela Cidadania dos "Homossexuais"' (Master's Thesis, Universidade Federal do Rio de Janeiro, 1993).

Robert Howes

Mason, Angela (b. 1944), British activist. Mason was involved on the left of radical gay/lesbian and feminist activism in the early 1970s, and other left politics before that. She was one of eight activists accused of conducting a bombing campaign in the early 1970s directed at right-wing targets, and was one of four acquitted at the end of the long trial. At the time she was at the London School of Economics, and then went on to lecture in sociology, and eventually to the study of law (which she then practised). It was at the LSE that she met her long-time partner Elizabeth Wilson, a writer and academic.

At the end of 1992, the mainstream lobby group Stonewall selected Mason as Executive Director, despite the *Daily Telegraph* 'exposing' her radical past. Stonewall had been formed in 1989 to maintain an ongoing lobbying presence in governmental and parliamentary circles. It had quickly established a reputation for cross-party effectiveness, and under Mason's direction it acquired an even stronger reputation. It took a leading role in parliamentary campaigning for an equal age of consent in 1994 and 1998, in mobilising British lesbians and gays to contact parliamentarians, and in helping to generate strategic legal challenges against statutory discrimination.

Under Mason's leadership, Stonewall has sometimes slipped into acrimonious disagreement with the more confrontational group OutRage!, but it has also earned widespread respect as an effective advocate for equality. The group's initial campaign on the age of consent was regarded as a textbook example of how to mobilise support for equality, even though unable to gain a parliamentary majority for such equality. Mason is particularly well regarded by mainstream activists representing all political parties, as well as by a wide range of parliamentarians and media observers.

Angela R. Wilson (ed.), *A Simple Matter of Justice?* (London, 1995); Emma Healey and Angela Mason (eds), *Stonewall 25: The Making of the Lesbian and Gay Community in Britain* (London, 1994).

David Rayside

Matlovich, Leonard (1943–88), American air force officer and activist. When his picture appeared on the cover of *Time* magazine in 1975, Air Force Sergeant Leonard Matlovich was catapulted to fame, becoming the most recognisable homosexual in the United States. Yet being the first 'openly' gay person to appear on the magazine cover, and the first to challenge directly the military's exclusion of homosexuals, was ultimately an ambivalent personal accomplishment.

Matlovich was born into a military family stationed in Georgia; his father was a career Air Force officer. After graduation from high school he enlisted in the Air Force in 1965. On his third tour of duty in Vietnam, Matlovich was injured by a land mine and received the Purple Heart medal. He then began teaching at various military bases; his courses in race relations became so respected that he won an Air Force award for his work. Matlovich also began to confront his own homosexuality. Barely a year after his first homosexual experience, Matlovich contacted gay activist Franklin KAMENY in Washington DC; Kameny had been quoted in an Air Force publication arguing that the time was right for a gay serviceperson to challenge the military's exclusionary policy. Kameny, Matlovich and a lawyer from the American Civil

Liberties Union decided to take a pre-emptive strike at the policy.

In a 1975 letter, Matlovich disclosed his homosexuality to his superiors as he asked for an exemption from the military's anti-gay policies. The military refused and instead initiated proceedings to discharge Matlovich. The case became a *cause célèbre* and a media deluge followed. For instance, a made-for-television movie of Matlovich's life appeared in 1978, and Matlovich's case concerning his dismissal moved from the military to civilian courts. Matlovich also was attempting to build his personal life and like thousands of gay men, moved to San Francisco in the late 1970s. He was soon convinced by a number of conservative gays to stand for the seat on the Board of Supervisors that fell vacant after Harvey MILK's assassination. But Matlovich was not interested in progressive coalition-building and he lost miserably to Harry Britt.

In 1980, the United States Court of Appeals ordered the Air Force to reinstate Matlovich and give him back pay. Admitting defeat, the military offered Matlovich a cash settlement if he would not return to the service. In the context of an appeal by the Air Force to the United States Supreme Court, marked by a growing conservatism, Matlovich took the money and ended his five-year long court battle. He donated a portion of the $160,000 settlement to gay community organisations, but also purchased a pizza parlour near San Francisco. Matlovich sold his business in 1984 and returned to the city, where he once again became marginally involved in politics and activism. He learned he had AIDS in September 1986 and died less than two years later.

Mike Hippler, *Matlovich: The Good Soldier* (Boston, 1989); Randy Shilts, *Conduct Unbecoming: Lesbians and Gays in the U.S. Military, Vietnam to the Persian Gulf* (New York, 1993).

Martin Meeker

Matos, Nemir (b.1949), Puerto Rican poet. Born in Puerto Rico, Matos resides in New York. The author of two poetry collections, she is one of the first Puerto Rican poets to speak openly on lesbian issues on the island.

Three key features of her poetry are the explicit lesbian eroticism, the use of colloquial language and a political agenda. In Matos's erotic discourse, the speaker pays a great deal of attention to her lover's body as well as to her own and the couple's reciprocal desires. Her poetry contains strong erotic images and comparisons with elements of nature, specifically elements of marine geography. An example is her poem 'Oleajes' ('Ocean Swells') from the collection *Las mujeres no hablan así*, in which the description of a sexual act between two women takes place.

In Matos's lesbian discourse, the use of a colloquial language to speak about sex as a way to challenge the poetic language and the oppression of women's sexuality is central. The openness of the language defies social conventions and it is a political strategy to undermine the status quo. The political aspect of Matos's poetry not only refers to the explicitness of the erotic discourse, but also to sociopolitical issues, such as the condemnation of the Vietnam War and the struggle for Puerto Rico's independence. In 'Canto a las mujeres tierra', a poem from *Las mujeres no hablan así*, through the inventory of women and the oppression they suffer, the speaker makes a claim for women's liberation from patriarchal as well as imperialistic domination.

Las mujeres no hablan así (Río Piedras, 1981); *A través del aire y del fuego pero no del cristal* (Río Piedras, 1981); Carlos Rodríguez Matos, 'Nemir Matos', in David William Foster (ed.), *Latin American Writers on Gay and Lesbian Themes: A Bio-Critical Sourcebook* (Westport, CT, 1994), pp. 216–17; Aurea María Sotomayor (ed.), *De lengua, razón cuerpo: Nueve poetas*

contemporáneas puertorriqueñas (San Juan, 1987), pp. 54–7.

Elena M. Martínez

Matthiasen, Niels (Peter Jacob) (1924–80), Danish politician. As an adopted child and youth, Matthiasen, in his parents' home, met the leading politicians of the Social Democratic Party as well as a great many authors, artists and actors. He was included in parties, theatre outings, and at the table of artists in restaurants. This unruly life was probably part of the reason for his leaving school at an early age. From 1939 to 1957 he worked for his father's publishing company, from 1954 as managing director. Matthiasen organised the election campaign for the Social Democratic Party in 1957, and in 1961 he was elected Party Secretary. As such he modernised the organisation of Denmark's largest political party. He also became a public figure. His tall stature, handsome features and outgoing manner were combined with a ready wit and a noticeable fondness for representative duties. He attached importance to being well-dressed on any occasion.

He was a member of Parliament from 1960 to 1973, 1975 to 1977 and 1978 to 1980; as Minister for Cultural Affairs (1971–73 and 1975–80), Matthiasen was able to make the most of his unbounded appetite for culture and art in all its forms. His political acumen and his enthusiasm overcame budgetary obstacles as well as resistance from local governments. The guiding principles of his politics of culture were democratisation, decentralisation and dissemination of art and culture, socially and geographically. This applied to both the elitist and to the more popular forms of culture, e.g. sport. By the time of his death Matthiasen, nicknamed 'Niels Culture', was regarded by many as almost the national embodiment of culture.

Matthiasen was often seen, and reported in the newspapers as seen, in public life, in the theatre, at exhibitions and at other cultural events in the company of the prominent ballet dancer Kirsten Simone. It was not generally known that he was a homosexual and he probably had real political reasons for staying in the closet. However, in journalistic and cultural circles, in Parliament and in the higher echelons of the Social Democratic Party, as well as in the gay subculture, his 'secret' was well known. In spite of all Matthiasen had going for himself as a public figure, it did cramp his style during the decade of Gay Liberation that he was, and probably realised that he was, Denmark's number one closet queen.

Søren Sørensen, 'Niels Matthiasen', *Dansk Biografisk Leksikon*, Vol. 9 (Copenhagen, 1981), pp. 471–2.

Wilhelm von Rosen

Maugham, Robin (1916–81), British writer. The son of the Lord Chancellor of England (whose viscountcy he inherited) and nephew of the writer W. Somerset Maugham, Robert Cecil Romer Maugham was born in London. He was educated at Eton and Cambridge University, then read law at Lincoln's Inn and was admitted to the bar. He served with British forces in North Africa during World War II, sustaining injuries which subsequently kept him from practising law, and turned his attentions to literature; his first works were about his wartime experiences.

Maugham became a prolific and popular novelist and short-story writer, though never so accomplished as his uncle. His wealth, family connections and celebrity allowed him to roam the world, finding both materials for his writing and personal companions (and also indulging in much socialising and drinking). Homosexuality is a regular theme in his works. *The Wrong People* (1967) centres on the efforts of a wealthy European expatriate in North Africa to procure as a sexual partner an ideal young man from England through the efforts of a visiting Englishman, himself a teacher enamoured of an Arab lad. A section of *Search for Nirvana*

(1975) – a title which could stand as Maugham's motto – describes an oasis in the Libyan desert where Maugham claimed homosexuality was guiltlessly practiced. Stories such as 'The Boy from Beirut', 'The Tea Planter' and 'The Senussi Soldier' continue the exploration of homosexuality in exotic foreign places. *Escape from the Shadows* (1972) and his other autobiographical works chronicle Maugham's own sexual itinerary. Other works address heterosexuality, but often in the context of inter-ethnic relationships.

Maugham's writings, his life and mentality, and his travels to Africa, Asia and Australasia situate him at the junction between an older homosexual attraction to imperial outposts (as seen in his uncle's works) and a newer sort of homosexual tourism in the post-colonial world. The open way in which his fast-paced, arresting works discuss homosexual themes make him worthy of greater attention than he usually receives.

Robin Maugham, *The Boy from Beirut and Other Stories*, ed. Peter Burton (San Francisco, 1982).

Robert Aldrich

Maupin, Armistead (b. 1944), American author. Like the main characters in his *Tales of the City* series, Maupin is a transplant who found a true home in San Francisco, the locale for these six novels. Born in Washington, DC, he grew up in Raleigh, North Carolina. After graduation with honours and a major in English from the University of North Carolina, he served in the US Navy in the Mediterranean and then in Vietnam. Following his discharge, he worked in Southeast Asia as a volunteer, building housing for disabled Vietnamese veterans, and then as a reporter in Charleston, South Carolina and, finally, in San Francisco.

In 1976, he began writing a daily serial for the *San Francisco Chronicle*, the city's morning newspaper. Although the initial response was rather cool, its popularity quickly spread and the series grew into six novels: *Tales of the City* (1978), *More Tales of the City* (1980), *Further Tales of the City* (1982), *Babycakes* (1984), *Significant Others* (1987) and *Sure of You* (1989). They have also been collected into two volumes: *28 Barbary Lane* (1990) and *Back to Barbary Lane* (1991). Collectively titled 'Tales of the City' the episodes explore the lives of the inhabitants of the apartment house run by Anna Madrigal at 28 Barbary Lane, a fictional address on Russian Hill. The landlady dispenses hope, care and home-grown joints to her carefully chosen tenants, who become each other's family. The family of choice, one of the chief themes of post-Stonewall gay literature, creates a haven for those cast out by their family of blood. But, in contrast to many other works on this theme, Maupin's series brings the two families together, showing the possibility that love and tolerance can bridge differences. The author described his intent: 'From the very beginning, my goal has been to create a framework which is large enough to include most of humanity.'

This perhaps utopian vision accounts for some of these novels' enormous and long-lasting popularity. They are also enormously funny: not only does Maupin poke fun at gays and straights equally, but his plots teem with improbable coincidences like a Feydeau farce. His style makes the books highly readable: the chapters are short, and the story is carried on in dialogue and description that capture the essence of gay American life from the mid-1970s to the late 1980s. The serial nature of the works enabled Maupin to weave in current events such as the Jonestown massacre in Guyana or Anita BRYANT's anti-gay crusade, and this added to readers' interest in following the next instalments.

But probably the central reason why so many people – no matter the categories of sexual orientation, ethnicity, class or nationality which they might otherwise inhabit – read these books and have

watched the two television mini-series made from the first two volumes (1993, 1998) lies in the fact that Maupin truly does give insight into the human condition. One reader's reaction to the illness of the chief gay character (Michael 'Mouse' Tolliver) illustrates this: 'I'm nothing but a middle-aged housewife from Moraga, with two little machos of my own, but if you kill Michael Mouse I'll never subscribe to the *Chronicle* again.'

Maupin made gay and lesbian people real and treated all his characters as equal at a time when one read largely in vain for such depictions in literature. He spoke for and of the actual experience of gays and lesbians, as in the often anthologised 'Letter to Mama' (from *More Tales of the City*), Michael Tolliver's tender yet uncompromising coming out to his parents.

After concluding the *Tales* series, Maupin published another novel, *Maybe the Moon* (1992). Here he turned his satirical attention to Hollywood, writing in the voice of another outsider, the 31-inch tall actress Cadence Roth. Maupin has also been active in a wide variety of gay and lesbian causes, striving to turn that dream of equality and tolerance from his fiction into concrete reality.

Barbara Kaplan Bass, 'Armistead Maupin', in Emmanuel S. Nelson (ed.), *Contemporary Gay American Novelists* (Westport, CT, 1993), pp. 254–9; Jean W. Ross, 'Interview', *Contemporary Authors*, Vol. 130 (Detroit, 1990), pp. 308–11.

James W. Jones

McCaskell, Tim (b. 1951), Canadian activist. McCaskell has been one of Canada's most prominent gay activists since the 1970s, and one who has consistently incorporated race and class issues into his liberationist outlook. He was a member of the editorial collective of *The Body Politic*, Canada's most important gay magazine until its demise in 1987. In the early 1980s, he was also an important member of the Right to Privacy Committee, at the time the country's largest activist group, organised in response to police raids on gay bathhouses. Later in the decade, he was a founding member of the Simon NKOLI Anti-Apartheid Committee, and was active in other networks opposing South African apartheid.

McCaskell's highest profile activism began in 1989, when he helped found AIDS ACTION NOW!, a Toronto-based direct action group that was the most visible in Canada, pressing for changes in the way that treatments for AIDS were researched and disseminated. The group was particularly notable in combining confrontational tactics, diligent research and strategic lobbying, and had marked success in forcing shifts in government policy. McCaskell was appointed to the Ontario Advisory Committee on HIV and AIDS in 1992.

For many years, McCaskell worked for the Toronto Board of Education on anti-racist and other intitiatives. He contributed to the development of programming on sexual diversity that for a time put the Toronto Board within the small vanguard of North American school boards taking up this issue.

For years, he has been partner to Richard Fung, a Trinidadian-Chinese-Canadian filmmaker sharing his interest in anti-racist initiatives.

Barry Adam, *The Rise of a Gay and Lesbian Movement*, rev. edn (Boston, 1995); David Rayside and Evert Lindquist, 'AIDS Activism and the State in Canada', *Studies in Political Economy*, No. 39 (Autumn, 1992), pp. 37–76; Gary Kinsman, 'Managing AIDS Organizing', in William K. Carroll (ed.), *Organizing Dissent*, 2nd edn (Toronto, 1997).

David Rayside

McCullers, Carson (1917–67), American novelist, playwright. Born Lula Carson Smith in Columbus, Georgia, McCullers died from a stroke in Nyack, New York. As a child she studied piano and planned to become a concert pianist, but by the age

of 17 had decided to become a writer instead. She studied writing at Columbia University and New York University from 1934 until 1936; illness forced her to return to Columbus, establishing a pattern of returning home to recuperate that would continue throughout her life. She published her first novel, *The Heart Is a Lonely Hunter*, in 1940 to much acclaim. Other works include the novels *Reflections in a Golden Eye* (1941), *The Member of the Wedding* (1946), and *Clock without Hands* (1961); the collection *The Ballad of the Sad Café and Other Works* (1951); and the plays *The Member of the Wedding* (1951) and *The Square Root of Wonderful* (1958). The recipient of numerous awards, including two Guggenheim fellowships, she was also elected to the National Institute of Arts and Letters in 1952.

In 1937, she married Reeves McCullers and in 1940 they moved to New York. Though married, she described herself as an 'invert', and both she and her husband were apparently bisexual or at least troubled by a complicated sexual identity. Husband and wife were involved in more than one love triangle, one of the most serious with David Diamond, the composer. Though these triangles were not necessarily sexual liaisons, they were intense, romantic, and often the cause of jealousy.

McCullers and her husband separated and reunited several times, even divorcing and remarrying. They lived in France during their last days together in 1952–53. She left him after he had twice threatened a double suicide. (She herself had once tried committing suicide, in 1948.)

McCullers developed serious attractions for several women, and her friendships with both men and women were often deeply intense. One of her most important was with Annemarie Schwarzenbach (1908–42), a beautiful, unhappily married Swiss writer, to whom McCullers dedicated *Reflections in a Golden Eye*. Like most of the women with whom McCullers fell in love, Schwarzenbach was not prepared to form a long-term commitment and left her, breaking her heart. Most of McCullers's many infatuations with women were unreciprocated. She energetically sought out such disparate women as Katherine Anne Porter, Greta Garbo and a woman dancer in the New York City Ballet. She also had attractions to a few other men, including Arnold Saint Subber, with whom she conducted an intense liaison during 1955–57.

In the early 1940s, after separating from her husband the first time, McCullers lived in a house in Brooklyn Heights with George Davis, W. H. Auden, Gypsy Rose Lee, and at various times Chester Kallman, Benjamin BRITTEN and Peter PEARS – several of the housemates and visitors were prominent gay artists and intellectuals. Later, she became a close friend of the famous writer and fellow Southerner Tennessee WILLIAMS and she recommended the young Truman CAPOTE to her publisher.

McCullers's great themes were love and the rejection of the lover by the beloved, but her life and work cannot be quite so simply reduced to any single theme. Her ambivalence towards the American South was largely fuelled by concern about injustice. When her hometown library asked whether she would donate her manuscripts to its collection, she refused, saying that as long as the doors of the main library were closed to the black residents of Columbus, she did not feel she could do that. She shared a fierce compassion for the oppressed, the marginalised and the misunderstood. This concern appears strikingly in her portrayals of the injustices suffered by blacks in American society, her treatment of the problem of class and the plight of the working poor, and her vivid renditions of the marginalisation of those who resisted gender expectations. She and her best-known female protagonists – Mick Kelly, Frankie Addams, and Amelia – were tomboys or adult women who liked wearing clothing tailored for men. The search for identity was a major concern in much of her work. Her characters often felt themselves to be different from others, sometimes physically, usually emotionally and spiritually. Her works explored the moral and spiritual isolation that frustrated the need, as Frankie Addams put it in *Member of the Wedding*, to find 'the we of me'.

Virginia Spencer Carr, *The Lonely Hunter: A Biography of Carson McCullers* (New York, 1975); Carson McCullers, *The Mortgaged Heart*, ed. Margarita G. Smith (Boston, 1971).

Karen Lee Osborne

McKellen, Sir Ian (b. 1939), British actor. Born in Burnley, England, McKellen was educated at Wigan Grammar and the Bolton School, and later St Catharine's College, Cambridge, completing studies there in 1962.

His stage debut was at Coventry in 1961, in *A Man for All Seasons*, and he first appeared on the stage in London two years later, in *A Scent of Flowers*, for which he won the Clarence Derwent Award for best actor and an invitation to join the National Theatre. He went on to establish a reputation as one of England's finest actors, winning numerous awards, including the Lawrence Olivier Award for best actor in 1979 for his performance in Martin Sherman's searing drama about gays in a Nazi concentration camp, *Bent*. In 1979 he was made a Commander of the Order of the British Empire.

It was in 1988, at a time of increasing harassment of gays and lesbians by Margaret THATCHER's Tory goverment, that McKellen came out. He became increasingly involved in gay rights activities, often as a public speaker. In 1991 he was awarded a knighthood for services to the theatre. This generated some controversy, with the filmmaker Derek JARMAN, among others, condemning McKellen for accepting honours from a government that persecuted gays. However, this attack led to a surge of support for McKellen, with many other leading actors also choosing to 'come out', arguing that it was important that the public know that homosexuals could and did hold leading places in the creative worlds.

Among McKellen's recent works has been a highly-praised performance as the gay filmmaker James Whale in *Gods and Monsters*.

International Dictionary of Theatre, Vol. 3, *Actors, Directors and Designers* (Detroit, 1996).
Garry Wotherspoon

Meier, Karl ('Rolf') (1897–1974), Swiss actor, journalist. Born in St Gallen, Switzerland, he died in Zurich. The illegitimate son of Elisabeth Rheiner (who later married an Italian and disappeared from view), he was adopted at the age of 15 by Johann Thomas and Wilhelmina Meier. He followed an early desire to become an actor and appeared on the Swiss stage from 1920 to 1924; from 1924 to 1932 he toured the German provinces. After returning to Switzerland, in 1934 he joined the newly opened cabaret 'Cornichon' in Zurich and remained with it for thirteen years, taking part in probably 4,000 performances. After leaving Cornichon, Meier continued his career as actor on stage, radio, film and television. He was also successful as a director, particularly in the Swiss folk theatre.

Meier was of international importance as editor-in-chief of the homosexual cultural periodical *Der Kreis* from 1943 until its demise in 1967, during which time he always used the pseudonym Rolf. Begun in Zurich in 1932 as the joint lesbian and gay male publication *Freundschafts-Banner*, under the editorship of Anna 'Mammina' Vock, the name was changed to *Menschenrecht* (*Human Rights*) in 1937. Rolf, who had collaborated on the periodical since 1934, again changed the name to *Der Kreis* (*The Circle*) when he took over in 1943; thence it contained no more lesbian content. During World War II *Der Kreis* was the only 'gay' journal in the world, and with contributions in French from 1941 and in English from 1952, it continued to be unique as the only such trilingual journal. Photographs were included from 1940 and attracted many readers.

Although homosexual sex was legal in Switzerland for adult men, i.e. from age 20 (effective 1 January 1942), social oppression continued. Through *Der Kreis* and correspondence with readers Rolf helped many to overcome their isolation and strengthen the bonds of what he saw as an international 'homoerotic' (his preferred word) community. Although contributors to *Der Kreis* were not paid, it was an important outlet, e.g. for the homoerotic photographs of George Platt Lynes and was the beginning of successful writing careers, e.g. of Samuel M. STEWARD.

Under Rolf's leadership, the local collaborators of *Der Kreis* formed a club in Zurich that in addition to regular meetings became internationally known for its autumn and spring festivals, as well as the religiously-tinted Christmas celebrations. Naturally Rolf took an active role in the presentations, e.g. as director and actor in the first performance in 1955 (of one act) of the play *Game of Fools* by James BARR. Rolf's firm influence on *Der Kreis* is seen in the constant high ethical tone of the journal; although a (liberal Protestant) Christian, he allowed the publication of various opinions, while promoting his own view of the ideal gay man as one in a faithful, responsible and reciprocal relationship with another.

When Scandinavian magazines began publishing full frontal nudes and explicit sex scenes in the 1960s, readership of *Der Kreis* (which allowed neither) decreased; it folded for lack of funds in December 1967. But the long-running periodical, especially in the twenty-five years that Rolf was editor, made a lasting contribution to gay liberation and culture.

André Salathé, 'Karl Meier "Rolf" (1897–1974): Schauspieler, Regisseur, Herausgeber des "Kreis"', in *Thurgauer Köpfe 1*, ed. by André Salathé (Frauenfeld, Switzerland, 1996), pp. 203–14.
Hubert Kennedy

Meinhof, Ulrike (Marie) (1934–76), German political figure. Meinhof was born in Oldenburg, Germany, her parents died while she was still young, and she and her sister were brought up by Renate Riemack, a friend of their mother's and a committed socialist.

As a student Meinhof edited the left-wing student newspaper *konkret*, and she married her co-worker, Klaus Rainer Röhl. In 1962 she gave birth to twin girls, Bettine and Regine. But by the late 1960s, Meinhof had become involved with the more radical fringe of the student movement, and had split up with Röhl, making her name as a radical political journalist. In May 1970 she was, famously, part of a group that organised the escape from prison of Andreas Baader, a political arsonist involved in a series of attacks on Frankfurt department stores: the Baader–Meinhof Group was thus formed, also known in Germany as the *Rote Armee Fraktion*, or RAF. Despite the conjunction of her name with Baader's, Meinhof was not, as is often assumed, one of the group's leaders. But she did spend the next two years on the run, participating in politically motivated robberies and bombings until she was captured on 15 June 1972, and subsequently imprisoned. She is believed to have hanged herself in her cell on 9 May 1976.

Meinhof's concern for social justice led her to consider the role and meaning of homophobic oppression in capitalist society. The systematic repression of same-sex love in teenage girls is brought to the fore especially in her script for a television drama, *Bambule: Fürsorge – Sorge für wen?* (*On the Rampage: The Caring State – Caring for Whom?*). *Bambule* was written in the early months of 1970. It is a broadly non-fictional drama set in a (real) home for girls in West Berlin. This was not the first time that Meinhof had concerned herself with the problems of corrective institutions for children – she had previously worked with escapees from such 'homes' and had participated in radio broadcasts on the subject. In the institution depicted in *Bambule*, lesbian love is discouraged because of the feelings of bonding or solidarity it might awaken among the inmates, which would interfere with the process of their social subjugation. In fact one escapee from the home returns voluntarily because of her love for another girl. Another inmate, Monika, describes her experiences in a convent where the girls from 'difficult' backgrounds are not allowed to mix with each other, and from which she was finally expelled for kissing another girl. Monika makes the assumption that the one supervisor in the Berlin home who is supportive must also be a lesbian, because she is so clearly different from the others.

The play was filmed in April 1970, with most of the girls playing themselves. It was due to be broadcast on German television in May; but by this time Meinhof was under suspicion of participation in Baader's escape, and the broadcaster cancelled the screening. Another planned broadcast was cancelled in April 1971.

Meinhof's writings include numerous essays and articles on the political and social situation in Germany of the late 1960s and early 1970s.

Stefan Aust, *The Baader–Meinhof Group: The Inside Story of a Phenomenon*, transl. Anthea Bell (London, 1987); Ulrike Marie Meinhof, *Bambule: Fürsorge – Sorge für wen?*, ed. Klaus Wagenbach (Berlin, 1978); Mario Krebs, *Ulrike Meinhof: Ein Leben im Widerspruch* (Reinbek, 1995).

Sarah Colvin

Melo, Guilherme de (b. 1931), Mozambican/Portuguese journalist, novelist and activist. Guilherme de Melo was born into a white family in Maputo, then named Lourenço Marques, the capital of the Portuguese colony of Mozambique. After school he entered his chosen career of journalism and soon rose to be editor-in-chief of the main newspaper, *Notícias*. In 1964 the protracted guerrilla war of liberation from Portuguese rule led by FRELIMO broke out. Newspapers were heavily censored by the represssive Salazar/Caetano regime and generally followed a pro-government line. In April 1974 a revolution in Portugal led to the suspension of military activities in the colonies. A failed attempt to declare independence by Portuguese settlers in Mozambique following the example of Rhodesia led to a mass exodus of whites, including Melo and his family. Arriving virtually destitute in Portugal, a country he scarcely knew, Melo managed to obtain work as a journalist on the leading daily newspaper, *Diário de Notícias*, where he continued to work until retirement.

Melo came out as gay while still in Mozambique, going out openly with his partner. According to his own testimony, although his decision caused some raised eyebrows at first, his refusal to hide his sexuality while avoiding scandalous behaviour soon earned him respect and allowed him to continue his career. In Mozambique he published two books of stories and a novel, *As Raízes do Ódio* (*The Roots of Hatred*), an attempt to explore the differences between the Portuguese and Africans, which was seized by the secret police. In 1981, after his move to Portugal, he published *A Sombra dos Dias* (*Shadow of the Days*). This long novel is narrated in the third person but appears to have a strong autobiographical element, with a certain amount of gentle self-criticism and self-justification. It is a remarkable account of growing up gay in the privileged environment of a white family in colonial Mozambique before the outbreak of war and of leading an openly gay lifestyle against the background of an increasingly bitter anti-colonial war. The main character, Guy, is sensitive and lonely as a child, before becoming a professionally and socially successful journalist. After a failed attempt at marriage, he accepts his homosexuality and comes out as gay. The novel recounts the hero's relationships with a number of men, most of

whom are basically bisexual: several of them later get married and have children, although remaining friendly with Guy (in an interview, Melo later noted his own tendency to be attracted to masculine men and the problems which it caused him). The novel describes gay and intellectual life in Lourenço Marques during the anti-colonial wars, recording the false sense of security and well-being created by war-time prosperity, the censored media and the easy availability of lonely soldiers far from home. The most gripping part of the novel is the description of the dramatic events which brought all this to an end and led to the Portuguese exodus. It is a remarkable record of a society which has disappeared for ever, seen through the eyes of a gay man.

The success of this work, one of the first novels published in Portugal about homosexuality by an openly gay man, made Melo famous. He wrote a report on what it meant to be homosexual in Portugal and appeared on television programmes as a spokesman for the gay cause. Melo wrote two more novels with a gay theme, both set in Portugal. *Ainda Havia Sol* (*There was Still Sunshine*, 1984) intercuts the story of a 50-year-old gay man who is trying to come to terms with the end of an affair by analysing his feelings and his need to be loved by younger men and that of a young woman who is trying to rebuild her life after discovering that her husband has been having an affair with another woman. *O Que Houver de Morrer* (*He Who Has to Die*, 1989) has as its hero a young straight middle-class man, who discovers that his dead father was having an affair with a man. He sets out to destroy his father's lover but then finds himself befriending and finally having a sexual relationship with the gay man. In *Como um Rio sem Pontes* (*Like a River without Bridges*, 1992), Melo deals with the question of AIDS, although in this case the hero is a young heterosexual drug addict who has returned from Mozambique. These novels provide an interesting insight into life in Portugal in the 1980s but lack the dramatic background and sense of a world irrevocably gone for ever which is so powerful in *A Sombra dos Dias*. Melo is generally more successful at describing events than at characterisation or suggesting emotions, particularly hatred and evil.

Melo has also written works dealing with Africa and the position of women. He continues to encourage the development of the gay movement and the gay press in Portugal which, after a late start, has begun to emerge more strongly in the late 1990s.

Guilherme de Melo, *Ser Homossexual em Portugal* (Lisbon, 1983); Isidro Sousa, 'Guilherme de Melo: um Lutador pela Causa Homosexual', *Korpus* (Lisbon), no. 5 (1998), pp. 29–31.

Robert Howes

Mendicutti, Eduardo (b. 1948), Spanish writer. Mendicutti belongs to the extremely small group of Spanish intellectuals who do not hesitate to identify themselves as gay. He is never embarrassed to acknowledge his homosexuality when appearing in the media, and his fiction takes homosexual culture, identities and lifestyles as a source of inspiration. He has written a number of novels, including *Siete contra Georgia* (1987), *Una mala noche la tiene cualquiera* (1988), *Tiempos mejores*, (1989) *Los novios búlgaros* (1993) and *Qué culpa tengo yo de haber nacido tan sexy* (1997). His trademark is a bitchy sense of humour and a profound familiarity with gay slang as used by assertive, strong-willed drag queens. He has a good ear for the linguistic idiosyncrasies of his characters, and their wit and richness places them above stereotypes. Through the point of view of furiously life-affirming protagonists, he constructs stories of defiance and survival. In this sense, perhaps *Tiempos mejores* is his best work: the story of Antonio 'Maridiscordia', told in the first person, works as a reflection on the fate of political dissidents in the 1960s:

at that time, the protagonist worked in a union against the dictates of the regime and discovered love and sex in difficult conditions. Twenty years later, he is a successful interior decorator with a sharp tongue and a lot of attitude, who outrageously and provocatively expresses his sexuality unconcerned by the shock this may cause. Antonio's friend Enrique ('Queta') has become assimilated into the Socialist Party and stays largely in the closet. Through the evolution of their friendship and different attitudes toward life, Mendicutti constructs a powerful allegory of self-assertion and survival.

The same awareness of the links between sexuality and politics appears in *Una mala noche la tiene cualquiera*, the story of a hapless transvestite in Madrid on the night of 23 February 1981, when the still young Spanish democracy was endangered by the *coup d'état* attempted by the reactionary General Tejero: sexual freedom and the expression of homosexuality is clearly put forward as one of the achievements of democracy. *Siete contra Georgia* consists of seven monologues by professional drag queens relating their sexual experiences as an act of aggressive defiance of homophobic legislation in the state of Georgia (US). The narratives are both funny and sexy, and homosexual activity, against the general trend, is never presented as pathological or grim. Drag queens, gays and transexuals are shown as sensual individuals and, as often in his work, a sense of a close-knit community is projected.

Qué culpa tengo yo de haber nacido tan sexy marks a new direction in Mendicutti's narrative. Although the central character is still the sharp-tonged sexual dissident (a transexual who calls herself Rebecca de Windsor), the author abandons his usual urban setting for a plot reminiscent of a road movie which explicitly takes two references from Spanish classical literature: mysticism and the story of *Don Quixote*. When she discovers that youth is quickly becoming a distant memory, the protagonist searches for religious enlightenment and travels from one monastery to another in the company of a sexy but intellectually-challenged 'muscle mary'. As so often in Mendicutti's work, Rebecca's attitude is irreverent, and in the end she will come to realise that it is in herself that she must find the strength to face the disasters of age.

Mendicutti's popularity shows that homosexuality does not damage a writer's reputation and that there is a wide audience for gay fiction. Of course it could be argued that the version he often presents is easy to accept by the average reader: even for conservatives, the drag queen is a harmless and relatively 'safe' image of homosexuals. Many Spanish gays prefer to dissociate themselves from what they perceive as a stereotype. Yet Mendicutti is subtler than that: his outrageous characters present homosexuality as attractive and life-affirming, and they never refrain from behaviour that is bound to shock conservative minds. A typical representative of Spanish attitudes, Mendicutti does not seem to embrace the Anglo-American model that defends the need for a 'respectable' gay identity, but perhaps his work should be considered as a serious contribution to the debates surrounding the politics of homosexuality, a contribution that certainly can bring fresh air and a 'queer' sense of humour to some Mediterranean manifestations of sexual dissidence.

Alberto Mira

Mercury, Freddie (1946–91), British entertainer. Born Frederick Bulsara to a government accountant of Parsi extraction in Zanzibar, he migrated to England where, while having a degree in graphic design and illustration, he pursued his interest in music, becoming keyboardist in a band called Wreckage. In 1971 he was invited to join a new band, Queen, and their combination of 'bravado sound coupled with a campy style', along with undoubted musical ability, saw them ride the wave of popularity to international stardom. Hits such as 'Killer Queen' (1974), 'Bohemian Rhapsody' (1975) – which became the longest-running number one hit in the UK in twenty years – 'We are the Champions' (1977), and 'Another One Bites the Dust' (1980) exemplify their range and appeal. They wrote and performed the music for the movie *Flash Gordon* (1980).

In 1991, after years of rumours, Mercury admitted that he had AIDS, dying of bronchopneumonia the day after the press announcement revealed his illness. Yet his iconic status – and talents – lived on to beneficial purposes: the re-release of 'Bohemian Rhapsody', soon after Mercury's death, saw it rise to the top of the pop charts and raise desperately needed money for AIDS research. A concert in his memory, the 'Concert For Life', was also a huge AIDs fundraiser.

David Evans and David Minns, *Freddie Mercury: The Real Life* (Netherfield, 1997); *Contemporary Musicians*, Vol. 6 (Detroit, 1992).

Garry Wotherspoon

Merrill, James (1926–95), American writer. Chiefly known for his poetry, one of the master poets of his generation and one of the most famous and acclaimed members of the New York school, Merrill also wrote essays, a memoir, short stories, novels and plays. His poetry, 'chronicles of love and loss', twice won him the National Book Award (1967, 1979), the Bollingen Prize for Poetry (1973) and the Pulitzer Prize (1977). He was regarded as a master of style, with critics evoking Henry James and Marcel Proust when they talked of his sensibility and his themes: love, the evocation of memory, the contrast of art and life. His first book, *First Poems*, appeared in 1951. In an epic trilogy, *The Changing Light at Sandover* (1982), he explored the occult. He and his lifelong companion, David Jackson, presumed communication with spirits using a Ouija board.

Born in New York City, son of the financier Charles Merrill and his second wife, Helen Ingram, Merrill depicted his family fictionalised as the Tannings in his novel *The Seraglio* (1957). In *A Different Person: A Memoir* (1993), he wrote openly about his homosexuality, which is a recurrent but not obvious theme in much of his poetry.

David Kalstone, *Five Temperaments* (Oxford, 1977); Richard Howard, *Alone with America* (New York, 1980); Ross Labrie, *James Merrill* (Boston, 1982).

Seymour Kleinberg

Metcalfe, Robin (b. 1954), Canadian gay activist, writer, curator. Born in Chester, Nova Scotia, of Cape Breton and Acadian parents, Metcalfe got his first lesson in political struggle at the age of 9 when he came out – in Newfoundland's church-run schools – as a non-believer. Later, as a socialist and out gay man, he joined Halifax's Gay Alliance for Equality. For a quarter-century Metcalfe has been marching, organising, speaking and writing as perhaps the most visible queer spokesperson in Atlantic Canada.

Between 1976 and 1995, in addition to serving four times as chair of Gay Alliance Toward Equality (GATE) (later the Gay and Lesbian Association of Nova Scotia), Metcalfe organised or assisted with national and regional lesbian and gay conferences, represented GATE at three international ones, and was its presenter at broadcast and immigration hearings. From 1991 to 1994 he was Nova Scotia coordinator of Day Without Art and in 1995 presided over the Wilde in the Streets festival in Halifax.

A prolific writer, Metcalfe has contributed to gay journals ranging from *The Body Politic* (Canada), to *Gay Scotland*, *Revolt* (Sweden) and *OutRage* (Australia). His short stories have appeared in anthologies edited by John Preston and Alberto Manguel. He has written for more than twenty Canadian arts and literary journals, and been editor or publisher of several magazines, beginning with *Making Waves: an Atlantic quarterly for lesbians*

and gay men in 1981. He is currently regional editor of *C: International Contemporary Art*.

Metcalfe has been a frequent commentator on public affairs and the arts for the radio service of the Canadian Broadcasting Corporation. In 1992 he produced a five-part series on the Halifax lesbian and gay communities. He has lectured widely on art, craft and visual culture, on topics ranging from Nova Scotian queer history to embroidery art and 'Nudity, Heroism and Lust'.

Since the mid-1980s, Metcalfe has worked as an independent critic, curator and cultural activist. Several of his exhibitions have dealt with lesbian and gay themes, including 'Art by Gay Men' with James MacSwain (1982–1986), two exhibitions of Micah Lexier, and 'Queer Looking, Queer Acting: Lesbian and Gay Vernacular' (1997). His recent works have been particularly concerned with representations of the body and social construction of gender.

Robin Metcalfe vertical file, Canadian Lesbian and Gay Archives, Toronto; *Pink Ink* (August, 1983).

Harold Averill

Meyer, Detlev (1950–99), German author. Born into the rebuilding, then-divided city of Berlin, Meyer writes of gay life with the metropolitan flair and often sarcastic wit that has characterised his hometown since the pre-war years when W. H. Auden and Christopher ISHERWOOD visited there in search of boys. He studied library science in Berlin and in Cleveland, Ohio. In Toronto he worked as a librarian, and then served as a volunteer aid worker in Jamaica before returning to Berlin. Since the early 1980s, his career as an author has found success. Meyer is best known for his volumes of poetry (e.g. *Versprechen eines Wundertäters (Promises of a Miracle Worker*, 1993) and *Schöne Aussichten (Beautiful Views)*, published shortly before his death), his trilogy of stories collected under the title *Biographie der Bestürzung* (*Biography of Dismay*, 1985, 1987, 1989), and for his columns about gay life, published in Berlin's gay journals (*Siegessäule*, *magnus*) as well as in mass-market newspapers and journals (e.g. *Stern*). He also collaborated with Germany's most popular gay author, the cartoonist Ralf KÖNIG, on a very well-received book about gay love relationships, *Heiße Herzen* (*Hot Hearts*, 1990).

Critics point to Meyer's ability to describe gay life simultaneously at a distance and with intimacy as one of his defining characteristics. It is no surprise that irony and wit are hallmarks of this intimate distance. Typical of his style is the short piece *Which Man to Which Wine?* (1988): he uses the vocabulary of wine selection to describe a suitable male for the appropriate 'course', be it enjoyed in the dining room or in another setting. His wit, like Oscar Wilde's, views metropolitan life from under a raised eyebrow and above a slightly upturned smile. But Meyer's writing goes beyond the Irishman's rather distanced stance toward sex: Meyer's fictional characters and his poems describe the, for him, characteristically gay movement back and forth between the sublime realm of aesthetic enjoyment and the lustful touch between men.

One of Meyer's most highly praised talents is his stylistic brilliance. He not only loves words but can use the syntax and semiotics of the written word to shed a different light and even to create new meaning. Word plays and word translations into German, along with English or French phrases and quotations from literary greats, enliven his poetry and prose.

The trilogy *Biographie der Bestürzung* follows the relationships between two lovers, Dorn and Viktor, and their best friend, a woman named Todora. Dorn fancies himself an author, but life and lust usually keep him from the writing desk. The first two volumes, *Im Dampfbad greift nach mir ein Engel* (*In the Sauna an Angel Reaches out to Me*) and *David steigt aufs Riesenrad* (*David Climbs upon the Ferris Wheel*), focus on their escapades in and outside Berlin. The third, in which Dorn finds he is HIV-positive, *Ein letzter Dank den Leichtathleten* (*A Final Thanks to the Track Athletes*), describes various attempts to cope with the AIDS crisis, as Dorn tries to write a story about living with AIDS.

Meyer returns to this character, Detlev Dorn, in the novel *In meiner Seele ist schon Herbst* (*Autumn Is Already in My Soul*, 1995), but at a much earlier point in Dorn's life than in the trilogy. What appears at first to be a description of the infatuation one 17-year-old boy/pseudo-poet (Dorn) feels for a classmate, who now and then responds to Dorn's ardour, turns into something much deeper. In the latter part of the book, composed of Dorn's letters, poems and journal entries, Dorn finally has sex with another boy, the younger but more experienced Kevin. This relationship changes Dorn's life, for it allows Dorn to conceive of and to begin to live out a gay identity.

Detlev Meyer's poems, stories and prose pieces combine to become a voice of a gay man speaking both to and for gay men. That voice—in turn witty and sad, lustful and yearning—acknowledges the fears, despair and pessimism of love and death in the era of safe sex. But ultimately his texts speak optimistically, giving courage, laughter and hope.

Detlev Grumbach, 'Ich schreibe, also lebe ich'. Ein Gespräch über literarische Strategien im Umgang mit HIV und AIDS', *FORUM: Homosexualität und Literatur* no. 20 (1994), pp. 71–82; Dirck Linck, 'Detlev Meyer: "In Treue, Euer Hermann Löns"', *FORUM: Homosexualität und Literatur* no. 28 (1997), pp. 87–92.

James W. Jones

Michals, Duane (b. 1932), American photographer. Born in McKeesport, Pennsylvania, of working-class parents, Michals was initially raised by his Czechoslovakian grandmother. After graduating with a

Bachelor of Arts degree from the University of Denver in 1953, he was drafted into the US army and served as a second-lieutenant in Germany. On his discharge in 1956 he enrolled at the Parsons School of Design in New York, where he trained as a graphic artist but left to become assistant art director for *Dance* magazine. In 1958 he took up a job as a designer in the publicity department of Time, Inc. That year Michals made a three-week tourist trip to the Soviet Union, taking a borrowed camera with him. The striking quality of the photographs he took there encouraged him to pursue photography seriously and in 1959 he participated in his first group exhibition at the Image Gallery in New York.

By 1960 Michals was working as a commercial fashion and portrait photographer for magazines such as *Esquire* and *Mademoiselle* and, subsequently, for *Vogue*, *The New York Times* and *Scientific American*. Despite the success of his commercial work, its primary purpose was to support him while he pursued his own photography. Inspired by the evocative photographs of late nineteenth-century Paris by Eugène Atget, Michals produced the series *Empty New York* in 1964, which was followed in 1966 by the first of his serial photographic sequences, or 'photo-stories', titled *The Woman is Frightened by the Door*. Impatient with the idea that photography should be concerned solely with the mechanical transcription of a visible reality and frustrated by the limitations of the single image, Michals uses sequences or photo-narratives to explore subjective aspects of experience such as memory, feelings, desires and dreams as well as more metaphysical concerns relating to mortality, time and the nature of reality. Never simply linear narratives, but instead recalling the evocative paintings of René Magritte (whom he has also photographed), Michals's staged photo-sequences often depict allegorical or mythic narratives, personal and familial relations (especially between fathers and sons), and enigmatic encounters and situations. Despite the religious titles of much of his work, e.g. *The Fallen Angel* (1968), *The Voyage of the Spirit After Death* (1971), *Paradise Regained* (1973) and *Christ in New York* (1981), Michals's concerns are spiritual rather than conventionally religious. So too, while eschewing conventional gay imagery and graphic sexuality, Michals has examined erotic desire between men throughout his work. Although homoeroticism was only implicit in the early work, e.g. *Chance Meeting* (1970) and *The Enormous Mistake* (1976), Michals addressed it more overtly in *Homage to Cavafy* (1978), and a lyrical treatment of homosexuality remains an enduring concern, e.g. *Salute, Walt Whitman* (1996).

Combining text and image (Michals typically writes titles, commentaries and poems by hand on his prints), dispensing with the single photograph and unconcerned with technical perfection, Michals has broken with many of the conventions of fine art photography. Yet in doing so he has opened up new possibilities for photography as an expressive and poetic medium capable of suggesting rich metaphorical allusions and complex subjective associations. Michals has exhibited widely internationally, including major shows in Paris, Hamburg and Oxford (with accompanying catalogues), but principally uses book publishing as a vehicle for his photography; his many publications include *Take One and See Mt. Fujiyama* (1976), *The Nature of Desire* (1986) and *Eros and Thanatos* (1992). He lives and works in New York.

Duane Michals: Photographs/Sequences/Texts 1958–84 (Oxford, 1984); Max Kozloff, *Duane Michals: Now Becoming Then* (Altadena, California, 1990); Marco Livingstone, *The Essential Duane Michals* (London, 1997).

David L. Phillips

Midler, Bette (b. 1945), American entertainer. Born and raised in Hawaii, Midler had experience in a folk group and as a bit player in the movie *Hawaii* before moving to California in the late 1960s. She ended up in New York, and by 1971 was playing the role of the Acid Queen in a production of *Tommy*.

Midler first came to wider attention around 1970, when she began singing in the Continental Baths, a gay men's sauna in New York. Here, accompanied by Barry Manilow on piano, she developed certain specialised routines that endeared her to her gay audiences: Andrews Sisters send-ups, campy comedy routines and tear-jerker show stoppers. Commonly referred to as 'The Divine Miss M. – Flash with class and sleaze with ease' – she quickly achieved iconic status in the gay sub-culture, with characters based on her appearing in books and a movie, *The Ritz*. As a guest on various TV shows, she soon developed a wider audience, and her first album went gold. She won a Grammy Award for best new artist and appeared on the cover of *Time* magazine. In 1979 she made the successful biopic, *The Rose*, loosely based on the life of the rock star Janis Joplin; for this she received both an Academy Award nomination and a Grammy Award for the best female vocalist.

Despite a career slump in the early 1980s, over the next few years Midler made a range of movies that somewhat restored her public image; among the best are the farces *Down and Out in Beverley Hills* and *Ruthless People* (both 1986), *Outrageous Fortune* (1987) and *Big Business* (1988), this last with Lily Tomlin.

As she has become more mainstream, Midler has lost her cult status among gay communities, although she is still fondly remembered as the zany star who entertained gay audiences around the world with her spectacular stage shows, in which, dressed as a mermaid, she whizzed around the stage in a motorised wheelchair.

Contemporary Musicians, Vol. 8 (Detroit,

1993); Bette Midler, *A View from a Broad* (New York, 1980).

Garry Wotherspoon

Mieli, Mario (1952–83), Italian writer, activist. More than any other figure, Mario Mieli represented the arrival of an impassioned, radical and theoretically grounded gay activism in Italy in the 1970s. He embodied a rare combination of far-sighted intellectual power and a courageous (and sometimes outrageous) public persona, all of which ensure that his contributions to the gay cause in Italy are particularly memorable. When he took his own life in 1983, one early obituary summed up Mieli's profile perfectly, mourning the loss of an 'irreplaceable provocateur'.

Mieli was born into a large and prosperous family in Milan, but he lived for the first sixteen years of his life in the countryside near Lake Como. In 1968 the family moved back to Milan and Mieli, politically precocious, threw himself into the student uprisings of that year. This was the beginning of a long commitment to revolutionary causes. In 1971 he moved to London, where he joined the Gay Liberation Front. He spent time in London intermittently until 1975, but in 1972 he based himself in Milan, where he studied at university and became a founding member of one of the first Italian gay-rights groups, FUORI! (OUT! – but also Fronte universale omosessuale rivoluzionario italiano). When FUORI! placed itself under the political auspices of the Radical Party in 1974, Mieli left the group in protest. He had no doubt that the world needed to be changed, but he eschewed any particular party line. After 1974 he continued his activism with COM (Collettivi omosessuali Milanesi) and joined a radical theatre group, 'La traviata norma', as an actor and playwright.

By 1976 Mieli had graduated and was revising his thesis for publication. *Elementi di critica omosessuale* was published by Einaudi in 1977, and it is this work which established Mieli's reputation as one of the founders of Italian gay liberation. The book's central question is simple, and particularly for an Italian university student, courageous: why does society marginalise and repress homosexual behaviour? What follows is an astonishingly acute analysis of the need of capitalist society to encourage conformist sexual behaviour based on heterosexual marriage and the reproduction of family life, with its predictable range of needs. Naturally Mieli's work does not miss the role of religion in this process, but overall his work owes much to Marx, and perhaps most of all to KINSEY. The conclusion is a vision of a new sexual utopianism, where the enforcement of a heterosexual norm through the removal of other components on the erotic spectrum is regarded as deeply oppressive of human nature. Along the way the book makes prescient observations on a range of subjects, from the subversive value of transsexuals to the crucial importance of women's liberation, from the hypocritically latent homoeroticism of organised sports to anti-gay violence as a negative expression of censored homosexual desire. While much of what Mieli writes is familiar in the 1990s, for a 24-year-old Italian in the mid-1970s, it was a noteworthy performance.

There was an unstable element to Mieli, and he was well aware of what he openly referred to as his schizophrenia. Once he had published *Elementi di critica omosessuale*, he told interviewers from the budding gay press that he had chosen to dedicate himself to love, and also to alchemy. He promised that he would write an autobiographical novel that would reveal his alchemical discoveries. In the late 1970s Mieli did not altogether give up his rather personal crusade for the cause of a revolution based on the recognition of a broad range of sexualities, and he maintained a presence as a contributor to the radical press. But by 1981 he confessed that he had become extremely pessimistic about his cause, and at that stage he became involved in environmental and anti-nuclear politics. He did write the promised autobiographical novel but, in a psychological state which has not been fully understood, he peremptorily withdrew it from the press as it was about to be printed. This was a few days before he committed suicide on 12 March 1983.

Mieli's name lives on through the Circolo Mario Mieli, Rome's largest gay and lesbian organisation. This was being formed at approximately the same time as Mieli died, and it was named in recognition of his special role in Italian gay liberation. The group is particularly active in AIDS education and political lobbying.

In 1994 Mieli's novel, *Il risveglio dei Faraoni*, was published in Milan. The original writing had been recovered (except for one page) by a group of the author's friends after he died. The book was withdrawn from sale at the request of Mieli's family and is no longer available.

Mario Mieli, *Elementi di critica omosessuale* (Turin, 1977).

Mark Seymour

Milk, Harvey (1930–78), American politician and activist. In 1977, Harvey Milk won a seat on San Francisco's city council (Board of Supervisors), and thus became one of the first openly gay politicians to be elected in the US, and one of the highest profile activists in the country. Within a year, in November 1978, he (along with Mayor George Moscone) was assassinated by former supervisor Dan White, and came to be seen as a martyr to the movement in which he saw himself so deeply rooted.

Milk was born in New York State into a family of Russian-Jewish immigrants. In the 1950s, he was discharged from the navy because of his homosexuality, and then he worked in New York City at jobs as various as theatrical production and stock brokerage. He moved to San Francisco in 1969, and soon afterwards opened a camera store on Castro Street – at the time becoming more and more central to gay life in the city. He threw himself into politics almost immediately, and ran for the Board of Supervisors in 1973 and again two years later, and for the California legislature in 1976. By this time, his energy, good humour and activist commitment had gained him a reputation in the Castro, but not enough to secure him anything like the votes he needed to win. His chances were significantly improved in the 1977 election for Board of Supervisors. He had increased his support base in the gay and lesbian community, and had developed standing in other minority communities and organised labour. The connection to unions was solidified by Milk's support for a lesbian/gay boycott of the fiercely right-wing and anti-labour Coors brewing company. Just as important in boosting his chances was the shift in the city's electoral system from 'at-large' races to separate district elections, giving Milk's Castro Street home base added weight. That same election saw victories for other supervisors representing the politically marginalised, and for progressive mayor George Moscone.

Milk proved a skilful political broker while still being a tribune for sexual diversity and other progressive causes. He spoke regularly and inspiringly about the importance of coming out and of activist engagement. He publicly and effectively fought against an anti-gay referendum initiated in 1978 by California State Senator John Briggs (the ballot measure being lost that autumn). He also engineered the passage of an anti-discrimination measure for the city, gaining the support of all of his council colleagues except for Dan White, an ex-policeman with whom Milk had crossed swords on other fronts.

Milk's cold-blooded assassination provoked an outpouring of grief. Several months later, after White's murders led only to a conviction for manslaughter and a relatively modest sentence, grief turned to the intensely angry 'White Night' riots.

White was released in 1984 and committed suicide a year later.

Milk had a strong enough sense of the danger created by his high profile and outspokenness to tape-record a political will, once again urging the breaking down of closet doors, and discussing possible candidates for his political replacement. One of those mentioned favourably was a relatively unknown Harry Britt. Having worked with Milk in previous elections, he rapidly gained standing among San Francisco progressives. In the 1980 election, once again contested in city-wide races rather than district elections, Britt won a substantial enough vote to secure easy election – a sign of the extent to which the city's gay and lesbian population had become integral to the urban political landscape. Britt was sometimes frustrated at the criticism he occasionally faced from his own lesbian/gay constituency. To some extent, Milk himself was spared such scrutiny by his own remarkable political savvy, and the brevity of his time in office. Other openly gay and lesbian politicians have often enough faced pressures from movement activists impatient with the brokerage and compromise that go along with legislative politics, and have found themselves caught between the sometimes conflicting roles of movement representative and elected politician.

The progressive politics that Milk and Britt represented had never been uncontested, and became less secure in the years to follow. The Harvey Milk Gay Democratic Club became one of California's largest Democratic organisations, and not surprisingly came to be more dominated by the politics of brokerage and compromise than Milk himself would have been comfortable with. Despite Britts's success, the at-large electoral system generally encouraged more centrist candidacies, although still on the left more than the right.

In death Milk has remained an icon – as Randy SHILTS has written, he was the first martyr of the young gay movement: 'Milk was a gay leader who talked about hope, struggled for his political successes against all odds, and won.... That Harvey Milk's killer should be an all-American boy and ex-cop added poetic embellishment to this tale, for the thousands who had come to revere Harvey Milk as a martyr knew all too well that hating homosexuals is a solid part of the all-American ethos.'

Randy Shilts, *The Mayor of Castro Street: The Life and Times of Harvey Milk* (New York, 1982); Mark Thompson, *Long Road to Freedom: The Advocate History of the Gay and Lesbian Movement* (New York, 1994); Michael Tyrkus (ed.), *Gay and Lesbian Biography* (Detroit, 1997); David Rayside, *On the Fringe: Gays and Lesbians in Politics* (Ithaca, NY, 1998).

David Rayside

Millet, Kate (b. 1935), American scholar and writer. In both her political writing and her intense autobiographical essays and books, Millett has demonstrated, above all else, the ways in which politics, sexuality and the personal enter into a complex relationship in both feminist and gay and lesbian writing.

Born in St Paul, Minnesota, Millett first came to international attention with the publication of *Sexual Politics* in 1970. Based on her Columbia Ph.D. thesis, *Sexual Politics* electrified the field of literary studies with its innovative and even at times near-sacriligious rereadings of such authors as Norman Mailer, D. H. Lawrence and Henry Miller. Millett's rereading of Lawrence, for example, as deeply anti-feminist typified her energetic disputation of the subordinate role of women in libertine literary traditions, and her work recast their reception for the next two decades.

Millett's prominent activism was further complicated when she was 'outed' as a lesbian at a time when the role of lesbians within feminism was contentious amongst feminists and lesbians alike, and

when gay liberation had a similarly complex status for many women. Her response was the extraordinary autobiographical exercise *Flying* (1974), which documents in encyclopaedic detail the vicissitudes of her life at this time. Marked by a powerful poetic prose style and stream-of-consciousness explorations of memory, event, time and place, *Flying* provides a panoramic view not only of Millett's daily life but of a sexual and political life that was destined to pass by the early 1980s. Her follow-up volume, *Sita* (1977), concentrates on the passage of a love affair, but already shadows the passing of a political culture and lifestyle associated with the explosion of second-wave feminism.

Millet has also written a number of fiercely polemical essays which combine non-fiction and personal narrative to analyse social and power relations. *The Basement* (1979) chronicles the career of Gertrude Baniszewski, the 'torture mother' who murdered her lodger Sylvia Likens with the help of her children; *The Prostitution Papers* (1975) polemicised the state of the sex industry. In *The Politics of Cruelty: An Essay on the Literature of Political Imprisonment* (1994), Millett detailed in comprehensive and polemical prose the nature of political imprisonment and torture as state-sanctioned practices throughout the twentieth century. Published in 1990, *The Loony-Bin Trip* narrates Millett's experience of the interventions of psychiatry through her involuntary hospitalisation and subsequent treatment with anti-psychotic drugs. Millet's autobiography made a powerful intervention in support of anti-psychiatry movements and her combination of polemic and painful personal revelation typifies her insistence on the interrelated nature of the personal and the political. With *A.D.* (1995), Millett returned to the more narrowly autobiographical to tell the story of her relationship with her Aunt Dorothy, a memoir that ranges across her experiences as a young lesbian and the familial pressures that were generated by her passionate and ambivalent relationship with her aunt.

Millett's diverse output may be best understood as an elaborate engagement with the relationship between politics and the deeply personal. The twin volumes *Flying* and *Sexual Politics* addressed, in diverse but complementary ways, the question of literary language and its implication in the depiction of the vagaries of sexual subjectivity. Their appearance was timely in redefining some of the issues that haunted feminist thinking in this era: the relationship between gay liberation and feminism, the problem of depicting sexuality in aesthetic texts, and the everyday experience of a deeply committed political life. Above all, *Flying* remains a unique document in the history of gay liberation and feminist self-consciousness. Its high-seriousness may better be read now as a documentary-like odyssey within avant-garde, lesbian, gay and feminist circles in New York and elsewhere through the early 1970s, as well as a remarkable examination of the role of personal history in the construction of a sexual self.

Melissa Hardie

Minton, John (1917–57), British painter, illustrator. Born near Cambridge, England, Minton was the second of three boys in a well-to-do family. After the death of their father, a London solicitor, their mother's parents took over their upbringing. The wealth which later provided Minton with an independent income came from his mother's family's connection with clothing and haberdashery stores.

From school Minton, who showed talent for drawing, went to St John's School of Art, London, 1935–38. In 1938 he visited Paris with fellow student Michael Ayrton, the first of several emotional attachments to men who could not or would not respond to his advances. In 1941 when Minton was establishing his reputation as a painter they collaborated on designs for sets and costumes for John Gielgud's production of *Macbeth*.

In 1939 Minton, to his grandmother's disapproval, registered as a conscientious objector and was called up to the Pioneer Corps in the British Army in December 1941. He decided to transfer to the infantry but had a breakdown during training and was discharged.

The early influences on Minton's work were an English romantic painter Samuel Palmer, de Chirico, the Russian Ballet, Russian neo-romantic artists living in Paris and Graham Sutherland. He readily absorbed the styles of others. His ability to draw, and to compose inventively set him apart from other illustrators.

In 1943–46 Minton shared a house with the inseparable Scottish artists Robert Colquhoun and Robert MacBryde, and taught drawing and illustration at Camberwell School of Arts and Crafts. He then taught drawing at the Central School of Art in 1946–48 and painting at the Royal College of Art in 1948–56. Minton encouraged painter Keith VAUGHAN to continue his career and they shared a house together in 1946–52. Apart from their homosexuality and painting, they had little in common. Vaughan was irritated by Minton's social success, extrovert behaviour and carelessness.

Minton's early success as an illustrator was due to support and commissions from publisher John Lehmann for work in 'Penguin New Writing', illustrations for the classic *Treasure Island* and Elizabeth David's *A Book of Mediterranean Food*. He followed his own advice to students never to turn down any offer of work. During the late 1940s and early 1950s he exhibited regularly and his work was included in exhibitions, publications and institutional collections of contemporary British art.

During the 1950s Minton travelled in the West Indies, Morocco and Spain, drawing and painting scenes for later exhibitions. The neo-romantic pictorial tradition in which he worked was now overtaken by other styles and approaches as the art centre shifted from Europe to New York. He spoke bitterly about the futile direction of 'modern' art. Minton was distressed by the increase in arrests for homosexual offences in Britain after 1953 and is said to have destroyed his own erotic drawings. His sense of isolation was intensified when he felt abandoned by close male friends as they formed other relationships and moved on.

During the 1950s the size and compositional complexity of his paintings increased but critics remained indifferent to this work. One of his last large-scale paintings was *The Death of James Dean* (1957). Minton accurately described himself as a decorator and muralist, but he also created powerful figure and portrait paintings, especially his lonely male figures in bleak post-war dockland London. Minton died at home of an overdose of prescription drugs.

F. Spalding, *Dance Till the Stars Come Down: A Biography of John Minton* (London, 1991).

Ian Maidment

Mirguet, Paul (b. 1911), French politician. Mirguet was the author of the so-called 'Mirguet Amendment' declaring homosexuality a 'social scourge' in July 1960. Born into a family of farmers in Lorraine (now in eastern France, but then part of the German Empire), he served in the French army from 1932 to 1937 and again in 1939–40. Demobilised, he worked for the Resistance from 1941 to 1944, then rejoined the regular army until 1946. After the war, he pursued a business career and was elected a municipal councillor in Metz. In 1958 Mirguet won election to the National Assembly as a candidate for Charles de Gaulle's newly formed Union for the New Republic. During his single term in the Assembly (1958–62), he paid special attention to economic and agricultural legislation.

Mirguet is known best for his intervention in a debate in the Assembly on 18 July 1960. The deputies were considering a government bill to give the cabinet extraordinary power for three months to act by decree against the 'social scourges' of tuberculosis, alcoholism and prostitution. Mirguet moved an amendment to authorise the government to take, in addition, 'all appropriate measures to combat homosexuality'. He told the Assembly, 'You are all conscious of the seriousness of this scourge that is homosexuality, a scourge against which we have the duty to protect our children.' Adopted almost unanimously amidst good-humoured laughter, the amendment became part of the Law of 30 July 1960.

Mirguet justified his position in a television broadcast in 1975. Evoking the 'despair of fathers' who learn that their adolescent sons have been lured into homosexuality, he declared: 'What I wanted to do above all was to protect minors.' Mirguet was also 'haunted by the falling birth rate' in the West, which he blamed in part on homosexuality. He predicted that the Earth's population would grow to eight billion by AD 2000, but a shrinking proportion of these would be white, which meant that 'our [European] civilization is doomed in the short term'. Although Mirguet never explained clearly how he expected the government to discourage homosexuality, he always insisted that he never envisaged repressive measures. But on 25 November 1960, the French cabinet used its new authority under the law to issue an ordinance revising Article 330 of the Criminal Code so as to double the penalties for public offences against decency when these involved homosexuals. (Parliament repealed this discriminatory revision in November 1980.)

The Mirguet Amendment did not otherwise affect French homosexuals in their daily lives, but it contributed to their stigmatisation and convinced many of the need for radical political and social change. It thus helped to spark the gay liberation movement of the late 1960s. Significantly, one of the first radical gay newspapers in 1972 called itself *Le Fléau social* (*The Social Scourge*). Mirguet today lives in retirement in Metz. His opinions on homosexuality have not changed.

Who's Who in France; Archives of the National Assembly; correspondence between Mirguet and the author.

Michael Sibalis

Mishima, Yukio (1925–70), Japanese writer. Born Hiraoka Kimitake in Tokyo, the son of a senior civil servant and grandson of a former provincial governor, he published his first short story when he was 16, using the *nom de plume* that was to become his signature. Thereafter he wrote and published profusely.

During World War II, he worked in a factory and continued to write. Fame came with his second novel, *Confessions of a Mask* (1949), a largely autobiographical account of the life of a young man with homosexual desires. While Japanese critics tended to praise its erudition and sensitivity, and ignore the writer's sexuality, Western readers – especially gay ones – were taken with it, particularly for its exoticism, its explicit sexual descriptiveness and its emphasis on masculinity. Mishima despised effeminate men, and his devotion to the cult of machismo and bodybuilding were central to both his life and his writings.

Other novels include *Forbidden Colours* (1953), *The Temple of the Golden Pavilion* (1959) and *The Sailor Who Fell From Grace with the Sea* (1963). His most famous work was the series of novels *The Sea of Fertility* (1969–71). He also directed and acted in a film, *Patriotism* (1966), which valourised *seppuku* (ritual suicide).

At a time when there was still hostility to overt homosexuality being represented positively in novels in the West (the outcry over Gore Vidal's 1948 *The City and the Pillar* springs to mind), Mishima's work found a resonance with Western readers, and he developed a loyal following, particularly because of his focus on 'forbidden' behaviours.

In later life, Mishima cultivated a fascist ideology which, not unlike some aspects of early Nazi beliefs, combined a fierce nationalism with a worship of virile manhood. Indeed, his death reads like a plot from one of his novels. With young followers from the Shield Society, a private army of 100 members he had formed to protect Japan against the destruction of its traditional values, he broke into the National Defence Headquarters in Tokyo, and harangued the several thousand serviceman assembled there on the loss of the country's spiritual values (including, one presumes, the strong homosexual strand among the samurai), urging them to rise up and overthrow the government. Receiving little support, he then himself committed seppuku, the *coup de grâce* being delivered by his reputed lover, Morita.

Peter Wolfe, *Yukio Mishima* (New York, 1989); John Nathan, *Mishima: A Biography* (Rutland, 1975).

Garry Wotherspoon

Moix, Ana Maria (b. 1946), Spanish writer. Moix officially came out of the closet in 1997 in a lifestyle magazine (*Dunia*), together with her brother (Terenci MOIX, also a writer) in a touching interview in which they exchanged experiences about childhood games and about growing up in the repressive atmosphere of the 1950s and the 1960s.

Moix is a poet and fiction writer. Her childhood seems to have been a difficult one judging from her own account. She was included in the legendary poetic anthology *Nueve novísimos* (1970), which introduced a new generation of poets who broke with the rules of Francoism. Against the convoluted rhetoric and seriousness of the previous generation, Moix and others (also included were Vicente Molina FOIX and Manuel Vázquez Montalbán) used supposedly 'trivial' subjects and included numerous references to pop culture. Her poetry was later collected in the volume *A imagen y semejanza* (1983). But it was in the field of fiction that Moix gained major critical recognition.

Her sexual identity was never explicit and even in her work lesbianism appears wrapped in ambiguity. Her first novel, *Julia* (which appeared in 1970 and was dedicated to Esther TUSQUETS), dealt with a young woman who has an intense relationship with her literature teacher (Eva). Their *liaison* is never clearly sexual, but, in line with narratives typical of feminist writing, their bond is valued and has a political value: one sleepless night, Julia recalls how she was raped during her childhood and this turned her off men. Eva is for Julia a mother, a sister and a friend. There is an attempt to 'explain away' lesbianism not as desiring women, but as fear of men (which would today be regarded as conservative). Moix avoids easy classification and wants to present these women 'just as individuals', something too frequent among Spanish gay artists. However, the censors were not fooled and required forty-five excisions from the first edition. The character of Ernesto, Julia's brother, is a gay man inspired by Terenci Moix. Her second novel was *Walter ¿Por qué te fuiste?* (1974), in which several characters reflect on another one, following a similar strategy to that used by Virginia Woolf in *The Waves*. Childhood appears again as an important topic, and as the source of anguish and unhappiness in later life. Children in her work inhabit a world of nightmare and sexual repression. When they become adults, homosexuality is presented as a way of self-assertion and growth. Lesbianism in particular is a practice rather than an 'identity', and it is never something fixed. Her latest novel is *Vals negro* (1994), a fiction work about the figure of Princess Elisabeth of Austria. Moix is also a translator of, among others, Marguerite Duras, Samuel Beckett and Michel Leiris.

Alberto Mira

Moix, Terenci (b. 1942), pseudonym of Ramón Moix Messeguer, Spanish writer.

Writing in Spanish and Catalan, Moix claims to have been the first intellectual to come out as a gay man in Spain in the 1960s. Since then, he has kept a hilarious and somehow iconoclastic public persona, using the media to project a witty, surrealist and camp image. In the course of a TV interview for a national channel, Moix invited the interviewer to ask him whether he was homosexual, to which his disarming answer was, 'No, I'm videosexual'. Although he has been accused by gay activists of superficiality and excessive mannerism, Moix was an important gay voice in the years 1968–78, when gays and lesbians initiated the long process towards normalisation of homosexuality in the main urban areas of Spain, especially Barcelona. It must be noted that in Catalonia gay liberation was intimately linked to Catalan nationalism, and therefore Catalan, rather than Spanish, was the language used by most gay intellectuals.

Disdain for labels and categories is one of Moix's most apparent features: both in his public life and in his novels, big passions and melodrama, together with a well-crafted sense of humour, overtake logic and intellectual discussion. However, he has made clear remarks about his understanding of (homo)sexuality in short but important articles; by and large, he uses an aesthetic frame of thought to address the issue – aestheticism – which for some readers may come closer to a camp sensibility than to a serious attempt to filiate homosexual experience. Some of his early short stories (*La torre dels vicis capitals*, 1967) were censored and homosexual relations had to be camouflaged as heterosexual. Censure also affected the first edition of his 1970 important novel *El dia que va morir Marilyn*. His Catalan-language novel *El sexe del àngels* was denied an important prize in 1969 because of its strong criticism of the Catalan cultural milieu; eventually, Moix would become more uneasy within Catalan letters, and his production in Spanish would give him national and international relevance. When the same novel was awarded, in 1992, the prestigious Ramon Llull prize for novels in Catalan, Moix declared that his text was an attempt to understand his own frustrations regarding Catalan culture.

In Moix's novels, homosexuality is an unproblematical and joyous fact of life; more than a topic, it is an element of the background. However, most of his gay characters are troubled, unbalanced people who very rarely reach their ideal of sentimental happiness or sexual fulfilment. This tension between comic pose and tragic pathos is indeed one of the most salient features of Moix's gay-related novels.

Moix has written extensively on imperial Egypt and on classic Hollywood movies, two of his lifetime passions. As a movie commentator he currently writes for the magazine *Fotogramas*. He has referred extensively to his passion for cinema, which, allegedly, would have saved him from boredom and insubstantiality in his youth, when the Spanish cultural scene was controlled and dictated by state bureaucrats. An assiduous newpaper essayist, he published in 1995 a collection of his weekly *El País* articles under the title *Sufrir de amores*.

In 1990 Moix started publishing his long autobiography, *El peso de la paja*, whose first part was significantly titled as *El cine de los sábados*; subsequent volumes were *El beso de Peter Pan* (1993) and *Extraño en el paraíso* (1988). They were particularly interesting to gay readers for his accounts of different experiences as an openly gay writer both in the last years of Franco's dictatorship and during the country's transition to democracy and new ethic values.

Other works of interest to gay readers include: *Món mascle* (1971), *La caiguda de l'imperi sodomita* (1976), *La increada consciència de la raça* (1976), *Nuestro Virgen de los Mártires* (1983), *Amami, Alfredo!* (1984), *Garras de astracán* (1991), *El sexe del àngels* (1992).

Robert Richmond Ellis, *The Hispanic Homograph: Gay Self-Representation in Contemporary Spanish Autobiography* (Champaign-Urbana, Ill., 1997); Paul Julian Smith, *Laws of Desire: Questions of Homosexuality in Spanish Writing and Film 1960–1990* (Oxford, 1992).

Alfredo Martínez Expósito

Moldenhauer, Jearld (b. 1946), American-Canadian activist and bookseller. Born in Niagara Falls, NY, Moldenhauer attended Cornell University, where he studied biological sciences. In 1967 he helped to form the Cornell Student Homophile League, the second homophile group organised at an American university. After graduation, Moldenhauer emigrated to Canada in 1969 and found work as a research assistant at the University of Toronto. In October 1969 he called a meeting that led to the formation of the University of Toronto Homophile Association (UTHA), the first post-Stonewall gay organisation in Canada and the first at a Canadian university. Over the next several years Moldenhauer emerged as an architect of the early gay liberation movement in Canada and was instrumental in founding several important institutions, including *The Body Politic* (1971), Toronto Gay Action (1971), Gay Alliance Toward Equality (GATE) Toronto (1973) and the Canadian Gay Liberation Movement Archives (now the Canadian Lesbian and Gay Archives, 1973). During this period he encouraged public demonstrations and helped to initiate several civil rights-oriented projects. For Moldenhauer, the personal became political. Meetings were often held at his home, which came to serve as the first headquarters for some of these fledgling organisations.

In 1970 Moldenhauer decided to start Glad Day Bookshop after noticing that Toronto's booksellers were averse to selling the rapidly growing range of gay- and lesbian-positive books and magazines. He started selling books out of a knapsack at meetings and rallies, and through mail order. Soon Glad Day was a storefront operation, and Moldenhauer began to devote his energy to building the business. Within a few years Glad Day grew into one of the most comprehensive gay and lesbian bookstores in the world. Moldenhauer opened a second Glad Day in 1979 in Boston (and rebuilt after it was destroyed by arson in 1987). The bookshops became a magnet for gay writers, readers and activists, and a training ground for other gay booksellers. They also attracted the attention of the authorities. From as early as 1974 through the 1990s Canadian Customs officials regularly detained and seized imported shipments of books and periodicals bound for Glad Day in Toronto on the grounds that they offended community standards and were obscene under the Canadian Criminal Code. Glad Day challenged these decisions in the press and in court, sometimes successfully, and Moldenhauer emerged as a leading figure in the fight against Customs censorship.

Gerald Hannon, 'Who We Were, Who We Are: Jearld Moldenhauer', *The Body Politic*, No. 80 (1982), p. 32; H. J. Kirchhoff, 'A Sad Chapter in "Homophobia",' *Globe and Mail* (Toronto), 14 July 1990, p. C9; Jearld Moldenhauer, 'Victim of Myopia (or, "Gerald, Bring Me the Axe")', *The Body Politic*, No. 82 (1982), p. 7; Glenn Wheeler, 'Border Bannings: Gay Bookstores Bear the Brunt of Canada Customs Seizures', *Quill & Quire*, Feb. 1991, pp. 10, 34.

Donald W. McLeod

Monette, Paul (1945–95), American writer and activist. In his National Book Award-winning *Becoming a Man: Half a Life Story* (1992), Monette vividly describes how the closet enveloped and inhibited him. He detailed not only his experience of 1950s America, his education (at preparatory schools and Yale University), and his futile attempts at heterosexuality but also falling in love with a man and finally coming out. He sees the second half of his life as the life he truly lived, free of internal homophobia and empowered through love to take on societal homophobia.

Monette's first publication was a book of poems, *The Carpenter at the Asylum* (1975), and one of his final works was also a collection of poems, *West of Yesterday, East of Summer* (1994). In them, his mastery of language – its rhythms, syntax and images – evokes a world in which passion and understanding rewrite human experience, searching for a communion with another.

But Monette wanted to speak to a wider public, especially to other gays and lesbians. He wrote six novels, but even he admitted his limitations in this genre. Although perhaps too reliant on rather improbable plot devices, these stories first humanised gay men and then, in the 1990s, people with AIDS. His early novels, such as *Taking Care of Mrs. Carroll* (1978) and *The Gold Diggers* (1979), each place a pair of gay lovers at the centre of stories revolving around women friends and elaborate deceptions.

It was the AIDS crisis that enabled Monette to develop his artistic voice to its fullest. What he wrote before 1986 was a prelude, at best. When his longtime lover Roger Horwitz was diagnosed with AIDS and suffered from a variety of AIDS-related diseases in the mid-1980s, Monette at first could not write. But from that anguished silence came two of the most powerful pieces of AIDS literature: his account of their relationship and their experience together of AIDS – *Borrowed Time: An AIDS Memoir* (1988), and the poems he wrote while working on that book of non-fiction – *Love Alone: 18 Elegies for Rog* (1988). These intensely personal works both commemorate the love of the two men for each other and express the vast emotions of loss and anger that Monette felt. These twin needs of mourning and catharsis gave voice to what many gay men at that time were experiencing and made the books, especially *Borrowed Time*, not just popular but helpful in the best sense of that word.

After Horwitz's death, Monette increasingly explored, in his writing and in social activism, the ways in which the social-political climate shaped the personal, individual experience both of sexuality and of AIDS. Monette used book tours, speeches accepting awards or honorary degrees, and his role in ACT-UP as opportunities to educate non-gays about gay and lesbian life and about AIDS issues, and as ways to encourage gay and lesbian audiences to join in his vision of a more tolerant, more loving community. The author himself was diagnosed with AIDS in 1991 and died of complications from AIDS. Nonetheless, Monette's final years were filled with love (he formed long-term relationships with Stephen Kolzak, who died in 1990, and then with Winston Wilde) and were amazingly productive (he published novels, essays and poems). His collection of essays, *Last Watch of the Night* (1994), not only gives the reader insight into the heart and hope that motivated Monette, but it also completes the trilogy of books that tell his life story (along with *Becoming a Man* and *Borrowed Time*).

In his last two novels, Monette explored the themes of death and love, through gay men who have AIDS. *Afterlife* (1990) follows the ways in which three 'AIDS widowers' create lives on their own – this stands in stark contrast to the previous view of an AIDS diagnosis as a death sentence. Praising it, David Roman said this novel 'reads like Jane Austen in West Hollywood – courtship, social critique, irony, and, of course, AIDS'. *Halfway Home* (1991) is probably Monette's best novel, perhaps because it is the one closest to his vision. He described it: 'I really did get to write the gay love story I always wanted to do. It feels like my best book. I was not afraid to have lesbian characters. I exulted in them. The chosen family wins hands-down. I was able to generate a story that, even in the midst of death, could make the connection of intimacy.'

In an interview, Monette described why

he wrote *Borrowed Time*, but his words are true of all his writing and of his activism as well: 'I wanted to write something that would break hearts because it would show how much gay people loved each other [and I wanted] to give my people the record of who we were.' Elsewhere, Monette described himself this way: 'I'd rather be remembered for living well than for writing well, and for being a witness to the calamity that has engulfed my people.' No one was a better or more passionate lover and witness than Monette.

Malcolm Boyd, 'Paul Monette', in Sharon Malinowski (ed.), *Gay and Lesbian Literature* (Detroit, 1994), pp. 272–4; Joseph Cady, 'Immersive and Counterimmersive Writing about AIDS: The Achievement of Paul Monette's *Love Alone*', in Timothy F. Murphy and Suzanne Poirier (eds), *Writing AIDS: Gay Literature, Language, and Analysis* (New York, 1993), pp. 244–64; 'Paul Monette,' in James P. Draper (ed.), *Contemporary Literary Criticism*, Vol. 82 (Detroit, 1994), pp. 313–35; David Roman, 'Paul Monette', in Emmanuel S. Nelson (ed.), *Contemporary Gay American Novelists* (Westport, CT, 1993), pp. 272–81.

James W. Jones

Monferrand, Hélène de (b. 1947), French novelist. Born in Paris to a family of impoverished minor nobles, de Monferrand spent her childhood as a privileged European in pre-independence Algeria. Back in Paris, she attended the prestigious Lycée Jules Ferry, followed by university studies at Nanterre and the Sorbonne. Her academic qualifications include a first degree in classics and a postgraduate diploma in accountancy. Formerly head of financial services at a Parisian hospital, she now works in the French press. She also works, unpaid, as an editor and as treasurer of *Lesbia Magazine*, a buoyant French lesbian magazine of eighteen years' standing. She has lived with her present female partner for nine years. Her first novel, *Les Amies d'Héloïse* (*Héloïse's Friends*, 1990), which explicitly portrays multiple lesbian relations, defied marketing theories of segmentation through its warm reception by lesbian readers, a wider popular readership and also the Paris literary establishment (receiving the *Prix du Premier Roman* from the august Académie Goncourt).

In her trilogy – *Les Amies d'Héloïse*, *Journal de Suzanne* (*Suzanne's Diary*, 1991), and *Les Enfants d'Héloïse* (*Héloïse's Children*, 1997) – de Monferrand follows the fortunes of an (imaginary) network of upper-class, cosmopolitan girls and women, dominated by aristocratic family ties and lesbian tastes. With the exception of one character (Héloïse's son in *Les Enfants d'Héloïse*), de Monferrand's novels give overwhelming precedence to the point of view of female characters, and portray remarkable understanding and complicity both between straight and gay women and between younger and older women. Thus, aspects of identity often viewed as divisive – sexual orientation and age – are de-dramatised, presented not as barriers but rather as simple, relatively conflict-free givens.

Lesbians within de Monferrand's fiction are socially successful and fully integrated within mainstream society, rather than a ghettoised minority. They enjoy relationships of warmth and integrity with heterosexual friends and family members. A possible objection to this portrait might be that her lesbian characters' successful social functioning relies on discretion about their sexual orientation, a strict discontinuity between the public and the private, and that this amounts to nothing more than endorsement of the closet. Such an objection is over-schematised and reductive, for these lesbian characters, though closeted to the outer circle of society, are unostentatiously but unmistakably out to those who matter to them: family and friends. This ideological refusal to politicise sexuality, this preference for social pragmatism are complemented by de Monferrand's characteristic style: exuberant, hard-headed, resilient, at the antipodes of alienated contestation or of radical identity politics.

Essentially, the action of *Les Amies d'Héloïse*, an epistolary and diary-form novel, consists of Erika (29 years) seducing a young (15 year-old) but eminently responsive Héloïse, Héloïse eventually seducing Erika's former lover Suzanne (46 years), Erika shooting Héloïse in a fit of passionate jealousy, Héloïse's self-sacrificial marriage following Suzanne's suicide, and the reconciliation of and renewed passion between Erika and a widowed Héloïse after a 10-year split. It thus has the makings of a melodramatic, even farcical romance, but avoids such bathetic form by rejecting hackneyed formulas and by deploying sharp wit, humour and psychological authenticity in its construction of characters.

While refusing the conventional language of sexual politics, and displaying conspicuous reserves about conventional feminism (to the point of caricaturing it), this first novel nonetheless does problematise gender, gender relations and heterosexuality. The theory of maternal instincts as integral to women's identity, for instance, is given short shrift. Heterosexual marriage, for its part, is presented as an inevitable and sometimes satisfactory family unit, but also, significantly, as a utilitarian institution whose main function is to ensure reproduction and continuation of family lines.

The fact that this novel contains no working-class lesbians may alienate certain readers, but *Les Amies d'Héloïse* has no pretensions to be socially inclusive; instead, it concentrates on lesbianism within one narrowly delineated section of society, the section known best by the author. She takes the risk of ventriloquising her own politically incorrect views through her character Héloïse in the latter's defence of the anti-independence OAS group, derision of de Gaulle and passionate commiseration with the French colonisers ejected from Algeria after its independence in 1962. De Monferrand's right-wing image is mentioned by sociologist Frédéric Martel, who himself could hardly be seen as a left-wing radical. Clearly, she is in something of a minority within a minority; fellow stable-mates are thin on the ground in the contemporary period, when most lesbian and gay writers' allegiance is to the (symbolic, rather than party-political) left. In fact, the closest parallel is not with any other French lesbian writer, but with a gay male writer, Roger PEYREFITTE.

Les Enfants d'Héloïse has three main foci: the development of Héloïse's three children; her daughter Mélanie's growing awareness of her own lesbian orientation; and Héloïse's relationships with long-term partner Erika and clandestine lover Fédora. It thus yokes two categories usually seen as irreconcilable – those of sexually active lesbian and of mother. It is one of the few French works depicting a family consisting of children, biological mother and biological mother's female partner. Although the lesbian couple do not come out to their children, the latter discover their parents' secret in their teenage years, and by the end of the novel the daughter who has also identified as gay (Mélanie) expresses optimism about her future as a lesbian, feeling that she has been fortunate in having had good examples set by her mother and her mother's partner. This third novel in de Monferrand's trilogy implicitly vindicates a marginalised, socially unvalidated family unit, without employing politicised jargon. Indeed, like her previous two novels, it is stylistically classical, limpid, and highly elegant, some might even say mannered; marked, for instance, by a fetish for imperfect subjunctives, that other persecuted minority.

Frédéric Martel, Le Rose et le Noir (Paris, 1996), pp. 161, 201–2, 434.

Lucille Cairns

Monroe, Armand (b. 1935), Canadian entertainer, actor, activist. Monroe was born in Montreal as Armand Larivée. Although the city in which he grew up was known for its risqué night life, police raids on the bars that drew a gay clientele were a regular occurrence. Men dancing together was a legal offence, and treated as such.

In 1957 the flamboyant young man was asked by a bar owner if he would organise evenings that would attract a gay clientele to the Downbeat Club. Now known as La Monroe, he showed films, held bingo games and staged amateur nights and muscleman contests. Most of all, he hosted drag shows with quick wit and aggressive repartee, all the while dressed by the best couturiers. Monroe was not complacent about discriminatory practices: he encouraged men to slow-dance together in defiance of the law; he pressured management to hire gay staff at a time when establishments attracting gay clientele refused to do so.

By the end of the 1970s, Monroe was a media personality. He hosted shows called Côte à côte on both radio and television. His persona started making appearances in the works of Jean-Paul Daoust, Michel TREMBLAY and other writers. He played 'Dr Frank'n'furter' in a 1978 production of The Rocky Horror Show. In 1994, the National Film Board of Canada released Lois Siegal's film Lip Gloss, a documentary on transvestites in which Monroe makes frequent appearances and on which he worked as researcher and creative spirit. The film has been shown at film festivals in Montreal, Toronto and London, and has been aired on television across Canada.

Monroe carried the gay banner at the head of Montreal's first Gay Pride Parade, held in 1979.

Michael Hendricks

Monsiváis, Carlos (b. 1938), Mexican writer. Monsiváis was born in Mexico City and has lived there most of his life except for short stints visiting Harvard University and the University of California (Santa Clara). Sometimes described as a Huguenot Aztec, an outsider in an orthodox society, Monsiváis has consistently supported lesbian and gay artists as well as other progressive causes. Writing columns for the leftist daily *La Joranada* and appearing regularly on television, Monsiváis has championed the cause of striking teachers in Oaxaca, the student insurgents (gunned down during a 1968 demonstration in Tlatelolco Square), the Zapatistas in Chiapas and many other causes.

Monsiváis began as a protégé of Salvador Novo (1904–74) who led avant-garde, artistic and gay circles in Mexico City. In 1966, Monsiváis edited an important anthology of twentieth-century Mexican poetry and has since followed Novo in chronicling the quotidian city life in Mexico. While Novo concentrated on official events, Monsiváis has pursued the city's underbelly. Crime chronicles, beauty contests (for both sexes), movie stars, millenarian preachers, holidays and other remarkable happenings attract him and his readers. *Scenes of Modesty and Lasciviousness* (1981) surveys the punk phenomenon, funky bars, dancing, burlesque shows and much more inside Mexico City's onanistic abundance. His celebration of Mexican popular culture falls somewhere between kitsch, camp and reverence.

As a writer, Monsiváis's greatest contribution to gay liberation has been his bringing a gay sensibility to the study of poetry, art, literature and popular culture. Using humour, sarcasm and wit liberally, he follows the awesome contortions of sex symbols, both male and female. He explains, 'Those in control of society know that in the self-delusions of *machismo* (in the fascination of being defenceless before one's most deplorable fantasies) there lies an endless source of control.'

Since the deaths of Novo (1974) and Octavio Paz (1998), Monsiváis has become Mexico's leading intellectual and reaches a large domestic audience. Beyond television, newspapers and magazines, his books have appeared in many printings and editions. For instance, the wry and wonderful *New Catechism for Remiss*

Indians (1982) has been reprinted in editions for the parlour table as well as for the masses. The Mexican National Council for Culture and the Arts gave the work canonical status by including it in their series of classic Mexican texts.

Monsiváis waits to find an audience outside Mexico. John Kraniauskas recently translated a selection of his writings as *Mexican Postcards* (London, 1997) which would 'establish Monsiváis's rightful place in the pantheon of Latin America's greatest writers'. Monsiváis's interesting blend of leftist politics, popular culture, photography, art, poetry and other media offer rich texts for international readers.

Charley Shively

Montagnier, Luc (b. 1932), French medical researcher. With Robert GALLO, Montagnier is considered to be a co-discoverer of the human immunodeficiency virus (HIV) – the virus many believe causes acquired immune deficiency syndrome (AIDS). In 1990 he was appointed head of the Department of AIDS and Retroviruses at the Pasteur Institute; he has been awarded the Legion of Honour and the National Order of Merit by the French government.

In the late 1970s Gallo, a researcher at the American National Cancer Institute, was credited with the discovery of a human virus (HTLV) that could be transmitted through sexual contact and through contaminated blood. Gallo's work created immense interest among researchers at the Pasteur Institute in Paris. The Institute created a new unit for the study of oncogenic viruses in 1982: Montagnier was appointed its first director. Montagnier and his team attempted to replicate the findings of Gallo concerning the link between HTLV and AIDS. They were unsuccessful in this attempt; however, in April 1984 they isolated a new virus, Lymphadenopathy Associated Virus (LAV), which they considered to be the cause of AIDS. Later research has proved that LAV and HTLV are identical viruses.

S. Connor and S. Kingman, 'The Search for the Virus', in M. D. Grmek, *History of Aids: Emergence and Origin of a Modern Pandemic* (Princeton, 1990).

Mark Edwards

Mossop, Brian (b. 1946), Canadian activist, translator. Born in London, England, Mossop moved with his parents to Toronto in 1950. He joined the Communist Party in 1967 while a student at the University of Toronto, where he was deeply involved in the student movement. His life changed dramatically in the summer of 1974 when, in the space of two months, he quit university to become a translator, came out, joined the gay movement and met Ken Popert. Mossop's relationship with Popert has survived, but he was expelled from the Communist Party in 1976 'for advocating homosexuality'.

Mossop joined the Gay Alliance Toward Equality (Toronto) which Popert had helped found in 1973. GATE, the successor to Toronto Gay Action in organizing around civil rights issues, was a major force in gay liberation activities in Ontario. Mossop was GATE's representative at the National Gay Rights Coalition and president from 1977 to 1980. He was a founder of the Coalition for Gay Rights in Ontario (1975) and later its chairperson. He was also active in the anti-Anita BRYANT coalition and helped organise two national conferences.

In 1978 Mossop helped found the Right to Privacy Committee, formed to assist people arrested in a police raid on a gay sauna, and served on its executive until 1981. From 1981 to 1984 Mossop sat on the executive of the Gay Community Council which focused on community–police relations in the aftermath of the massive bath raids of 6 February 1981, when 286 people, including Mossop, were charged as found-ins.

In 1985 Mossop launched a grievance-at-work for not being granted bereavement leave to attend the funeral of his lover's father. He took the matter to the Canadian Human Rights Commission, citing discrimination based on family status. Seven years later, the Supreme Court of Canada agreed to hear the case. It found against him in a split decision but left the door open to other challenges.

Since 1984 Mossop has devoted his time to his profession – translating, training translators and writing articles. He has also sung in gay choirs since 1989.

Brian Mossop vertical file, Canadian Lesbian and Gay Archives, Toronto; Donald W. McLeod, *Lesbian and Gay Liberation in Canada* (Toronto, 1996).

Harold Averill

Mott, Luiz (b. 1946), Brazilian anthropologist, historian and activist. Mott was born into a large lower middle-class family in the industrial city of São Paulo. His father was Italian while his mother was Brazilian and a writer. He attended a Dominican seminary for his secondary education and then studied social sciences in the University of São Paulo. He took a Masters in Ethnology at the Sorbonne in France (1969–71), and obtained his Doctorate in Anthropology from the University of Campinas in 1975. He married in 1972 and had two daughters but divorced in 1978. The following year Mott took up a post at the Federal University of Bahia in Salvador.

In 1980 Mott founded the Grupo Gay da Bahia (GGB) as a social, consciousness-raising and campaigning organisation. It was the first Brazilian group to be officially recognised and to be given representation on an official AIDS prevention body. The GGB's first major successful campaign was to have Paragraph 302.0 of the World Health Organisation's International Classification of Diseases, which described homosexuality as a sexual deviation and disorder, declared invalid in Brazil. The group also successfully lobbied Brazilian scientific bodies to recognise gay rights. The GGB regularly appealed to the media, sometimes courting controversy by asserting that various Brazilian national heroes were homosexual, and organised a protest against the extreme anti-gay stance of the main local newspaper, *A Tarde*.

With the onset of the AIDS epidemic, Mott organised the first distribution of AIDS-prevention leaflets in 1982. The GGB has continued to take a proactive position towards AIDS, organising awareness campaigns, distributing condoms and putting pressure on politicians and officials to increase the resources dedicated to combatting AIDS. In 1987 Mott helped found the Bahian Anti-AIDS Centre and the following year was appointed a member of the National Aids Commission of the Brazilian Federal Ministry of Health.

In 1985 Mott met his partner, Marcelo Cerqueira. The couple were married in a religious ceremony by a Protestant minister in 1992. Although not recognised by the civil authorities, the event was reported by the media.

In the 1990s Mott became increasingly concerned with the question of human rights for lesbians and gays in Brazil. For some years the GGB had been collecting newspaper cuttings and publishing lists of lesbians and gay men who had been assaulted and murdered, either by robbers or police. The sheer number of these tragic events gave the lie to the common stereotype of Brazil as a gay paradise. In 1992 Mott gave a series of lectures in the US at the invitation of Amnesty International and in 1993 became the secretary for human rights of the Brazilian Association of Gays, Lesbians and Transvestites. In 1996 he wrote a booklet which catalogued the abuses to which lesbians and gays were subject, developing the notion of homophobia to show that these were not random acts of violence but an inevitable outcome of *machista* culture. In 1998 Mott's efforts were officially recognised in his adopted home when he was made an honorary citizen of Salvador.

In parallel with his activities in the gay movement, Mott has continued to build a career as an academic researcher. His main area of interest is sexual transgression and racial relations during Brazil's colonial period. For this he has used the records of the Portuguese Inquisition, which have survived in the Lisbon archives. For much of its history the Inquisition actively persecuted sodomites, and its legalistic methods, with their copious documentation, provide an insight into the gay subcultures of early modern Portugal and Brazil which is unrivalled in other European countries. Mott's publications have helped to make sexuality a subject for serious study, while his position as a respected academic has added stature to his political campaigns.

His energy has made the GGB, of which he remains the convenor, the most active and longest-lived of the Brazilian groups, in an area of the country renowned for its laid-back attitudes. The GGB is unusual, both in Brazil and elsewhere, in attracting members mainly from the poorer classes rather than the middle class. It has spread AIDS-awareness to lower-class gay men, male prostitutes and transvestites. Mott has been able to build on his academic research and international contacts to develop political and social campaigns which produce practical results in the Brazilian context. This has not been without its dangers: he has received threats and had his house and car daubed with anti-gay graffiti. Together with a handful of other gay activists, however, he has been able to seize an historical moment, when Brazil was rebuilding its civil society after years of military dictatorship, and ensure that gay rights are now firmly on the political agenda.

Luiz Roberto Mott, *Epidemic of Hate: Violations of the Human Rights of Gay Men, Lesbians, and Transvestites in Brazil* (Salvador/San Francisco, 1996); *Escravidão, Homossexualidade e Demonologia* (São Paulo, 1988); *O Lesbianismo no Brasil* (Porto Alegre, 1987); *O Sexo Proibido: Virgens, Gays e Escravos nas Garras da Inquisição* (Campinas, 1989); James N. Green, 'More Love and More Desire: The Building of a Brazilian Movement', in Barry D.

Adam, Jan Willem Duyvendak and André Krouwel (eds), *The Global Emergence of Gay and Lesbian Politics: National Imprints of a Worldwide Movement* (Philadelphia, 1999), pp. 91–109.

Robert Howes

Moura, Federico (1952–88), Argentinian singer. The leader of the pop band 'Virus' died of AIDS in his mother's arms. The irony of his death was concordant with the musical approach of his band during its nine years of existence.

Moura was a symbol of Argentine rock, albeit different from his musical contemporaries. During the 1980s, when most musicians concentrated on clearly defined social and political issues, the mordancy and irony in Virus's pop tunes proved it was possible to put together danceable music with ideas.

Virus came from La Plata, a neighbouring city to Buenos Aires, and during its life, the group was emblematic of the potential of rock and pop music in Argentina. The band's style was techno-pop that played a constant game of seduction and ambiguity with its audience. That ambiguity generated both strong adhesions and rejections among the audience. Moura came out as a gay man in 1987, the same year he was diagnosed with AIDS. His coming-out was not a surprise to anyone. As his brother Marcelo Moura (a member of the band) explains, 'Federico was gay, therefore his aesthetic make-up was gay as well. He was not interested in promoting or prioritizing it. He just acted the way he was.' There are many examples of this attitude embedded in the lyrics of their songs, the productions of their shows and the packaging of their albums.

Carlos Schröder

Mozetič, Brane (b. 1958), Slovenian writer and activist. Mozetič writes poetry, short stories and essays, and his translations from French include the books of Arthur Rimbaud, Jean GENET, Michael FOUCAULT and Amin Maalouf. He edits the Slovene gay and lesbian magazine *Revolver* and has edited an anthology of twentieth-century homoerotic poetry, *Drobci stekla v ustih* (*Pieces of Glass in the Mouth*, 1989), and an anthology of Slovenian homoerotic writing, *Modra svetloba* (*Blue Light*, 1990). He has won the award of the city of Ljubljana and the Zlata ptica, the highest award for young artists, as well as the French FALGWE award.

Mozetič has published nine books of poetry, a book of short stories, entitled *Pasijon* (*Passion*, 1993), and a novel, *Angeli* (*Angels*, 1996). His most important poetry collections are *Mreža* (*The Net*, 1989), *Pesmi za umrlimi sanjami* (*Poems for the Dead Dreams*, 1995) and a selection of earlier published poetry, *Obsedenost* (*Obsession*, 1991), published simultaneously in Ljubljana and Paris. His poetry has been translated into Serbian, French, English and German.

Mozetič joined the gay and lesbian movement in 1988 and in 1990 he was among the founders of the new gay and lesbian organisation Roza klub, whose aim is to end discrimination based on sexual orientation. Roza klub was founded as a political organisation, and Mozetič was on the List of Independent Social Movements candidates in the first democratic elections in 1990. He has been Roza klub's chairperson since then and he has initiated or cooperated on various projects, including the Ljubljana Gay and Lesbian Film Festival, conferences, (the tenth ILGA conference for Eastern, Southeastern and Central Europe in 1996), safer sex education and HIV/AIDS prevention; Mozetič is also a member of the Slovenian Council for HIV/AIDS prevention at the Ministry of Health.

His successes in politics include a ban on discrimination based on sexual orientation in the Slovenian Penal Code, equalisation of punishment for rapes in the Penal Code regardless of the victim's gender, and some developments in drafting a Registered Partnerships bill.

Aleš Pečnik

Mujica Lainez, Manuel (1910–84), Argentinian writer. Mujica Lainez represents a classic strand of Latin American narrative that seems to stand outside the frantic avant-garde of other well-known writers such as Julio Cortázar or Mario Vargas Llosa. In relation to the left-wing feel of these authors, Mujica's techniques and concerns seem closer to the bourgeois tradition whose summit might be represented by Proust. Indeed, there are a number of Proustian elements both in his life and his work. He belonged to a wealthy family of Buenos Aires society and was educated in Europe. His literary models are mostly European and, rather than turning his mind to a specifically Latin American reality, he set some of his most important narratives in Europe. Whenever he concentrated on Buenos Aires, it is the bourgeois metropolis aiming to reproduce European society that he is interested in, rather than the country of political turmoil and uncertain identity of the turn of the century. Houses, buildings and objects become precious in his narratives, and his passionate commitment to the past is hardly ever burdened with contemporary relevance. In this way, Mujica Lainez does not seem to belong to the Latin American tradition. However, all of these features do place him specifically within an international 'gay' tradition, a fact that heterosexist critics are reluctant to notice (and, it must be added, neither are gay critics: in a way, Mujica appears as a 'conservative' and therefore apropriation for the gay canon seems problematic).

Both in his life and in his writing, Mujica Lainez shows the features of the dandy tradition: elegant, precious style, interest in form, society and furniture, an apparent attempt to escape social reality, the placing of artistic endeavour at the centre of life. Coming out seems to have been a difficult process for him, but, as Oscar Hermes Villordo's biography subtly illustrates, he came to terms with his feelings and acknowledged his love for Guillermo Whitelow, whom he met in the early 1950s. Naturally, Mujica was not one to make it public, and this is reflected in the appearance of homoeroticism in most of his works. In the mysterious world of Buenos Aires society, there are secrets in all families, and stories such as *El retrato amarillo* (first published in 1956) seem to hint towards homosexuality as the ultimate secret. Homoerotic attachments or descriptions appear in some of his longer works, but it is very seldom that the gap between the homosocial and the homosexual is actually crossed. The one exception is his late novel *Sergio* (1976), a picaresque fantasy in which a beautiful youth is pursued by a host of rapacious adults of both sexes. In a weird finale, he meets two equally beautiful siblings, male and female, with whom he seems to share some transitory happiness. As is the case with Forster's *Maurice*, *Sergio* was Mujica's attempt to present a positive portrayal of homoeroticism (but not a too successful one at that).

Alberto Mira

Murray, Stephen O. (b. 1950), American scholar. Murray was born in St Paul, Minnesota. He was awarded a Ph.D. in sociology from the University of Toronto in 1979 and was then a postdoctoral fellow in medical anthropology at the University of California, Berkeley, following which he was employed as a project director evaluating San Francisco County mental health programmes. As an independent scholar, over the past decade, Murray has had a prolific output of books and articles mainly examining same-sex relations in different cultural contexts. Murray seeks to explain observed differences from a structural perspective and is critical of the view that there was no patterned homosexuality before the forensic medical discourse of the late-nineteenth century invented it.

In addition to assembling and comparing writing about homosexuality around the world, Murray has conducted ethnographic fieldwork in Canada, the United States, Guatemala, Mexico and Taiwan.

After producing a series of books assembling information on homosexuality region by region (a very broadly defined Oceania, Latin America, the Islamic world, sub-Saharan Africa and 'modern gay' America, with a special focus on ethnic differences), his book, *Homosexualities* (2000), is organised according to Barry ADAM's three major types (age-role-structured, gender-role-structured, not status-structured) of same-sex sexuality, and cross-tabulates the recorded presence of a type of homosexuality with variables such as modes of production, sexual division of labour, inheritance patterns, relative freedom of movement of women, religious specialisations, urbanisation and stratification. With such broad coverage, Murray's work necessarily relies on the compilation and interpretation of others' observations of many of the societies he examines, and he is more interested in establishing patterns than exploring specificities.

Murray has also published research in sociolinguistics, including work on lexicons for 'homosexuals', and gay ritual insults. He was a founding member of the Sociologists' Gay Caucus (1974), the Toronto Gay Academic Union (1975) and the Anthropologists' Research Group on Homosexuality (1978). Murray is or has been on the editorial boards of *History of Sociology, Encyclopedia of Homosexuality, Journal of Homosexuality* and *Sexualities*.

Stephen O. Murray (ed.), *Oceanic Homosexualities* (New York, 1992), and *Latin American Male Homosexualities* (Albuquerque, 1995); Stephen O. Murray and Will Roscoe (eds.), *Islamic Homosexualities* (New York, 1997); and *Boy Wives and Female Husbands: Studies in African Homosexualities* (New York, 1998).

Gerard Sullivan

Musiał, Grzegorz (b. 1952), Polish eye doctor, poet, novelist and literary translator. Born in Bydgoszcz (northern Poland) where he still lives, Musiał is a recluse, as he wrote in an autobiographical novel,

Czeska biżuteria (*Czech Jewellery*, 1983): 'I don't think that among other biographies my life could be something truly absorbing'. Musiał's work encompasses five volumes of poetry, including *Kosmopolites* (1980) and *Berliner Tagebuch* (1989), and four novels, the last of which, *Al fine*, was published in 1997. Musiał writes clearly under the influence of Marcel Proust, James Joyce, Witold GOMBROWICZ and Gertrude Stein, though decidedly in a style of his own. His often ironical, experimental style is full of sophisticated allusion and erudite knowledge requiring an equally vast knowledge from his readers. An eminent literary critic, Michał Głowiński, called *Al fine* 'an incessant debate on the metaphysical issues and the situation of man in the modern world, the richness of which overwhelms as apart from autobiographical traits it includes erotic, Jewish, musical and other subplots'.

Musiał is also a translator. Among other, mainly American works, he translated into Polish the poems of Allen GINSBERG. An active propagator of gay literature, Musiał published a very personal anthology of contemporary American poetry, *Ameryka! Ameryka! Antologia wierszy poetów amerykańskich po 1940 roku* (1994), where among 55 entries he included 12 gay and 4 lesbian poets.

Marcin Krzeszowiec, 'Poeta wzgardy', in *Inaczej*, vol. 1, no. 91 (1998), pp. 19–20.

Krzysztof Fordonski

Myles, Eileen (b. 1949), American poet and activist. Myles has been in the vanguard of experimental writing and performance, art criticism and lesbian feminist activism in New York since the 1970s. Born in Cambridge, Mass., she was educated at Catholic schools and the University of Massachusetts (Boston) before moving to Manhattan. Since then she has been a significant and versatile figure in the downtown arts scene, especially associated with the 'New York School' and St Mark's Poetry Project, which she directed from 1984 to 1986. Like the late Allan GINSBERG, Myles is a virtuoso poet-performer-activist of the East Village, producing work that is at once politically engaged, erotic, stylish and funny. She has edited little magazines (*Dodgems*, and the women-only *Ladies Museum*, both in 1977), and writes regular art criticism for the *Village Voice* and *Art in America*. Her books include *Not Me* (1991), *Chelsea Girls* (1994), *Maxfield Parrish* (1995), *School of Fish* (1997) and, as editor, *The New Fuck You: Adventures in Lesbian Reading* (1995). In 1992 she was a write-in candidate for the presidency of the United States.

Steven Clay and Rodney Phillips, *A Secret Location on the Lower East Side*, (New York, 1998); *Postmodern American Poetry*, Paul Hoover, ed. (New York, 1994); David Lehman, *The Last Avant-Garde: The Making of the New York School of Poets* (New York, 1999).

Kate Lilley

N

Nájera, Francisco (b. 1945), Guatemalan author. Nájera was born in Guatemala and now resides in New York City. A poet and a fiction writer, he investigates in his works the relationship between gender categories, eroticism and the process of writing. Throughout his works, the notion of the openness of love and that of the literary discourse are reclaimed. Nájera presents heterosexual, homosexual and bisexual forms of love and passion. In addition, religious rituals and traditional taboos are transgressed.

Con la libertad del amor (1987), a collection of twenty of Nájera's short poems, deals with the relationship of an older man and a young man, a relationship imbued with great tenderness and a delicate sensibility. In *Los cómplices*, a book of poetic stories, he explores homosexual as well as heterosexual love.

In the story 'No me despiertes' (Do Not Wake Me Up) from *Los cómplices*, one finds echoes of Borges, as in many of the poems and the stories of Nájera. This Borgesian echo is specifically because of the representation of time and space as well as the continuing reflection upon the process of writing. Here, the narrator, like the narrator in 'The Circular Ruins', is dreaming another reality – and the story itself is the account of that experience.

In *Cuerpo* (1996), Nájera investigates the process of writing, 'cuerpo' (body) and text are interchangeable. Moreover, the desire to interchange the poems is obvious in the loose arrangement of the twenty-nine poems – not bound, but rather collected without numbers and titles, thus claiming their changing positions within the literary discourse.

Dante Liano, *Rassegna Iberistica*, vol. 27 (1986), pp. 56–7; Ana Sierra, 'Francisco Nájera', in D. W. Foster (ed.), *Latin American Writers on Gay and Lesbian Themes: A Bio-Critical Sourcebook* (Westport, CT, 1994), pp. 278–81.

Elena M. Martínez

Navarre, Yves (1940–94), French author. Navarre was born in Condom, in the Gers region of Gascony. He was the son of a tyrnannical father, René Navarre, the Director-General of the French Oil Institute, and an affectionate but weak mother who was obliged to live in the shadow of both her husband and her overbearing mother-in-law. The family moved to Paris and Navarre was sent to the Lycée Pasteur in Neuilly-sur-Seine, where he was consistently bullied until well into his teens. He was an outstanding student with a flair for languages, but ended up attending the École des Hautes Études Commerciales du Nord. From there he went into a series of advertising jobs, between 1965 and 1970. His real desire, however, was to be a writer, and when his seventeenth novel, *Lady Black*, was finally accepted and published in 1971, he was able to devote himself to writing as a career. He went on to publish over thirty novels and plays, of which *Le Jardin d'acclimatation* (1980) won the Prix Goncourt. He was made a Chevalier of the Légion d'honneur and in 1992 he received an accolade for his collected works from the Académie Française. This sort of success did not satisfy him. At the beginning of the 1990s he moved to Montreal in an effort to escape his growing sense of ennui, but failed to find fulfilment there. He committed suicide in Paris.

Many of his novels are focused on homosexuality, particularly those he wrote in the 1970s, and have a highly autobiographical input: *Killer* (1975), for example, is based on his own experiences during a stay in Oxford. He also gave a frank account of his orientation in *Biographie* (1981), the third-person autobiography which he deliberately labelled 'novel' to highlight the complex relationship between self-narration and self-creation. His father had done his best to 'save' the young Yves from his sexual orientation, largely because he was afraid that a homosexual son would hinder his (largely mythical) political aspirations. He even went so far as to try to have the boy lobotomised as part of a so-called cure but was mercifully stopped by other members of the family, an incident which lies behind the prize-winning *Jardin d'acclimatation*. In *Les Loukoums* (1973) and *Killer*, Navarre explores the limits of promiscuous gay eroticism as a materialistic and destructive 'consumption' of other people's bodies. In *Le Petit Galopin de nos coeurs* (1977), on the other hand, he wrote one of the most romantic accounts of a long-lasting physical and emotional passion between two men ever produced in any language. In *Hotel Styx* (1989) and more specifically in *Ce sont amis que vent emporte* (1991), he broached the subject of AIDS, but the latter is still very much a novel about love. What links his more heterosexually-focused works to his gay-centred writing is in general the same questions of identity, emotional relationship and family pressures, all of them clearly growing out of his own experience.

Yves Navarre, *Biographie* (Paris, 1981).

Christopher Robinson

Navratilova, Martina (b. 1956), Czech-American athlete. Although Navratilova's parents lived in the Krkonose Mountains of Czechoslovakia, her mother went to Prague for her birth in 1956, the year Russians occupied Hungary, and twelve years before the same thing happened in Czechoslovakia. When Martina was three, her parents divorced and she and her mother moved in with another family at Revnice, just outside Prague. Their room overlooked a red clay tennis court. Her grandmother had been a national standard tennis player. Her mother, also a tennis player, gymnast and volleyballer, remarried a man she had met at the local tennis courts in 1961.

Navratilova was granted asylum in the US at 18 years of age, in 1975, though there was a statutory period of five years before citizenship was granted; homosexuality was not only illegal in many states but could be the sole grounds for denying citizenship. Nevertheless, she was granted citizenship in 1981 after declaring that she was 'bisexual'.

Navratilova learnt to play tennis as a child and was coached by her stepfather until nine years old, when she entered an after-school programme by George Parma, a leading Czech player. She won the Czech national championships in 1972 and was 'allowed' to play the circuit in the US in 1973, at the age of 16. She won her first professional tournament in 1974 and sent money home for her parents to buy their first car. She won her first Wimbledon singles title in 1978, defeating Chris Evert, and was then ranked number one for the first time in her career. Navratilova holds the record for the most singles titles, having won 166 during her career, and the record for doubles titles, at 163. She won 54

Grand Slam titles in singles, mixed and doubles.

Navratilova had crushes on women and teachers whilst growing up. However, once on tour in the US when she was about 19, she knew she liked 'the company of women better'. Her first affair with a woman lasted six months. Then, Rita Mae BROWN, the lesbian novelist, was introduced to Navratilova in 1978, whilst she was writing a novel with a Czech character in it. Early the following year the relationship became serious with daily phone calls, and they then lived together until early 1981.

Beginning in 1984 and lasting until 1990, Navratilova had a relationship with Judy Nelson, whom she had met when Nelson had organised the ball girls and ball boys for a tournament. It was her presence in Navratilova's 'box' at the French open and with her during Wimbledon in 1984 which meant lesbianism first became an ongoing topic of the media's coverage of Navratilova. Their break-up was also a very public affair, not the first time sporting journalists linked Navratilova's on-court performances with her personal emotional life. Not long after this, she had a relationship with champion skier Cindy Nelson until it was reported she was seeing the singer k.d. LANG.

Navratilova played a very different style of tennis – an energetic, net rushing, attacking style – which previously had only been used by men such as Rod Laver. During her career she developed a serious and scientific approach to her preparation and training as an athlete. She developed a muscular physique and was often berated by other women players and the press for looking and playing 'like a man'. It was her on-court style, her outstanding athletic achievements coupled with her public love for women, with lovers often sitting courtside, which kept her a prominent public figure throughout the 1980s into the 1990s.

Navratilova is arguably the most significant lesbian of the second half of this century in terms of visibility, material success, challenges to ideologies about women (and women in sport), as well as the physical embodiment and representation of alternatives to the hegemony of 'traditionally feminine body builds and physical style' based on heterosexuality and the fashion industry. As one of the greatest athletes of the century she was widely known almost from the beginning of her career as a lesbian – and rich and famous. Her success, coupled with the liberationist movements for women and gays and lesbians, made the options of professional sport for women and public lesbianism significant and viable for all those who come after her. Her prominence in such a popular cultural form has probably brought some measure of acceptance of lesbianism.

She has been the most public, most continually visible lesbian in mainstream culture, via the media, because of the dominant place sport occupies in globalised popular culture which transcends national boundaries and social characteristics such as age, gender, class and ethnicity. The fact that the women's international tennis circuit became very big business during her playing career (thanks to the work of Billie Jean KING) means there is an economic imperative to cover the lives of the 'stars' and 'personalities' on and off the court. Navratilova's years of rivalry with the traditionally 'feminine' Evert could be seen as the ongoing battle of 'sexualities', particularly as the nature of the circuit required the creation of a source of 'rivalry' to create public interest in the outcome of matches which were played between the same players, month after month. She has constantly made and kept lesbianism visible and discussable because she had been so public about her love of women, as well as being self-consciously an activist about AIDS, homophobia and legal issues in the US. Her financial success through endorsements and sponsorships would have been even greater had she been able to act on the advice of many to be 'discreet' about her personal life and loves. She carried the public and private burden of every prejudice and stereotype about lesbians in general and professional women athletes in particular.

Martina Navratilova with George Vecsey, *Being Myself* (London, 1986); Diane Hamer and Belinda Budge (eds), *The Good, the Bad and the Gorgeous: Popular Culture's Romance with Lesbianism* (London, 1994).

Helen Waite

Negrón-Muntaner, Frances (b. 1966), Puerto Rican poet, critic, filmmaker. Born in Santurce, Puerto Rico, Negrón-Muntaner moved to Philadelphia, where she resided until 1997; currently, she lives in Florida. She has been active in the American East Coast-Latino literary movements since the 1980s. Her poetry has appeared in journals such as *Conditions, The Evergreen Chronicles, The Painted Bride Quarterly, Centro* and *Heresies*. The publication of *Shouting in a Whisper/Los límites del silencio: Latino Poetry in Philadelphia / Poesía Latina en Filadelfia* (1994), an anthology edited by Negrón-Muntaner, attests to her commitment and interest in broadening the perspective of the Latino experience, to make it more inclusive for Afro-Latinos as well as gay and lesbian Latinos.

Indeed, Negrón-Muntaner's commitment to enhance the Latino experience to make it more inclusive for gay and lesbian issues is evident in her film *Brincando el charco* (*Crossing the Waters*, 1994). As the film's title suggests, it deals with the incessant displacement of Puerto Ricans between the island and mainland. Interestingly, in *Brincando el charco*, the issue of immigration is connected with sexual identities as the main character is a Puerto Rican lesbian who resides in the United States.

Anatomía de una sonrisa: Poemas anoréxicos, a collection of 69 poems, is deeply concerned with the issues of sexual and cultural identities. Thus, being a les-

bian and a Puerto Rican living in the United States and navigating between two cultures and two languages are central to this book.

Zoé Jiménez-Corretjer, 'Poetas de la "última" generación', *Claridad (En Rojo)*, 2 Dec. 1988, p. 22; Carlos Rodríguez-Matos, 'Frances Negrón-Muntaner', in D. W. Foster (ed.), *Latin American Writers on Gay and Lesbian Themes* (Westport, CT, 1994), pp. 288–90.

Elena M. Martínez

Neill, A(lexander) (Sutherland) (1883–1973), British educationalist. Neill went to a small school in Kingsmuir, near Forfar in Scotland. Despite being taught there by his father, a stern Calvinist, Neill trained as a teacher himself. After earlier experiments in Germany and Austria, Neill founded his co-educational 'free' school in England, moving in 1927 to Suffolk, where the school became famous as 'Summerhill'. Neill was influenced by Ibsen, Shaw and Nietzsche, but his ideas stemmed most directly from the psychological theories of Freud and Reich. He advocated a permissive and child-centred education, aiming to avoid, in particular, any repression of the child's sexuality. Left to their own 'self-regulation', children would, he supposed, develop into healthy adolescents without the prurient interest in sex produced by a repressed upbringing. Unfortunately, Neill's faith in the goodness of unrepressed human sexuality did not prevent him from being homophobic. The self-regulating child is also supposed to lack any 'perverted tendencies'. 'I do not know', writes Neill, 'what early repressions lead to homosexuality, but it seems quite certain that they must have originated in very early childhood. Summerhill nowadays does not take children under five, and therefore we have often had to deal with children who were wrongly handled in the nursery. Nevertheless, over a period of forty years, the school has not turned out a single homosexual. The reason is that freedom breeds healthy children.' The healthy child naturally conforms to traditional standards of sexual morality. Even more disturbingly, it becomes clear that the supposedly 'spontaneous' harmony between healthy human nature and conventional morality is really imposed: 'Some years ago, a new boy fresh from a public school tried to introduce sodomy. He was unsuccessful. Incidentally, he was surprised and alarmed when he discovered that the whole school knew about his efforts.' We can imagine how the other children behaved.

A. S. Neill, *Summerhill* (London, 1962); Ray Hemmings, *Fifty Years of Freedom: A Study in the Development of the Ideas of A. S. Neill* (London, 1972).

David West

Nestle, Joan (b. 1940), American author and activist. Born into a working-class family in New York, Nestle was educated at Queens College of the City University of New York and later taught English there. She is best known as a writer, having published *A Restricted Country* (1987), a collection of short stories, an important and controversial article on 'butch-femme relationships', which appeared in 1981, and a number of edited works. With Naomi Holoch, she has edited three anthologies of lesbian fiction, published from 1990 to 1996, and, with John Preston, *Sister and Brother: Lesbians and Gay Men Write about Their Lives Together* (1994). She also edited *The Persistent Desire: A Femme-Butch Reader* (1992).

In 1973, Nestle was one of the founders (with Deborah Edel) of the Lesbian Herstory Archives of New York City, the largest and oldest lesbian archive in the world. The Archives now have over 20,000 volumes, 12,000 photographs, 300 special collections and 1,600 periodical titles.

www.datalounge.net/network/pages/lha

Robert Aldrich and Garry Wotherspoon

Newton, Esther (b. 1940), American scholar. Born in New York and educated at the University of Michigan and the University of Chicago, since 1971, Newton has taught at the State University of New York College at Purchase, where she is now Professor of Anthropology. In a series of important books, she has explored lesbian and gay studies, anthropology and homosexuality, history and human rights. They include *Mother Camp: Female Impersonators in America* (1972), *Amazon Expedition* (edited with Bertha Harris, Jill Johnston and Jane O'Wyatt, 1973), *Womenfriends* (with Shirley Walton, 1976) and *Cherry Grove, Fire Island: Sixty Years in America's First Gay and Lesbian Town* (1993); forthcoming publications include *Margaret Mead Made Me Gay: Personal Essays, Public Ideas* and *My Butch Career*. A founding member and co-chair of the Committee for the Center for Lesbian and Gay Scholarship at the City University of New York's Graduate Center, she has also served on the editorial boards of a number of scholarly journals and as an adviser for documentary films.

Robert Aldrich and Garry Wotherspoon

Nkoli, Tseko Simon (1957–98), South African activist. Nkoli was born in Soweto in a seSotho-speaking family. He grew up on a farm in the Free State and his family later moved to Sebokeng. Nkoli became a youth activist against apartheid, with the Congress of South African Students and with the United Democratic Front. In 1983 he joined the mainly white Gay Association of South Africa (GASA), and after coming out in an interview with *City Press*, he formed the Saturday Group, the first black gay group in Africa. After speaking at rallies in support of rent-boycotts in the Vaal townships, he was arrested in 1984 and faced the death penalty for treason with twenty-one other political leaders in the Delmas trial. By courageously coming out while a prisoner, he helped change the attitude of the African National Congress to gay rights. While many gay groups around the world wrote to him and supported his defence, the GASA and white-dominated gay organisations in South Africa refused to support someone charged with political crimes. He was acquitted and released from prison in 1988.

He founded the Gay and Lesbian Organisation of the Witwatersrand (GLOW) in 1988, and was later involved in black gay choirs and sports groups. He travelled widely and was given several human rights awards in Europe and North America. He was a member of the ILGA board, representing the African region. He was one of the first gay activists to meet with President MANDELA in 1994. As one of the leading personalities in the National Coalition for Gay and Lesbian Equality, he helped in the campaigns to retain the inclusion of protection from discrimination in the Bill of Rights in the 1994 South African constitution, and for the May 1998 repeal of the sodomy laws. He helped establish Soweto's Township AIDS Project in 1990, and worked there on community education campaigns until 1996. After becoming one of the first publicly HIV-positive African gay men, he initiated the Positive African Men group based in central Johannesburg. In the months before his death, supported by his British lover Rod Sharp, he was writing his memoirs, and was concerned with the anti-homosexual campaigns in neighbouring Zimbabwe, Namibia, Swaziland, Botswana and Zambia. Nkoli died in hospital in Johannesburg on the eve of World AIDS Day, on 30 November 1998. Memorial services for him were held in Sebokeng, and in the Anglican cathedrals in Johannesburg and Cape Town. The September 1999 Pride March in Johannesburg was dedicated to his memory, and a downtown street was renamed in his honour.

Edwin Cameron and Mark Gevisser (eds), *Defiant Desire* (Johannesburg, 1993); Mathew Krouse, *The Invisible Ghetto* (Johannesburg, 1993).

Ken Davis

Noble, Elaine (b. 1944), US politician. In 1974, Noble became the first openly lesbian or gay candidate to win electoral office at the state level in the United States, and among the first to even contest electoral office as uncloseted.

Noble first won election to the Massachusetts House of Representatives in 1974, from a Boston area district, instantly becoming a role model for many lesbians and gay men. She won re-election easily in 1976. During her second term, Anita BRYANT began her anti-gay crusade, and Noble came under more pressure than ever to speak out on behalf of lesbians and gays. The legislative and constituency demands to take up a wide range of issues made the pressure to focus more on sexual orientation difficult. Her sense that she could never do enough to please community members who wanted her to be 'the gay politician' contributed to a decision not to seek re-election in 1978, though she also faced a tough race as a result of major redistricting. Barney FRANK then contested and won the State House seat created in that boundary change. In 1980, she sought the Democratic nomination for the US Senate, but lost to the then-newcomer Paul Tsongas, and twice ran unsuccessfully for city council in the city of Cambridge (1991 and 1993), next door to Boston. When not in politics, she has worked in health-care administration and consulting.

Mark Thompson (ed.), *Long Road to Freedom*: The Advocate *History of the Gay and Lesbian Movement* (New York, 1994); Michael J. Turkus (ed.), *Gay and Lesbian Biography* (Detroit, 1997).

David Rayside

Norris, David (b. 1944), Irish political figure. A traditional education led to a degree in English from Trinity College Dublin, and a lectureship in the same institution as a popular Joyce scholar. He challenged the constitutionality of Irish anti-homosexual legislation (inherited from the British) and having lost in the Irish courts (there is no access to European courts until all domestic remedy is exhausted), took his case to the European

Court of Human Rights. He was represented by Mary Robinson, later to be Ireland's first woman President and an exact coeval of Norris's in Trinity. Though judgement was given in Norris's favour in 1988, effect was only given to this decision in 1993, after a procedural device was found that would not force deputies to endanger their electoral chances by being seen to vote for homosexuality (the Bill was presented, and by common consent, no one challenged it, so that a vote was avoided). Norris's razor wit, tempered (at least in his later years) by a reluctance to wound, won him wide popularity, and he was elected to the Irish Senate to represent the University of Dublin (regularly topping the poll) and became a broadcaster and public personality. He has many interests, including the preservation of Georgian architecture and the rights of travelling people. He is fond of saying that had he not been gay, he would have been unbearably conservative.

The Criminal Law (Sexual Offences) Act 1993, repealing old British legislation, was signed into effect on 7 July 1993 by President Robinson, so eliminating from the criminal law all discrimination against homosexuality. The age of consent is set at 17 for all sexual acts, and there are no restrictions on privacy that obtain for only one sexual group. The measure was steered through parliament by Ireland's first female Minister for Justice, Maire Geoghegan Quinn. Norris declined to support the Bill of which he was so widely considered the architect when it came to the Senate, because it included other provisions (increasing the penalties for prostitution): he said he could not 'accept my liberation without a murmur at the expense of the victimisation of another vulnerable group'. An important first step towards liberalisation had been taken in 1988, when the Incitement to Hatred Act, which makes it an offence to incite hatred or violence against certain groups, was amended at the last minute, at Norris's instigation, by including a reference to

sexual orientation. Though protections for sexual minorities in the workplace are planned, this is still not enacted. In housing, for example, there is still nothing to prevent discrimination against gay men in the provision of mortgages, which usually takes the form of a declaration that one is not gay, and an AIDS test before obligatory insurance cover is granted.

Victoria Freedman, *The Cities of David: The Life of David Norris* (Dublin, 1995); Maryann Gialenella Valiulis, *Gender and Sexuality in Modern Ireland* (Amherst, MA., 1997); Eibhear Walshe, *Sex, Nation and Dissent in Irish Writing* (Cork, 1997).

David Parris

Nureyev, Rudolf (1938–93), Russian dancer and choreographer. Even the birth of Rudolf Hametovich Nureyev, unquestionably one of the most dynamic personalities in twentieth-century dance, was dramatic: he was born on a trans-Siberian train, near Irkutsk, Siberia. Nureyev studied folk dance and ballet in Ufa, and later at the Leningrad Choreographic School. Word of his meteoric rise through the ranks of the Kirov Ballet within three short years reached the West prior to his Paris debut in 1961. His sensational reception by Parisian audiences inevitably led to his defection at Orly Airport as he was about to be recalled to the Soviet Union. He immediately found guest appearances with European ballet companies including Britain's Royal Ballet, where he met Erik BRUHN, the world's reigning *premier danseur noble*. Despite an instant artistic rivalry, the two men formed an immediate and durable yet frequently stormy, artistic and intimate relationship.

Nureyev's peripatetic career was driven by an insatiable desire to perform and to explore all aspects of his art. Although he found a permanent home between 1962–77 as Guest Artist with the Royal Ballet, Nureyev performed extensively throughout the United States, continental Europe and Australia, frequently staging his versions of classic full-length nineteenth-century ballets. His desire to extend his artistic range led to work with leading contemporary and modern dance choreographers including Martha Graham, Paul Taylor, Maurice Béjart, Rudi VAN DANTZIG, Glen Tetley, Jiri Kiljyan and Twyla Tharp.

A palpable animal magnetism and brooding sexuality, catalysed by his early partnership with legendary British *prima ballerina* Dame Margot Fonteyn, made Nureyev possibly the dance world's first true male superstar of the twentieth century. Within his first decade in the West, he became one of the most recognised personalities in the world, appealing to all ages and sexes – an androgynous pop culture icon as well as one of the great performing artists.

While fierce individuality made Nureyev a mesmerising performer of unique dramatic intensity and feral sensuality, he was never a multifaceted interpretive artist of particular sensitivity or depth. Although he worked with every major choreographer, he frequently was criticised for highly personal interpretations often in opposition to the choreographer's original intent. These disparities only intensified with advancing age and the waning of his technical prowess. With the exception of Frederick Ashton's *Marguerite and Armand*, a showcase for the sublime Nureyev–Fonteyn partnership, none of Nureyev's collaborations generated a significantly inspired work.

The reflected glory of his celebrity, however, reaped benefits for choreographers as well as for international ballet companies, especially the National Ballet of Canada and the Australian Ballet, which after serving as background for the superstar earned international reputations of their own. Although fiercely jealous of his own stardom, Nureyev fostered several major international careers of his ballerina partners, including Karen Kain, Noella Pontois and Sylvie Guillem and the emerging male stars Frank Augustyn, Patrick Dupond and Charles Jude.

In the 1970s and early 1980s, Nureyev made numerous European and US television appearances both as dancer and guest star, including *Sesame Street* (1977), and made critically disastrous appearances in the Ken Russell films *Valentino* (1977) and *Exposed* (1983). From 1983 to 1989, Nureyev served a stormy tenure as artistic director of the Paris Opera Ballet, which he nevertheless succeeded in restoring to its previous artistic prominence and international reputation.

After Bruhn, whose death in 1986 deeply affected him, Nureyev's most significant intimate relationships were with the *auteur* filmmaker Wallace Potts (*Le Beau Mec*), and dancer and author Robert Tracy. While involved in Nureyev's life for many years, Tracy reportedly ended their physical relationship when Nureyev refused to abandon promiscuity despite the threat of AIDS. In the early 1990s, Tracy, now HIV-positive, brought a palimony suit against the dying Nureyev and accepted an undisclosed financial settlement. Despite intense, occasionally physical, relationships with many women, including Fonteyn, Nureyev unquestionably preferred uncomplicated, immediately gratifying sexual relationships with men. Yet he never came out as a homosexual.

The effects of AIDS, diagnosed in 1985, and age diminished his once formidable dancing powers but not his tempestuous nature or obsession for work. Nureyev survived nearly eight more years in a whirlwind of performing, choreography, an ill-advised tour in *The King and I*, and, in his last years, orchestral conducting. He left an estate of nearly $US 40 million to two Nureyev Foundations in Europe and the United States, charities created for the support of young dancers and to underwrite scientific and medical research.

Peter Watson, *Nureyev: A Biography* (London, 1994); Otis Stuart, *Perpetual Motion: The Public and Private Lives of Rudolph Nureyev* (New York, 1995): Diane Solway, *Nureyev: His Life* (New York, 1998).

A.M. Wentink

O

Ocaña, José Pérez (1947–83), Spanish drag artist. Perhaps the best way to understand the importance of 'Ocaña' is to place him in the context of the Spanish transition. They were the best of times, they were the worst of times: a sense of freedom was combined with political uncertainty; there was a strong pressure to forget about the dark events of the past (all the deaths, betrayals, abuses, imprisonments of people just because they were different or they thought differently) and in the process the present situation was neglected. Thus whereas anything human, any 'deviant' from the norm, was regarded as acceptable, there was a strong resistance to giving specificity and political substance to particular ways of deviation. It is as if tolerance required one to forgo analysis. But between 1976 and circa 1980 there seemed to be a window of opportunity where everything was possible and everybody seemed to have a voice.

Ocaña was born in a small Andalusian village and from childhood experienced abuse and marginalisation for not conforming to expected gender stereotypes. His soft demeanour, his 'artistic' tastes, his inclination to 'dress up' put him in the public eye of intolerance, which, unusually, contributed to reinforcing his sense of identity. He moved to Barcelona in 1971, and started a process of creating a public identity which by the end of the 1970s would become legendary. He created a character that would become his masterpiece: more than a transvestite, he was an artist of the self. Ocaña performed his fantasies in the streets, in the public eye. His imaginative attire and his play with influences from popular culture made him a recognisable figure. Among such influences was religious art. The artist recognised the oppressive nature of religion in Spanish society and was aware of the way it was used against homosexuals, but at the same time recognised its sensual and emotional aspects. Religion and other Spanish traditions became for Ocaña the stuff of camp performance. The Ramblas was his favourite haunt and soon a number of other similarly-minded individuals followed him. His popularity was such that he even became a character in the comic books of gay cartoonist Nazario. Gay Catalan filmmaker Ventura Pons also paid homage to Ocaña in an impressive, fascinating short film made in 1978: *Ocaña, retrato intermitente* (*An Intermittent Portrait*).

As with many other protagonists of the Spanish sexual revolution of the 1970s, in Ocaña's public declarations we find a strong rejection of homosexuality as a category. He sees himself as an essentially individual person, and only asks to be allowed self-expression. Categories and fixed concepts such as 'gay culture' for him would be ways of reducing the complexity of his uniqueness. It is important, from an

Anglo-American perspective, to listen to such voices (something similar can be found in the work of many other Spanish and Latin American homosexual intellectuals): they may have a point and this can be helpful in escaping the over-determined nature of contemporary urban gay identities. However, the fact that Ocaña can be reduced to camp, the fact that he chose to express himself using imagery that had attracted other Spanish homosexuals and that had been consistently rejected by straight males, also points out some gaps in his argument and the beginning for a deconstruction of an identity too easily presented as 'essential'. Ocaña died as a result of an AIDS-related disease.

Teresa M. Vilarós, *El mono del desencanto. Una crítica cultural de la transición española* (Madrid, 1998).

Alberto Mira

Omann, Sven, a.k.a. Wanda Liszt (b. 1950), Danish activist and theatre manager. After secondary school Omann sailed for a year as a mess boy to the Far East and to the US West Coast. He returned to high school in 1969 but dropped out and moved to Copenhagen in 1971. He first lived and worked in the Socialistisk Plakatgruppe (Socialist Printers' Commune) where communal sleeping was *de rigueur*, then in Copenhagen's first gay collective, the Stormly. From 1974 to 1975 Omann travelled in India, the first of several extensive explorations of the sub-continent (1976–77, 1984, 1994, 1995), usually accompanied by activists from the Gay Liberation Front. Since 1987 Omann has lived in the Konesumpen (The House-wives' Swamp), a commune situated in Christiania, a hippie town founded in 1971 on an area of Copenhagen's eastern ramparts, formerly military barracks.

Early in 1973 Omann joined the Copenhagen Gay Liberation Front (Bøssernes Befrielses Front) which had started up in 1971. His acute powers of observation and analysis and his bewitching sense of hu-

mour together with a marked capability for discreet leadership soon made him a pace-setting activist. His steadying influence and tenacious vision of gay politics became an important and inspirational ingredient in the surge of gay liberation in Denmark in the 1970s. In 1976, during the height of gender-fuck activism, he took the name Wanda Liszt.

In April 1976 the Gay Liberation Front moved to its own premises, the Gay House (Bøssehuset) in Christiania. Over the following years its large hall was regularly used to stage more or less improvised revues, partly inspired by visiting theatre groups: *Brühwarm* (Berlin), *Blue Lips* (London), and *Hot Peaches* (New York). The Gay House also ran a non-licensed bar that on weekends drew an audience of gradually more sedate former gay liberationists hungering for sexually incorrect entertainment. By 1980 the Gay Liberation Front had metamorphosed into a theatre group, the Gay House, which has since staged a large number of plays and revues. Wanda has continued to play a central role as an author of revues, and as director and actor. His one-act play *Wanda's International Television Cooking* (1986), was a tribute to 'panic sexuality' and post-homosexual self-deconstruction of sexual identity, envisioned as the laying of eggs and the preparation of Christmas pudding.

Besides the staging of plays by or adapted from, among others, Jean GENET, Molière, the Marquis de Sade and Oscar Wilde (*The Importance of Being Earnest*, 1995, with Wanda as Lady Bracknell), mention should be made of Wanda's adaptation of William BURROUGH's *The Wild Boys* ('Just Call Me Joe', 1987), and Rainer Werner FASSBINDER's *Das Kaffeehaus* ('Sort Kaffe', 1990). Wanda's adaptation of the latter was later staged at the Royal Theatre. Although The Gay House in general has succeeded in staging plays and revues that were decidedly unfit for presentation elsewhere, the revue *Bruno's Kids' Band* (1985), about the stages of a normal male homosexual's life, ran successfully in a theatre in Copenhagen proper. Recently Wanda has authored several of the songs with paedophile themes performed by the Gay House group, *Schwanzensängerknaben* (in cooperation with Bent Jacobsen, a.k.a. Britta), and the revue *Inside the Bunker: Adolf's and Eva's Last Christmas* (1998), a comment on genetics and the Danish policy of immigration.

The AIDS epidemic of the 1980s took a heavy toll among the members of the Gay House. On a number of occasions not plays but funerals were staged. Wanda is the author of the harrowingly morbid and funny AIDS revues *All Is Quiet On The Pestern Front* ('Intet Nyt fra Pestfronten', 1987), and *Gone With The Plague* ('Borte Med Pesten', 1991).

Knud Vesterskov Video, *Bøssehuset Live* (Copenhagen, 1989); *Schwanzensängerknaben*, CD (Copenhagen, 1998).

Wilhelm von Rosen

Orton, Joe (1933–67), British author. Orton was called 'the Oscar Wilde of Welfare State gentility' and noted for his darkly witty plays, which often contained homosexual subtexts and innuendo.

Orton's first West End success, *Entertaining Mr. Sloane* (1964), concerns a sexy young amoral thug (Sloane) lusted after by his middle-aged landlady, Kath, and her brother, Ed, a shady businessman. The conniving Sloane exploits Ed's and Kath's desire, playing the combined role of son/lover/protégé to his advantage. This advantage shifts when Sloane kills Kath's and Ed's father (who is a witness to an earlier murder by Sloane), and they work out an arrangement with the pragmatic Sloane by which they will take turns sharing him sexually in exchange for covering up the murder.

Orton's last play, *What the Butler Saw* (1969), is a riotous farce set in a mental institution. Although employing traditional farcical devices (multiple doors, clothes-switching, assumed and mistaken

identities), the conventional lightness of the farce is transformed by Orton during the course of the play into a darkly funny frenzy of Dionysian excess. Orton remarked regarding the tone of this play: 'As I understand it, farce was originally very close to tragedy and differed only in the treatment of its themes – themes like rape, bastardy, prostitution' – all of which are addressed in the play, as well as blackmail, substance abuse, nymphomania, homosexuality, transvestitism, fetishism, incest, adultery and murder. His other published works are a novel, *Head to Toe* (1971), an unproduced screenplay commissioned by the Beatles, 'Up Against It' (1979), and two early unproduced plays, 'Fred and Madge' (1959) and 'The Visitors' (1961).

Since the publication of John Lahr's biography – *Prick Up Your Ears* – the basis for the 1987 film of the same name, directed by Stephen Frears and starring Gary Oldman – and the publication of *The Orton Diaries*, Orton's life as a sexual adventurer and his grisly death at the hands of his partner Kenneth Halliwell (who committed suicide) have become well known. However, Lahr's 'morality tale' misrepresents the nature of the relationship between Orton and Halliwell by reading their life together as little more than a preparation for the murder–suicide, the result of, in Lahr's opinion, Halliwell's failure as a writer and his jealousy of Orton's success. Simon Shepherd argues that society's homophobia and heterosexism, which allowed no role or recognition for Halliwell in Orton's public life in the theatrical world, strained the relationship and led to Halliwell's psychosis and their deaths.

Joe Orton, *The Complete Plays* (London, 1976); John Lahr (ed.), *The Orton Diaries* (New York, 1986); John Lahr, *Prick Up Your Ears* (New York, 1978); Simon Shepherd, *Because We're Queers: The Life and Crimes of Kenneth Halliwell and Joe Orton* (London, 1989).

Jason Boyd

Ottinger, Ulrike (b. 1942), German film-maker. The avant-garde filmmaker was born Ulrike Weinberg in Konstanz, Germany. She had no formal training in film, but studied art in Munich and Paris, and has been living in Berlin since 1973. During the rise of women's film in Germany during the 1970s, Ottinger was one of the few filmmakers directly to address lesbian themes. Her first film, *Laokoon und Söhne* (*Laokoon and Sons*), was made in 1972, in collaboration with the writer-actress Tabea Blumenschein. Ottinger uses surrealism, exaggeration and satire in her films, seeking to alienate the viewer's gaze and thus sharpen our consciousness of how society and its power structures work. She is particularly interested in what potential might exist for women within these structures.

Her best-known work is *Bildnis einer Trinkerin* (*Portrait of an Alcoholic*, 1979), an episodic account of the exploits of a rich and beautiful woman who goes to Berlin to drink herself to death. But a kind of cult status has been achieved by her earlier film *Madame X – eine absolute Herrscherin* (*Madame X – An Absolute Ruler*, 1977), in which a tyrannical female pirate takes on board a crew of women who are rebelling against convention. After a promising start, hierarchical power structures prevail, and the women slaughter each other. Her recent film, *Exile Shanghai* (1996) is a documentary of over four and a half hours in length, focusing on the Hongkew Jewish ghetto and including recollections of gay Shanghai.

Ottinger's work has been described as a basis for erotic women's cinema. At the other end of the scale she has found herself a target for feminist criticism because of her unwillingness – especially obvious in *Madame X* – to believe in a glorious triumph of female community. She has also staged theatre productions in collaboration with Elfriede Jelinek, the Austrian dramatist who is notorious for her use of shocking and grotesque material. Other films include *Die Betörung der Blauen Matrosen* (*The Bewitching of the Blue Sailors*, 1975), *Freak Orlando* (1981), a free interpretation of Virginia Woolf's novel, *Dorian Gray im Spiegel der Boulevardpresse* (*Dorian Gray as Mirrored in the Tabloids*, 1984), *China – die Künste, der Alltag* (*China – The Arts and Everyday Life*, 1985), *Joan of Arc of Mongolia* (1988), and *Taiga* (1991–2).

Sandra Frieden, 'Ulrike Ottinger', in Friederike Eigler and Susanne Kord (eds), *The Feminist Encyclopedia of German Literature* (Westport, CT, 1997); Sandra Frieden *et al.* (eds), *Gender and German Cinema*, 2 vols (Providence, RI, 1993); Petra Lüschow, 'Ulrike Ottingers Kino', *Rundbrief Film, Filme im Lesbisch-Schwulen Kontext* (Oct./ Nov. 1995).

Sarah Colvin

P

Panero, Leopoldo María (b. 1948), Spanish poet. The ways in which a given author's sexual orientation find their way into his or her work are not predictable. Homoeroticism, camp or insistent representation of homosexuality are typical ways in which this happens, but they are by no means the only possibilities. Something in the writing of Leopoldo María Panero is closely related to his sexuality, and yet the articulation between the former and the latter is by no means easy to define.

Panero belongs to a wealthy family strongly identified with Francoism. His father was Leopoldo Panero, one of the most important Spanish poets under the regime, whose work unambiguously supported the fascist ethos. He was a severe, often violent man, perceived by his children as a threatening patriarchal figure: strong and distant, fascinating and forbidding. Leopoldo María's mother, Felicidad Blanc, was also a strong personality: fiercely defensive of her class values, manipulative and egotistical, she attempted to preserve her world view at all costs and impose it on others, most significantly on her children. The intensity of the young poet's relationship with both parents, who in different ways represent both the law and death, are the key references in his work. He suffered from strong psychological pressures and asked to be interned in an asylum, which he came to regard as a protective shell against the chaos of the external world. His relationship with language is conflictual, and his work explores the limits of meaning when the law of the father has to be rejected in order to achieve survival and self-realisation. Castrating mothers and vampire-like lovers, lustful and incestuous, can be made out both in his poetry and in his short narrative pieces (see, for instance, the poem entitled 'Ma mère', in which the poet's mother laughs as she sees her son's dismembered body being devoured by eagles and snakes). The landscape of Panero's imagination is that of the family as Oedipal nightmare re-worked as a gothic plot. On the other hand, his poetry show a fondness for the world of childhood. Alice and Peter Pan are recurring images, figures in a paradise that never existed and that will eventually prove impossible. Homosexuality in his work is therefore articulated in terms of rebellion against the Oedipal law. Given the strongly subjective character of his poems, homosexuality is hardly presented as something desirable or even erotic: in Panero's emotional shipwreck it is enough if it helps to give some sense of selfhood, to keep the head above water. In spite of all this, an undercurrent of playful humour permeates his work and is a sign of his survival. Around himself, he gathers fragments of literature that are meant to protect him from annihilation, and among these literary references is a clear preference for the world of children's books or gay authors. His poetry has been collected in *Un agujero llamado Nevermore* (1992), and *El lugar del hijo* (1976) gathers most of his chilling shorter fiction.

Leopoldo María Panero, *Un agujero llamado Nevermore* (Madrid, 1992).

Alberto Mira

Parker, Pauline Yvonne (b. 1938), and **Hulme, Juliet** (b. 1938), New Zealand murderers. Parker was born in Christchurch, New Zealand, to Honora Parker and Herbert Rieper, who were living falsely as a married couple although Rieper had not divorced his first wife. The Riepers were working-class, Herbert managing a small local fish shop and Honora housing boarders in the family home. Hulme was born in Liverpool, England, and was the daughter of wealthy parents. Her father, Henry Hulme, after lecturing in mathematics at the University of Liverpool, served as Chief Assistant at the Royal Observatory, Greenwich, from 1936 to 1938. In 1948, he was appointed Rector of Canterbury University College, Christchurch, New Zealand. Hilda Hulme, Juliet's mother, was the daughter of an Anglican minister. After settlement in Christchurch, she became involved in the Marriage Guidance Council and served as the Council's representative on the Canterbury Council of Social Services.

Parker and Hulme met in 1952 at Christchurch Girls' High School, where they formed an immediate and intense friendship. Pauline's diaries for 1953 and 1954 recorded their activities together, which included the usual schoolgirl activities but also included a remarkable amount of writing, including six co-authored novels, numerous plays, poetry and an opera. They constructed an elaborate fantasy world and acted out the parts of their characters' romances. Most of their activities took place at the Hulmes', as the Riepers' home had little privacy and Pauline's relationship with her

mother was turbulent. Medical advice was sought after concerns were raised about the girls sleeping and taking baths together. In late 1953, Henry Hulme and the Riepers discussed how the relationship might be broken apart, and Honora Parker took Pauline to a doctor, who informed her that he thought Pauline was going through a homosexual phase.

The crisis which immediately precipitated the murder arose when the Hulmes' marriage disintegrated, after Henry Hulme had been forced to resign following the deterioration of his relationship with the college and Hilda Hulme had revealed that she had been having an affair. Henry Hulme announced his intention to take Juliet with him to England. Pauline in particular was upset by this, because she had grown attached not only to Juliet but also to the Hulmes and their lifestyle. She and Juliet had plans to travel together to America. Pauline regarded her mother as the main obstacle to her being able to leave with Juliet, and in April 1954 she began to consider murder. She announced her plan to Juliet, who was concerned but not opposed.

On 22 June 1954, the two girls murdered Honora Parker during a stroll in the woods. Their manner after the murder was sufficiently unusual to make them immediate suspects, and the discovery of Parker's diary containing plans for the killing resulted in their speedy arrest. The trial of Parker and Hulme focused on the relationship between them. The prosecution argued that the murder was the premeditated act of two girls who saw their victim as an obstacle to their remaining together. The defence argued that it was a case of *folie à deux* or joint insanity. Both sides agreed that Pauline and Juliet were homosexual, the prosecution suggesting that it was a schoolgirlish phase of little import, the defence arguing that it was an element of their insanity. The girls were found guilty and sentenced to imprisonment, having avoided the death penalty by virtue of their youth. They were kept in separate prisons until they both were released in 1959 with new identities. Juliet left for England to join her mother, and Pauline remained in New Zealand on probation until 1965, after which she also left the country.

The Parker and Hulme case was immortalised in film with the release in 1994 of Peter Jackson's *Heavenly Creatures*, an examination of the imaginary world the two friends created and the events leading up to the murder itself. The publicity surrounding the film led to the discovery by journalists of Juliet Hulme, now living in Britain as the internationally renowned mystery writer Anne Perry, and Pauline Parker, also residing in Britain, under the name Hilary Nathan. When interviewed about the case, Perry firmly denied that there was ever a lesbian component to the relationship. Nathan has declined to comment. Despite Perry's assertion that the girls were not lesbian, it may nevertheless be said that the Parker/Hulme case is an important part of New Zealand lesbian history because the relationship was interpreted as lesbian at the time and was used as a symbol of the evils of lesbianism in the decades that followed. Pauline Parker's diaries featured in both the defence and the prosecution, and much was made in the courtroom and the media about those entries which seemed to suggest not only that the girls had slept together, but also that they had at least simulated lovemaking and had been aware that caution was required lest the Hulmes discover what they were doing. The prosecution was to call them 'two highly intelligent and perfectly sane but precocious and dirty-minded girls'. The link that was made between lesbianism and murder in the Parker – Hulme case was repeated in subsequent decades in the media and in the cautionary tales told to young lesbians by their parents.

Julie Glamuzina and Alison J. Laurie, *Parker & Hulme: A Lesbian View* (Auckland, 1991).

Karen Duder

Pasolini, Pier Paolo (1922–75), Italian writer, film director, critic. To call Pier Paolo Pasolini the *enfant terrible* of Italian post-war culture would understate the extent to which he was a perpetual thorn in the side of the Italian establishment, and would efface the complex mixture of admiration and revulsion which surrounded Pasolini both when he was alive and after his death. Pasolini, in short, was one of Italy's most controversial twentieth-century cultural figures, and also one of Italy's best-known gay men.

Pasolini was born in Bologna in the same year that Mussolini came to power, into a family whose middle-class status consisted of a precarious balance: his father came from an aristocratic family but had gambled away his small patrimony and had a career in the army; his mother's family had peasant origins, and she worked as a primary school teacher. The family moved frequently for the first 14 years of Pasolini's life, but resettled in Bologna in 1936. It was here that Pier Paolo finished high school and began his university career in the early 1940s.

As a student Pasolini was passionately interested in literature and poetry, and in 1941 he founded a journal of poetry with three friends. They called it *Eredi*, to express the four founders' sense that they were heirs of the great Italian poets such as Ungaretti and Montale. In 1942 Pasolini used his own money to publish a volume of poems, *Poesie a Casarsa*. Casarsa was his mother's home town, in the north-eastern province of Friuli, where the family used to take holidays. The poems made extensive use of the Friulian dialect that was peculiar to the province. Pasolini's interest in dialect as the expression of 'the people' was to become a motif of his later work. It was also the reason why the volume only received notices in a Swiss newspaper, since the fascists frowned on dialects as un-Italian and unpatriotic.

In 1943 Pasolini was briefly drafted into the army, but after the Allied liberation of southern Italy and the collapse of the fascist regime in September, he joined his mother in Friuli. He completed his university thesis on the poetry of Pascoli and took his degree in November 1945. For the next five years Pasolini taught literature at various schools, but did not get a stable job. He was swept up in the political uncertainty and excitement of those years, and joined the Communist Party, which for a brief moment in the mid-1940s seemed poised to inherit the mantle of the Italian anti-fascist Resistance, and with it the chance to shape society anew.

It was also during the late 1940s that Pasolini's homosexuality helped ensure that he did not remain a little-known left-wing school teacher in the provinces. He enthusiastically pursued the sexual opportunities offered by the Friulian *ragazzi di vita*, the adolescent street boys and peasants who for Pasolini embodied both the innocence and sensuality of a sub-proletariat untainted by the strictures of bourgeois morality. But by October 1949 Pasolini had been caught by those strictures: a local priest denounced him to the authorities and he was charged with corrupting minors and committing obscene acts in public places. As a result, Pasolini lost his job, and the communist newspaper, *L'Unità*, announced his ejection from the party, for 'moral and political indignity'. Pasolini swore that he would remain a communist despite party edicts.

In the winter of 1949 Pasolini fled to Rome. The following year the prosecution failed for lack of evidence, but the Italian justice system was to hound Pasolini throughout his life and even beyond (he was at the centre of no fewer than thirty-three judicial proceedings between 1950 and 1977). Eking out an initially miserable living in Rome giving private lessons and proof-reading, Pasolini began to enter Rome's cultural circles and he continued to write. In 1948 he had written *Amado mio*, about the love of the protagonist, Desiderio, for the very young Benito. *Amado mio*, although then unpublished, had been followed by *Atti impuri* (1949) and *Ali*

degli occhi azzurri (1950). In each of these novels the author was preoccupied with the now classic Pasolinian subject of adolescent males, and he used dialect both as an escape from what he saw as the traditional linguistic prison, and as a metaphor for an escape from traditional morality. Pasolini later developed these themes in a Roman context with *Ragazzi di vita* (1955) and *Una vita violenta* (1959). These novels, set largely in the contemporary Roman *borgate* (the squalid peripheral estates built to house the postwar homeless), represent the successful transfer from Friuli to Rome of the author's continuing fascination with those who struggled for existence, their locales, their language and their sensuality.

Although Pasolini's literary works attracted the attention of critics and a discerning public, their audience was restricted, and it was through the film world that he became a major cultural figure. In Rome he had become friends with the novelist Giorgio Bassani, and in 1953 Bassani found Pasolini some script-editing work in the film industry. Pasolini went on to work with several important directors, and gave advice about Roman dialect to Fellini for *Le notti di Cabiria* (1956) and *La notte brava* (1959). As well as a gradual shift in interest to the film world, the 1950s were also a period of mutation in Pasolini's political outlook. This essentially stemmed from an ideological crisis engendered by Pasolini's disillusionment with the USSR, coupled with an emerging sense of the inexorable power of the capitalist system to absorb all social classes through consumerism. The work which best expresses this turning point in Pasolini's political outlook is *Le ceneri di Gramsci*, effectively a novel in verse, which won Pasolini the prestigious Viareggio prize and established his position among Italy's intellectual elite.

This position made it easier for Pasolini to branch out on his own into the film world, and throughout the 1960s he was almost exclusively involved in film and theatre. He directed *Accatone* in 1961 – Accatone being the protagonist, a character of Rome's periphery, rough and primordial, acting principally on his physical instincts. The film caused a sensation when it was first shown at the Venice film festival. It was followed by *Mamma Roma* (1962), and *La Ricotta* (1963), and these films of the early 1960s represent the first phase of Pasolini's career in film. By the end of the 1960s the ideological crisis expressed in *Le ceneri di Gramsci* had matured into the mourning for a lost subproletariat class, which Pasolini felt had been beguiled by consumerism, and his later work reflects this shift. Although all his films are to some extent critiques of the bourgeois world, they became more introspective, religious and influenced by Freudian theory. Among his noteworthy productions were *Oedipus Rex* (1967), *Teorema* (1968), *Medea* (1970), and the *Trilogy of Life – The Decameron* (1971), *The Canterbury Tales* (1972) and *The Thousand and One Nights* (1974). Pasolini's last film was *Salò or the 120 Days of Sodom* (1975). Released posthumously, it was also his most controversial film, representing quite graphically the writings of the Marquis de Sade set against the last days of Italy's fascist regime.

Although film became Pasolini's primary medium, he continued to write, particularly on literary and film theory. *Empirismo eretico* (1972) is a collection of many of his essays published between 1964 and 1971, chiefly on questions of linguistics and semiology. He also wrote several plays, and his *Manifesto per il nuovo teatro* (1968) presents his theoretical position on the theatre. In 1972 Pasolini began to write a new novel, *Petrolio*, intended to be both an autobiographical work as well as an apocalyptic vision of Italy in the early 1970s. The draft of the novel lay unfinished when Pasolini died, and was only published in 1992.

Between the late 1960s and 1975 Pasolini raised his already controversial public profile with regular contributions to the mainstream press, waging a personal campaign against what he saw as the ills of Italian (and Western) society. He was a political renegade who refused to toe any particular party line. For example, during the student protests in 1968 he sided with the police (whom he regarded as the true sons of the poor) rather than the students (whom he considered spoiled bourgeois brats). In early 1975 he declared himself against abortion, claiming that the so-called sexual revolution was part of the bourgeoisification of the masses. His peculiar position against sexual liberation, especially in view of his own homosexuality, has engaged many subsequent critics, and has ensured that the debate about Pasolini continues. But his intervention on the subject was one among many, his preferred subjects being the themes of cultural homogenisation, consumerism, neocapitalism and the disappearance of the 'pure' sub-proletariat. Pasolini was always polemical, and he always received attention. His best articles were collected and published as *Scritti corsari* (1975).

At dawn on 2 November 1975, Pasolini's body was found by the police near a wharf in Ostia, on the outskirts of Rome. His body had been run over by his own car after his murder, and although it was established that the culprit had been a young man whom Pasolini had picked up for sex, controversy has always surrounded Pasolini's death: many were convinced that the half-heartedness of the trial suggested that this brilliant but uncomfortable cultural thorn had been 'removed' from the side of the Italian establishment, and that there was more to his death than a random act of violence.

Stefano Casi (ed.), *Desiderio di Pasolini. Omosessualità, arte e impegno intellettuale* (Turin, 1990); Naomi Greene, *Pier Paolo Pasolini: Cinema as Heresy* (Princeton, 1990); Luigi Martellini, *Introduzione a Pasolini* (Roma, 1989); Enzo Siciliano, *Vita di Pasolini* (2nd edn, Florence, 1995).

Mark Seymour

Pasqual, Lluís (b. 1951), Spanish stage director. Pasqual's production of Federico García Lorca's *El público* in 1987 was a milestone in twentieth-century Spanish theatre. Not only this was the first 'official' performance of an obscure text by a canonical Spanish playwright, but Pasqual's innovative work dared to make explicit the play's homoeroticism. As is often the case with Spanish critics, homosexuality was ignored in reviews, but audiences could not help being faced with images that referred to love between men. Whereas a later British production of the same work used a 'gay identity' approach (through the use of camp language, boas, in-your-face effeminacy), Pasqual just represented the sexual acts, coming perhaps closer to Lorca's intentions. Although he has never overstated his sexual identity, he has never made any efforts to conceal it, and an appearance on a television programme with a T-shirt with a printed pink triangle was enthusiastically commented on by Spanish gay critics. Pasqual is representative of the relaxed (but still silent) attitude the Spanish theatrical world has towards homosexuality: at one point in the late 1980s, it seemed that all the major figures in stage direction (with the exception of Alfonso Marsillach) happened to be gay or bisexual.

Pasqual studied humanities in Barcelona and started working in the theatre as an actor. He joined small touring companies in Catalonia (La Tartana-Teatre Estudi, Grup d'Estudis Teatrals d'Horta). Later he became a diction teacher at the Escola de Teatre de l'Orfeó de Sants. In the 1970s he worked with several Catalan singers, such as Lluis Llach and Maria del Mar Bonet, whose concerts he directed. During that period, he represented Spain in several international conferences on theatre. As a director, he built his reputation on his work for the Teatre Lliure (Barcelona) in the early 1980s. He also spent study periods in Poland, where he collaborated with the National Theatre of Warsaw. In the early 1980s he moved to Madrid to become director of the National Theatre, and in 1991 he was made director of the Théâtre de l'Odéon in Paris, where he designed programming and directed several well-received productions. He has worked on a Brecht adaptation of Marlowe's *Edward II* (1978), in which he emphasised the homoerotic attraction of Gaveston. Among his most important productions are Chekhov's *Three Sisters* (1978), an extraordinary version of Jean GENET's *The Balcony* (1980), Calderón's *La hija del aire* (1981) and Shakespeare's *As You Like It* (1982), which he recreated in Paris ten years later. He has also been successful in directing opera, and his production of Verdi's *Don Carlo* was widely acclaimed.

Alberto Mira

Pastre, Geneviève (b. 1924), French writer and publisher. A Frenchwoman born in Germany, Pastre earned the highest teaching qualification in France (the *agrégation*); for many years she taught classics in school and also directed a theatre company. She was married for eight years, but by the mid-1970s had begun to live and write as a lesbian, though at first not openly; she also became involved in the women's liberation movement. In 1980, she published *De l'Amour lesbien* (*On Lesbian Love*), a pioneering philosophical and anthropological study. Several years later she became president of Fréquence Gaie, a gay and lesbian radio station. She then created the Association des Octaviennes, a society of women writers, many of whom were lesbian, which later became the publishing house Les Octaviennes. In 1987, she published *Athènes et le péril saphique* (*Athens and the Sapphic Peril*), which Lionel Povert says was intended as a response to Michael FOUCAULT's history of sexuality; Pastre accused Foucault of having a faulty knowledge of both the ancient Greek language and lesbianism. In 1990, Pastre organised a festival of European gay and lesbian writers.

Pastre is one of a small number of

lesbian theorists in the world of letters in France; others include Monique WITTIG and Marie-Jo BONNET. Her writing, publishing and activism have made her one of the best-known and most respected lesbian public figures there.

Lionel Povert, *Dictionnaire Gay* (Paris, 1994), pp. 363–5; Frédéric Martel, *Le Rose et le noir. Les homosexuels en France depuis 1968* (Paris, 1996).

Robert Aldrich

'Patient Zero' (a.k.a. Gaëtan Dugas) (dates uncertain), Canadian AIDS figure. There is no doubt that Gaëtan Dugas led a very interesting life which would provide the material for a readable biography, but he was in many ways a very ordinary gay man of the late twentieth century. In the 1970s, the French-Canadian was employed as an international airline steward. Thus he was a young man able to travel the world in search of adventure and romance and, from his own accounts, he found both in abundance and had a number of sexual partners around the globe. There was nothing remarkable at all about his life until he became the central figure in the American hunt for the origin and cause of HIV/AIDS.

The Dugas story has two origins, depending on the source, though the scenarios overlap – just where will remain a matter of conjecture. In both, Dugas is the central figure and fills the role of a very convenient scapegoat for a society seeking an explanation for the advent of a new disease. In the East Coast version, in September 1979 Dr Linda Laubensten at the New York University Medical Centre examined a young man who had developed a purplish lesion on his neck: this was later diagnosed as Kaposi's Sarcoma (KS). Prior to the advent of AIDS, KS was considered to affect only older men of Mediterranean origin. Laubensten referred her patient to a colleague, Dr Kenneth Hymes. Two weeks later Hymes examined a 37-year-old man who had also

been diagnosed as having KS. Following further discussions, Laubensten discovered that both men had a sexual partner in common, Gaëtan Dugas.

In the West Coast story, in the early 1980s two Center for Disease Control investigators (Bill Darrow, a sociologist, and David Auerbach, an epidemiologist) were investigating the incidence of gay-related immune deficiency (GRID – an early name for AIDS) in Los Angeles. One of their interviewees reported that 'there are two other guys in the hospital with the disease right now, and I know they had sex with my lover'. Further investigation showed that many of the men in Los Angeles affected by GRID were sexually linked. Two of the men, who were unacquainted, independently mentioned a handsome French-Canadian flight attendant: Gaëtan Dugas.

Both versions explain the origins of the invention of 'Patient Zero'. Whilst investigation of the origins and transmission of disease is an epidemiologist's legitimate pursuit, the search for 'Patient Zero' went well beyond mere scientific investigation. During the initial years of the epidemic the medical and scientific communities knew little about AIDS: this lack of knowledge fuelled community conjecture and heightened the public's fears about the disease. In the early days of the epidemic it was clearly established that AIDS was linked in some way to urban gay men living in the industrialised nations. Commentators and politicians conveniently speculated that lifestyle choices of gay men – such as promiscuity, drug usage and 'unnatural' acts – led to the development of what was initially know as GRID. Whilst it is true that this speculation was later proved to have some scientific basis, much of the conjecture was directly targeted at further sullying public impressions of gay men. One of the most spurious suggestions was that the disease had a racial origin – gay men visiting Haiti had supposedly contracted the disease during their visits to the country. It was in this search for a cause and even a scapegoat that the 'Patient Zero' story gained prominence in several scientific and government circles.

As Dugas was a common link between many of the first cases of AIDS, some people concluded that in fact he started AIDS. That he and his contacts were homosexual led to a perception that the disease was limited to male homosexuals. As we now know, most of this speculation was not only wrong in fact, but also flawed in terms of scientific rigour. In many ways Dugas was a 'perfect' find for those seeking a scapegoat. During interviews he displayed considerable 'candour and swagger', he seemed 'unconcerned' about what he had 'done' and was able to recall many of his sexual exploits and brag about anticipated future encounters. He was a very marketable media product and reportedly enjoyed his media exposure.

For some, Gaëtan Dugas or 'Patient Zero' became a very convenient but short-lived scapegoat. History has shown that he was just a small but significant piece in the AIDS jigsaw. His story is important in that scientists were able to confirm the notion that AIDS was spread through sexual contact.

M. D. Grmek, *History of Aids: Emergence and Origin of a Modern Pandemic* (Princeton, 1990); R. Shilts, 'Patient Zero: The Man who Brought the AIDS Epidemic to California', *California*, Oct. 1987, pp. 96–9, 149, 160; L. Garrett, *The Coming Plague: Newly Emerging Disease in a World Out of Balance* (Harmondsworth, 1995).

Mark Edwards

Patrioli, Tony (Antonio) (b. 1941), Italian photographer. Patrioli was born in Manerbio (Brescia) and lives in Milan. He began to take pictures as an amateur in 1965, choosing the male nude as his subject and using his lovers as models. When he received an offer to publish his photographs commercially in the mid-1970s, Patrioli completed a course in advertising photography in Milan.

'I began as an erotic photographer and I make no apologies for it', Patrioli says. Unlike other Italian photographers of male nudes, such as Angelo Fallai, Giampaolo Barbieri and Dino Pedriali, Patrioli from the outset, and explicitly, directed his work at a gay audience, and came out as homosexual in *Homo* in the 1970s. The same magazine published his first softcore photographs (and later hardcore ones). From 1976 to 1986 Patrioli produced photographs for this and other Italian and international magazines (especially in northern Europe). 'Erotic photos were the only nude photos for which there was a market at this time. There were no books of nude photos, and no market for them', he remembers.

Patrioli nevertheless took an interest in nude photos of a more artistic sort, initially inspired by the work of Wilhelm von Gloeden, 'partly because Gloeden was the only photographer of the male nude who was not banned in Italy at the time, partly because his fantasies coincided with my own. The physical culture photos from America seemed too far from the world and the youths which I saw all around me'. Patrioli thus portrayed and documented the last stage of a particular Mediterranean culture which disappeared in Italy in the wake of the 'sexual revolution' – young men who, although always heterosexual, were available for homo-erotic activities if they had no access to heterosexual ones. In his work, they were always youths from the south of Italy, clearly amused by the narcissistic game of posing for the photographer yet anxious about exhibiting their sexual desirability to those who, according to the mores of the time, had no right to their bodies.

Changes in the market for photographs allowed Patrioli to publish his first book of male nudes, *Mediterraneo*, in 1984; it went through two Italian and two American editions. In the book, Patrioli created a precise typology from the youths whom he photographed: around 18-years old, with olive skin, both wild and playful and, above all, very 'Mediterranean'. This image appealed to the market and Patrioli followed with other books of photographs published in Italy, France and the United States, including *Garçons de la Mediterranée (Ragazzi)* (1985), *La specchio di Narciso* (1987), *Ragazzi (2): Garçons des deux Siciles* (1987), *Ephebi* (1989), *Sunbeams* (1989), *Cartoline* (1991) and *Made in Italy* (1994).

The disappearance of the very Mediterranean society in which these works were produced, as well as a move away from softcore pictures in erotic publishing and, in particular, the triumph of American musclemen in gay photography, led Patrioli to retire, and he now takes pictures only for his own enjoyment.

Giovanni Dall'Orto

Pears, Peter see BRITTEN.

Pegge, John (1944–95), South African activist. Pegge was first and foremost an HIV/AIDS activist. In the early 1980s, together with Gordon Isaacs, he started a gay support group called GASA-6010. With the first reported cases of AIDS in South Africa, circa 1983, they initiated an education campaign alerting the gay community to the dangers of HIV. GASA-6010, in which Pegge was a driving force, started education and training programmes which extended beyond the gay community. Homosexuality in South Africa was illegal at the time, yet Pegge managed to get the Department of Health to supply the organisation with condoms via a circuitous route. As early as 1985, he and others, through national and international lobbying attempts, tried to alert South Africans to all areas which would be affected by HIV/AIDS. These warnings however fell on deaf ears. Pegge was a tireless campaigner for the rights and dignity of persons with HIV/AIDS.

Gay and Lesbian Archives, University of the Witwatersrand Libraries, Johannesburg.

Graeme Reid

Penna, Sandro (1906–77), Italian poet. Penna was probably the only modern Italian poet who unabashedly expressed homoerotic love in his poetry. Penna was also unusual for the extent of his estrangement from developments in poetry such as hermeticism, neo-realism and avant-gardism, all of which exerted a strong influence on most Italian poets during Penna's lifetime. Because he has not been considered 'representative' by critics, for a long period he occupied only a marginal place in Italian literary criticism, despite winning several major prizes for his work. In recent years though, his poems have attracted renewed interest, and his entry into the canon of Italian poets was symbolised by a retrospective exhibition in Rome in 1997, held to commemorate the twentieth anniversary of his death.

Penna was the eldest of three children in a middle-class family which ran a reasonably successful shop in Perugia, central Italy. He was a sickly, delicate child, and he suffered emotionally as a result of his parents' unhappy marriage. In 1916, when Sandro was 10, his father returned from the war with syphilis, and his parents' arguments worsened. In 1920 his mother left her husband and went to live in Rome, leaving the children with their father. Penna felt the absence of his mother very much, and dedicated some of his earliest verses to her. He had to miss a period of school in his mid-teens because he became ill with pleurisy, and he stayed with his mother in Rome. The discovery of Italy's capital at the age of 16 enchanted Penna, and from then on he spent as much time there as possible. In 1925 he completed high school, and was qualified to work as a clerk.

Penna's first job was in his father's shop, but the unsettled mood of his childhood did not leave him as he entered adulthood. He suffered from long periods of depression, and felt that he had been psychologically disturbed as a result of being torn away from his mother as a child. He had become aware of his attraction to wild young boys through his 12-year-old cousin Quintilio, the first boy to be mentioned in Penna's diary. And by the late 1920s it was clear that he was having regular encounters with *ragazzi*. For example, he became infatuated with Ernesto, a Jewish boy of 15 whom Penna had met on a tram in Rome. The many letters he wrote to Ernesto, but never sent, are testimony to the desperation of his attraction. Although Penna did not appear to have suffered guilt as a result of his feelings for boys, those feelings certainly contributed to his sometimes overwhelming sense of being an outsider, someone who was unable to resign himself to the norm. A constant characteristic of Penna's poetry is a sense of the pressing urge to understand his place in the world, and to come to terms with a haunting and uncontrollable alternation between happiness and sadness.

Nevertheless, he did not simply resign himself to his emotional problems. After his father sacked him from his job in 1929, Penna moved to Rome permanently, where he lived with his mother and worked in a series of clerical jobs. He wrote to a medical doctor about his problem seeking advice, particularly on the question of homosexuality. At a time when it was still considered a disease, Penna wrote touchingly that what he felt was no different from what other men felt for women. In 1930 he underwent analysis by a Freudian doctor, but the most important result of the analysis was the fact that his doctor introduced Penna to the well-known poet Umberto Saba. This was Penna's introduction to the world of Italian letters, and in 1932 he had two poems published on the front page of the important journal *L'Italia letteraria*. Penna's talent was immediately recognised and much appreciated by writers like Carlo Emilio GADDA and Eugenio Montale, with whom he soon became friends.

Recognition, and increasingly, publication, did not help Penna's chronic depression or indigence. Throughout the 1930s Penna scraped a living out of odd jobs and the charity of his new-found literary friends. He worked briefly as an editor for *L'Italia letteraria*, and in 1936 a clerical job enabled him to rent a private room where he could write, though he continued to live with his mother. But these jobs never lasted long because Penna could not bear working to a predetermined rhythm. He had more success when he started to deal in rare books, for which he discovered a particular flair, and later he moved on to dealing in paintings. He continued dealing in books and paintings, with varying degrees of success, for the rest of his life. Nevertheless, Penna was always financially insecure, and always depended on the care of his friends. Later in his life, when he became quite well known, he even installed a collection box in the café beneath his apartment labelled 'Donations for Sandro Penna'.

Penna's not-of-this-world air also necessitated the tutelage of his friends when it came to publishing his poems. From the very beginning of their friendship, Montale advised Penna about which of his poems might run into censorship problems. And when, in 1939, Meridiana published a small volume of Penna's poems entitled *Poesie*, Montale had made sure that it contained no risky ones. The publication of *Poesie* ensured the recognition of Pennas's unique poetic voice, and prompted letters of admiration from people like De Pisis and COMISSO, who also became his friends. During the war Penna wrote less poetry, and he was reduced to selling soap and second-hand clothes to earn a living. Once the war was over Penna returned to writing, and in 1950 he published 37 poems in a volume entitled *Appunti*. Pier Paolo PASOLINI wrote a glowing but acute review for *Il Popolo*, discerning the sadness hidden beneath the apparently boyish happiness of the poems. Penna and Pasolini became firm friends from that point, spending much time wandering Rome in search of boys.

In 1956 Penna published another collection of poems, *Una strana gioia di vivere*.

Only 500 copies were printed, and the volume attracted little attention in the mainstream press. But it catered to Penna's growing audience of dedicated readers, and won him the Le Grazie prize. The judges included Piero SANTI and Carlo Gadda. The following year, Penna published a second volume with the title *Poesie* (the first volume of this name had appeared in 1939), containing many of the poems written between 1927 and 1957, including those which had been left out of the original volume. The new collection caused a stir in Italian literary circles, and even before any reviews had been published, it was announced that Penna would share the Viareggio prize with Pasolini and Mondadori. In the prevailing cold war climate, the choice of Penna and Pasolini caused a scandal, and was denounced on the Right as the decadent triumph of leftist pornography.

In 1956 Penna met the 14-year-old Raffaele, a street boy who had run away from home at the age of six. They became lovers and the boy moved in with Penna and his begrudging mother. It was a stormy, intense relationship which suffered several ruptures before Raffaele's final departure, but it also gave much pleasure and solace to Penna. He and Raffaele bought a German Shepherd puppy which they named Black, and once Raffaele was old enough to drive, Penna bought a car. This enabled them to spend many idyllic afternoons walking the dog in the countryside outside Rome. When, after fourteen years of intermittent cohabitation, Raffaele left to get married, all he took with him was Black. During subsequent years he granted Penna access to Black on a limited basis, as if she were their child. Penna whimsically thought that Black offered much of what he sought but did not find in boys: innocence, absolute faith and a complete absence of jealousy or malice.

Throughout the 1960s and 1970s Penna became increasingly eccentric in his personal habits, but also increasingly well known as a poet. In 1970 Garzanti reissued all Penna's previously published poems. These were read by a wide audience and the publication garnered him the Fiuggi prize that year. It is difficult to discern the extent to which the homoerotic themes that are undoubtedly central to Penna's poetry attracted or disturbed the Italian reading public. What does seem clear is that the poems transcended the banality of sex and entered another realm. Certainly, young boys occupy pride of place in Penna's poems, but they do so as symbols of innocence and naturalness, in a way which makes it clear that they are not subject to the laws of civilisation. The sense of freedom from these laws which pervades Penna's poetry, as well as their beautiful, limpid wording and structure, goes a long way towards explaining their appeal – and perhaps ironically, towards explaining why the poet himself largely escaped proscription.

Penna died in Rome, just a few days after winning the prestigious Bagutta prize for *Stranezze*, a collection of 119 previously unpublished poems written between 1957 and 1976.

Gualtiero De Santi, *Sandro Penna* (Florence, 1982); Elio Pecora, *Sandro Penna. Una biografia* (Milan, 1990).

Mark Seymour

Penteado, Darcy (1926–87), Brazilian author, painter and activist. Born in the state of São Paulo, Darcy Penteado had a successful career as a painter, society portraitist, stage designer and book illustrator. In the late 1970s and 1980s he became a spokesman for the emerging Brazilian lesbian and gay movement, giving interviews and appearing in newspaper and magazine articles. He was one of the founding members of the editorial board of *Lampião*, the first Brazilian gay newspaper, which appeared regularly between April 1978 and June 1981.

In later life Penteado turned to literature, publishing three collections of stories, a novel and a book of childhood recollections. These appeared at a critical time in the history of the Brazilian gay community, between the liberalisation of the repressive military regime of the early 1970s and the onset of the worldwide AIDS epidemic in the early 1980s. Although not great works of literature, they are representative of their period, one of political optimism and sexual freedom. Penteado's short stories are generally light-hearted, humorous and fantastic, with the conscious aim of depicting a positive image of contemporary gay life. Mostly they present an amusing picture of the lifestyle of the affluent middle-class gay male, leavened with touches of irony and the occasional encounter with the other world of poverty, hustling and homophobia. Although some verge on banality or didacticism, the more successful ones show an awareness of the underlying social reality. Several have been translated into English and published by Gay Sunshine Press in two anthologies of Latin American gay literature, *Now the Volcano* and *My Deep Dark Pain is Love*.

'Conto de Fadas Número Dois' (translated as 'Snow White Revisited') recounts with tongue-in-cheek irony how a queen builds a glass-fronted tomb in the woods where he goes cruising; after his death the tomb becomes a tourist attraction and then a place of religious pilgrimage. 'Jarbas o Imaginoso' (Jarbas the Imaginative) describes how a young gay man creates a series of fantasies for the amusement of his older lovers. In 'Bofe a Prazo Fixo' (Part-time Hustler) Penteado successfully treats a potentially difficult theme with a mixture of humour and light sentimentality: Angelo, a young straight worker, has sex with a rich homosexual in order to make enough money to marry; after the marriage they remain good friends and Angelo invites his ex-partner to be god-father to his first child.

Other stories have a more serious undertone. 'Capim Australiano, ou o Amor para Toda a Vida' (Australian Grass, or a Love to Last a Lifetime) portrays an experienced middle-aged gay man who cruises the bars, picking up partners. His relationships are transitory but not entirely devoid of emotion. He falls in love with a gymnastics teacher, but when the latter is not available he is quite content to go off with someone else. In other stories, a more sombre reality intrudes in the form of a delinquent hustler, a disabled black man or an unemployed worker forced to prostitute himself.

In two works which have not been translated, Penteado makes a sustained effort to create a utopian vision of gay life. 'Espartanos' (Spartans), a novella, paints an idyllic picture of three generations of masculine gay men who live together in harmony, ignoring social conventions and personal jealousies. The work is self-consciously optimistic and visionary but the absence of conflict results in a lack of tension which detracts from its effect aesthetically.

Penteado's most ambitious work was the full-length novel *Nivaldo e Jerônimo* (1981). Set in the dark days of the military regime, it describes the relationship between Jerônimo, a committed left-wing guerrilla, and Nivaldo, an attractive but apolitical younger man, who fall in love with each other. Despite their dangerous situation, they manage to spend some ecstatic days together, aided by sympathetic straight people, but when the older man appears to be killed in an ambush, Nivaldo attempts to commit suicide and then drifts into a life of prostitution and drugs. He ends up performing in a transvestite show where he catches sight in the audience of Jerônimo, who has survived his ordeal. The novel frequently descends into sentimentality and melodrama, and the ending is unconvincing. But it nevertheless represents an interesting attempt in fiction to bridge the gap between class and sexual politics. It aims to show that, in the political context of Brazil, homosexuals suffer from a repressive regime as much as the heterosexual population, and to portray a gay man who fights courageously for a political cause and for his own personal and sexual fulfilment.

Darcy Penteado, 'Australian Grass, or a Love to Last a Lifetime', 'Part-time Hustler', in Winston Leyland (ed.), *My Deep Dark Pain is Love: A Collection of Latin American Gay Fiction* (San Francisco, 1983), pp. 225–44; 'Snow White Revisited', 'Jarbas the Imaginative', in Winston Leyland (ed.), *Now the Volcano: An Anthology of Latin American Gay Literature* (San Francisco, 1979), pp. 237–53; David William Foster, *Gay and Lesbian Themes in Latin American Writing* (Austin, TX, 1991), pp. 76–80.

Robert Howes

Pereleshin, Valery (pseudonym of Valery Frantsevich Salatko-Petrishche) (1913–92), Russian poet. Born in Irkutsk, Siberia, into the family of a civil servant, he found himself at the age of seven, with his mother and brother, in Harbin, Manchuria, one of the main centres of Russian émigré life after the Bolshevik revolution. In 1935 he received a law degree from the local Russian-language university, where he stayed on as a researcher; however, the university was closed by Manchuria's Japanese occupying authorities in 1937. In 1938, he took monastic vows and soon moved to Beijing, where he worked at the Russian church mission, at the same time pursuing studies of Chinese language and literature. In 1943, he moved to Shanghai, where at the end of World War II he renounced his monastic vows and briefly worked for the Soviet news agency, TASS. In 1950, he attempted emigrating to the US, but was deported back to China on suspicion of being a communist sympathiser. In 1953, after many travails, he arrived with his mother in Rio de Janeiro, where he lived for the rest of his life. His first years there were extremely difficult and spent in poverty; his life acquired a degree of stability only in the 1960s, when he began an appointment at the local office of the British Council.

Pereleshin's first poem was published in a Harbin Russian-language newspaper in 1928; his first collection of poetry, *On My Way*, came out in 1937, followed by three more books of poems, in 1939, 1941 and 1944; in the 1940s, he also published several poetic translations from Chinese and English. After a prolonged silence, he then returned to writing in the late 1960s, with the publication of his fifth collection of poems, *A Southern Home* (1968). However, in the 1970s Pereleshin's talent developed with a truly explosive strength. Over the next two decades, he published eight collections of original poetry, a book-length *Poem Without a Subject* (1989), as well as memoirs on Russian literary life in China in the 1930s and 1940s and numerous translations of classical Chinese poetry into Russian, and of Russian poetry into Portuguese (most notably *The Alexandrian Songs* of Russia's greatest gay poet, Mikhail Kuzmin).

Pereleshin's poetry is unusual in the Russian tradition in its combination of conservative strict metric forms and of a very contemporary, lively and rich vocabulary. He was also unique due to his combination of cultural backgrounds (Russian, Chinese, Brazilian) and his outspokenness in his writing about his sexual feelings towards other men. His ninth and arguably best book of poems, *Ariel* (1976), a collection of sonnets inspired by an epistolary love affair with a young literary scholar in Moscow, offers some of the most inspired gay love poetry in Russian, ranging in its tone from tender to sado-masochistic. His other books offer fascinating examples of cross-cultural dialogue, describing his relationships with Chinese and Brazilian men. A poet of great technical skill and passion, Pereleshin was the leading Russian gay writer of the generation shaped by the revolution of 1917. Writing in distant China and Brazil, he formed a bridge between the flowering of Russian gay literature at the beginning of the century and the rebirth of gay writing in Russia in the final years of the Soviet empire.

Thomas Hauth (ed.), *Russian Literary and Ecclesiastical Life in Manchuria and China from 1920 to 1952: Unpublished Memoirs of Valerij Perelesin* (The Hague, 1996); Jan Paul Hinrichs (ed.), *Russian Poetry and Literary Life in Harbin and Shanghai, 1930–1950: The Memoirs of Valerij Perelesin* (Amsterdam, 1987); Jan Paul Hinrichs, 'Introduction', in Valerii Pereleshin, *Russkil poet v gostiakh u Kitaia, 1920–1952: Sbornik stikhotvorenii* (The Hague, 1989); Iurii Linnik, 'Valerii Pereleshin', *Navyi Zhurnal*, no. 189 (1992), pp. 227–56; Kevin Moss (ed.), *Out of the Blue: Russia's Hidden Gay Literature; An Anthology* (San Francisco, 1997); Aleksis Rannit, 'O Poezii I poetike Valeriia Pereleshina; Shesi' pervykh sbornikov poeta (1937–1971)', *Russian Language Journal*, no. 106 (1976), pp. 79–104.

Vitaly Chernetsky

Peri Rossi, Cristina (b. 1941), Uruguayan writer. The recipient of numerous important literary awards, Peri Rossi has resided in Spain since the early 1970s. In 1969, her book *Los museos abandonados* received the award for young writers from Arca Editorial; she also won the Marcha's Prize for her novel *El libro de mis primos* (1969). Peri Rossi's writing distinguishes itself for its criticism of social and political institutions as well as gender constructions and sex roles. Keeping the sexual meanings ambiguous and the presence of transgressive acts – such as incestuous relationships – characterise her works.

Her poetry and fiction deal extensively with issues of sexual identities. Peri Rossi's poetry collection *Evohé* (1976) encodes lesbian eroticism through the use of male and female pronouns. This gesture of articulating lesbian eroticism through the use of male and female pronouns allows the speaker to discuss lesbian erotic desire in the form of heterosexual desire.

The collection intertwines lesbian eroticism with a self-reflexive discourse. The speaker establishes a connection between the female body, language and poetry, words and women, the poet and the lover. The collection emerges from the pain of the separation of the lovers, and the male speaker states that he has found refuge in words after disappointments with women. Not willing to be seduced by the charm of words, he connects women's seductive powers with those of the words. Throughout the collection, the words 'woman' and 'language' are interchangeable.

In *Descripción de un naufragio* (1975), the female lover is identified with marine geography and the speaker uses marine metaphors to speak of the female body. In one of the poems of *Diáspora* (1976), the speaker confronts a male-oriented tradition that has objectified women by presenting a woman who makes public her lesbian identity. Here, the objectified woman assumes the role of the subject by making a political statement. She declares her sexual orientation as a way to re-affirm her existence.

In *Lingüística general* (1979), Peri Rossi investigates, as in *Evohé*, the relationship of language, meanings, grammar and gender categories. Whereas in the latter Peri Rossi uses a system of encoding lesbian eroticism and love, the theme of lesbianism is openly addressed in *Lingüística general*. *Desastres íntimos* (1997), Peri Rossi's latest collection of short stories, deals with the themes of love, desire, gender constructions and subjectivity.

Peri Rossi's presentation of lesbian and gay themes and issues challenge traditional views on identity, thus proclaiming the need to break away from established forms and the status quo.

Carmen Domínguez, 'Cristina Peri Rossi', in David William Foster (ed.), *Latin American Writers on Gay and Lesbian Themes: A Bio-Critical Sourcebook* (Westport, CT, 1994), pp. 316–21.

Elena M. Martínez

Perry, Troy D. (b. 1940), American cleric. Perry is a Christian in spite of Christianity: he was thrown out of two Protestant denominations for being gay, yet ended up founding a Christian church – the largest of its kind – that primarily serves the needs of gay men and lesbians, the Universal Fellowship of Metropolitan Community Churches.

Perry was born in Florida and grew up there and in Georgia and Texas. Familiar with both Pentecostal and Baptist traditions, by the age of 15 he was licensed to preach by a local Baptist church. After he was expelled from his second Pentecostal denomination for being gay (and having his wife – a minister's daughter – and children leave him), in 1968 he held a worship service for a dozen people in his home in Huntington Park, California, the beginning of the Metropolitan Community Church (MCC). In an interview in *The Christian Century* in 1996, Perry recalled: 'If you had told me 28 years ago that the largest organization in the world touching the lives of gays and lesbians would be a church, I would not have believed you. So many members of the lesbian and gay community feel that they have had violence done to them by religious groups that it is very difficult to evangelize any members of our community. But we do evangelize.' Yet, in 1992, the American National Council of Churches denied not only membership to the Metropolitan Community Church but also observer status. But Perry did not take that as a bad sign, the MCC being granted observer status with the World Council of Churches.

The MCC has the oldest ongoing AIDS ministry of any Christian denomination in the United States. Members of the MCC are unashamed to be both gay and Christian. According to Perry, 'I am very hopeful about our future. I used to say years ago that we were working to put ourselves out of business . . . . I see now that we will not be shutting our doors, and that there is a need for our church. Today there are gays and lesbians in church groups outside of my own denomination, but there are tens of thousands [over 46,000] who want to be part of the Universal Fellowship of Metropolitan Community Churches. We continue to expand and grow and carry

the good news that Jesus died for our sins, not our sexuality.'

Troy D. Perry, *Don't Be Afraid Anymore: The Story of Reverend Troy Perry and the Metropolitan Community Churches* (New York, 1990); *The Lord is My Shepherd and He Knows I'm Gay: The Autobiography of the Reverend Troy D. Perry* (Los Angeles, 1972); 'Gays and the Gospel: An Interview with Troy Perry', *The Christian Century*, vol. 113. no. 27 (1996), p. 896.
Lee Arnold

Pet Shop Boys (Chris Lowe, b. 1959, and Neil Tennant, b. 1954). English pop group the Pet Shop Boys command an impressive critical and popular following, having honed – in the words of one critic – 'disco music with an intensely intellectual appeal'. They have also consistently – if unintentionally – imbued their music with the 'open secret' of homosexuality, while maintaining an ambivalent public stance in relation to gay culture.

Lowe grew up in Blackpool, and played in a seven-piece jazz band, 'One Under The Eight', in the late 1970s. Tennant was raised a Catholic in Newcastle, and was a contributor and deputy editor for British pop magazine *Smash Hits*. The pair met in a hi-fi store in the early 1980s, and were soon writing songs together. Although they had originally intended to search for another singer, Tennant's provisional vocals on early recordings became the rule. They parted company with their first producer Bobby 'O' Orlando after the general failure of their debut single, 'West End Girls'. The same song, however, earned the duo widespread recognition when it was re-produced by Stephen Hague, who also helmed the debut album *Please* (1986). On this and subsequent albums – such as *Actually* (1987), *Behaviour* (1989) and the critically lauded *Very* (1993) – Tennant's penchant for classical music neatly dovetailed with Lowe's interest in contemporary dance genres, an effective combination on the dance-oriented economy of the English pop market.

From the onset, the Pet Shop Boys rejected several facets of traditional rock music aesthetics. Tennant boasted about his vocal limitations, while Lowe proudly highlighted programming tricks on their recordings; both were resolutely opposed to the contrived mystique which many rock musicians still perpetuate. Most significantly, their output disrupted conventional codes of gender and sexuality, with allusions to homsexuality proliferating. The single 'So Hard' (1991) calculatedly appropriated the polished synthesiser and drum programming which characterised 1970s Giorgio Moroder/Donna Summer records (the apotheosis of gay disco). On its B-side, 'It Must Be Obvious', Tennant represented his love in the image of social disorder ('oh no, I will upset the status quo'). Just as telling as their actual music has been their choice of collaborators over the years: 'What Have I Done To Deserve This?' (1987) was a successful duet with Dusty SPRINGFIELD; Liza Minelli's 1989 album *Results* was written and produced by Lowe and Tennant. The latter admits: 'The idea of the Pet Shop Boys recording with Liza Minelli is camp in itself'.

The duo have attracted adverse publicity from gay critical quarters, with several journalists decrying their public reticence on all matters sexual. Tennant eventually relented by officially 'coming out' to British gay magazine *Attitude* in August 1994; Lowe remained typically taciturn. The singer drew a useful distinction between the outlook of gay activist Jimmy SOMERVILLE (who had been one of their detractors) and the Pet Shop Boys: whereas the former used pop simply as a political platform, the latter's primary concern was producing pop music. And if Tennant's lyrics could be construed as discernably 'homosexual', then this was simply because 'I have written songs from my own point of view'. The duo's 'outing' process is overtly paralleled on recent recordings. *Bilingual* (1996) eschews the ironic detachment of years gone by (1987's

'Rent', for example) in favour of a new-found earnestness ('Metamorphosis'). The lyrics of 'A Red Letter Day' dedicate the song to 'all of those who don't fit in/Who follow their instincts and are told they sin'.

It could be argued that this banal univocality exemplifies the incommensurability of socio-political commentary and pop music. But perhaps Lowe's and Tennant's significance lies more in their ability to infuse pop musical tropes with a contemporary gay sensibility, particularly in an era when the conservative cultural agenda of Thatcherite England is still being felt.

Paul Burston, 'Neil Tennant: Honestly', *What Are You Looking At?: Queer Sex, Style and Cinema* (London, 1995) pp. 80–91; John Gill, 'Pet Shop Boys: Naturally', *Queer Noises: Male and Female Homosexuality in Twentieth-Century Music* (London, 1995), pp. 1–9; Chris Heath, *Pet Shop Boys, Literally* (Middlesex, 1991).

Adrian Renzo

Peyrefitte, Roger (b. 1907), French author. Born at Castres in the south-western department of Tarn, Peyrefitte was educated in Catholic boarding schools in that region, then briefly studied agriculture in Montpellier before finally graduating from the prestigious École libre des sciences politiques in Paris in 1930. He went into the diplomatic service and was embassy secretary in Athens from 1933 to 1938. He then returned to Paris, and in October 1940 resigned after a near-scandal involving an adolescent boy. He joined the service again in 1943 and was appointed to a post in Paris, where he stayed until expelled by a tribunal in 1945 on suspicion of collaboration. That decision was annulled in 1960. In 1944–45 he launched his literary career with his best known work, *Les Amitiés particulières*, for which he was awarded the Prix Renaudot. The personal history of his pederasty, of which he made little secret after 1945, he finally committed to paper in his *Propos* *secrets* (1977), where he describes his puritanism as a schoolboy, his initiation into anal sex with partners of both genders, and his final confirmation of his preference for adolescent boys during his secondment to the Athens embassy. On his return to Paris, he decided to renounce cruising after one or two brushes with the Paris police, but seems to have had no difficulty in pursuing his interests in private. He was a member of André BAUDRY's organisation Arcadie and supported the discreet pressures of that organisation for homosexual law reform. The love of his life appears to have been Alain-Philippe Malagnac, the schoolboy who played the role of Alexandre in the 1964 film of *Les Amitiés particulières*. Their relationship gave rise to another novel, *Notre amour* (1967), which itself became a subject of scandal. At the age of 16, having completed his *baccalauréat*, Malagnac became Peyrefitte's secretary for the period when he composed *Des Français*, *La Coloquinte* and *Manouche*. They also travelled together, following in the footsteps of Alexander the Great. Peyrefitte's writings have been prolific, though none have attained the stature or popularity of his first novel. His waspish taste for *romans à clefs* was indulged in such works as *Les Ambassades* (1951) and *La Fin des Ambassades* (1953), based on his experiences in the diplomatic corps, *Les Juifs* (1965) and *Des Français* (1970). His particular bugbear is the Catholic Church and its hypocritical attitude to homosexuality in general and pederasty in particular; he has tirelessly propagated the rumour of the homosexuality of Paul VI. His most consistently pederastic book is *Roy* (1979), which describes in explicit detail the sexual escapades of a Californian teenager from a rich family, who prostitutes himself for fun to a number of powerful men, starting with the Los Angeles chief of police. It is a work which well illustrates the relationship between pederasty and social rank which Peyrefitte has consistently exploited in his own life. There have also been

further autobiographical revelations in his *L'Innominato: Nouveaux propos secrets* (1989).

Roger Peyrefitte, *Propos secrets* (Paris, 1977).

Christopher Robinson

Picano, Felice (b. 1944), American writer. Born the son of a grocer in New York, Picano was educated at the City University of New York, and travelled to Europe. He settled in Greenwich Village in the early 1960s, and had a varied career, as a social worker, assistant editor and bookstore manager, before venturing into freelance writing. He was a founding member of the Violet Quill club, a group of young gay writers in New York in the 1970s, who gave each other critical and emotional support at a time when writing gay literature and getting it published was anything but easy.

Picano has been active in gay politics – he was a member of the Gay Activists Alliance – and in gay publishing: he was the founder and publisher of The Sea Horse Press (the first gay publishing house on the US east coast), and cofounder and co-publisher of Gay Presses of New York.

He has published some seventeen books, authoring fifteen, ranging from thrillers such as *The Lure* (1979) (which catapulted him to fame), to self-help books such as *The New Joy of Gay Sex* (with Charles Silverstein, 1992). Other titles include *The Deformity Lover and Other Poems* (1978), *Ambidextrous: The Secret Lives of Children* (1985), and *Men Who Loved Me* (1989). His books have charted gay life in the US over the past few decades – at precisely the time when the lesbian and gay subcultures have experienced a previously unimaginable flowering – and will provide an excellent resource for future historians. His own attempt at an historical novel, *Like People in History* (1995), charts the lives of two gay cousins over the last four decades, covering everything from the emergence of the Counterculture to the impact of the AIDS epidemic.

Contemporary Authors (NRS), vol. 52 (Detroit, 1996).

Garry Wotherspoon

Pierre & Gilles (Pierre Commoy and Gilles Blanchard) (b. *c.* 1950), French pop artists. Their art is instantly recognisable and it turns up everywhere in the gay world, not only on gallery walls, but also on advertising posters, magazine covers and record albums. The men themselves, however, remain almost entirely unknown. Both were born in western France in the early 1950s, Pierre in La Roche-sur-Yonne and Gilles in Le Havre. Pierre studied photography in Geneva, served in the army and settled in Paris in 1973, where he worked as a photographer for music and fashion magazines. In the same year, after studying painting in Le Havre, Gilles also came to Paris and found work as an illustrator. The two men met at a party in 1976, went home together that very night and have been inseparable ever since: 'We were different, but complementary. We got on so well that our work gradually overlapped and blended together. It just felt better that way.'

Most of their work takes the form of portraits of friends and celebrities. They produce two or three a month. They plan the decors, costumes and make-up together. Pierre then takes the photographs, which Gilles carefully retouches and transforms with bright acrylic paint 'in order to soften a contrast, to idealize, to whiten a tooth'. This creates striking images with an artificial and dreamlike quality: a sexy young toreador ringed with bright red roses; the singer BOY GEORGE as a blue-tinged Hindu god; the porn star Aiden Shaw, naked with his penis erect, ensconced on a pile of plush toy animals.

According to art critic Dan Cameron, 'While maintaining a resolutely homosexual stance, their art borrows shamelessly from pictorial conventions of the nineteenth century, the twenties, the fifties, and even the seventies.' Many describe their work as camp or kitsch and see in it a loosely defined 'gay aesthetic' of flamboyance, superficiality, artificiality, sentimentality, sexiness and glamour. But there is no conscious irony or derision in their images. Pierre & Gilles's commitment to their art is wholly sincere. They say that their work is 'sentimental' – 'we invent a more beautiful world' – but deny that it is camp or kitsch. 'For us, it's a whole: life, work, friends, models . . . In what we express through our work and our way of life, we show who we are. It's a way of being militant.'

In 1993 the City of Paris awarded them its Grand Prix de la Photographie. In 1996, for the twentieth anniversary of their meeting, the Maison Européenne de la Photographie in Paris mounted a retrospective exposition of their work.

Pierre et Gilles: un naturel confondant: entretien avec Michel Nuridsany (Paris, 1994); Stéphane Trieulat, 'Pierre & Gilles', *Têtu* (Dec. 1996); 'Pierre et Gilles ont 20 ans!', *Idol* (Nov. 1996); Barnard Marcadé and Dan Cameron, *Pierre et Gilles: The Complete Works* (Cologne, 1997).

Michael Sibalis

Piñera, Virgilio (1912–79), Cuban writer. Piñera's work is quickly regaining the prestige and reputation it reached in the late 1940s, when his play *Electra Garrigó* (1948) became an international success. His work for the theatre, his short stories and novels, together with his autobiographical writings, show a world in which a paranoid fear of the body is crossed with high camp. Such an irreverent combination can be read as a way of standing up to official realities through mockery, which has been read as essentially Caribbean. His fate as a writer under Castro sadly illustrates the bleakest side of the Cuban revolution. He was born into the utmost poverty, something too common in pre-Castro Cuba. In this sense,

Piñera is a representative of the class whose fate should have been improved by the Revolution, a cause he embraced (somewhat sceptically, it is true). Yet, his writings were forbidden in 1968, he was silenced, forced to earn a living as a translator, and would die in misery, lonely and forgotten. What happened in the intervening years is one more reminder of the flaws of a revolutionary creed that, at the very best, felt embarrassed by homosexuality and at worst made clear that gays could never be part of the New Cuba. Homophobia (supported, one must add, by intellectual stupidity and lack of a sense of humour) became stronger than any political ideology.

Homosexuality does not appear in Piñera's fiction writings, and this has led critics to suggest that he was a closeted gay who concealed his sexual identity: if there is a homosexual point of view in his work, this is expressed through fear of both discovery and of his own body. This opinion is actually open to discussion and reveals the flaws of projecting an Anglo-American theoretical framework (dominated by issues of 'homosexual identiti(es)') onto a Caribbean writer. In this context, the limits of the closet are blurred. In his autobiography, Piñera clearly says that from a very early age, he was aware of three 'gorgons' that would haunt him all of his life: the first was poverty, the second homosexuality, the third his artistic inclinations. This has been read as a manifestation of homosexual self-hate which is very off-the-mark in the context of Piñera's reflections. The three 'gorgons' are oppressive, it is true, and this shows unease about homosexuality. But it is important to notice that oppression is not rooted in self-hate, but in social intolerance. Piñera did not consider homosexuality bad in itself, but as something that could bring him trouble. And it did. Most importantly, he proceeds to link homosexuality to artistic impulses (he tells the reader how he used to like to read out poetry attired in drag before he managed

to become sexually active). From his own account, one may come to the conclusion that it was not his homosexuality that made him into a sad person (maybe quite the opposite). Reinaldo ARENAS included a moving account of Piñera's personality in his own autobiographical *Before the Night Falls*.

Piñera left the village where he was born to explore both his artistic instincts and his homosexuality: he went to Havana where he started a career in the theatre. He belonged to the main intellectual coterie of his time and befriended José LEZAMA LIMA, with whom he would develop a sometimes problematic relationship. When the triviality of his circle and his own artistic failure became unbearable, he travelled to Buenos Aires, where he met Jorge Luis Borges in 1946. It is interesting to notice how he disliked him for 'taking art too seriously'. Again, this is a mark of the sense of mockery that runs through all of his work. At that time, he also met the Polish writer Witold GOMBROWICZ, with whom, according to Arenas, he went out at night looking for sex. On his return to Cuba, he achieved theatrical success and wrote for several intellectual magazines before the Revolution. Publication of his novella *Presiones y diamantes* (1968) made him suspect of dissidence, and for the remainder of his life he became a nonperson, officially banned from work and under constant threat of imprisonment. His writing does show a bleak view of life, most obvious in the short stories and in novels such as *La carne de René* (*René's Flesh*), and a painful, disturbing view of the body is central to his aesthetics. But despair is not exclusive to homosexuals. Even those living in Cuba.

José Quiroga, 'Fleshing Out Virgilio Piñera from the Cuban Closet', in Emilie L. Bergmann and Paul Julian Smith *¿Entiendes? Queer Readings, Hispanic Writings* (eds), (Durham, 1995).

Alberto Mira

Pittenger, (William) Norman (1905–97), American theologian and educator. Born into a prosperous Episcopalian (Anglican) family in New Jersey, United States, he received his schooling in Princeton. He then worked as a freelance journalist and, although not an enrolled student, attended some classes at Princeton University and Princeton Theological Seminary. In 1933 he commenced training for the priesthood in the Episcopal Church at General Theological Seminary in New York and in 1937 was ordained priest. He was awarded the degree of Master of Sacred Theology in 1940 but never completed his doctoral thesis in the philosophy of religion. Subsequently he was awarded honorary doctorates in theology by Berkeley Divinity School (1949) and General Theological Seminary (1966).

For thirty years Pittenger taught theology at General Theological Seminary; first, from 1935, as an instructor, then as a fellow and finally as a professor. From 1952 until his retirement in 1966 he was the Charles Lewis Gomph Professor of Apologetics. He was also active in many Anglican and ecumenical organisations. In 1966 he moved permanently to England where he became a senior member of King's College, Cambridge. Although he never held an academic post in the college, he made much of his connection.

Pittenger was an enthusiastic teacher; he loved talking. Between 1936 and 1983, he recalled, he delivered 5,297 lectures, addresses and sermons and lectured in some 220 academic institutions. He wrote more than eighty books. His written work fell broadly into two areas: the Christian understanding of Jesus Christ and the relation between the Christian faith and modern culture. Many of his writings were fluent rather than profound; in jest he claimed he was the Barbara Cartland of theology.

In his theology Pittenger saw himself as a liberal in the Catholic tradition of Anglicanism. He regarded some of the traditional Christian doctrines as incompatible with modern knowledge; on several occasions conservative Anglicans accused him of heresy. During the 1940s Pittenger was converted to process theology, a radical theological movement of philosophical theology originating in the US that emphasises the processive or evolutionary nature of God, the creation and humanity. It was on the basis of process theology that he later developed a theology of sexuality which challenged many of the prohibitions of traditional Christianity.

The first of Pittenger's writings on homosexuality was an essay in an English journal in 1967 which led to a booklet called *Time for Consent? A Christian's Approach to Homosexuality*. Although ignored by the English church press, it brought him a large correspondence. In 1970 it reappeared in a revised and enlarged edition under the same title but without the question mark. *Time for Consent* was notable as the first work in the English language by a prominent theologian that argued for the full acceptance of homosexual relationships by the Christian Church. As such it was influential among a generation of gay Christians. After the publication of this book Pittenger became open about his own homosexuality. He established his first long-term gay relationship with Carlo [surname unknown], whom he met in Italy, and quietly supported the gay movement.

R. A. Norris (ed.), *Lux in Lumine: Essays to Honor W. Norman Pittenger* (New York, 1966); Norman Pittenger, 'An Unimportant Life: Memories of Persons, Places, and Work' (1985), unpublished typescript, St Mark's Library, General Theological Seminary, New York; Norman Pittenger, *Time for Consent: A Christian's Approach to Homosexuality* (London, 1970); obituaries, *Church Times* (London), 11 July 1997, and *The Independent* (London), 28 June 1997.

David Hilliard

Pizarnik, Alejandra (1936–72), Argentinian writer. Pizarnik was born in Buenos

Aires to a Jewish family that had immigrated from Eastern Europe. She began writing poetry in her teens; she studied philosophy, literature and journalism. In 1955 she began to paint under the tutelage of the Uruguayan artist Juan Batlle Planas; a sense of the visual is omnipresent in all her writing (poetry, prose, diary and correspondence). That same year she produced translations of the French Surrealists Paul Eluard and André Breton with her professor and mentor, Juan Jacobo Bajarlía, who – just as Pizarnik was beginning to be claimed by some of her critics for the emerging canon of queer writers in Latin America – published in 1998 a 'tell-all' memoir about his supposed romance with the teenaged budding poet.

In 1960 Pizarnik travelled to Paris, where she lived for four years, some of the most productive and creative of her short life. She wrote for literary magazines, translated French writers into Spanish, dabbled in coursework at the Sorbonne, and befriended important literary and cultural figures, such as Mexican poet Octavio Paz and Argentinian novelist Julio Cortázar. In the late 1960s, back in Buenos Aires, Pizarnik began to receive important recognition (the Buenos Aires First Prize for Poetry in 1966; a Guggenheim Fellowship in 1968; a Fulbright scholarship in 1971). Paradoxically, she manifested increasingly acute symptoms of the mental disorders which had begun, perhaps, many years before: cyclical anxiety and depression. After attempting to take her own life several times and being hospitalised in a psychiatric clinic, she died of an overdose of seconal.

Whether the overdose was intentional or not may never be known; however, as Ana María Fagundo has pointed out (and many other critics have echoed), Pizarnik's poetry 'was "death-driven" from the very start'. To the extent that Pizarnik is known at all, it has been, until recently, overwhelmingly as myth or persona, rather than as poet. She has been grouped with

other famous women writers who have committed suicide, such as Alfonsina Storni, Violeta Parra, Sylvia Plath, Anne Sexton and Virginia Woolf. Pizarnik has also been read as 'a *maudite* poet'; her biographer Cristina Piña places her in the line of the '*poètes maudits*' of the nineteenth century: Rimbaud, Lautréamont, Baudelaire, Mallarmé and Nerval. She was also deeply influenced by Surrealists, especially Antonin Artaud.

Pizarnik's own words seductively lead critics to this kind of attribution of mythic or '*maudit*' status to her work, as she frequently cites or alludes to poets such as Rimbaud in her poetry and journals. She shared the Surrealist notion of converting life into a poetic act, and made a number of well-known suggestive statements to this effect, such as: 'I wish I could live only in ecstasy, making the body of the poem with my body.'

Although several critics have pointed to a kind of double silencing – Pizarnik's texts do not contain obvious signs of her sexual orientation and most critics until recently have assiduously avoided this topic – the importance of Pizarnik for gay and lesbian history should not be underestimated. She had relationships with (mostly, significantly older) men – during her adolescence especially – as well as with women, during her stay in Paris and toward the end of her life. Piná confirms that her 'last and greatest love' was a woman. Perhaps the most obvious place to look for signs of lesbianism is in Pizarnik's 'unauthorised' or private writing, best known through the posthumous volume *Textos de Sombra* (*Shadow Texts*), of 1982, and published fragments of her diaries. The publication of a substantial volume of her correspondence is inestimably important in this regard.

The disturbing and beautiful *La condesa sangrienta* (*The Bloody Countess*) (1965), a series of prose vignettes about the (historical) Hungarian countess Erszebet Báthory, who sexually tortured and murdered over 600 young women in a frenzied attempt to quell her melancholia and find eternal youth, is the text in which several critics have identified Pizarnik's most graphic representation of lesbianism. Nevertheless, hints of a queer sexuality can be found in several of the seven volumes of lyric poetry published during her lifetime, dating from *La tierra más ajena* (*The Most Alien Land*) (1955) through *El infierno musical* (*Musical Hell*) (1971). These signs are most pronounced in the last two books, *Extracción de la piedra de locura* (*Extraction of the Stone of Folly*) (1968) and *El infierno musical*; however as early as *Arbol de Diana* (*Diana's Tree*), from 1962, the final poem reads, 'This repentant song, watchtower behind my poems: / this song conceals me, silences me'.

By recontextualising Pizarnik's recognisable motifs and signs (dolls, little girls, ladies, queens, wolves and more abstract images such as the colour blue, night, invisibility, the forbidden, shadows, cage, mirror and mask), domesticated by earlier critics under the less threatening rubrics of the death wish, her persona *maudite*, her refusal to grow up and live in (adult) reality, madness and silence, one can read both the repudiation and the inscription of lesbian sexuality.

Susana Chávez Silverman, 'The Look that Kills: The "Unacceptable Beauty" of Alejandra Pizarnik's *La condesa sangrienta*', in Emilie Bergmann and Paul Julian Smith (eds), *Entiendes? Queer Readings, Hispanic Writings*, (London, 1995), pp. 281–305; David William Foster, 'The Representation of the Body in the Poetry of Alejandra Pizarnik', *Hispanic Review* vol. 62 (1994), pp. 319–47; Delfina Muschietti, 'Alejandra Pizarnik: La niña asesinada', *Filología*, vol. 24 (1989), pp. 231–41; Cristina Piná, *Alejandra Pizarnik* (Buenos Aires, 1991).

Susana Chávez Silverman

Plummer, Kenneth (b. 1946), British scholar. Plummer studied at Enfield College and the London School of Economics and Political Science, and has lectured at the Middlesex Polytechnic, London (1968–74), and the University of Essex (1975–).

Plummer has written on homosexuality from a symbolic interactionist perspective. Symbolic interactionism is concerned with the ways in which people make sense of their own lives in the process of interacting with their immediate surroundings and larger cultural discourses. Plummer is particularly concerned with the processes of interaction (such as 'coming out') that precede the formation of a homosexual identity. In his first work on homosexuality, *Sexual Stigma* (1975), he examines the social meanings attached to a range of sexual behaviours, how they are constructed and what constraints are placed upon them. Plummer argues that it is crucial to examine views of homosexuality on each social level – that of society, the homosexual community and the homosexual individual.

In *Telling Sexual Stories* (1995), Plummer examines the contemporary obsession with talking about sexuality and expressing one's personal experiences in public, from television talk shows to tell-all autobiographies. He is interested in how such narratives are produced, how they change, and what roles they play in social and political spheres. Plummer argues that sexuality, and the identities and narratives surrounding it, are taking on a social and political importance never before witnessed, something he terms 'intimate citizenship'. Intimate citizenship involves 'concerns over the rights to choose what we do with our bodies, our feelings, our identities, our relationships, our genders, our eroticisms and our representations'. These concerns, Plummer argues, have taken on great political importance and have become, for many gays and lesbians, among others, a new means of organising our lives and effecting change.

Trent Newmeyer

Pombo, Álvaro (b. 1939), Spanish writer. Pombo is the son of wealthy parents belonging to the Francoist bourgeoisie. He graduated in philosophy in Madrid before moving to London, where he lived for eleven years between 1966 and 1977. The experience of exile is explored in his early narrative. Lonely characters, displaced both geographically and emotionally, wander around the city and find themselves unable to satisfy the demands of challenging situations. The difficulties of coming to terms with homosexuality are the focus of a number of narratives in one of his best works, the short story collection *Relatos sobre la falta de sustancia* (*Stories on the Lack of Substance*, 1977). 'El parecido de Ken Brody' ('Ken Brody Lookalike') tells the story of a strange love affair between two men, and fictions such as 'Regreso' ('Return Home') and 'El tío Eduardo' ('Uncle Edward') offer poignant pictures of homosexuality as the cause for estrangement from family and friends. Homosexual characters in his early works find it difficult to establish a smooth relationship with the world and live in a state of permanent inner exile. Another example of this somewhat grim view of homosexuality is his novel *Los delitos insignificantes* (*Insignificant Misdemeanours*, 1979), in which the middle-aged writer Ortega discovers sexual passion in his relationship with Quirós, an attractive, confused and violent young man who takes advantage of him and will eventually drive him to suicide.

In the light of these works, Pombo has been criticised for a depressing portrait of homosexual characters that does not seem to go beyond pre-Stonewall stereotypes: dissatisfied and immature, these men do not stand a chance of being happy. He has defended himself against these accusations, replying that it is the worldview reflected in these fictions that is bleak: homosexual characters just happen to inhabit this depressing world. But it would be a mistake to judge his work simply by these examples. Álvaro Pombo is also among the wittiest, funniest writers in contemporary Spanish literature. At his best, he can be considered as an inheritor to Valle-Inclán's

acute sense of the grotesque and of Goya's imagination to create distorted images that symbolically recreate the country's imaginative landscape. His mature work, from the 1980s onwards, is characterised by a sardonic, tongue-in-cheek intelligence and a baroque style that places characters in twilight worlds, where sexual indiscretion is only half-revealed and cleverly hinted at. Perhaps the best example of his mature mode is *El héroe de las mansardas de Mansard* (1983), a family saga set in Santander in the years following the civil war. A climate of secrecy and suspicion is bitingly conveyed. The central character is Kus-Kús, an elf-like child who stands at the centre of the family's intrigues and plays an active part in trading with their secrets. Pombo's recent fiction includes *Donde las mujeres* (1987). Progressively, his world has become less obsessive, more under control. He is the recipient of numerous literary awards in Spain, including the Herralde prize, which he won in 1983, and his work has been translated into English, German, Swedish and Italian.

Alberto Mira

Popp, Wolfgang (b. 1935), German scholar. Born in Bavaria, Popp studied music, German literature and philosophy at the Universities of Hamburg, Freiburg, Kiel, Münster and Konstanz. Since 1971, he has been Professor of German Language and Literature and Didactics at the University of Siegen. In the 1970s, he published mainly on the theme of teaching, but then developed interests in peace education as part of teachers' education and studies of homosexuality. In 1987, with colleagues, he founded the review *Forum: Homosexualität und Literatur*, now one of the major international journals of lesbian and gay studies. At Siegen, he established an institute of literary studies of homosexuality, the Rosa Flieder archive of homosexual journals, the August von Platen foundation and library, and an archive of unpublished scholarly works on homosexuality. The institute, in addition to regular conferences, publishes an annual *Lexikon Homosexuelle Belletrisik*, a book series on gay and lesbian studies, and a series of research bibliographies. Popp is the author of *Männerliebe. Homosexualität und Literatur* (1992).

Robert Aldrich and Garry Wotherspoon

Poulenc, Francis (1899–1963), French composer. Poulenc's early mentors included a bachelor uncle, and the pianist Ricardo Viñes (friend of Debussy and Ravel). After three years military service (fortunately immediately after World War I), his attempts to gain a broader technical musical education were at first foiled by a refusal from Paul Vidal of the Paris Conservatoire, who dismissed Poulenc as a disciple of Stravinsky, and his music as worthless. By this time he was already identified as a member of the so-called 'Les Six', a group of young and mildly iconoclastic Parisian composers of diverse stylistic interests also including Auric, Durey, Honnegger, Milhaud and Tailleferre. In the early 1920s his homosexual circle included Jean Cocteau (with whom he would collaborate later in life) and his lover, the novelist Raymond Radiguet, patron-of-the-arts Winaretta Singer (Princesse Edmond de Polignac), and the virtuoso harpsichordist Wanda Landowska. The heir to a small independent income from a family pharmaceutical company, in 1927 Poulenc bought a country house at Noizay in the Touraine, where much of his music was composed. Despite an earnest proposal of marriage to a close friend, Raymonde Linossier, in 1928, he was openly homosexual, and acknowledged his first serious relationship with the painter Richard Chanelaire. In a copy of his *Concerto Champêtre* (dedicated to Landowska, and one of his first major works) given to Chanelaire, he wrote: 'You have changed my life, you are the sunshine of my thirty years, a reason for living and working'.

Until the mid-1930s, Poulenc's music is characterised by a lightness of tone and almost picture-postcard naivety. From then onwards, his lifelong musical partnership with the singer Pierre Bernac (with Poulenc as accompanist) inspired a steady output of exquisite and sometimes deeply-felt songs. The macabre death of an acquaintance in a road accident inspired a sort of religious conversion (Poulenc, a dedicated hypochondriac, probably saw this as a premonition of his own mortality) and introduced the more serious, somewhat nostalgic voice first heard in his *Litanies à la vierge noire* (1936). However, though devoutly interested in Catholic faith, his surviving writings suggest he was never wholly won over to its certainties. The main sexual relationship of Poulenc's mid-life was with Raymond Destouches, a bisexual chauffeur from Noizay, who remained a close friend even after marriage. Destouches was unwittingly the muse for the surrealistic opera *Les Mamelles de Tirésias* (1944), in which an abandoned husband dresses up in his wife's clothes and miraculously gives birth to 40,000 children. Poulenc demonstrated his own sexual versatility when, a year later, he himself fathered a child (mother and daughter retain their anonymity). A chance meeting on a train in 1950 marked the start of a troubled five-year relationship with Lucien Robert, a travelling salesman from Marseilles. Poulenc was working on the final stages of his masterpiece, the tragic opera *Dialogues des Carmélites*, while nursing Destouches, seriously ill with pleurisy. The composition score was completed on the same evening as his lover's death in October 1955. From 1956 until his own death in 1963, Poulenc's partner was Louis Gautier, a young soldier. Poulenc duly wrote that his *Flute Sonata* (1956) was 'proof of the French Army's generosity to an old maestro's morale'. One of his most popular works is the brilliant but also wistful *Gloria* (1959), its soprano solo conceived for the voice of Leontyne Price.

Throughout his career, Poulenc cultivated public contacts with other homosexual artists. He collaborated with writers such as Max Jacob on *Le Bal masqué* (1932), Cocteau on the opera *La Voix humaine* (1958), and more than once performed his own *Concerto for Two Pianos* in concert with BRITTEN. In private, his innate love of gossip is attested to in numerous surviving letters. Meanwhile, gossip about him (for instance, in the diaries of the American composer Ned ROREM) inevitably focuses on his habitual sexual encounters with, ideally, uniformed men in Paris's *pissotières*. Of the dual religious and erotic impulses in his life and music, he once assured a friend: 'You know that I am as sincere in my faith, without any messianic screamings, as I am in my Parisian sexuality.'

Benjamin Ivry, *Poulenc* (London, 1996); Francis Poulenc, *Journal de mes mélodies*, ed. R. Machart (Paris, 1993).

Graeme Skinner

Praunheim, Rosa von (b. 1942), German filmmaker. Born in Riga, Latvia, as Holger Mischwitzky, Rosa von Praunheim chose his name to remind people of the pink triangle ('Rosa Winkel') that homosexuals had to wear in Nazi concentration camps. He grew up in Praunheim, a suburb of Frankfurt, Germany. Since Rainer Werner FASSBINDER's death in 1982, he is Germany's most prolific filmmaker, with forty films up to his mock autobiography *Neurosia* (1995) and still counting. His newest projects are *The Einstein of Sex: The Life and Work of Dr Magnus Hirschfeld* and *The History of Homosexuality from Stonehenge to Stonewall and Beyond*.

Praunheim initiated his artistic career as a student of painting (1961–67). In the late 1960s he began experimenting in film (with the gay filmmaker Werner Schroeter). Praunheim's teamwork with the lesbian filmmaker Elfi Mikesch (co-director with Monika Treut of *Seduction: The Cruel Woman*) similarly began in the late 1960s, and she has been his cinema-

tographer for several films, including *Horror Vacui* (1984), *A Virus Knows No Morals* (1985) and *Anita: Dances of Vice* (1988).

Praunheim's breakthrough came in 1970 with *Die Bettwurst*, a hilarious parody of bourgeois marriage. But his most renowned work, *It's Not the Homosexual Who is Perverse, but the Situation in Which He Lives* (1971), truly launched his career, as well as the gay movement in Germany, through the public debates that accompanied its screenings. Distribution of the film brought him to the United States, where he contributed to the gay liberation and AIDS activist movements in a number of significant documentaries, including *Army of Lovers or Revolt of the Perverts* (1972–76), *Positive* (1990) and *Silence = Death* (1990). Attuned to the seriousness of AIDS at an early date, Praunheim had already produced the feature-length part-musical, part-morality play *A Virus Knows No Morals* (1985). One of his most well-known features, *I am My Own Woman* (1992), is on the Berlin male-to-female transvestite Charlotte von Mahlsdorf. His most recent feature-length documentaries continue this thought-provoking tradition: *Transsexual Menace* (1996) presents transgender activism in the United States, while *Gay Courage* (1997) reviews, as its subtitle indicates, '100 Years of the Gay Movement in Germany and Beyond'. The latter film developed from the exhibition held in Berlin in 1997 on the same topic, for which von Praunheim curated several events.

Praunheim is also Germany's most prominent gay activist, a controversial status, not least because it is perceived that he sets himself up as the spokesman for the gay community. The German gay press, for instance, has called him a gay Führer and 'Gummi-Rosa' (Rubber Rosa), for his loud pleas for safe sex. In addition, he has aroused the anger of both gays and straights for outing several show-business personalities and politicians. He is currently helping to organise a large exhibition to be held in Berlin in 2001 on gays and lesbians in the Third World.

Alice A. Kuzniar, *The Queer German Cinema* (Stanford, 2000).

Alice A. Kuzniar

Premsela, Benno (1920–97), Dutch interior decorator and activist. Premsela grew up as the third child in a well-to-do progressive, humanistic environment. His parents had exchanged the old Jewish religion for socialism. His father was a physician and the first Dutch sexologist, who, in the 1930s, wrote several books on sexuality in which he pleaded for less rigid attitudes. Unlike most of his colleagues, he stated that homosexuality should not be looked upon as a perversity; the hostile reaction of society was the main problem. Of the Premsela family, only Premsela himself and his brother survived the Shoah. His feelings of guilt made him conscious that he had a mission in life. Being condemned to death once, he could not accept the fact that public ostracism was condemning him to social death for being a homosexual. So Premsela, as many survivors, flung himself into his work, being swung back and forth between feelings of rebelliousness and resignation, persistence and disillusion, and he dedicated himself to an ideal cause. From 1953 until 1976 he was a member of the board of the COC (Centre for Culture and Recreation, the Dutch homosexual and lesbian movement), during which period he was chairman for nine years. After his withdrawal from the board, he continued to play an active role in the organisation. In the late 1970s and during the 1980s he became involved as an adviser and member of the jury of the Homomonument foundation and as chairman of the foundation Gay and Lesbian Film Festival.

In 1947, shortly after its founding, Premsela became a member of the COC. Although he enjoyed the hidden subculture with its bars and parties, Premsela lacked positive role-models. He saw the COC as the instrument to build up a positive lifestyle and by doing so he defined the path of emancipation. For instance, although most of the members used an alias, Premsela always appeared under his own name. At the end of the 1940s with some other intellectuals – he always said that he could not have done it without others – he started the Small Circle, which became the advance guard of the COC in the 1950s and 1960s, with Premsela as one of its major spokesmen. Premsela and his supporters tried to increase the involvement of women – the COC was a mixed organisation – but failed to do so. Years later Premsela explained that they probably did not offer what women were looking for. In his eyes the emancipation of women was at the same time the emancipation of men, but it was too big a task for the COC to succeed in both, where society in general had failed.

Premsela stressed that the COC should not be just a place where people could enjoy themselves, but that the association had a duty to try to change society. He was not interested in scientific explanations about what caused homosexuality; for him homosexuality was nothing more than a 'normal human phenomenon'. It was, however, a social problem; homosexuals and lesbians had to accept themselves and be open about their lifestyle because only a positive attitude towards one's own homosexuality could establish a positive attitude by the outside world. Homosexuals were the only ones who really benefited from ending their position as second-class citizens and the discrimination they endured every day; they thus had to dedicate themselves totally to this cause. Premsela often said that he did not understand that homophiles – as the progressive term was in those days – lamented their fate. In his eyes every homophile was forced to emancipate himself, whereas most heterosexual men lived without any self-reflection. A member of a minority has the chance to get the most out of life. Yet Premsela realised that it sounded weird that he considered his being a homophile and a Jew as a double advantage.

With the election of Premsela as chairman in 1962, the COC entered a new phase. The association wanted its members to be open about their homosexuality – it changed its name in 1964 to the Dutch Society for Homophiles – and it founded the magazine *Dialoog* which aimed to start a dialogue between homosexuals and heterosexuals. The COC wanted to confront society with the hypocritical fact that people said that they did not mind if a person was a homophile so long as they were not confronted with men being openly intimate with one another. Premsela himself became the 'talk of the town' in 1964 when his face appeared on national television and he spoke without any reservation about his homosexuality.

In the following years Premsela led the COC into openness. The goal was to change society in such a way that it would no longer be of any importance if one was homosexual or heterosexual, man or woman; borders would disappear. By confronting heterosexuals with lesbians and homosexuals who were just 'ordinary human beings', homosexuality was to be integrated into society. The confrontation would establish understanding, and prejudices would disappear. In this process of bringing about a new society, homosexuals, lesbians and heterosexuals worked together. Some progressive heterosexuals even became members of the board of the COC, and the association again changed its name, to the Dutch Society for Integration of Homosexuality. Contrary to the development of the gay liberation movement in the United States, the COC did not want to establish a 'homosexual identity'. The American gay liberation movement was seen as oldfashioned and revengeful, and pursuing separatism.

Premsela participated from 1971 until 1976 in the foreign committee of the COC. He tried to get its ideas accepted in other countries, but the goal was too abstract and too idealistic, and the American concept of gay liberation became more influential. Even in the Netherlands, the whole concept of integration proved to be too big a step. When Premsela left the COC in 1976 openness about one's own homosexuality had become more common, but at the same time homosexuals and lesbians started to call themselves 'gays' and 'dykes' and strove for their own identity.

The cause of openness had succeeded in making homosexual men and lesbians more accepted by society But the emancipation process was not yet complete. Until the end of his life Premsela kept pointing out that though the Dutch parliament had banned several forms of discrimination by law – for instance since 1974 homosexuality has no longer been a reason to be rejected for military conscription – it would take generations to alter people's thoughts and attitudes.

Self-acceptance, openness and the struggle for emancipation had to be continued; there still was a long road ahead before reaching equality. Premsela saw religion as one of the main obstacles to this achievement. According to him, humans are always searching for a safe anchorage and find this in religion. Religious dogmas therefore have regularly led to prejudice and intolerance.

Hans Warmerdam

Prinsloo, Koos (1957–95), South African writer. Born in Kenya, Prinsloo migrated to South Africa in 1962. He studied Afrikaans at the University of Pretoria. He has published short stories and novels, including *Jonkmanskas* (1982), *Die hemel help ons* (1988) and *Slagplaas* (1993). His short story 'Border Story' was included in *Invisible Ghetto* (1993), South Africa's first anthology of gay and lesbian writing, and a memoir of childhood, 'Promise You'll Tell No-one', in *Defiant Desire* (1994). Prinsloo died of AIDS.

Edwin Cameron and Mark Gevisser (eds), *Defiant Desire* (Johannesburg, 1993); Mathew Krouse, *The Invisible Ghetto* (Johannesburg, 1993).

Ken Davis

Puig, Manuel (1932–90), Argentinian writer. Manuel Puig's *Kiss of the Spider Woman* (1976) is, for better or worse, the most widely disseminated text representing Hispanic homosexuality. A Hollywood film, a theatre adaptation and even a Broadway musical starring the legendary Chita Rivera attest to the popularity of this text. The musical was a messy affair which only touched on some of the novel's issues and distorted most of it, but Puig, who had a life-long fascination for larger-than-life divas and tinseltown glamour, would have loved Rivera's central performance and its final anthem to escapism.

The writer's early years in a small provincial town in the middle of the Argentinian *pampa* seem to be marked by the need to escape from dull, eventless reality into the realm of sophistication offered by the movies. The role of imagination in coping with oppression (whether sexual or political) was one of the recurring topics in Puig's fiction beginning with some of his earliest work, *La traición de Rita Hayworth* (*Betrayed by Rita Hayworth*, 1968) and *Boquitas pintadas* (1969). But far from just singing the praises of cheap emotions and popular entertainment, Puig creates a complex narrative framework, displaying an amazing array of techniques and intertextual influences, which contributes to seeing the character's love affair with these popular artifacts as flawed. Puig distances himself from the characters' plights and dreams, and is therefore able to show their delusions and, most importantly, the way dreams themselves can be oppressive. *Betrayed by Rita Hayworth* is probably the clearest statement in this sense: the narrative is set in an Argentinian village and deals with the petty dreams and barbed relationships between the bourgeois characters. In *Boquitas pinta-*

das, the world of lyrical masculinity of the tango and the sentimental masochism of the emotional songs of the 1940s is set against the background of the social novel.

Kiss of the Spider Woman reworks all of the former elements to construct a real web of feelings, delusions and betrayals. The narrative presents two characters sharing a prison cell in an abstract Latin American country. Molina is an effeminate homosexual; Valentín, a virile left-wing political prisoner. The clash between them is shown both through their conversations and through documents and pieces of straightforward narrative. Playing a modern-day Scheherazade, Molina keeps on entertaining Valentín by telling him convoluted narratives from old movies. Valentín's initial resistance is softened gradually as he suffers torture. What he does not know is that these stories carry with them poisonous betrayal: Molina is meant to gain Valentín's trust and use it to learn the names of fellow revolutionaries. At the same time, he will be trapped (and similarly 'betrayed') by the very stories he is telling, in which reactionary structures are concealed under cheap emotions.

The novel has been criticised for a less than positive portrayal of a Latin American queen, and there remains an effort to be made on the side of Hispanicists to create a reading framework that escapes the rhetoric of 'positive images'. In any case, one has to take into account that Puig left Argentina as early as 1955, and therefore his views have been influenced by homosexual identities from the places where he subsequently lived: Rome, Paris, London and, ultimately, New York.

Political and sexual repression go hand-in-hand in the rest of his work. After failed attempts to become a filmmaker (he studied in the Centro Sperimentale di Cinematografia in Rome), he concentrated on fiction-writing and became associated with other writers of the Latin American 'boom' of the 1960s. Even if he belongs very clearly in a notional 'gay' tradition (camp, drag, melodrama and homoeroticism are recurring elements in his fiction), he never really came out as a gay man and his work shows some degree of mistrust for fixed identities. However, as the Colombian writer Jaime Manrique Ardila wrote in an article on Puig published in *The Advocate*, Puig had no problem in dealing with his sexual orientation in everyday life. Manrique Ardila's article also stated what had so far been an open secret: that Puig had died of an AIDS-related disease.

Among the rest of Puig's work, *The Buenos Aires Affair* (1973) and *Pubis angelical* (1979) are especially interesting in the way they deal with sexual roles and oppressions. Both portray the way power permeates sexual liaisons, giving way to pain and lies.

Lucille Kerr, *Suspended Fictions: Reading Novels by Manuel Puig* (Urbana, IL, 1987); Norman Lavers, *Pop Culture into Art: The Novels of Manuel Puig* (New York, 1988); Jonathan Tittler, *Manuel Puig* (New York, 1993).

Alberto Mira

Punshon, Monte (Ethel May) (1882–1989), Australian public figure. Born in Ballarat, Australia, into a middle-class family, Punshon became a teacher but aspired to be an actress. She joined J. C. Williamson's Theatre Company as a teacher and toured with them, working under the pseudonym 'Miss Montague', as her father was strongly opposed to the theatre. Punshon also worked in radio and as an artist in a photographic studio. During World War II she joined the Australian Women's Army Service, and worked in the Tatura alien internment camp. After the war, she taught English at Bonegilla migrant camp and continued teaching for most of her life. Punshon, who learnt Japanese in the 1930s and had a lifelong interest in Japan, was awarded the Order of the Sacred Treasure by the Japanese government in 1988 for promoting cultural exchange and understanding between the two countries for sixty years. Punshon was also appointed Honorary Australian Ambassador for the 1988 World Expo in Queensland. This account is the public image Punshon presented in media interviews and in her published memoirs, *Monte-San: The Times Between, Life Lies Hidden*.

However, Punshon's private life is another story. She had intense long-term relationships with women from 1910 onwards. Through her involvement in radio and theatre, she met homosexual men and became involved in Melbourne's 'camp' sub-culture in the 1920s–1940s, on one occasion being best 'man' to the groom at a 'high camp' wedding. Punshon adopted the boyish fashions of the 1920s with enthusiasm. By the 1930s she dressed more mannishly – wearing a tie and jacket with skirts, or even leggings or jodhpurs – had her hair cut short and stood out in public as different. Punshon created two scrapbooks from newspaper cuttings from the 1920s–1940s of adventurous, 'single' (white) women who rejected conventional feminine roles and dress and expectations of motherhood and domesticity. They also contained stories about theatrical cross-dressing, male impersonators and women passing as men – including the 1929 English Colonel Barker case – and a review of Radclyffe Hall's 1928 lesbian novel *The Well of Loneliness*. The scrapbooks indicate the popularly circulating images Punshon drew on to construct her identity as an independent 'modern woman' who desired women, in an era of immense silence about female homosexuals.

Punshon gave an interview to a gay magazine in 1985 in which she talked of her love for women and her relationships in the early twentieth century. Yet she did not use sexual language to describe her relationships, nor did she use the words 'lesbian' or 'gay' to describe herself. Rather, she used the older language of female passionate friendship and romantic love, commenting 'in intimate circumstances, I prefer to be with women'. Punshon spoke of her 'friendship', her 'one and only love' and recalled the pain and heartbreak she felt when it ended: 'Debbie and I were very possessive of each other and never went out alone. After twelve years' friendship, Debbie left me for another life. I was heartbroken'.

The separation between her public image and her private life was blown apart in 1987 when her sexuality was bought to the notice of the morally conservative Bjelke-Petersen Queensland Government. Questions were asked about the suitability of Australia being represented by 'a lesbian' as an Australian ambassador – even if she was 105 years old and had been at the 1888 Exhibition. Punshon's sexuality became the centre of media attention.

When asked on national television how she felt being reported as a life-long lesbian, Punshon vehemently rejected labelling her sexual identity but reaffirmed her love for women: 'I'm not. I'm not labelled anything. I'm just me myself. I hate that name. I say that I like being with women because I feel more comfortable. They're a different species.'

Ruth Ford, 'Speculating on Scrapbooks, Sex and Desire: Issues in Lesbian History', *Australian Historical Studies*, vol. 27, no. 106 (1996), pp. 111–26; Monte, 'In Love with a Memory', in Margaret Bradstock and Louise Wakeling (eds), *Words from the Same Heart* (Sydney, 1987); Ethel May Punshon, *Monte-San: The Times Between, Life Lies Hidden* (Kobe, 1987).
                                    Ruth Ford

R

Rame, Knud, a.k.a. Kim Kent (b. 1935), Danish publisher and astrologer; educated as a bookseller. As a very young man Rame in 1952 met Helmer FOGEDGAARD, editor and founder of *Vennen* (*The Friend*), the first homophile magazine in Scandinavia. Inspired by Fogedgaard's vision of homophile emancipation, Rame, under the pseudonym Zedix, immediately began to contribute articles and short stories to *Vennen*.

In 1958 Rame, under the pen-name Kim Kent, began publication of the monthly magazine *Eos*. The name of the magazine referred to the Greek word for 'dawn' as well as to the Latin (accusative) pronoun 'them'. Originally the editorial policy of *Eos* was to avoid criticism of the authorities and concentrate on erotic entertainment (short stories, photos, personal ads). Over the years the emphasis of the erotic entertainment changed from romantic love to authoritarian relationships. In 1963 *Eos* introduced the American author Samuel M. STEWARD (Phil Andros) to Danish homophile readers. From 1962 Rame also published the monthly *Amigo* as a foreign language parallel (German and English) to *Eos*.

Although *Eos* and *Amigo* remained glossy and hedonistic magazines, they did not completely disregard homophile politics and the wider social issues of homophilia. In the late 1950s and early 1960s *Eos* – and its competitor, *Vennen* – were the voice of Denmark's homophile subculture during a period of virulent anti-homosexuality. Fogedgaard wrote a personal column in *Eos* until 1963. Bored with what Rame now characterises as 'brainwashing', he discontinued publication of *Eos* and *Amigo* in 1975. From 1980 to 1987 Rame contributed articles, serials and artwork to the international gay magazines *Revolt*, *Toy* and *Mr. S/M*, published in Sweden by Michael Holm.

Rame's wife, and joint owner of *Eos*, was also his closest collaborator, editorially and practically. His main inspirers, however, were Fogedgaard and the Danish philosopher Martinus, both of whom became central to Rame's life, personally and professionally. In 1973–77 he published *Occulta: Den skjulte verden* (*The Unseen World*), a quarterly devoted to spiritualism and New Age philosophy. Rame is also the author of *Astrologi fra A to Z* (*Astrology from A to Z*), 10 vols (1972–78). In 1970 he founded the *Astrologisk Akademi*, and since 1980 he has owned a bookshop in central Copenhagen specialising in alternative knowledge.

On a visit to the Mediterranean island of Malta in 1973, Rame experienced what he claims to be a revelation from a prehistoric Maltese incarnation. He has studied archaeology at the University of Malta and participated in excavations of ancient Maltese temples. At present he is preparing a thesis on Mediterranean Neolithic architecture.

In 1957 he married Ellinor Friang (b. 1926); the marriage was dissolved in 1973. He has been in a registered partnership (since 1991) with his companion since 1989, the painter and visual artist Carsten Pihl (b. 1959).

Wilhelm von Rosen

Rauset, Øyvind (b. 1952), Norwegian graphic artist, composer and musician. Educated at the Art Academy of Oslo, he had his debut at the State Autumn Exibition in 1973. He participated in and organised the first Scandinavian exhibition of gay and lesbian art, 'Night and Day', in Oslo, Copenhagen and Stockholm (1985), and had a separate exhibition at the famed Gallerie Janssen in Berlin (1988).

His main form is portraits and other drawings, often dwelling on the role of the modern boy and man. As a musician, Rauset has participated in the nationally famed folk-rock groups Folque and Ym-Stammen, who have appeared at the Danish Roskilde Festival. As a solo artist he has written music for TV and films and has recorded the solo albums *Landskap Med To Figurer* (*Landscape with two figures*, 1982) with the British musician Richard Burgesss, and *13 Impossible Dreams* (*plus one improbable*) 1988, rev. edn, 1992. In 1997 he was elected Norwegian cultural ambassdor to ILGA, and was awarded the Swedish Tupilak Prize.

Svend Erik Løken Larsen

Reagan, Ronald (b. 1911) and **Margaret Thatcher** (b. 1925), American and British politicians, respectively. Ronald Reagan, President of the United States from 1981 to 1989, and Margaret Thatcher, British Prime Minister from 1979 to 1991, appear here not because of any hint of personal sexual unorthodoxy, but because of what they represent. Reagan and Thatcher have come to symbolise in their respective countries 'the 1980s', a period when conservative reaction against the social

liberalism of the 1960s and 1970s produced a militant right-wing political movement which dominated the decade. Homophobia was a powerful element in the ideology which brought them to power, and this was reflected in their actions (and inactions) in office. Sadly, this had a disastrous effect on the way their governments responded to the emerging crisis of HIV/AIDS.

Thatcher was born in Grantham, Lincolnshire, the daughter of a grocer. She graduated from Oxford University in both law and science and worked as a research chemist before entering Parliament in 1959. She was a minister in the Heath government (1970–74) and became leader of the Conservative Party in 1975. Her base was the socially conservative Tory rank-and-file, who resented the party's gradual accommodation with social liberalism under her bachelor predecessor, Ted Heath. In 1979 she led the Tories to a smashing victory, and won two more elections against a divided and demoralised Labour Party. She was eventually undone by her unyielding opposition to British participation in the European Union and by the unpopular 'poll tax'. She was deposed as Tory leader in 1991 and created Baroness Thatcher.

Reagan was born in Tampico, Illinois, the son of an irregularly employed Irish Democrat father and an ambitious mother, who ensured he went to college. He early discovered a gift for talking and became a radio sportscaster before moving to Hollywood to make his fortune in 1937. He made a successful career as an actor in 'B' movies, with occasional breaks into better films which never quite led to stardom. After a failed marriage to Jane Wyman, he married Nancy Davis, an ambitious Republican. In the late 1950s, his acting career fading, he turned to politics, and was taken up by a group of wealthy conservatives. In 1966 and 1970 he was elected Governor of California, and in 1968 and again in 1976 he ran unsuccessfully for President. In 1980, aged nearly 70, he ran again, defeating the discredited Jimmy Carter, and presided over eight years of conservative government, partly inspired by Thatcher's success in Britain. His second administration was tainted by the Iran–Contra scandal, but he retained his remarkable popularity until his retirement.

Thatcher and Reagan successfully articulated the resentment of conservatives at the deep and rapid social changes which took place in Britain and the United States in the 1960s and 1970s. These included, among other things, changes in attitudes towards gender and sexuality, and particularly the gay rights revolution which began in 1969. Although this was not a dominant issue in the election which brought Thatcher to office – the power of the trade unions was far more important – she skilfully exploited it during her years in power, aided by a deeply homophobic tabloid press. At a Tory party conference Thatcher denounced the 'fact' that 'Children who need to be taught to respect traditional moral values are being taught that they have an inalienable right to be gay'.

In 1988 Thatcher enacted the notorious Section 28 of the Local Government Act, which made it illegal for any council or government body to 'intentionally promote homosexuality, or publish material with the intention of promoting homosexuality'. It also banned government schools from teaching anything which might be seen as 'promoting' homosexuality. While enforcement of the Section was sporadic, it served its purpose of embarrassing the Labour Party (which controlled most of the offending councils) and rallying a homophobic public behind the Tory party. Thatcher's years in office also saw increased censorship of gay-related material, enforced by a zealous Customs service, and increased persecution of gay men and lesbians in the Defence Forces.

No one has ever doubted that Thatcher's rhetoric reflected her deeply-held personal views. But Reagan is a different story. Many have remarked on the strange dichotomy between Reagan's public positions and his personal attitudes. A divorced movie actor who was estranged from his children and seldom attended church became the standard-bearer of the Christian Right's family values crusade. A longtime Hollywood resident, who knew many gay men and lesbians socially and professionally, he became the darling of Deep South and Midwest homophobes. The suspicion was widespread that Reagan's social conservatism was a cynical sham, designed first to win the Republican nomination and then the Presidency. If so, it was a sham he successfully maintained through eight years in office, and which the many genuine homophobes in his administration were happy to put into effect.

Among Reagan's Hollywood friends was Rock HUDSON, who was diagnosed with AIDS in 1985. Hudson was the first 'celebrity AIDS case', and his death was also the first occasion on which Reagan publicly acknowledged the existence of AIDS, which by that time had killed over 6,000 Americans, most of them gay men. Although government agencies such as the Centers for Disease Control had done excellent work in the scientific response to AIDS, the Administration's homophobia had prevented any useful educational or social policy response. AIDS education which 'promoted' homosexuality or drug use was banned, gay community AIDS organisations could not get funding or meet officially with the government. The Reagan Administration's response to AIDS was a national scandal, and one which cost thousands of lives. It is doubtful how much Reagan personally had to do with this, but he set the tone for his Administration and appointed its key personnel.

The great paradox of the Reagan and Thatcher years was that despite the best efforts of their two governments, and despite the terrible losses caused by AIDS, the gay and lesbian communities in both the United States and Britain continued to grow in size, confidence and visibility all through this period. Indeed the absence of government assistance in dealing with AIDS spurred the gay communities to feats of organisation and self-help that were without precedent, and that have subsequently served as a model for community mobilisation in many other contexts. There was in fact a growing split between British and American society as Thatcher and Reagan conceived it and as it actually was – Thatcher indeed denied that there was any such thing as society.

The sharp polarisation that Reagan and Thatcher's political rhetoric created around the issue of homosexuality actually assisted the political development of the gay communities in both countries. This, coupled with the impact of AIDS, meant that gay political activism increasingly concentrated on securing influence in the opposition parties – the Democrats in the United States, Labour in Britain – and in working to defeat Reagan's and Thatcher's rather less effectual successors, George Bush and John Major. The victories of Bill Clinton in 1992 and Tony Blair in 1997 were in part the result of this activism, and brought the gay and lesbian communities back into the political mainstream. While political homophobia in the United States and Britain is far from dead, it is unlikely ever again to be as triumphant as it was in the Reagan and Thatcher years.

Randy Shilts, *And the Band Played On* (New York, 1987); Garry Wills, *Reagan's America: Innocents at Home* (London, 1988); Hugo Young, *One of Us: A Biography of Margaret Thatcher* (London, 1990).

Adam Carr

Rechy, John (b. 1934), American author. Born in Texas of Mexican-American parentage, Rechy was educated at Texas Western College, and later served with the US Occupation Forces in Germany. Apart from his writing, Rechy has taught film and literature classes at the University of Southern California.

Rechy will always be remembered for his first two novels, *City of Night* (1963) and *Numbers* (1967). The former, described by one writer as 'a study of miscellaneous homosexuality and narcissism in American cities', deals openly with gay male cruising, while the latter chronicles the increasingly obsessive sexual activity of its protagonist, but set in a different milieu. Other works include *This Day's Death* (1969), *The Sexual Outlaw: A Documentary* (1977) and *Rushes* (1979).

Rechy's novels attracted a wide gay readership, not only because of their raunchy sexual material, but also because their internal debates reflected the concerns of many gay men of the time, of balancing the conflicts between the wholesale availability of sexual gratification and an awareness that there must be more to life: Rechy's anti-heroes tended to succumb to the former. From a late twentieth century perspective, his books – although often condemned for their bleak portrayal of aspects of gay life – chart a 'golden age' of sexual activity before the impact of HIV/AIDS.

Contemporary Authors (NRS), vol. 64 (Detroit, 1998).

Garry Wotherspoon

Reed, Lou (b. 1943), American singer/ songwriter. Born in New York, Reed's work is synonymous with the city where he and his band, the Velvet Underground, helped to create an alternative musical sound to that of the West Coast. By the time they came into contact with Andy WARHOL, the Velvet Underground had written 'Venus in Furs', based on Sacher-Masoch's novel, and Reed had begun to write songs about transvestism, homosexuality, bisexuality and drag – some performed with the Velvet Underground, and many recorded on a trio of albums from the beginning of his solo career, *Transformer* (1972), *Berlin* (1973) and *Rock 'n' Roll Animal* (1974). While *Berlin*, with its ISHERWOOD-like cabaret atmospherics, is arguably his best work, it is for 'Walk on the Wild Side' on *Transformer* (produced by David BOWIE) that Reed is best known. Although the song's lyrics deal with transvestism, it received some radio play in the US when it was first released. It has since become one of his signature tunes.

Reed has admitted to experimenting with homosexuality, and his concert tours in the early 1970s were known for their heavy borrowing from both gay culture and Glitter Rock performance styles. By 1982 and *The Blue Mask*, however, he had adopted the persona of the happily married straight man. Though Reed briefly reunited with the other members of the Velvet Underground for a European tour in 1993, the band broke up before embarking for North America. His status as a rock influence firmly established, Reed's solo work in the 1970s remains one of the most successful attempts at an American form of Glitter Rock, a style of music indebted to the Velvets' own work, and has served as an example for several generations of alternative rock bands.

Lou Reed, *Between Thought and Expression: Selected Lyrics of Lou Reed* (New York, 1993).
Shelton Waldrep

Reinig, Christa (b. 1926), German writer. Reinig was born in Berlin; her mother supported herself and her illegitimate daughter by working as a cleaner. Reinig grew up under the National Socialist regime. Her early aspiration was to become a gardener, but after an aborted apprenticeship in a flower shop she found work as an office assistant during the war. After World War II she laboured with the *Trümmerfrauen* among the ruins of the city, and then in an East German factory. Through evening classes Reinig was able to enter East Berlin's Humboldt University, where she studied archaeology and art history; this took her into a job as an archivist in an East German museum, and from 1948 she did editorial work on a satirical magazine called *Ulenspiegel*. Reinig was never accepted into the state-

monitored Writers' Society of the German Democratic Republic; she published with Fischer, a West German publisher, and after winning the prestigious Bremen Prize for Literature in 1964 for a collection of poems called, simply, *Gedichte* (*Poems*) she emigrated to West Germany. She now lives in Munich.

In 1971 Reinig was permanently disabled after a fall; this accident and its effects on her life became an important element in her first novel, *Die himmlische und die irdische Geometrie* (*The Geometry of Heaven and Earth*, 1975). Having been discouraged by both male and female friends from doing so, she did not make a lesbian agenda part of her work until after the sensationalised trial in Itzehoe in northern Germany of two lesbians, Marion Ihns and Judy Anderson, in 1974. Both were sentenced to life imprisonment for effecting the murder of Ihns's husband, but the gutter press took the opportunity of inflaming popular feeling against lesbianism and the developing women's movement. Reinig's reputation as a lesbian-feminist writer took off with the publication of her 1976 novel, *Entmannung* (*Emasculation*), the central chapter of which is concerned with the trial of Ihns and Anderson. *Entmannung*, which has the subtitle *Die Geschichte Ottos und seiner vier Frauen* (*The Story of Otto and his Four Women*), centres on a destructive, brutal professor, whose 'emasculisation' has been taken to represent Reinig's own struggle to free herself from masculinist thought patterns. Within the novel only Wölfi, a lesbian character (the fifth woman of the the story), is able to resist destruction by Otto. Like Reinig, Wölfi is a refugee from the GDR. The reader is confronted with the irony that Otto is granted full social access to the women he destroys, an access that Wölfi does not have.

After *Entmannung*, Reinig's work became progressively more lesbian-centred, and in her volume of essays *Der Wolf und die Witwen* (*The Wolf and the Widows*,

1980), the author describes herself as 'a member of the lesbian nation'.

Critical reception of Reinig has tended to concentrate either on the period before or on the period after her literary 'coming out' as a lesbian feminist; this has been called the 'phenomenon of the "divided Reinig"' (Marie Luise Gansberg). Her other works of prose fiction include *Drei Schiffe* (*Three Ships*, 1959), *Orion trat aus dem Haus* (*Orion Stepped out of the House*, 1969), *Mädchen ohne Uniform* (*Girls out of Uniform*, 1979 inspired by Christa Winsloe), *Die ewige Schule* (*The Eternal School*, 1982), *Nobody* (1989), and *Glück und Glas* (*Fortune and Glass*, 1991). She has also published poetry, radio plays and essays.

Jeannette Clausen, 'Christa Reinig', in Friederike Eigler and Susanne Kord (eds), *The Feminist Encyclopedia of German Literature* (Westport, CT, 1997); Cäcilia Ewering, *Frauenliebe und -literatur: (un)gelebte (Vor)Bilder bei Ingeborg Bachmann, Johanna Moosdorf und Christa Reinig* (Essen, 1992); Madeleine Marti, *Hinterlegte Botschaften: Die Darstellung lesbischer Frauen in der deutschsprachigen Literatur seit 1945* (Stuttgart, 1992); Catherine Winkelmann, 'Christa Reinig's Lesbian Warriors', in Christoph Lorey and John L. Plews (eds), *Queering the Canon: Defying Sights in German Literature and Culture* (Columbia, SC, 1998), pp. 234–47.

Sarah Colvin

Rekola, Mirkka Elina (b. 1931), Finnish poet. Rekola is one of the most respected modernists in Finnish poetry – although she feels rather outside such categorisations herself.

Already as a child in the industrial town of Tampere, Rekola made keen observations about the unjust divisions in the world around her. She suffered both from the ideological abyss left by the civil war of 1918 and from the amazing difference that gender made; to her surprise she was not the boy she thought she ought to have been. Her persistent illnesses separated her from her peers during her youth, and made her retreat into art, music and literature instead.

Homosexual acts for both women and men were illegal in Finland until 1971. At an early age, Rekola realised that it was not safe to speak of her feelings for other women, and she fell into a complete silence. The silence was broken with her first original poetry collection *Vedessä palaa* (*Burning/Returning in the Water*, 1954). It was also during this time that she moved to Helsinki, where she was intrigued, despite warnings, by the small literary circle gathered around the poet Helvi Juvonen (1919–59). Juvonen was known as a 'deviant', and in this circle Rekola found both like-minded writers and her first lover.

Rekola went on to write reviews and translations, while continuing with her own poetry. She speaks of having had paranoid anxieties at this time; she gradually overcame these through her writing, and she started to open herself to others and to the world. In her poetry, she cultivated her style of tension between emptiness and overflow, studied the possibilities of linguistic experiences, and kept writing puzzling verses which, in their ambiguity, opened new insights and ways of thinking for the reader. Her style sought unity between the dichotomies, and it was often considered difficult by those who were used to thinking only along such divisions. Yet she kept on encouraging her readers: 'It's all there, in the poem. Just ask it the simple questions.'

Besides the poetry, the reclusive Rekola in 1969 published *Muistikirja* (*A Notebook*), a collection of aphorisms, and in 1987 *Maskuja*, 'short stories as long as the life', written for her own pleasure about a creature of an unknown gender called Masku. (Note that, in Finnish, no gender distinction is made between personal pronouns.) Masku 'runs to a barber. "Do you have time, can you do something about this hair?" He/She raised his/her cap. "Look, their other end is totally loose".'

Unlike most Finnish lesbians and gays of her generation, Rekola, after protecting her parents for decades, started to come out publicly as a lesbian. The process began with an autobiographical poem about her silenced lesbianism included in a lesbian poetry collection, *Ääriviivasi ihollani* (*Your Contours On My Skin*, 1991) published by a newly-founded lesbian publishing house, Meikänainen. She gave an interview for the womens's magazine *Anna* in 1996, where she commented not only on her own 'orientation', but also criticised the hostility evident in the public discussion about the registration of same-sex relations. She also granted a personal interview for the lesbian and gay magazine *Z* in 1997.

Already an award-winning author, Rekola received the prestigious Suomi prize, the highest national cultural award, for 'changing the traditions of both writing and reading' in 1995. 'The poet of the poets' continues to write and publish, her latest collection being *Taivas päivystää* (*The Sky on Duty*, 1996).

With her ingenious usage of the shamanistic qualities of the Finnish language, Rekola's texts resist the trials of translation. However, the late Jean-Jacques Lamiche has succeeded in translating some of her poems into French (*Joie et asymétrie*, in *Revue Rivages*, no. 2 (1987)). Translations of Rekola's work are also available in English Anselm Hollo in *88 Poems*, Published in Helsinki in 2000.

Liisa Enwald, *Kaiken liikkeessä lepo. Monihahmotteisuus Mirkka Rekolan runoudessa* (*There is Rest in all Motion. Ambiguity in the poetry of Mirkka Rekola*) (Helsinki, 1997); Mirkka Rekola, *Tuoreessa muistissa kevät. Aforistiset kokoelmat* (*In Fresh Memory the Spring. Aphoristic Collections*) (Porvoo-Helsinki-Juva, 1987); Mirkka Rekola, *Virran molemmin puolin. Runot 1954–1996* (*Along Both Sides of the River. Poetry*) (Porvoo-Helsinki-Juva, 1997).

Tuula Juvonen

Renault, Mary (1905–83), British-South African novelist. Renault was born Mary Challans in London, the daughter of a doctor. She was educated at St Hugh's College, Oxford, intending to be a teacher. But having decided to be a writer, she trained in nursing to broaden her experience of life, and she worked as a nurse through World War II. During this period she published a series of novels, one of which, *Kind Are Her Answers*, featured a lesbian nurse.

After the war Renault and her lover, Julie Mullard, migrated to South Africa, and she lived in Cape Town for the rest of her life. She travelled widely in Africa and Europe, and her visits to Greece aroused her interest in classical civilisation, about which she acquired a formidable knowledge. In 1953 she published *The Charioteer*, a novel daring for its time, based on the lives of several gay men in wartime London. Although she showed an uncritical acceptance of Freudian theories about homosexuality, she also broke new ground in describing gay Spitfire pilots and Dunkirk heroes. This was her last novel set in the modern world, but far from the last to deal with male homosexuality.

Renault's fame rests on her series of historical novels set in ancient Greece. The series began with *The King Must Die* (1958) and *The Bull From the Sea* (1962), careful and believable reconstructions of the Theseus myth, complete with labyrinth and Minotaur. In *The King Must Die* she describes the matriarchal society of early Greece, and its overthrow by the patriarchal order personified by Theseus. These novels established her reputation as a historical novelist.

Her high reputation with gay men began with *The Last of the Wine* (1965) and continued with *The Mask of Apollo* (1966) and *The Praise Singer* (1978). These novels were all set in the classical Greek world, and all have strong male homosexual themes. *The Last of the Wine* is set in Athens during the Peloponnesian War

(433–404 BC), and a homosexual relationship forms its central storyline. *The Mask of Apollo* is set a little later and concerns the relationship between Plato and Dion. These novels showed not only Renault's wide classical scholarship, but her sensitivity. Male sexuality is dealt with in a direct but delicate manner. The culmination of Renault's career was her trilogy based on the life of Alexander the Great: *Fire From Heaven* (1970), *The Persian Boy* (1972) and *Funeral Games* (1981), the first two following Alexander's career from childhood, the third describing events after his death. In *Fire From Heaven* Alexander's lifelong relationship with Hephaistion, who later became one of his generals, is described. *The Persian Boy* is narrated by Bagoas, a Persian eunuch who became Alexander's lover after his conquest of the Persian empire. The novels show Alexander as a recognisably modern gay man, a view Renault pursued in her non-fiction work, *The Nature of Alexander* (1975).

The paradox of Renault's work is the fact that her Greek novels contain very few women of any note, and most of them are essentially negative characters, such as Olympias, Alexander's domineering mother (more Freudian influence is detectable here). That a woman and a lesbian should devote her literary career to male characters set in male-dominated societies does require some explanation, particularly since Renault was not alone in this: Marguerite Yourcenar's *Memoirs of Hadrian* (1954), a novel in the form of an autobiography, describes the relationship of the Emperor Hadrian and his lover Antinoüs. It seems likely that several factors motivated Renault. She evidently wanted to stay away from the traditional themes of 'women's novels' (family, marriage, scandal), and to tackle grand historical themes. The facts of history being what they are, she may have felt a lack of grand historical themes featuring women. She loved ancient Greece and wanted to write about it, but any novel set in a patriarchal society must perforce be male dominated.

She may also have found male homosexuality personally easier than lesbianism for her to address in her novels. Some of these issues are addressed in Ruth Hoberman's recent study of women novelists and the ancient world.

Although Renault's novels popularised ancient Greece and were well grounded in the scholarship of her time, her rather rosy view of the nature of male homosexuality in Greek society is now rather dated. More recent scholarship, such as that of Kenneth Dover and Eva Keuls, has demolished the idea of an ancient Greek sexual utopia, and also the view that Greek public men such as Plato and Alexander were 'gay' in the modern sense. Her portrait of Alexander in particular is somewhat romanticised: his arrogance, cruelty and self-indulgence are glossed over – perhaps as one would expect in a novel narrated by his lover. These weaknesses do not detract from the importance of Renault's novels for generations of modern gay men, who have been shown a vision of a society in which love between men was not only tolerated but exalted.

Renault and Mullard lived quietly in Cape Town for nearly forty years, and Renault was personally little known despite the success of her literary career. In the 1950s she was a member of the Black Sash, an anti-apartheid women's group, but she later withdrew from all public involvements, a choice which drew some criticism in the 1960s and 1970s.

David Sweetman, *Mary Renault: A Biography* (New York, 1993); Ruth Hoberman, *The Ancient World in Twentieth-Century Women's Historical Fiction* (New York, 1997); Eva C. Keuls, *The Reign of the Phallus: Sexual Politics in Ancient Athens* (Berkeley, 1985).

Adam Carr

Reve, Gerard (also Gerard Kornelis van het Reve) (b. 1923), Dutch author. Reve is one of the leading Dutch writers in the period after World War II. He was born into an Amsterdam communist family.

After the war, he became a journalist and in 1947 published his first novel, *De avonden (The Evenings)*. Most critics saw the book as an expression of youth's nihilism, which helped very much to establish its lasting success. In the 1950s Reve struggled with his work and his life. He married, but divorced and entered the gay world. His work stagnated although he published some superb short stories, several of which appeared in English at the time when he lived in London trying to make a new start. After he returned to Amsterdam, his work became explicitly homosexual and sadomasochistic. His favourite scene, which is repeated in many versions in his work, is a triangle named 'revism': the beloved young man punishes an impertinent lad while Reve assists the bully. Spanking on corduroy butts is the preferred form of castigation.

His books of letters, *Op weg naar het einde (Towards the end*, 1963) and *Nader tot U (Closer to you*, 1966), became big hits. Other than sexual themes, his topics are his alcoholism, his hatred of the working class and his conversion to the Catholic Church, as indicated in the book-titles. Just before he sought refuge in Mother Church, he was involved in the so-called 'donkey-scandal'. Reve had become one of the editors of the Dutch gay journal *Dialoog*. In an article for this magazine he expressed his love for God, who had descended from heaven in the form of a donkey which Reve fucked. As possible blasphemy, it became a court case in three stages that each time hit the front pages of the Dutch newspapers. In the last instance, at the Dutch Supreme Court, Reve was acquitted because this tale of heavenly bestiality was deemed to be his way to express his beliefs. Although Reve has since always posed as a devout Catholic and a faithful follower of pope and church, because of the sexual explicitness of his work relations were not optimal.

Reve adorned his series of lovers with the names of beasts of prey: wolf, tiger, fox. With one of them he staged a marriage-like celebration in a Catholic church and at a later point he maintained a household with two lovers. The work and life of Reve offered a mind-blowing experience to many young men coming out in the 1960s and 1970s.

Reve wrote his best work in the 1960s. In the late 1960s he moved to Frisia, leaving the city he hated. Since 1970 he has lived in France, in England, and once more in the Netherlands, and has ended with his lover, 'Sailor Fox', an avowed paedophile, in Belgium. The many novels he has written since the 1960s are of varying quality, repeating the basic sombre schema of his first books, and always with a good dose of 'revism'. Translating his books is difficult because of his old-fashioned, ironic style. Two of his books, *Lovely Boys* and *The Fourth Man*, have been made into movies. For his work Reve received the most prestigious literary prizes of the Netherlands. Apart from novels and short stories, he has written one unsuccessful play and a thin book of excellent poetry. In December 1998, the publication of his collected works began.

There are dozens of specialised publications on Reve, but no general introduction to his life and work.

Gert Hekma

Reznor, Trent (b. 1965), American singer. Born in rural Mercer, Pennsylvania, Reznor, a. k. a. Nine Inch Nails, is one of the most influential and controversial forces in North American popular music. His visceral fusion of industrial rock, wall of sound musical technology and the inner landscape of pain was let loose with NIN's 1989 debut, *Pretty Hate Machine*. Reznor established himself as one of the most exciting and intense live acts of the 1990s, as NIN infamously blew away the competition on both the 1991 Lollapalooza tour and 1994's Woodstock effort. The pitiless self-loathing of the 1992 EP, *Broken*, was followed in 1994 with *The Downward Spiral* – a terrifying journey through a man tearing pieces off himself and committing them to tape, and a devastating portrayal of tortured masculinity.

The explicit violence and sexual content of NIN's lyrics ('Wish' may well be the only Grammy award-winning song that mentions fist-fucking) and the images of S/M in some of their videos attracted the attention of conservative guardians of American morals, who have accused Reznor of promoting everything from suicide to Satan worship to deviant sexuality. Although not gay himself, some of Reznor's male fans have found his work and image provocative enough to declare their own desires toward their idol.

Fiona Buckland

Rich, Adrienne (b. 1929), American writer. Rich was born in Baltimore, Maryland, to a white southern Protestant mother, and a father of Ashkenazic and Sephardic Jewish descent. Much of Rich's writing, both her poetry and her essays, reflects poignantly on the position of women in patriarchal culture; her work critiques fixed notions of (hetero)sexuality, femininity and motherhood as oppressive to women and exposes these categories as political rather than as natural conditions for women. In its expression of sexual politics, drawing largely from her own experience as a Jewish lesbian and as a mother, Rich's work attempts to dismantle the traditional oppositions between art and politics, the personal and the political, the self and the world. Her poetry in particular has played an influential role in legitimising the politics of gender and sexuality as intimately connected to literature in opposition to humanist paradigms of literary study that view texts, writers and the act of reading as disembodied from specific social and material conditions.

In 1951, Rich graduated from Radcliffe College and two years later married the economist Alfred H. Conrad, an Orthodox Jew. As she reflects in 'Split at the Root: An Essay on Jewish Identity', Rich felt that her experience of motherhood,

especially through the 1950s and early 1960s while raising their sons, helped to radicalise her. After leaving her husband in 1966, moving to New York and becoming involved with many of the radical political movements of the 1960s, Rich became increasingly involved in feminism. Her essays from this period point to the ways in which women's experiences have been obliterated from history and have not only been misrepresented but misread in literature.

Rich's best known, yet controversial, contribution to lesbian studies is her essay 'Compulsory Heterosexuality and Lesbian Existence', first published in 1980. Speaking of lesbian existence through diverse historical periods and socio-geographical locations, Rich, through an emphasis on supportive relations between women, posits that all women can be located somewhere on the broad spectrum of lesbian identity whether or not they choose to identify as lesbians themselves. Rich's notion of a lesbian continuum has created controversy among some lesbian critics and theorists for blurring distinctions between lesbians and heterosexual women who are in supportive, non-sexual relationships with other women, and for diminishing the specificity of lesbian desire and the ways women relate to women sexually.

Other lesbian critics have argued that the idea of a lesbian continuum is not in itself problematic; while Rich's text allows for the substitution of 'lesbian' with 'woman', the problem lies in simplistic and self-serving interpretations of the essay that invoke 'woman' *instead* of 'lesbian' and reduce lesbianism to a sign of implicitly heterosexual resistance and desire. According to Teresa de Lauretis, in the late 1970s when Rich's essay was written, it was 'lesbian', not 'woman' that expressed Rich's vision and signified women's resistance to marriage and the institution of heterosexuality. Rich's continuum, de Lauretis argues, is a theoretical construct and should not be about who could or should be called a lesbian; the continuum is a conceptual space in which lesbian existence can be imagined in spite of what conspires to deny, omit or make it unimaginable. Rich herself has remarked on reappropriations of her notion of a lesbian continuum for ends other than she had anticipated. In *Blood, Bread, and Poetry* (1986), she observes that the idea of a lesbian continuum 'can be, is, used by women . . . as a safe way to describe their felt connections with women, without having to share in the risks and threats of lesbian existence'.

In her 'Twenty-One Love Poems', first published in 1976 shortly after beginning her relationship with novelist and poet Michelle CLIFF and later anthologised in *The Dream of a Common Language* (1978), Rich speaks specifically of her own passion for another woman. The poems can be read not only as a coming-out of an established figure in American poetry, but as an attempt to imagine two women together in, and perhaps apart from, a world that excludes them and reads the lesbian body grotesquely. Though Rich writes in her essays about female and lesbian invisibility in history and of the ways in which lesbian desire has been traditionally read as an aberration, these do not necessarily have the same shades of meaning in her poetry – female-centred sexuality, as it is captured in the unnumbered floating poem that interrupts the numbered sequence of the twenty-one poems in the series, exists in isolation from the rest of the world. Describing her lover's 'traveled, generous thighs / between which my whole face has come and come', and the 'insatiate dance of your nipples in my mouth', the floating poem ends with 'whatever happens, this is', showing, as Marilyn Farwell has argued, that the bodies of the lovers exist outside of history, outside of the narrative of the numbered poems that represent the body in pain, bodies separated physically in a homophobic social order. The lesbian body in the floating poem is cast as excess in relation to the numbered poems; while

it is a presence that may not fit into dominant narrative and discursive structures, it is nonetheless a presence that is felt and has impact on language and on the world. Rich has published several other volumes of poetry and prose. She and Cliff also edited the lesbian-feminist journal *Sinister Wisdom* from 1981 to 1983.

Teresa de Lauretis, *The Practice of Love: Lesbian Sexuality and Perverse Desire* (Bloomington, IN, 1994); Marilyn R. Farwell, 'The Lesbian Narrative: 'The Pursuit of the Inedible by the Unspeakable' ', in George E. Haggerty and Bonnie Zimmerman (eds), *Professions of Desire: Lesbian and Gay Studies in Literature* (New York, 1995), pp. 156–68.

William J. Spurlin

Rive, Richard (1931–89), South African writer. Rive was born in Cape Town in 1931 and grew up in the 'Coloured' and mixed-race area, District Six. He studied at Hewat Training College (where he also spent a large part of his working life as an English lecturer), the University of Cape Town, and then at Columbia University. He completed his doctorate on Olive Schreiner at Magdalen College, Oxford. He was a champion hurdler in his youth and was active in sport coaching and organisation throughout his life.

In the late 1950s he started writing short stories about the iniquities of the apartheid system and produced his first novel, *Emergency*, about the Sharpeville massacre, in 1963, and an autobiography, *Writing Black*, in 1981. He also compiled a pan-African anthology in English, *Modern African Prose*, which became a textbook in several countries. While he was one of the prominent black voices of literary protest, he never alluded in his work to his own homosexuality or to gay and lesbian issues. He was stabbed to death by a pair of 'rent boys' in his house just when an adaptation of his novel *'Buckingham Palace', District Six* (1986) was being staged to much acclaim at the Baxter Theatre in Cape Town, and just after his finishing another novel, *Emergency Continued*.

Mathew Krouse, *The Invisible Ghetto* (Johannesburg, 1993).

Ken Davis with Ann Smith

Robbins, Jerome (1918–98), American dancer, choreographer and director. Born Jerome Rabinowitz in New York, his family moved to Weehawken, New Jersey, where his father owned a delicatessen before moving into garment manufacturing. While enrolled at New York University (1935–38), he studied ballet and modern dance and by the late 1930s appeared both as an actor and dancer in summer stock and on Broadway. Robbins joined Ballet Theatre as a *corps de ballet* dancer in 1940, was promoted to soloist in 1942, and, in 1944, he created his first major ballet, *Fancy Free*, which received twenty-five curtain calls at its premiere. Less than a year later he choreographed *Interplay*, another hit ballet and, in collaboration with Leonard BERNSTEIN, Betty Comden, Adolph Green and Oliver Smith, created *On the Town*, a hit Broadway musical based on *Fancy Free*.

In the next decade, Robbins established himself as Broadway's dominant creative force with hits including *Billion Dollar Baby, High Button Shoes, Call Me Madam, The King and I, Peter Pan*, and *Bells Are Ringing*. Robbins reached the pinnacle of his popular success with his choreography and direction of *West Side Story*, the result of a collaboration of four Jewish gay men: Robbins, Leonard Bernstein, Stephen Sondheim and Arthur Laurents. Although some gays have claimed a homosexual subtext to the play and its lyrics, Sondheim rejected the assertion. Subsequent hits included *Gypsy, A Funny Thing Happened on the Way to the Forum* and *Fiddler on the Roof*. A 1989 retrospective of his unparalleled Broadway successes, *Jerome Robbins Broadway*, brought him his fourth Tony Award.

Robbins first left Broadway in 1949 to join George Balanchine's newly-formed New York City Ballet as a dancer and within a year was appointed associate director and choreographer, an association which endured for more than forty years. Among his ballets in the 1950s were *Age of Anxiety, The Cage, Fanfare, Afternoon of a Faun* and *Pied Piper*. In 1959, he left to form his own company, Ballets: USA, which toured the United States and Europe, and later returned to Broadway. In 1965 he returned to his balletic alma mater, Ballet Theatre, now American Ballet Theatre, to create his highly successful version of *Les Noces*. His true return to the world of ballet, however, was the creation of *Dances at a Gathering* for the New York City Ballet in 1969. Thereafter his career was committed to the ballet, offering an alternative to the unchallenged genius of Balanchine. With the impressive catalogue of new works created after his return to the New York City Ballet, it is safe to say that Robbins, along with Balanchine, had the longest continuous run of creative successes in twentieth-century ballet. Among important works of this second period were: *The Goldberg Variations, In the Night, Watermill, In G Major, Mother Goose, Other Dances, The Four Seasons, Opus 19: the Dreamer, Glass Pieces* and *I'm Old Fashioned*. With the death of Balanchine in 1983, Robbins was named co-Ballet Master-in-Chief of the New York City Ballet with dancer/choreographer Peter Martins. The relationship was tenuous and, after a stressful eight-year period, Robbins left New York City Ballet for the last time in 1990, although he continued to mount works for his favoured company, including a recension of *Les Noces*, shortly before his death. He died following a stroke in New York City.

Widely acknowledged as a theatrical genius, Robbins was one of the few ballet choreographers capable of creating truly comedic dance, e.g. *The Concert, Fanfare, Mother Goose, The Four Seasons*, as well as works of psychological intensity, though with more divergent success: *The Age of Anxiety, The Cage, The Dybbuk, Opus 19*. Despite unwaning popular acclaim, his work has been criticised as being superficially clever rather than genuinely innovative and iconoclastic like the neo-classic and abstract works of Balanchine, his only close contender for the label of genius in the history of American ballet. It also can be argued that Robbins, although widely acknowledged as being gay in theatrical and gay circles, never publicly admitted his orientation nor alluded to the gay experience in his work. As a rule, Robbins's ballets, even in their darkest moods, present a portrait of an idealised heterosexual world occupied by all-American boys and girls. Same-sex encounters in Robbins's ballets are relegated either to play, competition or asexual abstractions. His reputation for being unpredictably considerate or cruel may find its roots in his inability to admit his homosexuality. It has been argued that his 1953 appearance before the House Committee on Un-American Activities to name names of former colleagues in the Communist Party was based on his fear that exposure of his gay identity would jeopardise his ambitions for an imminent Hollywood career.

Charles Kaiser, *The Gay Metropolis* (New York, 1997).

A. M. Wentink

Roberts, Ian (b. 1965), Australian sportsman. Roberts was born in London, and moved with his family to Sydney, at the age of one. He grew up in the southern Sydney suburbs of Coogee and Maroubra, and starting playing rugby league for Maroubra Diggers as a child. Both epilepsy and recognition of his homosexuality nearly led to his giving up the game, but he persevered and began to play for the primarily working-class South Sydney league team in 1986. He gradually became one of the best forwards in Australia, transferred to Manly in 1989 (a move which created

acrimony, since the Manly 'silvertails' were the least working-class team in the country) to become the country's highest paid player. In 1995, after thirteen appearances for Australia, he joined the North Queensland club in Townsville, the same year that he declared that he was gay. Roberts is the only prominent Australian sportsman to have declared his homosexuality, and the only prominent rugby league player in the world to do so. In this particularly working-class game he received both abuse and considerable praise. Roberts battled with injuries, and retired from the sport in 1999, having gradually become something of a media celebrity and a supporter of various charities. His athletic physique also fitted him to enter a new profession of modelling for fashion and other advertisements.

Paul Freeman, *Ian Roberts – Finding Out* (Sydney, 1997).

John Connell

Robinson, Svend (b. 1952), Canadian politician. In 1988 Svend Robinson revealed on national television that he was gay, the first federal Member of Parliament to have ever come out, and for over a decade afterwards one of only two. From long before that, and through to the present, he has been an outspoken advocate for a variety of activist causes, including those which focus on sexual orientation.

Robinson was the son of an academic father and nurse mother who had left their native US in part because of the war in Vietnam. They moved to Burnaby, then a largely working-class suburb of Vancouver, in Canada's west coast province of British Columbia. Starting as a teenager, Robinson worked for the New Democratic Party (NDP), a social democratic party that was strong in provincial elections in a few of the country's western provinces, but generally only attaining minor party status at the federal level.

Robinson ran in his first federal election in 1979, at the age of 27, and won. There were enough rumours about his sexual orientation that his Conservative Party rival played on it in door-to-door campaigning. He was not yet convinced that his constituents would be ready to accept his homosexuality, though from the beginning he was an assertive advocate for lesbian and gay rights. He played an important role in legislative deliberations over a new Charter of Rights and Freedoms, approved in 1982, helping secure wording that would eventually be read by courts as protecting sexual minorities from discrimination. He was also a crucial player in a 1985 parliamentary inquiry that reported favourably on the importance of gay and lesbian rights.

Over the years, he has been a stong defender of the labour movement, feminism, aboriginal rights, environmentalism and a variety of other equity and civil liberties principles, invariably positioning himself on the left of his own party. From the beginning of his parliamentary career, in fact, he marked himself out as unusually independent, in a system generally characterised by tight party discipline. That, along with his articulateness and readiness to engage in extra-parliamentary activism, provided him with a high media profile that was exceptional for a Canadian legislator.

For some years, Robinson had been encouraged by gay and lesbian activists to come out. Early in 1988, knowing that his Conservative opponents would try to use the issue against him more than ever, and encouraged by the experiences of Chris SMITH in Britain and both Gerry STUDDS and Barney FRANK in the US, Robinson decided to make his announcement, once again making national news headlines. The Conservatives did indeed try to use the issue, but unsuccessfully.

Robinson was indefatigable in attending to constituency business. That, along with his principled independence and media visibility, bolstered his electoral strength at home. He won not only the election that immediately followed his coming out,

but the 1993 election, in which the NDP suffered enormous losses and a new right-wing party called Reform scored significant wins. He was re-elected in the 1997 election, fighting off a serious electoral challenge from the ruling Liberal Party.

In 1995, Robinson ran for the leadership of his own party. From the beginning, he staked out a position on the left, and drew together campaigners associated with a variety of the social movement causes that he had championed over the years. For a time, he was the front-runner in that campaign, though in the end he lost to Alexa McDonough. Robinson's gayness was not the most important of the factors that led to defeat, but it contributed to the view among significant numbers of the party faithful that he would damage the NDP electorally. What was more important was his unambiguously left position within the party, and the reputation he had among some party insiders for not being enough of a loyal team player. It was precisely that quality of independence that made him an exciting candidate for many activists inside and outside the party.

Robinson is widely considered one of the smartest and hardest-working parliamentarians in Ottawa. He also has earned virtual hero status among countless gays and lesbians across the country, many of whom he has addressed in countless speeches to local meetings. He gained respect among gays, lesbians, bisexuals and the transgendered largely because of his persistent willingness to identify with social movement activism even while operating within the constraints of a partisan legislative environment. His visibility has declined somewhat in recent years, in part a result of declining NDP strength in Ottawa, in part a result of his having developed more of a personal life. In the mid-1990s, he began a relationship with Max Riveron, and incorporated the partnership into his public presentation of himself, claiming benefits for Riveron that would normally accrue to a parliamentary 'spouse'. Robinson was seriously injured in a hiking accident at the end of 1997 – an accident that almost killed him – and the recovery from that contributed to a somewhat slower political pace in the following couple of years.

David Rayside, *On the Fringe: Gays and Lesbians in Politics* (Ithaca, NY, 1998).

David Rayside

Rochefort, Christiane (b. 1917), French author. Rochefort was born in Paris into a working-class family with socialist views: her father fought in the International Brigade against Franco in the Spanish Civil War. She worked as a journalist and spent fifteen years as a press attaché to the Cannes Film Festival. It was not until 1958 that she published her first novel, *Le Repos du guerrier*, which enjoyed a *succès de scandale* because its subject – the love affair between a middle-class girl and an alcoholic – was considered risqué. The novel was a commercial success too, and was made into a film starring Brigitte Bardot (1962). Her second novel, *Les Petits Enfants du siècle* (1961), about the horrors of childhood in the working-class suburbs of Paris, was shortlisted for the Prix Goncourt, won the Prix du Roman populiste and was also a best-seller. Thereafter her work has ranged widely from the social and psychological realism of *Les Stances à Sophie* (1963) to the feminist Utopian parable *Archaos ou le jardin étincelant* (1972). In 1988 she received the Prix Médicis for *La Porte du fond*. She has been reticent about her own private life – the autobiographical *Ma Vie revue et corrigée par l'auteur* (1978) is not designed to give access to her personal secrets. In her works, however, her treatment of gender and sexual orientation is notably progressive. In *Les Stances à Sophie* the only point at which the two married women at the centre of the novel ever experience really meaningful physical and emotional contact with anyone is during their brief mutual lesbian affair. Like Colette, Rochefort seems to envisage lesbianism as an im-

portant aspect of the potential experience of womanhood rather than as a separate identity. Similarly, in *Printemps au parking* (1969) Rochefort gives a masterly analysis of the emotional and sexual relationship between two young males – a student and a teenager – from which the notion of clearly categorisable sexual personas is excluded. In both *Les Stances à Sophie* and *Printemps au parking* sexual freedom is represented as the first weapon against the constrictions which bourgeois society has constructed around the individual. In *Archaos* Rochefort goes on to present a natural polysexuality as the necessary basis for the kind of direct communication, sincerity and solidarity essential to the construction of an alternative world. Her vision is perhaps more in accord with contemporary notions of 'queer' than with the gay liberationist ideals current in the 1970s when she formulated her position.

Margaret Ann Hutton, *Countering the Culture: The Novels of Christiane Rochefort* (Exeter, 1999); Christopher Robinson, *Scandal in the Ink* (London, 1995).

Christopher Robinson

Roffiel, Rosamaría (b. 1945), Mexican author, journalist. Born in Veracruz, Roffiel has worked as a journalist for *Excelsior* and the journals *Proceso* and *fem*.

Whereas her poetry is mainly concerned with issues of love, either heterosexual or lesbian, her prose deals with socio-political problems and specifically the oppression of women. In *Corramos libres ahora* (1986), a poetry collection, the themes of love, the female body and sexuality are central. *¡Ay, Nicaragua, Nicaraguita!* (1987) is a sociopolitical testimonial, a book that emerged during Roffiel's stay in Nicaragua during the Sandinista revolution and one that narrates her experiences during those years.

Amora, 'the first lesbian novel published in Mexico' (Foster), presents a lesbian discourse that affirms the value of women loving and working with other women. The novel starts with the meeting of Claudia and Lupe, testifies to the development of this relationship, the crisis that Claudia (a woman who is forcing herself to be heterosexual) experiences, the separation of the two women, and their final coming-to-terms with their sexuality.

One of the novel's chapters ('Hey, Aunt, What are lesbians like?') exposes and confronts the prejudices against lesbians. Lupe's niece asks her about the behaviour of lesbians while another young girl defends the stereotype of lesbians. The narrator makes a claim for lesbians' rights to their love and their sexuality.

Imbued with Mexican colloquialisms, the novel attacks the silencing and marginalisation of women in Latin American countries and states the need of working with other women toward a feminist agenda.

David William Foster, *Gay and Lesbian Themes in Latin American Writing* (Austin, 1991), pp. 114–18; Elena M. Martínez, Review of *Dos Mujeres* (Sara Levi Calderón) and *Amora* (Rosamaría Roffiel), *Letras Femeninas*, vol. 18. nos. 1–2 (Spring – Autumn 1992), pp. 175–9; Claudia Schaefer-Rodríguez, 'Rosamaria Roffiel', in David William Foster (ed.), *Latin American Writers on Gay and Lesbian Themes. A Bio-Critical Sourcebook.* (Westport, CT, 1994), pp. 382–5.

Elena M. Martínez

Rorem, Ned (b. 1923), American diarist and composer. Raised in Chicago by Quaker parents, Rorem studied at the Curtis Institute of Music and later at the Juilliard School in New York. By his mid-twenties he was winning acclaim for his song settings which, along with essays in other miniature forms, remain his most significant musical achievement. His music has been described as 'lean and elegant'.

Notoriety of a different order came to Rorem in the wake of the publication of his *Paris Diary* (1966). A chronicle of his late twenties, spent largely in Paris and Morocco, its provocative opening pages report a lunchtime discussion of masturbation, a meeting with Picasso and the first of many references to the writer's own (independently attested) physical beauty. With an engaging blend of candour, bravado and self-deprecation, Rorem goes on to detail such matters as his homosexuality and promiscuity; his drunken binges and hangovers; his work and extended bouts of laziness; and his many contacts with the famous (e.g. Cocteau, Alice B. Toklas, Gide), in a text liberally dotted with epigrammatic asides (e.g. 'The beautiful are shyer than the ugly, for they move in a world that does not ask for beauty'; and 'The same piece of music alters at each hearing. But oh, the need to repeat and repeat and repeat unchanged the sexual experience'). His later writings are even more candid in their revelations of Rorem's sexual contacts (e.g. Leonard BERNSTEIN, Noel Coward), and those whose advances he politely declined (Samuel Barber, Virgil Thomson), together with anecdotes about the proclivities of famous acquaintances (e.g. Francis POULENC and Julius Katchen), a handful of which must be counted as literary 'outings'.

Ned Rorem, *The Paris Diary of Ned Rorem* (New York, 1966), *The New York Diary* (New York, 1967), *Knowing When to Stop: A Memoir* (New York, 1994).

Graeme Skinner

Rosen, Wilhelm von (b. 1941), Danish scholar and activist. Wilhelm von Rosen was born and educated in Copenhagen, and took degrees from both Odense University and the University of Copenhagen. His thesis, for which he was awarded a D. Phil. from the latter university in 1994, was on Danish gay history from 1628 to 1912. He currently holds a position as Senior Researcher at the Danish National Archives, where he has worked as an archivist since 1970.

Rosen has been active in both gay politics and gay research. He was involved in the Copenhagen Gay Liberation Front from 1973 to 1977; arising from his initial thesis research, he has published articles in both Danish and English on Hans Christian Andersen, the politics of gay liberation, and Denmark's gay history, including, with Vagn Sondergaard, an edited book on gay life and gay writers for the high school curriculum.

Apart from his editing of the six-volume *Guide to the National Archives of Denmark*, from 1977 to 1983 he was co-editor of *Pan*, a monthly journal published by the Danish National Union of Gays and Lesbians, probably the longest-running extant publication for homosexuals.

He has been the recipient of various awards, including The Director of the National Archives Axel Lindvald's Memorial Prize in 1984.

Robert Aldrich and Garry Wotherspoon

Ross, Sinclair (1908–96), Canadian writer. Although not Canada's most read author – indeed, he tends to be little-known outside universities – James Sinclair Ross is perhaps the country's most canonised author. His 1941 novel, *As For Me and My House*, has garnered and generated a steady stream of criticism; most notably, critiques published just after Ross's death and posthumous 'outing' seek to examine his work with specific attention to the machinations of the writings' ambiguity, especially as such imputation underscores queerness and, particularly, homosexuality.

Ross's career as a writer had no auspicious beginning. He grew up on Saskatchewan farms, under the care of his mother, who had early on divorced her seemingly unstable husband. Ross was employed by the Royal Bank of Canada, stationed in various small prairie towns that would inform much of his early work, until he was transferred to Winnipeg in 1933. He was part of the war effort in England, from 1942 to 1946, and these years are reflected in some of his later fiction, such as 'Barrack Room Fiddle Tune' (1947). He spent the rest of his banking career in Montreal, until retiring in 1968. Abroad for twelve years, in Spain and Greece, Ross returned to Canada's west coast in 1980, living in Vancouver until his Parkinson's-related death.

In addition to *As For Me and My House*, Ross published three other novels – *The Well* (1958), *Whir of Gold* (1970), *Sawbones Memorial* (1974) – and two collections of short stories, including eighteen previously published stories, from the years spanning 1934 to 1972.

His earlier works, prior to 1945, feature mostly rural settings in which he thematically explored the sensitivities and sensibilities of boys and young men, especially as they struggle in (and often against) socially and environmentally challenging settings. *As For Me and My House*, for example, depicts the psychological resilience of a hypocritical small-town minister and his wife as they resist, with varying degrees of success, both the morally-freighted dictums of the prairie Bible-belt influence and the anxieties caused by hardships arising from the drought-ridden land in the Depression-era 1930s. The novel is rife with ambiguity such as the main male character's attachment to a pubescent boy. Other stories examine the lives of rather rough-hewn women – 'No Other Way' (1934); 'Nell' (1941) – whose gender attributes are clearly unstable, as are their marriages to rather effeminate, 'dandified' men. Later post-war works reveal a fascination with more intense psycho-pathological leanings – 'Jug and Bottle' (1949); 'Spike' (1967); 'The Flowers that Killed Him' (1972) – especially as the stories' characters may reveal a subtext of homosexuality as pathologically inspired. *Sawbones Memorial* features a gay-identified character, who is as 'out' as one might be in the small-town Saskatchewan of 1948. Yet he, too, despite his relative openness, appears to mirror the Freudian cliché of the domineering mother as having motivated her son's homosexuality.

Andrew Lesk

Rowse, A(lfred) L(eslie) (1903–97), British scholar. Born in Cornwall – where he later returned to live, and about which he often wrote – Rowse was educated at Christ Church, Oxford, and later became a fellow of All Souls' College there. Rowse was an eminent specialist of Elizabethan England, elected a Fellow of the British Academy and a Fellow of the Royal Society of Literature. He was the author of almost a hundred books, including studies of Elizabethan England, the Churchill family, the Puritan Revolution, the Tower of London, Westminster Abbey, Oxford, Milton, a biography of Marlowe, a memoir about W. H. Auden and several volumes of poetry and autobiography. He was widely acclaimed, in particular, as a Shakespearean scholar, and produced an annotated three-volume edition of his works and various other books on the Bard. Rowse argued that 'Shakespeare himself was even more than normally heterosexual, for an Elizabethan'. He discounted any homosexual aspects to Shakespeare's *Sonnets*, saying that it is 'wish fulfilment' to read homosexuality in the verses; 'Mr. W.H.', he asserted, was the publisher's dedicatee, not Shakespeare's.

In 1977, Rowse published *Homosexuals in History: A Study of Ambivalence in Society, Literature and the Arts*. The preface stated disarmingly, 'This book is decidedly *not* pornography. It is a serious study – or a series of studies – in history and society, literature and the arts,' which he hoped, 'may throw some light on the predisposing conditions to creativeness, in the psychological rewards of ambivalence, the doubled response to life, the sharpening of perception, the tensions that lead to achievement.' Rowse's work provided profiles of a large number of male figures, from the Renaissance to the twentieth century, mostly writers, who were sexually ambivalent and who had experienced homosexual emotions or relations. The book contained no notes or references, and Rowse's suggestions about the homosexuality of many figures on sometimes circumstantial evidence earned criticism from those who viewed his book as high-class gossip rather than serious research. His theory about connections between sexual ambivalence and creativity was not convincingly articulated, arch comments and idiosyncratic judgements put off some readers and, later, 'social constructionists' were at odds with his implicitly 'essentialist' views about homosexuality. Coming from such a renowned academic, however, the 'outing' of famous figures represented a forthright stance about the prevalence and importance of homosexuals in history, and may be seen, more generously, as a significant contribution to gay biography.

Rowse was somewhat coy about his private life. He was a friend of such ambivalent Oxonians as Graham Greene, Evelyn Waugh, Harold Acton, Christopher ISHERWOOD and Stephen Spender. Like the last two, Rowse spent a meaningful period in Weimar Germany. He formed a close attachment to a young German aristocrat, the son of a former minister to the Kaiser, Adam von Trott – described by Rowse as 'six feet five tall' and 'well aware of his shattering beauty', but 'fundamentally heterosexual'. In a volume of his autobiography, Rowse confessed that for him 'this was an ideal love-affair, platonic in the philosophic sense: we never exchanged a kiss, let alone embrace. We were both extremely high-minded, perhaps too much so'. Rowse helped von Trott earn a Rhodes Scholarship to Oxford, and the two remained friends until the German was killed fighting in the anti-Nazi Resistance.

A. L. Rowse, *A Cornishman Abroad* (London, 1976).

Robert Aldrich

Rule, Jane (Vance) (b. 1931), American-Canadian writer. 'Policing ourselves to be less offensive to the majority is to be part of our own oppression'. Jane Rule's potent effect on lesbian and gay culture is due to this determination to be unabashedly herself, as a writer, a citizen and a person.

Born in Plainsfield, New Jersey, Rule was educated in California and England. In 1956, she moved to Vancouver, British Columbia, where she became affiliated with the University of British Columbia, working there until 1974 as a periodic and visiting lecturer in English and Creative Writing. Here also, she met Helen Sonthoff, her partner and helpmate for over forty years, with whom she shared a home on Galiano Island until Sonthoff's death in 1999.

Her first novel, *The Desert of the Heart*, published in 1964, features Evelyn, who is in Reno ending a sixteen-year marriage, and Ann, who is a change-maker in a casino. Rule's story of how these two very different women found each other and fell in love was a rare affirmation of lesbian loving in its day. Its ending, realistic but notably lacking in tragedy, instilled hope in the hearts of many a young lesbian. (Donna Dietch adapted the novel into the film *Desert Hearts*.) Rule had a difficult time finding a publisher for the book. No US publishers would risk it, and even when Macmillan Canada finally accepted it in 1961, it took another three years for publication. Her second novel, *This Is Not For You*, suffered a similar fate but was finally published in 1970.

Rule's twelve-book output includes the novels *The Young in One Another's Arms* (winner of the Canadian Authors' Association Award for Best Novel of 1978), *Contract with the World* and *After the Fire*, as well as several books of short stories and essays. She has been represented in a number of anthologies and has published articles and stories in magazines ranging from *Chatelaine* to *The Body Politic*. Her writing, whether in fiction or essay, has met with mixed critical reaction. Of *Lesbian Images* (a study of lesbian writers), a *Times Literary Supplement* critic said, 'There is little new that can be said in a

few pages about Radclyffe Hall and Gertrude Stein', while a *Publisher's Weekly* reviewer called the book 'nicely balanced, feeling, instructive and altogether very worthwhile'.

Throughout her career, reviewers have made reference to her lesbianism, whether it is to note that she has 'put her own moral vision ahead of conventions that please critics' or to say that her essays are 'unabashedly clubby' or simply to suggest that her work 'belongs in all lesbian fiction collections'. Given that she has been openly lesbian since her first book, this is not surprising but it does not seem to have marginalised her work. In the early 1990s, Rule stopped writing fiction, stating publicly that she had said all that she needed to say. She has devoted her energies since then to participation in literary events and gay rights issues. Her eloquent testimony in the case of Little Sisters Book and Art Emporium against Canada Customs helped the Vancouver lesbian and gay bookstore win its limited victory.

Her commitment to 'change the social climate' for lesbians and gays has been consistent and clear throughout her more than forty years as a literary figure. In a review of Rule's last novel, Bill Schermbrucker of *Quill and Quire* said: 'Rule's career, like her life, has involved a persistent and articulate assertion of herself in the face of the ignorance, bigotry and denial that surrounds lesbians and books about relationships between women'.

Flaunting It! A Decade of Gay Journalism from The Body Politic (Vancouver, 1982); *Contemporary Canadian Authors*, vol. 1 (London, 1996).

Deborah Thomas

Russell, Craig (1948–90), Canadian female impersonator. Born in Toronto, Russell Craig Eadie was fascinated by the glamour of show business from an early age. When he was 13 and still in high school, he formed the Mae West International Fan Club. By the age of 15, Eadie had moved to

Los Angeles to work for West, a pivotal experience in his show business education. He soon returned to Toronto to finish high school but dropped out for good, working as an insurance clerk before returning to California in 1967. Eadie moved in with West, becoming her personal secretary for seven months, assisting with her fan mail and honing his impersonations of her. In 1968 Eadie returned to Toronto and enrolled in hairdressing school; he worked as a professional hairdresser from 1969 to 1971.

By late 1971 Eadie was performing his female impersonations at gay clubs in Toronto under the name Craig Russell. Soon he was travelling the North American club circuit and gathering a cult following for his repertoire of realistic impressions of famous ladies: from Peggy Lee and Judy Garland to Carol Channing and Barbra Streisand, and of course, his favourite, Mae West. Craig Russell became an international star after the release of the semi-autobiographical film *Outrageous* in 1977, which provided a vehicle for his impersonations and for which he won the Silver Bear award for Best Actor at the Berlin Film Festival in 1978. During the late 1970s Russell toured extensively and played larger venues internationally, but his performances became increasingly erratic due to substance abuse and psychological demons.

In 1980 Russell gave a disastrous performance at Carnegie Hall in New York that affected his career. In an attempt to escape the pressures of celebrity, Russell moved to Munich, Germany, in 1982, and surprised many by marrying Lori Russell. He spent the next several years expanding his act before returning to Toronto in 1986 to film the sequel to *Outrageous*, entitled *Too Outrageous!*. The film received mixed reviews and was unsuccessful at the box office. Russell's psychological and substance abuse problems were by this point barely controllable, and his career spiralled down until his death from AIDS-related complications.

Brice Rhyne, 'Craig Russell: Outrageous Is an Understatement', *Mandate*, Jan. 1979, pp. 39–44, 46; Jay Scott, 'Nothing Too Outrageous for Craig Russell', *Globe and Mail* (Toronto), 13 Nov. 1986', p. D1; Michael Valpy, 'Outrageous Life Was Fable for the Lost and Fragile', *Globe and Mail* (Toronto), 6 Nov. 1990, p. A2.

Donald W. McLeod

Russo, Renato (1960–96), Brazilian rock singer and songwriter. Russo, whose real name was Renato Manfredini Júnior, was born into a family of Italian descent in Rio de Janeiro. His father was an economist with the Bank of Brazil and his mother an English teacher. From age 7 to 10 Russo lived with his family in New York, where he soon became fluent in English. Returning to Brazil, the Russos settled in Brasília, leading a comfortable upper-middle-class lifestyle.

In 1978 Russo formed a punk band which was named Aborto Elétrico (Electric Abortion). Then, after a spell as solo artist, he formed Legião Urbana (Urban Legion) in 1984. The music of this band was loud and aggressive, appealing strongly to the younger generation brought up under the military regime, which was then relinquishing power. At huge shows in football stadiums the band exchanged insults with the audience and several finished in riots. The band had a series of hit albums which turned Legião Urbana into the most popular Brazilian rock band. *The Four Seasons* sold over three-quarters of a million discs, more than double that of any of its rivals. The band's last album was *O Descobrimento do Brasil* (*The Discovery of Brazil*), which appeared in 1993.

In 1989, Russo's adoptive son was born; around the same time, he began to talk about his bisexuality and later came out as gay in an interview. In 1989 he met an American in a gay bar in the US but the two-year relationship was traumatic due to his lover's drug addiction. Russo fell into a downward spiral of alcoholism, heroin addiction and depression. In 1990 he was diagnosed as HIV-positive, although he never publicly acknowledged his illness. By 1994 he was recovering from his alcohol and drug dependency. He became active in supporting AIDS prevention, the gay movement and the fight against drugs. He was one of the few major figures of Brazilian popular culture to be openly gay. He actively supported gay causes and his frankness about his sexuality served as an inspiration to isolated gays throughout the country. In 1996, Russo died of AIDS in Rio de Janeiro.

The traumas of the latter part of Russo's life were reflected in his music. The chorus of one of his songs, 'Meninos e Meninas' (Boys and Girls), was widely sung at the time he was acknowledging his bisexuality: 'I like boys and Girls.' From 1990 on, when he went solo again, he surprised critics and audiences with a more serious, melodious style, drawing partly on classical music and literature for inspiration. In 1993 he issued his first solo album, with an English title and sung in English. *The Stonewall Celebration Concert* was inspired by his American lover, who had died, and the gay movement. The disc bears a prominent pink triangle and a quotation from Auden: 'If equal affection cannot be / let the more loving one be me.'

Renato Russo, *Conversações com Renato Russo* (Campo Grande, 1996); Chris McGowan and Ricardo Pessanha, *The Billboard Book of Brazilian Music: Samba, Bossa Nova and the Popular Sounds of Brazil* (Enfield, 1991). 'O Novo Rei do Rock' *Veja*, 17 Oct. 1990, pp. 58–62; articles in *Sui Generis*, No. 4 (June 1995) and No. 17 (1996).

Robert Howes

Russo, Vito (1946–91), American author and film historian. Russo is a good example of the activist/writer whose writing was part of their activism, and whose activities from the 1970s played such an important part in opening up our knowledge of homosexuality in the past. In Russo's case, this was on how homosexuality had been dealt with in US films since the start of the motion picture industry.

Growing up in New York and New Jersey, Russo was able to experience at first hand gay life in and around Greenwich Village and Fire Island. While working in film distribution in the early 1970s, he became involved in Gay Activists Alliance (GAA), and began showing 'gay' films at the GAA Firehouse from 1971. His interest in the portrayal of lesbians and gays developed rapidly, leading to his slide shows and presentations, with which he travelled the world. His researches culminated in a book, *The Celluloid Closet: Homosexuality in the Movies* (1981; rev. edn, 1987), the definitive and enormously influential exposé of how homosexuality had been treated in (predominantly) American movies, for which he received the Gay-Book-of-the-Year Award from the American Library Association. The book was said to have been rejected by twenty-two publishing houses before it was finally published. He himself appeared in several documentaries, including *Common Threads: Stories From the Quilt* (1989), whose directors went on to make a film, *The Celluloid Closet* (1995), based on his book.

He died of AIDS-related complications.

Contemporary Authors, vol. 107 (Detroit, 1983).

Garry Wotherspoon

S

Saint Laurent, Yves (b. 1938), French fashion designer. Born in Algeria to French parents, Saint Laurent moved to Paris in 1954 where, soon after, he was employed by Christian Dior, the most successful fashion designer of the period. Although Dior was homosexual, the relationship with his young assistant was of a strictly professional nature, and Saint Laurent cites Dior as a major influence on his own work. After Dior's death in 1957, the 21 year-old was appointed chief designer of the Dior company, then France's largest and most prestigious fashion house.

In 1958, Saint Laurent met and fell in love with the entrepreneur Pierre Bergé. This lifelong personal association rapidly became a professional one, as Bergé assumed the financial, marketing and day-to-day affairs of a new venture, established in 1961, and centred around the *haute couture* house named after Saint Laurent. Bergé's business acumen is responsible for the creation of an international, multi-million dollar enterprise around Saint Laurent's prodigious talent. In 1971, even an image of the designer himself, posed provocatively in the nude, was the focus of an advertising campaign launching the company's first men's perfume. The creation of an international chain of boutiques, retailing exclusive, ready-made garments under the label Saint Laurent Rive Gauche (established in 1966) was the best organised and most successful effort among their Paris contemporaries.

Saint Laurent presented his first collection in 1962. In the following three decades, he had a decisive influence on women's fashion: highlights included the influential 'Trapeze' silhouette (1958) – a subtle tent-shape denoting a freer and more youthful trend; the 'Mondrian' dresses (1965) recreating the crisp, colour blocking of the Dutch Modernist painter; the 'Ballets Russes' collection (1976), featuring designs inspired by Russian folk costume; and the equally opulent 'Chinese' collection (1977). This foreshadowed a return to ostentation and formality in dress during the 1980s, as well as the use of *haute couture* shows as a promotional tool for the mass-marketing of designer perfumes, cosmetics and other licensed products bearing the designer's name.

Saint Laurent's most significant contribution to the vocabulary of women's fashion is a set of forms – especially jacket and trouser shapes – borrowed directly from men's tailoring. These include the sailor's navy wool pea-coat (1962), 'Le Smoking' (1966) and the plain and pinstripe suit (1971). In each case, Saint Laurent has naturalised each of these familiar forms into a convincing, transgendered garment for the late twentieth-century woman without sacrificing the power, sobriety, luxury and practicality of men's suits.

Other areas in which Saint Laurent has

achieved considerable success include theatre and film design as well as men's fashion. For all his success, Saint Laurent is painfully shy and reclusive by nature. One senses that an impetus for his work is the desire to project a confident and outgoing image of himself on the cat-walk, dressed in one of his own perfectly proportioned, androgynous suits.

The Metropolitan Museum of Art, *Yves Saint Laurent* (New York, 1984); Marguerite Duras, *Yves Saint Laurent: Images of Design, 1958–1988* (New York, 1988); Laurence Benaïm, *Yves Saint Laurent* (Paris, 1993).

Roger Leong

Saisio, Pirkko Helena (b. 1949), Finnish actress, writer and playwright. Among her other literary works relating to homo-sexuality, Pirkko Saisio has authored the first Finnish-language lesbian novel. The climate earlier had not been favourable for such an endeavour. For example, novelist Helvi Hämäläinen had planned to publish in 1928 a novel on the close friendship of two women. Apparently, the manuscript was conceived of as a lesbian love story and the publishers rejected it. There was an explicitly lesbian novel published in Finland but written in Swedish, by Nalle Valtiala (*Lotus*, 1973). Short stories and poems with lesbian themes were also pub-lished in Finland before Saisio's novel *Kai-nin tytär* (*Daughter of Cain*, 1984) finally became the first novel in Finnish which dealt openly with a lesbian relationship as its main theme.

Homosexuality has been one theme throughout Saisio's literary production. Social differences, homophobia and vio-lence are described in her novel *Betoniyö* (*The Concrete Night*, 1981). She also dis-cussed lesbian love in her play *Hissi* (*The Lift*, 1987, produced by Kom Theatre in Helsinki), which is set in a prison.

In the late 1980s and the early 1990s, Pirkko Saisio was using the pseudonyms 'Jukka Larsson' and 'Eva Wein'. The name 'Eva Wein' can be pronounced so that, in Finnish, it means 'Just Eve'. Using the male pseudonym 'Jukka Larsson', Saisio received positive reviews for her trilogy *Kiusaaja* (*The Tormentor*, 1986), *Viettelijä* (*The Tempter*, 1987), and *Kantaja* (*The Bearer*, 1991), which is inspired by biblical texts. When the media tried to find out the identity of the author, there was specula-tion as to which one of the Finnish male (sic!) authors was lurking behind the pseudonym. Together with her female partner, Pirjo Honkasalo, a filmmaker, Saisio created an outward appearance for the fictive 'Jukka Larsson'. They even took photographs of Saisio with a false mous-tache. Finally, Saisio revealed the truth about 'Jukka Larsson' in an interview. Sai-sio has later described how liberating it can be to write using a pseudonym. She also had an opportunity to see how differ-ently male and female authors are treated by critics. When 'Eva Wein' debuted with the work *Puolimaailman nainen* (*Woman of the Half-World*, 1990), the critics were partly negative. However 'Eva Wein's' sec-ond work, *Kulkue* (*The Procession*, 1992), was nominated for a coveted literature prize, the Finlandia award. Again Saisio revealed the hoax, but only when going to the press conference for the nominees.

Saisio has written novels and plays, plus a travel story (this with her partner Hon-kasalo). Saisio has also been involved in theatre and drama for television. Hon-kasalo and Saisio have together parented Pirkko Saisio's biological daughter Elsa. Elsa Saisio debuted as an actress in the movie *Tulennielijä* (*The Fire-Eater*, 1998), written by Saisio and directed by Hon-kasalo. In the mid-1990s Saisio came out in the media as a lesbian mother when public discussion for legislation of same-sex marriages and gay and lesbian adoption rights was raised in Finland.

Presently Saisio has a fixed-term post as a professor in the Theatre Academy of Finland.

Pirkko Saisio, 'Contrapuntal Dialogue: An Ex-tract from the Novel *Kainin tytär (Daughter of*

Cain)', Books from Finland, no. 2 (1985), pp. 129–35.

Johanna Pakkanen

Sánchez, Luis Rafael (b. 1936), Puerto Rican essayist, short-story writer, playwright, novelist. Born in a coastal town to a middle-class family, Sánchez took degrees at the University of Puerto Rico, New York University and the University of Madrid. While he has taught Latin American and Spanish Literature at the University of Puerto Rico, he is best known as a novelist and an essayist because of his novels *La guaracha del Macho Camacho* (*Macho Camacho's Beat*, 1976), *La importancia de llamarse Daniel Santos* (*The Importance of Being Named Daniel Santos*, 1988) *La guagua áerea* (*The Air Bus*, 1994) and in the story 'Jum!' *En cuerpo de camisa* – (*Body Show*, 1966).

Sánchez's work shows three themes: an existentialist anguish (mainly in his drama), Puerto Rican popular culture (in his novels and short stories), and the construction of a Puerto Rican identity through 'the other' (the Anglo-Saxon) in essays and novels. Sánchez's most common literary technique is the use of a polyphony of voices that at an allegorical level represent the voices of the different Puerto Ricans that have been juxtaposed in the island. Myths, popular music, humour, colloquial and formal language, trips, sarcasm, body language, use of one's own body and traffic jams show the construction and the establishment of a nationalist ideology.

Sánchez presents a discourse of homosexuality in *La guaracha*, *La importancia* and particularly in 'Jum'. On a literal reading Sánchez introduces the theme of homosexuality through the use of a discourse of masculinity and a rejection (homophobia) of queer practices. Through a discourse of masculinity he aims to praise and accept male chauvinism as a trait of the Puerto Rican popular culture, as can be seen in *La importancia* ('the orthodoxy of living manly' and 'My

semen belongs to whoever wants it'). The author also presents the discrimination against homosexuality.

On an allegorical level, Sánchez reflects on the social, political, ideological, sexual and identity crisis the nation was facing in the 1960s and 1970s, as it was trying to build an identity based on the ideology of 'manhood and male chauvinism'. In 1974 Congress approved a new penal code for Puerto Rico in which homosexual practices were given a specific criminal status. Therefore, Sánchez's depiction of homosexuality represents not only a discourse of homophobia, but also a challenge and a space for gay individuals who want to satisfy their homoerotic needs and sexual fantasies without being marginalised or silenced.

In addition, Sánchez is important because before the 1970s his short story 'Jum!' was the only work with a gay theme in Puerto Rican literature. Then ten years later, he returned to the same theme in his novel *La guaracha*. Here Sánchez introduces the *loca* character, embodying gender crossing and a discourse of transvestism. Sánchez succeeds not only in representing and narrating the homosexuality/queer practices through the hatred '*maricón/loca*', but also at an allegorical level representing both the lack of identity – the concept of being torn apart between two cultures – and the rejection of homosexual individuals, and the degree of marginalisation and subalternity of homosexuals in a society where maleness is based on a male chauvinist concept.

Arnaldo Cruz Malavé, 'Toward an Art of Transvestism: Colonialism and Homosexuality in Puerto Rican Literature', and Agnes I, Lugo-Ortiz, 'Community at its Limits: Orality, Law, and the Homosexual Body in Luis Rafael Sánchez's "Jum!"', in Emilie L. Bergmann and Paul Julian Smith (eds), *¿Entiendes?: Queer Readings and Hispanic Writings* (Durham, NC, 1995), pp. 137–67; David William Foster, 'Luis Rafael Sánchez', *Latin American Writers on*

Gay and Lesbian Themes: A Bio-Critical Sourcebook. (Westport, CT, 1994), pp. 401–4.

Juan Antonio Serna

Sanders, Douglas Esmond (b. 1938), Canadian activist and scholar. Sanders was a founding member and the second president of the Vancouver-based Association for Social Knowledge (ASK), Canada's first lesbian and gay rights organisation (formed in 1964 and lasting four years). Representing ASK, he was secretary for a period of the North American Conference of Homophile Organizations.

In 1991, he co-founded (with Christine Morrissey) the Lesbian and Gay Immigration Task Force (LEGIT). The following year, representing the International Lesbian and Gay Association (ILGA), he was the first 'out' person to speak at the United Nations, in the annual session of the Sub-Commission on Prevention of Discrimination and Protection of Minorities. In 1997, he played a central role in redrafting ILGA's constitution, and was elected to its Board. In 1998, representing the Canadian organisation EGALE (Equality for Gays and Lesbians Everywhere), he received funding from the Canadian International Development Agency for work towards a regional conference of lesbian and gay leaders in south-east Asia.

Sanders began teaching law in 1969, first in Ontario and then at the University of British Columbia. In 1990, he began teaching a course on lesbian and gay legal issues there, this being one of the first such law courses in the country. He has published law journal articles on lesbian/gay rights in Canada and in the international arena.

D. Sanders, 'Constructing Lesbian and Gay Rights', *Canadian Journal of Law and Society*, vol. 9, no. 2 (1994), pp. 99–143; 'Getting Lesbian and Gay Issues on the International Human Rights Agenda', *Human Rights Quarterly*, vol. 18 (1996), pp. 67–106; Gary Kinsman, *The Regulation of Desire: Homo and Hetero Sexualities*, (Montreal, 1996); Don McLeod,

Lesbian and Gay Liberation in Canada (Toronto, 1996).

David Rayside

Santi, Piero (1912–90), Italian writer. Born into a family of modest means at Volterra, Santi moved to Florence with his family when he was six years old. Apart from brief sojourns in Rome, Milan and Paris, he lived in Florence, the city he both loved and hated, all his life. He gained degrees in letters and jurisprudence, and worked for some years as a teacher, but the world of the school never particularly interested him. He started to write towards the end of the 1930s, initially as a critic of art and literature. By the beginning of the 1940s he had become an indefatigable leader of cultural life in Florence, and friend of the major intellectual figures of the time, who met regularly at the famous 'Giubbe Rosse' café. Among his many activities, he founded an art gallery, L'Indiano, and directed the literary journal *Cabalà*. At least among his friends, Santi never hid his homosexuality, and from an early date his stories featured adolescents coming to terms with the discovery of sex, and included specific allusions to homoerotic desire. This sets him apart from many of his friends, from Ottone Rosai to Palazzeschi to GADDA, all of whom were particularly careful not to reveal their sexual inclinations, and made Santi one of the most courageous writers of his time.

In the 1950s Santi published an autobiographical work which portrayed the search, sometimes obsessive, for sexual partners in public places, such as on the banks of the Arno river or at certain cinemas. He was particularly fascinated by cinemas as meeting places, and in 1954 began a project on the history of Florence's cinemas, *Ombre rosse*, in which he details the rituals of cinema cruising, effectively evoking the sense of complicity and the overcoming of inhibitions in those shadowy contexts. It was in the 1960s that Santi produced his two major novels, *Il sapore della menta* and *Libertà condizionata*.

But Santi was essentially an auto-biographical writer and his best work is to be found in his *Diario* of 1950, later expanded and republished with the title *La sfida dei giorni* in 1968, and in *Cronos Eros* in 1990.

Also of particular interest are two short stories, from the collection *Avventure nel parco* (1942), and *Due di loro* (1971). The latter presents a typically pagan, Mediterranean and Italian form of homoeroticism: two 'heterosexual' friends find themselves in the same bed (to protect the honour of their fiancées), discover the possibility of having sex together, but never for a moment suspect that either may be homosexual. They each marry their fiancées that same day but continue to be friends and to have sex 'at least once a week', while their wives continue to be wives.

Somewhat removed from fashion and success, Santi always put honesty to himself ahead of social gratification, even though this approach had its price. Notwithstanding authoritative critical recognition, his works were usually published by small houses, and remained in some ways 'clandestine'. They never reached a wide public, probably precisely because they treated homosexuality without the veils and mediation which until recent years were *de rigueur* in Italy.

Always fascinated by youth and beauty, Santi spent his final years surrounded by young and affectionate friends. He died in Florence.

Giovanni Dall'Orto, *La pagina strapata* (Turin, 1987); Andrea Papi (ed.), *Intorno al cuore di Piero Santi, in Quaderni di critica omosessuale*, no. 6 (Bologna, 1989).

Francesco Gnerre

Sapphire (Ramona Lofton) (b. 1950), American writer. Sapphire was one of four children born to an army family in California. During her early twenties, Sapphire lived in San Francisco before moving to New York City in 1976 where she currently lives and works. In New York, inspired by the work of Ntozake Shange and the Black Arts Movement, she set up NAPS, the first known black lesbian performing arts group in the United States, with Aida Mansuer and Irare Sabasu. Sapphire's first poem was published in 1977 in *Azalea: A Magazine by and for Third World Lesbians*. In 1990 Sapphire decided to concentrate on her writing and later completed an MFA in the writing programme at Brooklyn College where she was the 1994 recipient of the Macarthur Foundation Scholarship in Poetry.

Her work has appeared in several anthologies including *Angry Women, Research Series* (1991); *Women on Women: An Anthology of Lesbian Short Fiction* (1990); *Queer City: The Portable Lower East Side* (1992) and *Loving in Fear: An Anthology of Lesbian and Gay Survivors of Child Sexual Abuse* (1992). Sapphire's first collection of poetry and prose, *American Dreams*, was published in 1994. Sapphire's poetry explores themes of sexual abuse and healing and issues of racism and denial at the heart of the American dream. Her poetry has also been reported to Scotland Yard's Obscene Publications squad because it 'celebrated her sexuality'. In addition, the publication of her poem 'Wild Thing' in the Queer City edition of *The Portable Lower East Side*, a poem written from the perspective of a young black man convicted of the rape of a white female Central Park jogger in 1989, provoked a highly public Congressional controversy over funding offered by the National Endowment of the Arts.

Sapphire's poetry performances and *American Dreams* have earned her a large international audience, and she was offered a two-book contract with her novel *Push* published in 1996. The novel also explores themes of incest, racism, sexuality and writing.

Andrea Juno and V. Vale, *Angry Women* (San Francisco, California, 1991); Jewelle Gomez, 'Cutting Words', *Lambda Book Report*, vol. 4, no. 10 (1995), pp. 6–8; Kelvin Christopher James's interview with Sapphire in *Bomb*, no. 57 (Fall 1996).

Kate Pearcy

Sarduy, Severo (1937–93), Cuban writer. Sarduy's writing provides an interesting starting point for the discussion of homosexuality and identity in the context of Caribbean literature. Like a number of intellectuals outside English-speaking academia, Sarduy mistrusts categories. In one interview he said homosexuality was something he was not interested in. Homosexuality is just a word to fix human nature, and identities are essentially fluid. Following this, characters in his fiction defy categorisation: drag queens, perverse polymorphs and transexuals wander in and out of his narratives as if in a never-ending carnival where meanings resist any fixity. Of course in this world governed by a free libido homosexuality is just an old-fashioned thing, conservative at heart.

Sarduy, who spent most of his professional life in Paris and frequented poststructuralist circles (he wrote several pieces for the journal *Tel Quel*), used postmodern literary theory in support of floating identities and a free-wheeling libido. It is not a coincidence that Roland BARTHES was among his friends and one of his major influences. In both cases, one can choose to praise their honesty or else to read them as exponents of the closet. Neither came out, and the question of whether the theory was just an excuse for a stronger closet has been formulated. In the case of Sarduy, his personal circumstance makes his opinions even more suspect. As a homosexual in a country where men who acted out their homoerotic desires were put in prison, he must have been slightly concerned with his. He was in an ideal position to acknowledge that homosexuality is not about desire, but about politics. If one takes into account that he was more or less a supporter of Castro's regime (as long as his support could take place abroad), things are further complicated. The rejection of a homosexual culture from somebody who met and worked with Virgilio PIÑERA, José LEZAMA LIMA and Reinaldo ARENAS is somewhat puzzling, a case of theory working as a religious creed that blurs experience and depoliticises it.

He was born in Camagüey, a small village; his parents, like most people at the time, were very poor. His literary inclinations were not encouraged, and he decided to study medicine, even if he kept on publishing articles in the journal *Ciclón*, which had been founded by Lezama. He was very much on the side of the Revolution, like many intellectuals of the time. But soon after Castro reached power, Sarduy left for Paris. In spite of repeated invitations, he stayed there. His narrative, though, remains essentially Caribbean. One of the techniques he uses is a reproduction of the 'choteo', a way of speaking characterised by logorrhea, richness of popular vocabulary and constant surrealistic associations. Sarduy's characters, for instance in *De donde son los cantantes* (*Where the Singers Come From*, 1967) talk incessantly, and their words are the only fixed objects in a world where everything else, including personal identity, seems to be provisional. *Cobra* (1972) features prostitution and carnivalesque drag in a plot where characters appear and disappear and change in the baroque world of the tropical jungle. *Colibrí* (*Hummingbird*, 1983), with a plot which turns around a beautiful boy, is perhaps the most homoerotic of his fiction. Sarduy also wrote collections of poetry and literary criticism. His last work, *Pájaros en la arena* (*Birds on the Sand*, 1993), is among his most heartfelt: at last, Sarduy seems to step out of his carnivalesque voice in order to deal with AIDS, something which is both a fixed reality and a social topic. Sarduy died in Paris after complications of an AIDS-related illness.

Óscar Montero, 'The Name of the Game:

Writing/Fading Writer', in *De donde son los cantantes* (Chapel Hill, 1988).

Alberto Mira

Sargeson, Frank (1903–82), New Zealand writer. Sargeson was born Norris Davey in the town of Hamilton, New Zealand. His father was Town Clerk and he grew up in a Methodist family with due respect for the Bible and for books generally, though his father kept a close eye on what young Norris borrowed from the public library and often advised the librarian that the books he had borrowed should not be available for loan. Norris was, however, able to read Walt Whitman's poems without his father becoming suspicious and he delighted in recognising their true meaning.

Davey trained as a solicitor and then travelled to Europe for two years, but on his return to New Zealand, working in Wellington in 1929, a crucial event occurred in his life. He was caught by the police in a sexual encounter with a man the police already had their eye on. The matter was taken to court, the police assuming that Davey, as the younger man, was preyed on by the older, something he played along with. Davey's role in this case was to impact on his life considerably. He could no longer practise law and he spent the months following on the farm of his bachelor uncle for whom he had a considerable respect and affection (both the man and his lifestyle). Here he established patterns of writing which were to continue throughout his life. To help assume a new identity when he moved to Auckland, he took on his uncle's surname (Sargeson) as well as changing his first name to Frank.

Sargeson lived for the rest of his life in simple accommodation on the North Shore of Auckland and adopted a lifestyle of poverty of material possessions, which was for the most part very necessary. However, he also maintained this manner of living through periods when there was not absolute need. Sargeson was very generous in support of younger writers, providing them not only with advice but also with accommodation to enable them to focus on their work. It was here that his companion and lover Harry Doyle, a jockey, frequently stayed from 1935 until Doyle's death in 1971. Following that, Sargeson established another close companionable relationship with a woodsman.

Sargeson was a prolific writer of short stories through the 1930s and 1940s. He described himself as an 'aural writer who writes by ear and appeals more to the ear than the eye' and, using this talent, he captured well a special idiom to translate the experience of the ordinary person. Sargeson said that he 'aimed to write rhythmical ear-taking sentences which would not exactly duplicate any other sentences ever written', reflecting, imparting and enhancing a human condition which could only be that of New Zealand. He succeeded. He was also something of a puritan, challenging New Zealand society's excesses, and very regretful that it had lost its way and was a poor reflection of 'what it might worthily have been'.

A homoerotic thread is evident in a great deal of his writing, the admiration that 'mates' have for one another, their physical strength, their masculine ruggedness and their laconic dialogue, though it is probably fair to state that most readers approaching his work as it was published would not have detected the homosexual masculinity amongst the realistic stories of manly activity.

Through the 1950s Sargeson experienced a more arid period in his writing and then, suddenly, it seemed, in the 1960s and 1970s he experienced a period of enormous productivity, with three volumes of autobiography in which his skills as a writer of fiction were quite evident, volumes of short stories and some novels. In his three volumes of autobiography, *Once is Enough* (1973), *More than Enough* (1975) and *Never Enough* (1977), which are a crowning achievement describing his discovery of his true identity and career in a somewhat hostile environment, Sargeson refers to himself as bisexual but the only evidence of his expressed sexuality places him clearly in the homosexual camp. In common with Paul BOWLES'S autobiography *Without Stopping*, Sargeson is discreet about the more tender and intimate moments of his life, but he also expressed the general view that sexual explicitness was destroying literature by leaving nothing to the imagination. Sargeson's biographer, Michael King, in 1995, proved adept at uncovering a great deal which Sargeson did not publicly admit to in his lifetime and thereby gave a comprehensive picture focusing on his life rather than his work.

Among Sargeson's volumes of short stories are: *Conversation with my Uncle and Other Sketches* (1936), *A Man and his Wife* (1940), *That Summer and Other Stories* (1946), and *Collected Stories, 1935–1963* (1964). His short novels include *When the Wind Blows* (1945), *I for One* (1954), and *Man of England Now* (1972). Sargeson's longer novels include *I Saw in my Dream* (1949), which is without doubt semi-autobiographical at least in its first section, *Memoirs of a Peon* (1965), *The Hangover* (1967), *Joy of the Worm* (1969), and *Sunset Village* (1976).

Michael King, *Sargeson: A Life* (Auckland, 1995).

Michael Wooliscroft

Sarria, José (b. 1923), American performer and activist. Born in San Francisco, Sarria's biological family originated in Colombia and before that in Spain. His mother worked as a domestic servant and had to arrange for a second family to raise her son, born out of marriage. Sarria's 'third family' is one of his own invention: the fantastic royal family that became institutionalised as the Imperial Court System on Halloween 1965.

After serving in the army during World War II, Sarria attended university with the hopes of eventually becoming a school teacher. However, in 1952, he was arrested for solicitation at a prestigious San Francisco hotel bar famous as a gay cruising spot. Already interested in drag and performance, Sarria began to pursue entertainment as a career, working at the famed Black Cat Café; his performances became infamous by the end of the decade for campy renditions of *Carmen* and *Turandot*. The nascent political critique of Sarria's operas took place as the Mattachine Society and the Daughters of Bilitis were achieving some success at reforming the degraded image of homosexuals. Another development in San Francisco was the 'gayola' scandal of 1960 when gay bar owners revealed that they had been the victims of extortion at the hands of city officials. The episode inspired Sarria to stand for a seat on the San Francisco Board of Supervisors in 1961 and in so doing to become the first 'openly-gay' candidate for public office in the United States. Though he did not win, he did garner almost 6,000 votes, providing activists with the notion that gays might best agitate for their rights in electoral politics.

Sarria also became involved with setting up a social network which combined the fanciful royal drag culture from the 1950s with the aspects of the homophile movement in which he participated; the goal was to arm gays with self-respect (campy and overblown, but with irony) as well as to raise money for community organisations. This was the 'Imperial Court System', in which he crowned himself Empress. The group agitated for gay rights, held fund-raisers, provided an arena for active gays to speak in the public sphere, and spread beyond San Franscisco.

Nan Alamilla Boyd, 'San Francisco Was a Wide-Open Town: Charting the Emergence of Gay and Lesbian Communities through the Mid-Twentieth Century' (Doctoral Thesis, Brown University, 1995); John D'Emilio, *Sexual Politics, Sexual Communities: The Making of a Homosexual Minority in the United States, 1940–1970* (Chicago, 1983); Michael Gorman, *The Empress is a Man: Stories from the Life of José Sarria* (Binghamton, NY, 1998).

Martin Meeker

Sarton, May (1912–95), American writer. Born in Belgium in 1912 to George Sarton, a historian of science and Mabel Sarton, an English artist and designer, May Sarton moved to Massachusetts at an early age when her father took a job as a Harvard professor. She lived in New England most of her life. Her early passion was the theatre. After high school she joined a repertory theatre company and within two years had formed her own theatre company and worked with them as director, actress and producer for four more years. At this time as well, she began writing poetry and when her first book of poetry, *Encounter in April*, was published in 1937, Sarton had refocused her considerable energies on writing.

She was the author of more than fifty volumes of poetry and prose, including eight journals. Her journals seemed to touch her many admirers the most. She received countless letters from people young and old, who were touched by her open recording of feelings, dark and light. 'The journals are a way of finding out where I really am', said Sarton. 'I've tried to be honest. It's harder than it looks in a book that you know is going to be published to find the right line between indiscretion [and] to be absolutely open and transparent.' Her last journal, *At Eighty-Two*, was written the year before her death and recounts in vivid detail the brutal realities of illness and old age mixed with the singular and simple joys left to her – her cat, good friends and her home. Her poetry also contained elements of this 'transparency' and of another characteristic she valued highly – 'primary intensity'. In her book, *May Sarton: A Self Portrait*, she said, 'You write poetry for yourself, and God . . . you write novels as a dialogue . . . with other people.' Her earlier novels, such as *Joanna and Ulysses* (1963) and her most well-known novel, *Mrs. Stevens Hears the Mermaids Singing* (1965), certainly contained more of that 'primary intensity' than her later novels. By contrast, *The Education of Harriet Hatfield* (1985)

takes the promising premise of a 60-year-old woman confronting homophobia for the first time after the death of her lover of many years, and delivers it so unevenly – pedagogical passages followed by moments of satisfying insight – that it disappoints as a novel and just barely gets across a successful message.

Sarton admitted to having loved many people in her lifetime. Her lovers, including Juliette Huxley (wife of Julian Huxley of whom she was also lover), were her poetic muses and she sought them and discarded them frequently. She had one long relationship, with Judith Matlack, 'for whom I did not write a great many poems, I am sorry to say'. Many of her former lovers remained dear friends throughout her life. She died surrounded by them in her New England home.

May Sarton, *From May Sarton's Well: Writings of May Sarton* (Watsonville, CA, 1994); Margot Peters, *May Sarton: A Biography* (New York, 1997).

Deborah Thomas

Sartre, Jean-Paul (1905–80), French philosopher and writer. Sartre, who was born in Paris, was the most eminent public intellectual of post-World War II France. Writing prolifically in almost every medium, including novels, short stories and plays, essays, politically engaged journalism and polemic, literary criticism, biography and autobiography, he is best known as the philosopher of French existentialism. In contrast to much philosophy in the English-speaking world, Sartre's 'phenomenological' approach to philosophy offers striking descriptions of the complete range of human experience including love, sexuality and even homosexuality.

At the heart of Sartre's existentialism is a radical conception of human freedom. In his most important and difficult work, *Being and Nothingness* (1943), Sartre describes how, as conscious beings, we partake in the mysteriously undetermined 'nothingness' of the 'for-itself' or consciousness, which exists in radical opposition to the causally determined, objective 'being' of mere things or the 'in-itself'. The 'nothingness' of consciousness is at the heart of human freedom, our ability to transcend the causally determined realm of material things. But with absolute freedom comes absolute responsibility. The burden of responsibility is so arduous that we are forever trying to deny it by denying our freedom. In what Sartre calls 'bad faith' we insist on seeing ourselves as having no choice – whether as a result of biology, character or circumstances – but to be who we are and to act the way we do. As an example of bad faith Sartre discusses a certain homosexual who, though repeatedly acting on his inclinations, guiltily denies that he is 'a pederast'. However, it is *not* the homosexual who is in bad faith but his 'critical' acquaintance, who demands a sincere 'confession' of his sinful nature. In fact, by refusing to identify himself as being a certain kind of person – a homosexual – the homosexual shows a confused understanding of the true nature of his freedom to be or not to be whatever he chooses. The critic, on the other hand, is really asking the homosexual to *deny* his freedom by explaining his actions as the result of his being homosexual rather than simply things he chose to do.

In effect, Sartre's conception of bad faith anticipates queer criticisms of any identity politics that assumes a fixed or 'essential' identity. Rather than *being* gay or lesbian, to be queer is *not to be* confined to any fixed identity or normative sexuality. Writing some decades before gay liberation, Sartre also provides unflattering but acute descriptions of the alienated and, above all, isolated condition of the 'pederast' in a homophobic society. In *Saint Genet*, Sartre wrote: 'The homosexual never thinks of himself when someone is branded in his presence with the name *homosexual*. ... His sexual tastes will doubtless lead him to enter into relationships with this suspect category, but he

would like to make use of them without being likened to them. Here, too, the ban that is cast on certain men by society has destroyed all possibility of reciprocity among them. Shame isolates'. But neither homophobe nor homosexual can be reduced to their social conditioning. Sexuality remains, for Sartre, always a matter of free choice: 'I maintain that inversion is the effect of neither a prenatal choice nor an endocrinal malformation nor even the passive and determined result of complexes. It is an outlet that a child discovers when he is suffocating.' The homosexuality of the child in question, Sartre's heroic anti-hero Jean GENET, is a response to an impossible childhood and an unbearable society, his stubborn assertion of freedom.

Jean-Paul Sartre, *Being and Nothingness: An Essay on Phenomenological Ontology*, trans. Hazel E. Barnes (London, 1958); J-P. Sartre, *Saint Genet: Actor and Martyr* (New York, 1963).

David West

Saslow, James M. (b. 1947), American scholar. Born in Newark, New Jersey, Saslow was educated at Princeton University, Harvard University, the School of the Museum of Fine Arts in Boston and Columbia University, taking degrees in architecture and art history. He taught at Vassar College and Columbia University, and is presently Professor in the Department of Art at Queens College of the City University of New York. He has published widely on Italian Renaissance art and literature. His *Ganymede in the Renaissance: Homosexuality in Art and Society* (1986) was one of the first scholarly works on the theme of homosexuality in art, and Saslow has now published *Pictures and Passions: A History of Homosexuality in the Visual Arts* (1999), a survey of all periods of Western art, plus a chapter on non-Western cultures. He has also published *The Poetry of Michelangelo* (1991), an annotated translation, and was editor-in-chief of the *Bibliography of Gay and Lesbian Art* (1994). He was founding secretary of the executive committee of the Center for Lesbian and Gay Studies in New York. In 1986, he organised and chaired a symposium on gay art history at the College Art Association convention which introduced the 'new scholarship' and modern approaches to history and sexuality; he also helped establish the gay and lesbian caucus of the association.

Robert Aldrich and Garry Wotherspoon

Schwarzer, Alice (b. 1942), German activist. Probably Germany's best-known feminist activist, Schwarzer was born in Wuppertal in the Rhineland. She was the illegitimate child of her 22-year-old mother, and was brought up by her maternal grandparents, forming a particularly strong attachment to her grandfather who, she claims, raised her to be neither a girl nor a boy, but a human being.

After leaving school at 16, Schwarzer took an office job. Two years later she moved to Düsseldorf to work as a secretary in an advertising agency, then to Munich, and finally in 1964 to Paris. After three years in the French capital, she returned to Düsseldorf to train as a journalist with a local newspaper; she had failed the entrance exam for a college course. She also did work for the left-oriented satirical magazine *Pardon* before returning to France (where the student movement had opened some universities to those without passes in the higher school-leaving exams) to study philosophy and sociology at Vincennes.

In the midst of the student movement in Paris, Schwarzer was active in the women's group Mouvement de Libération des Femmes (MLF). In 1970 she met the *grande dame* of French feminism, Simone de Beauvoir, whom she greatly admired. By 1971 she was back in Germany, organising the notorious 'Aktion 218' as part of a campaign against paragraph 218 of the German constitution, which severely limited women's access to legal abortion. 'Aktion 218' took the form of a feature in the German news magazine *Der Stern* in

June 1971, in which 374 women admitted to having obtained an illegal abortion. In 1974, Schwarzer reported for the television programme *Panorama* on doctors who performed abortions, and thus stirred up another scandal.

Her best-selling book, *Der kleine Unterschied und seine großen Folgen* (*The Small Difference Between the Sexes and its Great Consequences*, 1975) contained reports by women on sexual relations, violence and oppression in heterosexual partnerships. Two years later Alice Schwarzer founded *Emma*, the magazine that described itself as by women, for women; its success was immediate, and when the first 200,000 copies sold out, an extra 100,000 had to be printed. These days *Emma* sells only around 50,000 copies and appears with the subtitle 'by women, for people' ('von Frauen für Menschen'); since 1993 it has limited itself to six editions per year.

Schwarzer has campaigned not only on the abortion issue, but also – through *Emma* – against pornography and other forms of violence against women, and more recently for animal rights. She has also taken to appearing on game shows on German television. A controversial figure, she has been called 'a macho in a skirt' by fellow feminists, as well as an inspiring leader of the women's movement. Schwarzer has published biographies of other charismatic women (*Marion Gräfin Dönhoff*, 1996, and *Romy Schneider*, 1998), and very recently two accounts of her own life have appeared, one an authorised biography (Dünnebier and Paczensky), the other more controversial (Mika). Other books by Alice Schwarzer include *PorNo* (1994) and *So sehe ich das! Über die Auswirkung von Macht und Gewalt auf Frauen und anderen Menschen* (*This Is How I See It: On the Effects of Power and Violence on Women and Other Human Beings*, 1997).

Anna Dünnebier and Gerd von Paczensky, *Das bewegte Leben der Alice Schwarzer: Die Biographie* (Berlin, 1998); Gaby Helbig, 'Basha

Mika: Alice Schwarzer' (hamburg.gay-web, June 1998); Basha Mika, *Alice Schwarzer: Eine kritische Biographie* (Hamburg, 1998); WDR Cologne, 'Portrait-Gast: Alice Schwarzer' (broadcast 21.05.1996, internet transcript).

Sarah Colvin

Sedgwick, Eve Kosofsky (b. 1950), American scholar. Probably the most influential and ground-breaking of the so-called 'queer theorists' whose work recharted gay and lesbian studies in the 1990s, Sedgwick earned her Ph.D. at Yale, with a thesis which formed the basis of her first book, *The Coherence of Gothic Conventions* (1980). It reconsidered some of the conventional aspects of gothic fiction in a manner which forecast some of her later more well-known work, if not its preoccupation with sexuality.

With the publication of *Between Men* (1985), Sedgwick's ambitious recharting of the relationship between literary studies and questions of sex and gender became explicit. Sedgwick explored the nature of 'homosocial' relations: specifically, what constituted a basis for social relationship between men, and how social networks of male association both eschew and yet always signal an interest in the idea or figure of the homosexual. Sedgwick's work, which depended upon a series of exacting and creative interpretations of largely canonical literary texts, profoundly affected the way in which literary studies sought to define questions of narrative and the thematic elaboration of sexual issues. Her work similarly cast familiar texts in new light; in particular, her exploration of the interdependency of homosociality (masculine social bonding), homophobia and homosexuality as three relations which structure masculine contact recast the ways in which those topics were to be debated within literary studies for the next decade and beyond.

Between Men, as an innovative social as well as literary analysis, extended the reach of Sedgwick's work beyond the confines of literary scholarship, paving the

way for the 1990 publication of *Epistemology of the Closet*, her most famous work. Following the lead given by FOUCAULT's analysis in *The History of Sexuality* of the ways in which sexuality may be spoken of, Sedgwick makes the audacious claim that the idea of knowledge itself must be understood in terms of the question of sexual knowledge. For Sedgwick, our culture might best be understood through an epistemology of the closet, that is, through the cluster of secrets that revolve around the question of gay identity and self-identification. Sedgwick's claims are based on a series of axioms which both define and restructure the ways in which sexual identity might be understood. For example, she questions the very nature of sexual definition as it revolves around object-choice, rather than a host of other possible definitional parameters; for Sedgwick, the varieties of sexual subjectivities that may be available for the task of self-definition is matched only by the various different ways in which we might understand those sexualities. The closet, in Sedgwick's analysis, stands not merely for the concept of secrecy, but more interestingly for 'the secret of having a secret', or the 'telling secret'. In other words, secrets are interesting as much for what they reveal as for what they fail to disclose. Similarly, Sedgwick is interested in broadening our understanding of the relationship between power and knowledge to include an appreciation of the various kinds of epistemological and political powers vested in ignorance.

Sedgwick's work in *Epistemology of the Closet* was deepened and expanded in the essays collected as *Tendencies* (1993); whereas *Epistemology of the Closet* mostly consisted of extended readings of literary texts, *Tendencies* ranged more widely to consider the questions of autobiographical and ficto-critical writing as well as to further some of the earlier book's investigations of the matter of sexual identification and definition. *Tendencies* animated Sedgwick's familiar themes with extended meditations on 'queer' as both activist and contemplative.

Sedgwick's autobiographical writing, included in *Tendencies*, and her collection of poetry, *Fat Art, Thin Art* (1994), redirected attention to some of the assumptions, implicit and explicit, which are common in and around academic writing, including the question of self-identification, and the relationship between personal and academic writing. Co-editor of the influential Series Q, Sedgwick profoundly affected the burgeoning field of queer theory both in her practice and in her support of the work of other theorists. More recently she co-edited with Adam Frank *Shame and Its Sisters*, a selection from the writing of the psychologist Silvan Tomkins.

Melissa Hardie

Seel, Pierre (b. 1923), French public figure. Seel was the first Frenchman to be recognised officially as a wartime 'homosexual deportee'. Born in Haguenau in Alsace on 16 August 1923, Seel grew up in Mulhouse, where his parents owned a bakery. Sexually active at 17, he came to the attention of the police when he foolishly reported the theft of his watch during a homosexual encounter. The police kept a list of the city's homosexuals, which fell into German hands when Germany occupied France in 1940 and annexed Alsace. The Gestapo arrested Seel on 3 May 1941. After ten days of beatings, he and other local homosexuals were interned in the Vorbrück concentration camp at Schirmeck near Strasbourg. There Seel endured harsh conditions, gnawing hunger and strenuous forced labour – and witnessed scenes of appalling savagery – until unexpectedly released in November 1941. Drafted into the German army in March 1942, he fought unwillingly against the Russians on the Eastern Front.

After the war, Seel made a 'pact of silence' with himself and (as he later wrote) 'began eradicating my homosexuality from my life'. He married in August 1950 and raised three children. The family lived in various towns in France before finally settling in Toulouse in 1968. Seel's marriage broke down in 1978. In May 1981 he attended a lecture at a bookshop in Toulouse on the Nazi deportation of homosexuals from France. He afterwards approached the speaker and revealed his own past experiences. Seel gave an anonymous interview to the homosexual review *Masques* and began attending meetings of David et Jonathan, an organisation of gay Catholics.

In April 1981 the Archbishop of Strasbourg remarked at a press conference, 'I consider homosexuality a sickness.' Seel wrote a public response to the Archbishop in November 1981, and his secret was out. He was interviewed in the press, on television and on radio. He published his memoirs in 1994. Throughout most of the 1980s and early 1990s Seel sought official government recognition as a victim of Nazism both for his own sake and also to set the historical record straight. Recognition finally came in early 1995.

And yet Seel has since turned on those very gay militants who helped him to win his cause. He has charged that 'the gay lobby and the socialists' used him for their own ends, denounced gay representation at the annual ceremonies commemorating the Nazi deportations from France ('I want to tell them: you've got no bloody business at this monument! Leave the deportees in peace'), and ridiculed the annual Gay Pride Parade, in which he once took part: 'To show their pride in being homosexuals, the demonstrators walked around half naked; it was monstrous!' Seel, now retired, lives in Toulouse, where his notoriety has resulted in at least one beating by 'gay bashers'.

P. Seel, *I, Pierre Seel, Deported Homosexual*, transl. J. Neugroschel, notes by J. Le Bitoux (New York, 1995); E. Lette, 'Un ancien déporté homo accuse', *Minute*, 26 April 1995.

Michael Sibalis

Selvadurai, Shyam (b. 1965), Sri-Lankan-Canadian novelist. Sri Lankan born, Selvadurai migrated to Toronto with his family in 1983, following violent, ethnically based rioting in Columbo. Selvadurai acquired almost instant recognition with the 1994 publication of *Funny Boy*. The novel centres on the life of a young Tamil man born into middle-class privilege, who is exploring his homosexuality amidst the political turmoil and growing violence of the late 1970s and early 1980s Colombo. While a student in a school embodying the most repressive of colonial values, the novel's protagonist develops a relationship with a young Sinhalese classmate, crossing the ethnic divide that was at the time tearing his country apart. The fictional family's emigration to Canada in response to frighteningly violent developments within their own neighbourhood seems to have autobiographical echoes in the author's own life, as does the gayness of the principal character. There is much that is different, though. Selvadurai's parentage is in fact mixed, with a Sinhalese father and Tamil mother, and he describes them as having been much more accepting of difference than he depicts Arjie's parents in the novel. *Funny Boy* won a Lambda Literary Foundation award in 1994, and a Smithbooks/Books in Canada First Novel Award in the same year. It was also named an American Library Association Notable Book.

Selvadurai's second novel, *Cinnamon Gardens* (1998), is set in the Ceylon of the 1920s. It too features the homosexual desire of a young man, as well as the search for autonomy by a young woman in the same repressive family circle. To help prepare ground for the novel, Selvadurai again lived in Sri Lanka with his partner Andrew (to whom the book is dedicated), experiencing first hand the discomforts and risks associated with being a nonconformist in a country with persistently traditional and conformist norms about sexuality. He is virtually alone as an openly gay cultural figure in Sri Lanka, but he sees his first novel as having helped put the issue of homosexuality on the table.

Kamal Al-Solaylee, 'Atmosphere of Dignity', *Xtra! Magazine*, 5 Nov. 1998.

David Rayside

Sénac, Jean (1926–73), French-Algerian writer. Of Spanish ancestry and modest circumstances, like many other settlers in the Oran region of French colonial Algeria where he was born, Sénac's early years were marked by poverty, military service and tuberculosis. After the war, he became a radio broadcaster and began publishing poetry in Algiers magazines. In 1954, his first collection, *Poèmes*, was published in Paris thanks to the help of Albert Camus. The same year marked the beginning of an eight-year Algerian war of independence, which Sénac spent in France. He resolutely took the side of the Algerians against supporters of *Algérie française*. In 1962, he returned to independent Algeria, where he again found work with the radio, continued composing his own poetry and published anthologies of French-language Algerian writers. His increasingly strident criticisms of the Algerian regime, combined with his open homosexual poetry and life, brought him into conflict with authorities. He was killed in 1973, though interpretations differ as to whether or not he was assassinated for political reasons.

Sénac's prose writings include powerful denunciations of colonialism and manifestos in favour of the Algerian revolution. His poems, often in experimental form, touch on both politics and sexuality, championing Algerian nationalism (and denouncing its failures), lauding the adolescents to whom he was attracted, and evoking the Algiers landscape. In his works and his life, Sénac was one of the most overt homosexuals of his generation in French letters, and his radical position in the decolonisation of Algeria intentionally joined together his political and sexual sentiments and his literary endeavours.

Jean Sénac, *Oeuvres poétiques* (Arles, 1999);

Archives de la Ville de Marseille, *Poésie au Sud* (Marseille, 1983); Les Amis des Archives de la Ville de Marseille, *Le Soleil fraternel* (Marseille, 1985).

Robert Aldrich

Shelley, Martha (b. ?), American activist and writer. Shelley was co-founder, with Rita Mae BROWN and others, of the first lesbian feminist group, the 'Lavender Menace' (later renamed the 'Radicalesbians').

Lesbian feminism, as an autonomous movement and body of knowledge informed by both feminism and gay liberation, emerged in response to lesbians' problematic positioning within the gay and women's movements. Lesbians' marginalised position within the New York Gay Liberation Front had led Shelley, Brown and others to form a lesbian caucus, 'GLF Women'. Women from the GLF caucus, together with lesbians from the women's liberation movement, then formed the 'Lavender Menace' in 1970. This group is most famous for producing the first lesbian feminist manifesto, 'The Woman-Identified Woman' (reproduced in anthologies under the authorship of the 'Radicalesbians'), and for their 'zap' of the Second Congress to Unite Women, held in New York (1970). The zap, in which 'Lavender Menace' members disrupted the proceedings of the Congress, called for the women's movement to face its own homophobia and support lesbian rights. The pretext for this action (as it was for their name, the 'Lavender Menace') was the National Organisation for Women's recent purge of lesbian office holders (particularly of Brown), and characterisation of lesbians by the organisation's founder, Betty Friedan, as 'the lavender menace'. This epithet referred to the widely-held view at that time that the presence of lesbians in the women's movement undermined its credibility and that lesbian issues were a distraction (a 'lavender herring', according to Friedan) from the legitimate concerns of feminists and feminism. 'The Woman-Identified Woman'

challenged both the notion of sexuality as simply a 'bedroom issue' (or as a 'sexual preference') and the stereotype of lesbians as 'male-identified' by constituting lesbianism an act of political solidarity with other women in a patriarchal social order. Linking lesbianism and feminism in this way, lesbian sexuality could be understood as a basis of resistance to patriarchy, an idea which was developed by later groups into a lesbian separatist strategy of non-engagement with the enemy (men). The formulation of lesbianism as a feminist political practice also led to the contentious claim that to be a 'real' feminist, a woman must make the political choice to become a lesbian. In the two years following the manifesto and the zap, debates about 'political lesbianism' and separatism convulsed the women's movement. During that time, radical lesbian separatist groups formed and produced lesbian feminism's major theoretical works. In 1971, under increasing pressure from within and outside the women's and lesbian movements, the National Organisation for Women included lesbian rights in its charter.

Martha Shelley's influential writings in the late 1960s and early 1970s include: 'Notes of a Radical Lesbian', 'Gay is Good', and 'Lesbianism and the Women's Liberation Movement'.

Sidney Abbott and Barbara Love, *Sappho Was a Right-On Woman: A Liberated View of Lesbianism* (New York, 1973); Alice Echols, *Daring to be Bad: Radical Feminism in America, 1967–1975* (Minneapolis, 1989); Karla Jay and Allen Young, *Out of the Closets: Voices of Gay Liberation* (New York, 1972).

Carolyn Williams

Shepard, Matthew (Wayne) (1976–98), American public figure. On 12 October 1998, Shepard, a 21 year-old student at the University of Wyoming, died from the effects of being beaten, having his skull smashed with a gun butt, stripped naked, tied to a fence and left outside for almost eighteen hours in near freezing temperatures. Shepard – a diminutive but athletic young man from a middle-class background, who was studying politics, international relations and languages – had been taken from a bar by two other young men and attacked because he was openly gay. His two attackers were convicted of the murder and sentenced to life imprisonment, spared the death penalty by the intervention of Shepard's family. In an address to the court at the sentencing hearing for one of the convicted murderers, Dennis Shepard denounced the hate crime of which his son had been a victim and spoke movingly about the family's acceptance of Matthew's sexuality. He called for increasing vigilance against homophobia and hate crimes: 'Matt's beating, hospitalization, and funeral focused worldwide attention on hate.' Addressing his son's killer directly, he added: 'My son died because of your ignorance and intolerance . . . my son has become a symbol – a symbol against hate and people like you; a symbol for encouraging respect for individuality; for appreciating that someone is different; for tolerance.' Asking the judge not to impose the death sentence, Shepard concluded: 'I give you life in the memory of one who no longer lives. May you have a long life, and may you thank Matthew every day for it.'

The Shepard case, showing the violence and homophobia that seemingly permeate American society, sparked considerable public debate on hate crimes. Many politicians denounced the crime, though some religious groups and conservative politicians used the opportunity to express anew their vehement condemnation of homosexuality and gun control. Gay and lesbian groups, as well as other organisations, held public demonstrations in memory of Shepard and in support of gay and lesbian rights. Shepard's family set up the Matthew Shepard Foundation and fund 'with the aim of helping people to abandon ignorance, prejudice and hate'.

The killing of Shephard highlighted the continuing (and indeed increasing) problem of homophobia and its expression in verbal and physical violence around the world, whether in the 'gay ghettos' of large cities, small country towns or, in a more systematic way, under political and religious regimes which have adopted anti-homosexual positions as official policy. The response to his death, however, did demonstrate the ability of the gay and lesbian community and their supporters to defend human rights as well as growing acceptance among much of the population of homosexuality and of the need for anti-discrimination and anti-vilification legislation.

www.matthewsplace.com

Robert Aldrich

Shilts, Randy (1951–94), American journalist and writer. Shilts was born and grew up in Chicago. His parents were Methodists and political conservatives. He was educated at the University of Oregon with majors in English and journalism.

In 1975 he became the North-West correspondent for the gay publication *Advocate*. Shortly afterwards he was appointed a staff writer for the *Advocate* based in San Francisco: he resigned in 1978 following differences with his editor. Eagan notes that 'in retrospect, among his most important articles were several detailing the alarming spread of sexually transmitted diseases among gay men amidst the indifference of government, medical, and gay leaders'.

From 1977 to 1980 Shilts was a freelance reporter for San Francisco Bay area public and independent television stations, providing coverage on local politics and the gay community. The financial freedom generated by these activities allowed him to embark on a career as a freelance writer on gay and lesbian issues for a number of major newspapers and magazines. Shilts's first book, *The Mayor of Castro Street: The Life and Times of Harvey Milk* (1982), received critical acclaim in both mainstream and gay press in the US. The story line chronicled the life of the assassinated politician (see MILK) as well as gay politics in San Francisco in the 1970s.

When appointed to the *San Francisco Chronicle* in 1981, Shilts was the first openly gay reporter to be hired by a major American daily newspaper. His assignments included coverage of gay issues, with his articles on AIDS being among the first to appear in the mainstream press. Shilts had two main topics for comment: the indifference of the Reagan administration to the emerging issue of AIDS, and the sexual practices of gay men and their contribution in the spread of the disease. On the latter point Shilts was to incur the wrath of many in the local gay community, who saw his comments as a direct attack on their new-found political and sexual freedoms. The former point was to form the genesis for Shilts's book *And the Band Played On: Politics, People, and the AIDS Epidemic* (1987). When published, this major piece of investigative journalism represented the first attempt to chronicle the spread of AIDS in the US. In particular it demonstrated the appalling inactivity on the part of the US government combating this major medical crisis. *And the Band Played On* received considerable favourable treatment in the mainstream press, and literary awards, and was adapted for a movie which was released in 1988. The movie was a commercial success. Eagan notes that Shilts was disappointed that the book failed to bring about changes in either government action or lifestyle changes that may halt the spread of the virus.

Shilts's final book, *Conduct Unbecoming: Lesbians and Gays in the U.S. Military*, was released in 1993. It was another fine example of investigative journalism chronicling the place of homosexuals in the US military and the selective enforcement of its ban on homosexuality. Whilst it received favourable critiques in both the gay and mainstream press (it was on the *New York Times* best-seller list for six

weeks), Shilts was criticised by some in the gay community for not 'outing' some of his military sources who remained in the 'closet'.

In the years 1982–88 Shilts was awarded a number of major gay and mainstream awards for his non-fiction.

Shilts discovered that he was HIV-positive in 1986. He participated in a commitment ceremony with his lover, Barry Barbieri, in 1993. By 1992 Shilts had developed full-blown AIDS, from which he died.

J. M. Eagan, 'Randy Shilts', in M. Bronski, *Outstanding Lives: Profiles of Lesbians and Gay Men* (Detroit, 1997); Shilts's papers are held in the James C. Hormel Gay and Lesbian Center at the San Francisco Public Library.

Mark Edwards

Smart, Jeffrey (b. 1921), Australian painter. He was born, grew up and lived in Adelaide, South Australia, until 1948. Proud of his first son, his father, a real-estate developer, named a street in a new subdivision 'Jeffrey': the dogleg street later gave Smart the title of his autobiography, *Not Quite Straight*.

Smart's first ambition was to be an architect, and the relationship between the constructed environment and people has been a constant theme in his work. From 1939 to 1941 Smart studied at the Adelaide Teachers' College and the South Australian School of Art and Crafts. Literature, especially the poetry of T. S. Eliot, and classical music were also integral to Smart's aesthetic development. The Adelaide modernist painter Dorrit Black introduced Smart to the Greek geometric principle of the golden section to calculate the structure of his paintings. At this time Smart also acknowledged his homosexuality, although in conservative Adelaide he had to tread carefully. He joined and exhibited with the Royal South Australian Society of Arts and also joined the newly formed Contemporary Art Society. For five years from 1942 Smart taught art in schools for the South Australian Education Department.

Smart successfully exhibited regularly either on his own or with groups in Adelaide and Sydney during the 1940s. He was described by Adelaide art critic Lisette Kohlhagen as a 'romantic realist' with 'a strong feeling of construction in his work'. Like many other Australian artists of this time, he was anxious to go 'overseas'. In 1949 he travelled to the US, then to Britain and Europe. After living and studying in Paris, Smart spent a year with artist friends, including Donald FRIEND, in Ischia on the Bay of Naples before returning to Australia to live in Sydney. He won first prize of £500 in the Commonwealth Jubilee art competition in 1951, wrote art criticism for the *Daily Telegraph* from 1952 to 1954, and began a regular art segment in the Australian Broadcasting Commission's children's radio programme *The Argonauts Club*. Thousands of devoted children listened to his advice and information. Smart felt constrained in his private life while he was employed in 'The Children's Hour', but he and Donald Friend occasionally sought out like-minded men in the 'camp' quarters of Sydney.

By the early 1960s Smart was ready to leave Australia again. Many of his friends were now in Europe and he felt alienated by the popularity of abstract expressionism which dominated the Sydney art world. In 1963, therefore, he returned to Italy, where he has lived ever since. He held his first solo European exhibition in Rome in 1965, and from then on exhibited regularly in solo or group exhibitions in London, Rome, Sydney and Melbourne. At his home in Arrezzo some order and stability was established in 1976 when Ermes de Zan moved in. He was not only an assistant to help with painting, but he reorganised the garden, attended to practical matters and provided Smart with emotional support. Their relationship continues.

Smart was always a successful artist.

From the age of 48 he has been able to live from the sale of his painting. His is represented in many public and corporate collections. There is no overtly gay subject matter in his paintings, but they can be interpreted as a metaphor for his own, and many other gay men's, sense of isolation and alienation from their surroundings.

Edmund Capon, *Jeffery Smart Retrospective* (Sydney, 1999); John McDonald, *Jeffrey Smart: Paintings of the 70s and 80s* (Sydney, 1990); Jeffrey Smart, *Not Quite Straight* (Melbourne, 1996).

Ian Maidment

Smith, Ann (b. 1944), South African scholar and activist. Smith was born in Johannesburg; she married in 1965 (and has three children) and met her first woman lover in 1974. In 1982 she was a founder member of GASA, the first national gay association in South Africa; she has served as the first chairperson of the Witwatersrand branch, president and international secretary. She succeeded in having GASA affiliated to the International Lesbian and Gay Association in 1985 in spite of serious anti-South African antagonism at the time, provoked by the policy of apartheid. She appeared on national television in the first South African programme on gay rights in 1984. The same year, with Joan Bellis, she founded Womanspace, a lesbian support and social group.

An academic, in 1995 Smith offered the first course on lesbianism and literature at the University of the Witwatersrand. She also helped organise the first South African academic conference on gay and lesbian studies, which was held at the University of Cape Town, also in 1995.

Robert Aldrich

Smith, Chris (b. 1951), British politician. In 1984, a speech in the city of Rugby made Chris Smith the first British parliamentarian to be openly gay, and in 1997 a

Labour Party election victory made him the first cabinet minister to be openly gay.

Smith was born in North London to a civil servant father and teacher mother. He was active in the Labour Party, and Fabian circles in particular, from his undergraduate years at Cambridge, where he excelled as a student of English, eventually completing a doctorate. His political career began when he was elected in 1978 to the local council of the North London borough of Islington. He was active in the lesbian and gay committee of that council, and a member of the Campaign for Homosexual Equality. He had run for Parliament in 1979, but in a hopeless race. In 1983, he ran for his home constituency and this time won narrowly, though in an election in which Margaret THATCHER's Conservatives were re-elected.

Smith's decision to come out was motivated partly by the anti-gay sentiment whipped up by the tabloid press, and eagerly exploited by the Conservatives. He had already been willing enough to speak out on sexual orientation issues, but was now higher profile than ever on them, though like other openly gay and lesbian politicians he felt the need to insist on his not being a 'one-issue politician'. In fact, he soon established a reputation both in Islington and the House of Commons as an extremely dilligent and effective representative.

Smith was re-elected with a small but increased majority in 1987. His gayness did not loom large in local campaigning, although sexual orientation issues were incorporated into the Conservatives' anti-Labour arsenal nationally. When, later that year, the anti-gay Clause 28 was added to the government's Local Government Bill, he was an assertive tribune for the lesbian and gay cause, outspoken in his criticism of his own party's slow response to the measure. That measure was passed in 1988, signalling a major defeat for the political movement to which Smith had seen himself allied, though the setback helped galvanise political activists in the years to come. In the early 1990s, he was a strong supporter of and collaborator with the new lobbying group Stonewall, in which his long-time partner Dorian Jabri was also active.

Smith won the 1992 election with a very large majority, though the Conservatives under John Major won nationally. Between that election and the next, the ranks of openly gay parliamentarians were doubled, by the Conservative MP Michael Brown having been nudged out of the closet by the tabloid press. The 1997 election saw two other openly gay Labour candidates winning office, Ben Bradshaw in Exeter and Stephen Twigg in the London area (the Conservative Michael Brown losing). Since that time, others have joined them in coming out, including Angela Eagle, a junior minister in the government, and others essentially forced out by the media. Smith himself again won handily, by this time having acquired a significantly higher profile by virtue of having been a member of the Labour Party's 'shadow cabinet' in various social policy portfolios.

Smith was a supporter of the 'modernising' Tony Blair, though somewhat to the left of the most influential elements of the team that was put into power in 1997. Smith was named Heritage Secretary, which placed him in charge of a variety of cultural, media and sports portfolios. This was a lower profile ministry than he and his supporters had expected, although there were controversies enough (for example, over the Royal Opera House) to keep him in the press.

Smith's advocacy for sexual orientation causes has been less pronounced since he became a member of his party's 'front bench', in part because he has been so preoccupied with the business of his cabinet portfolios, and in part because he is even more pressured than before to display loyal solidarity with his party colleagues and the party leader. In the 1992 and 1997 elections, the Labour Party promised action on a number of policy fronts relevant for sexual diversity, though once in office they displayed that caution around what were thought to be electorally risky issues that had long been characteristic of Labour's approach. While in opposition, Blair had been a strong advocate of lesbian and gay equality, most notably in the 1994 parliamentary debate over equalising the age of consent for homosexual and heterosexual activity (a debate which led to defeat). In office, his government did take steps toward equality, including one on the age of consent. Smith's membership in the cabinet gives him access to ministers and officials, and his very presence constitutes a reminder of the need to fulfil promises, but that influence is not always visible to the general public and the activist movement.

Throughout his political career, Smith's intelligence, diligence and integrity have earned him great respect among gays and lesbians across Britain, and among fellow parliamentarians. Partisanship runs very deep in Britain, but he has succeeded far more than most in garnering admiration across party lines.

David Rayside, *On the Fringe: Gays and Lesbians in Politics* (Ithaca, NY, 1998); Stephen Jeffery-Poulter, *Peers, Queers, and Commons* (London, 1991).

David Rayside

Socarides, Charles (b. 1922), American psychiatrist. The scientific study of homosexuality has often been controversial, especially from the perspective of the behavioural disciplines. Psychiatry, psychology and social work all emphasise individual differences and are highly critical of stereotypes and generalisations. Folk psychologies, historical precedents, myths and stereotypes have all been challenged in an era of social change and increasingly rigorous scientific research. The main areas of contention in the study of homosexuality have been gender identity, attribution and differences; behaviour vs identity; and developmental issues, often referred to as Nature vs Nurture. So-

carides has focused on the nurture aspect, from interpretation of Freudian theory, claiming that if behaviour is learned, it can be changed. He has further asserted that in the case of homosexuality, the behaviour *should* be changed because it is intrinsically pathological and leads to other psychological and social ills. He has recently modified his position in the face of growing evidence to the contrary.

In *The Overt Homosexual* (1968) Socarides asserted that homosexuality is a borderline perversion which can be cured using psychoanalytic techniques: 'Homosexuality ... is filled with aggression, destruction and self-deceit. It is a masquerade of life ... [involving] only destruction, mutual defeat, exploitation of the partner and the self.' At the time of the American Psychiatric Association's decision (1972–80) to remove homosexuality as a mental illness, from its diagnostic and statistical manual (DSM), he ridiculed any evidence refuting his opinion as 'mere propaganda', irrelevant and 'behaviouristic'.

One of Socarides's earliest published works, *Theoretical and Clinical Aspects of Overt Male Homosexuality* (1960), is a report of a symposium on psychoanalysis and homosexuality. He recounts two notable presentations: one by Serota, and another by Edoardo Weiss. Serota urges the analysts to be clear that homosexuality is the result of conflict, and that heterosexual readjustment is both desirable and possible, regardless of what the patient may want. Socarides has followed this line, to his own detriment. He ignored Weiss, who claimed: 'There seem to be certain well-integrated productive individuals who although intensely homosexual, seem to be capable of prolonged love relationships rather than pursuing momentary gratification. A study of such individuals might lead to a revision of our concepts of male homosexuality.' This is exactly what has happened in the era following the sexual liberation movements, dating from the late 1960s. Gay Liberation for example, has placed much importance on the

'Coming Out Process' in order to dispel homophobia and illogical preconceptions.

This period in the development of psychoanalysis in the US was characterised by controversy surrounding Kinsey's findings that male homosexual behaviour, in varying degrees, was more widespread than previously thought. There was also a tendency in analytical circles to concentrate on case studies, and with exceptions like Glover and Weiss, but especially with Socarides, there has been a major departure from Freud, namely, that psychosexual development following Oedipal operations had several viable outcomes, including homosexuality. This was replaced by the notion that if such development was not stymied, the outcome would be heterosexual object choice. Hence psychoanalysis was promoted as a default mechanism to restore hetrosexuality. The main influences of this particular school may be traced through Rado to Krafft-Ebing, whom Freud deposed, and a particular American strand of psychoanalysis.

In the earlier period there was also a tendency to equate male homosexuality with femininity, despite Freud's warning that such teleological equations were 'clearly insufficient, empirical and conventional'; as he wrote in 1913, 'What we speak of in ordinary life as "masculine" or "feminine" reduced itself from the view of psychology to the qualities of "activity" and "passivity" – that is, to qualities determined not by the instincts themselves but by their aims.'

Socarides was influenced by Bieber and Stoller, who placed the aetiology of homosexuality not in Freud's Oedipus complex, but in earlier oral, anal and genital stages, thereby forging a link between homosexuality and severe psychopathology. He viewed homosexuality as a fusion of aggressive and libidinal impulses, resulting in the formation of a perversion, as a defence against psychosis, aggravated by primitive maladaptive mechanisms of introjection and projection. He fortified this opinion with his interpretation of Melanie Klein's depressive and paranoid/schizoid positions in infancy. The result was a split between object (the idealised nurturing male) and ego (two or more distinct ego states). He also extended Margaret Mahler's developmental model of separation and individuation, claiming that gay men perform a 'resolution of the separation from the mother by running away from all women'.

He identified three main determinants which took homosexuality away from classical Oedipal issues; primitive defence mechanisms, simultaneous fear of separation from the mother and a wish to join her, and narcissistic object choice. These symptoms were added to a list of 'causes' compiled by P. Miller, also using questionable methodology: a predisposition which resulted from parental rejection, a precipitating incident involving seduction, and a perpetuating cycle of dependency and ongoing feminine identification, in order to compensate for a lost masculinity. The implication was that gay men are intrinsically less masculine than their heterosexual brothers, and lesbians were either ignored or outrageously ridiculed: 'The family of the homosexual is usually a female-dominated environment wherein the father was absent, weak, detached or sadistic. This furthers feminine identification. The father's inaccessibility to the boy contributed to the difficulty in making a masculine identification.'

At the time he was unaware of the serious consequences of such a claim. His own son is a gay activist and the current US Presidential Adviser on Gay and Lesbian issues. Moreover, many parents tragically blame themselves for their child's homosexual orientation, and some even engage in splitting, and ostracise their offspring from family life altogether.

The studies Socarides cited used grossly disturbed case material and prison populations, where homosexual interaction is less likely to be representative of dynamics in society. These studies left the connection between psychosis and homosexuality, and homosexuality and anti-social behaviour, unexamined. Moreover the result was to reinforce the idea of the homosexual as a sick and vicious criminal, with little if no reference to individual differences.

By the time of the Second Symposia of the American Psychoanalytic Association (1962) there were serious doubts about the universal validity of Socarides's current claims, but this only made him more determined to set himself up as an expert. The result was the formulation of Gay Reparative Therapy, which was openly criticised by the American Psychiatric Association (1998) as leading to confusion and borderline symptoms. It appears that where such therapy is effective, there is usually an added religious element, namely that the individual wants to change sexual orientation because of deeply held spiritual beliefs.

Robert Pryde

Somerville, Jimmy (b. 1961), British singer. Born in Glasgow, Somerville has an amazing voice, a tenor with an ability to sing 'castrato-style'. With two other musicians, he formed Bronski Beat in London in 1984, and the group built up a cult following on the gay circuit. They were immensely popular, particularly since many of their songs were explicitly gay, as in 'Smalltown Boy'. Other hits included 'Tell Me Why', with a strong disco beat; a version of the Gershwin classic 'It Ain't Necessarily So'; and the Donna Summer anthem 'I Feel Love'. The group's popularity soon spread beyond the gay subculture, and they were launched on the road to international stardom.

In 1985 Somerville quit Bronski Beat, and then with friend Richard Coles formed a new band, the Communards, whose disco-styled 'You Are My World' was an instant hit, reaching the UK Top Thirty; other hits followed, including 'Don't Leave Me This Way' and 'So Cold The Night', and a revival of Gloria Gaynor's 'Never Can Say Goodbye'. Somerville has a loyal following worldwide, partly because of his musical

talents, and partly because of his gay activism, this latter expressed in both the lyrics to his music and his personal appearances at many gay fund-raising benefits.

D. Clarke (ed.), *The Penguin Encyclopaedia of Popular Music* (London, 1998); C. Larkin, *The Virgin Encyclopaedia of Eighties Music* (London, 1997).

Garry Wotherspoon

Spear, Allan (b. 1937), US politician. Spear was first elected to the Minnesota State Senate in 1972 as a progressive Democrat in a district that included the University of Minnesota. He had been teaching history at the University since 1964, at which time he was completing his Yale University doctorate. His thesis on 'Black Chicago' was published soon afterwards.

During the two years after his first election he became more involved in the gay/lesbian movement, and was publicly supportive of campaigns for gay rights ordinances in Minneapolis and neighbouring St Paul. In the course of that work, he decided to come out publicly, and did so through a sympathetic interview with a Minneapolis newspaper in December 1974. He was then re-elected in 1976 and in the several elections since then. In 1982 he shifted constituencies, as a result of redistricting, and won re-election in an area that included a substantial concentration of Minneapolis gays and lesbians, alongside relatively prosperous areas that are conservative on some issues but socially liberal.

In 1992, he ran for and won the Presidency of the State Senate, defeating an opponent who was among the most anti-gay in the chamber. In the following year, the two houses of the Minnesota legislature approved a measure prohibiting discrimination based on sexual orientation – a measure first introduced twenty years before and spearheaded by him ever since.

Over his legislative career, Spear

specialised in issues related to criminal law reform and human rights. He authored a number of crime bills over the late 1980s and 1990s which addressed such issues as sexual assault, at-risk children and hate crimes. He has also drafted or supported legislation on battered women's pro-grammes, aboriginal education and child care. He was a founding member of the International Network of Lesbian and Gay Officials.

David Rayside

Spellman, Francis Cardinal (1889–1967), American cleric. Spellman was born in Whitman, Massachusetts, to a small-town grocer. A rather undistinguished student, he graduated in 1911 from Fordham University and decided to enter the priest-hood. He studied at the North American College in Rome and was ordained in 1916. He then filled a variety of minor positions in the Boston archdiocese before landing a post in 1925 as an attaché in the service of the Papal Secretariat of State. In his diplomatic service, Spellman excelled at public relations (he helped establish the Vatican's first radio station in 1931) and at personal relations, forming close bonds with several powerful members of the church hierarchy, including the Papal Secretary of State, Cardinal Pacelli, who in 1939 was elected Pope Pius XII.

Although the ambitious Spellman had risen to the bishopric before the accession of Pius XII, the new pope rewarded his faithful friend by appointing him Arch-bishop of New York in 1939. In 1945, he was raised to the cardinalate. Spellman's administration of the diocese of New York was masterful: he doubled church membership between 1939 and 1967, undertook so many building projects that the Catholic Church was New York City's second largest employer, and quickly en-tered the public political spotlight as the spokesman for American Catholicism. He was so influential that his residence on Madison Avenue was known simply as The Powerhouse.

As a public figure, Spellman was well known for his political and social con-servatism. In 1949, he helped break a strike at Calvary Cemetery in New York by employing seminarians as strike-breaking gravediggers. An arch-anti-communist and powerful figure in the Republican Party, Spellman defended Senator Joseph McCarthy's 1953 investi-gations of subversives and homosexuals in the federal government. Spellman was also highly influential in foreign affairs, sup-porting the establishment of the state of Israel and American involvement in South Vietnam. Through all of these events, Spellman was particularly deft at painting his opponents as religious bigots and claiming the authority to speak for all American Catholics (until Vietnam-era anti-war Catholics challenged his leadership).

The details of Spellman's personal life are elusive. The Cardinal was known as 'Thelma' Spellman in some circles and was rumoured to enjoy an active sexual and social life in New York City, with a par-ticular fondness for Broadway musicals and their chorus boys. His biographer notes that many interviewees 'took his homosexuality for granted' but has not documented his relationships. It is likely that Spellman engaged in an active yet deeply closeted life much like that of his close personal friend Roy COHN.

John Cooney, *The American Pope: The Life and Times of Francis Cardinal Spellman* (New York, 1984); Francis Cardinal Spellman, *What America Means to Me* (New York, 1953).

Christopher Capozzola

Springfield, Dusty (1939–99), British singer. Dusty Springfield's distinctively husky voice and her elaborately con-structed image made her a much-loved soul diva among lesbians and gays.

Born Mary O'Brien in London, she and her brother Tom formed a folk trio, the Springfields, with Tim Field. After their first chart successes, the trio split up in

1963. Tom became a songwriter, including stints with the Seekers, while Mary went on to forge a solo career under the new name of Dusty Springfield.

In 1963–64 Springfield scored her first big hit, 'I Only Want to Be with You', a song which incorporated a soul sound which was more reminiscent of Motown than anything being produced in Britain at the time. This initial success was quickly followed by a string of other hits. In 1964, for example, she recorded Burt Bacharach's 'I Just Don't Know What to Do with Myself', and followed it up with the same writer's 'Wishin' and Hopin'', both of them achingly melodramatic songs which showcased perfectly her vocal and communicative talents. By 1966 'You Don't Have to Say You Love Me' was number one on the UK charts and number four in the US, and it was this song, more than any other, with which she was associated.

Increasingly she spent her time in the US, where in 1969 she recorded what is widely considered to be her best album: *Dusty in Memphis*. During the 1970s and 1980s she slipped from public view, living a reclusive life in the US, while periodically attempting comebacks on the cabaret circuit. In 1987 Neil Tennant persuaded her to record a single with the PET SHOP BOYS, and 'What Have I Done to Deserve this?' brought Dusty back to public prominence, this time on the dance charts on both sides of the Atlantic. She resumed her solo career and the collaboration with the Pet Shop Boys produced no fewer than four of the tracks on her 1990 album *Reputation*.

Persistent rumours about the singer's sexuality were neither confirmed nor denied, but she nevertheless maintained a loyal following among lesbians and gays. Drag queens, in particular, loved her distinctive 1960s image: the towering blond beehive, the dark mascara, the glamorous frocks and the expressive gestures. Her songs, with their suggestive lyrics and plaintive refrains, have been affectionately parodied and camped up by many a cabaret performer.

The Penguin Encyclopaedia of Popular Music (London, 1998).

C. Faro

Słarosta, Sławek (Sławomir) (b. 1965), Polish singer, musician, activist and editor. Born in Warsaw, he studied psychology and sociology but without taking degrees. In the 1980s and early 1990s Starosta sang, played keyboards and wrote lyrics for various pop and rock bands. His second album with a group called Balkan Electrique, *Piosenki o miłoœci* (*Love Songs*, 1994), included songs with Słarosta's gay and anti-AIDS lyrics later used in promotional campaign Kochaj Nie Zabijaj (Make Love, Don't Kill).

Since 1986 Słarosta has been a member of Warszawski Ruch Homoseksualny (Warsaw Homosexual Movement), the third gay organisation in Poland after FILO in Gdansk and ETAP in Wroclaw, which appeared after 1985 in reaction to police action directed against homosexuals. In 1989, he was one of the founders of Lambda, the Polish gay and lesbian association. In 1991, he became the chief editor of *Men*, a monthly gay magazine; since 1996, after an editorial split, he has been the editor of *Nowy Men*. Since 1999 he has been editor-in-chief of *Gejzer*. He is one of the leading personalities of the Polish gay movement – organiser of the Gay Mister Poland competition (since 1996), Gay Pride (since 1998) and the Gay Artists' Festival (since 1998). The only editor of an adult magazine (out of twenty published in Poland) accused of spreading pornography, he has been under threat of pending prosecution since 1996.

Katarzyna Adamska, *Ludzie obok. Lesbijki i geje w Polsce* (Toruń, 1988).

Krzysztof Fordoński

Stefan, Verena (b. 1947), Swiss-German novelist. Stefan was born and educated in Switzerland. After leaving school she moved to West Berlin, where she trained as a physiotherapist and studied sociology without taking a degree. She became an active participant both in the student movement of the later 1960s and the women's movement of the 1970s.

Stefan's first major work was *Häutungen* (1975): a literary collage of poetry, autobiography and feminist analysis, which was translated into English as *Shedding* (1978). The first edition of *Häutungen*, comprising 3,000 copies, had sold out within a month, and by 1979 the work had sold 140,000 copies in West Germany. A cult book in the German women's movement (although some critics have accused Stefan of reproducing gender stereotypes), it has appeared in twenty-two editions to date. Stefan's intimate, autobiographical approach had a revolutionary impact on West German women's writing, especially in its explicit investigations of women's subjectivity and sexuality.

One of Stefan's many projects in *Häutungen* was to expose the patriarchal values latent both in the left-wing politics of the student movement and in the illusion of sexual liberation. Her style is experimental – she dispenses, for example, with the standard capitalisation of nouns in German – and can be read as an attempt to write female experience in non-patriarchal language. Stefan writes in the foreword to *Häutungen* that she is 'speechless' regarding women's experience; in an attempt to find the language in which to express it, she takes recourse, among other things, to poetry. Her protagonist searches for a (sexual) identity, in encounters with men and women. In a gradual process she moves through bisexuality to lesbianism, finally rejecting masculinist heterosexuality with its latent and overt violence towards women.

Other works by Stefan include *Mit Füssen mit Flügeln. Gedichte und Zeichnungen* (*With Feet With Wings: Poems and Drawings*, 1980), *Wortgetreu ich träume. Geschichten und Geschichte* (1987),

published in English as *Literally Dreaming* with *Shedding* (1994), and more recently *Es ist reich gewesen: Bericht vom Sterben meiner Mutter* (*It Was Rich: An Account of my Mother's Death*, 1993) and *Rauh, wild & frei: Mädchengestalten in der Literatur* (*Rough, Wild, and Free: Girls in Literature*, 1997).

Georgina Paul, 'Inarticulacy: Lesbianism and Language in post-1945 German Literature', in David Jackson (ed.), *Taboos in German Literature* (Oxford, 1996), pp. 165–82; C. A. Costabile-Heming, 'Verena Stefan', in Frederike Eigler and Susanne Kord (eds), *The Feminist Encyclopedia of German literature* (Westport, CT, 1997); Susan L. Coralis and Kay Goodman (eds), *Beyond the Eternal Feminine: Critical Essays on Women and German Literature* (Stuttgart, 1982).

Sarah Colvin

Stefano, Joey (1968–94), American actor. At a time when actors in hardcore male sex films purported to be straight, Joey Stefano, both onscreen and off, was an eager – indeed voracious and pushy – bottom. Explicit representations of his 'if you're man enough, come and fuck me' sexuality were consumed by large audiences on videos made in 1989–90 and in personal appearances around the United States until his death in 1994 from a combination of cocaine, morphine, heroin and his favourite drug, Special K (ketamine). Before he moved to Hollywood and was discovered and given his '*nom de porn*', the drug of choice for the high-school-dropout, Philadelphia hustler Nicholas Anthony Iacona, Jr. was angel dust (PCP). Making money to buy downer drugs by renting his body was his established way of life before he appeared in any hardcore videos.

The condescending pathography *Wonder Bread and Ecstasy* recounts the short career of an uneducated, inarticulate waif with no sense of how to manage money and no ability to plan long-range, who rocketed to stardom, was almost immediately viewed as 'yesterday's news', and descended a bit more slowly than he rose, through a thicker haze of drugs, to an early death. That the locale is hardcore gay videos is the main difference between this book and shelves of other trashy biographies of movie stars who could not handle success and/or were desired to death by those confusing the screen image with the fragile human being who projects the image. Initially, Iacona was thrilled to have sex with hunks he had lusted after while watching hardcore videos, but he was increasingly unhappy that his sexual partners were expecting Joey Stefano, the premier sex object who was supposed to be as tough and invulnerable as his arse was hungry to be penetrated. Although his type was older, hypermasculine males, it was a drag queen, Chi Chi LaRue (né Larry Paciotti), who launched Joey Stefano, loved Nick Iacona and was still attempting to help keep both afloat the day Nick overdosed instead of showing up for film work. Stefano was probably infected with HIV before he understood the dangers of infection. Once he learned he was infected, he publicly acknowledged it and undertook to help others avoid becoming infected. As careless as he was with his own life (sharing needles as well as being fucked without condoms) and as uneducated and unintrospective as he was as Joey Stefano, he bravely took a very clear public stand for protected sex in film scenes against a reluctant industry and was also among the first porn stars to volunteer regularly for AIDS fund-raisers.

Charles Isherwood, *Wonder Bread and Ecstasy: The Life and Death of Joey Stefano* (Los Angeles, 1996).

Stephen O. Murray

Steward, Samuel (Morris) (1909–93), American author. Born in Woodsfield, Ohio, he died in Berkeley, California. He studied at Ohio State University, where he received a doctoral degree in English in 1934. His

teaching career, begun in 1934, was abandoned in 1954 in favour of a career as tattooist, which he had started in Chicago in 1952 under the name Phil Sparrow. In 1949, Steward met Alfred KINSEY and became an 'unofficial collaborator' in his research, remaining a friend until Kinsey's death in 1956. To his career as tattooist, he added that of gay writer in 1958 when he was invited to contribute to the trilingual Swiss journal *Der Kreis*; his association with *Der Kreis* lasted until its demise in 1967.

Steward used at least ten pseudonyms, but is best known as Phil Andros, the eponymous hero of several collections of witty and graphic stories of gay male sex, including *$tud* (1966), *The Joy Spot* (1969), *My Brother, the Hustler* and *Renegade Hustler* (1970), and *San Francisco Hustler, The Greek Way*, and *When in Rome . . . Do* (1971).

On a trip to Europe in 1937 Steward formed a friendship with Gertrude Stein and Alice B. Toklas, whom he visited again in 1939. He was unable to visit during World War II and returned to France only in 1950 to visit Toklas (Stein died in 1946), but thereafter spent many Christmas holidays with her until her death in 1967. Steward commemorated his friendship with the famous lesbian couple in *Dear Sammy* (1977), which told of his relationship with them, and later in three novels in which they appear as characters: *Parisian Lives* (1984), *Murder Is Murder Is Murder* (1985), and *The Caravaggio Shawl* (1989).

In the mid-1960s Steward had moved to California, continuing his tattooing in Oakland and his writing in Berkeley. *Chapters from an Autobiography* appeared in 1981. But Phil Andros was not forgotten, and more collections followed: *Below the Belt* (1981) and *Different Strokes* (1984). The very popular Phil Andros stories inspired a generation of younger gay writers.

Michael Williams, '*In Memoriam, Samuel*

Morris Steward, 1909–1993', Journal of Homo-sexuality, vol. 30, no. 3 (1996), pp. xiii–xv.

Hubert Kennedy

Stockwood, (Arthur) Mervyn (1913–95), British Anglican bishop. Born in Bristol into a middle-class family, his solicitor father was killed during World War I. As a schoolboy brought up in the Church of England, he was introduced to Anglo-Catholic worship at All Saints', Clifton, which reinforced his love of ritual and sense of the dramatic. Educated at The Downs School and Kelly College (a minor public school in Devon), in 1931 he entered Christ's College at Cambridge University, where he graduated BA in 1934. Having studied for the Anglican ministry at Wescott House theological college in Cambridge, he was ordained deacon in 1936, priest in 1937. He was curate of St Matthew's, Moorfields, in a poor area of Bristol, then vicar from 1941 to 1955. Having converted to socialism while at theological college, he joined the Socialist Christian League and the Labour Party.

In 1955 he was appointed vicar of Great St Mary's, the University Church, in Cambridge, where his preaching and gift for showmanship drew large congregations of undergraduates. He put the University Church on the ecclesiastical map and gained a national reputation. In 1959, at the suggestion of Archbishop Geoffrey Fisher, Tory Prime Minister Harold Macmillan appointed Stockwood to the see of Southwark in south London. Under Stockwood's leadership, Southwark became one of the best-known dioceses in the Church of England, a place where new ideas and new initiatives were encouraged. During the 1960s the term 'South Bank religion' became synonymous with radical theology and public controversy. Its most famous expression was the book *Honest to God* (1963), by John Robinson, whom Stockwood had appointed as suffragan bishop of Woolwich. Another controversial work was *No New Morality* (1964)

by Douglas Rhymes, a gay priest on the staff of Southwark Cathedral, which questioned the traditional view that Christian morality was based upon absolute laws.

Stockwood was homosexually inclined though almost certainly celibate. He was attracted by handsome teenage schoolboys and young men of the upper classes, but always in the role of father figure rather than lover. Within the Church of England, he was liberal in his view of the morality of homosexual behaviour. He spoke in favour of homosexual law reform, included gay couples among the guests at his dinner parties, and on at least one occasion blessed a gay relationship. As one of his fellow bishops recalled: 'He didn't mind his clergy having it off as long as there wasn't a scandal.'

As bishop of Southwark, Stockwood was a colourful and creative leader. Although sympathetic to the political left, he enjoyed mixing with members of the royal family, the rich and the famous. In 1980 he retired as bishop and went to live in Bath. Shortly before his death he was one of ten Church of England bishops 'outed' by a gay radical gay organisation because of their 'hypocrisy and homophobia'. Stockwood was neither hypocritical nor homophobic.

Obituary in *The Times*, 14 Jan. 1995; Michael De-la-Noy, *Mervyn Stockwood: A Lonely Life* (London, 1996); Mervyn Stockwood, *Chanctonbury Ring: An Autobiography* (London, 1982).

David Hilliard

Studds, Gerry (b. 1937), US politician. In July 1983, Studds became the first national politician in the US to come out as gay, continuing then to serve as a Democratic representative from Massachusetts until retiring in 1996.

Studds was first elected to Congress in 1972, representing a district that took in fishing communities and other coastal areas south of Boston, including Cape Cod. His first victory was an upset, but in the next few elections he built up ever larger majorities. He served constituency interests well, taking advantage of strategic committee assignments. Though at times perceived as 'patrician' in his demeanour, his campaigning effectiveness was bolstered by extraordinary rhetorical talent. In Washington, he held to progressive views on a variety of both domestic and international affairs. He was a co-sponsor of a 1975 gay/lesbian civil rights bill, and of many other Congressional initiatives on sexual orientation in the years to follow.

Studds was forced to come out in 1983 by revelations about a brief 1973 affair with a Congressional page, which eventually led to a 'censure' by his colleagues. He was not the first member of Congress to have been faced with disclosure of homosexual conduct, but he was the first to confront them by affirming his gayness. Later that summer, he was cheered by constituents in an annual parade of New Bedford's Portuguese Roman Catholics, and later that autumn re-elected. His long service in the House gave him access to important committee assignments, though his standing among colleagues was always somewhat tainted by the circumstances leading to his coming out.

In the early 1990s, Studds played a leading role in trying to end the US military's ban on lesbians and gays, forcing the publication of confidential reports favourable to lifting the ban. Though cautious about appearing too frequently to be a tribune for these causes, he was widely respected among activists, especially in Washington, and seen as an indispensable source of advice and assistance on Capitol Hill. In 1992, he became Chair of the Merchant Marine and Fisheries Committee of the House, and thereby a member of the Democratic leadership, though in 1994, the Republicans capture of a legislative majority stripped his party of committee chair positions. In 1996, he announced that he would not seek re-election.

Mark Thompson (ed.), *Long Road to*

Freedom: The Advocate History of the Gay and Lesbian Movement (New York, 1994); David Rayside, *On the Fringe: Gays and Lesbians in Politics* (Ithaca, NY, 1998).

David Rayside

Sullivan, Andrew (b. 1963). British-American author and editor. Born to a middle-class Irish Catholic family in a London suburb, Sullivan earned his undergraduate degree in modern history and modern languages at Oxford University, where he was Chair of the Oxford Union, the university's famed debating society. Winner of a prestigious Harkness Fellowship, Sullivan went to the United States and earned a master's degree in public administration and a Ph.D. in political science at Harvard University, writing a thesis on the conservative British philosopher Michael Oakeshott.

While a postgraduate, Sullivan embarked on a freelance writing career that led him in 1990 to a position as Washington columnist for *Esquire* magazine, and in 1991, at the precocious age of 28, to the editorship of *The New Republic*, America's leading journal of opinion. In this position, Sullivan – who has described himself as 'postideological' – continued the magazine's drift towards conservatism in foreign and domestic policy issues. Sullivan also introduced the magazine's readers to cultural politics, authored several pieces on gay and lesbian topics, and dealt with a media spotlight focused on the first openly gay editor of a mainstream American magazine.

In 1996, Sullivan stepped down as editor to devote more attention to his writing. Sullivan also publicly announced his HIV-positive status, although all involved denied that this was the cause of his resignation. Other rumours about political conflicts with editors and his inconsistent work ethic (likely related in part to the effects of HIV treatment) nonetheless dogged Sullivan's departure from the magazine. Since 1996, he has served as a contributing editor to *The New Republic* while pursuing independent writing and reviewing projects.

Sullivan has emerged as a prominent gay 'conservative', although his views on gay and lesbian politics cannot always be categorised under that label. His 1995 book *Virtually Normal: An Argument about Homosexuality* follows in the tradition of early Anglo-American liberalism, insisting on public tolerance of homosexuality while allowing for individual discrimination in the private sphere. This stance, as well as Sullivan's distance from the radical left traditions that have given rise to much gay and lesbian political thought, has drawn Sullivan extensive criticism. He has spoken out against 'outing', remains an active communicant in the Catholic Church, has recommended same-sex marriage for gay men as 'an essentially civilising activity', and was among the first to express hope for 'the end of AIDS' after the breakthroughs of multiple drug treatments beginning in 1996. His 1998 book *Love Undetectable: Notes on Friendship, Sex, and Survival* explores these issues as well as his own theories on the ethics of love and friendship.

Walter Kirn, 'The Editor as Gap Model', *New York Times Magazine* (7 March 1993), pp. 26–7; Thomas H. Stahel, S. J., 'I'm Here: An Interview with Andrew Sullivan', *America*, vol. 168 (8 May 1993), pp. 5–11; M. C. Williams, 'The Battle Hymn of the New Republic', *Vanity Fair*, no. 432 (August 1996), pp. 54 ff.

Christopher Capozzola

Sylvester (1947–88), American disco diva. Sylvester was one of the very first stars to completely eschew the confines of the pop music closet. Sassy, outrageously camp, and flamboyantly cross-dressed in a welter of sequins and shimmering turbans, he was completely comfortable with a public persona that was 'queer' two decades before the current re-invention of the term.

Born Sylvester James in Los Angeles, like many other African-American singers he first came to public attention as a child gospel star. Then in 1967 he moved to San Francisco, where he completely reinvented himself as a member of a wittily camp nightclub act, the Cockettes.

By the early 1970s Sylvester had a growing reputation as a solo performer, especially within the burgeoning gay subculture of San Francisco. His debut album, *Sylvester* (1977), was a huge hit with gay fans, mixing as it did the pulse of disco with more soulful ballads. Working with ex-Motown stalwart Harvey Fuqua, by the late 1970s Sylvester crafted a distinctive sound which gradually saw his fame transcend the gay cult following to reach mass appeal. Follow-up albums produced disco classics such as 'You Make Me Feel Mighty Real' and 'Do You Wanna Funk'.

After his mass appeal had waned somewhat in the 1980s, he remained an active and much-loved member of the gay community, generously donating his services particularly to AIDS-related work. In 1988 Sylvester himself died of AIDS-related illnesses. However, his memory remains very much alive through the legacy of his music. Dance-floors in gay and lesbian clubs the world over continue to erupt joyously at the sound of his distinctive voice as it launches into one of the disco anthems that defined an era.

Michael Heatley (ed.), *The Encyclopedia of Rock* (Melbourne, 1996).

C. Faro

T

Taktsis, Costas (1927–88), Greek author. Taktsis's fame rests about equally on his writing, his lifestyle and the manner of his death, and to all of these his sexuality was central. Born in Thessaloniki, but growing up in Athens, he led an adolescent existence as much disrupted by family circumstances (his upbringing was almost exclusively in the hands of a variety of female relatives) as by the German occupation of Greece and the Greek civil war which followed. The circumstances of his early life are very shadowy, and his autobiography *The First Step* (published posthumously in 1989) is written in such a way as to focus the reader on the discontinuities of his existence rather than to clarify his personal history, although it does give an amusing account of the variety of sexual possibilities open to a schoolboy bent on self-education in a period of great social upheaval. In the post-war period, his first publications, *Brazilian Symphony* (poems, 1954) and *Café Byzantium* (also poems, 1956), attracted no particular attention, and between 1954 and 1964 he left Greece altogether, moving between Western Europe, Africa, the US and Australia and keeping himself by methods that can only be guessed at. In 1963 he published, at his own expense, *The Third Wedding*, a blackly comic novel which devastatingly exposes the oppressive role of the family in Greece and explodes the traditional Greek mythology of motherhood. But even this novel, although translated into French and English in 1967, only really became widely known in Greece with its second edition (1970). It was followed by a similarly sophisticated but more elliptical exploration of comparable issues in his short-story cycle *Small Change* (1972). In the meantime Taktsis had begun to gain a reputation for himself as an amusing and scandalous wit in various Athenian cafés and *salons*. After the fall of the Colonels' dictatorship in 1974, he went on to make frequent contributions in the media, both in the press and on the air, on issues of Greek society and culture, and began to publish essays on the same topics. He made no secret of his homosexuality but declined to take an active part in the gay liberation movement, ostensibly because he believed that oppression of homosexuals could only be solved as part of a wider social liberation. Nonetheless, some of his journalistic contributions of the 1980s were very outspoken on the subject, such that rapidly Taktsis and homosexuality became virtually synonymous in the public mind. What was perhaps less widely known was that for many years he had also been practising as a transvestite prostitute, a profession which seems to have led eventually to his death, since he was probably murdered by a client. On this subject, as on all aspects of sexuality, his autobiography is entirely open, and if read in conjunction with it, his novel and story-cycle take on a new importance. Between the three works, Taktsis constructs a highly individual account of the fluidity of sexual identity, the ways in which society in general – and Greek society in particular – works to limit that fluidity for its own purposes, and the extent to which Greek literature has helped to 'fix' the gender values of its culture.

P. Mackridge, 'The Protean Self of Costas Taktsis', *The European Gay Review*, vol. 6/7 (1991), pp. 172–98; C. Robinson, 'Social, Sexual and Textual Transgression: Kostas Taktsis and Michel Tremblay, a comparison', in D. Tziovas (ed.), *Greek Modernism and Beyond* (Lanham, MD, 1997).

Christopher Robinson

Tatchell, Peter (b. 1952), British activist. Born into a working-class evangelical Christian family in Melbourne (Australia), Tatchell moved to Britain in 1971. Already an activist, he joined the Gay Liberation Front in London.

In 1983, Tatchell contested a by-election in Bermondsey as the official Labour Party candidate, though his association with extra-parliamentary left militancy incurred the wrath of the Party leadership. Though not out as gay at first, his sexuality provoked unceasing attacks from his opponents and the tabloid press, and he lost the election to the Liberals.

Tatchell was active in unsuccessful efforts to form the Organization for Lesbian and Gay Action in the mid-1980s, and then in the campaign to oppose the anti-gay Clause 28 of the 1988 Local Government Bill, prohibiting the 'promotion' of homosexuality. The failure to stop the passage of that legislation helped convince him and other activists to form OutRage! in 1990. This was a London group devoted to confrontational direct action on sexual orientation issues, its tactics contrasting sharply with those of the mainstream lobby group Stonewall (though in fact working towards some of the same legislative objectives). Tatchell's indefatigability,

his willingness to put himself on the front lines, and his knack for designing eye-catching stunts has contributed greatly to the high profile of OutRage! over most of the period since its foundation.

He has also participated in activist campaigns directed at the institutions of the European Union, and in 1992 published *Europe in the Pink: Lesbian and Gay Equality in the New Europe*. He has also published books on the Bermondsey by-election and other topics, and has been a prolific writer in the gay/lesbian and left press.

Tatchell has regularly created controversy within and beyond gay/lesbian/bisexual/transgendered circles. He has openly disdained the 'softly, softly' respectability of other activist groups. He has supported 'outing' in the face of widespread opposition from other activists, and has followed through by publicising the homosexuality of prominent figures in the Church of England. Still, Tatchell's creative civil disobedience has won him many admirers.

Peter Tatchell, *The Battle for Bermondsey* (London, 1983); Lesley White, 'Indecent Exposure', *The Sunday Times Magazine*, 25 April 1995; Ian Lukas, *OutRage: An Oral History* (London, 1998).

David Rayside

Taylor, Dame Elizabeth (b. 1932), British actor and AIDS activist. For most people Elizabeth Taylor is best known for her diamonds (the 33.19 carat Krupp diamond and the 69.42 carat Cartier diamond), her collection of husbands (eight marriages and eight divorces), her fragrances (three at last count), her operations (forty to date), her deaths (she is reported to have died twice and been revived twice) and, most significantly, her acting career. She was awarded two Oscars and was the first actress to earn US$1 million for a film.

In the 1980s she added another important dimension to her life when she became active in the community fight against

AIDS. In 1985 she helped found the American Foundation for AIDS Research (AmFAR). With the proceeds of the sale of photos of her latest wedding (to Larry Fortensky in 1991), she founded her own AIDS charity – The Elizabeth Taylor AIDS Foundation (ETAF). AmFAR is mainly involved in AIDS research, whereas ETAF is focused more on the provision of funding to AIDS service organisations throughout the world (which provide assistance to those living with HIV/AIDS). Whilst Taylor remains committed to supporting AmFAR (she remains its National Chairman), it seems that her favoured cause is ETAF, where she can more directly assist those living with HIV/AIDS. In 1993 Taylor received the Jean Hersholt Humanitarian Award from the American Academy of Motion Picture Arts and Sciences for her contribution to the fight against HIV/AIDS. She has also been awarded the Aristotle S. Onassis Foundation Award (1988) and the Legion of Honour (1987) and made a Commander of Arts and Letters (1985) by the French government.

Whilst it is true that Taylor blatantly exploits her celebrity status to raise funds for AIDS charities, her involvement in HIV/AIDS has not been limited to mere social engagements. She is well aware that her public profile gives her the opportunity and power to influence public opinion: this includes the power to influence political leaders. She often actively participates in the lobbying activities of AmFAR, dealing directly with members of the US administration. She has openly criticised the AIDS policies of both sides of American politics. For instance, in a speech to the National Press Club during the 1996 US Presidential campaign, she condemned the policy of both candidates to ban needle exchanges, stating that 'misunderstanding, social squeamishness and lack of compassion have prevailed over sensible public health practice'.

Taylor has encouraged many others within the 'entertainment industry' to take up the AIDS cause. She has admitted that she is 'very crass' when it comes to asking her fellow celebrities to open their chequebooks. Internationally, the entertainment industry has provided ongoing support for the cause: the most obvious symbol of that support has been the wearing of a red ribbon at such highly publicised events as the American Academy Awards and the Cannes Film Festival, as well as many and varied high exposure gala and first-night performances.

The active participation of the entertainment industry is not surprising, given that many involved in that industry are directly affected by AIDS either by being infected themselves or through personal and professional relationships with people infected. The participation of personalities such as Elizabeth Taylor has not only raised much needed cash for AIDS charities: it has also smoothed the way for mainstream public acceptance of people affected by the disease through demystifying many aspects related to AIDS. Taylor was the first celebrity to offer assistance to the AIDS cause. In 1985 she chaired the first major AIDS benefit – the Commitment to Life dinner which netted US$1 million for a Los Angeles community-based AIDS service organisation. *Vanity Fair* noted that 'Elizabeth Taylor brought AIDS out of the closet and into the ballroom, where there was money – and consciousness – to be raised'.

Taylor's association with AIDS was not just professional or philanthropic. She also had a very personal association with the disease. Her old friend and former co-star Rock HUDSON died from AIDS, her personal secretary Roger Wall committed suicide after learning that he was HIV-positive and her former daughter-in-law, Aileen Getty, also contracted the virus. The tabloid press even suggested that Taylor had AIDS in 1990 when she nearly died from an undiagnosable pulmonary virus. She has said that this experience galvanised her to do something important – 'I thought, I've got to do something to help people who are *really* sick'. In many ways Taylor's association with Hudson proved to be a catalyst for her involvement with the AIDS issue. Hudson's doctor was Michael GOTTLIEB, the physician who published the first article on AIDS in the *New England Journal of Medicine*, in 1981. Gottlieb was able to provide Taylor with factual information about AIDS – in turn she was able to relay this information to a wider audience, the American public. Gottlieb and Taylor collaborated in the establishment of AmFAR.

Hudson's illness highlighted the homophobia of Hollywood, and indeed that of mainstream America. In *Vanity Fair* Taylor is quoted as saying, 'I realized that this town . . . was basically homophobic, even though without homosexuals there would be no Hollywood, no show business! Yet the industry was turning its back on what it considered to be a gay disease.' It was this community attitude which prompted Taylor to become involved in her first AIDS activity.

Vanity Fair, Nov. 1992, pp. 103–5, 154–7.

Mark Edwards

Tennant, Neil See PET SHOP BOYS.

Testori, Giovanni (1923–93), Italian writer, critic. Widely known in Italy as a critic of art and contemporary culture, Testori was also a prolific author of novels, plays and poetry. Much less well known was the fact of his homosexuality, which, although the subject appeared frequently as a theme in Testori's works, was certainly not a publicised aspect of his personality. Testori was devoutly Catholic, and in many ways his life and work embody much of the tension between modern sexual emancipation and the Catholic religion. While some of his early works may have seemed to be leading towards the former, in later life Testori fervently embraced the latter.

Testori was born in one of the outer suburbs of Milan in 1923, the third of six children in a family of middle-class means.

His parents had moved to the city from the nearby countryside so that his father could take up a job overseeing production in a silk mill. Because the young Giovanni was a promising student he was sent to school in the centre of Milan, where he was initially teased for speaking his parents' provincial dialect. Nevertheless, he did well at school, showing a precocious interest in art, and at the age of 16 even publishing an article on an exhibition of Caravaggio's paintings. By the time Testori graduated from the Catholic University of Milan with a degree in philosophy (his thesis was on the aesthetics of surrealism), he had published several small articles and an essay on Matisse.

At university Testori made many friends among Milanese artistic and literary circles, and after graduating in 1947 he gravitated towards a full involvement in that world. Initially he worked as an assistant curating art exhibitions, an activity with which he was to be involved for many decades. He continued to write, too, and one of his early plays, *Caterina di dio* was produced in 1948. Critics noted the heavily Catholic emphasis on sin lived as guilt and self-laceration, a theme which was to become one of Testori's hallmarks. But he also worked in a neo-realistic vein, exemplified by his first published narrative work, *Il dio di Roserio* (1954), and the better-known collection of short stories, *Il ponte della Ghisolfa* (1958). Detailing life in Milan's industrial suburbs, the title story became the basis for VISCONTI's film *Rocco e i suoi fratelli* (1960). Testori was called upon to advise on Milanese dialect during the making of the film, and this began a long collaboration between the two men.

This collaboration also resulted in Testori's only real brush with scandal when, in 1960, Visconti produced Testori's latest play, *L'Arialda*. The production ran for fifty-three performances in Rome, but was closed down in Milan after one night, on the grounds that it was depraved. The principal reason for the prosecutor's concern was the main character's brother, a beautiful homosexual prostitute who made no secret of his tastes or his occupation. The cancellation of the play resulted in a clamorous public debate, and attracted the intervention of figures like PASOLINI, who said that although he did not like the play, the attempt to censor it was monstrous.

After *L'Arialda*, Testori gradually moved away from neo-realism in favour of the mystical, moralising and Catholic themes that were to become the main features of his later work. In 1965 he published a volume of poems, *I trionfi*, which indicated the change, although they also contained many allusions to homosexuality; 1967 saw another collaboration with Visconti, who produced Testori's play *La monaca di Monza*. It was also during this period that Testori began the relationship with the man whom he was later to describe as the love of his life, Alain. Several of Testori's published works were inspired by this relationship, including *L'Amore* (1968) and *Per sempre* (1969), both collections of poems. Somewhat later, *Alain* (1972) and *A te* (1973) were published in small print-runs not intended for sale. And it was over Alain that the long collaboration between Testori and Visconti came to an end: Alain had had a small part in the film *La caduta degli dei* (1969) but his appearance was edited from the final version. Acrimony over this led to the end of Testori's and Visconti's friendship.

Contrary to the general trend towards increasing sexual freedoms after 1968, and despite his own sexual tastes, Testori's view of homosexuality leant increasingly towards the Catholic view of non-procreative emission as a sin. Notwithstanding the moving intimacy of the small works inspired by Alain, Testori presented the public with a more tortured view of homosexuality as a damnation requiring spiritual redemption. This is one of the themes of the theatrical trilogy made up of *Ambleto* (1973), *Macbetto* (1974) and *Edipo* (1977), which detail the self-destructive voyage of an anarchic and tormented gay prince towards the void. And in the novel *La cattedrale* (1974), Testori skilfully intertwines the stories of an artist working in medieval Lombardy and a writer in twentieth-century Milan. Both characters are obsessed with and repulsed by sex with men, and in each case the resulting torments are only exorcised by death: the medieval character sacrificially murders the boy he has sex with; the modern character is killed in an accident.

In 1977 Testori's response to the death of his mother marked a definitive turn towards a more politically active fundamental Catholicism. That year he was also appointed as art critic for the major Milanese newspaper, *Il Corriere della sera*, a position he used to lament the corruptive effects of mass culture. He strongly emphasised what he saw as the damaging irony of Western culture being emptied of any real meaning just at the point when the instruments for its diffusion were becoming more powerful than ever. He increasingly used theatrical work as an opportunity to dramatise the Christian liturgy, his 1979 play *Interrogatorio a Maria* being a good example. He also took a stand on various social issues, and in 1981 he wrote *Factum est*, a programmatic manifesto against abortion.

Testori was active as a critic and writer well into his old age, although he occupied an increasingly isolated position. Notwithstanding his fervent Catholicism, his work was not surprisingly viewed as unorthodox by Catholics, but he was regarded with more hostility by gay intellectuals for his insistence on the idea of homosexuality being a damnation which could only be exculpated through Christianity.

Giovanni Cappello, *Giovanni Testori* (Florence, 1983); Francesco Gnerre, *L'eroe negato* (Milan, 1981).

Mark Seymour

Thandekiso, Tsietsi (1948–97), South African cleric. Tsietsi Thandekiso inspired the members of a small Christian prayer group in Johannesburg to transform themselves into a fully fledged church, the Hope and Unity Metropolitan Community Church, which was established in 1994. The church met the needs of a growing community of young Africans who were gay or lesbian, and located itself on the top floor of the Harrison Reef Hotel in the inner-city suburb of Hillbrow, Johannesburg, seven floors above one of South Africa's oldest existing gay bars, the Skyline. In 1995, during the period of negotiating a new constitution for a democratic South Africa, Thandekiso met with the Reverend Kenneth Meshoe, leader of the conservative and homophobic African Christian Democratic Party, in order to challenge his party's opposition to lesbian and gay equality. Thandekiso's funeral service took place in his former church, the Apostolic Faith Mission Church. The service included leading lesbian and gay activists – a fitting irony to the fact that he had been alienated from this homophobic church community and had established instead a church in which lesbian and gay identities were celebrated and affirmed – in his own words, 'the small flock that God has given me'.

Gay and Lesbian Archives, University of the Witwatersrand Libraries, Johannesburg.

Graeme Reid

Thatcher, Margaret See REAGAN.

Thesiger, Sir Wilfred (b. 1910), British explorer and writer. Thesiger was born in Addis Ababa, where his father was head of the British legation to Ethiopia; his uncle was Viceroy of India. As befitted such parentage, Thesiger was educated at Eton and Oxford after spending his early life in Africa. He returned to Ethiopia as a guest at the coronation of Emperor Haile Selassie, one of his heroes.

Thesiger explored Ethiopia in the early 1930s and fulminated against Mussolini's invasion of the country. Next he explored the Tibesti region in what was then the Anglo-Egyptian Sudan and the French African empire. He served in British forces during World War II, then explored the 'empty quarter' of the Arabian peninsula in the late 1940s. He lived with the 'Marsh Arabs' in southern Iraq in the 1950s and also travelled to India, Afghanistan and Iran. Thesiger's accounts of his adventures, including *Arabian Sands* (1959) and *The Marsh Arabs* (1964), made him a bestselling author and also won him accolades from geographical societies.

Thesiger has rightly been considered the last of the great imperial explorers. His works added greatly to knowledge of little-known regions, and he promoted the benefits of European expansion: 'The Empire was absolutely outstanding, and I was proud to have something to do with it.' Thesiger thus followed in the steps of such earlier explorers and writers as Richard Burton and Lawrence of Arabia, whom he also counted among his heroes. His writing shows an aristocratic commitment to duty, violent anti-modernism, pleasure in the challenges of old-fashioned exploration, and fortitude in enduring the hardships of desert life.

In his expeditions, Thesiger also enjoyed the companionship of the rugged young warriors who are admiringly portrayed in his writings and photographs. The virile comradeship of desert treks clearly provided Thesiger with his closest and most satisfying personal relationships: 'I'm not saying there is anything sexual in it,' Thesiger commented, 'but certainly you have this feeling of love for them and there you are.' He felt most at ease in the all-male world of Bedouin camps. Thesiger also told of performing countless circumcisions of young men on his travels. He never married.

Wilfred Thesiger, *The Life of My Choice* (London, 1987); Michael Asher, *Thesiger: A Biography* (London, 1994).

Robert Aldrich

Thorpe, Jeremy (b. 1929), British politician. Thorpe, the son of a Tory MP, was educated at Eton and Oxford, where he was President of the Union, and became a barrister in 1954. He was a brilliant scholar and a witty public speaker. He was active in the Liberal Party from his youth and in 1959 was elected MP for North Devon. Had he been born fifty years earlier, he would have been a cabinet minister before he was 40, but at this time the Liberals were at their lowest ebb, with only six MPs.

Thorpe succeeded Jo Grimond as Liberal leader in 1967, and in 1968 he married Caroline Allpass, with whom he had a son. Caroline Thorpe was killed in a car accident in 1970, and in 1973 Thorpe married Marion, Countess of Harewood, ex-wife of the Queen's cousin, the Earl of Harewood. Thorpe led the Liberals through three elections, during which the party's fortunes revived considerably, mainly due to his media skills and high public profile. In February 1974 he found himself with the balance of power in the House of Commons. He declined Ted Heath's offer of a Tory/Liberal coalition and supported a minority Labour government.

In October 1975 Norman Scott, a former model, alleged that Thorpe had hired a hitman, Gino Newton, who had tried to shoot him in an incident on Dartmoor, in which Scott's dog was killed. He alleged that he and Thorpe had had a homosexual affair in the early 1960s, and that Thorpe had threatened to kill him if he revealed this fact. It emerged that Scott had sold letters from Thorpe to tabloid newspapers, and also written to Thorpe's mother. Thorpe denied all these allegations, but the subsequent media scandal forced him to resign as Liberal leader in May 1976.

Scott found an ally in Peter Bessell, a former Liberal MP who said that there had been a conspiracy, involving Thorpe, to silence Scott, and that donations to the Liberal Party had been used by Thorpe to pay Newton. As a result Thorpe and two other men were charged in August 1978 with conspiring to kill Scott, and a committal hearing in December sent them to trial. Thorpe was released on £5,000 bail. The trial was set for March 1979, but was postponed because of the May general election, in which Thorpe contested his seat (against the wishes of the Liberal Party) but was defeated.

The trial of Thorpe and his alleged accomplices took place under intense media scrutiny, and this itself became an important point in the proceedings. Thorpe's counsel, Sir David Napley, accused Scott and Bessell of having a financial interest in Thorpe's conviction, since they would be able to sell their stories to the tabloids. Bessell, he said, had been offered £10,000 by the *Sunday Telegraph*, with a further £25,000 if Thorpe was convicted.

At the trial Scott alleged that Thorpe had seduced him in 1961, and that they had been lovers for three years. He related how he had bitten the pillow while Thorpe sodomised him – the Australian transvestite satirist Barry HUMPHRIES later popularised the term 'pillow-biters' for gay men. Thorpe's name for Scott had been 'Bunny'. After Thorpe became Liberal leader, he had become concerned that Scott would reveal their relationship, and had offered to find him jobs abroad to buy his silence. In 1968, when Scott had threatened to speak out, Thorpe had first considered having Scott killed.

Thorpe did not take the stand, but through his counsel he denied all Scott and Bessell's claims. He said he and Scott had been friends only, that he had tried to help Scott in his career, and that Scott had attempted to blackmail him on that basis. He agreed that he had discussed with his fellow defendants ways in which Scott might be 'frightened' into ceasing this blackmail, but denied that there had been any conspiracy to kill Scott (or his dog). After a month of proceedings and a long deliberation, all three were found not guilty.

Thorpe was greatly aided by the summing up of the trial judge, Sir Joseph Cantley, who told the jury that Scott was 'a warped, hysterical personality' and 'an accomplished sponger', a 'whiner and a parasite'. Bessell and Scott, he said, had a pecuniary interest in Thorpe's conviction, and this reduced their credibility. Bessell, said the judge, was 'a humbug', and Newton, the alleged hitman, was a 'chump'. Further, the judge said, Thorpe's failure to take the stand should be seen by the jury as 'totally neutral' and not as an admission of guilt.

The more respectable parts of the British media condemned the tabloid sensationalising of the trial, and also the chequebook journalism which, ironically, helped Thorpe's case by allowing his accusers to be depicted as corrupt. Why, it was asked, was the trial of a former leader of a minor party, who had never held office and was no longer even an MP, worth the constant attention of seventy journalists? The answer of course was that the real issue in the case was Thorpe's alleged homosexuality, and the British public's apparently insatiable appetite for gossip about the sexual lives of their rulers.

After the trial Thorpe disappeared from public life. It is important to note that since he was acquitted of all charges, none of Scott's accusations, including those concerning his alleged relationship with Thorpe, were proven to be correct. Thorpe has never made any statement about his sexuality, and since he is now 70 it seems unlikely he is going to do so. The retired Labour prime minister, Lord Wilson, later claimed that the allegations against Thorpe were fabricated by the South African secret police because of Thorpe's outspoken opposition to apartheid. This has never been proved. The case was kept alive for a while by the publication of two muck-raking books rehashing the events leading up to the trial, but with the perspective of twenty years the whole business now seems like a rather sordid storm in a teacup.

The Economist (London), 12 Aug., 25 Nov., 2 Dec., 9 Dec., 16 Dec. 1978; 12 May, 23 June, 30 June 1979; Auberon Waugh, *The Last Word: An Eye-Witness Account of the Trial of Jeremy Thorpe* (London, 1980).

Adam Carr

Tielman, Rob (b. 1946), Dutch scholar. Tielman has always considered the year in which he was born as a special one. The Dutch gay and lesbian movement COC (Culture and Recreation Centre), and the Humanistisch Verbond (Humanist League) were both founded the same year, and he played an active role in these organisations. Besides that he sees himself as a child of the Liberation. His father, a socialist, had been imprisoned during World War II by the Nazis; his mother had gone into hiding. At the age of 21, Tielman finally could become a member of the COC. Between 1911 and 1971 the Dutch Penal code forbade sexual contacts between adults, male and female, and minors under the age of 21 (Paragraph 248*bis* of the Criminal Code). The COC was thus afraid that the government would take measures if the society allowed those under 21 to become members. For these young men and women, the only way out was to start their own groups. In this way youth societies and student groups connected to the COC were founded. The groups allied in the Federatie Studenten Werkgroepen Homosexualiteit (Federation of Student Workgroups on Homosexuality, FSWH). Tielman became a member of a homosexual student group and played a dominant role in the federation, and criticised the policy of the COC in the late 1960s. The openness that was promoted by the chairman, Benno PREMSELA, did not go far enough and homosexual men and women were afraid to confront heterosexual people. Society would only change if homosexual men and women made clear that they were just 'fellow human beings'. The students' slogan was 'Integration through

Confrontation', and in their eyes this strategy should be part of the larger sexual revolution that was taking place. The confrontation would establish understanding, and prejudices would disappear. In the process of creating a new society, homosexuals, lesbians and heterosexuals worked together as the federation organised its first demonstration in January 1969. They went to Parliament, demonstrated against anti-homosexual laws and demanded the right of free love and self-determination. Premsela and the leading figures of the FSWH believed in the same goal. The union then changed its name to the Dutch Society for Integration of Homosexuality, and Tielman served as secretary (1971–75). At the same time, he started to work as a sociologist at the University of Utrecht. The policy of integration subsequently broke down in the mid-1970s, as heterosexual society was not changing rapidly enough. Small groups, inspired by gay liberation in the US, the UK, Germany and France, fiercely attacked the COC. In a few years the concept of a 'homosexual identity' was also accepted by the COC.

Most of the students who had been active in the COC in the 1960s and had changed the policy of the union were engaged in psychological, sociological and sexological research. By the early 1970s, a considerable amount of scientific work was produced in the Netherlands (regrettably hardly ever translated into a main European language). More and more homosexuals realised that they as scholars could do important research work and by doing so could improve the positions of lesbians and gay men. In 1978 they made a start with 'homostudies'. Tielman himself wrote his thesis on *Homoseksualiteit in Nederland* (*Homosexuality in the Netherlands*, 1982), in which he mainly focused on the twentieth century and the role of the COC, which he considered an emancipation movement comparable to those working for the emancipation of women and the working class. Tielman was one of the leading figures of Homostudies Utrecht (the gay studies unit at the University of Utrecht), serving as chairman from 1982 until 1992. It focused on the emancipation of homosexuals and lesbians and did mainly sociological and sexological research on discrimination, the position of homosexuals in the police force, the media and homosexuality, the legal position of homosexuals around the world, the legal position in the Netherlands and AIDS; some historical research was also done. It seemed that Homostudies Utrecht looked upon homosexuality as a 'biological construction', while Homostudies Amsterdam (the gay studies unit at the University of Amsterdam) saw it as a 'social construction'. The latter published more historical and philosophical works. But the difference was mainly that Utrecht was doing more practical research and Amsterdam more theoretical work. Today the interest in 'Homostudies' has faded, it seems, as a result of the improving position of homosexuals and lesbians. Few students take the courses and Utrecht's unit has been dissolved. Tielman, the COC and some other institutions are still trying, however, to establish a professorial chair in 'Homostudies'.

Apart from his work as a scholar, Tielman was active from 1987 until 1994 in the Nationale Commisie AIDS-Bestrijding (National Commission on the Fight against AIDS), which was set up by the Dutch government. For many years he was also an adviser to the World Health Organisation, for which he wrote *Bisexuality and HIV/AIDS*. He was a board member of several institutions, for instance, *Homologie*, a scientific, cultural and literary magazine; Vrolijk (Dutch for 'gay' in the old sense), a gay and lesbian bookshop; and Homodok, an important documentation centre on homosexuality. (*Homologie* ceased publication in 1997.) He is still active in the COC committee on national politics. Since 1992 he has worked as a professor of education. In his personal life, he and his partner of over twenty-seven years have been foster parents of homosexual teenagers for many years. In 1998, Tielman was awareded the Bob Angelo Medal – named after the founder of the COC, Nico ENGELSCHMAN, who used 'Bob Angelo' as a pen-name for his work.

Hans Warmerdam

Tippett, Sir Michael (1905–98), British composer. Summer 1923 was Tippett's first term as a student at the Royal College of Music in London, and saw his first overwhelming unrequited love affair for an attractive young (heterosexual) church musician, Herbert Sumsion. Through his cousin and friend, Phylliss Kemp, he met the choral conductor and folk-song researcher Francesca Allinson, who became one of his most intimate companions during the 1930s. With Allinson (who was also partly homosexual), he for a while contemplated marriage and childbearing (even by artificial insemination). In 1932 he met the young Bauhaus-trained painter Wilfred Franks, and later wrote (in 1991): 'Meeting with Wilf was the deepest, most shattering experience of falling in love; and I am quite certain that it was a major factor underlying the discovery of my own individual musical voice . . . all that love flowed out in the slow movement of my *First String Quartet* [1935].' However, the relationship was complicated from the first by Franks's reservations about homosexuality (he eventually married). Until this time Tippett had accepted his homosexuality 'without reservation, as something instinctive and therefore natural' (1991). But now, guided by his reading of Jung, he put himself through a prolonged period of dream therapy in an attempt to come to terms with his turbulent reactions to the isolating effects of difference. Late in life he identified with Nietzsche's line, 'One must have a chaos inside oneself to give birth to a dancing star.' And, indeed, he eventually abandoned therapy and embraced his personal turbulence as central to his creativity.

A growing political commitment was inspired by Tippett's strong sense of compassion and practical work on behalf of the underprivileged, notably war veterans, the unemployed (especially in Britain's impoverished north) and other victims of the capitalist economy. He briefly joined the British Communist Party in the mid-1930s, but, a Trotskyite by inclination, he was repelled by its strongly Stalinist stance. In the wake of these experiences, Tippett composed two of his most lastingly popular works, the *Concerto for Double String Orchestra* (1939) and the oratorio *A Child of Our Time* (1939–41). The inspiration for this modern secular 'passion' was the assassination of a German diplomat in Paris by a young Jewish boy, and the terrible pogrom against Jews that followed. Bowen has rightly called it 'a moving assertion of humanitarianism in an epoch of catastrophe'. Tippett always felt the piece was about scapegoats in general, and late in life, prompted by a German doctor researching AIDS, accepted that these included AIDS sufferers who, in the 1980s, were, as he wrote, 'victims of discrimination and ostracisation'. Tippett had originally approached T. S. Eliot to write the text of *A Child of Our Time*, but, upon being shown Tippett's detailed scenario, Eliot told the composer that he would be better to write the words himself, advice that he followed then and in five subsequent operas.

In 1943 Tippett became a conscientious objector to war service, and, despite character testimony on his behalf (by Vaughan Williams among others), was sent to prison for three months. His mother (who had once been briefly jailed for her participation in a suffragette protest) believed this to be his finest hour. A year earlier, Tippett had first met Benjamin BRITTEN and Peter PEARS, with whom for a while he developed a close friendship, sleeping once with Britten (though not having sex), and causing Pears some initial pangs of jealousy. Far more importantly, they shared pacifist and musical interests, notably in the then burgeoning Early Music revival. In 1945, Allinson, unable to face life as an invalid and Tippett's continuing failure to respond fully to her, both physically and in the emotional development of their relationship, committed suicide. The song cycle *The Heart's Assurance* (1951), to which he gave the subtitle 'Love under the Shadow of Death', is dedicated to her memory, and sets to music verses by two poets, Sidney Keyes and Alun Lewis, who had died in World War II. Through this time, Tippett was sharing a difficult relationship with John Minchinton, a young bisexual musician, who later married.

In the aftermath of the war, Tippett spent six years (1946–52) working on the libretto for an opera, 'a kind of modern *Magic Flute*'. *The Midsummer Marriage*, premiered at Covent Garden in 1955, both bemused and delighted its audience and critics for the narrative difficulties of its hermetic text and the ebullient optimism of its musical idiom (it has since had four-teen further productions). Since the war, Tippett had also been a regular lecturer, writer and broadcaster on musical subjects. He took six months off composing in 1958 to rework many of his previous presentations into a book, *Moving Into Aquarius* (1959), in which he considers the role of the composer in the light of a mil-lennial change. In 1957 Tippett renewed contact with Karl Hawker, a painter he had met before the war. Hawker had since married and had children, but when his marriage broke down, he came back to live with Tippett, acting partly as his secretary and assistant. Tippett later wrote: 'Any physical relations between us never lasted for long. Tensions developed, Karl would remain aloof and even wonder whether he was truly gay.' Meanwhile, a declamatory, tightly scored second opera, *King Priam* (1962), marked the advent of the more ur-gent, dissonant voice in Tippett's music, cemented in the *Second Piano Sonata* (1962), the *Concerto for Orchestra* (1963) and the oratorio *The Vision of St Augus-tine* (1966).

From the mid-1960s, as a long running pendant to his troublesome home-life with Hawker, Tippett carefully nurtured a new and rewarding relationship with an ideal-istic young music student, Meirion (Bill) Bowen. Refreshingly, Bowen was not only happily gay, but capable of being a close musical confidant, and their companion-ship – personal and professional – re-mained central, alongside other sexual relationships for both men, for the rest of Tippett's life. Very slowly, life with Hawk-er became untenable, a fact that Tippett, in his autobiography, appears to blame on Hawker's instability. However, Bowen in his Tippett obituary makes the general observation that 'few close relationships survived [Tippett's] ruthless creative ob-session'. From this time comes a third opera, *The Knot Garden* (1970), arguably his most original creation for the stage, en-larging the palette of *Priam* to reflect new interests in popular music and culture. In the wake of homosexual law reform and the abolition of theatrical censorship in Britain, it was also the first to contain homosexual characters, Dov, a composer, and Mel, a black writer. These changes were undoubtedly partly due to his con-tact with Bowen, who 'officially came into the foreground of my existence' in 1974, and partly a response to his first visit to the United States, where he was deeply impressed by more liberal attitudes toward sexuality among many young people.

The year 1977 saw the completion of the *Fourth Symphony*, and the fourth opera, *The Ice Break*, which deals with political and racial violence. The massive choral and orchestral work *The Mask of Time* (1983) has the air of a final summa-tion, and it was indeed Tippett's intention, following its completion, to reduce his composing load, and reap the rewards of fame, notably in the form of frequent travel. However, he also went on to com-pose a fifth and final opera, *New Year* (1986–88), perhaps his most whimsical work, clearly inspired by the multi-media age and by the musical and literary syntax of pop. Though Tippett's productivity was now severely curtailed by the frailties of age and poor eyesight, during the following years he laboured to produce three final major works, *Byzantium* (1989), a setting of Yeats's poem for soprano and orchestra, the *Fifth String Quartet* (1991–92) and *The Rose Lake* (1993), described as 'a song without words for orchestra'.

Tippett's homosexuality was an 'open secret' for much of his career, but it was not documented until as recently as Kemp's 1984 book, and more fully and candidly by Tippett himself (in 1991). The revised 1997 edition of Bowen's book further relates Tippett's sexuality to his music. Tippett rarely brought specifically gay issues into his work or writings; however, he was a pioneer of the open exploration of a wider spectrum of sexuality, especially in his stage works. As much as by his sexuality and left-leaning personal politics, Tippett's persona was characterised by an impatience with petty conventions and a love of fun, as attested to later in life by his large collection of colourful sneakers. In his last years he was reunited with Sumsion and Franks, both of whom were proud to acknowledge him once more as, respectively, friend and former lover. Tippett was knighted in 1966 and, on the recommendation of his friend William Walton, made a Companion of Honour in 1979.

Michael Tippett, *Moving into Aquarius* (London, 1959) and *Those Twentieth Century Blues: An Autobiography* (London, 1991); Meirion Bowen, *Michael Tippett* (London, 1982; rev. edn 1997); Ian Kemp, *Tippett: The Composer and His Music* (London, 1984).

Graeme Skinner

Tom of Finland (1920–91), Finnish artist. Born Touko Laaksonen in Kaarina in south-west Finland, he adopted the name Tom of Finland in 1957. The son of middle-class schoolteacher parents, Laaksonen moved to Helsinki in 1939 to study advertising. However World War II cut

short his studies when the USSR invaded Finland in November 1939. Finland was finally forced to sue for peace in March 1940, and in April Laaksonen was drafted into the army, where he was commissioned as a lieutenant in an anti-aircraft division. War resumed on the eastern front when Hitler initiated the Operation Barbarossa invasion of the USSR in 1941. Having formed a pact with Nazi Germany, Finland attacked the Soviet Union, although it was not until late 1944 that Laaksonen saw military action on the eastern front. In February 1945 Finland again surrendered to the Soviet Union, and he resumed his art studies in Helsinki while simultaneously studying piano at the Sibelius Academy of Music. In the years following the war, he worked as a freelance commercial artist and cabaret pianist, and in 1953 he met Veli, who was to be his partner for the next 28 years.

Although Laaksonen had been making what he described as his 'dirty drawings' since the 1940s, it was only in the late 1950s that he began publishing these hitherto secret pictures. On the suggestion of a friend, he sent some drawings to the Athletic Model Guild (AMG) photo agency and publishing company established in Los Angeles after the war by Bob Mizer, who used a drawing of a lumberjack on the cover of the Spring 1957 issue of *Physique Pictorial*. Because of the need to remain anonymous, and due to the unfamiliarity of his Finnish name for an American audience, Laaksonen signed the drawing 'Tom of Finland', this format being common amongst physique photographers (e.g. BRUCE OF LOS ANGELES, Kris of Chicago and Lon of New York). Despite the immediate popularity of his drawings, he was only able to give up his job in advertising in 1973 – the same year in which he had his first solo exhibition in Hamburg. By then he had already produced a substantial number of drawings and books including over 200 drawings for AMG as well as the comic-strip *Kake* series (originally published in Denmark in

1968 and which ran to over twenty titles) featuring the sexual escapades of its eponymous hero.

Although there are stylistic shifts across Tom of Finland's work (which comprises over 3,000 drawings) with, for example, the earliest drawings having a softer line (just as the men depicted are less rugged than in the later drawings), many of the key elements of his art were evident by the late 1950s. Laaksonen's wartime experiences, in particular the readily available sex during the Helsinki blackouts and the constant presence of men in uniform, were an especially formative influence. While only a few drawings of Nazi soldiers survive, uniforms remained an integral aspect of Tom of Finland's masculinist vision of homosexuality. Rejecting current identifications (in the 1950s and 1960s) of homosexuality with effeminacy and camp, Tom of Finland's men are typically working class or blue collar (e.g. lumberjacks, sailors, bikers, policemen and soldiers), and are depicted with a stock set of physical attributes – cropped hair, square jaws, broad chests, highly developed muscles, narrow waists and buttocks, and massive genitals. Deliberately producing a fantasy, almost caricatural, version of masculinity, this proletarian macho 'look' provided a specifically contemporary image of gay men and also shaped the emergence of the 'clone' in the 1970s (particularly in the US) as well as the iconography of gay leather and S&M culture. In spite of the self-consciously excessive machismo of this imagery, many of the drawings (especially those from the 1960s) have a humorous edge to them and depict a tender affection between men, which is often relayed through the exchange of looks rather than by overt sexual activity. As such, despite the apparent similarity of these (frequently uniformed) physical types to the hypermasculine figures of fascist art (such as Arno Breker's sculptures), the drawings undercut traditional notions of masculinity and power by overtly depicting sexual desire between men. By the early 1980s,

however, there was a greater aggressiveness in the drawings (paralleling, perhaps, the tenor of much US video pornography). So too, the photo-realist technique of the drawings (which were often based on photographs) also became harder and the musculature of the bodies more massive.

In 1978 Tom visited the US for the first time and, following the death of Veli in 1981, began regularly travelling between Finland and America, where he met Andy WARHOL and Robert MAPPLETHORPE. By this time his drawings were regularly exhibited in the US and Europe, in addition to their continued publication in numerous magazines and serials. Although Tom of Finland was not the only gay graphic artist working in the US – the physique artist George Quaintance (1915–57), also published by Mizer, was an important precursor, and artists such as Etienne, Rex and Blade were also significant contemporaries – he was the most prolific. Growing imitation and pirating of his work led to an association between the US businessman Durk Dehner and Tom, and in 1986 they established the Tom of Finland Foundation in Los Angeles, which is both the official archive of Tom's work (much of which has been published in several books of drawings) and a collection of gay erotic art. A documentary film of Tom's life and work, entitled *Daddy and the Muscle Academy*, directed by Ilppo Pohjola and partly financed by the Finnish Film Board, was released in 1991. Later that year Tom of Finland died of a stroke in Helsinki.

F. Valentine Hooven III, *Tom of Finland: His Life and Times* (New York, 1993), *Beefcake: The Muscle Magazines of America, 1950–1970* (Cologne, 1995); Michael Ramakers, *Tom of Finland: The Art of Pleasure* (Cologne, 1998).

David L. Phillips

Toms, Ivan (b. 1953), South African activist. Born in Cape Town, Toms served two years in the South African Defence Force, conscripted after completing medical training in 1976. A committed Anglican, Toms worked as a doctor for over a decade in the Crossroads squatter camp in the Cape Flats, and became active in the End Conscription Campaign (ECC). He was also active in the pioneering anti-apartheid Organisation of Lesbian and Gay Activists, and had met with leaders of the African National Congress in exile in Harare to discuss gay rights. Called up for periodic service in the Defence Force in July 1987, Toms refused and was charged, tried and sentenced to eighteen months, gaol. His case was reported widely in Europe and North America. Although his homosexuality was downplayed by the ECC, he was subject to a long and very public campaign of anti-gay vilification, graffiti and death threats. The prosecution raised the issue of his homosexuality in the trial, and his lawyer, Edwin CAMERON, called Anglican Bishop David Russell to testify on his behalf; he politely endorsed Toms' fight against gay oppression. Toms was released on bail after nine months in Pollsmoor prison, pending an appeal, which was successful. He has subsequently worked in progressive non-government organisations providing health and HIV services in Cape Town.

Edwin Cameron and Mark Gevisser (eds.), *Defiant Desire* (Johannesburg, 1993).

Ken Davis

Tondelli, Pier Vittorio (1955–91), Italian writer, critic. Tondelli's short life poignantly spanned the triumphs and tribulations of a generation of late twentieth-century youth, from the hopes and activism of the 1960s to the realities of AIDS in the 1990s, and his work, more than that of any other Italian novelist, captures the pleasures and anxieties of this generation. He came from a provincial middle-class family in central Italy, and studied under Umberto Eco in the 1970s at the University of Bologna. Although Tondelli is known principally as a

novelist, he was also an essayist and cultural critic (his most significant work was collected and published as *Un weekend post-moderno* in 1990), as well as an indefatigable crusader for youth culture: he was actively involved in the encouragement of young writers, and edited three anthologies of their work between 1986 and 1990.

Tondelli's literary legacy consists of four novels published between 1980 and 1990. The first, *Altri libertini* (1980), presents six separate episodes, each of which reveals a generation of uninhibited youth revelling in the discovery of literature, sex and the political activism of the 1970s. The exuberance of these episodes corresponds to Tondelli's own sense of freedom after he left the strictures of his own provincial background. Critics hailed the work as that of a fresh voice in Italian literature, and discerned the influence of several modern American novelists, including KEROUAC, BALDWIN and BURROUGHS. It is almost certain that failed attempts to censor the novel ensured its subsequent best-seller status, and in turn that success paved the way for the publication of later 'scandalous' novels in Italy by authors such as Aldo BUSI.

With *Pao Pao* (1982), Tondelli brought to centre stage the gay themes that had been implicit in his first novel. Clearly autobiographical, *Pao Pao* details the experiences of a group of young men during their twelve months of obligatory military service. The novel expresses a certain pride in the way homosexuality can form part of a broader political struggle, and in this case the gayness of the principal characters assures an ironic and liberating approach to military service, a lamented rite of passage in the life of Italian males. The next novel, *Rimini* (1985), departs from the autobiographical quality of the first two, and represents a new level of literary maturity. Set in the large Adriatic resort city of the title, the novel uses experimental narrative techniques to interweave myriad stories featuring the exaggeratedly exotic human fauna of the Adriatic coast in summer, including two male lovers.

Returning to an autobiographical strain, Tondelli's last novel, *Camere separate* (1989), is a dramatic story about two lovers, Leo and Thomas, experimenting with the freedom their gayness gives them to invent new forms of masculine identity, but also struggling with the difficulties, including, ultimately, AIDS. It was written when Tondelli discovered he had an AIDS-related illness, and a series of coded details reveals that the author is contemplating his own life in the third person through the character Thomas, who is the narrator Leo's dying lover. In this sense the novel can be read as an AIDS diary, something rare in Italian literature.

Tondelli did not intend the novel to make his own condition public, nor did it do so. Instead, he returned to his family to live the final two years of his life, and, perhaps surprisingly for one who had been so engaged in public debate, chose to remain silent about his illness.

Fulvio Panzeri, *Tondelli. Il mestiere di scrittore: una conversazione autobiografica* (Ancona, 1994).

Mark Seymour

Torfason, Hördur (b. 1945), Icelandic actor, songwriter, singer, director. Born in Reykjavík, Iceland, he studied at Iceland's National Theatre School in Reykjavík, from which he graduated in 1970. He was employed as an actor at the National Theatre in Iceland (1970–72), after which he worked as a freelance director, songwriter, singer and performer in Iceland and Denmark.

In August 1975 Torfason was the first Icelander ever to come out of the closet publicly as a gay man, in an interview with the Icelandic magazine *Samúel*. This had tremendous repercussions as he was already a popular performer in his home country. As a consequence his records were no longer played on radio (and thus stopped selling). Direct threats were made

on his life and he was generally ostracised by society. Following this, he fled into exile to Copenhagen, where he lived until 1991.

During his exile he returned to Iceland regularly, however, to work as a theatre director, and in 1978 took the initiative in the foundation of the Icelandic Organisation for Lesbians and Gay Men, Samtökin '78, which was formally established on 2 May 1978.

Torfason has made a large number of records, writing both music and lyrics, as well as performing to his own guitar accompaniment. His lyrics have often focused on controversial issues such as homosexual love, as well as gay and lesbian rights in general.

Haukur F. Hannesson

Tournier, Michel (b. 1924), French author. Born and brought up in Paris, Tournier was just too young to be actively engaged in World War II, but he experienced the realities of the Occupation. This was especially significant for him, as his family, though anti-Nazi, were pro-German. It also made him acutely aware of people's capacity for self-mythologisation, as he saw the realities of the co-existence of suffering and collaboration turned into the legend of heroic French Resistance. In 1946 Tournier set off for a 'brief visit' to the University of Tübingen which turned into a stay of almost four years, studying philosophy. On his return, however, he failed the *agrégation* in philosophy and abandoned plans for an academic career. Instead he went into the media, first to a publishing house, then into radio and television. It was only in 1967 that his first novel, *Vendredi, ou les limbes du Pacifique*, appeared, winning the Grand Prix du Roman of the Académie Française. With the publication of his second novel, *Le Roi des Aulnes*, in 1970, for which he won the Prix Goncourt, he established himself almost overnight as one of France's leading contemporary novelists. In 1972 he was elected to the Académie Goncourt. Since then his major literary works have included a literary autobiography, *Le Vent Paraclet* (1977), in which he uses an analysis of his writing career to project his own self-myth, a collection of short stories, *Le Coq de bruyère* (1978), and several novels, of which the most interesting are *Les Météores* (1975) and *La Goutte d'or* (1988).

Tournier's work as a whole is based on the transgression of the conventional boundaries between opposites: affirmation and negation, intellect and physicality, masculine and feminine, reality and fantasy. In exploring these boundaries he makes great use of marginality, particularly in issues of gender and sexuality, an emphasis probably due to his own homosexuality. At the heart of both *Vendredi* and *Le Roi des Aulnes*, the first with its suggestions of interracial desire (it is a revamped Robinson Crusoe narrative), the second with its overt reference to paedophilia, there is a sexual orientation which is other than the norm. *Le Coq de bruyère* extends the range of 'abnormalities' to androgyny and fetishism. In *Les Météores* above all there is a systematic rejection of the limits of conventional heterocracy, through the defiantly homosexual Alexandre and the more exotic homosexual bonding of the identical twins Paul and Jean. By using his characters to lay bare the absurdity of the distinct categories into which sexuality is conventionally divided, Tournier is dramatising the tension between man's overwhelming desire to categorise (and thus control) experience and his pleasurable sense of the uncategorisability of that experience.

W. Cloonan, *Michel Tournier* (Boston, 1983).

Christopher Robinson

Tratnik, Suzana (b. 1963), Slovenian activist. Tratnik started the first lesbian organization in Slovenia, LL (the abbreviation stands for Lesbian Lilit) in 1987. Before that she had cooperated with Magnus, a mostly gay male Slovenian organisation, and Lilit, a feminist group, from which LL evolved.

Most important among Tratnik's projects and achievements are co-editing the Slovenian gay and lesbian magazine *Revolver* and editing the lesbian bulletin *Pandora*. She has written *L* (the anthology of the Slovenian lesbian movement), and organised an international lesbian camp on Rab island (now in Croatia) and a week of lesbian films. She also contributed significantly to increasing the visibility of lesbians and changing society's attitude towards homosexuality by her public appearances and work with media. In 1998 Tratnik published her first novel, *Pod ničlo* (*Below Zero*).

Ales Pečnik

Tremblay, Michel (b. 1942), Canadian writer. Tremblay, born in Montreal, trained to become a typesetter like his father, but was noticed as a particularly gifted pupil in school, and books were always part of his home environment. Literary success came after a competition organised by Radio Canada. His production (over forty texts) divides into three parts, only partially according to chronology.

The first is a series of plays, of which *Les Belles Soeurs* (1972) is perhaps the most celebrated. Character (nearly always women's) is more important than plot: as there is little dramatic development, the texts tend to be short, though very cleverly constructed. In *À toi pour toujours ta Marie-Lou* (1972), an unhappily-married couple who committed suicide ten years earlier share the stage with their two surviving daughters, the two time-planes being separated by lighting; in *Albertine en cinq temps* (1984) the five characters are the same woman at different stages of her life.

The second series comprises the five novels of the *Chroniques du Plateau Mont-Royal*: these are, in effect, the prehistory of the plays, and explain the characters' earlier life. Although Tremblay's novels are increasingly written in Key West, the snug and reassuring atmosphere of the overcrowded apartment of his childhood has continued to haunt his imagination. The action begins in the year of Tremblay's birth, while he is still in the womb. His uncle Édouard's transvestite tendencies become ever more apparent, leading first to an outing in full drag, and then to a trip to France in an abortive attempt to acquire a cultural background befitting a duchess.

Lastly, there are a series of autobiographical texts showing a very ordinary kind of modern homosexuality. Some follow Tremblay's own development from first contact with an art-form to his own first work: theatre (*Les Douze Coups de théâtre*, 1992) or reading (*Un Ange cornu avec des ailes de tôle*, 1994) – his heroic, but unavailing attempts at borrowing from the public library what was supposed to be the first gay novel in Quebec (André Béland's *Orage sur mon corps*) recall a less liberal age. Undoubtedly, for any man who has ever taken out his unwanted chastity with the firm intention of losing it, *La Nuit des Princes charmants* (1995) deserves cult status. The first pick-up is to happen at the opera. Unfortunately, the narrator makes contact with two men, and occupies most of the night trying to choose: 'I lost my virginity just as the sun was rising; he lost his a few minutes later. Bingo! Mission accomplished! Victory!' This is as raunchy as Tremblay gets: the physical description of sex acts is taboo.

If Tremblay were not an important gay writer, he would be an important feminist writer, and in *Le Premier Quartier de la lune* (1989) and *Un Objet de beauté* (1997) tackles affectionately the difficult subject of schizophrenia. Insofar as he is political, he is a Quebec nationalist. He is not a 'one-issue' writer. On the other hand, his many books constitute a single universe, and the characters move from one to another in a twentieth-century *comédie humaine*.

Jean-Marc Barrette, *L'Univers de Michel Tremblay: dictionnaire des personnages* (Mon-

treal, 1996); Ginette Pelland, *Hosanna et les duchesses: étiologie de l'homosexualité masculine de Freud à Tremblay* (Quebec, 1994).

David Parris

Trifonov, Gennady Nikolaevich (b. 1945), Russian writer, editor, translator. Trifonov was born in Leningrad, and his mother, Yekaterina Trifonova, survived the 900-day blockade and earned medals during the war, while his father, Nikolai Rozentsveig, was a military doctor. Trifonov's studies at the Philology Faculty of Leningrad University were interrupted when he was called up for two years' service in the Soviet Army. He graduated in 1969.

From 1968 to 1973 Trifonov worked as the literary secretary of the writers Vera Panova and her husband, David Dar; the latter was also gay. Dar's and Panova's fame and status may have shielded Trifonov from KGB harassment. After Panova's death, however, the KGB heard that he had written articles on underground literature. Trifonov had begun writing in 1960, but he was not published in Russia until 1988. His verse made its way to the West beginning in the early 1970s, being published in English translation mostly in the United States. When he requested permission to emigrate to the United States in 1975, Trifonov attracted the attention of the KGB.

In 1976 a criminal case was fabricated against Trifonov by the KGB, and he was arrested, tried and sentenced to four years in the prison camps. In 1978 he sent a poem/letter to his friends in the West. To support Trifonov, several gay periodicals, including *Gay Sunshine*, published the poem and an article on Trifonov by Dar. Released from prison in 1980, Trifonov found it difficult to find work in literature, so he spent two years loading books for a bookstore. He continued to request permission to emigrate, and in 1986 the KGB again began criminal proceedings against him. This time friends in the United States launched a campaign to protect him, and the KGB left him alone. With the advent of

Gorbachev's *perestroika*, Trifonov was finally granted permission to travel abroad. Since 1988 he has visited the United States and Scandinavia.

Trifonov's literary works, many of which deal with gay themes, have for the most part been published outside Russia. His poems were published by gay journals in the 1970s. His first novel, *Lyova*, was published in Sweden in Swedish translation; the Russian manuscript has been lost. With Olga Zhuk, Trifonov founded the gay literary journal *Gay Slaviane! (Gay/ Hey Slavs!)*, in which he published fragments of his second novel, *Dva baleta Dzh. Balanchina (Two Ballets of G. Balanchine)*, parts of which have also been published in England and in the United States.

As of this writing Trifonov's prose is scheduled to be published by Glagol, the gay publishing house in Moscow run by Alexander Shatalov. A third novel, *Setka (Net)*, will also be published. It deals with Trifonov's prison camp experiences and impressions.

Trifonov has remained in Leningrad, now St Petersburg. He teaches Russian literature, history and English in a private high school. He has also taken up translation, translating two novels of American writer Kevin Esser. Trifonov now writes poetry rarely, but continues to write prose.

Kevin Moss

Trudeau, Pierre Elliot (b. 1919), Canadian politician. As Minister of Justice and then Prime Minister, Trudeau played a key role in two federal legislative advances relevant for sexual diversity.

Having been a prominent lawyer, academic and political writer in the province of Quebec for two decades, Trudeau first ran for office as a Liberal candidate in the 1965 federal election. He won, and in the following year he was appointed Parliamentary Secretary to Prime Minister Lester Pearson. In 1967 he entered the cabinet as Justice Minister, and in that capacity he proposed wide-ranging changes to criminal law that were eventually passed in 1969, including provisions that partially decriminalised abortion and male homosexuality. (Following the British pattern, Canadian law had never criminalised female homosexuality.) Gay sexual contact was made permissable if conducted in private between consenting adults of 21 years of age or more; the inequalities thus enshrined between homosexual and heterosexual activity were gradually eliminated over the course of the next twenty-five years.

In 1968, Trudeau successfully contested the leadership of the Liberal Party, his campaign and victory triggering widespread enthusiasm among younger voters in particular. His intellectual quickness and preparedness to challenge political norms won him many admirers in Canada and abroad, though his centralist policies provoked substantial resentment in his native Quebec and in the Western provinces. His advocacy of official bilingualism likewise earned him friends and foes. His declaration of the War Measures Act in October 1970, in response to the kidnapping of a Quebec cabinet minister and British diplomat, was widely supported at the time, but the limitations on rights that it imposed tarnished his long-standing reputation as a civil libertarian.

Nevertheless, it was his interest in the rights of individual citizens that led him to propose a constitutionally entrenched Charter of Rights and Freedoms. It was to be part of a larger political package that would 'patriate' the country's constitutional statutes from London, and create a formal process for amending such statutes. In the course of major controversy, with the Quebec provincial government refusing to agree to the package, the new constitutional order was approved in 1982.

The new Charter of Rights and Freedoms had provisions for equality rights that did not include sexual orientation explicitly, and an amendment on that subject had been rejected in the Canadian House of Commons. Those who might have thought that Trudeau and his Liberal government were supportive of equality for lesbians and gays were disabused of that notion. There were undoubtedly some Liberal parliamentarians who were favourably inclined, but of the federal parties only the New Democratic Party was on side.

Despite the lack of legislative and governmental support in 1982, by the 1990s Canadian courts were increasingly treating the Charter as if it included sexual orientation implicitly. By the end of the decade, the Supreme Court had enshrined such interpretation, securing protection against discrimination for gays and lesbians as individuals, and increasingly securing same-sex relationships from discrimination.

Trudeau served as Prime Minister from 1968 to 1979, and then again from 1980 to 1984, at which time he resigned from federal politics, returning to Montreal and the practice of law. He continues to intervene politically and to write, most notably in opposition to Quebec separation.

Christina McCall and Stephen Clarkson, *Trudeau and Our Times* (Toronto, 1994); Michael Mandel, *The Charter of Rights and the Legalization of Politics in Canada* (Toronto, 1989); W. A. Bogart, *Courts and Country* (Toronto, 1994).

David Rayside

Tsarouchis, Yannis (1910–89), Greek painter. Tsarouchis trained at the School of Fine Arts in Athens and in the studio of the neo-Byzantine painter Photis Kontoglou (1931). He was strongly influenced by a visit to Paris in the mid-1930s, where he added the influence of Matisse to those of Hellenistic art, Byzantine mosaic and Turner. From 1940 to 1960 many of his paintings make allusion to archetypes of Greek sculpture and vase painting but ally this to life-drawing and acute observation of the Greek environment. Already at this period his greatest work incorporates either uniformed figures – soldiers,

sailors, policemen – painted with great sensuality, such as *Sailor with Coffee-cup* (1954) and *Sailor Dreaming of Love* (1955), or male nudes, notably the striking *Nude* (1940) where the strong male figure is rendered vulnerable by a broken, bandaged thumb. Tsarouchis returned to Paris in the 1960s, remaining there until the end of the military regime in Greece in 1974. During these years he painted a series of large sensual canvases with an allegorical import, of which the best known is *The Martyrdom of St Sebastian* (1970), in which the saint is pierced by the arrows of contemporary Greek soldiers in green fatigues.

A gay sensibility is very evident throughout his work, notably in his instinct for blending conventional opposites. This is particularly true of his representation of gender. His portraits of women favour a look of raw strength, e.g. the series of four seasons (1970). Male figures on the other hand play off the associations of conventional masculine power, particularly uniforms and bodies with pronounced musculature and strong jawlines, against sinuous elements of posture conventionally seen as feminine, particularly in the placing of hands or the throwing of weight onto one hip. In paintings such as *Esprit ailé boutonnant son caleçon* (1966) or the soldiers with huge butterfly wings from his last years, the same effect is created by the juxtaposition of masculine strength and the gossamer beauty of the wings.

Tsarouchis – Peintures et gouaches (Paris, 1997); Philip Core, obituary, *The Observer*, Aug. 1989; Athena Schina, 'The Immortal Images of Yiannis Tsarouchis', *Athena Magazine*, July/Aug. 1989; Ivan Teobaldelli, 'Yannis Tsaruchis', *Babilonia*, no. 7 (1983).

Christopher Robinson

Tusquets, Esther (b. 1936), Spanish writer and publisher. When a recent Spanish lesbian *roman à clef*, Lola Van Guardia's *Con pedigree*, introduced a character described as the 'high priestess of dyke *belles lettres*', few were left in doubt as to the character's real alter-ego. Of course Tusquet's sexual identity is still open to speculation, and no clear statement identifies her with lesbian politics or lesbian desire. In fact she has been notoriously coy about the issue, often reluctant to speak about her personal input into her characters. To be fair, she does not even identify with feminist politics, following an all-too-recurrent trend in Spanish attitudes towards gender and sexuality: there cannot be a politics of sexuality because, proponents claim, sexuality is a highly subjective, personal issue; any attempt to 'fix' it, to give it a name, is also a step towards killing what is more individual, more vital about it. In the same line but maybe occasionally less coy are other defenders of apolitical ambiguity such as filmmaker Pedro ALMODÓVAR and singer Miguel Bosé. Of course, we could wonder whether in their attempts to escape simplistic characterisation, these artists are not actually impersonating the ultimate stereotype: the closet case.

In spite of all her attempts at tacit denial, some circumstances of Tusquets's life point toward a committed attitude towards gender issues. She comes from a wealthy Catalan family and went through a difficult marriage. She entered the publishing business, taking responsibility for Lumen in the 1970s, at the time a relatively small imprint specialising in religious books. Soon, the whole catalogue was renewed and Lumen started to include numerous women writers and more progressive titles. Tusquets scored a personal success at the helm of this publishing firm, something striking since publishing is (and, especially, was at the time) a strongly 'male' business. She started writing late in life, and her first novel is even more unusual than she is given credit for. *El mismo mar de todos los veranos* appeared in 1978 and is a milestone in Spanish lesbian fiction. Again, for a writer who claims to be 'outside' the feminist tradition, it is a very 'feminist' book. Not only does the plot tell

about a woman who finds a new sense of selfhood through an emotional and erotically charged relationship with another woman (even if the ending seems to cancel this out), but the style, narrative structure, voice and moods are indebted to what (with or without justification) was described in the 1970s as *écriture féminine*. Stream of consciousness, cyclical narrative, women-oriented plot and other features made this a favourite among lesbian readers (although at the time there was hardly any choice). The relationship between a mature woman (Elia) and a younger student is told with both detachment and passion, and the reader remains convinced that it is healthier than the stifling marriage the protagonist finds herself in. Most importantly for the time, no attempt is made at making Elia's lesbianism the result of a traumatic childhood or at explaining it away as pathology.

Similarly relaxed portrayals of relationships between women appear in Tusquets's following two novels: *El amor es un juego solitario* (1979) and *Varada tras el último naufragio* (1980). The first of these presents an emotional triangle with two female sides and in which feminity is the focus of eroticism; the second includes a young lesbian among its main characters, entangled in a complex web of feelings and betrayals. In neither of these can we find a 'lesbian identity' and it would be hard to set them up as examples of 'positive images' of lesbians, but nevertheless Tusquets's intelligence illuminates the conflicts in these women's lives and somehow it is difficult to 'blame' lesbianism for their unhappiness.

Sometimes the opposite seems to be true: lesbian relationships constitute a ray of hope in their lives. Tusquets's latest novel is *Con la miel en los labios* (1997), which presents a group of politically commited students against the background of the Spanish political transition to democracy and which again introduces lesbian characters and concerns.

Alberto Mira

Tutu, Desmond (Mpilo) (b. 1931), South African cleric. Born in Klerksdorp in the Free State, Tutu was ordained as an Anglican priest in 1961 and studied at King's College, London, until 1966. He became in turn Dean of St Mary's Cathedral in Johannesburg (1975), Bishop of Lesotho (1976), and General Secretary of the South African Council of Churches (1978). In 1986 he was enthroned as Archbishop of Cape Town and primate of the Church of the Province of Southern Africa, head of the Anglican church in South Africa, Namibia, Mozambique, Swaziland and Lesotho. He was elected president of the All-Africa Conference of Churches in 1987. He was a strong critic of apartheid, and an advocate internationally of sanctions against the regime. He won the Nobel Peace Prize in 1984. When he retired as archbishop in 1995 he was appointed head of the Truth and Reconciliation Commission.

Tutu many times spoke out strongly in South Africa, and on visits to the US and Australia, against persecution of homosexuals, and supported repeal of South Africa's anti-homosexual laws after the 1994 constitution was adopted. On many occasions he has challenged the Anglican and other churches: 'If the church, after victory over apartheid, is looking for a moral crusade, then this is it: the fight against homophobia and heterosexism.'

Desmond Tutu, *Rainbow People of God* (London, 1995); Mark Gevisser, 'Subtle Art of Being Gay the African Way', *Sunday Independent*, 26 Sept. 1999.

Ken Davis

U

Uys, Pieter-Dirk a.k.a. Evita Bezuidenhout (b. 1945), South African writer, satirist and performer. Born of Jewish and Afrikaner parents in Cape Town, since 1970 he has written over two dozen plays. His character Evita was originally created for a column in the Johannesburg *Sunday Express*, as a way of getting criticism of government policies printed despite censorship in the 1970s. Uys first publicly performed Evita, one of the world's most effective and popular cross-dressing interventions in national politics, in 1981. She was the wife of a Nationalist Member of Parliament. Later she became Ambassador to the 'independent homeland of Bapetikosweti', closely modelled on Boputhatswana. Uys published Evita's 'autobiography' in 1992, *A Part Love,*

A Part Hate. Uys has taken Evita to audiences in Canada, Australia, the UK, Germany and the Netherlands. After the election of the first democratic government in 1994, Evita broadcast on national television a series of humorous and humanising in-depth interviews with cabinet ministers of the Government of National Unity, baking *koeksisters* for Mandela, swimming with Slovo, and ballroom dancing with Naidoo. These interviews were subsequently published as *Funigalore* in 1995.

Pieter-Dirk Uys, *A Part Love, A Part Hate*, (Pretoria, 1994); Pieter-Dirk Uys, *Funigalore*, (London, 1995).

Ken Davis

V

Vallières, Pierre (1938–98), Canadian activist. Vallières emerged from a working-class background in Montreal to become a leading member of the Front de Libération du Québec (FLQ), a group with high profile in the 1960s and early 1970s, prepared to use violence to further the cause of independence. He joined the group in 1965, and spent four years in jail starting in 1966, for his role in a demonstration at the United Nations in New York and for accusations associated with an earlier bombing death in Montreal (for which he was first convicted and then acquitted on appeal). Vallières was the FLQ's most prominent writer, having been a contributor to various newspapers and magazines from the early 1960s, and most famously publishing *White Niggers of America* in 1968, widely read in Quebec as well as the rest of Canada. He renounced the FLQ's violence after adherents murdered a Quebec cabinet minister they had kidnapped in October 1970, and publicly supported the Parti Québécois (PQ), a political party that had been formed to lead the sovereigntist charge in provincial electoral politics (and which eventually formed the government). As the PQ moved closer to the centre, he renounced it, too, and remained uninvolved in the campaign for 'yes' votes in the pro-sovereignty referendum of 1995.

He returned to journalism in the years to follow, and retained an activist engagement with the disadvantaged, most energetically throwing his energies into publicising the plight of Bosnians and into shipping relief supplies to that region. Among the causes he devoted most energy to was gay rights, as he said, 'looking for maximum freedom for the individual, for individual sense of pride and self-esteem'.

Matthew Hays, 'Pierre Vallières', *Xtra! Magazine*, 14 Jan. 1998.

David Rayside

Van Beeren, Bet (1902–67), Dutch bar owner. Bet, the 'Queen of the Zeedijk', was the owner of the popular 't Mandje (the Basket) on the Zeedijk (sea dike) in Amsterdam. This street, close to the old harbour, has for long had a reputation for illicit pleasures, foremost among them prostitution and booze. It was the place for sailors to spend their money on arrival in Amsterdam.

In the 1930s, Chinese and Surinamese entered the district and introduced ethnic restaurants and jazz music. Drugs arrived some time later. In this street, several bars were tended by dykes who had made their money in prostitution. Some of these bars catered to a public not only of prostitutes and their johns, but also gays and lesbians. Gay men could take a chance with the sailors and working-class men who did not have enough money to pay for a whore or were too drunk to be accepted as a client.

Lesbians might pick up a prostitute or an adventurous lady.

Among the dykes of the dike Bet Van Beeren was by far the most famous. She was from a poor and large Jordaan family. After a labyrinthine career on and around the streets of central Amsterdam, she started her own bar, The Basket, in 1927. It was a typical small Amsterdam pub, at most 40 square metres overall. Only after World War II did the bar get a reputation in gay and lesbian circles. She herself made much of her support for the Dutch Resistance against the German occupation and the help she offered after the war to the poor children of the Zeedijk neighbourhood.

Van Beeren was instrumental in developing the reputation of her bar. She was the archetype of a gin-drinking, cigar-smoking and motorbike-riding dyke who wore leather jackets and sailor suits. She was a tough woman who defended both her many lovers against other pretenders as well as the gay boys against violent seamen or obtrusive police-officers. The great day at the Basket was Queen's Day, since 1948 celebrated on 30 April. This festive occasion had not yet developed into the big street party it is nowadays, but in some places gay men and women could go in drag and dance as same-sex couples (which was strictly forbidden on other days). The police checked bars regularly for the presence of gay and lesbian traces at that time, and if they found any, they would withdraw their licenses. Although gay drag and dancing were allowed in other venues on Queen's Day, The Basket became famous because of this. Normally, it was strictly forbidden by Van Beeren, who had rigid ideas about proper behaviour. Except for Queen's Day, kissing and touching were taboo for gay lovers. As with many so-called depraved women, Van Beeren was ambivalent about her own morality and developed a penchant for the good works of a largely sexophobic organisation like the Salvation Army, which she allowed to solicit in her bar.

The Basket was not a gay bar, as it attracted a mixed crowd. But it developed a gay and lesbian reputation at that time because of the availability of 'normal' men and women who did not object to a gay or lesbian trick. It was a time when 'normalcy' was an enticement for queens and butches. Van Beeren contributed much to the gay reputation of her bar by her overwhelming presence. She turned the Basket into an 'international museum'. Its walls were completely covered with memorabilia like pictures, cards and letters and its ceiling with cut-off ties and belts that were taken – willingly or unwillingly – from her clients. Many stories about her unpredictable behaviour added to her fame. She was said often to have disappeared for extended periods when she had found another 'femme'-lover.

Van Beeren was Amsterdam's most famous dyke of this century. After her death in 1967 her straight sister Greet continued The Basket in her spirit. With the invasion of drugs and criminality in the 1970s, she was no longer able to keep the bar open and closed it in 1983. Efforts to get the interior on the list of monuments and to establish a gay museum in the building failed. But the bar still exists as it was and was reopened in the week of the Amsterdam Gay Games in 1998, while a replica of the interior was exhibited in the city's Historical Museum. We still hope that the memory of Bet Van Beeren will be commemorated in the future by a new opening of her bar as a historic monument.

Tibbe Bosch (ed.), *Bet van Beeren: koningin van de Zeedijk* (Amsterdam, 1977).

Gert Hekma

Van Dantzig, Rudi (b. 1933) Dutch dancer, choreographer and ballet director. Born in Amsterdam, Van Dantzig studied with Ann Sybranda and Sonia Gaskell in Amsterdam, and later with Martha Graham. From 1952 to 1954, he was a dancer with Gaskell's Ballet Recital, rising to the rank of soloist with its successor, the Nether-lands Ballet, for which he created his first choreography. In 1959, he was a founding member of the Nederlands Dans Theater, but returned to the Netherlands Ballet the following year to become Associate Art-istic Director (to Gaskell) of the Dutch National Ballet, Co-Director with Robert Kaesen in 1969, and from 1971 to 1991, Artistic Director. Van Dantzig's inter-national reputation as the major choreog-rapher produced by the Netherlands was established through choreographies for American Ballet Theatre, Ballet Rambert, Britain's Royal Ballet, the Harkness Ballet, Israel's Bat-Dor Dance Company, the Royal Danish Ballet and the Paris Opera Ballet. Since his earliest choreographic es-says, his works have portrayed dramatic struggles between innocence and the evils of an insensitive, grasping materialistic world. In works such as *Monument for a Dead Boy* (1965), created for his longtime partner, the dancer/choreographer and de-signer Toer van Schayk, and *Songs of Youngsters* (1977), Van Dantzig was among the first choreographers openly to portray the homosexual struggle against an intolerant society. *Monument* created a sensation when performed by the Hark-ness Ballet in the late 1960s and was the first 'modern' ballet role offered to Rudolf NUREYEV, for whom Van Dantzig created three original works: *The Ropes of Time* (commissioned by the Royal Ballet, 1970), *Blown in a Gentle Wind* (1975) and *About a Dark House* (1978). Van Dantzig's versa-tility ranges from the profound *Four Last Songs* (1977), one of his most acclaimed works, to recensions of the full-length classics *Romeo and Juliet* (1967) and *Swan Lake* (1988). A preponderance of his works have been designed by Van Schayk.

In addition to his contributions to world dance, Van Dantzig has made a notable contribution to gay literature with his autobiographical novel *Voor een Verloren Soldaat* (*For a Lost Soldier*, 1986) which was made into Roeland Kerbosch's ac-claimed 1993 film of the same name

featuring Jeroen Krabbe, Maarten Smit and Andrew Kelley.

A. M. Wentink

Van Hattum, Jacob (1900–81), Dutch author. Van Hattum was born in Wom-mels, Frisia, where he had a happy childhood in a large family. His father was gardener for the mayor. The nude swimming of the local lads offered the first inspiration to the sickly boy. In 1913 the family moved to Elspeet in the eastern part of the country. Van Hattum studied to become a teacher, obtaining his first position in 1922, and from 1926 to 1956 he worked in Amsterdam, where he eventu-ally died.

Van Hattum was active in the Dutch Re-sistance during World War II. His first book of poetry, published in 1932, was of socialist inspiration. About fifty books of short stories and poems were published during his lifetime. The topics shifted from politics to education, nature, animal stories, fairy-tales and sex. He wrote some articles and stories for the general press. The content of some of his literary work is surprisingly cruel and homosexual. *Man-nen en katten* (*Men and Cats*, 1947), *De liefste gast* (*The Loveliest Guest*, 1961), *De wolfsklauw* (*The Wolf's Claw*, 1962) and *De ketchupcancer* (1965) contain the more famous gay and cruel work. Van Hattum's interest was in younger men and adoles-cents. The malignity is not in the sado-masochism, but in the vicious games people play with each other. Van Hattum belonged very much to the time of the closet. He was unhappy and insecure about his desires and probably lived the chaste life of a voyeur. In his home in the 1930s, he entertained a painting class for intimate friends. It was really for the nude male models that the men came together, not to learn to sketch. From the 1960s Van Hattum's mental abilities slowly declined while his work as a closeted gay man went out of fashion. He is perhaps most famous because of an S & M poem dedicated to him by Gerard REVE. The collected poems and stories of Van Hattum were published again in 1993–4 but found little acclaim. He has been surpassed by a new generation with Reve as its main hero.

T. Oegema van der Wal, *Van en over Jac. van Hattum* (Brussels, 1969).

                                                                    Gert Hekma

Vanggaard, Thorkil (1910–98), Danish psychiatrist. Vanggaard became a medical doctor in 1938, specialising in psychiatry at the University Hospital in Copenhagen, and graduated in 1951 from the New York Psychoanalytical Institute. From 1960 he was a consultant at the University Hospital. Vanggaard taught dynamic psychiatry at the University of Copenhagen (as associate professor, 1954–70) and other Scandinavian universities. He contributed to psychiatry with several important works on schizophrenic borderline states (1955), objectivity and causality in psychiatry (1959) and the concept of neurosis (1959, 1979). Vanggaard also served as vice-president of the International Psychoanalytical Association.

In 1962 Vanggaard published an article on male homosexuality in the *Medical Weekly* in which he argued that homosexuality was a property found in all men, the so-called 'Homosexual Radical'. What distinguished the 'normal man' from the 'homosexually inverted' was not homosexual behaviour and homosexual preparedness but heterosexual genital potency. Inverted homosexuals feared the female genitalia ('vagina dentata') and sought sexual and emotional compensation through their homosexual potency. One might interpret Vanggaard to mean that male homosexuality is a natural given while heterosexuality must be learned through the mature male's conquering his own fear of female genitalia. Inverted homosexuals were to be pitied as 'invalids' and should be treated by society with 'reasonable toleration'. Vanggaard explicitly criticised the chief of Copenhagen's Vice Squad, police superintendent Jens JERSILD,

who in several books had advocated a theory of seduction. Boys and young men could easily, Vanggaard wrote, be seduced to homosexual activities, but that did not make them homosexually inverted. The article was well-timed and politically motivated (as Vanggaard later accepted with a certain degree of self-satisfaction). It served as scientific legitimation for the abrogation, three years later, of the so-called 'Ugly Clause' which made it a criminal act to obtain sex for payment with a person of the same sex under 21 years of age.

Vanggaard's article included historical aspects and cross-cultural perspectives which in 1969 he expanded in his book, *Phallós: A Symbol and its History in the Male World* (translated into English, German, Dutch and Japanese). Here Vanggaard combined the 'Homosexual Radical' with male power and saw the phallus as the literal (rape) or symbolic/psychological instrument in the building and maintaining of male hierarchies. His historical material was inadequately researched. His theories caused controversy.

Vanggaard's views on the culture that was his own were both straight and straightforward. The conspiracy of silence on homosexuality and the widespread disgust for homosexuals, he wrote, had deep cultural roots which could not be changed. 'Boys and young men in our culture must learn to suppress their homosexuality, but this ought not to come about under severe inner conflict.'

Vanggaard's personality was that of a dominating male. He was married in 1938 to the opera singer Associate Professor Grethe Præstrud (1912–95).

Thorkil Vanggaard, *Phallós: A Symbol and its History in the Male World* (New York, 1972), and 'Homosexuality in Heterosexuals', *Borderlands of Sanity* (Copenhagen, 1979); Ebbe Linnemann, 'Thorkil Vanggaard', *Dansk Biografisk Leksikon*, vol. 15 (Copenhagen, 1984), pp. 278–9.

                                                                Wilhelm von Rosen

Vargas, Chavela (b. 1919?), Mexican singer. Chavela Vargas's fame is not limited, as in the case of other singers, to being a role-model or figure on to which fantasies are projected. Vargas is not a sphinx, nor a mere object of the homosexual gaze; her performances, and her life in general, illustrate the role of certain forms of pop music as vehicles of sexual trangression. Although born in Costa Rica, Vargas moved to Mexico in the 1950s. Her career in singing began in bohemian cabarets in Mexico City and her performances attracted attention for their originality. Vargas used changes of rhythm, guttural sounds and all the potential of her voice to produce impressive versions of Mexican songs. All these elements broke apart the classic, naturalistic form of the songs, and through the cracks between the pieces, a very human pain emerged. Vargas' voice and style constructed her songs as personal declarations of desire and passion, not simply performances. It is a quality shared with very few other singers and situates her among the legends of pop music along with Judy Garland, Billie Holiday, Edith Piaf, Janis Joplin, Maria CALLAS and a handful of other women in whose performances life and art came together in a painful manner. It is significant that Vargas chooses not to change the pronouns or the gender of the figures in her songs: she chooses songs written to be sung by a man to a woman and makes them her own. The eroticism of her version of 'Macorina', for example, earned its name when, in her interpretation of the phrase 'Put your hand here, Macorina', Vargas, long before MADONNA, placed her hand on her groin while she stared at a woman in the audience.

Vargas, a friend of Frida Kahlo and her husband Diego Rivera, became legendary for appearances with enormous motor-cycles or automobiles. Her behaviour on stage and off, her stormy relations with women led to her rejection by right-minded Mexican society (and even by professional associates such as Lola Beltrán,

who criticised her publicly). Her ostracism from major theatres forced her to perform in local cabarets and to travel constantly. An attempt to make a comeback in the 1970s was not a success, although her performances in a venue frequented by gays, El Hábito, in Cocoyán, were fascinating for those who attended them. In this context it is difficult to ignore the hypocrisy with which Vargas's later return to the stage in 1993, was greeted by those who lamented that she had been unjustly forgotten: euphemistic views which bespoke homophobia. Vargas has used the *bolero* and the *ranchera* in a series of four records which she has recorded since 1993. It is said that at this time she met the cinematographer Pedro ALMODÓVAR while singing in a low-life venue in Mexico City; he engaged her for a series of performances and a tour in Spain which scored a great success. In interviews she gave, Vargas spoke of the pains of the last twenty years, which she compared to a living death; reporters reponded with a prudishness that was meant to show friendliness but hid condescension. The sexual transgressions about which she spoke in these conversations formed a subtext that Vargas – at least the Vargas of her wild years – wanted to bring to light. Television programmes showed a woman who made an effort to remain tame but whose wisdom was radiant by contrast with the frozen smiles of other fellow performers. Vargas has been compared the other 'mother of the Mexican song', Lucha Reyes, of whom it was also said she was lesbian: in both cases, a fascinatingly 'machoist' perspective.

When singing, her perspective is not simply that of a man. In her songs Vargas is a 'macho' who loves delicate women, and like the males of Mexican folk songs, can be hurt by their arrogance or rejection. Musical modulation and emphasis place eroticism and desire in the foreground, never allowing us to forget that this is a woman who sings of her own pains. In her work Vargas communicates a stance of radical solitude and transgression. In an essay entitled 'Crossing the Border with Chavela Vargas: A Chicana Femme's Tribute', Yvonne Yarbro-Navajo has presented Vargas as an important model of butch identity in the imagination of the Latin lesbian. The heterosexist *machismo* of the songs is resisted by her positioning as a lesbian, providing a point of reference for other lesbians; Yarbro-Navajo reads her persona in terms of force, an active fight against the conventions of gender and society. In 1995, Almodóvar used, in *La flor de mi secreto*, a sequence of a television appearance by Vargas, in which she sings 'En el último trago', as a key episode in the story of his heroine. He thus explored the melodramatic value of Vargas, but not as a model of sexual transgression. Joaquín Sabina dedicated the song 'Por el boulevard de los sueños rotos' to Vargas, who (once again the object of some condescension) appears a sad and melancholy being.

Y. Yarbro-Navajoh 'Crossing the Border with Chavela Vargas: A Chicana Femme's Tribute', in Daniel Balderston and Donna J. Guy (eds), *Sex and Sexuality in Latin America* (New York, 1997).

Alberto Mira

Vaughan, (John) Keith (1912–77), British artist. Born in Selsey, Sussex, England, the eldest of two boys, he grew up in Hampstead, London. His father left the family in 1918. Vaughan was educated at Christ's Hospital, a public school at Horsham, where he was a boarder. His school-day memories were of sex, guilt and misery but also of inspiration from Frank Brangwyn's sixteen large tempera paintings in the school chapel.

Without formal training, in 1931 Vaughan joined Lintas (Lever International Advertising Services), London, as a trainee artist, where he worked until shortly before he was called up for war service. At Lintas he was remembered as a snappy dresser, preferring to talk about ballet and art. His interest in ballet, and

his photographic studies of performers were a response to his attraction to half-naked male dancers. Vaughan's ambitions as an artist were encouraged by Lintas art director Reg Jenkins, his artist wife Marjorie, and fellow worker, Australian artist Jack (John) Passmore.

Vaughan's recognition of his own homosexuality was a gradual process during the early 1930s. From 1939 to 1977 (with few breaks) he wrote a self-analytical journal which charted, in sixty-one volumes, his work and sexual exploits and fantasies.

At his call-up in 1940 Vaughan registered as a conscientious objector on humanitarian grounds. In 1941 he was assigned to the non-combatant Pioneer Corps in the British Army in which he undertook menial and monotonous work until his discharge in 1946. During this time his painting took on a sombre romanticism – typically, small male figures overwhelmed by ominous landscapes. Through a fellow conscientious objector he met the art patron Peter Watson and publisher John Lehmann. Lehmann commissioned illustrations and book jacket designs from Vaughan and also encouraged him to write for *Horizon* and *Penguin New Writing*. Vaughan was introduced by Watson to the neo-romantic English artist Graham Sutherland. He was especially influenced by Sutherland in the way he painted at this time and by his encouragement for him to pursue painting as a career.

Although he went through periods of doubt about his ability, Vaughan was included in all major exhibitions of contemporary British painting and held one-person exhibitions in Britain, Europe and America almost yearly from the 1940s to 1970s. He is now included in most public collections of British painting. The standing male nude was a continuing motif in his work. In the 1962 catalogue for a retrospective exhibition at Whitechapel Gallery, London, Vaughan acknowledged his debt to Brangwyn, Cézanne, the Diaghilev

Ballet, Picasso, Sutherland, Palmer, Braque, Matisse and de Staël. It was, however, the 1952 exhibition in London by de Staël that spurred Vaughan to re-evaluate his style.

The 1950s was the most successful and satisfying period of his life. He achieved some domestic stability with his partner, painting student Ramsay McClure. In the 1960s he received several significant appointments and awards, including a CBE in 1965. He continued to be included in surveys of British painting but he felt threatened by the younger generation of artists for whom he was now a role model. He did not share the left-wing, anti-nuclear stance of Patrick Proctor; he avoided the gay liberation rhetoric of Mario Dubsky; and he was uncomfortable with David HOCKNEY's insistence on 'coming out' in his own paintings and life. These three young artists all shared Vaughan's obsession with the male nude, but Vaughan was set in the restrictive culture of the British 1930s. In 1966 New York critics described him as the 'veteran' British painter.

Vaughan was a compulsive worker and claimed that if he could not sustain an erection he could not paint. After operations for cancer he could neither have sex nor paint, and took his own life.

Edward Lucie-Smith (introduction), *Keith Vaughan 1912–1977: Drawings of the Young Male* (London, 1991); Keith Vaughan, *Journal and Drawings, 1935–1965* (London, 1966); Malcolm Yorke, *Keith Vaughan: His Life and Work* (London, 1990).

Ian Maidment

Versace, Gianni. (1947–97), Italian fashion designer. During the heady 1980s and on into the more restrained 1990s, few fashion designers had quite as glamorous a profile as Gianni Versace. Beyond his assiduous cultivation of glamour and celebrity status, what made Versace stand out in the fashion world was his innovative fusion of high fashion with elements of popular culture. And in a business which is usually assumed to involve a high proportion of gay men, Versace was unusual not only for telling the world he was gay, but for incorporating images of the apparently harmonious life of his extended family into his own publicity.

Versace was born the poor southern Italian region of Calabria two years after the end of World War II, when the Italian economy had virtually ceased to exist. In many ways Versace's meteoric career in the fashion industry is emblematic of Italy's more general economic miracle in the post-war period. By the time Versace was in his teens, his family was reasonably well off: his father sold electrical appliances, and his mother ran a successful dressmaking shop. It was under his mother's supervision that Versace did his apprenticeship, but in 1972 he moved to Milan, where he worked for several important fashion houses before founding his own. Versace's entry into the industry coincided with the beginning of Italy's fashion boom, and after only a decade, he had entered into the top rank of designers.

The method which ensured Versace's success was a shrewd combination of daring design innovation, clever publicity and a traditional Italian reliance on family members to run the business. His designs were often more daring and sexy than those of his contemporaries, and he made extensive use of celebrities, from rock stars to royalty, to make sure his clothes attracted media and public attention. Versace played a large part in creating the new category of 'supermodel' in the 1980s, and was also at the forefront of another 1980s trend: the use of male bodies, often barely clad, in advertising. But Versace cleverly balanced the risqué, even outrageous publicity he employed to sell his fashion with carefully cultivated images of his own family life. His brother and sister were involved in the business from the early days, and because of the family's wealth and rather contrived dynastic image, not to mention the opulence of Versace's houses, they have often been regarded as Italy's modern Medici family.

Despite his public emphasis on the importance of family, Versace openly acknowledged his homosexuality by coming out in the North American press. The fact that many of his advertisements were effectively paeans to male beauty made more sense in this light, and the point was made even more explicit with the publication of *Men Without Ties*, a coffee-table book looking back over Versace's male fashion, with a clear emphasis on the homoerotic. Versace lived with his companion, Antonio D'Amico, from 1982 – the latter had been a model, and was involved in the business as a designer. Versace also associated himself with several AIDS charities, especially those connected with show-business celebrities such as Elton JOHN.

In July 1997 Versace was shot dead on the steps of his mansion in Miami, apparently by a crazed gay man, Andrew Cunanan, who was on the FBI's most-wanted list in connection with several murders. Cunanan committed suicide shortly after shooting Versace, and the motive for Cunanan's final murder, apart from a desire for notoriety, remains unclear. Versace's death was mourned throughout the world, especially in Italy and in fashion and celebrity circles.

Mark Seymour

Vicinus, Martha (b. 1939), American scholar. Born in Rochester, New York, and educated at Northwestern, Johns Hopkins and Wisconsin universities, Vicinus is Eliza M. Mosher Distinguished University Professor of English and Women's Studies at the University of Michigan in Ann Arbor. She is a leading specialist in nineteenth-century British history and a pioneering author of studies of lesbians. With Martin Bauml DUBERMAN and George CHAUNCEY, Jr., she edited *Hidden from History: Reclaiming the Gay and Lesbian Past* (1989), and she has edited *Lesbian Subjects: A*

Feminist Studies Reader (1996). Among her important articles on the history of sexuality are studies of university women in England, English boarding-school friendships, the historical roots of modern lesbian identity, the adolescent boy as '*femme fatale*' in the *fin de siècle*, and 'lesbian perversity' and Victorian marriage as revealed in the 1864 Codrington Divorce Trial. She has also written on lesbian historiography and is currently completing a book on *Romantic Friendships: Lesbian Identities, 1800–1930*.

Vicinus edited the journal *Victorian Studies* from 1970 to 1982, and is a member of the editorial board of *Feminist Studies*. She has been the recipient of fellowships from the American Council of Learned Societies, the Guggenheim Foundation, the National Endowment of the Humanities and the Australian Humanities Research Centre.

Robert Aldrich

Vidal, Gore (b. 1925), American writer. Born into a distinguished political family, Vidal has written novels, short stories, plays for stage, film and television, personal essays, political commentary and literary criticism; he has also written detective novels under the name of Edgar Box. His parents, Eugene and Nina Gore, divorced early, but Vidal was deeply influenced by his blind grandfather, Oklahoma senator Thomas Pryor Gore. Politics and society became one of his most abiding subjects, in his historical fiction as well as his plays, one of which, *The Best Man*, he wrote for television and adapted for the movies in 1964. Among his notable screenplays is the adaptation of Tennessee WILLIAMS's *Suddenly Last Summer* (1959). Williams was a friend, much as Truman CAPOTE was an enemy, and their emnity was aired on public talk shows, as were his quarrels with William Buckley and Norman Mailer. Vidal served in the armed forces during World War II, and his experience in the Aleutians in 1943 became the basis of his first novel, written at the age of 19.

His first two novels, *Williwaw* (1946) and *In a Yellow Wood* (1947), were both critically praised for the precocity of the author as well as the promise of work to come. In 1948, he published *The City and the Pillar*, an examination of the homosexual underworld of post-war New York City. Vidal set out to challenge stereotypes – the homosexual as effeminate, neurotic, unnatural – in an effort to view male homosexual love with seriousness and sympathy. Though the novel ends melodramatically, it was still an unprecedented effort. It was reissued, revised, in 1965 and again in 1995. The novel caused a scandal when it first came out. The *New York Times* gave the book a savage review, refused to accept any advertising for it, and either did not review or published very negative reviews of his next five novels. The scandal impaired his reputation for years (though it sold copies). Vidal has said that the experience has haunted his entire literary career.

Vidal's story 'Pages from an Abandoned Journal,' part of a volume of short stories, *A Thirsty Evil: Seven Short Stories* (1956), is a satiric image of international gay life before the Gay Liberation movement. In 1949, Vidal wrote *Season of Comfort*, a fictionalised autobiography, and in 1995 he published *Palimpsest*, an anecdotal account of his life. His novel *Myra Breckinridge* (1968), a best-seller, is the author's favourite work, an outrageous satire on sex, gender and American culture. In 1993, his collection *United States: Essays 1952–1992* won the National Book Award. His recent work includes *Hollywood* (1990), *Live from Golgotha: The Gospel According to Gore Vidal* (1992) and *Screening History* (1992). He contributes regularly to *The Nation*, *The Times Literary Supplement* and *The New York Review of Books*.

Vidal, who presently lives in Ravello, Italy, with Howard Austen, his companion of many years, has distanced himself from gay politics, suspicious of all activism in general, though he has been a trenchant critic of American politics and culture from the beginning of his public career, and he twice ran for congressional office (in 1960 and 1982). Described by critics as witty, cheerless, obstreperous and charming, he has said of himself: 'I am exactly as I appear. There is no warm loveable person inside. Beneath my cold exterior, once you break the ice, you find cold water.'

Robert Kiernan, *Gore Vidal* (New York, 1982); Jay Parini (ed.), *Gore Vidal: Writer Against the Grain* (New York, 1992).

Seymour Kleinberg

Viktiuk, Roman Grigorievich (b. 1936), Ukrainian theatre director, adapter, dramaturg. Born in Lvov, in the Ukraine, Viktiuk spoke German, Ukrainian and Polish before Russian. As a child he worked in the theatre in a Pioneer camp and in children's productions. At 18 he went to Moscow to enroll in GITIS (State Institute of Theatrical Arts), where he studied with Galina Rozhdestvenskaia. In 1958 he returned to Lvov, where he worked in the Youth Theatre and the Pioneer Palace. The tragic death of a young lover led Viktiuk to leave Lvov forever in 1967.

As a gay man with dissident leanings, Viktiuk often came into conflict with the conservative world of Soviet theatre. While director of a theatre in Kaliningrad (Tver) in 1968, he was expected to stage a work in honour of the centenary of Lenin's birth. Called to a meeting of the local party committee, he claimed to have found a letter from Klara Zetkin to Nadezhda Krupskaia which mentioned that Lenin 'wanted to see our youth play Schiller's *Kabale und Liebe*'. The production was approved, and the posters read 'For the Centenary of Lenin's Birth: Intrigue and Love'. A review stated that 'uncontrollable associations come up during the play', and Viktiuk was fired from the theatre with a black mark in his work record. When he was summoned to the Ministry of Culture in Moscow, he did not ask for a position. Instead he applied on his own to theatres in the Baltic Republics, and was hired in Vilnius (provincial theatres were often more liberal). He continued to subvert authority. When he presented a play by Goldoni, he interpolated material he claimed to have found in the author's diaries – material that even the play's translator had not heard of. In fact the material he inserted was from the dissident writers Sinyavsky and Solzhenitsyn!

Viktiuk returned to Moscow in 1977, where he has directed plays in various theatres and houses of culture. He was always a popular independent director in a system that rewarded stability and where most directors were attached to one theatre for life. He never became a party member or received honours, an apartment or travel abroad from the state.

In terms of gay themes, Viktiuk's work can be divided into three periods: Soviet, *glasnost* and post-Soviet. Viktiuk had a thriving career in the theatre even under Brezhnev. Because he was relatively marginal, either as a director in provincial theatres or as an invited guest rather than a member of a major theatre troupe, he probably came under less scrutiny by the censors. His camp sensibility and subversive subtexts could be read by some of those in the know.

But it was when Gorbachev relaxed the controls on what could be presented to the Soviet public that Viktiuk became more open in his stagings, if not in his interviews (homosexuality was not decriminalised until 1993). In the days of *glasnost* Viktiuk finally came into his own as a gay director. What had been a subtext in some of Viktiuk's productions could finally come out onstage. The hit of the 1988–89 theatre season was his production at the Satirikon theatre of GENET's *The Maids* with men cast in the roles of the women. The production combined elements of camp with extravagant costumes, exaggerated makeup and dance numbers to the music of Dalida (inclusion of pop music is

typical of Viktiuk's camp sensibility). Two other plays the same season – Tsvetaeva's *Phaedra* and an adaptation of Sologub's *Petty Demon* – were not overtly homosexual, yet Viktiuk's productions brought out the underlying homoerotic themes in them. Sexy bare-chested men cavorted on stage, the objects of the characters' and the audience's gaze. *Phaedra* was also typical Viktiuk in that it was a star vehicle for an actress (diva), Alla Demidova. Choreography, music and costumes (or the lack thereof for men) became as important as the text.

Liberalization under Gorbachev also allowed Viktiuk to travel. A turning point towards even more overtly gay theatre came when Viktiuk was invited to San Diego, California, in 1989 to direct Turgenev's *Month in the Country*. Instead he staged the first Soviet play to deal with a gay relationship, Nikolai Koliada's *Rogatka* (*Slingshot*). He produced the same play in Russia in 1993, after the fall of the Soviet Union. Again he incorporated dancelike movements of bare-chested men, this time to the music of Queen. Other Viktiuk productions with overtly gay themes include David Henry Hwang's *M. Butterfly*, in which the role of Song Liling was played by the counter-tenor Edik Kurmangaliev, who actually sang onstage, and an adaptation of Oscar Wilde's *Salome*, with interpolated scenes from Wilde's trials (this time to the music of Marilyn Manson and James Brown).

The theatre of Viktiuk is at the same time aesthetically oversaturated and spiritually charged. He plays at educating the prudish Soviet audience (a scene in his play on the Marquis de Sade was set in a schoolroom, with desks, blackboard and visual aids), yet at the same time he stops short of using full nudity in his productions. He wants to help people liberate themselves, and he does it by emphasising the mystery and cult aspects of theatrical ritual. His productions have earned him critical praise as well as *succès de scandale* and a large gay following.

Yuri Matthew Ryuntyu, *Roman Viktiuk: retsept dlia geniia* (Moscow, 1996).

Kevin Moss

Village People, The, American pop group. The Village People was an extraordinary confection of pop which combined all the theatricality and dress excesses of glam rock with the easy rhythms of disco. Of all the pop groups of the 1970s, none was so explicitly targeted at the flourishing gay subculture of the time as this group.

What was unique about their stage presence was their self-consciously macho image. Dressed in the codified gay fantasies of the era – construction worker, sailor, policeman, leatherman, 'Red Indian', etc. – the Village People also performed songs such as 'Fire Island', 'San Francisco' and 'Macho Man' which struck an immediate resonance with its gay target audience. Their biggest hit, 'YMCA' (1979), gave the group worldwide fame, and while an unsuspecting public sang along to the catchy tune, gay audiences delighted in the ironies of the lyrics and the stylised masculinity of the choreography.

Formed in 1977 under the direction of disco producer Jacques Morali, the original line-up of this pop group consisted of Victor Willis, Felipe Rose, Alexander Briley, Randy Jones, David Hodo and Glenn Hughes. In 1979 Ray Simpson replaced Willis as lead vocalist, and since then there have been a number of other changes in the line-up.

By the 1980s the group began to seem dated and clichéd. An attempt at changing their image – by adopting a 'Renaissance' look – proved unsuccessful. *Can't Stop the Music*, the 1980 feature film built around the pop group, was an excruciatingly inane – and dishonest – vehicle which served neither to resurrect the group's waning general popularity nor endear it to its core gay following.

The Village People's main historical significance lies in the group's portrayal of gay fantasies and styles of the mid- to late-1970s, and the translation of these subcultural preoccupations into music with a mass appeal. Jacques Morali, the group's main creative force, died of AIDS-related illnesses in 1991.

Michael Heatley (ed.), *The Encyclopedia of Rock* (Melbourne, 1996).

C. Faro

Villena, Luis Antonio de (b. 1951), Spanish writer. Novelist, poet, literary critic, essayist and journalist, Villena is one of the key personalities in Spanish contemporary gay culture. Outspoken and eminently 'visible', his newspaper columns and media appearances have for years contributed to raise consciousness of a gay presence, whereas his fiction and literary essays are an important step towards recovering the gay tradition in Spain. In this way, he was instrumental in getting the work of Colombian gay poet Porfirio Barba-Jacob published. Contrary to common practice in his country, Villena's introduction deals with his subject's homosexuality as an aspect relevant for a proper reading of his work. Similarly, he translated and edited Michelangelo's poems and included an introduction that made explicit the attempts at censorship these have suffered. As a scholar and literary critic, he has translated Greek pederastic poetry and helped stir public debate on the homosexuality of canonical poets such as Vicente ALEIXANDRE and Luis CERNUDA. He has written on little-known literary personalities such as Álvaro de Retana and Antonio de Hoyos. In all of these instances, a whole hidden history is coming to light.

Villena was born into a bourgeois family and received a good education in private schools. He has written an account of his adolescence in the autobiographical novel *Ante el espejo*; Villena appears as a young man notoriously lacking in inhibitions, taking advantage of the opportunities provided by the all-male environment of religious schools. His crushes on other students and his imaginative life, his explorations in the adult world, are carefully described. His early poetry made an impression on the critics, especially the volumes *Hymnica* (1978) and *Huir del invierno* (1981). Luis Cernuda is one of his poetic fathers, as one of the very few Spanish canonical poets who dealt with the eroticism of the young male body. Villena chooses to insert himself into a Hellenistic poetical tradition, centred around the Mediterranean world, and authors such as Cavafy are important influences. The Mediterranean works symbolically in his work as a sun-drenched landscape where eroticism and sensuality can be explored, whereas the northern countries are imagined in terms of 'winter', cold and darkness.

He is also the author of several works of fiction, often with a strong autobiographical element. *Amor pasión* (1983) is a brief novel (which he now considers slightly out of date) that compares sensible love for women to passionate love for young boys, taking inspiration from Greek pederastic writings. *Divino* (1994) revisits Madrid in the 1920s and the 1930s, and includes a rare peek into the intellectual landscape of the time, peopled with gay dandies. *Chicos* (1989) is far more explicit and consists of a series of character sketches of young boys, conveyed through a homoerotic perspective.

His attitude towards explicit identification with homosexuality has changed significantly: in the late 1970s he preferred not to speak about it and used the term 'ambiguity', resorting to the idea that sexuality is always fluid and necessarily outside the field of politics. However, in later years, he has lent unambiguous support to the homophile cause: he is a frequent contributor to gay publications and is often seen in gay political gatherings.

Juan Manuel Godoy, *Cuerpo, deseo e idea en la poesía de Luis Antonio de Villena* (Madrid, 1997); Christopher Perriam, *Desire and Dissent: An Introduction to Luis Antonio de Villena*, (Oxford, 1995); Luis Antonio de Villena, *Ante el espejo: Memorias de una adolescencia*, (Barcelona, 1982).

Alberto Mira

Visconti, Luchino (1906–76), Italian film-, theatre- and opera-director. The artistic career of Luchino Visconti spanned the great changes in European society between the 1930s and 1970s. The privileged milieu of his youth, his left-wing politics and his homosexuality combined to give him a particularly incisive view of those changes, while his independent wealth meant that he could afford to take artistic risks which others could not. The result was a legacy of films and theatrical productions which place Visconti securely among Europe's most prominent directors.

The fourth of seven children, Visconti was born into a rich and aristocratic Milanese family whose lifestyle epitomised the prosperity and privilege of the well-to-do during the Belle Epoque. The family lived in a grand palace in the centre of Milan, where Visconti was educated privately. He was not a particularly good student, but under the influence of his father, he became passionate about literature, and by an early age was familiar with a broad range of works from Shakespeare, Balzac and Stendhal to Dostoevsky, Gide and Proust. This passion for literature was to become one of the major influences on Visconti's work. But his education was not limited to books: he learnt to play the 'cello, and also to ride horses. When Visconti was 20 he began his military service at an elite cavalry school, where he later became an officer. He loved the military life, and spent some years in his early twenties winning prizes in riding competitions. In short, Visconti enjoyed the protected upbringing and privileged education of a young aristocrat, and the interests which he developed during that period are reflected throughout his career.

It was not a career which got off to a precocious start. Although Visconti bought himself a movie camera when he was in his early twenties, it was not until he was approaching 30 that he became involved in the making of films professionally. In the meantime, he travelled extensively, making use of the family's access to elite cultural circles, especially in Paris. Also in the early 1930s, he became romantically attached to Irma Windisch-Grätz, an Austrian princess. Though the romance was mainly conducted through letters, it is possible that the couple would have married, but for the disapproval of Irma's parents, and in 1935 the engagement was called off.

The following year, 1936, Visconti turned away from a dilettante phase and began to work in the film world in earnest. The turning point was a meeting with the Paris filmmaker Jean Renoir, to whom Visconti was introduced by their mutual friend Coco Chanel. Renoir had links to the French Communist Party and Léon Blum's Popular Front, and was at first suspicious of the dashing nobleman from fascist Italy. But he took him on as third assistant, and soon Visconti's hitherto ambiguous politics became firmly set to the left. The year 1936 also marked a turning point in Visconti's personal life: in Paris he met a handsome German of his own age, and they began an affair which lasted intermittently for three years, and a friendship which lasted until Visconti's death. The German was known simply as Horst, and went on to become a well-known fashion photographer in New York.

After assisting Renoir with *Une partie de campagne*, Visconti returned to Italy, where he designed some scenes and costumes for the theatre. But he was restless (and perhaps stultified by the strictures of fascist culture) and travelled extensively for the next two years, first to Greece, and then to the USA to see Hollywood. During the war, Visconti collaborated with a group centred around the journal *Cinema*, directed by Mussolini's son Vittorio. Despite the group's closeness to the upper echelons of the fascist hierarchy, its members apparently enjoyed some degree of freedom, and were even able to focus their attention on the problems of the proletariat. It was as part of this group that Visconti directed his first film, *Ossessione*.

Released in 1942, *Ossessione* was based on James Cain's novel *The Postman Always Rings Twice*, and it represents a landmark in Italian film history as well as in Visconti's career. A clear break from the triumphalist rhetoric of many fascist films, *Ossessione* examines the relationships between two men and a woman, and its gritty, natural style prefigures post-war neo-realism. One character is particularly significant: known only as the Spaniard (a reference to his having fought for the Republicans in the Spanish civil war), he is a sort of vagabond, representing freedom, democracy and independence of mind. His homosexuality is heavily hinted at, and his friendship with the other leading character, Gino, is laced with homoerotic innuendo. Needless to say, the film caused a scandal when it was released, and even though the fascist regime allowed it to circulate (since it did not specifically attack the government), local censorship meant that few people saw it.

From 1943, Visconti was heavily involved in the anti-fascist Resistance movement, whose energies, after the fascist government fell in September, were focused against the German occupation. Visconti's house in Rome became a nerve centre for anti-fascists and because of this he found himself in confinement briefly before the Allies liberated Rome. After the war Visconti was mainly involved in theatre, and between 1945 and 1947 he directed eleven plays. Particularly noteworthy was his production of Marcel Achard's *Adamo*, which treated the question of homosexuality explicitly. The play managed a season of twelve nights in Rome, but in Milan the production was closed by police and the same thing occurred in Venice.

Once the Catholic-based Christian Democratic party was established in power in 1947, anti-fascism started to become a less urgent issue, and public attention was focused towards the Soviet threat. As a result of this shift, cinema became a battleground between the forces of change and those favouring moderation. By 1948 Visconti had declared himself in favour of the Italian Communist Party, and started work on a film that was intended to assist the Communists in the election that year. The resulting film, *La terra trema* (1948), dealt with one of Italy's most serious problems, the question of southern poverty. The film, using Sicilian dialect, was not a success, and the two planned sequels were never made.

Despite the critical and commercial failure of *La terra trema*, it marked the beginning of an intensely productive period in Visconti's life. He continued to direct in the theatre, and introduced Italians to playwrights like Tennessee WILLIAMS and Arthur Miller. He also began to direct operas, and throughout the 1950s he had many successes at La Scala, where he frequently worked with Maria CALLAS. His next film was *Bellissima* (1952), neo-realist in style, and examining the effects of a frustrated mother living out her ambitions through her daughter. Well received, *Bellissima* was followed by *Senso* (which won the Silver Lion at the Venice film festival in 1954) and *Le notti bianche* (1957), an adaptation of a Dostoevsky novel. By the late 1950s Visconti's preferred themes were clear: close examination, often inspired by Freud, of interpersonal and often family tensions, played out against a backdrop of political and class conflict. These themes predominate in *Rocco e i suoi fratelli* (1960), which follows the fortunes of a southern Italian family living in Milan. Visconti focuses on the destructive transplantation of southern family mores into an industrial context, but the film is also noteworthy for its inclusion of a homosexual character, Morini. He is the boxer who trains one of Rocco's brothers, Simone. Although censorship laws prevented anything explicit, it is implied that Morini and Simone are more than just coach and athlete.

After *Rocco*, Visconti made four more films in the 1960s. *Il Gattopardo* (1963), based on Tomaso de Lampedusa's novel, is a sumptuous and historically detailed film about the Italian Risorgimento seen through the eyes of a noble Sicilian family. In 1965 Visconti won the Golden Lion he so coveted at Venice for *Vaghe stelle dell'Orsa*. Two years later, he released *La strega bruciata viva* (a classic vision of the family as both a lost refuge and a suffocating prison), and *Lo straniero*, based on the novel by Camus. *La caduta degli dei* (*The Damned*, 1969), was the last film Visconti made in the 1960s, but it began his famous German trilogy. Helmut Berger, who was also Visconti's lover, starred as the somewhat gender-confused scion of a powerful German steel-making family during the 1930s. The film examines the family's choice to support the Nazis, and in Visconti's own words, it depicts Nazism as a form of capitalism at the extremes of degradation.

The second film of the German trilogy was a project which had been dear to Visconti for many years: *Death in Venice* (1971). Based on Thomas Mann's famous novella, it is a poignant portrayal of the aging Professor Aschenbach's obsessive attraction to the beautiful adolescent Tadzio. The final film of the trilogy was *Ludwig* (1973), which marked a return to Visconti's interest in grand historical reconstructions, but continued the interest in sexuality displayed in the previous two films, since King Ludwig of Bavaria was homosexual. Visconti made two more films after Ludwig. *Gruppo di famiglia in un interno* (1974) and *L'Innocente* (1976, based on the novel by D'Annunzio). Neither treated specifically gay themes, but both represented Visconti's continuing fascination with family ties and intimate relationships.

Visconti was in some senses a child of the nineteenth century, and even though he picked up the grand themes of the twentieth century with ease, his view of homosexuality was not always a liberating one. But by being prepared to bring the idea up as early as 1942, and to make it a theme throughout his work in a deeply Catholic country where silence has so clearly impeded gay liberation, Visconti helped to break the silence.

Alessandro Bencivenni, *Luchino Visconti* (Milan, 1994); Renzo Renzi, *Visconti segreto* (Rome, 1994); Bruno Villien, *Visconti* (Milan, 1987).

Mark Seymour

Vriend, Delwin (b. 1967), Canadian public figure. Vriend is best known for launching a court case that resulted in a resounding victory for gay rights in Alberta and in Canada. In 1991 he was fired from his position as an instructor at the King's University College, a small Christian institution, because of his sexual orientation. Seeking a forum for grievance, Vriend took his complaint to the Alberta Human Rights Commission only to be told that sexual orientation did not fall under the purview of that province's human rights act. Vriend then took his case to court and won the right to be heard. The government of Alberta appealed and the first verdict was overturned. Vriend then appealed the case to the Canadian Supreme Court.

In April 1998 the Supreme Court ruled that the omission of sexual orientation from provincial human rights acts was in direct contravention to the Canadian Charter of Rights and Freedoms. The Court, rather than requiring Alberta to go through a lengthy process of amending its human rights act, 'read in' sexual orientation to the relevant legislation. This is a process whereby a new category, such as sexual orientation, is effectively incorporated into pertinent sections of legislation by court order. By this time, most Canadian provinces had included sexual orientation in their human rights codes by legislating change, beginning with Quebec in 1977. The Supreme Court ruling effectively required the few remaining provincial and territorial jurisdictions to follow suit.

Vriend continues to live in Edmonton and now teaches at the University of Alberta.

Didi Herman, *Rights of Passage: The Struggle for Lesbian and Gay Legal Equality* (Toronto, 1994); David Rayside, *On the Fringe: Gays and Lesbians in Politics* (Ithaca, NY, 1998).

Juliette Nicolet

W

Waddell, Tom (1937–87), American athlete. Born Tom Fluabacher in New Jersey, he took on the surname of his adoptive parents after his natural parents' divorce. Trained as a medical doctor, specialising in infectious diseases, he was drafted into the army during the Vietnam War, which he publicly criticised. After being demobbed, he moved to San Francisco.

He had a strong interest in, and talent for, gymnastics and athletics, competing in the decathlon in the 1968 Olympics, where he again became involved in controversy: he supported the two US athletes who gave the Black Power salutes during their medal award ceremony.

His name is now most associated with the Gay Games, which he and others helped organise, formed out of San Francisco Arts and Athletics (SFAA) (1980). Their use of the original title, Gay Olympics, was contested by the US Olympic Committee, which won a court case on the issue. There is a nice irony in that, at a time of massive controversy about the corruption and ticketing scandals engulfing the Olympic Games, the Gay Games' ideals of community inclusiveness and individual self-affirmation reflect most fully what both sets of games should be about.

Waddell died of AIDS-related complications.

Tom Waddell and Dick Schaap, *Gay Olympian:*
The Life and Death of Dr Tom Waddell (New York, 1996).

Garry Wotherspoon

Walsh, María Elena (b. 1930), Argentinian writer. Walsh has been a vibrant presence in Argentinian culture since the publication of her first book of poetry in 1947. Her language is colloquial, but the poetic form of her works is formal. Both as a writer, and as a singer for children and adults, she is renowned. But it is for her opposition to any form of discrimination or oppression, even during the harshest period of the Argentinian dictatorship (1976–83), that she is most respected. Her poems and songs became emblematic of the resistance exerted against totalitarian powers, and censorship of her work did not prevent it from being widely disseminated. Such songs as 'Canción de Caminantes', (Travellers' Song), 'Como la cigarra' (Like the Cicada), or her translation of 'We Shall Overcome' were popular during the dictatorship, and functioned as symbols of endurance and recognition. The generation that grew up listening to her children's songs was the generation disappearing under the dictatorship. Their acceptance of Walsh as one of their own socially legitimised her authorial voice.

Walsh has always been silent about her personal life. Although she has neither identified herself as a lesbian, nor produced 'explicit' lesbian literature, many of her writings, particularly her poems for adults, allow a lesbian reader to recognise herself within the texts. It is due to a combination of her silence about her personal life and her consistently supportive stance on human rights in general, and women's rights in particular, that Walsh has been perceived by the lesbian and gay population as 'one of our own'.

Her works have been translated into several languages, including French and Hebrew, but unfortunately, not English. Her poetry includes *Otoño Imperdonable* (1947), and most recently, *Cancionero contra el mal de ojo* (1976). Walsh has also published a novel, *Novios de antaño*.

Ilse A. Luraschi and Kay Sibbald, *María Elena Walsh o el desafío de la limitación* (Buenos Aires, 1993).

Carlos Schröder

Walter, Aubrey (b. 1944), British activist and publisher. Walter was born in London and grew up in Salisbury. His parents were members of the Communist Party, and Walter's first political activity was with the Campaign for Nuclear Disarmament. Through the Young Communist League he met his future partner, David Fernbach, with whom he has lived since 1964. In the late 1960s the pair were closely involved with the Vietnam Solidarity Campaign and the radical student movement. In the summer of 1970 Walter toured the US to make links with radical groups and the newly formed Gay Liberation Front. He took part with the New York GLF in the Revolutionary People's Constitutional Convention held in Philadelphia in September 1970, where he met Bob Mellors, also a student from England. On their return Walter and Mellors called a meeting to found a London GLF; Walter was a leading activist in the three years of its existence, and instrumental in starting the gay liberation newsheet *Come Together*.

After working for some years as a primary teacher, in 1979 Walter, together with David Fernbach and Richard Dipple,

founded the Gay Men's Press book publishing project; as one of GMP's first titles, he edited and introduced the London GLF anthology *Come Together*. Walter's publication in 1983 of the children's book *Jenny Lives with Eric and Martin* brought a storm of controversy, and was used by the Conservative Party in its 1987 election campaign. In 1981 Walter pioneered a gay art and photography series, which continues under the imprint *Editions Aubrey Walter*.

Garry Wotherspoon

Ware, John (b. 1939), Australian activist. Ware was co-founder, with Christabel Poll, of the Campaign Against Moral Persecution and first editor of its journal, *Camp Ink*. In mid-1970, Ware and a group of friends in Sydney decided to establish a small group to bring homosexual rights into the public sphere. The group was to monitor and respond to media coverage of homosexual issues and to provide speakers for community groups.

Ware and Poll were interviewed by the national daily, *The Australian*, in September 1970, becoming the first people to openly discuss their homosexuality in the mainstream press in a positive manner. The massive public response to the article shifted the founders' thinking and within a year the organisation had gone national, with 1,500 members and branches in most capital cities and at most universities. Ware himself travelled extensively, spreading the word and helping to found branches in other cities.

Ware was particularly concerned with psychiatric abuse of homosexuals (Sydney being at that time an important centre for aversion therapy and brain surgery directed at curing homosexuality) and remained active around this issue. He was also co-editor of *Camp Ink*, which reported events and debated the way forward for the fledgling movement, bringing these issues to the attention of the membership and to the wider layers of opinion-makers to whom the journal was distributed.

Ware's vision for the group owed much to the counter-cultural thinking of the time. For the first two years, CAMP had no formal leadership structure. Members of the various subgroups within CAMP carried on their own activities, pooling any funds, and distributing them by vote at monthly general meetings. By early 1972, however, pressures for a more formal structure had built up, and a constitution and elected co-presidents were instituted. Ware remained editor of *Camp Ink* until early 1974, when he finally withdrew.

Graham Willett

Warhol, Andy (1928–87), American artist. Born in Pittsburgh to a worker's family of Slovakian extraction, Andrew Warhola finished art school in his hometown in 1949 and moved to New York. From then on he used the name Andy Warhol.

Warhol began his professional career as a commercial artist designing advertisements for glossy magazines and glamorous shops. In his commercial artwork the 'blotted-line' technique became his trademark. In 1962 his artistic reputation reached international fame with his exhibitions *Campbell's Soup Cans* and *Andy Warhol*, showing paintings, rubber stamps, prints and silkscreens on canvas. The death, disaster and diva series made his artwork a pioneering icon of Pop Art. From then on, the character of Warhol developed into the Pope of Pop Culture in a wider sense.

In 1963 he acquired a 16mm movie camera, a Polaroid camera, a tape recorder and a huge loft that became legendary as the Factory (1963–74). These gains were major tools in Warhol's work. He shot his first film, *Sleep*, in 1963 in the Factory. His early unedited films, combining slow motion and close-up technique with low-tech realism and underground gutter glamour, depict an ever-expanding microcosmos of faces and figures without families. All the time Warhol's non-professional 'actors' lounged in settings stripped of fathers, mothers, sons and daughters, evoking a happening world without parents and children, reduced to the young and the youthful of all ages, Warhol's 'Superstars' ('Man is a Superstar'). The queerest among the Warhol films stem from the period 1963–67: *Blow-Job*, *Haircut*, *Couch* and other works.

Lonesome Cowboys was the last film completed before Warhol was shot in the Factory on 3 June 1968 by Valerie Solanas, author of the clever but fundamentalist feminist *SCUM-Manifesto* (Society for Cutting Up Men). After Warhol had turned down a Solanas filmscript and a role for the author in one of his own films, she decided to shoot him, notwithstanding her ideological considerations to spare an effeminate gay man her warfare against men. Warhol's later films from the period 1967–77, including *Fuck*, *Trash*, *Heat* and *Flesh*, were later edited by assistants.

During the late 1960s he organised parties and discotheques, produced albums, concerts and multimedia performances and started the magazine *Interview*. From 1972 through 1987 Warhol mainly focused on executing serial portraits of reigning queens, Communist leaders, species at risk, artists, Renaissance paintings, skulls, athletes, torsos, guns, dicks, cars, cats, dogs, myths, camouflages, sports, shadows, self-portraits and ads. In the 1980s he produced posters and explored fax- and copying-machineries and cable television. Silkscreens of Beethoven and Rado watches were the last canvases Warhol completed before his death.

Warhol's posthumous reputation, based on his voluminous output and his sense for commercial publicity and art marketing, easily outshines his impact in other domains of life. Apart from his numerous exhibitions, Warhol constantly explored public forms in exhibitionistic and voyeuristic communication, usually labelled Pop Art Underground And Hedonism.

Warhol's Factory represents one of the formative crossroads in the globalisation of public gay culture since the 1960s. In the Factory he set a dynamic model for gender desertion and sexual dissidence. Arrangements and activities there provoked gender renegation, cultivation of sexual diversity and transgression of regular body schemes. Within the reduced limits of the Factory in its heyday, conventional straight gender roles and nuclear family values were resisted if not rejected, giving way to the questioning and re-development of sex and gender scripts. The Factory confronted a generation of gays of all ages with the basic modern challenge of how to be gay in public beyond the limits of family values and prevailing gender schemes.

Warhol's Factory inspired and intensified the sensual revolution of the 1960s in many domains. It ruthlessly promoted the cult-image of parties, groupies, America's most beautiful new men and women, sex, drugs, music, arts, sleepless nights and days of fame and glamour. These turned the Factory's queer underground into a promised land for many.

However, for many inexperienced pioneers the Factory changed from a cockpit facing a glittering future into a pitfall without prospects. Too many characters associated with Warhol and the Factory live today in misery, poverty or isolation – or have disappeared because of AIDS, violence, drug-abuse, suicide, medical self-neglect or overestimation of their own abilities. Warhol's sudden death after a neglected health-crisis fits very well in this view. At the same time, the splendour-and-misery-fate resulting from the 1960s underground attitude to life, as actualised and pushed to art, sex and gender extremes in Warhol's Factory, fits into the wider image of dandyism. In a long-term retrospective from Beau Brummel through Oscar Wilde among others, Warhol counts as one of the twentieth century's most complex and complete dandies.

Public relations between Warhol's circle and the political gay movement were non-existent. Instead Warhol, on his own, presided over an underground circle which formed a queer movement. The combined meaning of these qualities has shaped Warhol's public importance in gay life and beyond.

Stephen Koch, *Stargazer, Andy Warhol's World and his Films* (New York, 1973); Victor Bockris, *Warhol* (London, 1989); Jennifer Doyle, Jonathan Flatley, Esteban Munoz Jos (eds), *Pop Out: Queer Warhol* (Durham, 1996).

Mattias Duyves

Waring, Marilyn (b. 1952), New Zealand scholar. Waring was born in northern New Zealand and holds a Ph.D. in political economy. In 1975, she became the youngest member of and the only woman in the New Zealand Parliament. In her maiden speech to the house, Waring indicated that she would use her position as a Member of Parliament to represent the women and the youth of New Zealand. In 1977 she was appointed Chair of the Public Expenditures Committee (PEC) which reviewed parliamentary budgets and expenditures. Waring was re-elected in 1978 and 1981, but left parliamentary politics in 1984 after campaigning against her own government on behalf of a nuclear-free New Zealand. The National Party government had been re-elected in 1981 with a majority of only two seats, and Waring's stand against the presence of nuclear-powered and armed ships in New Zealand territory rendered effective government impossible. A snap election was called in 1984, in which the Labour Party won predominantly on the issue of nuclear policy. Waring is now Senior Lecturer in Social Policy and Social Work at Massey University, Auckland.

Waring's research into national accounting systems, undertaken as part of her duties as Chairperson of the PEC and then continued after her departure from parliamentary politics, culminated in the publication of her ground-breaking work *If Women Counted: A New Feminist Economics* (1988), also published as *Counting for Nothing*. Waring's aim was to reveal the ways in which the United Nations

System of National Accounts by its very nature devalues the unpaid labour of women and children and ignores the environment. Waring demonstrates that environmental concerns and the work of women and children are not factored into calculations of Gross National Product unless they create surplus value and thus profit. Women's roles as subsistence producers and reproducers are, within modern economics, worthless. While feminists had long been arguing that women's work was regarded as less valuable than that of men, Waring was the first to show that this attitude is woven into the very fabric of economic theory and policy, and is incorporated structurally into the international rating of any country's economic worth.

In her introduction to Waring's *If Women Counted*, feminist author Gloria Steinem remarked that Waring, 'the rare expert who is also witty, a populist, and an excellent explainer ... not only puts human beings and human values into economics, but also vice versa'. Waring continued her focus on the status of women in *Human Rights* and *Three Masquerades: Essays on Equality, Work and Human Rights* (1996). In a damning indictment of modern equality and human rights discourses, *Three Masquerades* chronicles women's unequal status within 'equality', the continued devaluing of women's labour as something other than 'work', and the gendered bias of 'hu(man) rights'. The rights of lesbians and gay men have also featured in her political activism. Waring has been 'out' as a lesbian since the 1970s and speaks publicly on gay and lesbian issues. She currently campaigns in support of same-sex marriages being made legal in New Zealand and worldwide.

National Film Board of Canada, *Who's Counting? Marilyn Waring on Sex, Lies & Global Economics* (Montreal, 1995).

Karen Duder

Warner, Tom (b. 1952), Canadian activist. Born in Saskatchewan, Warner was educated primarily in Toronto, where he has been a prominent gay activist. Since the early 1980s, he has worked at the Institute of Chartered Accountants of Ontario, where he is now Registrar. He is also a Fellow of the Institute of Chartered Secretaries and Administrators in Canada, and in 1998 was made President.

His activism for sexual diversity causes dates from 1971, when he was a founding member of the Gay Students' Alliance at the University of Saskatchewan. On first moving to Toronto in 1973, he was a founding member and then president of the Gay Alliance Toward Equality (GATE). In subsequent years, he was active in such groups as the National Gay Election Coalition (1974), the Committee to Defend John DAMIEN (1975–86), The BODY POLITIC (1970s), the Right to Privacy Committee (1978–79), the Association of Gay Electors (1979–81), the Working Group on Police-Minority Relations (1979–80), the Committee to Elect George HISLOP (1980) and the Toronto Lesbian and Gay Community Council (1981–82),

His most long-standing and high-profile activism has been associated with the Coalition for Lesbian and Gay Rights in Ontario (CLGRO), of which he was a founding member in 1975. He has been its leading spokesperson through most of the group's history, most prominently during campaigns to add sexual orientation to the provincial human rights code (unsuccessfully in 1981, successfully in 1986). In 1994, working from his CLGRO base, he co-chaired the Campaign for Equal Families, in many ways an effective campaign group though unsuccessful in its immediate legislative objective. The passage of human rights legislation in 1986 provided CLGRO with a certain entry to provincial policy-making, and Warner was for a time a member of the Lesbian and Gay Advisory Committee to the Ontario Human Rights Commission. In 1993 he was made (by provincial cabinet appointment) a Commissioner for the Ontario Human Rights Commission, becoming the first openly gay man in Canada to be named to a statutory human rights body. He served in that position for three years. He has spoken widely on sexual orientation issues, and is frequently quoted in the national press on the subject.

Ed Jackson and Stan Persky (eds), *Flaunting It!* (Toronto, 1982); Donald McLeod, *Lesbian and Gay Liberation in Canada* (Toronto, 1996); Didi Herman, *The Rights of Passage* (Toronto, 1994).

David Rayside

Warren, Patricia Nell (b. 1936), American writer. The publication of Jacqueline Susann's *Valley of the Dolls* in 1967 ushered in a new wave of fiction: popular, controversial, and explicit. In the wake of Susann's bestseller, the popular novel addressed with renewed vigour the question of sexual identity, and the complicated relationship between culture, sexual experimentation and the delineation of new kinds of sexual identities. Not surprisingly, it became an ideal vehicle for gay liberation to represent its new politics of sexual emancipation, politicised militancy and vocal self-identification, and nowhere more so than in the fiction of Patricia Nell Warren, whose novel, *The Front Runner*, was published in 1974.

Warren, an editor at *Reader's Digest*, published *The Last Centennial* in 1971 under the pseudonym Patricia Kilina, but it was for *The Front Runner* that she became best known, and the novel has enjoyed a considerable following among gay men since its publication. The story of Billy Sive, the so-called 'front runner' whose track career is tragically curtailed by his assassination, the book recast gay male identity. Its world was the world of track and field, and of men whose gay identity is asserted along with their vigorous participation in a male-dominated culture of athletics and sporting competition where the assumption of heterosexuality is questioned with peril. Sive proposed a new identity for the young gay

man: Sive is 'masculine', competent, sexually self-aware and adventurous whilst observant of a strict code of ethical conduct in his sexual relationships. The novel also negotiated the question of changing sexual mores in American culture through the experiences of Harlan Brown, the ex-Marine coach whose divorce, work as a hustler and professional disgrace when his sexuality was revealed all chart the changing conditions in which gay male sexuality was expressed in post-war America. Harlan's encounter with Billy, and to a lesser extent the other gay runners in the novel, signals an historical shift in the nature of gay identity.

Warren's next two novels, *The Fancy Dancer* (1976), and *The Beauty Queen* (1978), pursued the issues of gay identity and lifestyle through their explorations of the impact of gay liberation on the popular imagination. *The Fancy Dancer* explores love between a motorcycle-riding hellion and a priest in a small-town setting somewhat reminiscent of Grace Metalious' *Peyton Place*, the novel that twenty years earlier had lifted the lid on small-town hypocrisy. *The Beauty Queen* traces the rise of anti-gay politics through the figure of Jeannie Laird Colter, an ex-beauty queen whose gubernatorial campaign pivots around anti-gay politics but whose private life is haunted by family secrets. Its story evokes the career of Anita BRYANT in particular, the singer whose anti-gay crusades were controversial accompaniments to the gains of gay liberation through the 1970s.

Warren returned to fiction in 1994 with *Harlan's Race*, a sequel to *The Front Runner*, which recasts gay politics in the light of a changed social climate through the 1980s, and the advent of HIV/AIDs-related illnesses. *Billy's Boy* (1998) continues the saga in a novel that explicitly addresses the concerns of younger gays and which is directly addressed to them, as well as to the many fans of *The Front Runner* and *Harlan's Race*. This shift in focus reflects Warren's own work as an advocate for the young, dealing with sexuality, education and other issues in the more conservative climate of the 1990s.

Melissa Hardie

Waters, John (b. 1946), American film director. Waters was born in Baltimore, Maryland, and, according to his 1981 collection *Shock Value*, a decision early on to pursue a career in film was inspired by the lists of forbidden films read to him by nuns at his Catholic Sunday school. Waters's obsession with the cinematic was accompanied by a fascination with bad taste, and this relationship underpins his cinematic output from his first film, *Hag in A Black Leather Jacket* (1964) to his most recent, *Pecker* (1998). Whilst Waters's work as a director has had a significant underground following since the 1970s, and retains its interest in subcultural style, his films since *Hairspray* (1988) have enjoyed wide cinematic release, as they parlay his typical preoccupation with trash, filth and bad taste – to him, what 'entertainment is all about' – in a more conventional cinematic register.

Made with stolen film stock and shot on the roof of his parents' home, *Hag in A Black Leather Jacket* inaugurated an early career which combined his loving exploration of Baltimore's blue-collar, bar and gay cultures with cinematic techniques indebted to the avant-garde cinema Waters discovered in New York in the 1960s. An habitué of 'adult' cinemas as well as a devotee of the avant-garde, Waters was mesmerised by subcultural style and sensational storylines. His work explored the gimmicky and the popular while engaging with the formally interrogative work of Andy WARHOL, Kenneth ANGER and other avant-garde filmmakers. Waters's films charted some now familiar associations between camp, the sexually outrageous and the cinematically self-conscious. *Multiple Maniacs* (1970), his first 'talkie', featured murder and a lobster-rape scene; *Pink Flamingos* (1972), a notorious scene of coprophagy; *Female*

Trouble (1975), the life and execution of a female criminal; *Desperate Living* (1977), the fantasy town of Mortville. *Polyester* (1981) gained a broader audience than Waters's mostly cult following, and was enhanced with 'odorama': audience members were distributed a 'scratch and sniff' card in homage to the gimmick-laden career of William Castle, one of Waters' heroes.

Fundamental to Waters's success was the development of a core group of actors in his films. Divine (Harris Glenn Milstead) was a lynchpin of Waters's films from his second, *Roman Candles* (1966), until Divine's death shortly before *Hairspray* was released. Also featured was Cookie Mueller, the writer (*Walking Through Clear Water*; *Ask Dr Mueller*), and more lately Ricki Lake, whose roles in *Hairspray* (1988) and *Cry-Baby* (1990) preceded her career as talkshow host. Since *Hairspray*, Waters's particular combination of Baltimore homage, wry nostalgia and filth has become a quirky accompaniment to the mainstreaming of camp in the 1980s. His recent films have had casts drawn from Hollywood as well as his staple *Dreamland* players; *Serial Mom* (1994) starred Kathleen Turner and Sam Waterson, as well as featuring Patty Hearst, the kidnap victim whose inclusion in Waters's films typifies his loving fascination with crime as well as the timely transgression of distinctions between the movies, entertainment and 'real life'.

These preoccupations are nowhere better documented than in his 1987 collection *Crackpot: The Obsessions of John Waters*, in which he discloses his love of the tabloid publication *The National Enquirer*, his fascination with crime and criminal trials, his daily routines and his cinematic debts. Waters's work has meanwhile branched into other media, with the publication of *Director's Cut* (1997), a series of photographic collages of favourite movies and actors that pay respect to the viewer–fan as 'director'.

John G. Ives and John Waters, *American*

Originals: John Waters (New York, 1992); *Desperate Visions: The Journal of Alternative Cinema*, Camp America, Volume 1: John Waters / John and Mike Kuchar.

Melissa Hardie

Watney, Simon, (b. ?) British AIDS and gay activist, cultural theorist, media analyst and art historian. From the early 1970s through the mid-1980s Watney taught cultural studies, with a special interest in photographic education, at the Central London Polytechnic. In the late 1970s he joined the editorial board of *Scope* magazine and wrote widely as an art critic and as a photographic historian.

Watney's involvement in gay and lesbian politics began in the early 1970s through his participation in a number of community organisations and regular contributions to the British gay press. His involvement with AIDS issues commenced in 1984. In 1986 he helped organise the first UK conferences on AIDS and the role of the media, thus starting an intermeshing of his professional career with his role as an AIDS activist.

Watney has written extensively on the history of the HIV/AIDS epidemic, with particular emphasis on the inability of governments and society to adopt appropriate measures to counter the spread of the disease and to support and care for those affected by HIV/AIDS. His books, including *Policing Desire: Pornography, AIDS and the Media* (1987), *Taking Liberties: AIDS and Cultural Polictics* (1989) and *Practices of Freedom* (1994), have received considerable critical acclaim. Watney is a director of the Red Hot AIDS Charitable Trust (based in the UK) which raises funds for community-based HIV prevention programs, and a long-term member of the Terrence HIGGINS Trust (UK).

Mark Edwards

Watson, Lex (b. 1943), Australian activist. Watson first encountered gay politics as a member of the Humanist Society in New South Wales in the late 1960s, when he was involved in its attempt to form a homosexual law reform society. The group had little success and was soon overtaken by the formation of the Campaign Against Moral Persecution (CAMP) which, by having openly gay spokespeople, rapidly became the premier Australian gay rights organisation. Watson soon joined and is credited by John WARE with giving the group its political edge, and with being instrumental in organising the group's first ever demonstration. He developed a national profile within the movement with his efforts to mobilise lobbying in support of the federal parliament's law reform motion in 1973. He achieved mainstream notoriety when, while speaking to a public meeting in Mt Isa, in outback Queensland, an angry opponent threw a bucket of what was discreetly described as 'excrement' over him.

Watson was, with Sue WILLS, first Co-President of CAMP (NSW) after it opted for a more formal structure, and he resigned, with her and others, over the organisation's drift away from politics and into welfarism.

In the early 1980s, he played a central role in the formation of the Gay Rights Lobby, which campaigned for homosexual law reform in New South Wales, though he fell out with the group as a whole over his preparedness to settle for something less than full equality on the age of consent. He was then involved in activism around AIDS as a founder of the AIDS Action Committee and as a member of the first advisory body set up by the federal minister of health.

He has written extensively over the years on issues such as law reform, psychiatry, the gay and lesbian media, and AIDS.

Graham Willett

Webb, Clifton (1891–1966), American dancer and actor. A former child actor, opera singer and dancer, Webb became a major box office star in his late forties and at one time was more popular than Tyrone

Power and Gregory Peck. Unmarried, he lived with his mother, a French poodle and a parrot. He 'enjoyed the company of young people'. His wispy elegance and overwhelming conceit gave him membership of the 1940s 'sissies club', which included actors such as George Sanders and Claude Rains who, in Vito RUSSO's words, were 'at times sophisticated but vaguely sinister outsiders . . . just a little deadly'. Yet, in the 1950s, he extended his appeal, without losing his bite, into less threatening environs.

After being shunned by Hollywood for years because of his sexuality, 20th Century Fox's Darryl F. Zanuck was persuaded against his better judgement by Otto Preminger to let Webb co-star in the 1944 thriller *Laura*. He was an instant hit as the acidulous and murderous friend/lover of the eponymous heroine. His third assignment, *The Razor's Edge* (1946), saw him playing a more explicitly gay role. He received Academy Award nominations for both films. Villainy and snobbery gave way to misanthropy with a comic intent. He was the babysitting bachelor writer who hated children in *Sitting Pretty*. Two more films featuring his apalling but appealing Mr Belvedere followed.

Webb was one of the few epicene character actors to be acceptable as bachelor or father, connoisseur of women or asexual. Always beautifully groomed, he was attractive to audiences as either confirmed bachelor or pillar of the community.

He certainly conforms to the sissy image of the 1930s, being superior, overly neat and with a detached attitude to life and women. There is something sinister about him yet something comfortable, too. There were other actors who matched him in detachment and style – George Sanders, Eric Portman, Anton Walbrook, Claude Rains, Dennis Price – who did play leading roles but none were ever major box office attractions. Only Vincent Price – who appeared with Webb in *Laura* – could parlay svelte over-sensitivity and a snide tongue into mass appeal, and that was mainly in the horror genre.

Keith Howes

Weeks, Jeffrey (b. 1945), British scholar. Born in Rhondda, Wales, Weeks was educated at University College London and the University of Kent at Canterbury. He has written and edited over a dozen books and more than sixty scholarly articles, many on the history of sexuality. He has held teaching and research positions at the London School of Economics, the Universities of Essex and Kent, Bristol Polytechnic and other institutions. Since 1994 Weeks has been Professor of Sociology at South Bank University in London, where he was Head of the School of Education, Politics and Social Science from 1995 to 1998 and is currently Dean of the Faculty of Humanities and Social Science.

In *Coming Out: Homosexual Politics in Britain from the Nineteenth Century to the Present* (1977; rev. edn, 1990), Weeks wrote a history of the homosexual emancipation movement from the time of John Addington Symonds, Havelock Ellis and Edward Carpenter to the present. It is considered a pioneering and authoritative work in gay history. Among Weeks's more recent publications are *Sex, Politics and Society: The Regulation of Sexuality since 1800* (1981; rev. edn, 1989); *Sexuality and Its Discontents: Meanings, Myths and Modern Sexualities* (1985), *Sexuality* (1986), *Between the Acts: Lives of Homosexual Men, 1885–1967* (with Kevin Porter, 1990; rev. edn, 1998), *Against Nature: Essays on History, Sexuality and Identity* (1991) and *Invented Moralities: Sexual Values in an Age of Uncertainty* (1995). He has edited books on social diversity and on sexual cultures, and co-authored a set of guides to sources in British political history. His published articles treat a variety of subjects – the women's movement, male prostitution, problems of older homosexuals, psychoanalysis and homosexuality, Michel FOUCAULT and AIDS issues. He has served on the editorial board of various journals, including *History Workshop Journal*, the *Journal of the History of Sexuality*, the *Journal of Homosexuality* and *Victorian Studies*.

Concerning his studies of the history and social organisation of sexuality, Weeks states: 'This has been the major focus of my work since the early 1970s . . . I have been particularly concerned with exploring the relationship between historical and sociological approaches in trying to understand the emergence of historically defined sexual categories. I have also explored the changing forms of social regulation of sexuality, the ideological debates on sexual behaviour, and the social policy implications of the recent rethinking of sexual values. More recently, this preoccupation has led to a concern with studying the historical roots, social impact and policy consequences of the HIV/AIDS epidemic.'

http://www.sbu.ac.uk/fhass/staff/
jeffreyweeks.shtml
		Robert Aldrich and Garry Wotherspoon

Weinberg, Martin (Stephen) (b. 1939), American scholar. Weinberg was educated at St Lawrence University, the University of Massachusetts and Northwestern University. He has taught at Rutgers University, New Jersey (1965–68), and since at Indiana University at Bloomington (since 1968). He was also a senior research sociologist at the Institute for Sex Research (1968–80).

Weinberg collaborated with Alan Bell to investigate the dimensions of what it means to be gay or lesbian in today's society. *Homosexualities: A Study of Diversity among Men and Women* (1978) involved face-to-face interviews with approximately 1500 people on a number of subjects, including sexual experience, sexual problems, acceptance of homosexuality, religiousness, social and psychological adjustment, and political beliefs. Weinberg and Bell found great diversity among their respondents and argued that race, sex, age and sometimes education must be

taken into account when examining gay and lesbian life experiences.

Weinberg, Bell and Sue Hammersmith's *Sexual Preference: Its Development among Men and Women* (1981) was groundbreaking in both its method and and its findings. In a controlled study, 979 gay men and lesbians were interviewed and compared to a group of 477 heterosexual men and women. The authors found that sexual preference was largely determined prior to adolescence and that homosexual feelings preceded homosexual activity by (on average) three years. They found no evidence to support the 'overbearing mother' hypothesis of causation; identification with a particular parent had no significant role in the development of sexual preference.

Weinberg, along with his colleagues, has helped to change the ways in which we view sexual preference and gay and lesbian identity. His *Dual Attraction: Understanding Bisexuality* (1994) (co-authoured with Colin Williams and Doug Pryor) continues work on this often neglected subject.

		Trent Newmeyer

West, D(onald) J(ames) (b. 1924), British criminologist and psychiatrist. West studied at the University of Liverpool and the University of London, taking degrees in medicine. He has also been awarded an Honorary Doctor of Letters (1978) from Cambridge University. Since 1960, West has held a professorship (and is currently a professor emeritus) at Cambridge University's Institute of Criminology.

The author of works on sexual crimes and victimisation, homosexuality, delinquency and male prostitution, West's *Homosexuality* (1955; published in the United States as *The Other Man*) was one of the first significant studies of homosexuality in contemporary Britain since Havelock Ellis's *Sexual Inversion* (1915). It is a wide-ranging and exhaustive text that begins by examining evidence of homosexuality in non-Western cultures, in different historical periods and within the animal kingdom. It carefully considers homosexuality in the context of the time (the Wolfenden Committee in Britain was in the midst of its review of the laws regarding homosexuality) through examinations of homosexual subcultures, the oft-neglected subject of lesbianism, and the legal, medical and social problems faced by homosexuals in Britain and other Western nations. The second half of the text is concerned with the question of causation (what produces homosexuality), and West considers hormonal, genetic and psychological interpretations of homosexuality. He also devotes attention to various theoretical explanations of lesbianism and bisexuality.

Although West clearly prefers a psychoanalytic approach, he also provides a sensitive and nuanced discussion of a number of psychological, biological, social and cultural approaches to homosexuality. This broad and balanced perspective leads him to stress that it is futile and misleading to develop an all-encompassing typology of homosexuality when evidence points to a wide variety of homosexual life experiences across and within historical, gendered, cultural and social spheres.

West's work was quite revolutionary for the time in that it called for the decriminalisation of homosexual acts, stressed the multiplicity of causes of homosexuality and assessed the variegated scientific evidence in an objective and rational manner. Unlike his American psychiatric counterparts Irving BIEBER and Charles SOCARIDES, who posited heterosexuality as the natural norm and homosexuality as an aberration, West did not reject Sigmund Freud's theory that all individuals are constitutionally bisexual: 'Exclusive preference for the opposite sex is an acquired trait, and involves the repression of a certain amount of homosexual feeling which is natural to the human being.' Heterosexuality was not a natural given but, like homosexuality, a result of life and family experiences during childhood and adolescence.

For West, an 'orthodox' Freudian, same-sex attraction was not pathological in and of itself. Although the exclusive homosexual, that is, one 'who is repelled rather than attracted by feminine charms, really suffers from an abnormal inhibition', individuals who have 'normal, happy relations with the opposite sex' and engage in 'occasional homosexual activities' are not 'necessarily psychologically ill'. Exclusive homosexuality is produced in early life and the aversion to heterosexual relations are formed much like other fears and inhibitions. Since the fear of heterosexual relations (i.e. exclusive homosexuality) is produced much like other phobias, West concludes that it could be 'cured' under ideal conditions (lengthy treatment, a strong motivation to change, the presence of heterosexual activities and dreams, and if this fear is not already deeply entrenched).

Although West entertained the notion of a possible treatment for homosexuality, unlike his American counterparts, he was extremely cautious regarding its application for all homosexuals. He also reviewed other non-psychoanalytic treatments, such as aversion therapy, and concluded that these approaches to 'curing' homosexuality did not significantly differ from psychoanalytic therapy in regard to their (equally low) success rates.

Homosexuality proved to be a lasting success and consistently in demand. A revised edition was published as a 'Pelican book' in 1960 and was followed by a second revised edition in 1968. The revisions primarily consisted of supplementing and expanding existing sections in light of recent scholarship (the 1968 edition, for instance, greatly expanded the discussion regarding lesbianism). The fourth edition was yet another revision, but, fundamentally reworked, it was published as *Homosexuality Re-examined* (1977).

Most significantly it included contemporary research on non-patient gays and lesbians (generally a better sample of the gay and lesbian population than psychiatric patients), advances and changes in psychological and psychiatric perspectives on homosexuality, and a significant addition of works on gay and lesbian communities, life experiences and identities written by gays and lesbians themselves. This effort, to examine how gays and lesbians view themselves, reveals West's willingness to admit that psychiatrists and other professionals were not (and should not be) the only authoritative voices on homosexuality.

A comparison of *Homosexuality Reexamined* with its predecessors not only reveals the ways in which society had changed *vis-à-vis* gays and lesbians but also documents changes in West's own conceptualisation of the issue.

His reappraisals can also be found in West's later works, such as *Male Prostitution* (1993), based on interviews with 133 current and former male sexworkers.

West continues to write on homosexuality and other issues related to sexuality. Most recently, he has co-edited, with Richard Green, *Sociolegal Control of Homosexuality: A Multi-nation Comparison* (1997).

Trent Newmeyer

White, Edmund (b. 1940), American writer. In 1988, *Newsweek* called White America's foremost gay novelist. White has defined himself not as a writer who happens to be gay, but as a gay writer, and has come to be regarded as an unofficial spokesman for the American gay community. Born in the Ohio to Edmund White, Sr. and Delilah Teddlie, he struggled for years in therapy before accepting his homosexuality. But by the early 1980s, he had become a gay activist, part of a group of writers who called themselves 'The Violet Quill', and, subsequently, one of the founders of The Gay Men's Health Center. In 1985, he announced that he had tested positive for the AIDS virus.

With Adam Mars-Jones, he published *The Darker Proof: Stories from a Crisis* (1987), fiction about the impact of AIDS

on gay life, and since then has edited the *Faber Book of Gay Short Fiction* (1991), *The Burning Library: Essays* (1994) and *Skinned Alive: Stories* (1995). These works are a chronicle of gay lifestyles and society's changing attitudes toward homosexuality, and are a contribution to contemporary social history. White's openly gay work began with his collaboration with Charles Silverstein, *The Joy of Gay Sex: An Intimate Guide* (1977), continued with *States of Desire: Travels in Gay America* (1980), and his autobiographical novels, *A Boy's Own Story* (1982), the sequel, *The Beautiful Room is Empty* (1988), and most recently, *The Farewell Symphony* (1997). In 1994, he received the National Book Critics Circle Award for *Genet: A Biography* (1993); he has also published *Proust* (1999). His earlier fiction includes *Forgetting Elena* (1973), *Nocturnes for the King of Naples* (1978) and *Caracole* (1985).

White has worked as an editor at *Time* magazine and *The Saturday Review of Literature*, and taught at Johns Hopkins, Columbia, Yale and Brown Universities. After many years residence in Paris he currently lives in New York, and teaches writing at Princeton University.

Larry McCaffrey, *Alive and Writing: Interviews* (Urbana, 1987).

Seymour Kleinberg

White, Patrick (1912–90), Australian writer. The only son of second cousins Ruth Withycombe and Victor Martindale White, Patrick White was born in London where his parents were on vacation. His was a privileged existence; as his biographer David Marr notes, 'The story of the Whites in Australia is the history of a fortune, a river of money that flowed through New South Wales.' In 1925 White was sent to Cheltenham College to be educated in upper-class English style, and it was there, in an atmosphere of extreme sexual repression, that he first became conscious of his homosexuality. This was not a happy discovery for White, and he accepted it in a fatalistic fashion. The poetry he wrote during his time at Cheltenham mirrored this: 'I am a stranger; / I must veil myself; / I must hide me'.

In 1932 White signed up for modern languages at King's College, Cambridge. His tutor in French was Donald Beves, a homosexual whose posthumous fame centred on unfounded accusations of treason. Whilst at Cambridge, White also met E. M. Forster, and fell in love with the evasive and reticent poetry of A. E. Housman.

He joined the Royal Air Force in 1940, and met his life-long love, Manoly Lascaris (then in the Royal Greek Army), in Alexandria in 1941. In February 1948 White returned to Australia for good, and was joined by Lascaris one month later. They set up house in Sydney, and remained there together until White's death in 1990.

Themes and issues relating directly or obliquely to homosexuality, and clearly or obtusely drawn homosexual characters, can be traced in all White's works. The reverberant ambiguity White so admired in Housman's poetry was to become a distinguishing feature of most of his fiction (this is all that David MALOUF, for example, saw, and concluded that White was unwilling to engage with the subject). Operating both as a closeting effect and a pleasurable thing-in-itself, White's homosexual evasiveness presents readers with a constant interchange between concealment and expression, surface and depth. The presence in his fiction of female characters who look like men (*The Aunt's Story*), and of male characters who look like women (*The Twyborn Affair*), of male characters who are effeminate (*The Solid Mandala*, *Riders in the Chariot*, *The Living and the Dead*), of female characters who are butch (*The Aunt's Story*), and of apparently asexual male bonding (*Voss*), all intimate tantalisingly – without necessarily signalling – the omnipresence of a homosexual (sub)text in White's works. Overall, the closet is a key trope in his fic-

tion and epitomizes the psychological and physical trauma of homosexual characters.

This expressive restraint on the subject of homosexuality in his writing was largely carried over into his actions. Although he lived openly in Sydney with Lascaris, White was not a champion of homosexual causes. From the late 1960s, when the move to reform anti-homosexual laws was accompanied by public outings, not only did he stay in the closet, he refused to offer any support. He reacted likewise to the 1971 demonstrations for homosexual rights. White's decision to distance himself thus must take into account his class and status position, and his sense of being an interloper in Australia by virtue of his education and his sexuality (he referred to himself as a 'veiled bride'). However, although White was not predisposed to public pronouncements and actions regarding his sexuality, he did make his own imaginative/literary contribution to the wave of cultural and social interrogation of 'norms'. *The Solid Mandala* (1966) is the first novel in which he clearly delineates a male homosexual, and elegantly traces the psychological and physical anguish of the closet. It is with this beautifully written and lyrically descriptive novel that White began the – publicly unacknowledged – process of deconstructing the literary closet.

In 1973, he won the Nobel Prize for Literature. He did not 'come out' until 1981 with his autobiography provocatively entitled *Flaws in the Glass* (White jokingly called it *The Poof's Progress* and, following publication, others called it *Claws in the Arse*). By this stage his reputation was clearly established; he had published fifteen novels and three collections of poems, and had several plays performed. Yet he still felt uneasy about possible reactions, a clear sign of the fear that a culture of censorship and repression continued to instil in him. However, it was with the publication of *Memoirs of Many in One* (1986) that White's homosexuality became controversial. The only one of his novels not to lend itself easily to the terms of canonical interpretations, *Memoirs* caused outrage amongst homophobic critics. As the novel that proclaimed White as a 'cross-dressed' author, it was fitting *Memoirs* should be his last.

White's pre-emptive involvement with many of the central tenets of gay, queer and gender studies highlights the all-too-often elided significance of his work. As a particularly consistent and comprehensive critic of sexual regulation, White in his literary works sought vigorously to emphasise the centrality of sexuality to subjectivity. His works offer new ways of theorising and resisting hegemonic control over the multiplicity of sexual and gender roles struggling for legitimacy.

Valerie Beattie, 'In Other Words: Homosexual Desire in the Novels of Patrick White' (Ph.D. Thesis, University of Edinburgh, 1996); David Marr, *Patrick White: A Life* (London, 1991).

Valerie Beattie

Whitehouse, Mary (b. 1910), British journalist and morals campaigner. She was born in Shrewsbury, England, and was brought up and educated in Chester. After training as an art teacher, she taught at a school in Wolverhampton from 1932 to 1940. During these years her religious commitment was strengthened and she became deeply involved in the Oxford Group, later called Moral Re-Armament. This movement had a powerful influence on her thinking. Through the Oxford Group she met Ernest Whitehouse, whom she married in 1940. Both were devout Christians: Mary was an Anglican and Ernest a Methodist. They settled in Wolverhampton and had three sons. In 1953 she returned to teaching and from 1960 to 1964 was a senior mistress, with responsibility for art and sex education, at a secondary modern school at Madeley. In 1975 from rural Worcestershire she moved closer to London, to Ardleigh in Essex.

Whitehouse's conservative Christian views were challenged by the social, moral and cultural changes that occurred in Britain in the late 1950s and 1960s. Like many others, she was appalled by the observed increase in sexual material, coarse language, violence and irreverent satire in the mass media, especially on television, which entered the home, corrupted the minds of children and desecrated the sacredness of sex. She saw these trends as a deliberate attempt to undermine the fundamental Christian values of society. In an attempt to stem the tide, in 1964 she was a founder of the Clean-Up TV Campaign. In 1965 this developed into the National Viewers' and Listeners' Association, which during the next decade became a well-organised and influential pressure group in support of 'Christian standards' and opposing sexual explicitness in broadcasting and television. As president of the association, Whitehouse became an experienced and confident campaigner and the subject of many newspaper articles. In 1971, with Malcolm Muggeridge and others, she founded the Festival of Light as a national organisation to campaign against pornography and 'moral pollution'. In 1980 she was made a Commander of the Order of the British Empire.

Whitehouse deplored the increasing visibility of homosexuals and public tolerance of homosexuality. She regarded homosexual behaviour as a perverse practice that was always contrary to God's law, but she denied that she condemned homosexuals as people. In the defence of traditional moral standards her primary concern was to protect their religious basis. This led her to invoke the ancient law against blasphemy. In 1977 she took legal action against the London paper *Gay News* for publishing, in June 1976, a poem by James Kirkup called 'The Love that Dares to Speak its Name'. This poem, described by Whitehouse as 'blasphemous and obscene', depicted a sexual relationship between a Roman centurion and the crucified body of Christ. The case aroused national attention and polarised opinion.

In her prosecution Whitehouse was widely supported by conservative Christians, though church leaders kept their distance. In July 1977 a London jury, by a majority verdict, found *Gay News* and its editor Denis Lemon guilty of publishing a blasphemous libel. Both were fined and Lemon received a suspended prison sentence. An appeal in 1978 against the sentence was dismissed.

Whitehouse opposed the aims of the gay movement and regularly attacked what she saw as the homosexual/intellectual/humanist lobby. For many gay people in Britain she became a symbol of conservative Christian authoritarianism and opposition to gay equality.

Max Caulfield, *Mary Whitehouse* (London, 1975); Michael Tracey and David Morrison, *Whitehouse* (London, 1979) and *Who Does She Think She Is?* (London, 1971); Mary Whitehouse, *Quite Contrary* (London, 1993).

David Hilliard

Whitton, Charlotte (1896–1975), Canadian social worker, politician. Whitton was born into a merchant family in Renfrew, Ontario, Canada. She excelled in her studies at the Renfrew Collegiate Institute and won numerous scholarships. She took her Bachelor of Arts at Queen's University, followed by a Diploma in Teaching. In 1918, having left Queen's, she took a position as Assistant Secretary to the Social Service Council of Canada. She became the assistant editor of the new journal *Social Welfare* and began organising the Canadian Council on Child Welfare as a volunteer. In 1926, she was appointed its director. In 1950, Whitton embarked on a career in politics and in 1951 was elected to the Ottawa Board of Control. In 1952, she served as the Canadian delegate to the Commission on Child Welfare at the League of Nations. She was mayor of Ottawa from 1952 to 1956, and again from 1960 to 1964. She retired from civic politics in 1972.

Whitton is remembered primarily as 'the old lady bitch mayor of Ottawa', but it was her activism for the cause of child welfare which, in the early twentieth century, saw her become one of Canada's most influential public figures. Her life's work was the improvement of the condition of children in Canada, and she campaigned tirelessly on the issues of juvenile delinquency and illegitimacy. In keeping with the feminism of her time, Whitton was simultaneously progressive and conservative, deploring society's differential treatment of the mothers and fathers of illegitimate children, while in the next breath arguing against the immigration of groups she regarded as undesirable. She alienated herself from many social workers in 1945 when she published a pamphlet arguing against what she considered the subsidisation by the state of the reproduction of 'defectives'.

Whitton was inspired by close relationships with women throughout her life. While at Queen's University, she had found a mentor in Professor Wilhelmina Gordon, becoming eventually somewhat of a protegée to Gordon. Gordon was disappointed by Whitton's decision in 1918 not to pursue graduate studies at Bryn Mawr and then Oxford, but rather to enter social work. They nevertheless remained friends. Whitton also maintained 'passionate friendships' with several female university friends. After she moved to Toronto, around 1918, Whitton met Margaret Grier, who worked for the Juvenile Court and Big Sisters. In 1922, Whitton and Grier moved to Ottawa, where Whitton took up positions as Secretary to the Minister of Trade and honorary secretary of the Canadian Council on Child Welfare, and Grier as Secretary of the Canadian Tuberculosis Association. They were to live together until Grier's death in 1947. Throughout their relationship, Whitton referred to Grier in terms common to the 'romantic friendships' of the nineteenth century; she wrote in words exalting Grier's beauty and expressed devotion and commitment to her companion.

Historians have debated whether or not the Whitton–Grier relationship was lesbian, and most argue that, because there is no evidence of a physical relationship between the two, it was not. Letters written by the two show that they did sleep together and were physically affectionate with one another. Regardless of the physical content of their relationship, it may be said that Whitton and Grier lived in a twentieth-century version of the 'romantic friendship', and may be included in a history of lesbianism by those who do not require of lesbian relationships a genital component. Even in the alleged absence of a physical relationship, Whitton and Grier were, in all other respects, in a same-sex 'marriage'. Their relationship is one of the few yet documented romantic friendships in Canadian history.

Patricia T. Rooke, 'Public Figure, Private Woman: Same-Sex Support Structures in the Life of Charlotte Whitton', *International Journal of Women's Studies*, vol. 6, no. 5 (1983), pp. 205–28; P. T. Rooke and R. L. Schnell, *No Bleeding Heart: Charlotte Whitton, A Feminist On the Right* (Vancouver, 1987).

Karen Duder

Wildeblood, Peter (b. 1923–99), British public figure. Wildeblood was one of the defendants in the 'Montagu case' of 1954, the most publicised trial involving homosexual offences in post-war, pre-Wolfenden Britain, and author of two books concerning his experiences, *Against the Law* (1955) and *A Way of Life* (1956).

Most accounts of the Montagu trials and the events that led up to them have been based upon Wildeblood's own account in *Against the Law*. However, Wildeblood is at times evasive and deliberately vague about details and, furthermore, devotes only a small portion of the book to the trial itself. Patrick Higgins examined the copious and detailed newspaper coverage of the trials, and found quite a different story than the one sketched by Wildeblood.

On 16 October 1953, Scotland Yard announced that Wildeblood's friend, Edward John Barrington Douglas-Scott-Montagu, third Baron Montagu of Beaulieu and a friend, assistant film director Kenneth Hume, were each to be charged with one count of committing an unnatural offence (sodomy) and one count of indecent assault against two members of the Boy Scout troop that acted as guides to Montagu's Palace House at Beaulieu when it was open to the public. On 3 August, Montagu and Hume had taken the two scouts for a swim near Beaulieu, and the scouts alleged that, after the swim, one scout had had sex with Montagu and the other with Hume in Montagu's beach-hut.

Montagu's trial opened in December 1953. Due to the lack of any conclusive medical proof of sodomy, and the scout's unconvincing testimony, Montagu was eventually acquitted of the charge of committing an unnatural offence, but, as the jury could not agree on the indecent assault charge, the Director of Public Prosecutions decided to retry him on this charge. However, before Montagu's retrial could take place, he, his cousin Michael Pitt-Rivers and Wildeblood were arrested in January 1954. Eventually all three were charged with a total of nineteen counts involving sodomy, attempted sodomy and gross indecency with Eddie McNally and John Reynolds, two Royal Air Force men. McNally was Wildeblood's lover and had introduced Reynolds to Montagu, with whom Reynolds claimed he had had sex a number of times. Reynolds also alleged that, while vacationing with McNally and Wildeblood at Montagu's beach-hut, he had been introduced to Pitt-Rivers; and that he, Pitt-Rivers, Wildeblood and McNally had gone to Pitt-Rivers's estate, Larmer Tree, and that he had had sex with Pitt-Rivers there and at his London flat a number of times.

The counts against the three men were linked by a charge of conspiracy, which allowed the prosecution to present to the jury the history of the interrelationships amongst the charged men: Montagu and Pitt-Rivers were charged with counselling and procuring homosexual acts, and Wildeblood was charged with aiding and abetting the commission of such acts. It is clear that the Crown, humiliated by their failure in Montagu's first trial, was using the charge of conspiracy to ensure that they would win a conviction. (It appears that Montagu was never retried for the incident involving the boy scout.)

The police had become aware of the connection between Montagu, Pitt-Rivers and the airmen at the time of Montagu's trial, when McNally, according to Higgins, was questioned in connection with an investigation into 'a homosexual network within the service'. McNally and Reynolds were undoubtedly pressured, probably even intimidated, into confessing and agreeing to give evidence (some of it possibly fabricated) against Montagu, Pitt-Rivers and Wildeblood. It was obvious that the goal, for the police, was evidence against Montagu, since although McNally and Reynolds confessed to having committed homosexual acts with a total of twenty-seven men, only Montagu, Pitt-Rivers and Wildeblood were ever charged, and both airmen were granted complete immunity from charges on all their confessed offences.

The trial began in March 1954. Evidence for the charges rested not only on the testimony of McNally and Reynolds, but also on letters between the parties (both suggestive and blatant) and the oddness of the association between men who seemed to have so little in common. Whereas Wildeblood admitted on the stand that he was an 'invert' and had had a relationship with McNally (although he claimed he could not have had sexual relations with McNally since he had been impotent for the past three years), Montagu and Pitt-Rivers not only denied knowing that Wildeblood, McNally and Reynolds were homosexuals, but denied the sugges-

tion that they were homosexual and the allegations that they had had sex with Reynolds. The three men were all found guilty. Montagu was sentenced to twelve months, Pitt-Rivers and Wildeblood to eighteen months. Wildeblood was released after serving a year of his sentence.

Against the Law, written and published before the law regarding homosexuality had changed, although making the courageous admission, 'I am a homosexual', is perhaps more satisfying as a record of prison life and conditions than as an account of a homosexual's life in post-war Britain. Wildeblood (by necessity and by design) was evasive about his homosexual activities and his participation in the homosexual subculture of the time. While it contains autobiographical and factual elements, *Against the Law* is primarily an example of early homosexual activism. The implicit thesis is that what he and his fellow defendants were charged, convicted and imprisoned for – consenting sexual relations between adult men in private – should not be a criminal offence.

Wildeblood was a vigorous participant in the struggle for law reform: he presented his book and gave evidence to the Wolfenden Committee and authored a pamphlet entitled *The Homosexual and the Law* (1959), sponsored by the Homosexual Law Reform Society.

Wildeblood's second book, *A Way of Life*, consists of a series of fictionalised histories of sexual misfits whom Wildeblood claims to have encountered due to his authorship of *Against the Law* and his co-ownership of a bar in one of London's seedier districts. This book is much less bitter and much more optimistic about the ability of homosexuals to lead happy and fulfilled (if unconventional) lives and is confident that the law and society will eventually change to the benefit of homosexuals.

Patrick Higgins, *The Heterosexual Dictatorship* (London, 1996).

Jason Boyd

Williams, Cecil (1909–79), South African activist. Born in Cornwall, Williams migrated to South Africa in 1929. He taught English literature at prestigious schools in Johannesburg, and volunteered to fight in World War II. During and after the war Williams was a leading activist in the anti-fascist Springbok League, in the South African Communist Party, and in the 1950s in the African National Congress-aligned Congress of Democrats. Williams was a prominent theatre director, his productions including the anti-apartheid 'Kimberly Train' in 1959. Driven 'underground' with Nelson MANDELA when the latter re-entered the country illegally from Botswana as head of the ANC's armed wing UmKhonto weSizwe, Williams was arrested near Pietermaritzburg in 1962. He fled with his Scottish boyfriend into exile in the UK and died there in 1979. He has been credited by ANC leaders, such as Albie Sachs, with having had a profound impact on their understanding of homosexuality, laying the groundwork for the ANC's adoption of gay rights policies in the late 1980s. The ANC dedicated its message to the first gay and lesbian pride march in Johannesburg in 1990 to Williams. He was the subject of a 1998 film, '*The Man Who Drove with Mandela*'.

Ken Davis

Williams, Kenneth (1926–88), British actor and comedian. Williams was born in London, the son of a Bloomsbury hairdresser. He trained as a lithographer, but discovered his comic talents in the Army during World War II, when he served in India, Malaya and Burma as part of the Combined Entertainments Unit. After the war he worked in repertory theatre for several years. He had the ability for a serious theatrical career – his early heroes were John Gielgud and Laurence Olivier, as well as Orson Welles and Noël Coward – but his genius as a comedian led him to leave the Old Vic to work in radio.

In the 1950s radio shows like Kenneth Horne's *Round the Horn* and *Beyond Our*

Ken and Tony Hancock's *Hancock's Half Hour* (where he first teamed up with Sid James and Hattie Jacques) made Williams a household name in Britain. His trademarks were an outrageously camp voice and an unending series of *double entendre* jokes: tame by 1990s standards but refreshingly shocking for the audiences of the post-war BBC. He also worked in live cabaret and later in television, where his mobile face and hand-flapping style earned him a cult following. By the late 1950s he was starring in his own shows, *The Kenneth Williams Show* and *Stop Messing About*.

At the same time Williams moved naturally into films, and began a long career in broad farce with *Carry On Sergeant* in 1958. This film brought together the 'Carry On' team, including Charles Hawtrey, Sid James, Hattie Jacques, Barbara Windsor and others, who were to make more than twenty-five films by the time the series died of boredom in the late 1970s. Their trademarks were feeble plots, an interchangeable cast, skilful slapstick, and an unending stream of very old jokes, mainly about sex, which became steadily cruder as censorship relaxed in the 1960s and 1970s. The 'Carry On films' were a goldmine for Williams, but eventually became a prison from which he could not escape.

Williams's success in comedy stereotyped him as a comic queen, and eventually he was allowed to play nothing else. He was a close friend of the playwright Joe ORTON, who cast him as Inspector Trusscott in the original production of *Loot*. But audiences had come to expect campery from Williams, and were uncomfortable when he gave them anything else. Eventually he withdrew from theatre, claiming he no longer liked the long hours. In fact he had become so badly typecast he could no longer get 'straight' roles.

Little seems to be known about Williams's personal (which is to say, sexual) life. When a friend, the Tory MP Gyles Brandreth, asked him point blank if he was homosexual, Williams answered: 'Mentally yes, spiritually yes, physically no'. He told Brandreth that he belonged to 'a more discreet generation: before the love that dare not speak its name started shouting the odds from the rooftops'. It is unlikely that this is the whole truth, but it does seem that Williams shared with some homosexual men of his generation an almost hysterical aversion to physical contact. He once said that the reason he rarely entertained at home was that he couldn't stand 'the thought of someone else's bottom on my loo'.

Williams was a prize example of a type which flourished in British popular culture from the 1920s to the 1970s: the obvious, but not open, homosexual man. Williams and other actors of this type, such as Hawtrey and Frankie Howerd, could be as camp as they liked, the camper the better, and audiences loved it – but they could never actually say: 'I am homosexual.' With the advent of openly gay actors and characters from the 1970s on, and with the demise of the puritanical pre-war culture which enjoyed being scandalised by their essentially harmless campery, this kind of comedy went into a sharp decline, a decline which (mercifully) killed the 'Carry On' films, but which also killed Williams's career.

By the 1980s Williams had become something of a relic, although he could still trade on his reputation to good effect: in 1983 London Weekend Television offered him £10,000 for An Audience With Kenneth Williams. He dutifully did the talk-show circuit, but he resented the fact that his career had become, in effect, mainly a process of parodying himself. His jokes became cruder and less funny, a process made worse by his drinking – he damaged several professionally-useful friendships by overplaying himself while under the influence. His health declined as he reached his sixties, and in 1988 he took an overdose of barbiturates, leaving a gloomy final diary entry which asked: 'Oh, what's the bloody point?' His father had also killed himself when his business failed.

Williams was a professional paradox: a hugely successful comedian with a cult following, who could no longer get fulfilling work because of the very success of the role he had created for himself. 'Contrary to several opinions, I don't believe he was tortured by his sexuality,' wrote Brandreth in a recent commemorative article. Maybe not, but the roots of his professional failure can be traced to his sexuality, or rather to his inability to express it. This may seem a strange observation about a man whose public persona was as a screaming queen. But in fact that overblown persona, camp yet closeted, foul-mouthed yet sexless, stood between Williams and any real self-expression. It was increasingly anachronistic in a new age of sexual openness which Williams could not cope with, personally or professionally.

R. Davies (ed.), *The Kenneth Williams Diaries* (London, 1993).

Adam Carr

Williams, Tennessee (1911–83), American writer. America's greatest playwright, he also wrote many short stories. His greatest play, regarded by many as the greatest play in American literature, *A Streetcar Named Desire* (1947), brought him fame and wealth and an international reputation. Williams complained that his early success was a burden, that celebrity and seriousness about work were incompatible, and while he was passionately devoted to work, it was clear that it suffered as his fame grew. He never recreated the brilliance of *Streetcar*, though for the next ten years he wrote many successful plays, among them, *Summer and Smoke* (1950), *The Rose Tattoo* (1951), *Cat on a Hot Tin Roof* (1955), *Sweet Bird of Youth* (1956), *Orpheus Descending* (1957), *Night of the Iguana* (1961), as well as fiction, short stories and a novel, *The Roman Spring of Mrs. Stone* (1950), but his artistic decline was irreversible. Williams attributed this decline to the hostility of the critics whom he accused of being homophobic (though he did not use the term), but his own dependence on alcohol and barbituates was at least equally culpable.

Born to Edwina Dakin, the Southern Belle daughter of a minister, and Cornelius Williams, a businessman, he was closest to his younger sister, Rose (there was a younger brother as well). His parents' marriage was very unhappy, and he sided with his mother, regarding his father as his enemy, the man who ridiculed him, calling him Miss Nancy. Later, he forgave his father and turned on his mother, who had had his beloved sister institutionalised and ordered her to undergo a lobotomy, a subject he explored in *Suddenly Last Summer* (1958). He never forgave his mother, and he undertook the care of his sister for the rest of her life. Rose's story inspired the largely autobiographical play, *The Glass Menagerie* (1945), his first Broadway success, which launched his dramatic career.

Two years after his death, his *Collected Short Stories* were published with a candid autobiographical preface Williams had written in 1960. Here in one volume were all of Williams's homosexual fiction, stories from his earliest years as a writer to the end of his career. Many of them are distinguished fiction, but all of them are bold and unapologetic (see especially 'Mysteries of the Joy Rio', 'Hard Candy', 'One Arm', 'Desire and the Black Masseur', 'Two on a Party'). Unlike his depiction of homosexuals in his plays, who are invariably unhappy as homosexuals, tragic or absurd, the men in his fiction are heroic in their pursuit of desire, the same driven, larger-than-life quality with which he endows his dramatic heroines. Even at the end of his career, after coming out publicly on television and in print as a gay man, making what Gore VIDAL would call a 'circus' of his life, in a late play, *Small Craft Warnings*, he has an aging homosexual, Quentin, deliver a long gloomy monologue about the perils of being gay.

Williams could never reconcile himself to his sexual persuasion, and his conflict about his sexuality was the dominant subject of both the fiction and, transformed into heterosexual terms, of his dramas. With his remarkable gift for lyric language, he created a literature whose style and sensibility were unmistakable; it was a sensibility formed by his closetry. No matter how public the knowledge of his private life became, he still could not utter the words 'homosexual' or 'gay' in his literary works. This disparity, between his public flaunting of his sexuality in interviews, in fiction, and in his memoir, and his deep uneasiness about naming himself as homosexual was a conflict that finally stifled him, and the loss of his career destroyed him, as it had Oscar Wilde. He died freakishly while inebriated, suffocated by the cap of a medicine bottle he had inadvertently swallowed throwing the capful of barbituates down his throat.

Lyle Leverich, *Tom: The Unknown Tennessee Williams* (London, 1995); Donald Spoto, *The Kindness of Strangers: A Life of Tennessee Williams* (Boston, 1985); Tennessee Williams, *Memoirs* (Garden City, NY, 1975).

Seymour Kleinberg

Wills, Sue (b. 1944), Australian activist. Wills was one of the early leaders of the gay and lesbian rights movement in Australia, an office-bearer in the Campaign Against Moral Persecution (CAMP) in New South Wales and a writer on various aspects of gay activism. Inspired to come out by an address by Dennis ALTMAN at Sydney University in 1972, she was one of a number of activists grouped around the Department of Government there. Drawn to CAMP rather than Gay Liberation, in part because she was able to locate the former, she is credited by founder John WARE with revitalising the group's interest in the abuse of homosexuals by the psychiatric profession and she wrote many articles on this topic. She was also involved in CAMP's Homosexual Guidance Service, which both campaigned and coun-selled. Wills was elected first Co-President with Lex WATSON and served two terms (1972–73 and 1973–74). She worked to fos-ter closer links and a better understanding between women's liberation and lesbian activists in CAMP. Her struggle to negoti-ate the tensions between men and women within the organisation, and her involve-ment with the CAMP Women's Associ-ation, centred on an effort to keep women within the group, fearing that if lesbians left, their political focus would be lost. In the end, it was a deepening depoliticisa-tion that led her, Watson and those closest to them to resign from the leadership.

Wills was subsequently involved as a re-searcher for the federal government's Royal Commission into Human Relation-ships, producing important insights into public thinking on the question of homo-sexuality. Her unpublished Ph.D. thesis, 'The Politics of Sexual Liberation', and the document collection she compiled as part of her research are invaluable sources for the early history of the movement in Australia.

Graham Willet

Wilson, Sir Angus (1913–91), British writer. Angus Frank Johnstone-Wilson was born in England to a landed, storytelling Scot-tish dynasty in decline, which his father accelerated with high and low living, gambling and debts. Wilson's mother was from a South African family who made good through trade, and settled in Eng-land. He spent part of his childhood in South Africa.

Back in England, Wilson found a stabil-ity at school and university that was not offered at home. Within these institutions he fashioned himself into a 'character'. His homosexuality soon became obvious and, as his pretty looks metamorphosed into oddity and campness, he created de-fences to protect himself. Taking pride in his differences and learning to clown, im-personate and tell stories enhanced his natural kindness and generosity, and at-tracted others to him. At Oxford he read history, kept up with other reading, espe-cially novels, and involved himself in drama and politics.

In 1937 he secured a job at the British Museum. From 1942 until after the war, Wilson worked at the Government Code and Cypher School as a decoder, though the work caused childhood traumas to resurface.

Wilson waited a long time for his sex-ual and emotional freedom, which came only when his dependent father died in 1938. (His mother had died in 1929.) Be-tween a number of affairs and a *ménages à trois*, Wilson met Tony Garrett, fifteen years his junior. From 1946 onwards, their relationship, based on friendship as well as mutual attraction, slowly developed until it became a strong, loving and re-spectful, though not always unproblem-atic, partnership that neither wanted to relinquish.

Some time after his post-war return to the British Museum, Wilson was given a job in the Reading Room. He rose to the position of Deputy Superintendent, then resigned in 1955 to devote his time to writing. Wilson thought of himself pri-marily as a novelist although he first found success in 1947 via the short story. He believed in the novel as a serious liter-ary form at a time of stagnation and de-cline, and amongst assiduous readers and critics was regarded as a saviour of the English novel. *Hemlock and After* (1952), Wilson's first novel, set the tone for the others. With its themes of homosexuality and abuse, it shocked readers into new fic-tional regions – glitter and glitz on the surface, darkness on the underside. Wil-son knew many men (and women), in-cluding Garrett and himself, who had been badly wounded by oppression, and his novels were an opportunity to investi-gate the nature of evil and to exorcise so-ciety's phantoms. *No Laughing Matter* (1967), a family saga, was regarded by many as his masterpiece. The phantoms lurking here were Wilson's own family and childhood. In this novel, as in life, parody is a gateway to reality and thence to compassion, which leads to forgiveness and resolution.

From the time Wilson left the British Museum, he lived an increasingly busy literary life, becoming mentor to many authors, writing book and television reviews and travel articles, speaking on radio and television, attending conferences and sitting on panels and committees. He worked as a guest lecturer, especially in America, and in 1963 became a senior lecturer at the University of East Anglia. He was honoured with a knighthood in 1980.

In the mid-1980s he began to suffer from dementia and was cared for by Garrett until his death.

Margaret Drabble, *Angus Wilson: A Biography* (London, 1995).

Susan Taylor

Wilson, Douglas (1950–92), Canadian activist, publisher and writer. Born in Meadow Lake, Saskatchewan, Wilson gained prominence in September 1975 in a fight for gay rights at the University of Saskatchewan. The Dean of the University's College of Education refused to allow Wilson, a postgraduate student in the Department of Educational Foundations, to go into the school system to supervise practice teachers because of his public involvement with the gay liberation movement. At that time Wilson was Vice-President of the Gay Community Centre Saskatoon and had been trying to start a gay academic union at the university. Although he was qualified to do the job, Wilson was disqualified solely on the basis of his sexual orientation. The decision was upheld by the President of the University of Saskatchewan. The Committee to Defend Doug Wilson was formed, and generated much support for Wilson across Canada. His appeal to the Saskatchewan Human Rights Commission for a hearing on the case was ultimately unsuccessful,

and by 1976 Wilson and the Committee had abandoned the case.

Wilson spent most of his life involved in human rights issues, gay activism and AIDS organising. He left the University of Saskatchewan in 1976 and in 1977 founded Stubblejumper Press, a small press dedicated to publishing works by Canadian lesbians and gay men. From 1978 to 1983 he served as the executive director of the Saskatchewan Association on Human Rights, a lobbying group.

In 1983 Wilson moved to Toronto, where he worked for the Toronto Board of Education as an adviser to the Race Relations and Equal Opportunity Office. In 1984, he was one of the founding members of the Rites Collective, publishers of *Rites: For Lesbian and Gay Liberation*.

Wilson's political career culminated in 1988 when he stood for Parliament as a candidate for the New Democratic Party in the Toronto riding of Rosedale. He was the first openly gay candidate to be nominated by a major political party in Canada. He fell ill during the campaign, however, and was diagnosed with AIDS. Wilson spent the rest of his life as an indefatigable AIDS activist. In 1988 he was a founding member of AIDS Action Now!, and became the founding chairperson of the Canadian Network of Organizations for People Living With AIDS.

Wilson was involved for more than twelve years in a relationship with the singer, songwriter and writer Peter McGehee. Wilson nurtured McGehee's creative talents, published his work and managed him as a singer and songwriter. The author of *Boys Like Us* (1991), a tragicomic novel tracing a group of gay male Toronto friends during the AIDS crisis, McGehee succumbed to the disease in 1991. During his own illness Wilson edited McGehee's posthumous novel *Sweetheart* (1992), and one month before his death completed his first novel (based on McGehee's notes), *Labour of Love* (1993), the third volume of McGehee's *Boys Like Us* trilogy.

Jeffrey Canton, 'Doug Wilson, October 11, 1950–September 26, 1992', *Xtra!* (Toronto), 2 Oct. 1992, p. 7; Donn Downey, 'Activist Championed Gay Cause at University of Saskatchewan', *Globe and Mail* (Toronto), 30 Sept. 1992, p. C5; Douglas Wilson papers, Canadian Lesbian and Gay Archives, Toronto.

Donald W. McLeod

Winkler, Josef (b. 1953), Austrian novelist. Winkler was born into a farming family in the small village of Kamering in Carinthia. He left school at seventeen with no qualifications – this, he said, was due to his being so absorbed in reading for his own pleasure that he had neither the time nor the inclination for school work. His reading of Jean GENET in particular brought about an intense literary awakening. The novels of the French author continue to inform Winkler's works.

In his homage to Genet, *Das Zöglingsheft des Jean Genet* (*Flowers for Jean Genet*), Winkler tells that after having stumbled by chance across *Notre-Dame-des-Fleurs* in a bookshop he gave away all the books that had until then made up his personal library and turned his attention to acquiring and consuming Genet's *oeuvre* instead. Of the personal implications of Genet's writing, Winkler writes: 'The feeling when I caress the naked body of a boy, of doing something sleazy and deplorable – even then society's moralistic clock was ticking in my head – left me utterly as I read *Notre-Dame-des-Fleurs*. All at once I even began to be proud of my homoerotic desire'.

Genet's novel *Pompes funèbres* (*Funeral Rites*) inspired Winkler to set down on paper a defining experience of his adolescence. Two of the author's teenage friends decided to hang themselves together and were discovered hanging intertwined from a beam in a farm building, embracing one another in death. This suicide pact between the teenage lovers Jakob and Robert becomes the theme of Winkler's first novel *Menschenkind*, and

also leaves its mark in the two subsequent novels of his trilogy *Das wilde Kärnten* (*Wild Carinthia*).

By exploring the rigid, patriarchal, oppressively Catholic and heterosexual power structures of the farming world in which he spent his formative years, and distilling from it a poeticisation of homosexuality with its implied contravention of all the rules of that world, Winkler establishes a new vision of humanity and a new morality. In the shape of the transvestite Jakob Menschikow – who draws strongly on Genet's Divine in *Notre-Dame-des-Fleurs* – Winkler creates in his trilogy an erotically-charged saviour figure, subverting the Catholic context from which such a figure is derived, and at the same time imbuing it with new meaning. As well as clearly displaying the influence of Genet, Winkler's novels are marked by allusions to the works of other gay authors, such as Pier Paolo PASOLINI, Hubert FICHTE and Oscar Wilde. The intellectual framework transcends parochial life and at the same time creates a cultural framework which makes village life more bearable for Winkler.

Winkler occupied various secretarial and administrative positions before the success of his trilogy of novels, since when he has lived as a novelist, spending most of his time in Carinthia. He has been awarded numerous literary prizes, most recently the 'Förderpreis des Großen Kunstpreises Berlin' (1994).

Dirck Linck, *Halbweib und Maskenbildner. Subjektivität und schwule Erfahrung im Werk Josef Winklers* (Berlin, 1993).

Andrea Capovilla

Winterson, Jeanette, (b. 1959), British writer. 'No-one working in the English language now comes close to my exuberance, my passion, my fidelity to words.' This 'heir to Virginia Woolf' – another of her self-characterisations – has upset many a literary arbiter with her habit of self-publicity, but her work has added a significant dimension, at once postmodern and post-national, to contemporary British letters.

Winterson was born in Lancashire, adopted and raised by Pentecostal evangelists and groomed for missionary work, a calling she failed to embrace. Prior to and after her Oxford degree, at St Catherine's, she held a variety of occupations, from funeral parlour cosmology to publishing, from ice cream sales to lesbian prostitution. Her rebellion against the constraints of her early upbringing is rendered in her first novel, *Oranges are Not the Only Fruit* (1985), which won the Whitbread award. This is an inventive and witty portrait of an artist as a young girl, as well as the story of an adolescent lesbian's coming-of-age. The *bildungsroman* structure is interspersed with brief parables which serve as commentaries on the heroine's sexual and spiritual crisis, and it is this component which rehearses Winterson's enduring interest in fairy-tale and myth. A fabulist at heart, she mischievously revisits the story of Noah in *Boating for Beginners* (1985), and evokes Woolf's *Orlando* in *The Passion* (1987), a fantasy of unrequited love, cross-dressing and androgyny, set in Venice during the Napoleonic Wars. Italo Calvino's influence is evident in *Sexing the Cherry* (1989), a novel anchored both in Restoration and contemporary London, where history merges with science and fairy-tale, where genders blur, and all manner of journeys can be undertaken. Metafictional anxieties, and intertextual ironies – a cheeky nod to Erich Segal's *Love Story* – define *Written on the Body* (1992), with its triangular relationship between the narrator, her heroine and the heroine's husband. Another triangle of desire governs *Gut Symmetries* (1997), a surreal, prophetic narrative which grapples with modern physics and metahistory, while *Art and Lies* (1994), barely a novel, introduces us to Sappho's ghost, a feminised Picasso and a gelded male of no particular distinction. The voice of the essayist informs almost all her fiction, but is formally on display in *Art Objects: Essays on Ecstasy and Effrontery* (1995). Her short stories are collected in *The World and Other Places* (1998).

The subjects Winterson identifies in her own writing – 'the nature of time; love between parent and child, woman and woman, woman and man; the journey; the quest for self; the outsider' – are explored with missionary zeal. She maintains a fiercely loyal readership and provokes scorn among those critics who prefer to see only an Edith Sitwell refashioned for the late twentieth century.

Laura Doan, 'The Fruits of Lesbian Desire: Jeanette Winterson's Sexing the Postmodern', in Laura Doan (ed.), *The Lesbian Postmodern* (New York, 1994); Carolyn Allen, 'Jeanette Winterson: The Erotics of Risk', *Following Djuna: Women Lovers and the Erotics of Loss* (Bloomington, 1996), pp. 46–80; Helena Grice and Tim Woods (eds), *'I'm Telling You Stories': Jeanette Winterson and the Politics of Reading* (Amsterdam, 1998).

Roger Bowen

Wittig, Monique (b. 1935), French writer. Born in Alsace, Wittig became an activist in the French feminist movement of the early 1970s, a celebrated writer of literary, theoretical and political texts (receiving the coveted Prix Médicis for her first novel in 1964), and, after emigrating to the United States in 1976, an academic within the North American university system. Her revolutionary work has inspired feminists and lesbians throughout the world to rethink the fundamental categories of gender which constitute and structure both human society and that invention of the late nineteenth century, sexuality.

Critique is the hallmark of all Wittig's texts. The first target is language in its patriarchial forms, and from this primary critique flow all the others: those of gender, heterosexuality, psychoanalysis, structuralism and, perhaps most surprisingly, *écriture féminine*.

Her literary work includes novels, short stories and plays. Notable amongst these are *L'Opoponax* (1964; transl. *The Opoponax*, 1966), *Les Guérillères* (1969), *Le Corps lesbien* (1973; transl. *The Lesbian Body*, 1975), *Virgile, non* (1985; transl. *Across the Acheron*, 1987) and *Le Voyage sans fin* (1985; transl. *The Constant Journey*, 1984). In these works, Wittig appropriates, redefines and reinvents traditionally masculine-dominated genres such as the Bildungsroman, the epic poem and even, in *Brouillon pour un dictionnaire des amantes* (1975; transl. *Lesbian Peoples: Material for a Dictionary*, 1979), the dictionary. Highly original and experimental in form, Wittig's literary writings can prove too reconditely challenging for some non-academic readers. However, their ideological underpinnings are often illuminated by the remarkable conceptual clarity of her theoretical and political writings, in particular *The Straight Mind and Other Essays* (1992). In these, the various critiques mentioned above become more explicit and accessible.

The assault on gender is the basis of her intriguingly polemical claim that lesbians are not women. By this she means that, in conventional patriarchal societies, women are defined essentially by their (subordinate) relation to men, that women are dependent on men not just for their material but also for their ontological status, and that, since lesbians do not define themselves in relation to men and thus elude gender, lesbians are not women. She exhorts gay people to stop conceiving of themselves as women and men, since in so doing they are instrumental in maintaining heterosexuality. Heterosexuality she sees not as an institution but, more disquietingly, as a political regime, 'which rests on the submission and appropriation of women'.

Wittig's problematisation of *écriture féminine* also derives from the founding critique of language and, more obviously, of the linguistically mediated myth of gender. Although at least two of her literary works, *Les Guérillères* and *Le Corps lesbien*, have been assimilated by many critics and readers to the category of *écriture féminine*, because of their strikingly experimental style and their vision of new relations between women, Wittig's epistemological framework in fact rejects the very binary division masculine/feminine on which the concept of *écriture féminine* depends. In particular, she is alert to the dangers of reductive biologism and essentialism inherent in the emphasis placed by *écriture féminine* on the metaphors of the maternal body.

Wittig's opposition to structuralism is based on its invocation of what she calls 'necessities', or structures, which escape the control of consciousness and therefore the responsibility of individuals. In her view, structuralism cynically posits unconscious processes, for example, the exchange of women as a necessary condition for every society, which helps to maintain intact social inequalities. She analyses the assertion of such necessary, trans-cultural structures as a political, oppressive discourse aimed at foreclosing the possibility of human agency.

Another equally political, equally oppressive and equally prestigious discourse deconstructed by Wittig is that of psychoanalysis, which since Lacan has, of course, been governed by structuralist premises. The reification of such concepts as Difference, Desire and the Name-of-the-Father is, in Wittig's view, characteristic of 'the straight mind'.

Her critique of the straight mind, that overarching ideology of our times, has enabled countless gay individuals to recognise the political and disciplinary nature of psychoanalytic, academic and populist-naturalist discourse, and to problematise the whole concept of 'knowledge' as value-free.

Jennifer Birkett, '*Sophie Ménade*: The Writing of Monique Wittig', in Alex Hughes and Kate Ince (eds), *French Erotic Fiction: Women's Desiring Writing* (Oxford, 1996); D. G. Crowder,

'Amazons and Mothers? Monique Wittig, Hélène Cixous and Theories of Women's Writing', *Contemporary Literature*, vol. 24, no. 2, (1983); Renate Günther, 'Are Lesbians Women? The Relationship between Lesbianism and Feminism in the Work of Luce Irigaray and Monique Wittig', in Owen Heathcote, Alex Hughes and James S. Williams (eds), *Gay Signatures: Gay and Lesbian Theory, Fiction and Film in France, 1945–1995* (Oxford, 1998); Erika Ostrovsky, *A Constant Journey: The Fiction of Monique Wittig* (Carbondale, IL, 1991).

Lucille Cairns

Wolfenden, John Frederick (Baron Wolfenden of Westcott) (1906–85), British educator. Wolfenden, whose name was to become a household word fifty years later, was born at Swindon, Wiltshire. He majored in philosophy at Queen's College, Oxford, graduating in 1928, and spent a postgraduate year at Princeton University in the US. He tutored in philosophy at Magdalen College, Oxford, 1929–34. In 1934 he began a sixteen-year career as a school headmaster. He was seconded to the Air Ministry in 1941 to establish and administer the Air Training Corps. In 1950 he was appointed Vice-Chancellor of Reading University. He left Reading in 1963 to become Chairman of the University Grants Committee (1963–68), and then Director of the British Museum (1969–73). As well as these formal positions, Wolfenden served on (and frequently chaired) numerous committees concerned with education and social service. During this long career in education and public service, he was awarded honorary doctorates from eight universities, received the CBE in 1942, was knighted in 1956 and was made a life peer in 1974.

Wolfenden's name became a household word, in some circles a notorious one, through his chairmanship of the Committee on Homosexual Offences and Prostitution (1954–57). At this time there was growing public disquiet about the brazen behaviour of female prostitutes soliciting for custom in the streets of major cities. While prostitution was not an offence, soliciting was, but attempts to control it were increasingly unsuccessful. In the matter of male homosexuality, which was an offence with penalties as high as life imprisonment, several recent court cases involving prominent men had created much scandal. There was increasing criticism of unsavoury police methods such as the use of *agents provocateurs*. Blackmail of homosexuals was not uncommon, but those being blackmailed were afraid to notify the police lest they be arrested and punished for the homosexual acts concerned. In these highly sensitive areas of sexual behaviour, involving conflicting issues both of morality and of legality, it was proving increasingly difficult to balance civil liberties and individual freedom against the need to preserve public order. The law and the police were being brought into disrepute and the government wanted an impartial and comprehensive review which would make recommendations for improvement.

Wolfenden said, perhaps disingenuously, that he did not know why he had been chosen to chair this inquiry, but he had become known to bureaucrats and others as an effective manager and a clear thinker. In common with most middle-aged people of his time he knew little about homosexuality but considered it distasteful, even disgusting. His own position was, in some ways, complicated by the recent distressing discovery that his 20-year-old son, Jeremy, was openly homosexual.

Wolfenden's committee comprised fifteen men and women, including judges, members of Parliament, doctors, lawyers and ministers of religion. Its terms of reference were: 'To consider (a) the law and practice relating to homosexual offences and the treatment of persons convicted of such offences by the courts; and (b) the law and practice relating to offences against the criminal law in connection with prostitution and solicitation for immoral purposes, and to report what changes, if any, are desirable.'

The Committee spent three years considering these matters, a period during which Wolfenden decided (after hearing some early evidence) that it would be prudent for him to avoid using public toilets!

The Committee's proposals with respect to homosexuality were revolutionary and highly controversial. Despite his personal opinions on the subject, Wolfenden had viewed the investigations of the Committee as a philosophical exercise and had been careful to confine them to considering the law, not morality. The Committee concluded that religious sanctions against homosexuality were not grounds for action by the secular courts, and that 'there must remain a realm of private morality and immorality which is, in brief and crude terms, not the law's business'. On this foundation the Committee constructed its core recommendation 'that homosexual behaviour between consenting adults in private be no longer a criminal offence'. To protect those who might not be able to protect themselves, 'adult' was defined as 21 years of age (although the female age of consent was then 16), and more stringent penalties were recommended for those who exploit minors or where consent was lacking.

A violent torrent of debate and criticism erupted when the Committee's Report was published. Many newspapers condemned it in sensational terms, one calling it 'the Pansies' Charter'. The finding that 'homosexuality cannot legitimately be regarded as a disease' provoked an outcry from psychiatrists for whom this was almost an article of faith. Religious interests predicted the end of civilisation. The Report became a best-seller.

Not surprisingly, the government, which had privately hoped for assistance in curbing homosexual behaviour, was in no hurry to legislate on the recommendations. The Home Secretary took the view that any change in the law might be regarded as tacit approval of homosexuality, and took no action. It was left to individual MPs to raise the matter in Parliament but whenever it came to a vote the majority wanted no change in the law. Gradually these majorities diminished until, in 1967, the Sexual Offences Act was passed which gave legal form to the Committee's recommendations. It had taken ten years, but Wolfenden was philosophical about the delay, recognising that if laws were to be respected they should generally follow public opinion rather than try to lead it. His Committee's thinking had been considerably in advance and one just had to wait for public opinion to catch up. One may speculate that another reason for the government's inaction was concern that if it became known that the chairman's son was an active homosexual the credibility of both the government and the Report would be damaged. If this was a complication, it was removed when Jeremy Wolfenden died in 1965.

The Wolfenden Report, as it quickly became known to the discomfort of its principal author and his family, had an influence far beyond the UK. For example, in 1961 the American Bar Association issued a draft Model Penal Code which omitted homosexual offences between consenting adults, and this gradually led to state legislatures decriminalising homosexuality. In 1969 the Canadian Parliament decriminialised homosexuality. In general, it could be argued that the greater tolerance for private consensual homosexual acts which developed during the 1960s and 1970s made possible the gay liberation movement by freeing homosexuals from the need for secrecy about their sexuality.

Read today the Report strikes one as conservative and old-fashioned, full of compromises, incongruities and inconsistencies. What could all the fuss have been about? But in the context of its times it was in many ways a courageous (some thought an outrageous) statement for re-

form and tolerance in a highly controversial area. Many of the case studies in
the Report, taken from police and court
reports, are both sad and appalling to
those accustomed to more liberal societal
attitudes to homosexuality. Wolfenden
and his Committee did courageous
pioneering work towards equality and
tolerance.

'Jeremy Wolfenden', in Sebastian Faulks, *The
Fatal Englishman: Three Short Lives* (London,
1996); *Report of the Committee on Homosexual Offences and Prostitution*, Sept. 1957
(Cmnd. 247); John Frederick Wolfenden, *Turning Points: The Memoirs of Lord Wolfenden*
(London, 1976).

Neil A. Radford

Wolff, Charlotte (1897–1986), German-
French-British writer, medical practitioner, cheirologist. Wolff was born into
a middle-class Jewish family in Riesen-
burg, West Prussia. The family moved to
Danzig in 1913, where Wolff attended a
prestigious grammar school. During a stay
with a cousin in Berlin, she became acquainted with the poet and dramatist Else
Lasker-Schüler. She later studied philosophy in Freiburg, Königsberg and
Tübingen, and philosophy and medicine
in Berlin, where she was awarded a medical doctorate in 1928. Around the same
time her early poems were published in a
literary journal called *Vers und Prosa*
(*Verse and Prose*).

Wolff's first medical post was at the Vir-
chow hospital in Berlin. She also worked in
family planning in some of the city's most
deprived areas. By 1932 anti-Semitism was
growing extreme in Germany, and Wolff
as a Jew was moved to a more sheltered
post in the district of Neukölln. But she
was nonetheless arrested, on charges of
espionage and wearing men's clothes, and
released only when a guard recognised and
defended her as his wife's doctor. Three
days later her apartment was searched,
and Wolff decided that it was time to leave

Germany. In May of 1933 she emigrated to
Paris.

In Neukölln, Wolff had begun to spe-
cialize in cheirology, the study of the
hand. The psychocheirologist Julius Spier
taught her to hand-read, and from this
Wolff developed a theory of diagnosis via
the hand. In exile in France and England,
she performed experiments, comparing
the hands of human beings and apes and
publishing her results. In 1941, in recognition of her work, she was made an honorary member of the British Psychological
Society.

In Paris, Wolff shared a flat with the
journalist Helen Hessel. Barred from
working as a doctor, she lived from reading hands, including those of the French
surrealists André Breton, Paul Eluard and
Antoine de Saint-Exupéry.

In 1936 she moved to London, with the
help of Aldous and Maria Huxley. It was
Maria who arranged a meeting with Virginia Woolf, whose hands Wolff analysed.
In return, Woolf invited Wolff to tea, and
presented her with a German translation
of *To The Lighthouse*.

Shortly after the completion of her
book manuscript, *The Hand in Psychological Diagnosis* (published in 1952),
Wolff was finally registed as a doctor in
Britain, and could practise again. Her research diversified into lesbianism and bisexuality, and she won international recognition in these areas, influencing particularly the German lesbian movement
of the 1970s. She continued to pursue a
literary as well as an academic career,
and in 1969 published her autobiographical memoirs, *On the Way to Myself*, in
which she maintains that 'homosexual
love is ideal twinship'. In 1978 she accepted an invitation from the lesbian
group L.74 (Lesbos 1974) to give a reading in Berlin, her first visit to the capital
since her emigration, and a year later returned again, this time to address a university summer course on 'Lesbian Love
and the Women's Movement'. Her autobiography, *Hindsight*, appeared in 1980,

and was published in German as *Augen-blicke verändern uns mehr als die Zeit* (1982).

Other works by Charlotte Wolff include her treatises *The Human Hand* (London, 1942), *Love Between Women* (London, 1971) and *Bisexuality: A Study* (1977), as well as the novel *An Older Love* (London, 1976).

Renate Wall, *Lexikon deutschsprachiger Schriftstellerinnen im Exil 1933 bis 1945* (Freiburg i. Br., 1995).

Sarah Colvin

Y

Young, Ian (b. 1945), Canadian writer, publisher and activist. Born in London, Young spent much of his childhood in South Africa before settling in Canada in 1957. During the 1960s he became involved with the civil rights movement while at the University of Toronto, and began to publish poetry. In 1969 he was one of the founders of the University of Toronto Homophile Association (UTHA), the first post-Stonewall gay organisation in Canada and the first formed at a Canadian university. During the 1970s Young devoted himself to writing and publishing. He founded Catalyst Press, the first gay literary publishing house, in 1970; it issued over thirty titles by Canadian, British and American writers before suspending publication in 1980. Young edited the pioneering gay poetry anthology *The Male Muse* (1973) and compiled one of the first gay literary reference works, *The Male Homosexual in Literature: A Bibliography* (1975; 1982). His erudite book review column 'The Ivory Tunnel' was a staple of the Canadian gay newsmagazine *The Body Politic* from 1975–85. During the 1970s and 1980s Young became increasingly interested in ceremonial magic; in 1981, he co-founded the Hermetic Order of the Silver Sword. He continued to publish poetry, including *Son of the Male Muse* (1983) and *Sex Magick* (1986). By the 1990s his attention turned to the study of alternative or dissident theories of AIDS. Young compiled two of the leading studies in this field: *The AIDS Dissidents: An Annotated Bibliography* (1993), and, with John Lauritsen, *The AIDS Cult: Essays on the Gay Health Crisis* (1997). Young's *The Stonewall Experiment: A Gay Psychohistory* (1995) was a meditation on the psychic life of gay men from the age of Whitman to the AIDS crisis. In 1997, Young co-founded the Toronto branch of Health Education AIDS Liaison (HEAL), a non-profit, community-based education network dedicated to challenging the HIV-=AIDS hypothesis and the efficacy of HIV-based treatment protocols.

Andy Quan, 'Years of the Quiet Son: The Continuing Legacy of Ian Young', *ARC: Canada's National Poetry Magazine*, no. 32 (Spring 1994), pp. 19–25; Ian Young, 'A Canadian Catalyst Presses for Change', *Advocate*, no. 315 (1981), pp. 23–26; Ian Young, *Ian Young: A Bibliography 1962–1980* (Toronto, 1981); Ian Young papers, Canadian Lesbian and Gay Archives, Toronto.

Donald W. McLeod

Z

Zapata, Luis (b. 1951), Mexican author. Zapata is an open gay writer who discusses gay issues in his novels and short stories. His first novel, *Hasta en las mejores familias* (*Even in the Best of Families*, 1975), belongs to the literary movement of *La Onda* (Mexico's New Wave). It is a first-person introspective account of middle-class values and the role of homosexuality in Mexican society. *Las aventuras, desaventuras y sueños de Adonis García, el vampiro de la colonia Roma* (*Adonis García: A Picaresque Novel*, 1979) is a celebration of homosexual love in the streets of Mexico City. It is an excellent novel, written in the form of the illogical stream of consciousness that was fashionable in the 1970s, and tells in vivid conversations what it is to be a poor, gay prostitute in a big, contemporary city. *De pétalos peremnes* (*Perennial Petals*, 1981) is a brief study of desire and social class in present-day Mexico: a maid and her employer share the same lover, each trying to fill a vacuum in their lives. *En jirones* (*In Tatters*, 1985), an explicit gay novel, tells the impossible love story between Sebastián and A. Sebastián's love and desire for A. drive him to insanity and make him incapable of functioning as a social being. A. at the same time cannot conceptualise his homosexuality and marries a woman of his own social status. The literary use of pornography, the deliberate attempt to arouse the reader with the explicit sexual scenes, and the melodramatic and soothing effect of using Juan Gabriel's songs make this novel one of the most interesting texts ever written in Latin America.

Ese amor que hasta ayer nos quemaba (*That Love that Was Burning Us Until Recently*, 1989) is a collection of short stories, the oldest from 1975; some had already appeared in *De amor*. *La hermana secreta de Angélica María* (*Angélica María's Secret Sister*, 1989) is a minor masterpiece, a portrayal of what it means to be a sexual outcast in rural Mexico, and the brutal division between reality and the world of fantasy and dreams of pop culture. *¿Por qué mejor no nos vamos?* (*Why Don't We Just Leave?*, 1992) is an explicit novel about a sceptical, middle-aged man who tells of his life as a *joto* ('faggot') in Mexico; the novel explores the cultural, ethnic and class differences between *joto* and *gay*. *La más fuerte pasión* (*The Strongest Passion*, 1995) is a more cynical approach to the meaning of love. It tells of the relationship between the middle-aged and rich Santiago, and the handsome and young Arturo. Arturo's mother, Sarita, arranges the relationship between the two men: Arturo will get a good education thanks to Santiago's money and good taste, and Santiago will be able to enjoy Arturo's body, love and company.

Zapata's ability to put together oral language (most of his texts are conversations of people from all social classes without direct information about the background and the setting of the conversation), Mexican (and American) popular culture, high- and low-brow culture, rural and urban milieus and gender issues make him one of the best contemporary Mexican writers.

Salvador A. Oropesa

Zaremba, Eve (b. 1930), Canadian writer, activist. Zaremba is the creator of Helen Karemos, the first-ever lesbian detective in a series. Karemos is the central character of (so far) six books beginning with *A Reason to Kill* (1978). Zaremba also wrote *Privilege of Sex: A Century of Canadian Women* (1972), a pioneering book about women in Canada. She has, in the past, also owned a used-book store and publishing enterprise in Toronto.

As is the case with many lesbian feminists, much of her activism has been embedded in feminism and in building a women's movement in Toronto and Canada. Working in collective structures she co-founded Women's Place, the first women's centre in Canada (1972), helped set up the Women's Credit Union (1974), and co-founded *Broadside*, a feminist newspaper (1978). Zaremba also fought for an autonomous lesbian movement and helped establish the Lesbian Organization of Toronto (LOOT) in 1976. Her previous experience in advertising, market research and business consulting added much-needed practical skills into an atmosphere of heady idealism.

World War II was a pivotal event for Zaremba, who left Poland in 1940. She attended secondary school in Scotland and England and emigrated to Canada in 1952.

Becki L. Ross, *The House that Jill Built: A Lesbian Nation in Formation* (Toronto, 1995).

Maureen FitzGerald